GCSE
Combined Science
Higher Level

Here it is, your dream come true! No, not a never-ending pizza buffet, or the secret to eternal youth, it's something much better — it's CGP's GCSE Combined Science guide!

It's the ultimate revision triple-threat — everything you need to know for Combined Science Biology, Chemistry and Physics. Plus, there are exam-style questions for every topic, a full set of practice papers, <u>and</u> a free online edition.

You'll also find links to our fantastic online content, with video solutions for practice questions, as well as Retrieval Quizzes to help you nail down all the facts you need to learn.

Unlock your free online extras!

Just go to **cgpbooks.co.uk/extras** and enter this code or scan the QR codes in the book.

4043 1222 8637 1341

By the way, this code only works for one person. If somebody else has used this book before you, they might have already claimed the Online Edition.

Complete
Revision & Practice
<u>Everything</u> you need to pass the exams!

Contents

Working Scientifically

The Scientific Method 2
Models and Communication 3
Issues Created by Science 4
Risk 5
Designing Investigations 6
Processing Data 9
Presenting Data 10
More on Graphs 11
Units 12
Converting Units 13
Drawing Conclusions 14
Uncertainty 15
Evaluations 16

Topic B1 — Cell Biology

Cells 17
Microscopy 19
Warm-Up & Exam Questions 22
Cell Differentiation and Specialisation 23
Cell Specialisation 24
Stem Cells 25
Chromosomes and Mitosis 27
Warm-Up & Exam Questions 29
Diffusion 30
Osmosis 31
Active Transport 33
Exchanging Substances 34
More on Exchanging Substances 36
Warm-Up & Exam Questions 38
Exam Questions 39

Topic B2 — Organisation

Cell Organisation 40
Enzymes 42
Investigating Enzymatic Reactions 44
Enzymes and Digestion 45
More on Enzymes and Digestion 46
Food Tests 47
Warm-Up & Exam Questions 49
Exam Questions 50
The Lungs 51
Circulatory System — The Heart 53
Circulatory System — Blood Vessels 54
Circulatory System — Blood 55
Warm-Up & Exam Questions 56
Exam Questions 57
Cardiovascular Disease 58
Warm-Up & Exam Questions 61
Health and Disease 62
Risk Factors for Non-Communicable Diseases 64
Cancer 66
Warm-Up & Exam Questions 67
Plant Cell Organisation 68
Transpiration and Translocation 69
Transpiration 70
The Rate of Transpiration 71
Measuring Transpiration and Stomata 72
Warm-Up & Exam Questions 73
Exam Questions 74

Throughout this book you'll see grade stamps like these:

These grade stamps help to show how difficult the questions are.
Remember — to get a top grade you need to be able to answer **all** the questions, not just the hardest ones.

In the real exams, some questions test how well you can write (as well as your scientific knowledge).
In this book, we've marked these questions with an asterisk (*).

Topic B3 — Infection and Response

Communicable Disease..75
Viral and Fungal Diseases...................................77
Protist and Bacterial Diseases.............................78
Preventing Disease...79
Warm-Up & Exam Questions................................80
Fighting Disease...81
Fighting Disease — Vaccination..........................82
Fighting Disease — Drugs...................................84
Developing Drugs...86
Warm-Up & Exam Questions................................87
Exam Questions..88

Topic B4 — Bioenergetics

Photosynthesis...89
The Rate of Photosynthesis................................90
Measuring the Rate of Photosynthesis................93
Ideal Conditions for Photosynthesis....................95
Warm-Up & Exam Questions................................96
Exam Questions..97
Respiration..98
Metabolism...99
Aerobic and Anaerobic Respiration...................100
Exercise..101
Warm-Up & Exam Questions..............................102
Revision Summary for Topics B1-4....................103

Topic B5 — Homeostasis and Response

Homeostasis..104
The Nervous System..105
Reflexes..107
Investigating Reaction Time.............................108
Warm-Up & Exam Questions..............................109
The Endocrine System.....................................110
Comparing Nerves and Hormones.....................111
Controlling Blood Glucose................................112
Diabetes...113
Warm-Up & Exam Questions..............................114
Puberty and the Menstrual Cycle......................115
Controlling Fertility..117
Adrenaline and Thyroxine................................120
Warm-Up & Exam Questions..............................121

Topic B6 — Inheritance, Variation and Evolution

DNA..122
Reproduction...124
Meiosis...125
X and Y Chromosomes.....................................126
Warm-Up & Exam Questions..............................128
Genetic Diagrams..129
More Genetic Diagrams....................................131
Inherited Disorders..133
Warm-Up & Exam Questions..............................135
Exam Questions...136
Variation...137
Evolution..139
Warm-Up & Exam Questions..............................141
Selective Breeding...142
Genetic Engineering..143
Warm-Up & Exam Questions..............................145
Fossils..146
Antibiotic-Resistant Bacteria............................147
Classification..148
Warm-Up & Exam Questions..............................150

Topic B7 — Ecology

Competition..151
Abiotic and Biotic Factors................................152
Adaptations..154
Food Chains...155
Warm-Up & Exam Questions..............................156
Using Quadrats...157
Using Transects..158
The Water Cycle...159
The Carbon Cycle...160
Warm-Up & Exam Questions..............................161
Exam Questions...162
Biodiversity and Waste Management.................163
Global Warming..165
Deforestation and Land Use.............................167
Maintaining Ecosystems and Biodiversity..........169
Warm-Up & Exam Questions..............................171
Revision Summary for Topics B5-7....................172

Topic C1 — Atomic Structure and the Periodic Table

Atoms 173
Elements 174
Isotopes 175
Compounds 176
Formulas and Equations 177
Warm-Up & Exam Questions 179
Exam Questions 180
Mixtures 181
Chromatography 182
Filtration and Crystallisation 183
Distillation 185
Warm-Up & Exam Questions 187
The History of the Atom 188
Electronic Structure 190
Development of the Periodic Table 191
The Modern Periodic Table 192
Warm-Up & Exam Questions 193
Metals and Non-Metals 194
Group 1 Elements 195
Group 7 Elements 197
Group 0 Elements 199
Warm-Up & Exam Questions 200
Exam Questions 201

Topic C2 — Bonding, Structure and Properties of Matter

Ions 202
Ionic Compounds 205
Warm-Up & Exam Questions 207
Covalent Bonding 208
Warm-Up & Exam Questions 211
Polymers 212
Giant Covalent Structures 213
Allotropes of Carbon 214
Metallic Bonding 216
Warm-Up & Exam Questions 217
States of Matter 218
Warm-Up & Exam Questions 221

Topic C3 — Quantitative Chemistry

Relative Formula Mass 222
The Mole and Mass 223
Warm-Up & Exam Questions 226
The Mole and Equations 227
Concentration and Limiting Reactants 228
Warm-Up & Exam Questions 230

Topic C4 — Chemical Changes

Acids and Bases 231
Strong Acids, Weak Acids and their Reactions ... 232
Warm-Up & Exam Questions 235
Metals and their Reactivity 236
Redox Reactions 239
Warm-Up & Exam Questions 241
Electrolysis 242
Electrolysis of Aqueous Solutions 244
Warm-Up & Exam Questions 246

Topic C5 — Energy Changes

Exothermic and Endothermic Reactions 247
Bond Energies 249
Warm-Up & Exam Questions 251
Revision Summary for Topics C1-5 252

Topic C6 — The Rate and Extent of Chemical Change

Rates of Reaction 253
Factors Affecting Rates of Reaction 254
Measuring Rates of Reaction 256
Rate Experiments 258
Finding Reaction Rates from Graphs 260
Warm-Up & Exam Questions 261
Exam Questions 262
Reversible Reactions 263
Le Chatelier's Principle 265
Warm-Up & Exam Questions 266

Topic C7 — Organic Chemistry

Hydrocarbons 267
Fractional Distillation 269
Uses and Cracking of Crude Oil 270
Warm-Up & Exam Questions............................ 271
Exam Questions.. 272

Topic C8 — Chemical Analysis

Purity and Formulations.................................. 273
Testing for Gases... 274
Paper Chromatography 275
Warm-Up & Exam Questions............................ 277

Topic C9 — Chemistry of the Atmosphere

The Evolution of the Atmosphere 278
Climate Change and Greenhouse Gases 280
Carbon Footprints 282
Air Pollution 284
Warm-Up & Exam Questions............................ 285

Topic C10 — Using Resources

Finite and Renewable Resources...................... 286
Sustainability 287
Recycling 288
Life Cycle Assessments 289
Warm-Up & Exam Questions............................ 291
Potable Water and Water Treatment 292
Warm-Up & Exam Questions............................ 295
Revision Summary for Topics C6-10 296

Topic P1 — Energy

Energy Stores 297
Work Done 298
Kinetic and Potential Energy Stores................. 299
Specific Heat Capacity 300
Investigating Specific Heat Capacity 301
Warm-Up & Exam Questions............................ 302
Conservation of Energy and Power 303
Conduction and Convection............................. 304
Reducing Unwanted Energy Transfers 305
Efficiency 306
Warm-Up & Exam Questions............................ 307
Energy Resources and their Uses 308
Wind and Solar Power..................................... 309
Geothermal and Hydro-electric Power 310
Wave Power and Tidal Barrages 311
Bio-fuels 312
Non-Renewable Resources 313
Trends in Energy Resource Use 314
Warm-Up & Exam Questions............................ 315

Topic P2 — Electricity

Current and Circuit Symbols............................ 316
Resistance 317
Investigating Resistance 318
I-V Characteristics 319
Warm-Up & Exam Questions............................ 320
Circuit Devices.. 321
Sensing Circuits 322
Series Circuits 323
Parallel Circuits 325
Circuits and Resistance 326
Warm-Up & Exam Questions............................ 327
Electricity in the Home 328
Power of Electrical Appliances......................... 329
More on Power.. 330
The National Grid.. 331
Warm-Up & Exam Questions............................ 333

Topic P3 — Particle Model of Matter

Particle Model 334
Density 335
Internal Energy and Changes of State 336
Specific Latent Heat 337
Particle Motion in Gases 338
Warm-Up & Exam Questions 339
Exam Questions 340

Topic P4 — Atomic Structure

Developing the Model of the Atom 341
Isotopes 343
Ionising Radiation 344
Nuclear Equations 345
Half-Life 346
Irradiation and Contamination 348
Warm-Up & Exam Questions 350
Exam Questions 351
Revision Summary for Topics P1-4 352

Topic P5 — Forces

Contact and Non-Contact Forces 353
Weight, Mass and Gravity 354
Resultant Forces 355
More on Forces 357
Warm-Up & Exam Questions 358
Forces and Elasticity 359
Investigating Springs 361
Warm-Up & Exam Questions 363
Distance, Displacement, Speed and Velocity 364
Acceleration 365
Distance-Time Graphs 366
Velocity-Time Graphs 367
Drag 368
Terminal Velocity 369
Warm-Up & Exam Questions 370

Newton's First and Second Laws 371
Inertia and Newton's Third Law 372
Investigating Motion 373
Warm-Up & Exam Questions 375
Stopping Distances 376
Reaction Times 377
Braking Distances 378
Momentum 379
Warm-Up & Exam Questions 380

Topic P6 — Waves

Wave Basics 381
Transverse and Longitudinal Waves 382
Experiments with Waves 383
Refraction 385
Warm-Up & Exam Questions 387
Electromagnetic Waves and Uses of EM Waves 388
Uses of EM Waves 389
Dangers of Electromagnetic Waves 392
Infrared Radiation and Temperature 393
Investigating Emission 394
Warm-Up & Exam Questions 395
Exam Questions 396

Topic P7 — Magnetism and Electromagnetism

Magnets 397
Magnetism 398
Electromagnets 399
Warm-Up & Exam Questions 400
The Motor Effect 401
Electric Motors 403
Warm-Up & Exam Questions 404
Revision Summary for Topics P5-7 405

Practical Skills

Measuring Techniques 406
Safety and Ethics... 409
Setting Up Experiments.. 410
Heating Substances 412
Working with Electronics.. 413
Sampling 414
Comparing Results... 415

Practice Exams

Biology Practice Paper 1 416
Biology Practice Paper 2 428
Chemistry Practice Paper 1 440
Chemistry Practice Paper 2 452
Physics Practice Paper 1 464
Physics Practice Paper 2 477

Answers... 489
Glossary 523
Index 537
The Periodic Table and Physics Equations Sheet................ 542

You'll see **QR codes** throughout the book that you can scan with your smartphone.

A QR code next to a tip box question takes you to a **video** that talks you through solving the question. You can access **all** the videos by scanning this code here.

A QR code on a 'Revision Summary' page takes you to a **Retrieval Quiz** for that topic. You can access **all** the quizzes by scanning this code here.

You can also find the **full set of videos** at cgpbooks.co.uk/GCSEScienceHigher/Videos
and the **full set of quizzes** at cgpbooks.co.uk/GCSEScienceHigher/Quiz

For useful information about **What to Expect in the Exams** and
other exam tips head to cgpbooks.co.uk/GCSEScienceHigher/Exams

---

Published by CGP

From original material by Richard Parsons.

Editors: Emily Garrett, Rob Hayman, Paul Jordin, Sharon Keeley-Holden, Luke Molloy, Rachael Rogers and Sarah Williams.

Contributors: Mike Bossart, Paddy Gannon and Barbara Mascetti.

With thanks to Emily Smith for the copyright research.

Data used to construct a table on page 286 © Crown Copyright, courtesy Forestry Commission (April 2021), licensed under the Open Government Licence v3.0. http://www.nationalarchives.gov.uk/doc/open-government-licence/version/3/

Stopping distance data used on page 376 from the Highway Code. Contains public sector information licensed under the Open Government Licence v3.0. http://www.nationalarchives.gov.uk/doc/open-government-licence/version/3/

With thanks to SCIENCE PHOTO LIBRARY for permission to reproduce the image of a contraceptive implant on page 437.

Renewables data on page 473 contains public sector information licensed under the Open Government Licence v3.0. http://www.nationalarchives.gov.uk/doc/open-government-licence/version/3/

Data used to construct braking distances table on page 485 from the Highway Code. Contains public sector information licensed under the Open Government Licence v3.0. http://www.nationalarchives.gov.uk/doc/open-government-licence/version/3

Printed by Elanders Ltd, Newcastle upon Tyne.
Clipart from Corel®

Illustrations by: Sandy Gardner Artist, email sandy@sandygardner.co.uk

Text, design, layout and original illustrations © Coordination Group Publications Ltd. (CGP) 2021
All rights reserved.

Photocopying more than 5% of this book is not permitted, even if you have a CLA licence.
Extra copies are available from CGP with next day delivery • 0800 1712 712 • www.cgpbooks.co.uk

Working Scientifically

The Scientific Method

*This section **isn't** about how to 'do' science — but it does show you the way **most scientists** work.*

Scientists Come Up With **Hypotheses** — Then **Test** Them

1) Scientists try to explain things. They start by observing something they don't understand.

2) They then come up with a hypothesis — a possible explanation for what they've observed.

3) The next step is to test whether the hypothesis might be right or not. This involves making a prediction based on the hypothesis and testing it by gathering evidence (i.e. data) from investigations. If evidence from experiments backs up a prediction, you're a step closer to figuring out if the hypothesis is true.

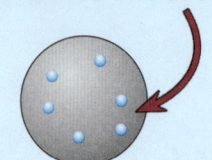

About 100 years ago, scientists hypothesised that atoms looked like this.

Several Scientists Will Test a Hypothesis

1) Normally, scientists share their findings in peer-reviewed journals, or at conferences.

2) Peer-review is where other scientists check results and scientific explanations to make sure they're 'scientific' (e.g. that experiments have been done in a sensible way) before they're published. It helps to detect false claims, but it doesn't mean that findings are correct — just that they're not wrong in any obvious way.

3) Once other scientists have found out about a hypothesis, they'll start basing their own predictions on it and carry out their own experiments. They'll also try to reproduce the original experiments to check the results — and if all the experiments in the world back up the hypothesis, then scientists start to think the hypothesis is true.

4) However, if a scientist does an experiment that doesn't fit with the hypothesis (and other scientists can reproduce the results) then the hypothesis may need to be modified or scrapped altogether.

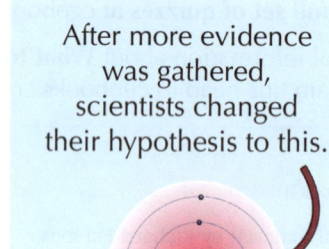

After more evidence was gathered, scientists changed their hypothesis to this.

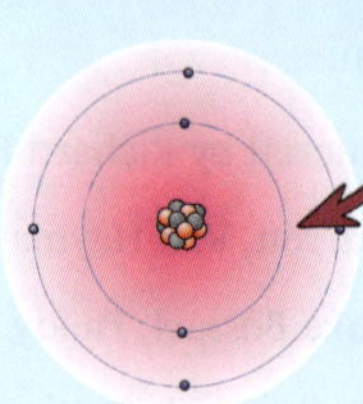

If **All** the **Evidence** Supports a Hypothesis, It's **Accepted** — For Now

1) Accepted hypotheses are often referred to as theories. Our currently accepted theories are the ones that have survived this 'trial by evidence' — they've been tested many times over the years and survived.

2) However, theories never become totally indisputable fact. If new evidence comes along that can't be explained using the existing theory, then the hypothesising and testing is likely to start all over again.

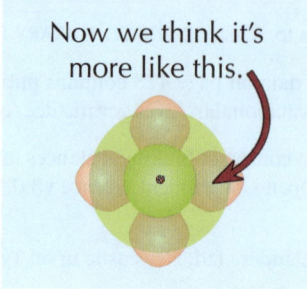

Now we think it's more like this.

Scientific models are constantly being refined...

The scientific method has been developed over time. Aristotle (a Greek philosopher) was the first person to realise that theories need to be based on observations. Muslim scholars then introduced the ideas of creating a hypothesis, testing it, and repeating work to check results.

Working Scientifically

Models and Communication

*Once scientists have made a **new discovery**, they **don't** just keep it to themselves. Oh no. Time to learn about how scientific discoveries are **communicated**, and the **models** that are used to represent theories.*

Theories Can Involve Different Types of Models

1) A representational model is a simplified description or picture of what's going on in real life. Like all models, it can be used to explain observations and make predictions. E.g. the Bohr model of an atom is a simplified way of showing the arrangement of electrons in an atom (see p.189). It can be used to explain trends down groups in the periodic table.

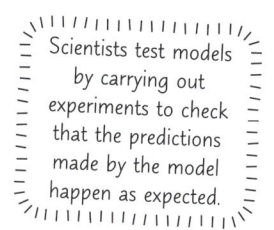
Scientists test models by carrying out experiments to check that the predictions made by the model happen as expected.

2) Computational models use computers to make simulations of complex real-life processes, such as climate change. They're used when there are a lot of different variables (factors that change) to consider, and because you can easily change their design to take into account new data.

3) All models have limitations on what they can explain or predict. E.g. ball and stick models (a type of spatial model) can be used to show how ions are arranged in an ionic compound. One of their limitations is that they don't show the relative sizes of the ions (see p.205).

Scientific Discoveries are Communicated to the General Public

Some scientific discoveries show that people should change their habits, or they might provide ideas that could be developed into new technology. So scientists need to tell the world about their discoveries.

Gene technologies are used in genetic engineering to produce genetically modified crops. Information about these crops needs to be communicated to farmers who might benefit from growing them and to the general public, so they can make informed decisions about the food they buy and eat.

Scientific Evidence can be Presented in a Biased Way

1) Scientific discoveries that are reported in the media (e.g. newspapers or television) aren't peer-reviewed.

2) This means that, even though news stories are often based on data that has been peer-reviewed, the data might be presented in a way that is over-simplified or inaccurate, making it open to misinterpretation.

3) People who want to make a point can sometimes present data in a biased way (sometimes without knowing they're doing it). For example, a scientist might overemphasise a relationship in the data, or a newspaper article might describe details of data supporting an idea without giving any evidence against it.

Companies can present biased data to help sell products...

Sometimes a company may only want you to see half of the story so they present the data in a biased way. For example, a pharmaceutical company may want to encourage you to buy their drugs by telling you about all the positives, but not report the results of any unfavourable studies.

Working Scientifically

Issues Created by Science

*Science has helped us **make progress** in loads of areas, from medicine to space travel. But science still has its **issues**. And it **can't answer everything**, as you're about to find out.*

Scientific Developments are Great, but they can Raise Issues

Scientific knowledge is increased by doing experiments. And this knowledge leads to scientific developments, e.g. new technologies or new advice. These developments can create issues though. For example:

> Economic issues: Society can't always afford to do things scientists recommend (e.g. investing in alternative energy sources) without cutting back elsewhere.

> Social issues: Decisions based on scientific evidence affect people — e.g. should fossil fuels be taxed more highly? Would the effect on people's lifestyles be acceptable?

> Personal issues: Some decisions will affect individuals. For example, someone might support alternative energy, but object if a wind farm is built next to their house.

> Environmental issues: Human activity often affects the natural environment. For example, building a dam to produce electricity will change the local habitat so some species might be displaced. But it will also reduce our need for fossil fuels, so will help to reduce climate change.

Science Can't Answer Every Question — Especially Ethical Ones

1) We don't understand everything. We're always finding out more, but we'll never know all the answers.
2) In order to answer scientific questions, scientists need data to provide evidence for their hypotheses.
3) Some questions can't be answered yet because the data can't currently be collected, or because there's not enough data to support a theory.
4) Eventually, as we get more evidence, we'll answer some of the questions that currently can't be answered, e.g. what the impact of global warming on sea levels will be. But there will always be the "Should we be doing this at all?"-type questions that experiments can't help us to answer...

> Think about new drugs which can be taken to boost your 'brain power'.
> - Some people think they're good as they could improve concentration or memory. New drugs could let people think in ways beyond the powers of normal brains.
> - Other people say they're bad — they could give some people an unfair advantage in exams. And people might be pressured into taking them so that they could work more effectively, and for longer hours.

There are often issues with new scientific developments...
The trouble is, there's often no clear right answer where these issues are concerned. Different people have different views, depending on their priorities. These issues are full of grey areas.

Working Scientifically

Risk

*Scientific discoveries are often great, but they can prove **risky**. With dangers all around, you've got to be aware of hazards — this includes **how likely** they are to **cause harm** and **how serious** the effects may be.*

Nothing is Completely Risk-Free

1) A hazard is something that could potentially cause harm.

2) All hazards have a risk attached to them — this is the chance that the hazard will cause harm.

3) The risks of some things seem pretty obvious, or we've known about them for a while, like the risk of causing acid rain by polluting the atmosphere, or of having a car accident when you're travelling in a car.

4) New technology arising from scientific advances can bring new risks, e.g. scientists are unsure whether nanoparticles that are being used in cosmetics and suncream might be harming the cells in our bodies. These risks need to be considered alongside the benefits of the technology, e.g. improved sun protection.

5) You can estimate the size of a risk based on how many times something happens in a big sample (e.g. 100 000 people) over a given period (e.g. a year). For example, you could assess the risk of a driver crashing by recording how many people in a group of 100 000 drivers crashed their cars over a year.

6) To make decisions about activities that involve hazards, we need to take into account the chance of the hazard causing harm, and how serious the consequences would be if it did. If an activity involves a hazard that's very likely to cause harm, with serious consequences if it does, that activity is considered high risk.

People Make Their Own Decisions About Risk

1) Not all risks have the same consequences, e.g. if you chop veg with a sharp knife you risk cutting your finger, but if you go scuba-diving you risk death. You're much more likely to cut your finger during half an hour of chopping than to die during half an hour of scuba-diving. But most people are happier to accept a higher probability of an accident if the consequences are short-lived and fairly minor.

2) People tend to be more willing to accept a risk if they choose to do something (e.g. go scuba diving), compared to having the risk imposed on them (e.g. having a nuclear power station built next door).

3) People's perception of risk (how risky they think something is) isn't always accurate. They tend to view familiar activities as low-risk and unfamiliar activities as high-risk — even if that's not the case. For example, cycling on roads is often high-risk, but many people are happy to do it because it's a familiar activity. Air travel is actually pretty safe, but a lot of people perceive it as high-risk.

4) People may underestimate the risk of things with long-term or invisible effects, e.g. using tanning beds.

The pros and cons of new technology must be weighed up...
The world's a dangerous place and it's impossible to rule out the chance of an accident altogether. But if you can recognise hazards and take steps to reduce the risks, you're more likely to stay safe.

Working Scientifically

Designing Investigations

*Dig out your lab coat and dust off your badly-scratched safety goggles... it's **investigation time**.*

Evidence Can Support or Disprove a Hypothesis

1) Scientists observe things and come up with hypotheses to test them (see p.2). You need to be able to do the same. For example:

   Observation: People with big feet have spots. Hypothesis: Having big feet causes spots.

2) To determine whether or not a hypothesis is right, you need to do an investigation to gather evidence. To do this, you need to use your hypothesis to make a prediction — something you think will happen that you can test. E.g. people who have bigger feet will have more spots.

3) Investigations are used to see if there are patterns or relationships between two variables, e.g. to see if there's a pattern or relationship between the variables 'number of spots' and 'size of feet'.

Evidence Needs to be Repeatable, Reproducible and Valid

1) Repeatable means that if the same person does an experiment again using the same methods and equipment, they'll get similar results.

2) Reproducible means that if someone else does the experiment, or a different method or piece of equipment is used, the results will still be similar.

3) If data is repeatable and reproducible, it's reliable and scientists are more likely to have confidence in it.

4) Valid results are both repeatable and reproducible AND they answer the original question. They come from experiments that were designed to be a fair test...

Make an Investigation a Fair Test By Controlling the Variables

1) In a lab experiment you usually change one variable and measure how it affects another variable.

2) To make it a fair test, everything else that could affect the results should stay the same — otherwise you can't tell if the thing you're changing is causing the results or not.

3) The variable you CHANGE is called the INDEPENDENT variable.

4) The variable you MEASURE when you change the independent variable is the DEPENDENT variable.

5) The variables that you KEEP THE SAME are called CONTROL variables.

> You could find how temperature affects the rate of an enzyme-controlled reaction. The independent variable is the temperature. The dependent variable is the rate of reaction. Control variables include the concentration and amounts of reactants, pH, the time period you measure, etc.

6) Because you can't always control all the variables, you often need to use a control experiment. This is an experiment that's kept under the same conditions as the rest of the investigation, but doesn't have anything done to it. This is so that you can see what happens when you don't change anything at all.

Working Scientifically

Designing Investigations

The Bigger the Sample Size the Better

1) Data based on small samples isn't as good as data based on large samples. A sample should represent the whole population (i.e. it should share as many of the characteristics in the population as possible) — a small sample can't do that as well. It's also harder to spot anomalies if your sample size is too small.

2) The bigger the sample size the better, but scientists have to be realistic when choosing how big. For example, if you were studying the effects of living near a nuclear power plant, it'd be great to study everyone who lived near a nuclear power plant (a huge sample), but it'd take ages and cost a bomb. It's more realistic to study a thousand people, with a range of ages and races and across both genders.

Your Equipment has to be Right for the Job

1) The measuring equipment you use has to be sensitive enough to measure the changes you're looking for. For example, if you need to measure changes of 1 cm^3 you need to use a measuring cylinder that can measure in 1 cm^3 steps — it'd be no good trying with one that only measures 10 cm^3 steps.

2) The smallest change a measuring instrument can detect is called its resolution. E.g. some mass balances have a resolution of 1 g, some have a resolution of 0.1 g, and some are even more sensitive.

3) Also, equipment needs to be calibrated by measuring a known value. If there's a difference between the measured and known value, you can use this to correct the inaccuracy of the equipment.

Data Should be Repeatable, Reproducible, Accurate and Precise

1) To check repeatability you need to repeat the readings and check that the results are similar. You need to repeat each reading at least three times.

2) To make sure your results are reproducible you can cross check them by taking a second set of readings with another instrument (or a different observer).

3) Your data also needs to be accurate. Really accurate results are those that are really close to the true answer. The accuracy of your results usually depends on your method — you need to make sure you're measuring the right thing and that you don't miss anything that should be included in the measurements. E.g. estimating the amount of gas released from a reaction by counting the bubbles isn't very accurate because you might miss some of the bubbles and they might have different volumes. It's more accurate to measure the volume of gas released using a gas syringe.

4) Your data also needs to be precise. Precise results are ones where the data is all really close to the mean (average) of your repeated results (i.e. not spread out).

Repeat	Data set 1	Data set 2
1	12	11
2	14	17
3	13	14
Mean	13	14

Data set 1 is more precise than data set 2.

Working Scientifically

Designing Investigations

You Need to Look out for **Errors** and **Anomalous Results**

1) The results of your experiment will always vary a bit because of random errors — unpredictable differences caused by things like human errors in measuring. The errors when you make a reading from a ruler are random. You have to estimate or round the distance when it's between two marks — so sometimes your figure will be a bit above the real one, and sometimes it will be a bit below.

2) You can reduce the effect of random errors by taking repeat readings and finding the mean. This will make your results more precise.

3) If a measurement is wrong by the same amount every time, it's called a systematic error. For example, if you measured from the very end of your ruler instead of from the 0 cm mark every time, all your measurements would be a bit small. Repeating the experiment in the exact same way and calculating a mean won't correct a systematic error.

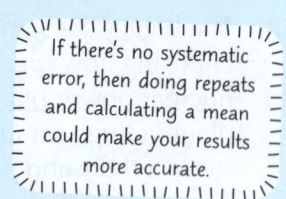

If there's no systematic error, then doing repeats and calculating a mean could make your results more accurate.

4) Just to make things more complicated, if a systematic error is caused by using equipment that isn't zeroed properly, it's called a zero error. For example, if a mass balance always reads 1 gram before you put anything on it, all your measurements will be 1 gram too heavy.

5) You can compensate for some systematic errors if you know about them, e.g. if a mass balance always reads 1 gram before you put anything on it, you can subtract 1 gram from all your results.

6) Sometimes you get a result that doesn't fit in with the rest at all. This is called an anomalous result. You should investigate it and try to work out what happened. If you can work out what happened (e.g. you measured something wrong) you can ignore it when processing your results.

Investigations Can be **Hazardous**

1) Hazards from science experiments might include:

- Microorganisms, e.g. some bacteria can make you ill.
- Chemicals, e.g. sulfuric acid can burn your skin.
- Fire, e.g. an unattended Bunsen burner is a fire hazard.
- Electricity, e.g. faulty electrical equipment could give you a shock.

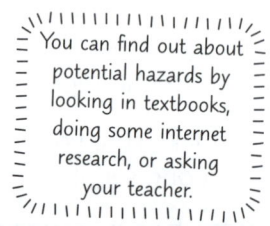

You can find out about potential hazards by looking in textbooks, doing some internet research, or asking your teacher.

2) Part of planning an investigation is making sure that it's safe.

3) You should always make sure that you identify all the hazards that you might encounter. Then you should think of ways of reducing the risks from the hazards you've identified. For example:

- If you're working with sulfuric acid, always wear gloves and safety goggles. This will reduce the risk of the acid coming into contact with your skin and eyes.
- If you're using a Bunsen burner, stand it on a heat proof mat. This will reduce the risk of starting a fire.

 **Designing an investigation is an involved process...**
Collecting data is what investigations are all about. Designing a good investigation is really important to make sure that any data collected is accurate, precise, repeatable and reproducible.

Working Scientifically

Processing Data

*Processing your data means doing some **calculations** with it to make it **more useful**.*

Data Needs to be Organised

1) Tables are dead useful for organising data.
2) When you draw a table use a ruler and make sure each column has a heading (including the units).

There are Different Ways of Processing Your Data

1) When you've done repeats of an experiment you should always calculate the mean (average). To do this add together all the data values and divide by the total number of values in the sample.

2) You might also need to calculate the range (how spread out the data is). To do this find the largest number and subtract the smallest number from it.

Ignore anomalous results when calculating the mean and the range.

EXAMPLE The results of an experiment to find the volume of gas produced in an enzyme-controlled reaction are shown below. Calculate the mean volume and the range.

Repeat 1 (cm^3)	Repeat 2 (cm^3)	Repeat 3 (cm^3)	Mean (cm^3)	Range (cm^3)
28	37	32	(28 + 37 + 32) ÷ 3 = 32	(37 − 28) = 9

3) You might also need to calculate the median or mode (two more types of average). To calculate the median, put all your data in numerical order — the median is the middle value. The number that appears most often in a data set is the mode.

If you have an even number of values, the median is halfway between the middle two values.

E.g. If you have the data set: 1 2 1 1 3 4 2
The median is: 1 1 1 2 2 3 4. The mode is 1 because 1 appears most often.

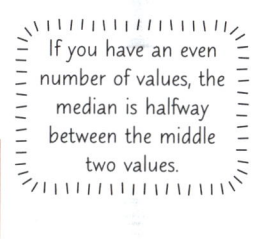

Round to the Lowest Number of Significant Figures

The first significant figure of a number is the first digit that's not zero. The second and third significant figures come straight after (even if they're zeros). You should be aware of significant figures in calculations.

1) In any calculation where you need to round, you should round the answer to the lowest number of significant figures (s.f.) given.
2) Remember to write down how many significant figures you've rounded to after your answer.
3) If your calculation has multiple steps, only round the final answer, or it won't be as accurate.

EXAMPLE The mass of a solid is 0.24 g and its volume is 0.715 cm^3. Calculate the density of the solid.

Density = 0.24 g ÷ 0.715 cm^3 = 0.33566... = 0.34 g/cm^3 (2 s.f.)

2 s.f.   3 s.f.   Final answer should be rounded to 2 s.f.

Don't forget your calculator...

In the exam you could be given some data and be expected to process it in some way. Make sure you keep an eye on significant figures in your answers and always write down your working.

Working Scientifically

Presenting Data

Once you've processed your data, e.g. by calculating the mean, you can present your results in a nice **chart** or **graph**. This will help you to **spot any patterns** in your data.

If Your Data Comes in Categories, Present It in a Bar Chart

1) If the independent variable is <u>categoric</u> (comes in distinct categories, e.g. flower colour, blood group) you should use a <u>bar chart</u> to display the data.

2) You also use them if the independent variable is <u>discrete</u> (the data can be counted in chunks, where there's no in-between value, e.g. number of protons is discrete because you can't have half a proton).

3) There are some <u>golden rules</u> you need to follow for <u>drawing</u> bar charts:

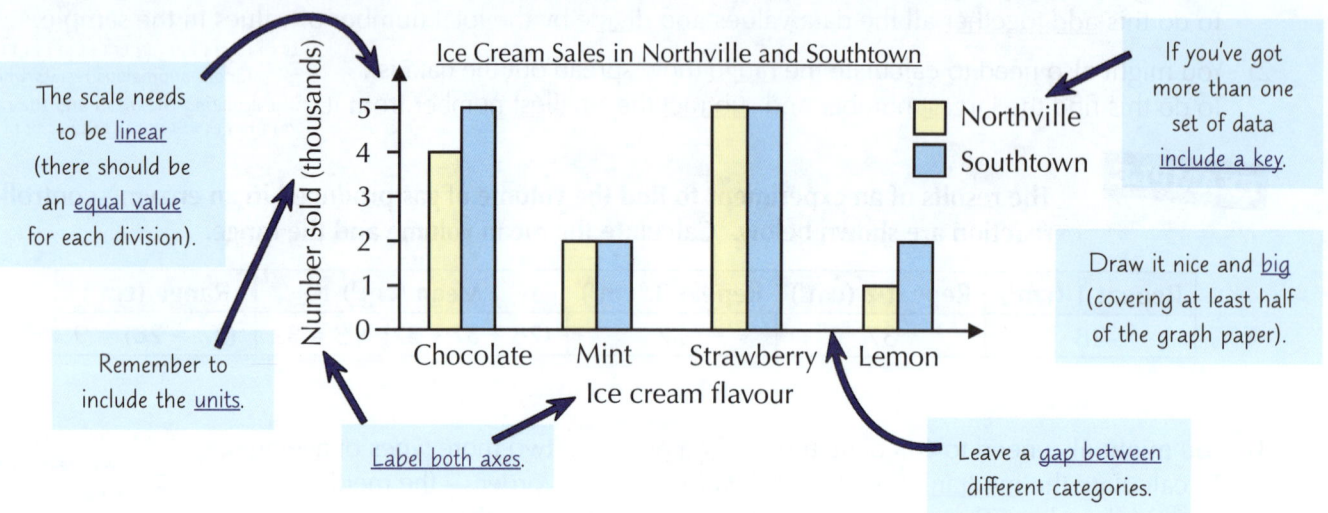

The scale needs to be <u>linear</u> (there should be an <u>equal value</u> for each division).

Remember to include the <u>units</u>.

<u>Label both axes</u>.

If you've got more than one set of data <u>include a key</u>.

Draw it nice and <u>big</u> (covering at least half of the graph paper).

Leave a <u>gap between</u> different categories.

If Your Data is Continuous, Plot a Graph

1) If both variables are <u>continuous</u> (numerical data that can have any value within a range, e.g. length, volume, temperature) you should use a <u>graph</u> to display the data.

2) Here are the <u>rules</u> for plotting points on a graph:

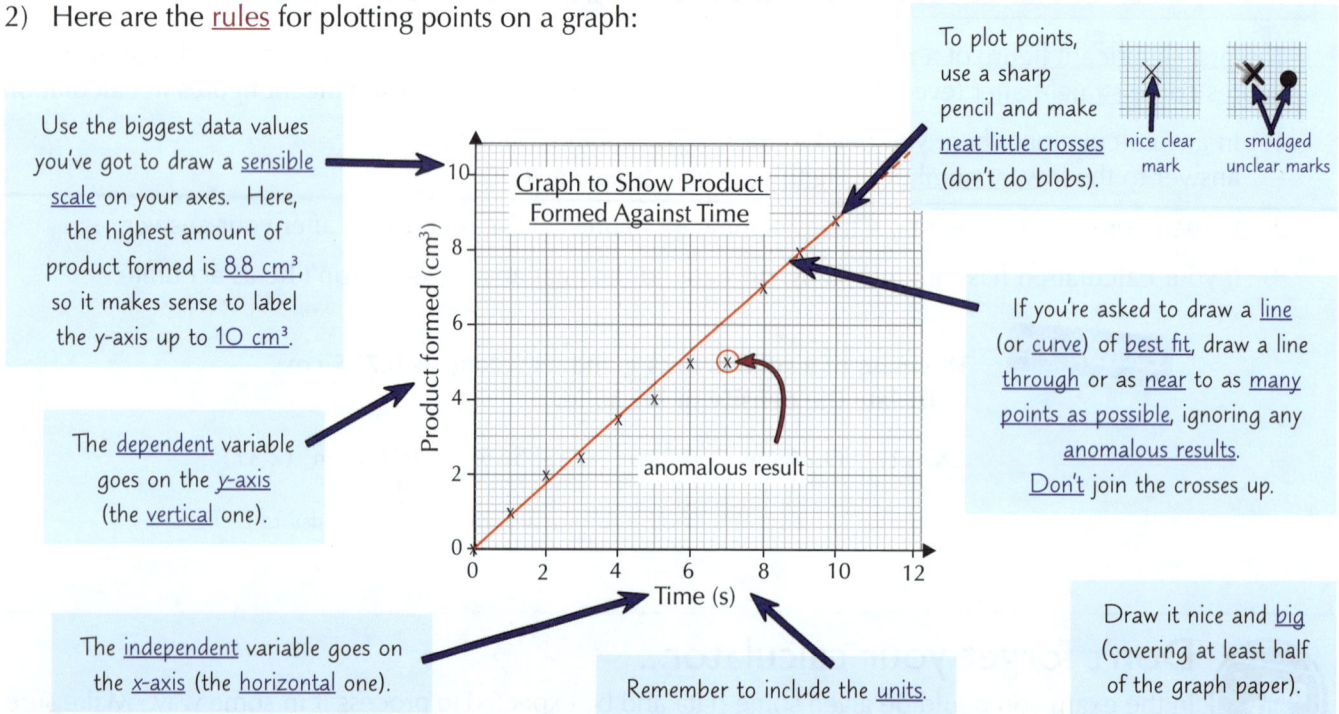

Use the biggest data values you've got to draw a <u>sensible scale</u> on your axes. Here, the highest amount of product formed is <u>8.8 cm³</u>, so it makes sense to label the y-axis up to <u>10 cm³</u>.

The <u>dependent</u> variable goes on the <u>y-axis</u> (the <u>vertical</u> one).

The <u>independent</u> variable goes on the <u>x-axis</u> (the <u>horizontal</u> one).

Remember to include the <u>units</u>.

To plot points, use a sharp pencil and make <u>neat little crosses</u> (don't do blobs). nice clear mark / smudged unclear marks

If you're asked to draw a <u>line</u> (or <u>curve</u>) of <u>best fit</u>, draw a line <u>through</u> or as <u>near</u> to as <u>many points as possible</u>, ignoring any <u>anomalous results</u>. <u>Don't</u> join the crosses up.

Draw it nice and <u>big</u> (covering at least half of the graph paper).

Working Scientifically

More on Graphs

*Graph's aren't just fun to plot, they're also really useful for showing **trends** in your data.*

Graphs Can Give You a Lot of Information About Your Data

1) The gradient (slope) of a graph tells you how quickly the dependent variable changes if you change the independent variable.

$$\text{gradient} = \frac{\text{change in } y}{\text{change in } x}$$

You can use this method to calculate any rates from a graph, not just the rate of a reaction. Just remember that a rate is how much something changes over time, so x needs to be the time.

The graph below shows the volume of gas produced in a reaction against time. The graph is linear (it's a straight line graph), so you can simply calculate the gradient of the line to find out the rate of reaction.

1) To calculate the gradient, pick two points on the line that are easy to read and a good distance apart.

2) Draw a line down from one of the points and a line across from the other to make a triangle. The line drawn down the side of the triangle is the change in y and the line across the bottom is the change in x.

Change in y = 6.8 − 2.0 = 4.8 cm   Change in x = 5.2 − 1.6 = 3.6 s

$$\text{Rate} = \text{gradient} = \frac{\text{change in } y}{\text{change in } x} = \frac{4.8 \text{ cm}^3}{3.6 \text{ s}} = 1.3 \text{ cm}^3/\text{s} \text{ or } 1.3 \text{ cm}^3\text{s}^{-1}$$

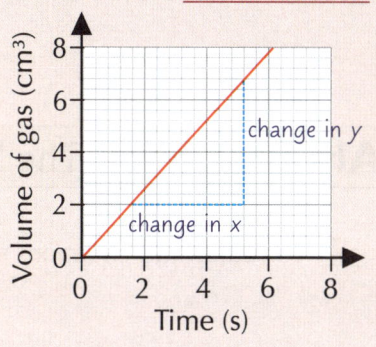

The units of the gradient are (units of y)/(units of x). cm^3/s can also be written as cm^3s^{-1}.

2) If you've got a curved graph, you can find the rate at any point by drawing a tangent — a straight line that touches a single point on a curve. You can then find the gradient of the tangent in the usual way, to give you the rate at that point.

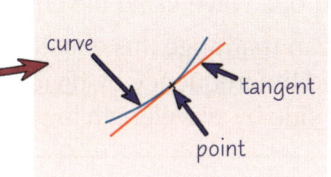

3) The intercept of a graph is where the line of best fit crosses one of the axes. The x-intercept is where the line of best fit crosses the x-axis and the y-intercept is where it crosses the y-axis.

Graphs Show the Relationship Between Two Variables

1) You can get three types of correlation (relationship) between variables:

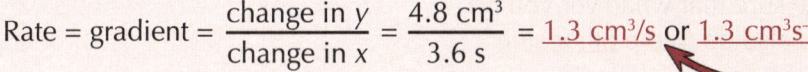

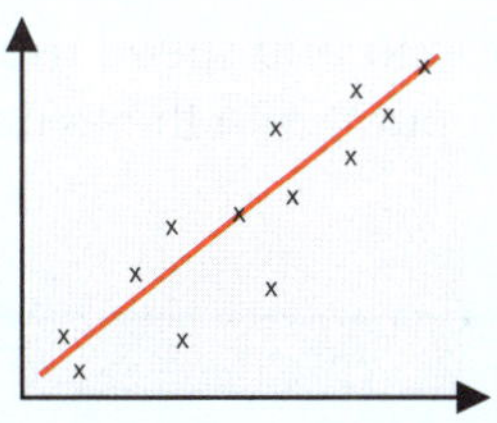

POSITIVE correlation: as one variable increases the other increases.

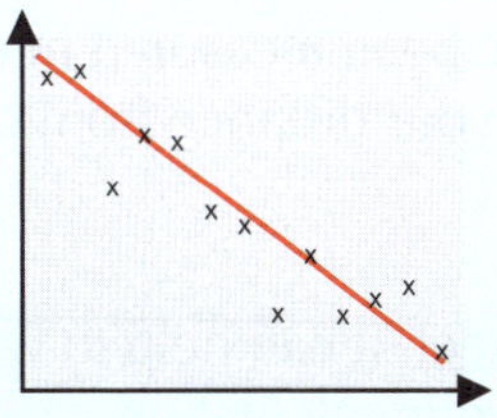

INVERSE (negative) correlation: as one variable increases the other decreases.

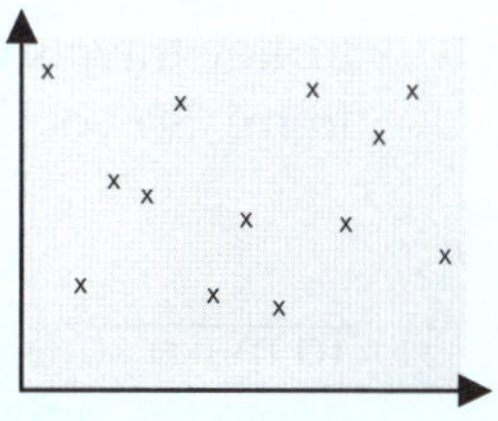

NO correlation: no relationship between the two variables.

2) Just because there's correlation, it doesn't mean the change in one variable is causing the change in the other — there might be other factors involved (see page 14).

Working Scientifically

Units

*Graphs and maths skills are all very well, but the numbers don't mean much if you don't get the **units** right.*

S.I. Units Are Used All Round the World

1) It wouldn't be all that useful if I defined volume in terms of bath tubs, you defined it in terms of egg-cups and my pal Fred defined it in terms of balloons — we'd never be able to compare our data.

2) To stop this happening, scientists have come up with a set of standard units, called S.I. units, that all scientists use to measure their data. Here are some S.I. units you'll see in GCSE Science:

Quantity	S.I. Base Unit
mass	kilogram, kg
length	metre, m
time	second, s
amount of substance	mole, mol
temperature	kelvin, K

Always Check The Values Used in Equations Have the Right Units

1) Formulas and equations show relationships between variables.

2) To rearrange an equation, make sure that whatever you do to one side of the equation you also do to the other side.

> For example, you can find the speed of a wave using the equation: ⟶ wave speed = frequency × wavelength
> You can rearrange this equation to find the frequency by dividing each side by wavelength to give: ⟶ frequency = wave speed ÷ wavelength

3) To use a formula, you need to know the values of all but one of the variables. Substitute the values you do know into the formula, and do the calculation to work out the final variable.

4) Always make sure the values you put into an equation or formula have the right units. For example, you might have done an experiment to find the speed of a trolley. The distance the trolley travels will probably have been measured in cm, but the equation to find speed uses distance in m. So you'll have to convert your distance from cm to m before you put it into the equation.

5) To make sure your units are correct, it can help to write down the units on each line of your calculation.

S.I. units help scientists to compare data...
You can only really compare things if they're in the same units. E.g. if the rate of blood flow was measured in ml/min in one vein and in l/day in another vein, it'd be hard to know which was faster.

Working Scientifically

Converting Units

*You can **convert units** using **scaling prefixes**. This can save you from having to write a lot of 0's...*

Scaling Prefixes Can Be Used for Large and Small Quantities

1) Quantities come in a huge range of sizes. For example, the volume of a swimming pool might be around 2 000 000 000 cm³, while the volume of a cup is around 250 cm³.

2) To make the size of numbers more manageable, larger or smaller units are used. These are the S.I. base units (e.g. metres) with a prefix in front:

Prefix	tera (T)	giga (G)	mega (M)	kilo (k)	deci (d)	centi (c)	milli (m)	micro (μ)	nano (n)
Multiple of Unit	10^{12}	10^{9}	1 000 000 (10^{6})	1000	0.1	0.01	0.001	0.000001 (10^{-6})	10^{-9}

3) These prefixes tell you how much bigger or smaller a unit is than the base unit. So one kilometre is one thousand metres.

4) To swap from one unit to another, all you need to know is what number you have to divide or multiply by to get from the original unit to the new unit — this is called the conversion factor.

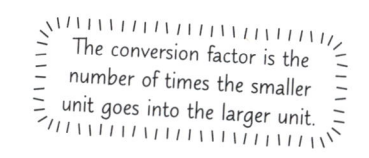

The conversion factor is the number of times the smaller unit goes into the larger unit.

- To go from a bigger unit (like m) to a smaller unit (like cm), you multiply by the conversion factor.
- To go from a smaller unit (like g) to a bigger unit (like kg), you divide by the conversion factor.

5) Here are some conversions that'll be useful for GCSE Science:

Length can have lots of units including mm, μm and nm.

mm ⇄ μm ⇄ nm (× 1000 / ÷ 1000)

Mass can have units of kg and g.

kg ⇄ g (× 1000 / ÷ 1000)

Volume can have units of m³, dm³ and cm³.

m³ ⇄ dm³ ⇄ cm³ (× 1000 / ÷ 1000)

Energy can have units of J and kJ.

kJ ⇄ J (× 1000 / ÷ 1000)

MATHS TIP — To convert from bigger units to smaller units...

...multiply by the conversion factor, and to convert from smaller units to bigger units, divide by the conversion factor. Don't go getting this the wrong way round or you'll get some odd answers.

Drawing Conclusions

*Once you've carried out an experiment and processed your data, it's time to work out **what your data shows**.*

You Can **Only Conclude** What the Data Shows and **No More**

1) Drawing conclusions might seem pretty straightforward — you just look at your data and say what pattern or relationship you see between the dependent and independent variables.

The table on the right shows the rate of a reaction in the presence of two different catalysts:

Catalyst	Rate of Reaction / cm³/s
A	13.5
B	19.5
No catalyst	5.5

CONCLUSION: Catalyst B makes this reaction go faster than catalyst A.

2) But you've got to be really careful that your conclusion matches the data you've got and doesn't go any further.

You can't conclude that catalyst B increases the rate of any other reaction more than catalyst A — the results might be completely different.

3) You also need to be able to use your results to justify your conclusion (i.e. back up your conclusion with some specific data).

The rate of this reaction was 6 cm³/s faster using catalyst B compared with catalyst A.

4) When writing a conclusion you need to refer back to the original hypothesis and say whether the data supports it or not:

The hypothesis for this experiment might have been that catalyst B would make the reaction go quicker than catalyst A. If so, the data supports the hypothesis.

Correlation **DOES NOT** Mean **Cause**

If two things are correlated (i.e. there's a relationship between them) it doesn't necessarily mean a change in one variable is causing the change in the other — this is REALLY IMPORTANT — DON'T FORGET IT. There are three possible reasons for a correlation:

1) CHANCE: It might seem strange, but two things can show a correlation purely due to chance.

For example, one study might find a correlation between people's hair colour and how good they are at frisbee. But other scientists don't get a correlation when they investigate it — the results of the first study are just a fluke.

2) LINKED BY A 3RD VARIABLE: A lot of the time it may look as if a change in one variable is causing a change in the other, but it isn't — a third variable links the two things.

For example, there's a correlation between water temperature and shark attacks. This isn't because warmer water makes sharks crazy. Instead, they're linked by a third variable — the number of people swimming (more people swim when the water's hotter, and with more people in the water you get more shark attacks).

3) CAUSE: Sometimes a change in one variable does cause a change in the other. You can only conclude that a correlation is due to cause when you've controlled all the variables that could affect the result.

For example, there's a correlation between smoking and lung cancer. This is because chemicals in tobacco smoke cause lung cancer. This conclusion was only made once other variables (such as age and exposure to other things that cause cancer) had been controlled.

Uncertainty

*Uncertainty is how sure you can really be about your data. There's a little bit of **maths** to do, and also a formula to learn. But don't worry too much — it's no more than a simple bit of subtraction and division.*

Uncertainty is the Amount of Error Your Measurements Might Have

1) When you repeat a measurement, you often get a slightly different figure each time you do it due to random error (see page 8). This means that each result has some uncertainty to it.

2) The measurements you make will also have some uncertainty in them due to limits in the resolution of the equipment you use (see page 7).

3) This all means that the mean of a set of results will also have some uncertainty to it. You can calculate the uncertainty of a mean result using the equation:

$$\text{uncertainty} = \frac{\text{range}}{2}$$

The range is the largest value minus the smallest value (see p.9).

4) The larger the range, the less precise your results are and the more uncertainty there will be in your results. Uncertainties are shown using the '±' symbol.

EXAMPLE

The table below shows the results of a respiration experiment to determine the volume of carbon dioxide produced. Calculate the uncertainty of the mean.

Repeat	1	2	3	mean
Volume of CO_2 produced (cm^3)	20.1	19.8	20.0	20.0

1) First work out the range:

   Range = 20.1 − 19.8 = 0.300 cm^3

2) Use the range to find the uncertainty:

   Uncertainty = range ÷ 2 = 0.300 ÷ 2 = 0.150 cm^3

   So the uncertainty of the mean = 20.0 ± 0.150 cm^3

5) Measuring a greater amount of something helps to reduce uncertainty.

> For example, in a rate of reaction experiment, measuring the amount of product formed over a longer period compared to a shorter period will reduce the uncertainty in your results.

The smaller the uncertainty, the more precise your results...

Remember that equation for uncertainty. You never know when you might need it — you could be expected to use it in the exams. You need to make sure all the data is in the same units though. For example, if you had some measurements in metres, and some in centimetres, you'd need to convert them all into either metres or centimetres before you set about calculating uncertainty.

Working Scientifically

Evaluations

*Hurrah! The end of another investigation. Well, now you have to work out all the things you did **wrong**. That's what **evaluations** are all about I'm afraid. Best get cracking with this page...*

Evaluations — Describe How Investigations Could be Improved

An evaluation is a critical analysis of the whole investigation.

1) You should comment on the method — was it valid? Did you control all the other variables to make it a fair test?

2) Comment on the quality of the results — was there enough evidence to reach a valid conclusion? Were the results repeatable, reproducible, accurate and precise?

3) Were there any anomalous results? If there were none then say so. If there were any, try to explain them — were they caused by errors in measurement? Were there any other variables that could have affected the results? You should comment on the level of uncertainty in your results too.

4) All this analysis will allow you to say how confident you are that your conclusion is right.

5) Then you can suggest any changes to the method that would improve the quality of the results, so that you could have more confidence in your conclusion. For example, you might suggest changing the way you controlled a variable, or increasing the number of measurements you took. Taking more measurements at narrower intervals could give you a more accurate result. For example:

> Enzymes have an optimum temperature (a temperature at which they work best). Say you do an experiment to find an enzyme's optimum temperature and take measurements at 10 °C, 20 °C, 30 °C, 40 °C and 50 °C. The results of this experiment tell you the optimum is 40 °C. You could then repeat the experiment, taking more measurements around 40 °C to a get a more accurate value for the optimum.

6) You could also make more predictions based on your conclusion, then further experiments could be carried out to test them.

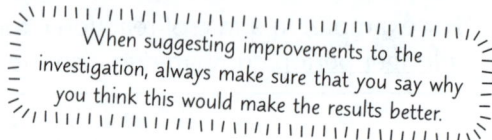
When suggesting improvements to the investigation, always make sure that you say why you think this would make the results better.

Always look for ways to improve your investigations

So there you have it — Working Scientifically. Make sure you know this stuff like the back of your hand. It's not just in the lab or the field, when you're carrying out your groundbreaking investigations, that you'll need to know how to work scientifically. You can be asked about it in the exams as well. So swot up...

Working Scientifically

Topic B1 — Cell Biology

Cells

*When someone first peered down a microscope at a slice of cork and drew the **boxes** they saw, little did they know that they'd seen the **building blocks** of every organism on the planet...*

Organisms can be Prokaryotes or Eukaryotes

1) All living things are made of cells.

2) Cells can be either prokaryotic or eukaryotic. Eukaryotic cells are complex and include all animal and plant cells. Prokaryotic cells are smaller and simpler, e.g. bacteria (see next page).

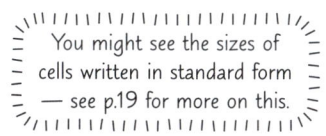
You might see the sizes of cells written in standard form — see p.19 for more on this.

3) Eukaryotes are organisms that are made up of eukaryotic cells.

4) A prokaryote is a prokaryotic cell (it's a single-celled organism).

Plant and Animal Cells have Similarities and Differences

Animal Cells

The different parts of a cell are called subcellular structures.
Most animal cells have the following subcellular structures — make sure you know them all:

1) Nucleus — contains genetic material that controls the activities of the cell.

2) Mitochondria — these are where most of the reactions for aerobic respiration take place (see page 100). Respiration transfers energy that the cell needs to work.

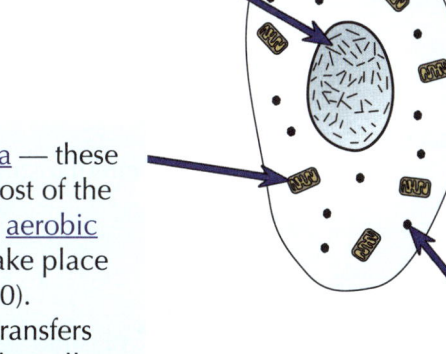

3) Cytoplasm — gel-like substance where most of the chemical reactions happen. It contains enzymes (see page 42) that control these chemical reactions.

4) Cell membrane — holds the cell together and controls what goes in and out.

5) Ribosomes — these are where proteins are made in the cell.

Subcellular structures are all the different parts of a cell

Make sure you get to grips with the different subcellular structures that animal cells contain before you move on to the next page. There are more subcellular structures coming up that you need to know...

Cells

Plant Cells

Plant cells usually have all the bits that animal cells have, plus a few extra things that animal cells don't have:

The cells of algae (e.g. seaweed) also have a rigid cell wall and chloroplasts.

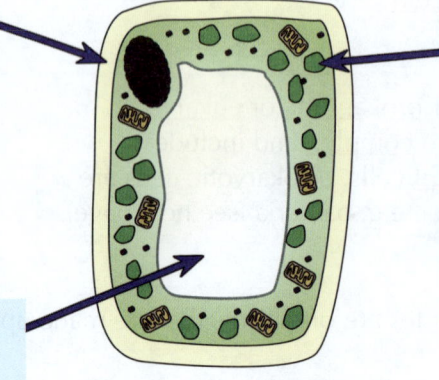

1) Rigid cell wall — made of cellulose. It supports the cell and strengthens it.

2) Chloroplasts — these are where photosynthesis occurs, which makes food for the plant (see page 89). They contain a green substance called chlorophyll, which absorbs the light needed for photosynthesis.

3) Permanent vacuole — contains cell sap, a weak solution of sugar and salts.

You could get asked to estimate the area of a subcellular structure. If you do, treat it as a regular shape. For example, if it's close to a rectangle, use the area formula 'area = length × width'.

Bacterial Cells Are Much Smaller

1) Bacteria are prokaryotes.
2) Bacterial cells don't have a 'true' nucleus — instead they have a single circular strand of DNA that floats freely in the cytoplasm.
3) They may also contain one or more small rings of DNA called plasmids.
4) Bacteria don't have chloroplasts or mitochondria.

Here's what a bacterial cell might look like:

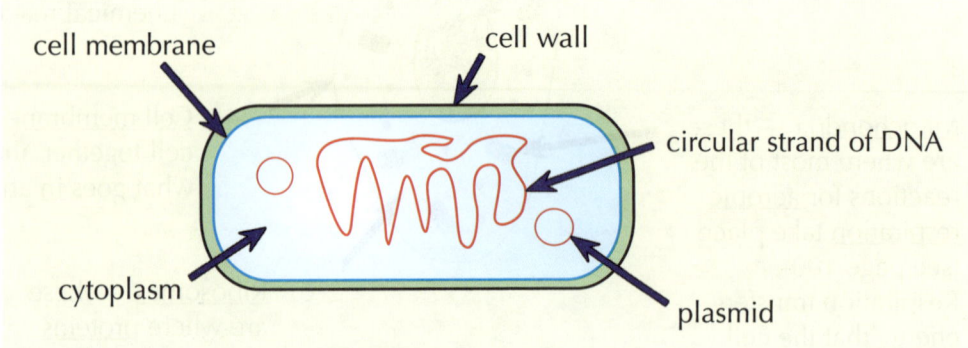

There's quite a bit to learn in biology — but that's life, I guess...

REVISION TIP: On these pages are a typical animal cell, plant cell and bacterial cell. Make sure you're familiar with all their structures. A good way to check that you know what all the bits and pieces are is to copy out the diagrams and see if you can remember all the labels. No cheating.

Topic B1 — Cell Biology

Microscopy

Microscopes are pretty important for biology. There's a lot you need to know about them...

Cells are **Studied** Using **Microscopes**

1) Microscopes let us see things that we can't see with the naked eye. The microscopy techniques we can use have developed over the years as technology and knowledge have improved.
2) Light microscopes use light and lenses to form an image of a specimen and magnify it (make it look bigger). They let us see individual cells and large subcellular structures, like nuclei.
3) Electron microscopes use electrons instead of light to form an image. They have a much higher magnification than light microscopes.
4) They also have a higher resolution. (Resolution is the ability to distinguish between two points, so a higher resolution gives a sharper image.)
5) Electron microscopes let us see much smaller things in more detail, like the internal structure of mitochondria and chloroplasts. They even let us see tinier things like ribosomes and plasmids.

See pages 20-21 for how to use a light microscope.

You Need to be Able to Use the **Formula** for **Magnification**

You can calculate the magnification of an image using this formula:

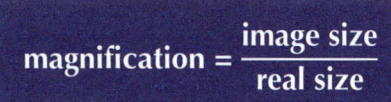

Both image size and real size should have the same units. If they don't, you'll need to convert them first (see page 13).

 A specimen is 50 μm wide. Calculate the width of the image of the specimen under a magnification of × 100. Give your answer in mm.

1) Rearrange the formula.   image size = magnification × real size
2) Fill in the values you know.   image size = 100 × 50
3) Remember the units in your answer.   = 5000 μm
4) Convert the units.   = 5 mm

Remember, to convert from micrometres (μm) to millimetres (mm), you need to divide by 1000 (see p.13). E.g. 5000 μm ÷ 1000 = 5 mm

You Need to Know How to Work With Numbers in **Standard Form**

1) As microscopes can see such tiny objects, sometimes it's useful to write numbers in standard form.
2) This is where you change very big or small numbers with lots of zeros into something more manageable, e.g. 0.017 can be written 1.7×10^{-2}.
3) To do this you just need to move the decimal point left or right.
4) The number of places the decimal point moves is then represented by a power of 10 — this is positive if the decimal point's moved to the left, and negative if it's moved to the right.

 A mitochondrion is approximately 0.0025 mm long. Write this figure in standard form.

1) The first number needs to be between 1 and 10 so the decimal point needs to move after the '2'.
2) Count how many places the decimal point has moved — this is the power of 10. Don't forget the minus sign because the decimal point has moved right.

0.0025

2.5×10^{-3}

Check the units used in that equation are both the same

Q1 A cheek cell is viewed under a microscope with × 40 magnification. The image of the cell is 2.4 mm wide. Calculate the real width of the cheek cell. Give your answer in μm. [2 marks]

Topic B1 — Cell Biology

Microscopy

It's all very well knowing what microscopes *do* — you also have to know how to actually **use** one.

You Need to **Prepare** Your **Slide**

If you want to look at a specimen (e.g. plant or animal cells) under a light microscope, you need to put it on a microscope slide first. A slide is a strip of clear glass or plastic onto which the specimen is mounted. For example, here's how to prepare a slide to view onion cells:

1) Add a drop of water to the middle of a clean slide.

2) Cut up an onion and separate it out into layers. Use tweezers to peel off some epidermal tissue from the bottom of one of the layers.

3) Using the tweezers, place the epidermal tissue into the water on the slide.

4) Add a drop of iodine solution. Iodine solution is a stain. Stains are used to highlight objects in a cell by adding colour to them.

5) Place a cover slip (a square of thin, transparent plastic or glass) on top. To do this, stand the cover slip upright on the slide, next to the water droplet. Then carefully tilt and lower it so it covers the specimen. Try not to get any air bubbles under there — they'll obstruct your view of the specimen.

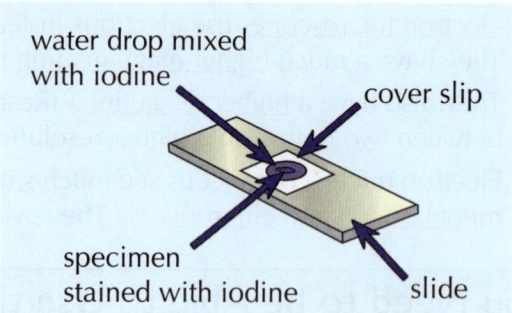

Know the Parts of a **Light Microscope**

To look at your prepared slides, you need to know how to use a light microscope. Here are the main parts you'll use:

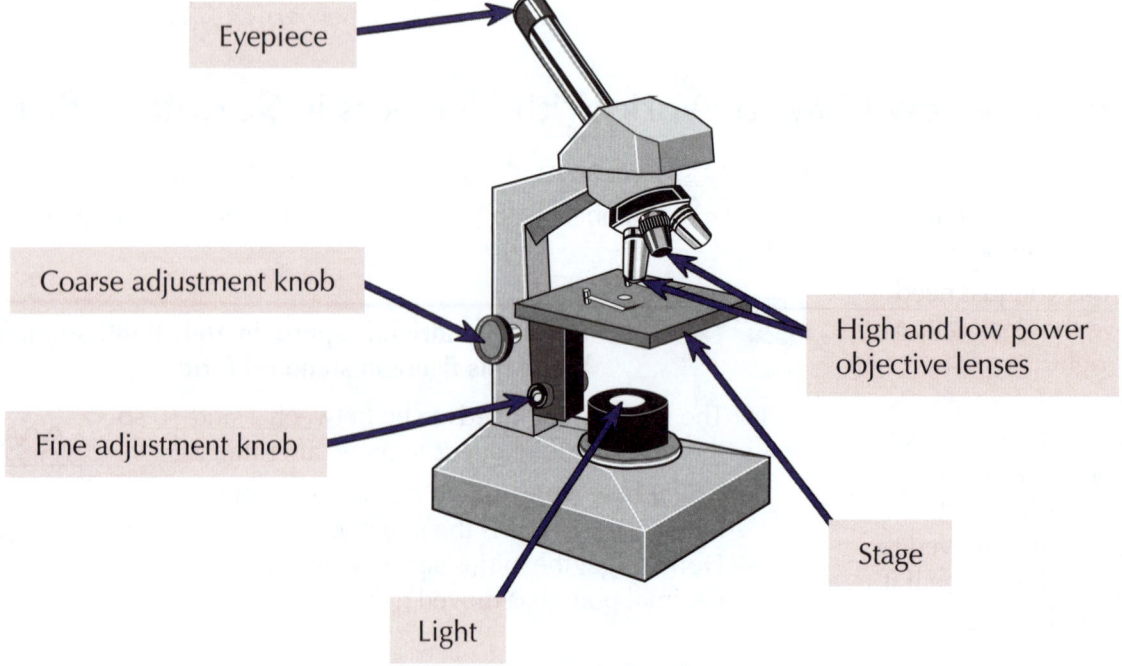

Stains can make subcellular structures easier to see

Carry on to the next page for how to use the microscope above to view your specimen.

Topic B1 — Cell Biology

Microscopy

Use a **Light Microscope** to Look at Your **Slide**

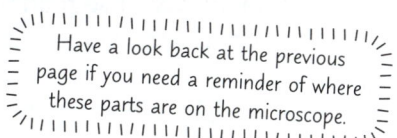
Have a look back at the previous page if you need a reminder of where these parts are on the microscope.

1) Clip the slide you've prepared onto the stage.

2) Select the lowest-powered objective lens (i.e. the one that produces the lowest magnification).

3) Use the coarse adjustment knob to move the stage up to just below the objective lens.

4) Look down the eyepiece. Use the coarse adjustment knob to move the stage downwards until the image is roughly in focus.

5) Adjust the focus with the fine adjustment knob, until you get a clear image of what's on the slide.

6) If you need to see the slide with greater magnification, swap to a higher-powered objective lens and refocus.

Draw Your Observations **Neatly** with a **Pencil**

1) Draw what you see under the microscope using a pencil with a sharp point.
2) Make sure your drawing takes up at least half of the space available and that it is drawn with clear, unbroken lines.
3) Your drawing should not include any colouring or shading.
4) If you are drawing cells, the subcellular structures should be drawn in proportion.
5) Remember to include a title of what you were observing and write down the magnification that it was observed under.
6) Label the important features of your drawing (e.g. nucleus, chloroplasts), using straight, uncrossed lines.

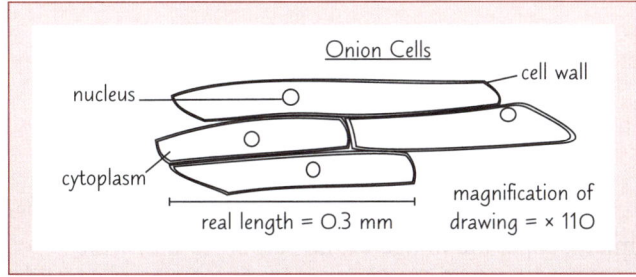

You can work out the real size of a cell by counting the number of cells in 1 mm of the sample (see p.408). You can work out the magnification of your drawing using this formula:
magnification = length of drawing of cell ÷ real length of cell.
So here, magnification = 33 mm ÷ 0.3 mm = × 110.

Your microscope might look a bit different
The appearance of light microscopes can vary (e.g. they might have two eyepieces rather than one) but they should have the same basic features shown on the previous page.

Topic B1 — Cell Biology

Warm-Up & Exam Questions

So, hopefully you've read the last five pages. But could you cope if a question on cells or microscopes came up in the exam? With amazing new technology we can simulate that very situation...

Warm-Up Questions

1) Name the subcellular structures where aerobic respiration takes place.
2) Give three ways in which animal cells are different from plant cells.
3) Give two differences in structure between prokaryotic and eukaryotic cells.
4) What type of microscope should be used to look at the internal structure of chloroplasts?
5) Write the number 0.00045 μm in standard form.

Exam Questions

1 Which of the following subcellular structures would you not expect to find in a prokaryotic cell? Tick **one** box. *(Grade 4-6)*

☐ plasmid   ☐ nucleus   ☐ cell wall   ☐ cell membrane

[1 mark]

2 **Figure 1** shows a typical plant cell. *(Grade 4-6)*

Figure 1

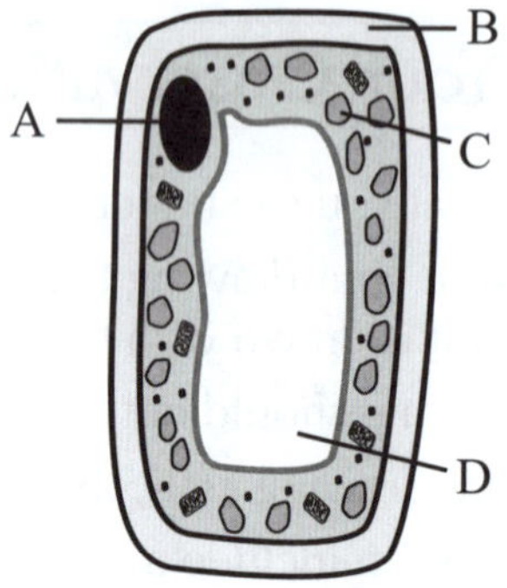

2.1 Which label points to a chloroplast? Tick **one** box.

☐ A   ☐ B   ☐ C   ☐ D

[1 mark]

2.2 What is the function of a chloroplast?

[1 mark]

2.3 **Figure 1** also shows ribosomes.
What is the function of a ribosome?

[1 mark]

PRACTICAL

3 A light microscope can be used to observe a layer of onion cells on a slide. *(Grade 6-7)*

3.1* Describe how you would use a light microscope to view onion cells.
Include how you would prepare the slide.

[6 marks]

3.2 When the onion cell is viewed through the light microscope, the image of the cell is 7.5 mm wide. The real width of the onion cell is 75 μm.

Calculate the magnification used to view the cell using the formula:

$$\text{magnification} = \frac{\text{image size}}{\text{real size}}$$

[2 marks]

Topic B1 — Cell Biology

Cell Differentiation and Specialisation

*Cells **don't** all look the **same**. They have **different structures** to suit their **different functions**.*

Cells **Differentiate** to Become **Specialised**

Differentiation is the process by which a cell changes to become specialised for its job.

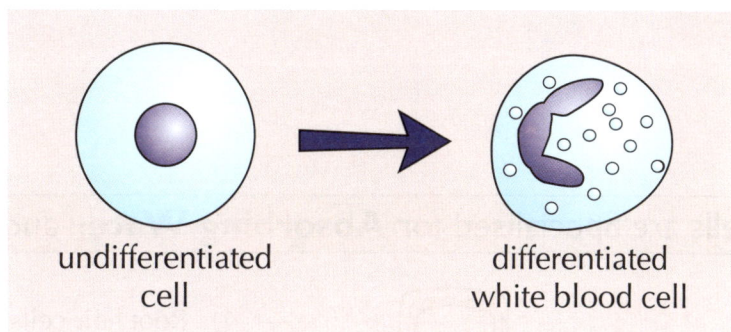

undifferentiated cell

differentiated white blood cell

1) As cells change, they develop different subcellular structures and turn into different types of cells. This allows them to carry out specific functions.

2) Most differentiation occurs as an organism develops. In most animal cells, the ability to differentiate is then lost at an early stage, after they become specialised. However, lots of plant cells don't ever lose this ability.

3) The cells that differentiate in mature animals are mainly used for repairing and replacing cells, such as skin or blood cells.

4) Some cells are undifferentiated cells — they're called stem cells. There's more about them on page 25.

You Need To Know These **Examples** of **Specialised Cells**

Sperm Cells are Specialised for **Reproduction**

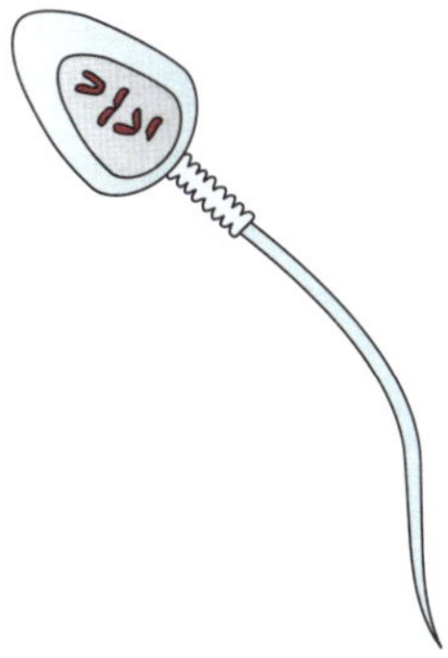

1) The function of a sperm is basically to get the male DNA to the female DNA.
2) It has a long tail and a streamlined head to help it swim to the egg.
3) There are a lot of mitochondria in the cell to provide the energy needed.
4) It also carries enzymes in its head to digest through the egg cell membrane.

Nerve Cells are Specialised for **Rapid Signalling**

1) The function of nerve cells is to carry electrical signals from one part of the body to another.
2) These cells are long (to cover more distance) and have branched connections at their ends to connect to other nerve cells and form a network throughout the body.

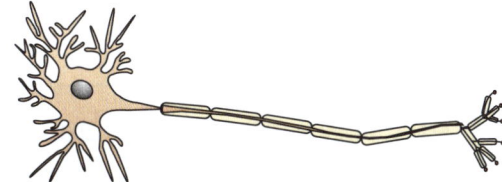

Topic B1 — Cell Biology

Cell Specialisation

Muscle Cells are Specialised for Contraction

1) The function of a muscle cell is to contract quickly.
2) These cells are long (so that they have space to contract) and contain lots of mitochondria to generate the energy needed for contraction.

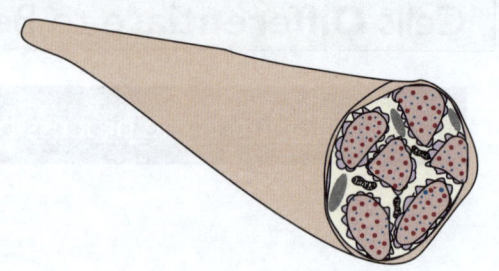

Root Hair Cells are Specialised for Absorbing Water and Minerals

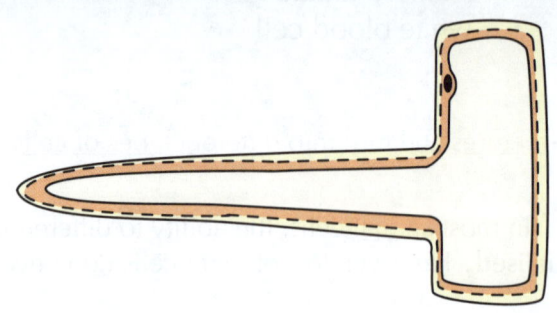

1) Root hair cells are cells on the surface of plant roots, which grow into long "hairs" that stick out into the soil.
2) This gives the plant a big surface area for absorbing water and mineral ions from the soil.

Phloem and Xylem Cells are Specialised for Transporting Substances

1) Phloem and xylem cells form phloem and xylem tubes, which transport substances such as food and water around plants.
2) To form the tubes, the cells are long and joined end to end.
3) Xylem cells are hollow in the centre and phloem cells have very few subcellular structures, so that stuff can flow through them.

phloem   xylem

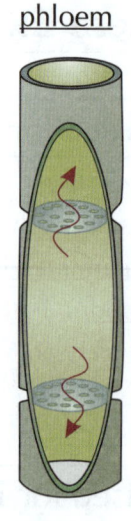 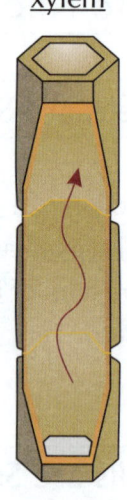

There's more about phloem and xylem on page 69.

Cells have the same basic bits but are specialised for their function

Not all cells contain all of the bits shown on pages 17-18. This is because some specialised cells don't have a use for certain subcellular structures — it depends on their function. For example, root hair cells grow underground in the soil, so they don't need chloroplasts because they don't photosynthesise.

Topic B1 — Cell Biology

Stem Cells

*Stem cell research has exciting **possibilities**, but it's also pretty **controversial**.*

Embryonic Stem Cells Can Turn into ANY Type of Cell

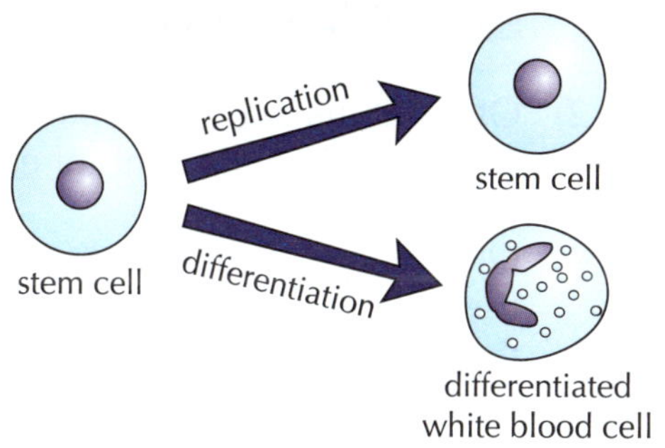

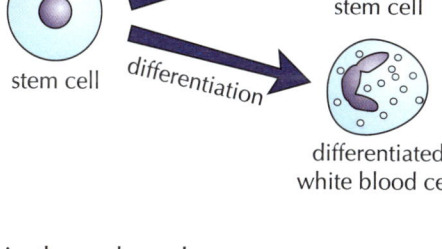

1) Differentiation is the process by which a cell changes to become specialised for its job — see p.23.
2) Undifferentiated cells, called stem cells, can divide to produce lots more undifferentiated cells. They can differentiate into different types of cell, depending on what instructions they're given.
3) Stem cells are found in early human embryos. They're exciting to doctors and medical researchers because they have the potential to turn into any kind of cell at all. This makes sense if you think about it — all the different types of cell found in a human being have to come from those few cells in the early embryo.
4) Adults also have stem cells, but they're only found in certain places, like bone marrow.
5) Unlike embryonic stem cells, adult stem cells can't turn into any cell type at all — only certain ones, such as blood cells.
6) Stem cells from embryos and bone marrow can be grown in a lab to produce clones (genetically identical cells) and made to differentiate into specialised cells to use in medicine or research.

Stem Cells May Be Able to Cure Many Diseases

1) Medicine already uses adult stem cells to cure disease. For example, stem cells transferred from the bone marrow of a healthy person can replace faulty blood cells in the patient who receives them.
2) Embryonic stem cells could also be used to replace faulty cells in sick people — you could make insulin-producing cells for people with diabetes, nerve cells for people paralysed by spinal injuries, and so on.

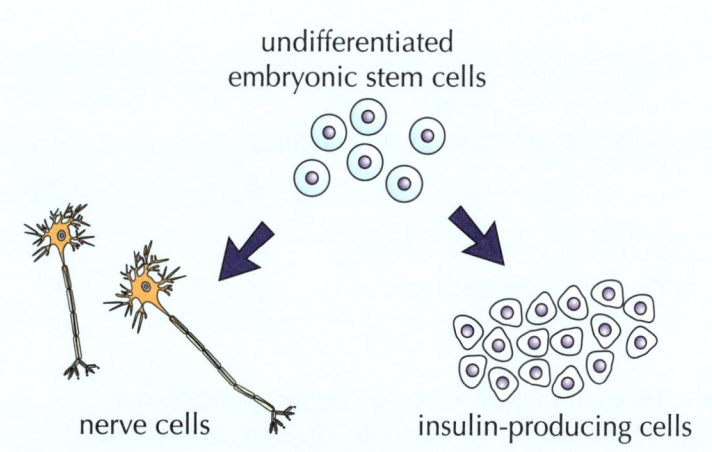

3) In a type of cloning, called therapeutic cloning, an embryo could be made to have the same genetic information as the patient. This means that the stem cells produced from it would also contain the same genes and so wouldn't be rejected by the patient's body if used to replace faulty cells.
4) However, there are risks involved in using stem cells in medicine. For example, stem cells grown in the lab may become contaminated with a virus which could be passed on to the patient and so make them sicker.

Topic B1 — Cell Biology

Stem Cells

Some People Are Against Stem Cell Research

1) Some people are against stem cell research because they feel that human embryos shouldn't be used for experiments since each one is a potential human life.

2) Others think that curing patients who already exist and who are suffering is more important than the rights of embryos.

3) One fairly convincing argument in favour of this point of view is that the embryos used in the research are usually unwanted ones from fertility clinics which, if they weren't used for research, would probably just be destroyed. But of course, campaigners for the rights of embryos usually want this banned too.

4) These campaigners feel that scientists should concentrate more on finding and developing other sources of stem cells, so people could be helped without having to use embryos.

5) In some countries stem cell research is banned, but it's allowed in the UK as long as it follows strict guidelines.

Stem Cells Can Produce Identical Plants

1) In plants, stem cells are found in the meristems (parts of the plant where growth occurs — see p.68).

2) Throughout the plant's entire life, cells in the meristem tissues can differentiate into any type of plant cell.

3) These stem cells can be used to produce clones (identical copies) of whole plants quickly and cheaply.

4) They can be used to grow more plants of rare species (to prevent them being wiped out).

5) Stem cells can also be used to grow crops of identical plants that have desired features for farmers, for example, disease resistance.

Some species of orchid are endangered in the UK. Many can be successfully reproduced by cloning using stem cells.

Alternative sources of stem cells would avoid the controversy

Research has been done into getting human stem cells from other sources — e.g. it may be possible to 'reprogramme' differentiated adult cells back to an undifferentiated stage. But whatever your opinion of stem cell research is, it's good to know what their uses are and the arguments for and against using them.

Topic B1 — Cell Biology

Chromosomes and Mitosis

*In order to survive and grow, our cells have got to be able to **divide**. And that means our DNA as well...*

Chromosomes Contain Genetic Information

1) Most cells in your body have a nucleus. The nucleus contains your genetic material in the form of chromosomes.
2) Chromosomes are coiled up lengths of DNA molecules.
3) Each chromosome carries a large number of genes. Different genes control the development of different characteristics, e.g. hair colour.
4) Body cells normally have two copies of each chromosome — one from the organism's 'mother', and one from its 'father'. So, humans have two copies of chromosome 1, two copies of chromosome 2, etc.
5) The diagram shows the 23 pairs of chromosomes from a human cell.

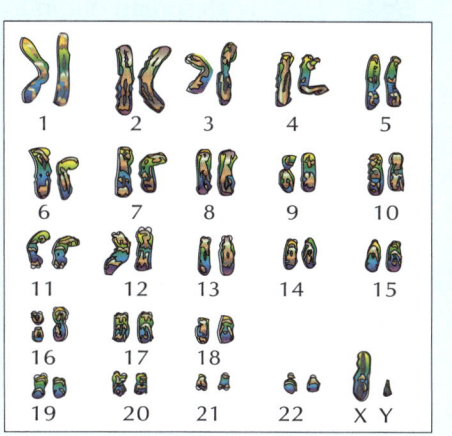

The Cell Cycle Makes Cells for Growth, Development and Repair

1) Body cells in multicellular organisms divide to produce new cells as part of a series of stages called the cell cycle.
2) The stage of the cell cycle when the cell divides is called mitosis.

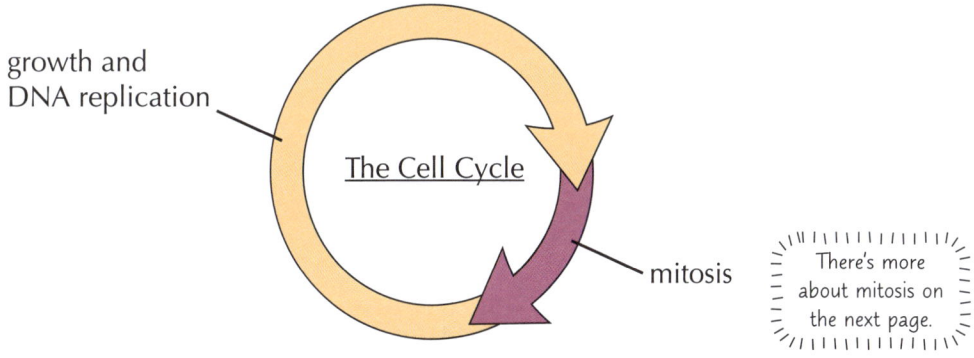

There's more about mitosis on the next page.

3) Multicellular organisms use mitosis to grow and develop or replace cells that have been damaged.
4) The end of the cell cycle results in two new cells identical to the original cell, with the same number of chromosomes.

The cell cycle is important for growth and repair

Not all cells are going through the cell cycle at the same time, but when a cell does go through these stages, you end up with two cells where you originally had just one. The body closely controls which cells divide and when — if this control fails, it can result in cancer (see page 66).

Topic B1 — Cell Biology

Chromosomes and Mitosis

There are two main stages of the cell cycle...

Growth and DNA Replication

In a cell that's not dividing, the DNA is all spread out in long strings.

Before it divides, the cell has to grow and increase the amount of subcellular structures such as mitochondria and ribosomes.

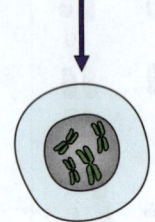

It then duplicates its DNA — so there's one copy for each new cell. The DNA is copied and forms X-shaped chromosomes. Each 'arm' of the chromosome is an exact duplicate of the other.

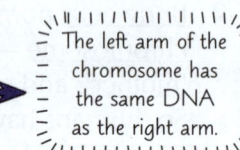 

The left arm of the chromosome has the same DNA as the right arm.

Mitosis

Once its contents and DNA have been copied, the cell is ready for mitosis...

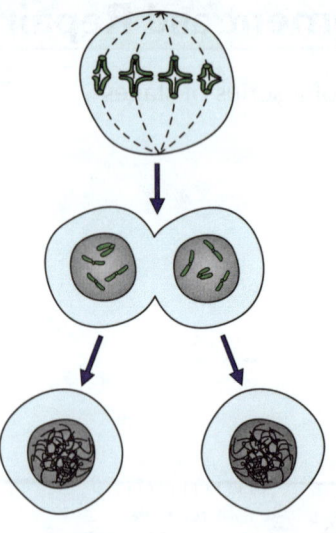

The chromosomes line up at the centre of the cell and cell fibres pull them apart. The two arms of each chromosome go to opposite ends of the cell.

Membranes form around each of the sets of chromosomes. These become the nuclei of the two new cells — the nucleus has divided.

Lastly, the cytoplasm and cell membrane divide.

The cell has now produced two new daughter cells. The daughter cells contain exactly the same DNA — they're identical. Their DNA is also identical to the parent cell.

Mitosis produces two identical daughter cells

Mitosis can seem tricky at first. But don't worry — just go through it slowly, one step at a time.

Q1   A student looks at cells in the tip of a plant root under a microscope.
She counts 11 cells that are undergoing mitosis and 62 cells that are not.
     a) Calculate the percentage of cells that are undergoing mitosis.   [1 mark]
     b) Suggest how the student can tell whether a cell is undergoing mitosis or not.   [1 mark]

Q1 Video Solution

Topic B1 — Cell Biology

Warm-Up & Exam Questions

There's only one way to do well in the exam — learn the facts and then practise lots of exam questions to see what it'll be like on the big day. We couldn't have made it easier for you — so do it.

Warm-Up Questions

1) What does cell 'differentiation' mean?
2) Describe how a root hair cell is specialised for its function.
3) How can stem cells be used to preserve rare plant species?
4) Where in the cell are chromosomes found?
5) True or false? The cells produced in mitosis are genetically identical.

Exam Questions

1   **Figure 1** shows how the amount of DNA per cell changes as a cell undergoes two cell divisions by mitosis. Point **C** is the time when the chromosomes first become visible in the cells.

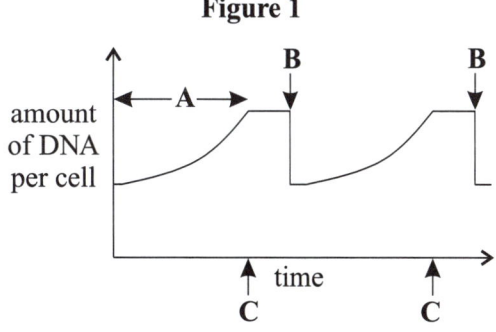

Figure 1

1.1 Describe what is happening to the DNA during stage **A**.
    Suggest why this needs to happen.

[2 marks]

1.2 Suggest what happens at time **B**.

[1 mark]

1.3 How many cells are there after the first cell division?

[1 mark]

2   Adult stem cells have already been used to cure disorders, and it is thought that embryonic stem cells have the potential to treat many more disorders.

2.1 Describe how stem cells could be used to treat disorders.

[1 mark]

2.2 Explain why embryonic stem cells have the potential to treat more disorders than adult stem cells.

[1 mark]

2.3 Give **one** place where adult stem cells are found in the body.

[1 mark]

Topic B1 — Cell Biology

Diffusion

Diffusion is really important in living organisms — it's how a lot of **substances** get **in** and **out** of cells.

Don't be Put Off by the Fancy Word

1) Diffusion is simple. It's just the gradual movement of particles from places where there are lots of them to places where there are fewer of them.
2) That's all it is — just the natural tendency for stuff to spread out.
3) Unfortunately you also have to learn the fancy way of saying the same thing, which is this:

> Diffusion is the spreading out of particles from an area of higher concentration to an area of lower concentration.

4) Diffusion happens in both solutions and gases — that's because the particles in these substances are free to move about randomly.
5) The simplest type is when different gases diffuse through each other. This is what's happening when the smell of perfume diffuses through a room:

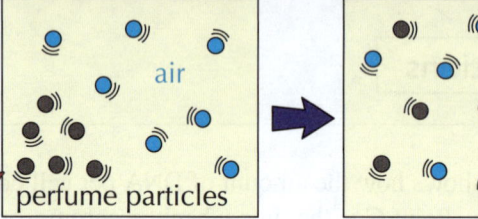

The bigger the concentration gradient (the difference in concentration), the faster the diffusion rate. A higher temperature will also give a faster diffusion rate because the particles have more energy, so move around faster.

Cell Membranes Are Kind of Clever...

1) They're clever because they hold the cell together but they let stuff in and out as well.
2) Dissolved substances can move in and out of cells by diffusion.
3) Only very small molecules can diffuse through cell membranes though — things like oxygen (needed for respiration — see page 100), glucose, amino acids and water.
4) Big molecules like starch and proteins can't fit through the membrane:
5) Just like with diffusion in air, particles flow through the cell membrane from where there's a higher concentration (a lot of them) to where there's a lower concentration (not such a lot of them).

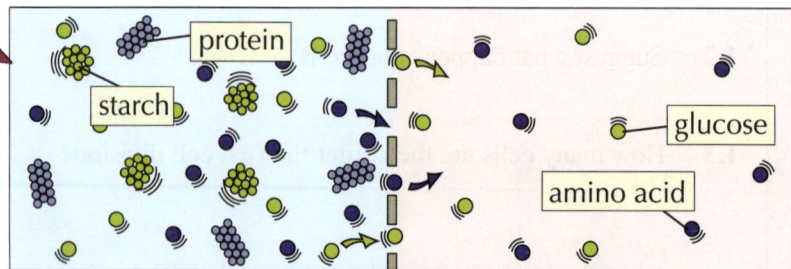

6) They're only moving about randomly of course, so they go both ways — but if there are a lot more particles on one side of the membrane, there's a net (overall) movement from that side.

> The larger the surface area of the membrane, the faster the diffusion rate because more particles can pass through at once — see page 35.

Diffusion is just particles spreading out

Really tiny particles can go through cell membranes to even up the concentration on either side.

Q1 A student adds a drop of ink to a glass of cold water.
   a) What will the student observe to happen to the drop of ink. Explain your answer. [2 marks]
   b) How might the observation differ if the ink was added to a glass of warm water?   [1 mark]

Topic B1 — Cell Biology

Osmosis

*If you've got your head round **diffusion**, osmosis will be a **breeze**.
If not, have another look at the previous page...*

Osmosis is a Special Case of Diffusion, That's All

Learn this definition of osmosis:

> Osmosis is the movement of water molecules across a partially permeable membrane from a region of higher water concentration to a region of lower water concentration.

1) A partially permeable membrane is just one with very small holes in it. So small, in fact, only tiny molecules (like water) can pass through them, and bigger molecules (e.g. sucrose) can't.

2) The water molecules actually pass both ways through the membrane during osmosis. This happens because water molecules move about randomly all the time.

3) But because there are more water molecules on one side than on the other, there's a steady net flow of water into the region with fewer water molecules, i.e. into the stronger sugar solution.

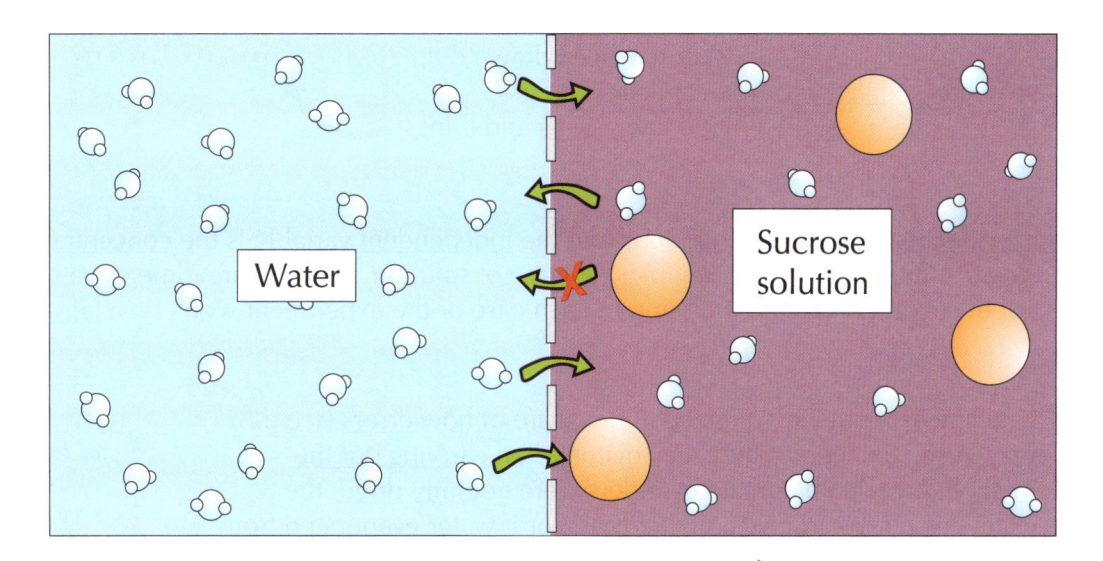

[Diagram: Water on left side, Sucrose solution on right side, with a partially permeable membrane between them. Net movement of water molecules is from left to right.]

4) This means the strong sugar solution gets more dilute. The water acts like it's trying to "even up" the concentration either side of the membrane.

5) Osmosis is a type of diffusion — passive movement of water particles from an area of higher water concentration to an area of lower water concentration.

Diffusion is movement from where there's lots to where there's few...

...so osmosis is really just a fancy word for the diffusion of water molecules. It's simple really.

Topic B1 — Cell Biology

PRACTICAL — Osmosis

There's an experiment you can do to show osmosis at work.

You can Observe the Effect of Sugar Solutions on Plant Tissue

1) Cut up a potato into identical cylinders, and get some beakers with different sugar solutions in them. One should be pure water and another should be a very concentrated sugar solution (e.g. 1 mol/dm³). Then you can have a few others with concentrations in between (e.g. 0.2 mol/dm³, 0.4 mol/dm³, 0.6 mol/dm³, etc.)

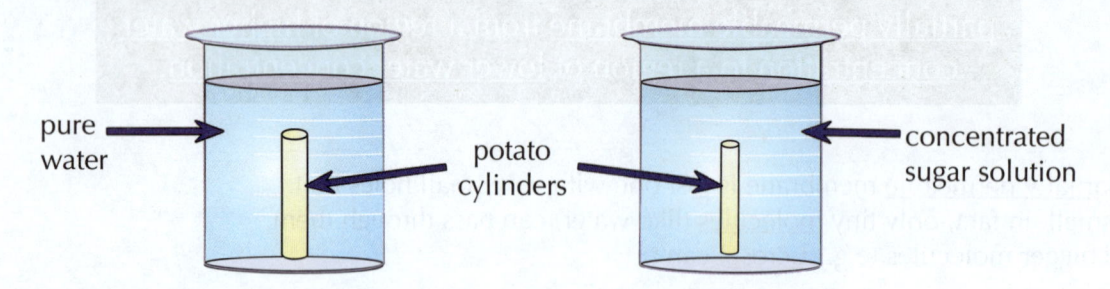

2) You measure the mass of the cylinders, then leave one cylinder in each beaker for twenty four hours or so.

3) Then you take them out, dry them with a paper towel and measure their masses again.

4) If the cylinders have drawn in water by osmosis, they'll have increased in mass. If water has been drawn out, they'll have decreased in mass. You can calculate the percentage change in mass, then plot a few graphs and things.

By calculating the percentage change (see p.415), you can compare the effect of sugar concentration on cylinders that didn't have the same initial mass. An increase in mass will give a positive percentage change and a decrease will give a negative percentage change.

The dependent variable is the chip mass and the independent variable is the concentration of the sugar solution. All other variables (volume of solution, temperature, time, type of sugar used, etc.) must be kept the same in each case or the experiment won't be a fair test.

Like any experiment, you need to be aware of how errors (see p.8) may arise. Sometimes they may occur when carrying out the method, e.g. if some potato cylinders were not fully dried, the excess water would give a higher mass, or if water evaporated from the beakers, the concentrations of the sugar solutions would change. You can reduce the effect of these errors by repeating the experiment and calculating a mean percentage change at each concentration.

You could also carry out this experiment using different salt solutions and see what effect they have on potato chip mass.

You could do a similar experiment to work out the rate of osmosis by leaving the potato cylinders for 30 minutes, then dividing the change in mass (in grams) by the time taken (in minutes). So the units for the rate would be g/min.

Osmosis is the reason why it's bad to drink sea-water...

The high salt content means you end up with a much lower water concentration in your blood and tissue fluid than in your cells. All the water is sucked out of your cells and they shrivel and die.

Q1 Explain what will happen to the mass of a piece of potato added to a concentrated salt solution. [2 marks]

Topic B1 — Cell Biology

Active Transport

*Sometimes substances need to be absorbed against a concentration gradient, i.e. from a lower to a higher concentration. This process is referred to as **active transport**.*

Root Hairs Take In Minerals and Water

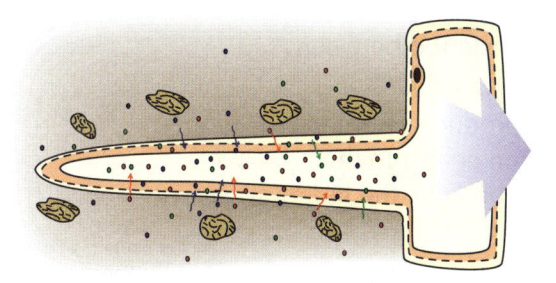

Root Hair Cell

1) As you saw on page 24, the cells on plant roots grow into "hairs" which stick out into the soil.
2) Each branch of a root will be covered in millions of these microscopic hairs.
3) This gives the plant a large surface area for absorbing water and mineral ions from the soil.
4) Plants need these mineral ions for healthy growth.
5) The concentration of minerals is usually higher in the root hair cells than in the soil around them.
6) So the root hair cells can't use diffusion to take up minerals from the soil.

Root Hairs Take in Minerals Using Active Transport

Water is taken into root hair cells by osmosis (see page 31).

1) Minerals should move out of the root hairs if they followed the rules of diffusion. The cells must use another method to draw them in.
2) That method is a process called "active transport".
3) Active transport allows the plant to absorb minerals from a very dilute solution, against a concentration gradient. This is essential for its growth. But active transport needs energy from respiration to make it work.
4) Active transport also happens in humans, for example in taking glucose from the gut (see below), and from the kidney tubules.

We Need Active Transport to Stop Us Starving

Active transport is used in the gut when there is a lower concentration of nutrients in the gut, but a higher concentration of nutrients in the blood.

1) When there's a higher concentration of glucose and amino acids in the gut they diffuse naturally into the blood.
2) BUT — sometimes there's a lower concentration of nutrients in the gut than there is in the blood.
3) This means that the concentration gradient is the wrong way.
4) The same process used in plant roots is used here — active transport.
5) Active transport allows nutrients to be taken into the blood, despite the fact that the concentration gradient is the wrong way.

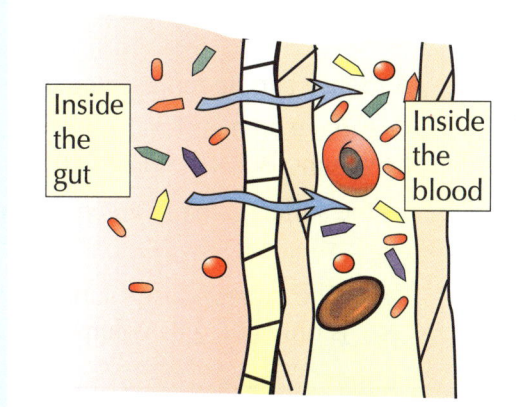

This means that glucose can be taken into the bloodstream when its concentration in the blood is already higher than in the gut. It can then be transported to cells, where it's used for respiration (see p.98).

Active transport uses energy

An important difference between active transport and diffusion is that active transport uses energy.

Topic B1 — Cell Biology

Exchanging Substances

*How easily stuff **moves** between an **organism** and its **environment** depends on its **surface area to volume ratio**.*

Organisms Exchange Substances with their Environment

1) Cells can use diffusion to take in substances they need and get rid of waste products. For example:

   - Oxygen and carbon dioxide are transferred between cells and the environment during gas exchange.
   - In humans, urea (a waste product produced from the breakdown of proteins) diffuses from cells into the blood plasma for removal from the body by the kidneys.

2) How easy it is for an organism to exchange substances with its environment depends on the organism's surface area to volume ratio (SA : V).

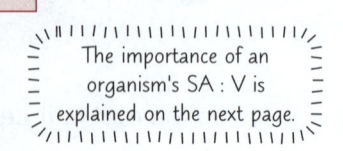

The importance of an organism's SA : V is explained on the next page.

You Can Compare Surface Area to Volume Ratios

A ratio shows how big one value is compared to another. The larger an organism is, the smaller its surface area is compared to its volume. You can show this by calculating surface area to volume ratios:

A hippo can be represented by a 2 cm × 4 cm × 4 cm block.

The area of a surface is found by the equation: LENGTH × WIDTH

So the hippo's total surface area is:
   (4 × 4) × 2 (top and bottom surfaces of block)
   + (4 × 2) × 4 (four sides of the block)
   = 64 cm².

The volume of a block is found by the equation: LENGTH × WIDTH × HEIGHT
So the hippo's volume is 4 × 4 × 2 = 32 cm³.

The surface area to volume ratio of the hippo can be written as 64 : 32.
To simplify the ratio, divide both sides of the ratio by the volume.

So the surface area to volume ratio of the hippo is 2 : 1.

A mouse can be represented by a 1 cm × 1 cm × 1 cm block.
Its surface area is (1 × 1) × 6 = 6 cm².
Its volume is 1 × 1 × 1 = 1 cm³.

So the surface area to volume ratio of the mouse is 6 : 1.

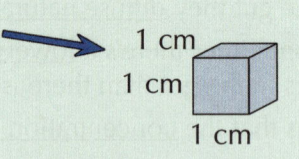

> The cube mouse's surface area is six times its volume, but the cube hippo's surface area is only twice its volume. So the mouse has a larger surface area compared to its volume.

Surface area to volume ratios crop up a lot in biology...

...so it's a good idea to try to understand them now. Remember that, generally speaking, a smaller object has a larger surface area to volume ratio than a bigger object.

Q1   A bacterial cell can be represented by a 2 μm × 2 μm × 1 μm block.
Calculate the cell's surface area to volume ratio.   [3 marks]

Topic B1 — Cell Biology

Exchanging Substances

Multicellular Organisms Need Exchange Surfaces

1) In single-celled organisms, gases and dissolved substances can diffuse directly into (or out of) the cell across the cell membrane. It's because they have a large surface area compared to their volume, so enough substances can be exchanged across the membrane to supply the volume of the cell.

2) Multicellular organisms have a smaller surface area compared to their volume — not enough substances can diffuse from their outside surface to supply their entire volume. This means they need some sort of exchange surface for efficient diffusion (see below and pages 36-37 for some examples). The exchange surface structures have to allow enough of the necessary substances to pass through.

3) Exchange surfaces are adapted to maximise effectiveness:

- They have a thin membrane, so substances only have a short distance to diffuse.
- They have a large surface area so lots of a substance can diffuse at once.
- Exchange surfaces in animals have lots of blood vessels, to get stuff into and out of the blood quickly.
- Gas exchange surfaces in animals (e.g. alveoli) are often ventilated too — air moves in and out.

Gas Exchange Happens in the Lungs

1) The job of the lungs is to transfer oxygen to the blood and to remove waste carbon dioxide from it.

2) To do this the lungs contain millions of little air sacs called alveoli where gas exchange takes place.

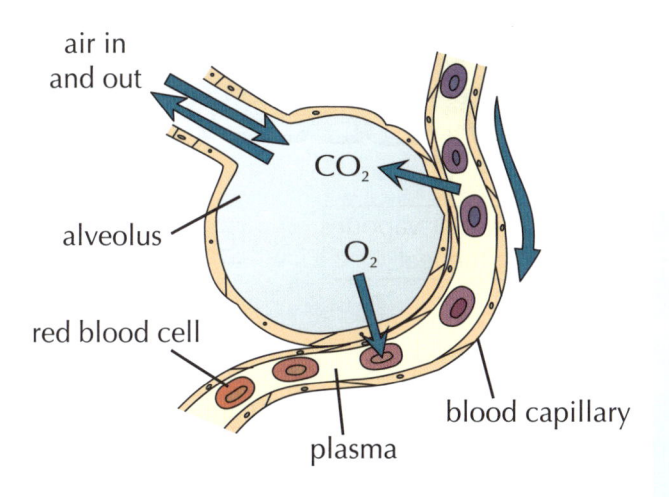

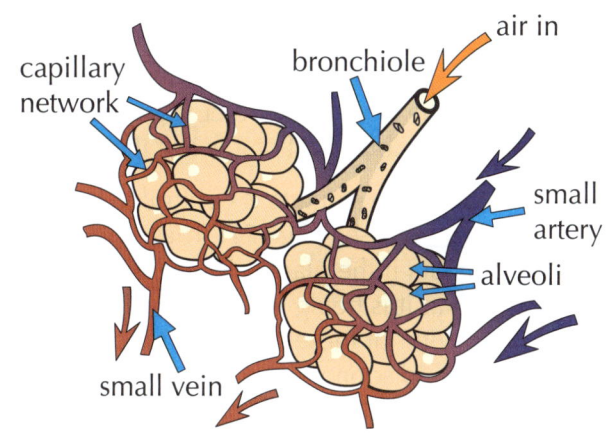

Blue = blood with carbon dioxide.
Red = blood with oxygen.

3) The alveoli are specialised to maximise the diffusion of oxygen and CO_2. They have:
- An enormous surface area (about 75 m^2 in humans).
- A moist lining for dissolving gases.
- Very thin walls.
- A good blood supply.

Humans need alveoli for gas exchange

You might well get asked to explain how the adaptations of the alveoli help gas exchange, so make sure you know what those adaptations are and why they affect the rate of diffusion. There are some more structures you need to know about coming up on the next couple of pages...

Topic B1 — Cell Biology

More on Exchanging Substances

The Villi Provide a Really Big Surface Area

1) The inside of the small intestine is covered in millions and millions of these tiny little projections called villi.
2) They increase the surface area in a big way so that digested food is absorbed much more quickly into the blood.
3) Notice they have:

- a single layer of surface cells
- a very good blood supply to assist quick absorption.

The digested food moves into the blood by diffusion and by active transport (see page 33).

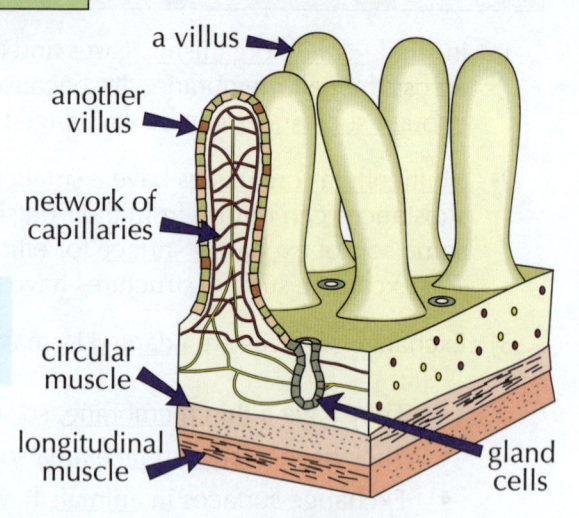

The Structure of Leaves Lets Gases Diffuse In and Out of Cells

Carbon dioxide diffuses into the air spaces within the leaf, then it diffuses into the cells where photosynthesis happens. The leaf's structure is adapted so that this can happen easily:

1) The underneath of the leaf is an exchange surface. It's covered in little holes called stomata which the carbon dioxide diffuses in through.

2) Oxygen (produced in photosynthesis) and water vapour also diffuse out through the stomata. (Water vapour is actually lost from all over the leaf surface, but most of it is lost through the stomata.)

3) The size of the stomata is controlled by guard cells — see page 72. These close the stomata if the plant is losing water faster than it is being replaced by the roots. Without these guard cells the plant would soon wilt.

4) The flattened shape of the leaf increases the area of this exchange surface so that it's more effective.

5) The walls of the cells inside the leaf form another exchange surface. The air spaces inside the leaf increase the area of this surface so there's more chance for carbon dioxide to get into the cells.

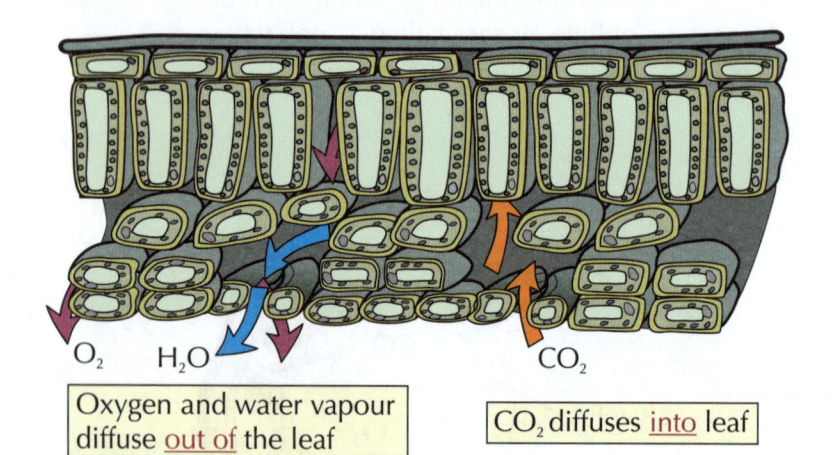

O_2 H_2O CO_2

Oxygen and water vapour diffuse out of the leaf

CO_2 diffuses into leaf

The water vapour evaporates from the cells inside the leaf. Then it escapes by diffusion because there's a lot of it inside the leaf and less of it in the air outside.

Big surface areas mean substances can diffuse through quickly

Q1 In terms of gas exchange, explain why the flat shape of a leaf increases the rate at which a plant can photosynthesise. [2 marks]

Q2 Coeliac disease causes inflammation of the small intestine, which can damage the villi. Suggest why a person with coeliac disease might have low levels of iron in their blood. [2 marks]

Topic B1 — Cell Biology

More on Exchanging Substances

*It's not just **humans** and **plants** that need specialised surfaces for gas exchange.
Fish need an exchange surface that allows them to **efficiently** exchange gases **underwater**.*

Gills Have a Large Surface Area for Gas Exchange

1) The gills are the gas exchange surface in fish.

2) Water (containing oxygen) enters the fish through its mouth and passes out through the gills. As this happens, oxygen diffuses from the water into the blood in the gills and carbon dioxide diffuses from the blood into the water.

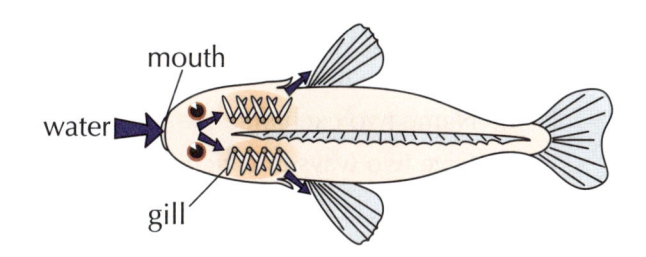

3) Each gill is made of lots of thin plates called gill filaments, which give a big surface area for exchange of gases.

4) The gill filaments are covered in lots of tiny structures called lamellae, which increase the surface area even more.

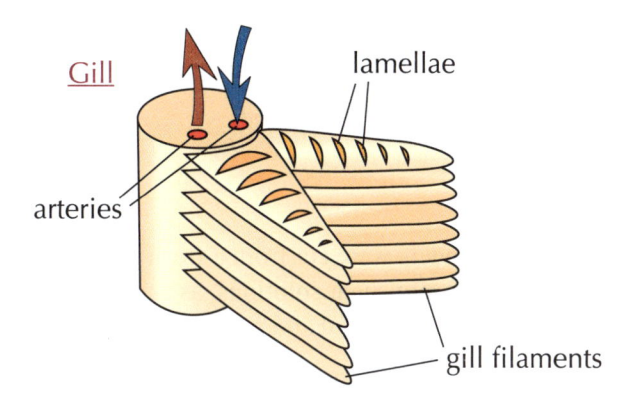

5) The lamellae have lots of blood capillaries to speed up diffusion.

6) They also have a thin surface layer of cells to minimise the distance that the gases have to diffuse.

7) Blood flows through the lamellae in one direction and water flows over in the opposite direction. This maintains a large concentration gradient between the water and the blood.

8) The concentration of oxygen in the water is always higher than that in the blood, so as much oxygen as possible diffuses from the water into the blood.

Exchange surfaces are specialised for efficient diffusion

Multicellular organisms are really well adapted for getting the substances they need to their cells. It makes sense — if they couldn't do this well, they'd die out. A large surface area is a key way that organisms' exchange surfaces are made more effective — molecules can only diffuse through a membrane when they're right next to it, and a large surface area means that a lot more molecules are close to the membrane.

Topic B1 — Cell Biology

Warm-Up & Exam Questions

Question time again — Warm-Up first, then Exam (or the other way round if you want to be different).

Warm-Up Questions

1) Explain why temperature affects the rate of diffusion.
2) Explain what is meant by a partially permeable membrane.
3) Other than diffusion, by what two processes do substances move across exchange surfaces?
4) Give four ways in which exchange surfaces in animals are adapted to maximise their effectiveness.
5) Name two exchange surfaces in humans.
6) Give two ways in which the structure of a gill is adapted for effective gas exchange.

Exam Questions

1   In a fume cupboard, a student injects a sample of ammonia gas into one end of a glass tube. A piece of damp litmus paper in the opposite end of the tube turns blue when the ammonia gas reaches it. It takes 35 seconds for the litmus paper to turn completely blue.

    Suggest what will happen to the length of time taken for the litmus paper to turn completely blue if the student injects a greater amount of the ammonia gas. Explain your answer.

    [3 marks]

PRACTICAL

2   In an experiment, four 5 cm long cylinders were cut from a fresh potato. The cylinders were then placed in different sugar solutions, as shown in **Figure 1**. After 24 hours the potato cylinders were removed and measured.

Figure 1

Tube A — distilled water
Tube B — 1.0 mol/dm³ sugar solution
Tube C — 2.0 mol/dm³ sugar solution
Tube D — 3.0 mol/dm³ sugar solution

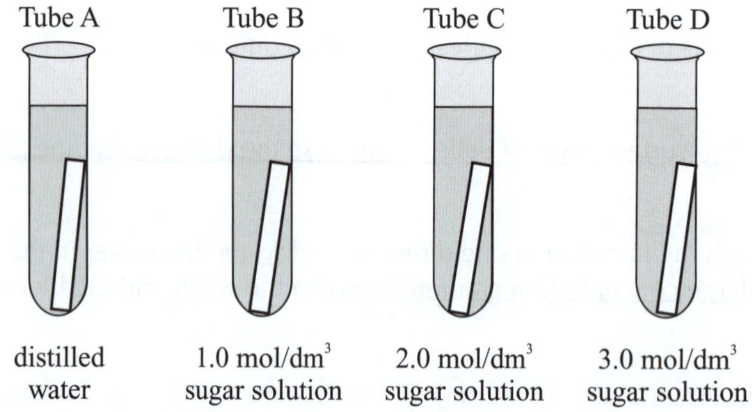

2.1   Which potato cylinder would you expect to be shortest after 24 hours? Explain your answer.

[2 marks]

2.2   The potato cylinder in tube A increased in length during the 24 hours. Explain why this happened.

[2 marks]

Topic B1 — Cell Biology

Exam Questions

3 **Figure 2** shows a villus from the small intestine.
Glucose and other products of digestion are absorbed into the blood through the villi.

Figure 2

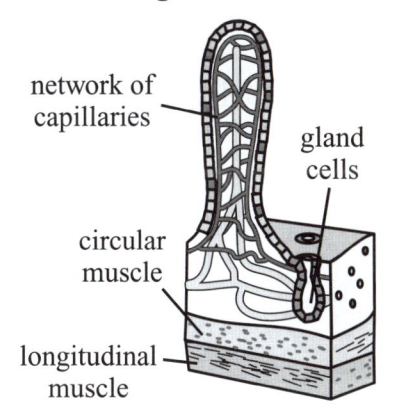

(Diagram of villus showing: network of capillaries, gland cells, circular muscle, longitudinal muscle)

3.1 Suggest how the products of digestion move into the blood.

[2 marks]

3.2 Explain how the structure of villi is related to their function.

[3 marks]

4 A student made up some gelatine with cresol red solution and ammonium hydroxide. Cresol red solution is a pH indicator that is red in alkaline solutions and yellow in acidic solutions. The student cut the gelatine into cubes of different sizes, and placed the cubes in a beaker of dilute hydrochloric acid. He measured how long it took for the cubes to change from red to yellow as the acid moved into the gelatine and neutralised the ammonium hydroxide. His results are shown in **Table 1**.

Table 1

Size of cube (mm)	Time taken for cube to become yellow (s)			
	Trial 1	Trial 2	Trial 3	Trial 4
5 × 5 × 5	174	167	177	182
7 × 7 × 7	274	290	284	292
10 × 10 × 10	835	825	842	838

4.1 Name the process by which hydrochloric acid moves into the gelatine cubes in this experiment.

[1 mark]

4.2 Calculate the mean time for a 10 × 10 × 10 mm gelatine cube to become yellow in this experiment.

[2 marks]

4.3 Calculate the surface area to volume ratio of a 10 × 10 × 10 mm cube.
Give the ratio in its simplest form.

[3 marks]

4.4 Describe and explain the relationship between the size of the gelatine cube and the time taken for the cube to become yellow.

[3 marks]

Topic B1 — Cell Biology

Topic B2 — Organisation

Cell Organisation

*Some organisms contain loads of **cells**, but how, you might wonder, do all these cells mean you end up with a working human... the answer's **organisation**.*

Large Multicellular Organisms are Made Up of Organ Systems

1) Cells are the basic building blocks that make up all living organisms.
2) As you know from page 23, specialised cells carry out a particular function.
3) The process by which cells become specialised for a particular job is called differentiation.

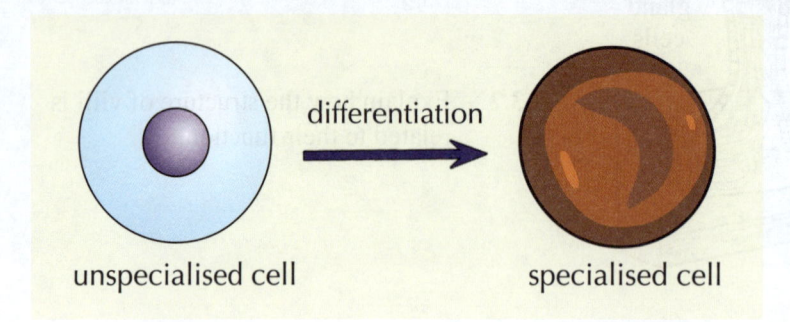

unspecialised cell → differentiation → specialised cell

4) Differentiation occurs during the development of a multicellular organism.
5) These specialised cells form tissues, which form organs, which form organ systems (see below and next page).
6) Large multicellular organisms (e.g. humans) have different systems inside them for exchanging and transporting materials.

Similar Cells are Organised into Tissues

1) A tissue is a group of similar cells that work together to carry out a particular function.
2) It can include more than one type of cell.
3) In mammals (like humans), examples of tissues include:

- Muscular tissue, which contracts (shortens) to move whatever it's attached to.
- Glandular tissue, which makes and secretes chemicals like enzymes and hormones.
- Epithelial tissue, which covers some parts of the body, e.g. the inside of the gut.

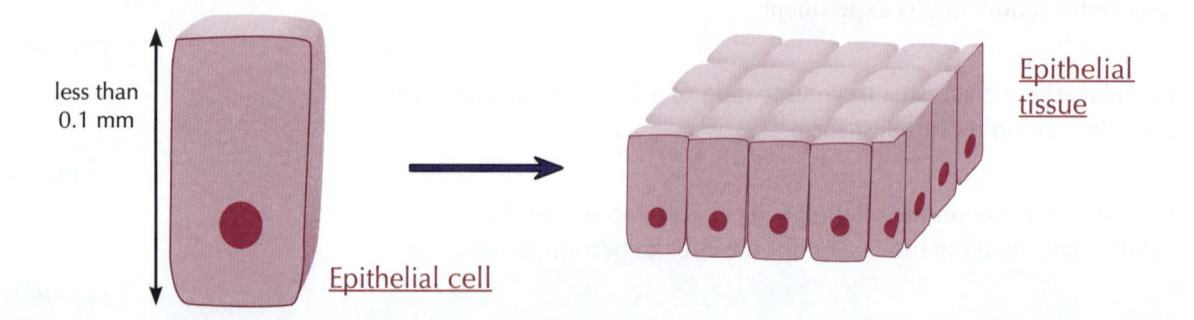

less than 0.1 mm

Epithelial cell → Epithelial tissue

Topic B2 — Organisation

Cell Organisation

*We left off at **tissues** on the previous page — now you need to know how they're organised...*

Tissues are Organised into Organs

An organ is a group of different tissues that work together to perform a certain function.

> For example, the stomach is an organ made of these tissues:
> - Muscular tissue, which moves the stomach wall to churn up the food.
> - Glandular tissue, which makes digestive juices to digest food.
> - Epithelial tissue, which covers the outside and inside of the stomach.

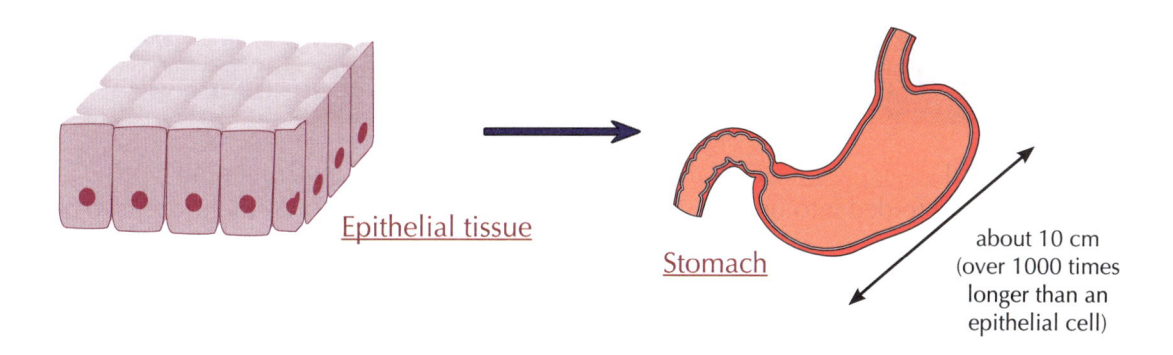

Epithelial tissue → Stomach

about 10 cm (over 1000 times longer than an epithelial cell)

Organs are Organised into Organ Systems

An organ system is a group of organs working together to perform a particular function.

> For example, the digestive system (found in humans and other mammals) breaks down and absorbs food. It is made up of these organs:
> 1) Glands (e.g. the pancreas and salivary glands), which produce digestive juices.
> 2) The stomach and small intestine, which digest food.
> 3) The liver, which produces bile.
> 4) The small intestine, which absorbs soluble food molecules.
> 5) The large intestine, which absorbs water from undigested food, leaving faeces.

Organ systems work together to make entire organisms.

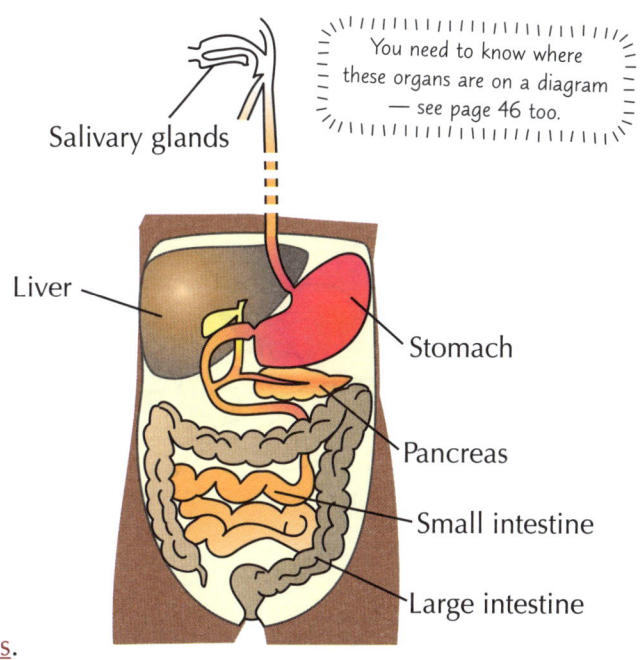

You need to know where these organs are on a diagram — see page 46 too.

Salivary glands
Liver
Stomach
Pancreas
Small intestine
Large intestine

Digestive system

Remember — cells, tissues, organs, organ systems

OK, so from the last couple of pages you know that cells are organised into tissues, the tissues into organs, the organs into organ systems and the organ systems into a whole organism.

Topic B2 — Organisation

Enzymes

Chemical reactions are what make you work. And *enzymes* are what make them work.

Enzymes Are Catalysts Produced by Living Things

1) Living things have thousands of different chemical reactions going on inside them all the time. These reactions need to be carefully controlled — to get the right amounts of substances.
2) You can usually make a reaction happen more quickly by raising the temperature. This would speed up the useful reactions but also the unwanted ones too... not good. There's also a limit to how far you can raise the temperature inside a living creature before its cells start getting damaged.
3) So... living things produce enzymes that act as biological catalysts. Enzymes reduce the need for high temperatures and we only have enzymes to speed up the useful chemical reactions in the body.

> A CATALYST is a substance which INCREASES the speed of a reaction, without being CHANGED or USED UP in the reaction.

4) Enzymes are all large proteins and all proteins are made up of chains of amino acids. These chains are folded into unique shapes, which enzymes need to do their jobs (see below).

Enzymes Have Special Shapes So They Can Catalyse Reactions

1) Chemical reactions usually involve things either being split apart or joined together.
2) Every enzyme has an active site with a unique shape that fits onto the substance involved in a reaction.
3) Enzymes are really picky — they usually only catalyse one specific reaction.
4) This is because, for the enzyme to work, the substrate has to fit into its active site. If the substrate doesn't match the enzyme's active site, then the reaction won't be catalysed.

The substance that an enzyme acts on is called the substrate.

5) This diagram shows the 'lock and key' model of enzyme action.

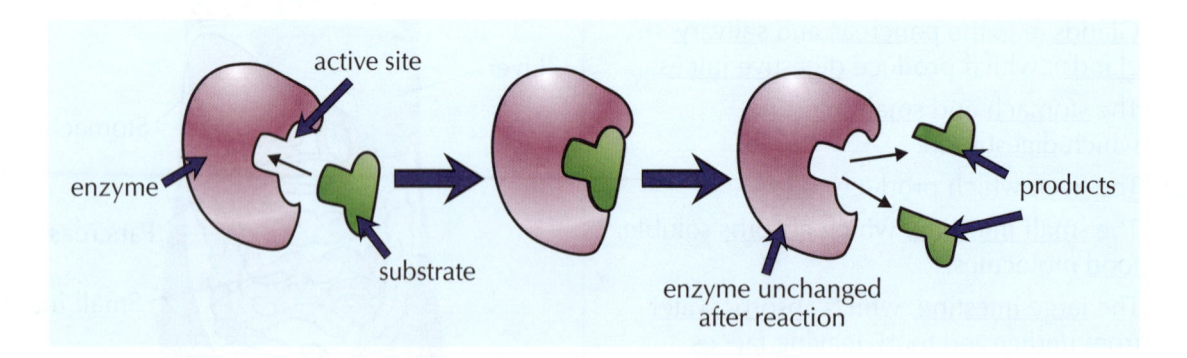

6) This is simpler than how enzymes actually work. In reality, the active site changes shape a little as the substrate binds to it to get a tighter fit. This is called the 'induced fit' model of enzyme action.

Enzymes speed up chemical reactions
Just like you've got to have the correct key for a lock, you've got to have the right substance for an enzyme. As you can see in the diagram above, if the substance doesn't fit, the enzyme won't catalyse the reaction...

Topic B2 — Organisation

Enzymes

*Enzymes are clearly very clever, but they're **not** very versatile. They need just the right **conditions** if they're going to work properly.*

Enzymes Need the Right Temperature...

1) Changing the temperature changes the rate of an enzyme-catalysed reaction.
2) Like with any reaction, a higher temperature increases the rate at first.
3) But if it gets too hot, some of the bonds holding the enzyme together break. This changes the shape of the enzyme's active site, so the substrate won't fit any more. The enzyme is said to be denatured.
4) All enzymes have an optimum temperature that they work best at.

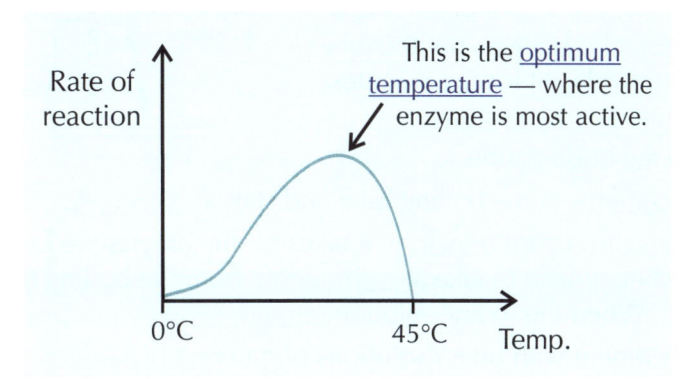

This is the optimum temperature — where the enzyme is most active.

... and the Right pH

1) The pH also affects enzymes. If it's too high or too low, the pH interferes with the bonds holding the enzyme together.
2) This changes the shape of the active site and denatures the enzyme.
3) All enzymes have an optimum pH that they work best at. It's often neutral pH 7, but not always — e.g. pepsin is an enzyme used to break down proteins in the stomach. It works best at pH 2, which means it's well-suited to the acidic conditions there.

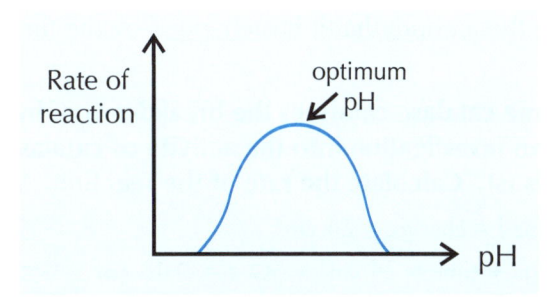

Most enzymes catalyse just one reaction

The optimum temperature for most human enzymes is around normal body temperature. And stomach enzymes work best at low pH, but the enzymes in your small intestine like a higher pH.

Topic B2 — Organisation

Investigating Enzymatic Reactions

You Can Investigate the Effect of pH on Enzyme Activity — PRACTICAL

The enzyme amylase catalyses the breakdown of starch to maltose. It's easy to detect starch using iodine solution — if starch is present, the iodine solution will change from browny-orange to blue-black. This is how you can investigate how pH affects amylase activity:

1) Put a drop of iodine solution into every well of a spotting tile.
2) Place a Bunsen burner on a heat-proof mat, and a tripod and gauze over the Bunsen burner. Put a beaker of water on top of the tripod and heat the water until it is 35 °C (use a thermometer to measure the temperature). Try to keep the temperature of the water constant throughout the experiment.
3) Use a syringe to add 1 cm³ of amylase solution and 1 cm³ of a buffer solution with a pH of 5 to a boiling tube. Using test tube holders, put the tube into the beaker of water and wait for five minutes.
4) Next, use a different syringe to add 5 cm³ of a starch solution to the boiling tube.
5) Immediately mix the contents of the boiling tube and start a stop clock.
6) Use continuous sampling to record how long it takes for the amylase to break down all of the starch. To do this, use a dropping pipette to take a fresh sample from the boiling tube every 30 seconds and put a drop into a well. When the iodine solution remains browny-orange, starch is no longer present.
7) Repeat the whole experiment with buffer solutions of different pH values to see how pH affects the time taken for the starch to be broken down.
8) Remember to control any variables each time (e.g. concentration and volume of amylase solution) to make it a fair test.

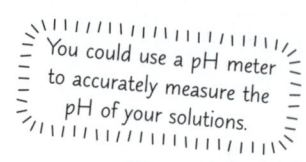

You could use an electric water bath, instead of a Bunsen and a beaker of water, to control the temperature.

You could use a pH meter to accurately measure the pH of your solutions.

Here's How to Calculate the Rate of Reaction

1) It's often useful to calculate the rate of reaction after an experiment. Rate is a measure of how much something changes over time.
2) For the experiment above, you can calculate the rate of reaction using this formula:
   E.g.

   $$\text{Rate} = \frac{1000}{\text{time}}$$

   At pH 6, the time taken for amylase to break down all of the starch in a solution was 90 seconds. So the rate of the reaction = 1000 ÷ 90 = 11 s⁻¹ (2 s.f.)

   The units are in s⁻¹ since rate is given per unit time.

3) If an experiment measures how much something changes over time, you calculate the rate of reaction by dividing the amount that it has changed by the time taken.

EXAMPLE
The enzyme catalase catalyses the breakdown of hydrogen peroxide into water and oxygen. During an investigation into the activity of catalase, 24 cm³ of oxygen was released in 50 seconds (s). Calculate the rate of the reaction. Write your answer in cm³ s⁻¹.

Amount of product formed = change = 24 cm³
Rate of reaction = change ÷ time = 24 cm³ ÷ 50 s = **0.48 cm³ s⁻¹**

cm³ s⁻¹ is another way of writing cm³/s.

You can investigate other factors too...

You could easily adapt this experiment to investigate how factors other than pH affect the rate of amylase activity. For example, you could use a water bath to investigate the effect of temperature.

Q1 An enzyme-controlled reaction was carried out at pH 4. After 2 minutes, 36 cm³ of product had been released. Calculate the rate of reaction in cm³/s. [1 mark]

Topic B2 — Organisation

Enzymes and Digestion

*The **enzymes** used in **digestion** are produced by **cells** and then released into the **gut** to mix with food.*

Digestive Enzymes Break Down Big Molecules

1) Starch, proteins and fats are big molecules. They're too big to pass through the walls of the digestive system, so digestive enzymes break these big molecules down into smaller ones like sugars (e.g. glucose and maltose), amino acids, glycerol and fatty acids. These smaller, soluble molecules can pass easily through the walls of the digestive system, allowing them to be absorbed into the bloodstream.

Carbohydrases Convert Carbohydrates into Simple Sugars

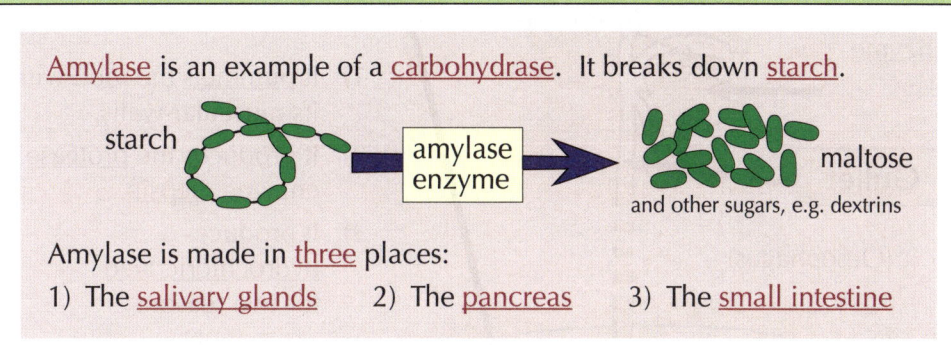

Amylase is an example of a carbohydrase. It breaks down starch.

starch → amylase enzyme → maltose and other sugars, e.g. dextrins

Starch is a carbohydrate.

Amylase is made in three places:
1) The salivary glands   2) The pancreas   3) The small intestine

Proteases Convert Proteins into Amino Acids

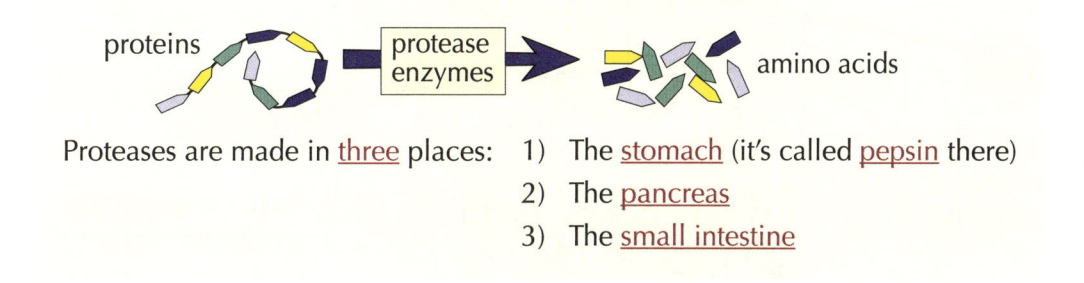

proteins → protease enzymes → amino acids

Proteases are made in three places:
1) The stomach (it's called pepsin there)
2) The pancreas
3) The small intestine

Lipases Convert Lipids into Glycerol and Fatty Acids

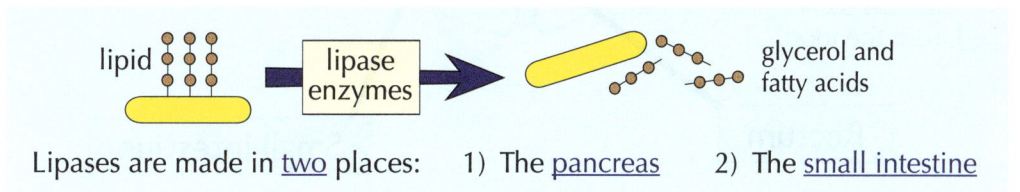

lipid → lipase enzymes → glycerol and fatty acids

Lipases are made in two places: 1) The pancreas   2) The small intestine

Remember, lipids are fats and oils.

2) The body makes good use of the products of digestion. They can be used to make new carbohydrates, proteins and lipids. Some of the glucose (a carbohydrate) that's made is used in respiration (see p.98).

Bile Neutralises the Stomach Acid and Emulsifies Fats

1) Bile is produced in the liver. It's stored in the gall bladder before it's released into the small intestine.
2) The hydrochloric acid in the stomach makes the pH too acidic for enzymes in the small intestine to work properly. Bile is alkaline — it neutralises the acid and makes conditions alkaline. The enzymes in the small intestine work best in these alkaline conditions.
3) It emulsifies fats. In other words it breaks the fat into tiny droplets. This gives a much bigger surface area of fat for the enzyme lipase to work on — which makes its digestion faster.

Topic B2 — Organisation

More on Enzymes and Digestion

So now you know what the enzymes do, here's a nice **big picture** of the **whole** of the digestive system.

The **Breakdown** of Food is Catalysed by **Enzymes**

1) Enzymes used in the digestive system are produced by specialised cells in glands and in the gut lining.
2) Different enzymes catalyse the breakdown of different food molecules.

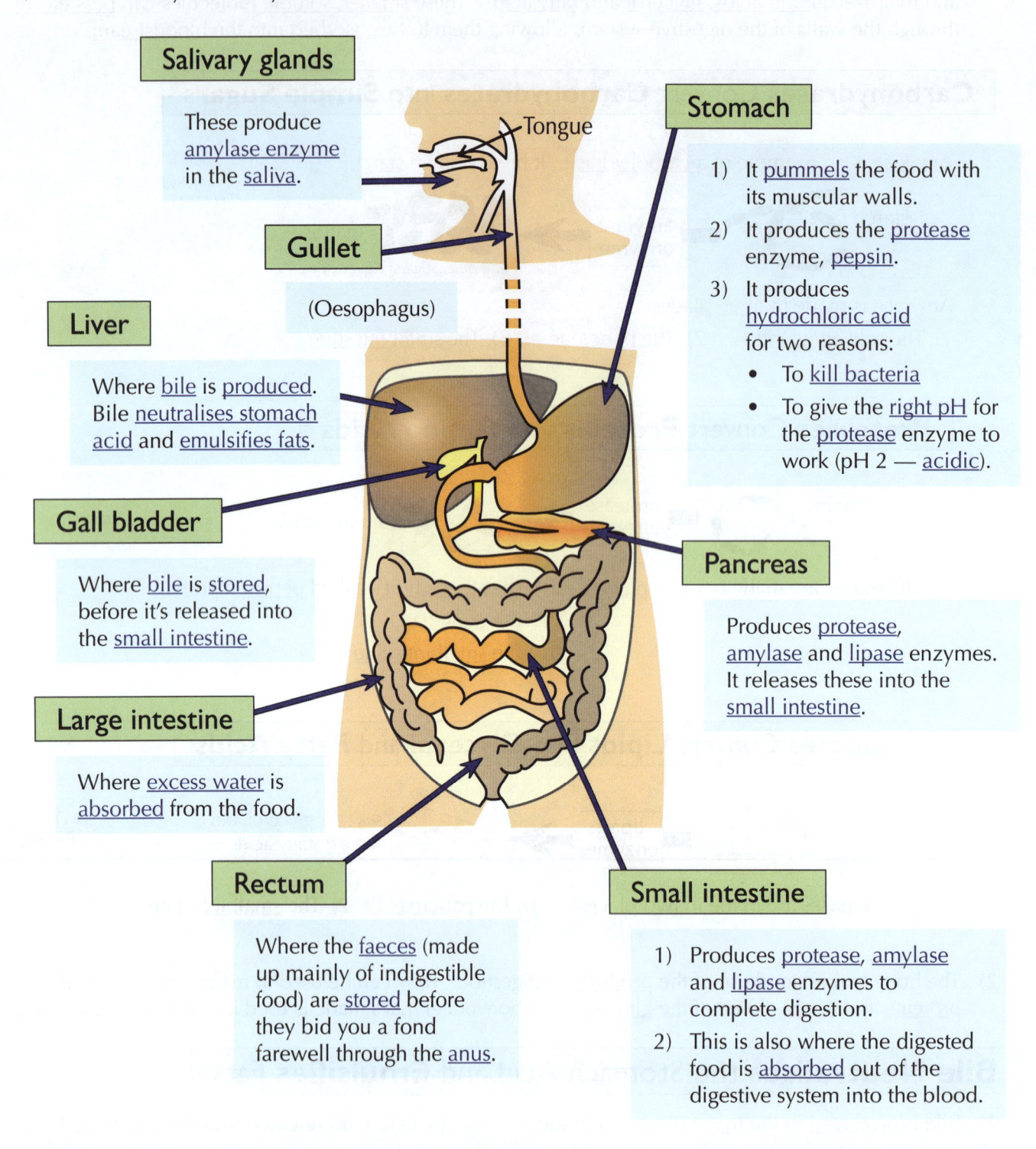

Salivary glands
These produce amylase enzyme in the saliva.

Gullet
(Oesophagus)

Liver
Where bile is produced. Bile neutralises stomach acid and emulsifies fats.

Gall bladder
Where bile is stored, before it's released into the small intestine.

Large intestine
Where excess water is absorbed from the food.

Rectum
Where the faeces (made up mainly of indigestible food) are stored before they bid you a fond farewell through the anus.

Stomach
1) It pummels the food with its muscular walls.
2) It produces the protease enzyme, pepsin.
3) It produces hydrochloric acid for two reasons:
   - To kill bacteria
   - To give the right pH for the protease enzyme to work (pH 2 — acidic).

Pancreas
Produces protease, amylase and lipase enzymes. It releases these into the small intestine.

Small intestine
1) Produces protease, amylase and lipase enzymes to complete digestion.
2) This is also where the digested food is absorbed out of the digestive system into the blood.

That's nine different bits of the digestive system with different jobs

Did you know that the whole of your digestive system is actually a big hole that goes right through your body? It just gets loads of food, digestive juices and enzymes piled into it...

Topic B2 — Organisation

Food Tests

PRACTICAL

*There are some clever ways to **identify** what type of **food molecule** a sample contains.
For each of the tests, you need to prepare a **food sample** first. It's the same each time though.*

Prepare Your Food Sample First

Before you can carry out any of the food tests on these pages, you need to prepare a food sample. Here's what you'd do:

1) Get a piece of food and break it up using a pestle and mortar.
2) Transfer the ground up food to a beaker and add some distilled water.
3) Give the mixture a good stir with a glass rod to dissolve some of the food.
4) Filter the solution using a funnel lined with filter paper to get rid of the solid bits of food.

Use the Benedict's Test to Test for Sugars

Sugars are found in all sorts of foods such as biscuits, cereal and bread. There are two types of sugars — non-reducing and reducing. You can test for reducing sugars in foods using the Benedict's test:

1) Prepare a food sample and transfer 5 cm³ to a test tube.
2) Prepare a water bath so that it's set to 75 °C.
3) Add some Benedict's solution to the test tube (about 10 drops) using a pipette.
4) Place the test tube in the water bath using a test tube holder and leave it in there for 5 minutes. Make sure the tube is pointing away from you.
5) If the food sample contains a reducing sugar, the solution in the test tube will change from the normal blue colour to green, yellow or brick-red — it depends on how much sugar is in the food.

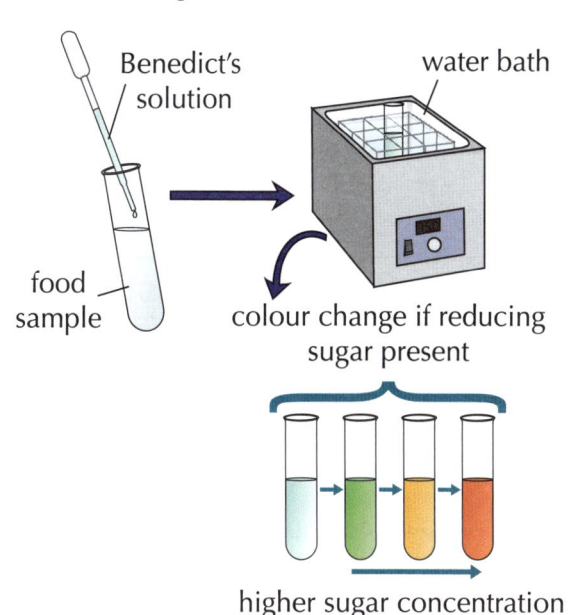

Benedict's solution → water bath → colour change if reducing sugar present

higher sugar concentration

Use Iodine Solution to Test for Starch

You can also check food samples for the presence of starch. Foods like pasta, rice and potatoes contain a lot of starch. Here's how to do the test:

1) Make a food sample and transfer 5 cm³ of your sample to a test tube.
2) Then add a few drops of iodine solution and gently shake the tube to mix the contents. If the sample contains starch, the colour of the solution will change from browny-orange to black or blue-black.

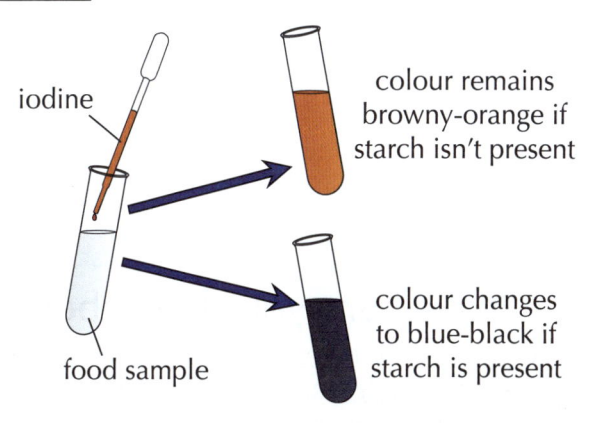

iodine → food sample → colour remains browny-orange if starch isn't present / colour changes to blue-black if starch is present

Topic B2 — Organisation

PRACTICAL: Food Tests

*There are a couple more **food tests** coming up on this page — for proteins and for lipids. As with the other tests, you need to use the method on the previous page to prepare a **sample** of your food first.*

Use the Biuret Test to Test for Proteins

You can use the biuret test to see if a type of food contains protein. Meat and cheese are protein rich and good foods to use in this test. Here's how it's done:

1) Prepare a sample of your food and transfer 2 cm³ of your sample to a test tube.

2) Add 2 cm³ of biuret solution to the sample and mix the contents of the tube by gently shaking it.

3) If the food sample contains protein, the solution will change from blue to purple. If no protein is present, the solution will stay blue.

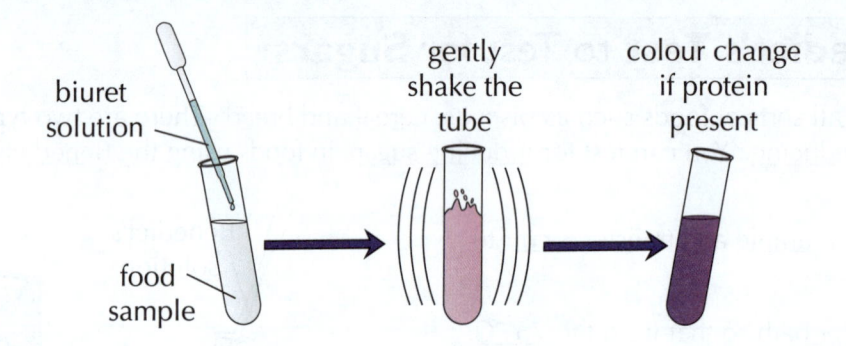

Use the Sudan III Test to Test for Lipids

Lipids are found in foods such as olive oil, margarine and milk. You can test for the presence of lipids in a food using Sudan III stain solution.

1) Prepare a sample of the food you're testing (but you don't need to filter it). Transfer about 5 cm³ into a test tube.

2) Use a pipette to add 3 drops of Sudan III stain solution to the test tube and gently shake the tube.

3) Sudan III stain solution stains lipids. If the sample contains lipids, the mixture will separate out into two layers. The top layer will be bright red. If no lipids are present, no separate red layer will form at the top of the liquid.

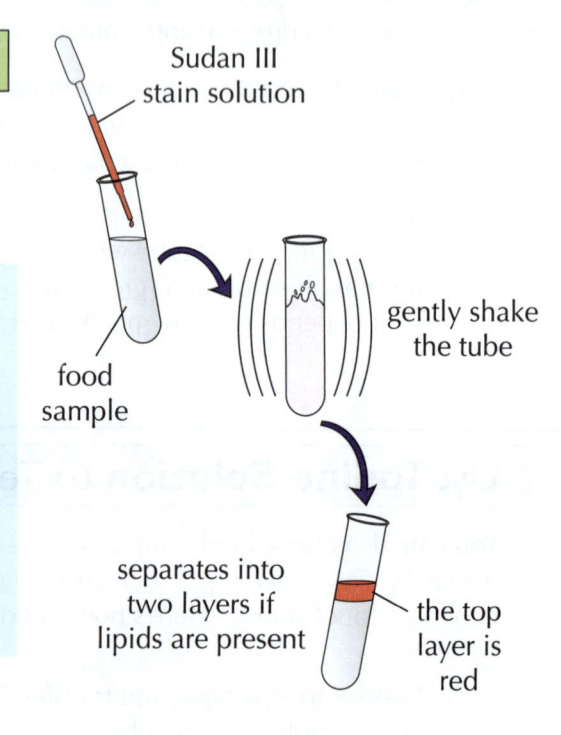

PRACTICAL TIP: Make sure you think about all of the hazards...

Iodine is an irritant to the eyes, and the chemicals in the biuret solution are dangerous, so wear safety goggles for food tests. If you spill any of the chemicals on your skin, wash it off straight away. Be careful around the water bath in the Benedict's test, too. And if that's not enough to be cautious about, Sudan III stain solution is flammable, so keep it away from any lit Bunsen burners.

Topic B2 — Organisation

Warm-Up & Exam Questions

Doing well in exams isn't just about remembering all the facts, although that's important. You have to get used to the way the exams are phrased and make sure you always read the question carefully.

Warm-Up Questions

1) What is an organ system?
2) What is meant by the optimum pH of an enzyme?
3) Which enzyme digests: (a) starch   (b) protein   (c) lipids?
4) What are the products of the digestion of: (a) starch   (b) protein   (c) lipids?
5) Name the three parts of the digestive system that produce protease enzymes.
6) Describe how you would prepare a food sample before testing it for the presence of different food molecules.

Exam Questions

1   **Figure 1** shows the human digestive system.   *Grade 4-6*

Figure 1

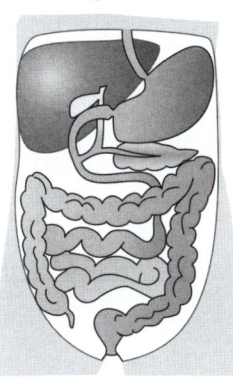

1.1   Label the place where bile is produced.

[1 mark]

1.2   Describe why bile needs to have an alkaline pH.

[1 mark]

1.3   Outline how bile helps with the digestion of fats.

[2 marks]

2   **Figure 2** represents the action of an enzyme in catalysing a biological reaction.   *Grade 4-6*

Figure 2

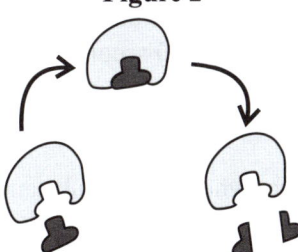

2.1   In terms of the enzyme's shape, explain why an enzyme only catalyses one reaction.

[1 mark]

2.2   The optimum pH of the enzyme is pH 7.
Explain what effect a very low pH would have on the activity of the enzyme.

[2 marks]

Topic B2 — Organisation

Exam Questions

3 Figure 3 shows the effect of temperature on the action of two different enzymes. *Grade 6-7*

3.1 What is the optimum temperature for enzyme **A**?
[1 mark]

3.2 One of these enzymes was extracted from human liver cells. The other was extracted from bacteria living in hot underwater vents.

Suggest which enzyme came from the bacteria. Give a reason for your answer.
[1 mark]

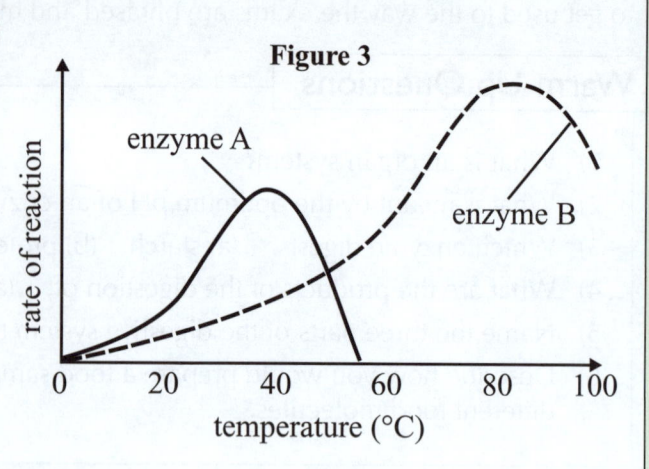

PRACTICAL

4 A student wanted to know which substances were present in a food sample. She prepared a solution containing the food, and added some of the solution to each of three test tubes. She then added iodine solution to test tube **A**, biuret solution to test tube **B** and Sudan III stain solution to test tube **C**. Her results are shown in **Table 1**. *Grade 6-7*

Table 1

Test tube	Description of solution in test tube
A	Blue-black
B	Blue
C	In two layers. Top layer red.

Describe what the student's results show about which substances are present in the food sample.
[3 marks]

PRACTICAL

5 A student was investigating the effect of pH on the rate of amylase activity. He used a syringe to put amylase solution and a buffer solution with a pH of 6 into a test tube. He then used a different syringe to add a starch solution to the boiling tube. He mixed the contents and then started a stop clock. Every 30 seconds he took a sample from the boiling tube and tested it for the presence of starch. When there was no starch present he stopped the stop clock. He repeated the experiment three times. *Grade 6-7*

5.1 Suggest why he used two different syringes when adding substances to the boiling tube.
[1 mark]

5.2 His experiment showed that the average time taken for the starch in the boiling tube to be broken down was 60 seconds. Calculate the rate of the reaction.
Give your answer in s^{-1} to 2 significant figures. Use the formula: $\text{rate} = \dfrac{1000}{\text{time}}$
[1 mark]

5.3 Describe what the student needs to do next in his investigation to determine the effect of pH on the rate of amylase activity.
[1 mark]

Topic B2 — Organisation

The Lungs

*When it comes to **breathing**, much more than just a pair of lungs is needed. There are some other vital parts that help to get the **oxygen** you need in, and the waste **carbon dioxide** out...*

The Lungs Are in the Thorax

1) The thorax is the top part of your body.

2) It's separated from the lower part of the body by the diaphragm.

3) The lungs are like big pink sponges and are protected by the ribcage. They're surrounded by the pleural membranes.

4) The air that you breathe in goes through the trachea. This splits into two tubes called bronchi (each one is a bronchus), one going to each lung.

5) The bronchi split into progressively smaller tubes called bronchioles.

6) The bronchioles finally end at small bags called alveoli where the gas exchange takes place (see next page).

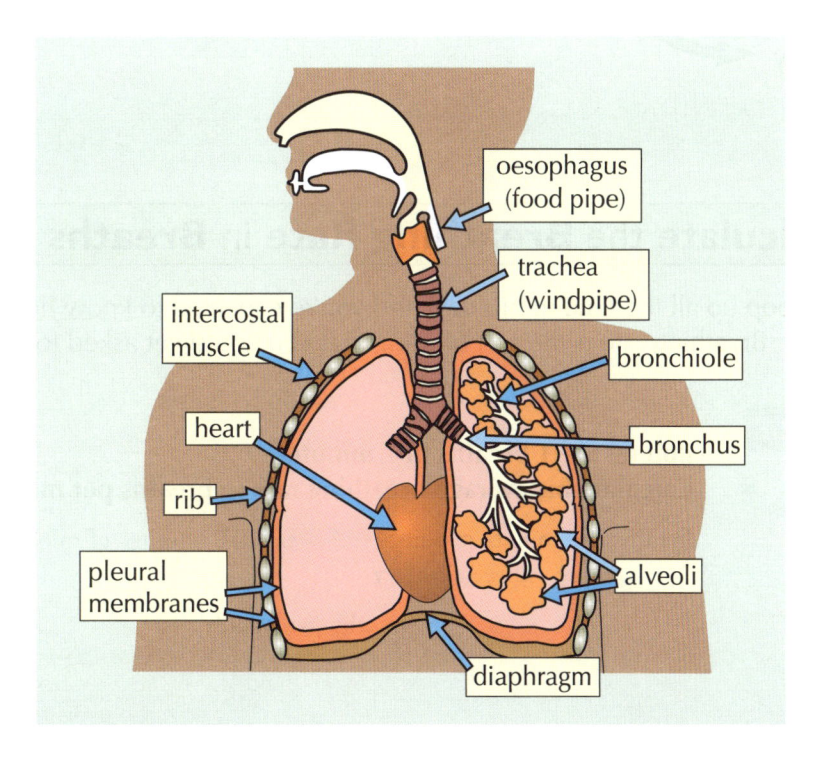

Take a deep breath...

...and make sure you get to grips with the layout of the innards of your chest. Try sketching the diagram and adding the labels until you think you've got it sussed. If you know where the trachea, bronchi, bronchioles and alveoli are, then you're making a pretty good start.

Topic B2 — Organisation

The Lungs

Now that you know where the alveoli are, it's time to find out what they do.

Alveoli Carry Out Gas Exchange in the Body

1) The lungs contain millions and millions of little air sacs called alveoli, surrounded by a network of blood capillaries. This is where gas exchange happens.
2) The blood passing next to the alveoli has just returned to the lungs from the rest of the body, so it contains lots of carbon dioxide and very little oxygen. Oxygen diffuses out of the alveolus (high concentration) into the blood (low concentration). Carbon dioxide diffuses out of the blood (high concentration) into the alveolus (low concentration) to be breathed out.

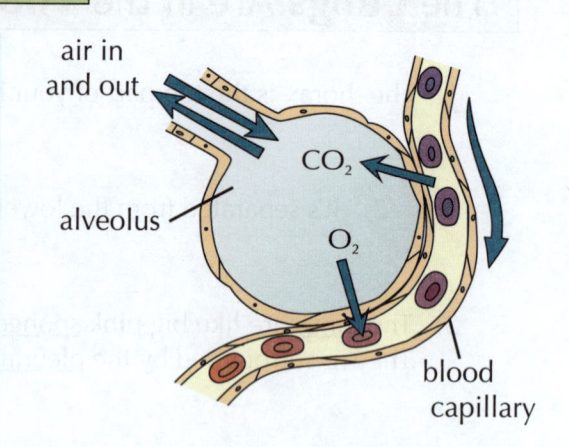

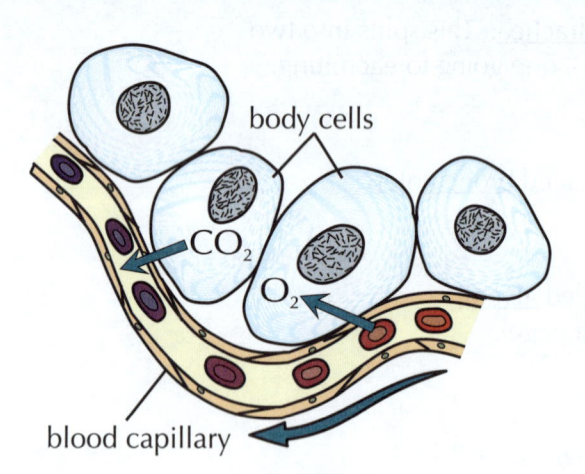

3) When the blood reaches body cells oxygen is released from the red blood cells (where there's a high concentration) and diffuses into the body cells (where the concentration is low).
4) At the same time, carbon dioxide diffuses out of the body cells (where there's a high concentration) into the blood (where there's a low concentration). It's then carried back to the lungs.

You Can Calculate the Breathing Rate in Breaths Per Minute

Rate calculations pop up all the time in biology, and you're expected to know how to do them — thankfully they're pretty easy. Breathing rate is the sort of thing that you could get asked to work out in your exam.

EXAMPLE

Bob takes 91 breaths in 7 minutes.
Calculate his average breathing rate in breaths per minute.

breaths per minute = number of breaths ÷ number of minutes
= 91 ÷ 7
= 13 breaths per minute

Alveoli are exchange surfaces

Back on page 35, you read about how exchange surfaces can be adapted to maximise their effectiveness. Alveoli have all of these adaptations to speed up the process of getting oxygen into the blood and getting the waste carbon dioxide out of the body — flick back to page 35 for a reminder.

Topic B2 — Organisation

Circulatory System — The Heart

*The circulatory system carries **food** and **oxygen** to every cell in the body. As well as being a delivery service, it's also a waste collection service — it carries **waste products** to where they can be removed from the body.*

It's a DOUBLE Circulatory System

The circulatory system is made up of the heart, blood vessels and blood. Humans have a double circulatory system — two circuits joined together:

1) In the first one, the right ventricle (see below) pumps deoxygenated blood (blood without oxygen) to the lungs to take in oxygen. The blood then returns to the heart.
2) In the second one, the left ventricle (see below) pumps oxygenated blood around all the other organs of the body. The blood gives up its oxygen at the body cells and the deoxygenated blood returns to the heart to be pumped out to the lungs again.

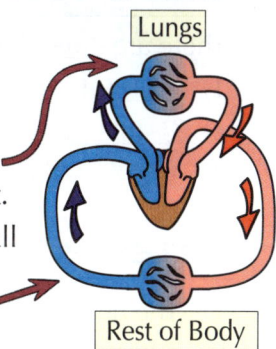

The Heart Contracts to Pump Blood Around The Body

1) The heart is a pumping organ that keeps the blood flowing around the body. The walls of the heart are mostly made of muscle tissue.
2) The heart has valves to make sure that blood flows in the right direction — they prevent it flowing backwards.
3) This is how the heart uses its four chambers (right atrium, right ventricle, left atrium and left ventricle) to pump blood around:

Atrium is when there is just one. Atria is plural.

1) Blood flows into the two atria from the vena cava and the pulmonary vein.
2) The atria contract, pushing the blood into the ventricles.
3) The ventricles contract, forcing the blood into the pulmonary artery and the aorta, and out of the heart.
4) The blood then flows to the organs through arteries, and returns through veins (see next page).
5) The atria fill again and the whole cycle starts over.

The heart also needs its own supply of oxygenated blood. Arteries called coronary arteries branch off the aorta and surround the heart, making sure that it gets all the oxygenated blood it needs.

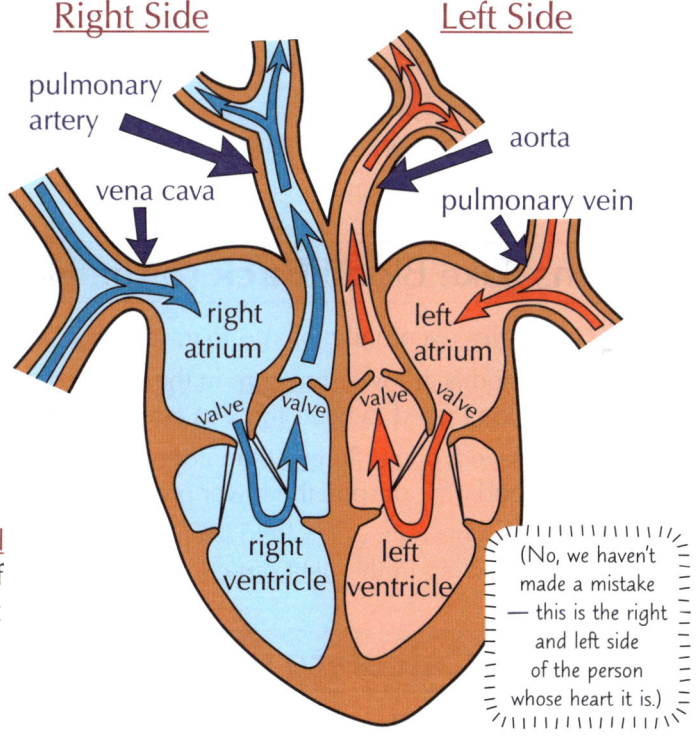

(No, we haven't made a mistake — this is the right and left side of the person whose heart it is.)

The Heart Has a Pacemaker

1) Your resting heart rate is controlled by a group of cells in the right atrium wall that act as a pacemaker.
2) These cells produce a small electric impulse which spreads to the surrounding muscle cells, causing them to contract.
3) An artificial pacemaker is often used to control heartbeat if the natural pacemaker cells don't work properly (e.g. if the patient has an irregular heartbeat). It's a little device that's implanted under the skin and has a wire going to the heart. It produces an electric current to keep the heart beating regularly.

Topic B2 — Organisation

Circulatory System — Blood Vessels

Blood needs a good set of 'tubes' to carry it round the body. Here's a page on the different types:

Blood Vessels are Designed for Their Function

There are three different types of blood vessel:
1) ARTERIES — these carry the blood away from the heart.
2) CAPILLARIES — these are involved in the exchange of materials at the tissues.
3) VEINS — these carry the blood to the heart.

Arteries Carry Blood Under Pressure

1) The heart pumps the blood out at high pressure so the artery walls are strong and elastic.
2) The walls are thick compared to the size of the hole down the middle (the "lumen").
3) They contain thick layers of muscle to make them strong, and elastic fibres to allow them to stretch and spring back.

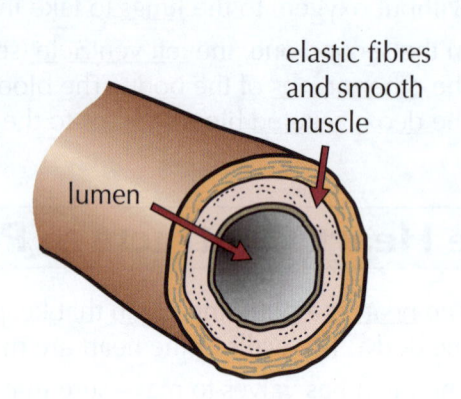

Capillaries are Really Small

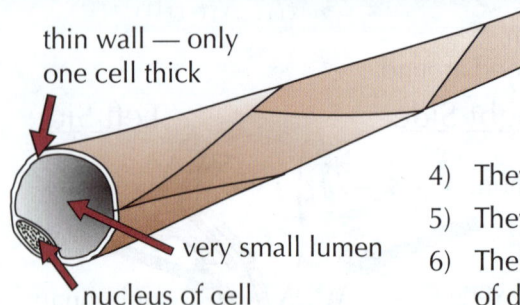

1) Arteries branch into capillaries.
2) Capillaries are really tiny — too small to see.
3) They carry the blood really close to every cell in the body to exchange substances with them.
4) They have permeable walls, so substances can diffuse in and out.
5) They supply food and oxygen, and take away wastes like CO_2.
6) Their walls are usually only one cell thick. This increases the rate of diffusion by decreasing the distance over which it occurs.

Veins Take Blood Back to the Heart

1) Capillaries eventually join up to form veins.
2) The blood is at lower pressure in the veins so the walls don't need to be as thick as artery walls.
3) They have a bigger lumen than arteries to help the blood flow despite the lower pressure.
4) They also have valves to help keep the blood flowing in the right direction.

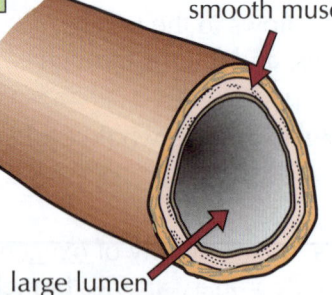

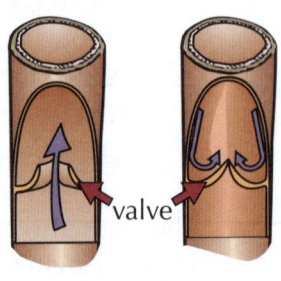

You Can Calculate the Rate of Blood Flow

You might get asked to calculate the rate of blood flow in your exam. Thankfully, it's not too tricky. Take a look at this example:

EXAMPLE 1464 ml of blood passed through an artery in 4.5 minutes. Calculate the rate of blood flow through the artery in ml/min.
rate of blood flow = volume of blood ÷ number of minutes
= 1464 ÷ 4.5 = 325 ml/min

Veins have valves — arteries carry blood away from the heart

Q1 2.175 litres of blood passed through a vein in 8.7 minutes.
    Calculate the rate of blood flow through the vein in ml/min. [2 marks]

Topic B2 — Organisation

Circulatory System — Blood

*Blood is a **tissue**. It's part of a huge **transport system**. There are four main things in blood...*

Red Blood Cells Carry Oxygen

1) The job of red blood cells is to carry oxygen from the lungs to all the cells in the body.
2) Their shape is a biconcave disc (like a doughnut) — this gives a large surface area for absorbing oxygen.
3) They don't have a nucleus — this allows more room to carry oxygen.
4) They contain a red pigment called haemoglobin.
5) In the lungs, haemoglobin binds to oxygen to become oxyhaemoglobin. In body tissues, the reverse happens — oxyhaemoglobin splits up into haemoglobin and oxygen, to release oxygen to the cells.

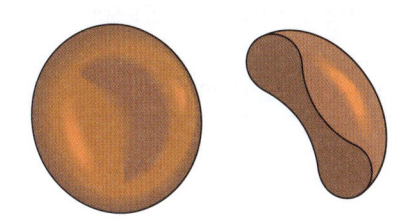

The more red blood cells you've got, the more oxygen can get to your cells. At high altitudes there's less oxygen in the air — so people who live there produce more red blood cells to compensate.

White Blood Cells Defend Against Infection

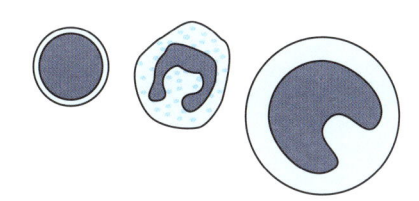

1) Some can change shape to engulf unwelcome microorganisms, in a process called phagocytosis.
2) Others produce antibodies to fight microorganisms, as well as antitoxins to neutralise any toxins produced by the microorganisms.
3) Unlike red blood cells, they do have a nucleus.

Platelets Help Blood Clot

1) These are small fragments of cells. They have no nucleus.
2) They help the blood to clot at a wound — to stop all your blood pouring out and to stop microorganisms getting in.
3) Lack of platelets can cause excessive bleeding and bruising.

Plasma is the Liquid That Carries Everything in Blood

This is a pale straw-coloured liquid which carries just about everything:

1) Red and white blood cells and platelets.
2) Nutrients like glucose and amino acids. These are the soluble products of digestion which are absorbed from the gut and taken to the cells of the body.
3) Carbon dioxide from the organs to the lungs.
4) Urea from the liver to the kidneys.
5) Hormones.
6) Proteins.
7) Antibodies and antitoxins produced by the white blood cells.

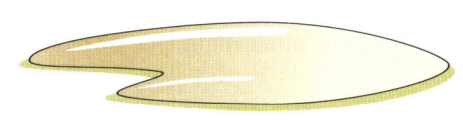

Blood — red blood cells, white blood cells, platelets and plasma

Blood tests can be used to diagnose loads of things — not just disorders of the blood. This is because the blood transports so many chemicals produced by so many organs.

Q1   Describe the purpose of platelets in blood.   [1 mark]

Q2   State the function of the cell labelled X in the image on the right.   [1 mark]

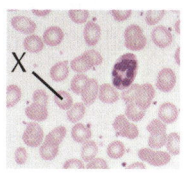

Topic B2 — Organisation

Warm-Up & Exam Questions

There are some nice diagrams to learn on the previous few pages. If you don't bother, you'll feel pretty silly if you turn over the exam paper and the first question asks you to label a diagram of the heart. Just saying... Anyway, let's see if these questions get your blood pumping...

Warm-Up Questions

1) What is the name of the tubes that the trachea splits into?
2) What is the function of the coronary arteries?
3) What is an artificial pacemaker?
4) What do veins do?
5) Which component of blood is made from small fragments of cells?

Exam Questions

1 A student ran for 12 minutes. *Grade 4-6*

1.1 During this 12 minute run, the student took 495 breaths.
Calculate his average breathing rate in breaths per minute.

[1 mark]

1.2 The student also measured his heart rate before and during his run.
Before his run, the student's heart rate was at its natural resting rate.
Outline how natural resting heart rate is controlled.

[1 mark]

2 The cell shown in **Figure 1** transports oxygen around the body. *Grade 6-7*

2.1 Explain how this cell's shape is adapted for transporting oxygen.

Figure 1

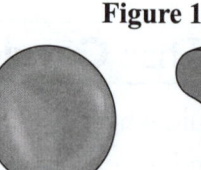

View from above   Cut through view

[1 mark]

2.2 Describe and explain **one** other way in which this cell is adapted for carrying oxygen.

[2 marks]

2.3 Name the other main type of blood cell, and state its function.

[2 marks]

Blood cells are carried in the bloodstream inside blood vessels.

2.4 Capillaries are one type of blood vessel.
Outline how the structure of a capillary enables it to carry out its function.

[4 marks]

2.5 Blood flows through different types of blood vessels at different rates.
The volume of blood that passed through an artery in 150 seconds was 1155 ml.
Calculate the rate of blood flow through the artery in ml/min.

[2 marks]

Topic B2 — Organisation

Exam Questions

3 **Figure 2** shows the human heart and four blood vessels, as seen from the front. The left ventricle has been labelled.

Grade 6-7

Figure 2

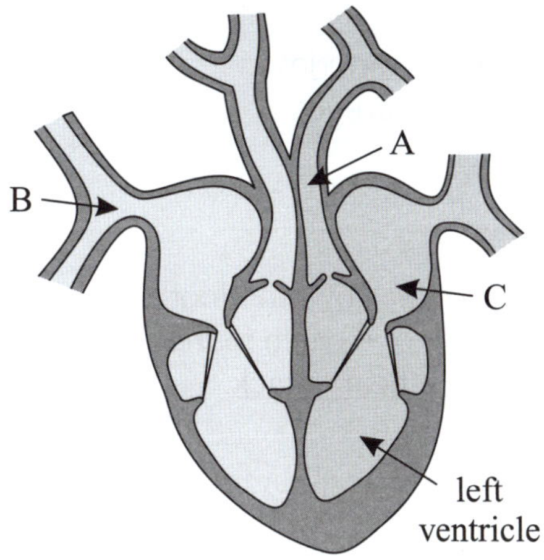

[Diagram of heart with labels A, B, C and left ventricle]

3.1 Name the parts labelled **A**, **B** and **C**.

[1 mark]

3.2 Describe the function of the left ventricle.

[1 mark]

3.3 What is the function of the valves in the heart?

[1 mark]

3.4* Describe how deoxygenated blood from the body passes through the heart to reach the lungs.

[4 marks]

4 A student did an experiment to compare the elasticity of arteries and veins. He dissected out an artery and a vein from a piece of fresh meat. He then took a 5 cm length of each vessel, hung different masses on it, and measured how much it stretched. His results are shown in **Table 1**.

Grade 7-9

Table 1

Mass added (g)	Length of blood vessel (mm)	
	Artery	Vein
0	50	50
5	51	53
10	53	56
15	55	59
20	56	-

4.1 Suggest **one** way in which the student could tell which was the artery and which was the vein when he was dissecting the meat.

[1 mark]

4.2 Which vessel stretched more easily? Suggest why this was.

[1 mark]

Topic B2 — Organisation

Cardiovascular Disease

Cardiovascular disease is a term used to describe diseases of the heart or blood vessels, for example coronary heart disease. This page tells you all about how **stents** are used to combat coronary heart disease.

Coronary Heart Disease is Life-Threatening

Coronary heart disease is when the coronary arteries that supply the blood to the muscle of the heart get blocked by layers of fatty material building up.

This causes the arteries to become narrow, so blood flow is restricted and there's a lack of oxygen to the heart muscle — this can result in a heart attack.

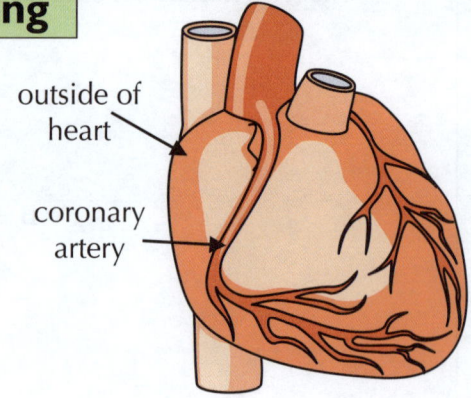

outside of heart

coronary artery

Stents Keep Arteries Open

1) Stents are tubes that are inserted inside arteries. They keep them open, making sure blood can pass through to the heart muscles. This keeps the person's heart beating (and the person alive).

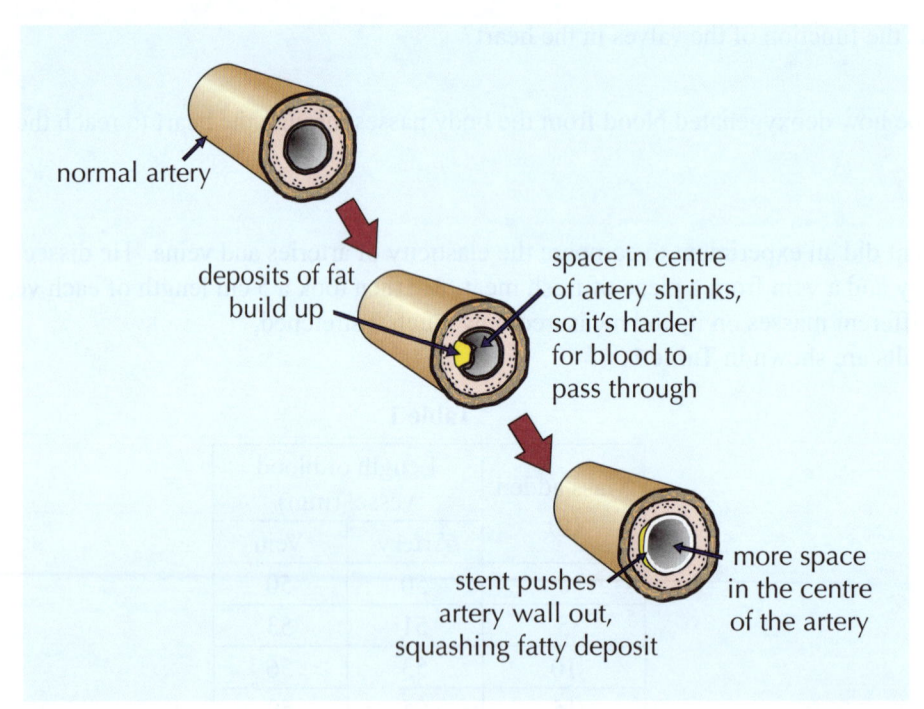

normal artery

deposits of fat build up

space in centre of artery shrinks, so it's harder for blood to pass through

stent pushes artery wall out, squashing fatty deposit

more space in the centre of the artery

2) Stents are a way of lowering the risk of a heart attack in people with coronary heart disease. They are effective for a long time and the recovery time from the surgery is relatively quick.
3) On the down side, there is a risk of complications during the operation (e.g. heart attack) and a risk of infection from surgery. There is also the risk of patients developing a blood clot near the stent — this is called thrombosis.

Coronary heart disease is a type of cardiovascular disease

Coronary heart disease is caused by the arteries being blocked by fatty material — if the heart muscle can't get enough oxygen, then it can't work properly. And if the heart can't work properly, well, you're in trouble.

Topic B2 — Organisation

Cardiovascular Disease

*You've read about stents, so now it's time for a second treatment for coronary heart disease — **statins**.*

Statins Reduce Cholesterol in the Blood

1) Cholesterol is an essential lipid that your body produces and needs to function properly. However, too much of a certain type of cholesterol (known as 'bad' or LDL cholesterol) can cause health problems.

2) Having too much of this 'bad' cholesterol in the bloodstream can cause fatty deposits to form inside arteries, which can lead to coronary heart disease.

3) Statins are drugs that can reduce the amount of 'bad' cholesterol present in the bloodstream. This slows down the rate of fatty deposits forming.

Statins Have Advantages and Disadvantages

Advantages

1) By reducing the amount of 'bad' cholesterol in the blood, statins can reduce the risk of strokes, coronary heart disease and heart attacks.

2) As well as reducing the amount of 'bad' cholesterol, statins can increase the amount of a beneficial type of cholesterol (known as 'good' or HDL cholesterol) in your bloodstream. This type can remove 'bad' cholesterol from the blood.

3) Some studies suggest that statins may also help prevent some other diseases.

Disadvantages

1) Statins are a long-term drug that must be taken regularly. There's the risk that someone could forget to take them.

2) Statins can sometimes cause negative side effects, e.g. headaches. Some of these side effects can be serious, e.g. kidney failure, liver damage and memory loss.

3) The effect of statins isn't instant. It takes time for their effect to kick in.

An Artificial Heart Can Pump Blood Around the Body

1) If a patient has heart failure, doctors may perform a heart transplant (or heart and lungs transplant if the lungs are also diseased) using donor organs from people who have recently died. However, if donor organs aren't available right away or they're not the best option, doctors may fit an artificial heart.

2) Artificial hearts are mechanical devices that pump blood for a person whose own heart has failed. They're usually only used as a temporary fix, to keep a person alive until a donor heart can be found or to help a person recover by allowing the heart to rest and heal. In some cases though they're used as a permanent fix, which reduces the need for a donor heart.

3) The main advantage of artificial hearts is that they're less likely to be rejected by the body's immune system than a donor heart. This is because they're made from metals or plastics, so the body doesn't recognise them as 'foreign' and attack in the same way as it does with living tissue.

4) But surgery to fit an artificial heart (as with transplant surgery) can lead to bleeding and infection. Also, artificial hearts don't work as well as healthy natural ones — parts of the heart could wear out or the electrical motor could fail. Blood doesn't flow through artificial hearts as smoothly, which can cause blood clots and lead to strokes. The patient has to take drugs to thin their blood and make sure this doesn't happen, which can cause problems with bleeding if they're hurt in an accident.

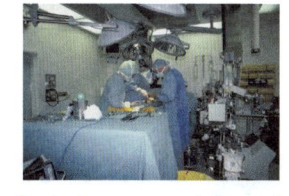

Replacing a person's heart is major surgery, which has risks.

Topic B2 — Organisation

Cardiovascular Disease

*One final page on cardiovascular disease. Having a heart transplant or getting an artificial heart fitted aren't the only surgeries for cardiovascular disease. Surgeons can do things like **replacing** just the **valves** in a heart.*

Faulty Heart Valves Can Be Replaced

1) The valves in the heart can be damaged or weakened by heart attacks, infection or old age.

2) The damage may cause the valve tissue to stiffen, so it won't open properly. Or a valve may become leaky, allowing blood to flow in both directions rather than just forward. This means that blood doesn't circulate as effectively as normal.

3) Severe valve damage can be treated by replacing the valve.

4) Replacement valves can be ones taken from humans or other mammals (e.g. cows or pigs) — these are biological valves. Or they can be man-made — these are mechanical valves.

5) Replacing a valve is a much less drastic procedure than a whole heart transplant. But fitting artificial valves is still major surgery and there can still be problems with blood clots.

Artificial Blood Can Keep You Alive In An Emergency

1) When someone loses a lot of blood, e.g. in an accident, their heart can still pump the remaining red blood cells around (to get oxygen to their organs), as long as the volume of their blood can be topped up.

2) Artificial blood is a blood substitute, e.g. a salt solution ("saline"), which is used to replace the lost volume of blood. It's safe (if no air bubbles get into the blood) and can keep people alive even if they lose 2/3 of their red blood cells. This may give the patient enough time to produce new blood cells. If not, the patient will need a blood transfusion.

3) Ideally, an artificial blood product would replace the function of the red blood cells, so that there's no need for a blood transfusion. Scientists are currently working on products that can do this.

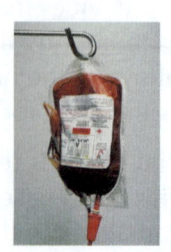

An artificial blood product that carries oxygen would replace the need for a blood transfusion from another person. This would have advantages such as decreasing the risk of diseases being passed on.

Don't lose heart...

EXAM TIP
You could be asked to evaluate treatments for cardiovascular disease. Don't panic — just use any information you're given and your own knowledge to weigh up the advantages and disadvantages. Make sure your answer doesn't just focus on one side — e.g. don't just talk about the advantages and ignore the disadvantages — and don't forget to include a justified conclusion.

Topic B2 — Organisation

Warm-Up & Exam Questions

Hopefully I've persuaded you by now that it's a good idea to try these questions. Believe me, when you're sitting with your real exam paper in front of you, you'll feel so much better knowing that you've already been through loads of practice questions. So off you go...

Warm-Up Questions

1) Which vessels are affected in coronary heart disease?
2) a) What device can be used to keep an artery open?
   b) Give three risks associated with getting one of these devices fitted.
3) What is an artificial heart?

Exam Questions

1 Coronary heart disease is the main cause of death worldwide. **Figure 1** shows a cross-section of a blood vessel in someone with coronary heart disease. *(Grade 4-6)*

Figure 1

1.1 Name the substance labelled **X** on **Figure 1**.
[1 mark]

1.2 Explain how the presence of this substance can affect oxygen delivery to the heart muscle.
[2 marks]

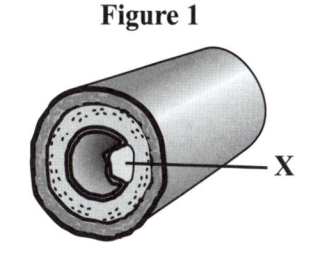

2 A patient is taken into hospital. They are diagnosed as having a leaky heart valve. *(Grade 6-7)*

2.1 Explain why a leaky valve could cause a health problem.
[2 marks]

The doctor decides that a surgeon should replace the valve.

2.2 Name and describe the **two** types of valve that the surgeon might use.
[4 marks]

2.3 Suggest **one** disadvantage of replacing the faulty valve.
[1 mark]

3 Some people with cardiovascular disease take statins. These are drugs that need to be taken every day. *(Grade 6-7)*

3.1 Outline why statins are sometimes used in the treatment of coronary heart disease.
[2 marks]

3.2 Suggest **one** disadvantage to a patient of taking statins.
[1 mark]

Topic B2 — Organisation

Health and Disease

*Try as we might, it's unlikely that we'll be in tip-top condition for all of our lives — **disease** tends to get us all at some point. There are lots of **different types** of diseases we could get...*

Diseases are a Major Cause of Ill Health

Health is the state of physical and mental wellbeing.
Diseases are often responsible for causing ill health.

Diseases Can be Communicable or Non-Communicable

1) Communicable diseases are those that can spread from person to person or between animals and people. They can be caused by things like bacteria, viruses, parasites and fungi. They're sometimes described as contagious or infectious diseases. Measles and malaria are examples of communicable diseases. There's more about them on pages 75-78.

2) Non-communicable diseases are those that cannot spread between people or between animals and people. They generally last for a long time and get worse slowly. Asthma, cancer and coronary heart disease (see page 58) are examples of non-communicable diseases.

Different Types of Disease Sometimes Interact

Sometimes diseases can interact and cause other physical and mental health issues that don't immediately seem related. Here are a few examples:

1) People who have problems with their immune system (the system that your body uses to help fight off infection — see p.81) have an increased chance of suffering from communicable diseases such as influenza (flu), because their body is less likely to be able to defend itself against the pathogen that causes the disease.

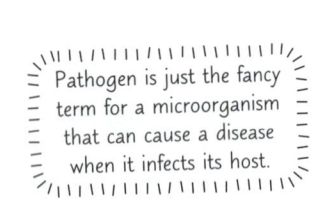

Pathogen is just the fancy term for a microorganism that can cause a disease when it infects its host.

2) Some types of cancer can be triggered by infection by certain viruses. For example, infection with some types of hepatitis virus can cause long-term infections in the liver, where the virus lives in the cells. This can lead to an increased chance of developing liver cancer. Another example is infection with HPV (human papilloma virus), which can cause cervical cancer in women.

3) Immune system reactions in the body caused by infection by a pathogen can sometimes trigger allergic reactions such as skin rashes or worsen the symptoms of asthma for asthma sufferers.

4) Mental health issues such as depression can be triggered when someone is suffering from severe physical health problems, particularly if they have an impact on the person's ability to carry out everyday activities or if they affect the person's life expectancy.

Communicable diseases can spread...

...but non-communicable diseases can't. Remember that — it's really important.

Topic B2 — Organisation

Health and Disease

Ill health isn't just about having a disease — there are plenty of **other causes**.
And then there's the **cost** of ill health to consider too — there might be more to it than you'd first thought...

Other Factors Can Also Affect Your Health

There are plenty of factors other than diseases that can also affect your health. For example:

1) Whether or not you have a good, balanced diet that provides your body with everything it needs, and in the right amounts. A poor diet can affect your physical and mental health.

2) The stress you are under — being constantly under lots of stress can lead to health issues.

3) Your life situation — for example, whether you have easy access to medicines to treat illness, or whether you have access to things that can prevent you from getting ill in the first place, e.g. being able to buy healthy food or access condoms to prevent the transmission of some sexually transmitted diseases.

Non-Communicable Diseases Can Be Costly

The Human Cost

1) The human cost of non-communicable diseases is obvious. Tens of millions of people around the world die from non-communicable diseases per year.
2) People with these diseases may have a lower quality of life or a shorter lifespan. This not only affects the sufferers themselves, but their loved ones too.

The Financial Cost

1) It's also important to think about the financial cost.
2) The cost to the NHS of researching and treating these diseases is huge — and it's the same for other health services and organisations around the world.
3) Families may have to move or adapt their home to help a family member with a disease, which can be costly.
4) Also, if the family member with the disease has to give up work or dies, the family's income will be reduced.
5) A reduction in the number of people able to work can also affect a country's economy.

Lots of things affect health, and ill health can be costly

A human cost is the effect something has on humans. A financial cost is to do with how much spending something results in. When you're studying biology, you'll come across lots of things that have a human cost or a financial cost (or both). Some things can have quite far-reaching knock-on effects.

Topic B2 — Organisation

Risk Factors for Non-Communicable Diseases

You've probably heard the term 'risk factor' before. These next couple of pages have lots of info on them. There's nothing too tricky, but there's quite a bit to read — take it slowly and make sure it goes in.

Risk Factors Increase Your Chance of Getting a Disease

1) Risk factors are things that are linked to an increase in the likelihood that a person will develop a certain disease during their lifetime. They don't guarantee that someone will get the disease.

2) Risk factors are often aspects of a person's lifestyle (e.g. how much exercise they do).

3) They can also be the presence of certain substances in the environment (e.g. air pollution) or substances in your body (e.g. asbestos fibres — asbestos was a material used in buildings until it was realised that the fibres could build up in your airways and cause diseases such as cancer later in life).

4) Many non-communicable diseases are caused by several different risk factors interacting with each other rather than one factor alone.

5) Lifestyle factors can have different impacts locally, nationally and globally. E.g. in developed countries, non-communicable diseases are more common as people generally have a higher income and can buy high-fat food. Nationally, people from deprived areas are more likely to smoke, have a poor diet and not exercise. This means the incidence of cardiovascular disease, obesity and Type 2 diabetes is higher in those areas. Your individual choices affect the local incidence of disease.

Some Risk Factors Can Cause a Disease Directly

Some risk factors are able to directly cause a disease. For example:

Smoking has been proven to directly cause cardiovascular disease, lung disease and lung cancer. It damages the walls of arteries and the cells in the lining of the lungs.

It's thought that obesity can directly cause Type 2 diabetes by making the body less sensitive or resistant to insulin, meaning that it struggles to control the concentration of glucose in the blood.

There's more about Type 2 diabetes on page 113.

Topic B2 — Organisation

Risk Factors for Non-Communicable Diseases

Here are a few more risk factors that can directly cause disease:

1) Drinking too much alcohol has been shown to cause liver disease. The liver breaks down alcohol, but the reaction can damage its cells.
2) Liver cells may also be damaged when toxic chemicals leak from the gut due to damage to the intestines caused by alcohol.
3) Too much alcohol can affect brain function too. It can damage the nerve cells in the brain, causing the brain to lose volume.

Smoking when pregnant reduces the amount of oxygen the baby receives in the womb and can cause lots of health problems for the unborn baby. Drinking alcohol has similar effects. Alcohol can damage the baby's cells, affecting its development and causing a wide range of health issues.

There's more about cancer coming up on the next page.

Cancer can be directly caused by exposure to certain substances or radiation. Things that cause cancer are known as carcinogens. Carcinogens work in different ways. For example, some damage a cell's DNA in a way that makes the cell more likely to divide uncontrollably. Ionising radiation (e.g. from X-rays) is an example of a carcinogen.

Risk Factors Can be Identified Using Correlation

1) Risk factors are identified by scientists looking for correlations in data. However, correlation doesn't always equal cause.
2) Some risk factors aren't capable of directly causing a disease, but are related to another risk factor that is.
3) For example:

See pages 11 and 14 for more about correlations.

A lack of exercise and a high fat diet are heavily linked to an increased chance of cardiovascular disease, but they can't cause the disease directly. It's the resulting high blood pressure and high 'bad' cholesterol levels (see p.59) that can actually cause it.

It's hard to avoid all risk factors of disease...

...but remember that risk factors that cause disease don't mean you'll definitely get the disease — they just increase the chance of it happening. Also, remember that not all risk factors cause disease. Many are just correlated with the disease, meaning there is a relationship between them.

Topic B2 — Organisation

Cancer

*The more we understand about **cancer**, the better our chances of **avoiding** and **beating** it. Hoorah.*

Cancer is Caused by Uncontrolled Cell Growth and Division

This uncontrolled growth and division is a result of changes that occur to the cells and results in the formation of a tumour (a growth of abnormal cells). Not all tumours are cancerous. They can be benign or malignant:

Benign
1) This is where the tumour grows until there's no more room.
2) The tumour stays in one place (usually within a membrane) rather than invading other tissues in the body.
3) This type isn't normally dangerous, and the tumour isn't cancerous.

Malignant
1) This is where the tumour grows and spreads to neighbouring healthy tissues.
2) Cells can break off and spread to other parts of the body by travelling in the bloodstream.
3) The malignant cells then invade healthy tissues elsewhere in the body and form secondary tumours.
4) Malignant tumours are dangerous and can be fatal — they are cancers.

Risk Factors Can Increase the Chance of Some Cancers

Anyone can develop cancer. Having risk factors doesn't mean that you'll definitely get cancer. It just means that you're at an increased risk of developing the disease. Cancer survival rates have increased due to medical advances such as improved treatment, being able to diagnose cancer earlier and increased screening for the disease.

Risk Factors Can Be Associated With Lifestyle

Scientists have identified lots of lifestyle risk factors for various types of cancer. For example:

1) Smoking — It's a well known fact that smoking is linked to lung cancer, but research has also linked it to other types of cancer too, including mouth, bowel, stomach and cervical cancer.
2) Obesity — Obesity has been linked to many different cancers, including bowel, liver and kidney cancer. It's the second biggest preventable cause of cancer after smoking.
3) UV exposure — People who are often exposed to UV radiation from the Sun have an increased chance of developing skin cancer. People who live in sunny climates and people who spend a lot of time outside are at higher risk of the disease. People who frequently use sun beds are also putting themselves at higher risk of developing skin cancer.
4) Viral infection — Infection with some viruses has been shown to increase the chances of developing certain types of cancer. For example, infection with hepatitis B and hepatitis C viruses can increase the risk of developing liver cancer. The likelihood of becoming infected with these viruses sometimes depends on lifestyle — e.g. they can be spread between people through unprotected sex or sharing needles.

Risk Factors Can Also Be Associated With Genetics

Sometimes you can inherit faulty genes that make you more susceptible to cancer. For example:

> Mutations in the BRCA genes have been linked to an increased likelihood of developing breast and ovarian cancer.

Topic B2 — Organisation

Warm-Up & Exam Questions

It's time for some more questions — don't just assume that you've remembered everything you just read on the past few pages. Give these a go, and then go back over anything that you struggled with.

Warm-Up Questions

1) What is meant by 'health'?
2) What does it mean if a disease is 'communicable'?
3) Give an example of a national financial cost associated with non-communicable diseases.
4) Give an example of a type of risk factor other than an aspect of a person's lifestyle.

Exam Questions

1 Many diseases have risk factors. *Grade 4-6*

1.1 What is meant by the term risk factor?

[1 mark]

1.2 Give **one** risk factor for lung disease.

[1 mark]

1.3 Name **one** carcinogen that is a risk factor for cancer.

[1 mark]

2 Cancer results from a tumour. *Grade 4-6*

2.1 What causes tumours to form? Tick **one** box.

☐ Uncontrolled cell division.

☐ Slow cell division.

☐ Cell division stopping.

☐ Cells dying.

[1 mark]

2.2 Name the type of tumour that causes cancer.

[1 mark]

2.3 Explain how secondary tumours form in the body.

[2 marks]

3 Diseases can be communicable or non-communicable. *Grade 6-7*

3.1 What is meant by a non-communicable disease?

[1 mark]

3.2 Influenza is a communicable disease.
Why might someone who has a problem with their immune system have an increased chance of suffering from influenza?

[1 mark]

Topic B2 — Organisation

Plant Cell Organisation

*You saw on pages 40-41 how animals keep their **specialised cells** neat and tidy — plants are in on the act too.*

Plant Cells Are Organised Into Tissues And Organs

Plants are made of organs like stems, roots and leaves. Plant organs work together to make organ systems. These can perform the various tasks that a plant needs to carry out to survive and grow — for example, transporting substances around the plant. Plant organs are made of tissues. Examples of plant tissues are:

1) Epidermal tissue — this covers the whole plant.
2) Palisade mesophyll tissue — this is the part of the leaf where most photosynthesis happens.
3) Spongy mesophyll tissue — this is also in the leaf, and contains big air spaces to allow gases to diffuse in and out of cells.
4) Xylem and phloem — they transport things like water, mineral ions and food around the plant (through the roots, stems and leaves — see next page for more).
5) Meristem tissue — this is found at the growing tips of shoots and roots and is able to differentiate (change) into lots of different types of plant cell, allowing the plant to grow.

For more on photosynthesis, see page 89.

The Leaf is an Organ Made Up of Several Types of Tissue

Leaves contain epidermal, mesophyll, xylem and phloem tissues.

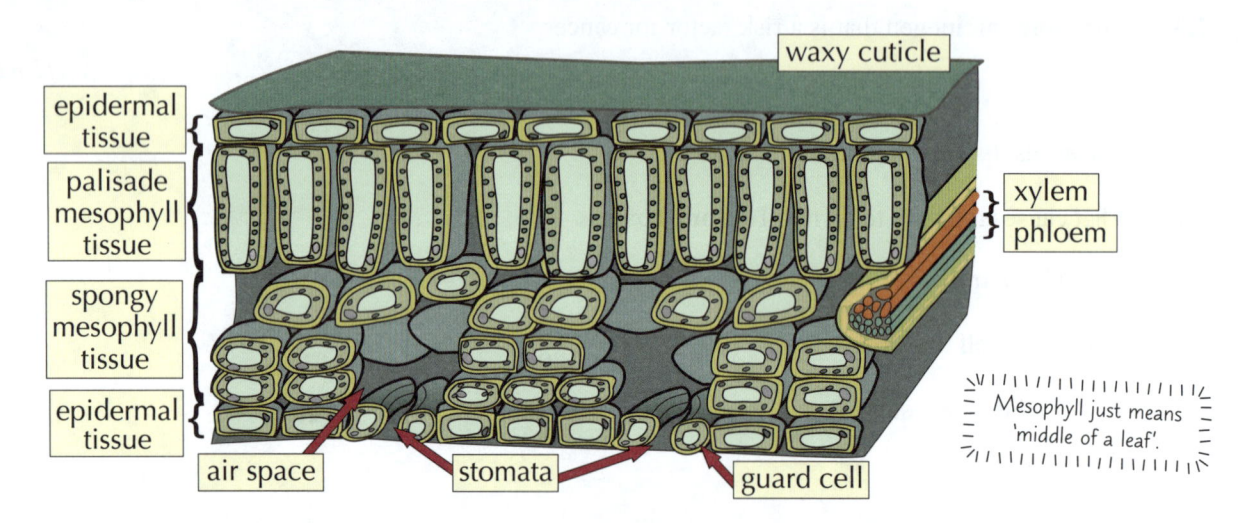

Mesophyll just means 'middle of a leaf'.

Here's how the structures of the tissues that make up the leaf are related to their function:

1) The epidermal tissues are covered with a waxy cuticle, which helps to reduce water loss by evaporation.
2) The upper epidermis is transparent so that light can pass through it to the palisade layer.
3) The palisade layer has lots of chloroplasts (the little structures where photosynthesis takes place). This means that they're near the top of the leaf where they can get the most light.
4) The xylem and phloem form a network of vascular bundles, which deliver water and other nutrients to the entire leaf and take away the glucose produced by photosynthesis. They also help support the structure.
5) The tissues of leaves are also adapted for efficient gas exchange (see page 36). E.g. the lower epidermis is full of little holes called stomata, which let CO_2 diffuse directly into the leaf. The opening and closing of stomata is controlled by guard cells in response to environmental conditions. The air spaces in the spongy mesophyll tissue increase the rate of diffusion of gases.

Topic B2 — Organisation

Transpiration and Translocation

*Flowering plants have **two** separate types of vessel — **xylem** and **phloem** — for transporting stuff around. **Both** types of vessel go to **every part** of the plant, but they are totally **separate**.*

Phloem Tubes Transport Food:

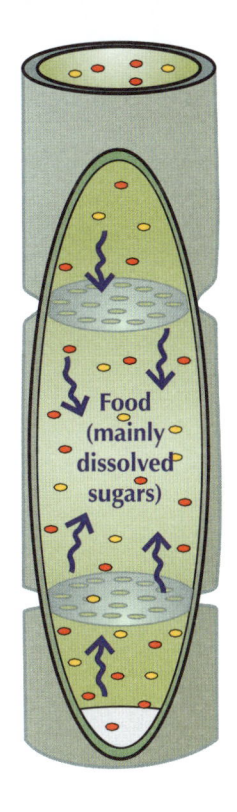

1) Made of columns of elongated living cells with small pores in the end walls to allow cell sap to flow through.

Cell sap is a liquid that's made up of the substances being transported and water.

2) They transport food substances (mainly dissolved sugars) made in the leaves to the rest of the plant for immediate use (e.g. in growing regions) or for storage.

3) The transport goes in both directions.

4) This process is called translocation.

Xylem Tubes Take Water Up:

1) Made of dead cells joined end to end with no end walls between them and a hole down the middle. They're strengthened with a material called lignin.

2) They carry water and mineral ions from the roots to the stem and leaves.

3) The movement of water from the roots, through the xylem and out of the leaves is called the transpiration stream (see next page).

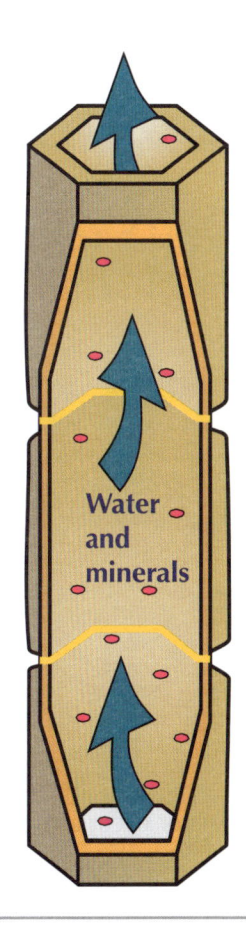

Xylem vessels carry water, phloem vessels carry sugars

Make sure you don't get your phloem mixed up with your xylem. To help you to learn which is which, you could remember that phl<u>o</u>em transports substances in b<u>o</u>th directions, but xylem only transports things upwards — x<u>y</u> to the sk<u>y</u>. It might just bag you a mark or two on exam day...

Topic B2 — Organisation

Transpiration

*If you don't water a house plant for a few days it starts to go all droopy. Plants need **water**.*

Transpiration is the Loss of Water from the Plant

1) Transpiration is caused by the evaporation and diffusion (see page 30) of water from a plant's surface. Most transpiration happens at the leaves.

2) This evaporation creates a slight shortage of water in the leaf, and so more water is drawn up from the rest of the plant through the xylem vessels to replace it.

3) This in turn means more water is drawn up from the roots, and so there's a constant transpiration stream of water through the plant.

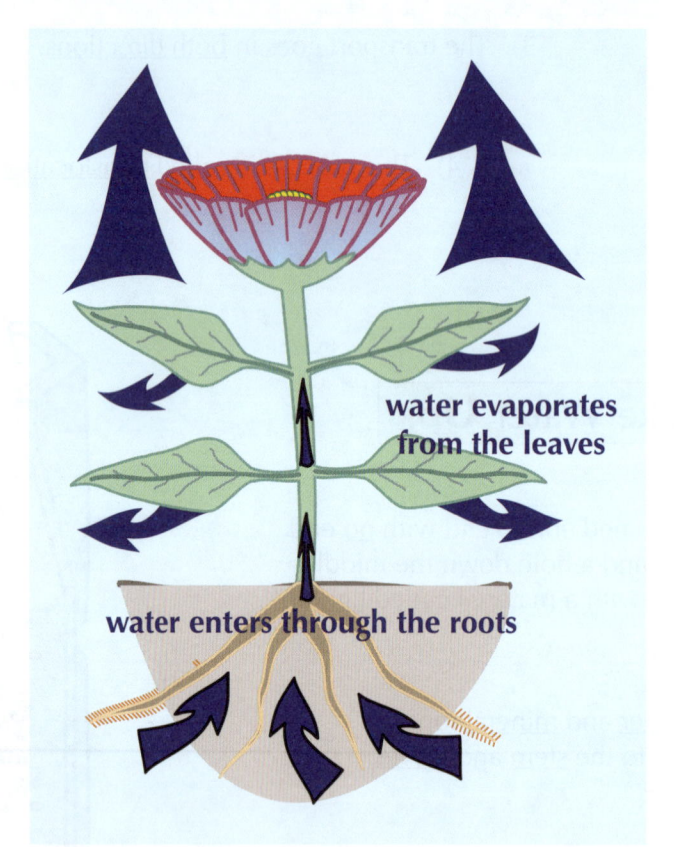

water evaporates from the leaves

water enters through the roots

Head back to page 24 to see how root hair cells are adapted for taking up water.

Transpiration is just a side-effect of the way leaves are adapted for photosynthesis. They have to have stomata in them so that gases can be exchanged easily (see page 36). Because there's more water inside the plant than in the air outside, the water escapes from the leaves through the stomata by diffusion.

Transpiration involves evaporation and diffusion

A big tree loses about a thousand litres of water from its leaves every single day — it's a fact. That's as much water as the average person drinks in a whole year, so the roots have to be very effective at drawing in water from the soil. Which is why they have all those root hairs, you see.

Topic B2 — Organisation

The Rate of Transpiration

*The **rate of transpiration** varies according to the **environmental conditions**...*

Transpiration Rate is Affected by Four Main Things

Light Intensity

1) The brighter the light, the greater the transpiration rate.
2) Stomata begin to close as it gets darker. Photosynthesis can't happen in the dark, so they don't need to be open to let CO_2 in. When the stomata are closed, very little water can escape.

Temperature

1) The warmer it is, the faster transpiration happens.
2) When it's warm the water particles have more energy to evaporate and diffuse out of the stomata.

Air Flow

1) The better the air flow around a leaf (e.g. stronger wind), the greater the transpiration rate.
2) If air flow around a leaf is poor, the water vapour just surrounds the leaf and doesn't move away. This means there's a high concentration of water particles outside the leaf as well as inside it, so diffusion doesn't happen as quickly.
3) If there's good air flow, the water vapour is swept away, maintaining a low concentration of water in the air outside the leaf. Diffusion then happens quickly, from an area of higher concentration to an area of lower concentration.

Humidity

1) The drier the air around a leaf, the faster transpiration happens.
2) This is like what happens with air flow. If the air is humid there's a lot of water in it already, so there's not much of a difference between the inside and the outside of the leaf.
3) Diffusion happens fastest if there's a really high concentration in one place, and a really low concentration in the other.

Topic B2 — Organisation

Measuring Transpiration and Stomata

*Sorry, more on **transpiration**. But then it's a quick dash through **stomata** and out of the other end of the topic.*

A Potometer can be Used to Estimate Transpiration Rate

1) You can estimate the rate of transpiration by measuring the uptake of water by a plant.
2) This is because you can assume that water uptake by the plant is directly related to water loss by the leaves (transpiration).
3) Set up the apparatus as in the diagram, and then record the starting position of the air bubble.
4) Start a stopwatch and record the distance moved by the bubble per unit time, e.g. per hour.
5) Keep the conditions constant throughout the experiment, e.g. the temperature and air humidity.

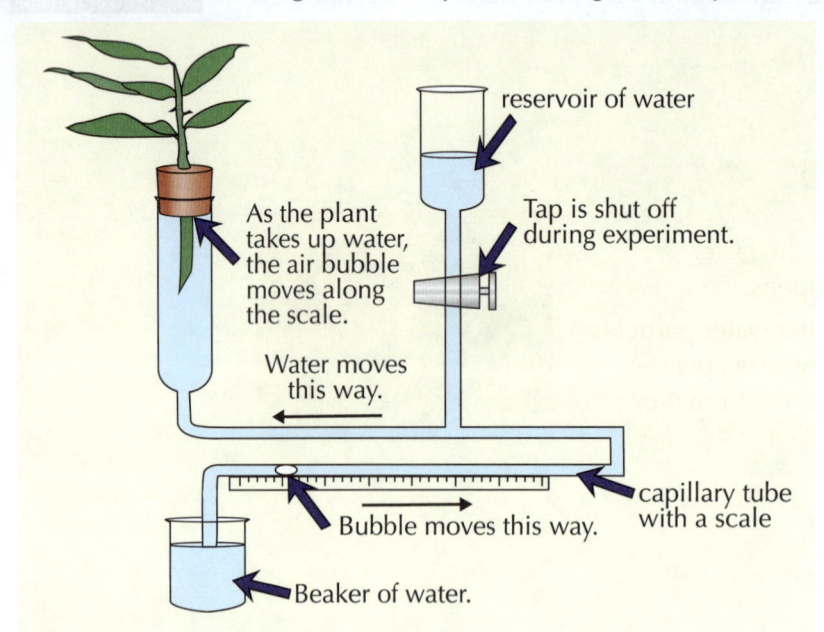

Diagram labels: reservoir of water; As the plant takes up water, the air bubble moves along the scale; Tap is shut off during experiment; Water moves this way; Bubble moves this way; capillary tube with a scale; Beaker of water.

This piece of apparatus is called a potometer. Setting it up is quite tough — there are some tips on page 410.

Guard Cells Are Adapted to Open and Close Stomata

1) They have a kidney shape which opens and closes the stomata (page 36) in a leaf.
2) When the plant has lots of water the guard cells fill with it and go plump and turgid. This makes the stomata open so gases can be exchanged for photosynthesis.
3) When the plant is short of water, the guard cells lose water and become flaccid, making the stomata close. This helps stop too much water vapour escaping.
4) Thin outer walls and thickened inner walls make the opening and closing work.
5) They're also sensitive to light and close at night to save water without losing out on photosynthesis.
6) You usually find more stomata on the undersides of leaves than on the top. The lower surface is shaded and cooler — so less water is lost through the stomata than if they were on the upper surface.
7) Guard cells are therefore adapted for gas exchange and controlling water loss within a leaf.

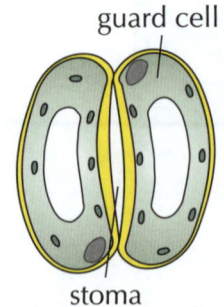

Diagram label: guard cell; stoma (plural — stomata)

The opening and closing of stomata allows plants to survive

Different leaves will have different distributions of stomata. You can peel the epidermal tissue off some leaves and then mount them on microscope slides (see page 19) to compare them.

Q1 Aloe vera plants grow in hot, dry areas. Primroses grow in cool, wet areas. Predict which plant will have fewer stomata per cm^2 on the underside of its leaves. Explain your answer. [2 marks]

Topic B2 — Organisation

Warm-Up & Exam Questions

Just a few simple Warm-Up Questions and a few slightly harder Exam Questions stand between you and mastering cell organisation and transport in plants...

Warm-Up Questions

1) Describe the characteristics of meristem tissue.
2) Which layer of plant tissue contains lots of chloroplasts?
3) True or false? Substances pass in both directions through xylem vessels.
4) State the four main factors that affect the rate of transpiration in plants.

Exam Questions

1 Leaves contain many types of tissue. *(Grade 4-6)*

Which type of plant tissue contains air spaces for the diffusion of gases?
Tick **one** box.

☐ epidermal tissue

☐ palisade mesophyll tissue

☐ spongy mesophyll tissue

☐ meristem tissue

[1 mark]

2 Plants absorb water and mineral ions through their root hair cells. *(Grade 4-6)*

2.1 Name the vessels that transport water and mineral ions from the roots of a plant to the leaves.

[1 mark]

2.2 Describe the structure of the vessels you named in **2.1**.

[3 marks]

2.3 Name the process of water transport through a plant.

[1 mark]

3 Aphids are insects which feed on plant cell sap. Cell sap is the name given to the liquids carried around the plant in transport vessels. *(Grade 6-7)*

3.1 The cell sap the aphids feed on contains sugars.
What type of transport vessel does the cell sap come from?

[1 mark]

3.2 Explain how the structure of these transport vessels is adapted to their function.

[2 marks]

3.3 Name the movement of cell sap through the plant's transport vessels.

[1 mark]

Topic B2 — Organisation

Exam Questions

4 A student used a rose plant in his garden to carry out some investigations. *(Grade 7-9)*

4.1 The student cut several stems from the plant and put them in a glass vase on his kitchen windowsill.
He added a layer of oil to the surface of the water to prevent evaporation.
Over the next few days, he noticed that the level of water in the vase gradually decreased.
How would the reduction of water in the vase differ if the kitchen was not as warm?
Explain your answer.

[3 marks]

4.2* The student investigated the appearance of guard cells on the underside of a rose leaf at different times on a humid day. He took a leaf from his rose plant at 10 am, 4 pm and 11 pm and immediately examined it under a microscope. He drew diagrams to show the appearance of the guard cells at each time, as shown in **Figure 1**.

Figure 1

A   B   C

Suggest which diagram (A-C), shows the appearance of the guard cells observed at 11 pm.
Explain your answer.

[4 marks]

5 A student was investigating transpiration in basil plants under different conditions. *(Grade 7-9)*
She used twelve plants, three plants in each of the four different conditions.
The plants were weighed before and after the experiment. She calculated the
% loss in the mass per day and recorded her results in **Table 1**.

Table 1

plant	in a room (% loss in mass)	next to a fan (% loss in mass)	by a lamp (% loss in mass)	next to a fan and by a lamp (% loss in mass)
1	5	8	10	13
2	5	9	11	15
3	4	11	9	13
mean	4.7	9.3		13.6

5.1 Calculate the mean % loss in plant mass for the three plants by a lamp.

[2 marks]

5.2 Explain why the plants located next to a fan lost more mass than those in a still room.

[3 marks]

5.3 The student then covered the undersides of the leaves with petroleum jelly.
Suggest how this would affect the rate of transpiration from the leaves.

[2 marks]

5.4 Suggest how you could alter the student's experiment to investigate the effects of humidity on the rate of transpiration in basil plants.

[2 marks]

Topic B3 — Infection and Response

Communicable Disease

*If you're hoping I'll ease you gently into this new topic... no such luck. Straight on to the **baddies** of biology.*

There Are **Several Types** of **Pathogen**

1) Pathogens are microorganisms that enter the body and cause disease.
2) They cause communicable (infectious) diseases — diseases that can easily spread (see p.62).
3) Both plants and animals can be infected by pathogens.
4) Pathogens can be bacteria or viruses (see below), or protists or fungi (see next page).

1. **Bacteria** Are Very Small **Living Cells**

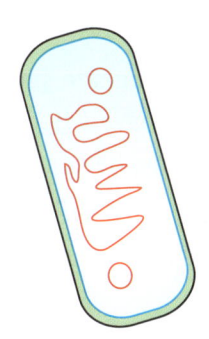

1) Bacteria are very small cells (about 1/100th the size of your body cells), which can reproduce rapidly inside your body.

2) They can make you feel ill by producing toxins (poisons) that damage your cells and tissues.

2. **Viruses** Are **Not** Cells — They're Much Smaller

1) Viruses are not cells. They're tiny, about 1/100th the size of a bacterium.

2) Like bacteria, they can reproduce rapidly inside your body.

3) They live inside your cells and replicate themselves using the cells' machinery to produce many copies of themselves.

4) The cell will usually then burst, releasing all the new viruses.

5) This cell damage is what makes you feel ill.

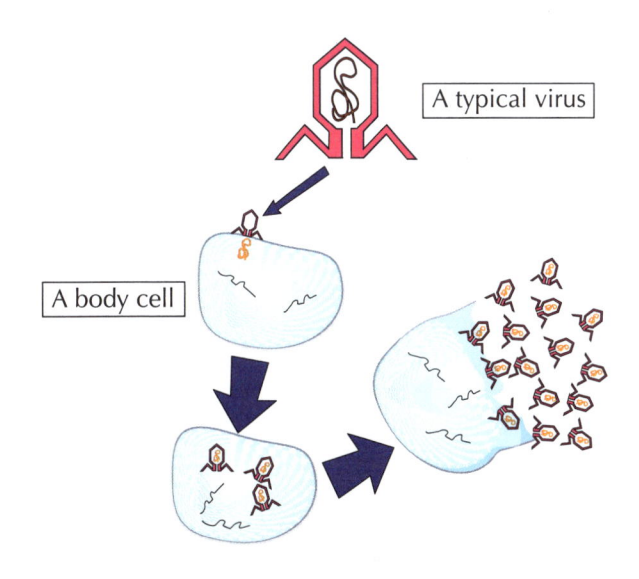

A typical virus

A body cell

Topic B3 — Infection and Response

Communicable Disease

3. Protists are Single-Celled Eukaryotes

1) There are lots of different types of protists. But they're all eukaryotes (see page 17) and most of them are single-celled.
2) Some protists are parasites. Parasites live on or inside other organisms and can cause them damage. They are often transferred to the organism by a vector, which doesn't get the disease itself — e.g. an insect that carries the protist.

4. Fungi Come in Different Shapes

1) Some fungi are single-celled.
2) Others have a body which is made up of hyphae (thread-like structures).
3) These hyphae can grow and penetrate human skin and the surface of plants, causing diseases.
4) The hyphae can produce spores, which can be spread to other plants and animals.

Pathogens Can Be Spread in Different Ways

Pathogens can be spread in many ways. Here are just a few...

Water
1) Some pathogens can be picked up by drinking or bathing in dirty water.
2) E.g. cholera is a bacterial infection that's spread by drinking water contaminated with the diarrhoea of other sufferers.

Air
1) Pathogens can be carried in the air and can then be breathed in.
2) Some airborne pathogens are carried in the air in droplets produced when you cough or sneeze — e.g. the influenza virus that causes flu is spread this way.

Direct Contact
1) Some pathogens can be picked up by touching contaminated surfaces, including the skin.
2) E.g. athlete's foot is a fungus which makes skin itch and flake off. It's most commonly spread by touching the same things as an infected person, e.g. shower floors and towels.

Watch yourself, there are a lot of nasties out there...

Plants need to be worried too, as you'll find out. It's strange to think such small things can have such massive effects on your body, but bacteria and viruses in particular can multiply extremely quickly.

Viral and Fungal Diseases

*There are heaps of diseases caused by **viruses** or **fungi** — here are four of them...*

Measles, HIV and TMV are Viral Diseases

1. Measles

1) <u>Measles</u> is spread by <u>droplets</u> from an infected person's sneeze or cough.
2) People with measles develop a <u>red skin rash</u>, and they show signs of a <u>fever</u> (a high temperature).
3) Measles can be very serious, or even fatal, if there are <u>complications</u>. For example, measles can sometimes lead to <u>pneumonia</u> (a lung infection) or inflammation of the brain (<u>encephalitis</u>).
4) Most people are <u>vaccinated</u> against measles when they're young.

2. HIV

1) <u>HIV</u> is a <u>virus</u> spread by <u>sexual contact</u>, or by exchanging <u>bodily fluids</u> such as blood. This can happen when people <u>share needles</u> when taking drugs.
2) HIV initially causes <u>flu-like symptoms</u> for a few weeks. Usually, the person doesn't then experience any symptoms for several years. During this time, HIV can be controlled with <u>antiretroviral drugs</u>. These stop the virus <u>replicating</u> in the body.
3) The virus attacks the <u>immune cells</u> (see page 81).
4) If the body's immune system is badly damaged, it <u>can't cope</u> with <u>other infections</u> or <u>cancers</u>. At this stage, the virus is known as <u>late stage HIV</u> infection, or <u>AIDS</u>.

3. Tobacco Mosaic Virus

1) <u>Tobacco mosaic virus</u> (<u>TMV</u>) is a <u>virus</u> that affects many species of <u>plants</u>, e.g. <u>tomatoes</u>.
2) It causes a mosaic pattern on the leaves of the plants — parts of the leaves become <u>discoloured</u>.
3) The discolouration means the plant can't carry out <u>photosynthesis</u> as well, so the virus affects <u>growth</u>.

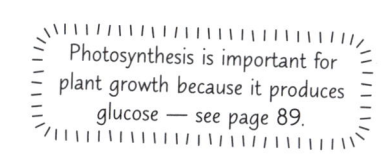

Photosynthesis is important for plant growth because it produces glucose — see page 89.

Rose Black Spot is a Fungal Disease

1) <u>Rose black spot</u> is a <u>fungus</u> that causes <u>purple or black spots</u> to develop on the <u>leaves</u> of <u>rose plants</u>. The leaves can then turn <u>yellow</u> and <u>drop off</u>.
2) This means that less <u>photosynthesis</u> can happen, so the plant doesn't <u>grow</u> very well.
3) It spreads through the environment in <u>water</u> or by the <u>wind</u>.
4) Gardeners can treat the disease using <u>fungicides</u> and by <u>stripping</u> the plant of its <u>affected leaves</u>. These leaves then need to be <u>destroyed</u> so that the fungus can't spread to other rose plants.

Topic B3 — Infection and Response

Protist and Bacterial Diseases

*Sorry — I'm afraid there are some more diseases to learn about here. This time, there's one disease caused by a protist and a couple caused by **bacteria**. I don't know about you, but I'm starting to feel a bit itchy...*

Malaria is a Disease Caused by a Protist

1) Part of the malarial protist's life cycle takes place inside a mosquito.
2) The mosquitoes are vectors (see page 76) — they pick up the malarial protist when they feed on an infected animal.
3) Every time the mosquito feeds on another animal, it infects it by inserting the protist into the animal's blood vessels.
4) Malaria causes repeating episodes of fever. It can be fatal.
5) People can be protected from mosquitoes using insecticides and mosquito nets.

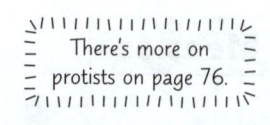

There's more on protists on page 76.

Salmonella and Gonorrhea Are Two Bacterial Diseases

1. *Salmonella*

1) *Salmonella* is a type of bacteria that causes food poisoning.
2) Infected people can suffer from fever, stomach cramps, vomiting and diarrhoea.
3) These symptoms are caused by the toxins that the bacteria produce (see page 75).
4) You can get *Salmonella* food poisoning by eating food that's been contaminated with *Salmonella* bacteria, e.g. eating chicken that caught the disease whilst it was alive, or eating food that has been contaminated by being prepared in unhygienic conditions.

2. Gonorrhoea

1) Gonorrhoea is a sexually transmitted disease (STD).
2) STDs are passed on by sexual contact, e.g. having unprotected sex.
3) Gonorrhoea is caused by bacteria.
4) A person with gonorrhoea will get pain when they urinate. Another symptom is a thick yellow or green discharge from the vagina or the penis.
5) Gonorrhoea was originally treated with an antibiotic called penicillin, but this has become trickier now because strains of the bacteria have become resistant to it (see page 84).
6) To prevent the spread of gonorrhoea, people can be treated with antibiotics and should use barrier methods of contraception (see page 118), such as condoms.

REVISION TIP

Hang in there, this stuff is pretty gross, but it's nearly over...
Try drawing out a table with columns for 'disease', 'type of organism it's caused by', 'symptoms' and 'how it's spread', then fill it in for all the diseases on this page and the previous one. See how much you can write down without looking back at the page.

Topic B3 — Infection and Response

Preventing Disease

*Pathogens can make life very **difficult**, but there are lots of things we can do to **protect** ourselves...*

The Spread of Disease Can Be Reduced or Prevented

There are things that we can do to reduce, and even prevent, the spread of disease. For example:

1. Being Hygienic

Using simple hygiene measures can prevent the spread of disease.

> Doing things like washing your hands thoroughly before preparing food or after you've sneezed can stop you infecting another person.

2. Destroying Vectors

1) By getting rid of the organisms that spread disease, you can prevent the disease from being passed on.
2) Vectors that are insects can be killed using insecticides or by destroying their habitat so that they can no longer breed.

> The spread of malaria (see previous page) can be reduced by stopping mosquitoes from breeding.

3. Isolating Infected Individuals

If you isolate someone who has a communicable disease, it prevents them from passing it on to anyone else.

4. Vaccination

Vaccinating people and animals against communicable diseases means that they can't develop the infection and then pass it on to someone else.

There's more about how vaccination works on page 82.

> For example, in the UK, most poultry (e.g. chickens and turkeys) is given a vaccination against *Salmonella*. This is to control the spread of the disease.

There you go, basic hygiene can be a real life saver...

There are lots of ways to prevent the spread of diseases and often the method used depends on the disease. As well as the methods on this page, don't forget about the different ways of preventing the spread of the diseases you learnt about on the previous two pages — e.g. using condoms.

Topic B3 — Infection and Response

Warm-Up & Exam Questions

Have a go at these questions to test whether you know about each of the diseases covered on the previous pages — their symptoms, how they are transmitted and how their spread can be limited.

Warm-Up Questions

1) What is meant by a communicable disease?
2) List three viral diseases.
3) What symptom of measles is shown on the skin?
4) What effect does rose black spot disease have on plants?
5) How is gonorrhoea transmitted between individuals?
6) How can vaccinations help to limit the spread of a disease?

Exam Questions

1   Diseases are often recognised by their symptoms. *(Grade 4-6)*

1.1   Describe the initial symptoms of HIV infection.

[1 mark]

1.2   Give **two** symptoms of gonorrhoea.

[2 marks]

1.3   A person has food poisoning caused by *Salmonella*. Give **two** symptoms that they may have.

[2 marks]

2   Viruses are a type of pathogen. They can infect every type of living organism. *(Grade 6-7)*

2.1   What is meant by the term 'pathogen'?

[1 mark]

2.2   The leaves of a tobacco plant can become discoloured if it is infected by a particular virus. Name the virus that affects tobacco plants in this way and describe what effect the discolouration of the leaves can have on a plant.

[2 marks]

2.3   HIV is a virus that can infect humans. Outline how HIV can be spread.

[2 marks]

3   The methods used to prevent the spread of a disease depend on how the disease is transmitted. *(Grade 6-7)*

3.1   It is important for chefs to wash their hands thoroughly before cooking. Suggest why.

[1 mark]

3.2   Explain why hand washing may not be helpful in limiting the spread of malaria.

[2 marks]

3.3   Suggest and explain **one** reason why efforts to limit the spread of malaria often focus on the mosquito.

[1 mark]

Topic B3 — Infection and Response

Fighting Disease

*The human body has some pretty neat features when it comes to **fighting disease**.*

Your Body Has a Pretty Sophisticated Defence System

1) The human body has got features that stop a lot of nasties getting inside in the first place.
2) The skin acts as a barrier to pathogens. It also secretes antimicrobial substances which kill pathogens.
3) Hairs and mucus in your nose trap particles that could contain pathogens.
4) The trachea and bronchi (breathing pipework — see page 51) secrete mucus to trap pathogens.
5) The trachea and bronchi are lined with cilia. These are hair-like structures, which waft the mucus up to the back of the throat where it can be swallowed.
6) The stomach produces hydrochloric acid. This kills pathogens that make it that far from the mouth.

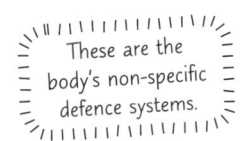

These are the body's non-specific defence systems.

Your Immune System Can Attack Pathogens

1) If pathogens do make it into your body, your immune system kicks in to destroy them.
2) The most important part of your immune system is the white blood cells. They travel around in your blood and crawl into every part of you, constantly patrolling for microbes. When they come across an invading microbe they have three lines of attack.

1. Consuming Them

White blood cells can engulf foreign cells and digest them. This is called phagocytosis.

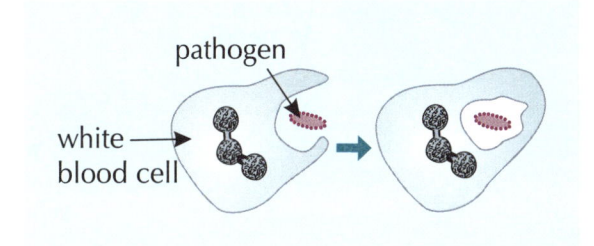

2. Producing Antibodies

1) Every invading pathogen has unique molecules (called antigens) on its surface.
2) When some types of white blood cell come across a foreign antigen (i.e. one they don't recognise), they will start to produce proteins called antibodies to lock onto the invading cells so that they can be found and destroyed by other white blood cells. The antibodies produced are specific to that type of antigen — they won't lock on to any others.
3) Antibodies are then produced rapidly and carried around the body to find all similar bacteria or viruses.
4) If the person is infected with the same pathogen again the white blood cells will rapidly produce the antibodies to kill it — the person is naturally immune to that pathogen and won't get ill.

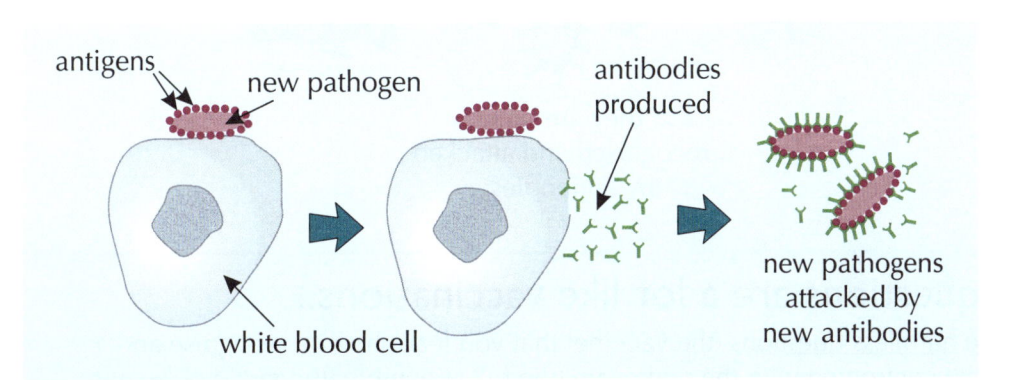

The white blood cells that produce antibodies are also known as B-lymphocytes.

3. Producing Antitoxins

These counteract toxins produced by the invading bacteria.

Topic B3 — Infection and Response

Fighting Disease — Vaccination

*Vaccinations have changed the way we fight disease. We don't always have to deal with the problem once it's happened — we can **prevent** it happening in the first place.*

Vaccination — Protects from Future Infections

1) When you're infected with a new pathogen, it takes your white blood cells a few days to learn how to deal with it. But by that time, you can be pretty ill.

2) Vaccinations involve injecting small amounts of dead or inactive pathogens. These carry antigens, which cause your body to produce antibodies to attack them — even though the pathogen is harmless (since it's dead or inactive).

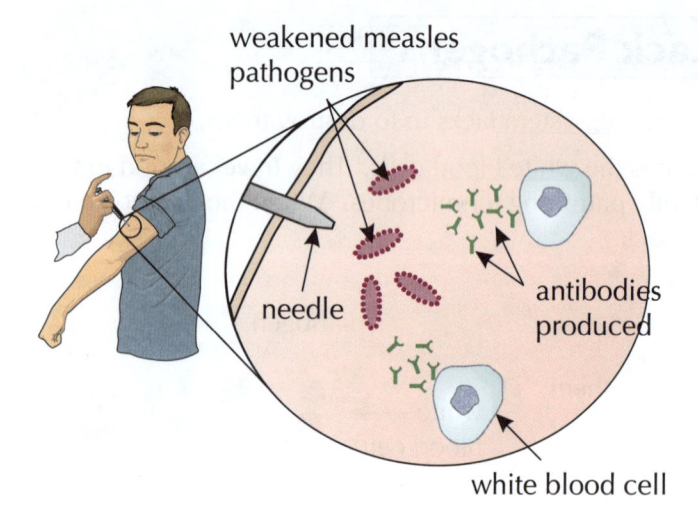

The MMR vaccine contains weakened versions of the viruses that cause measles, mumps and rubella (German measles) all in one vaccine.

3) But if live pathogens of the same type appear after that, the white blood cells can rapidly mass-produce antibodies to kill off the pathogen.

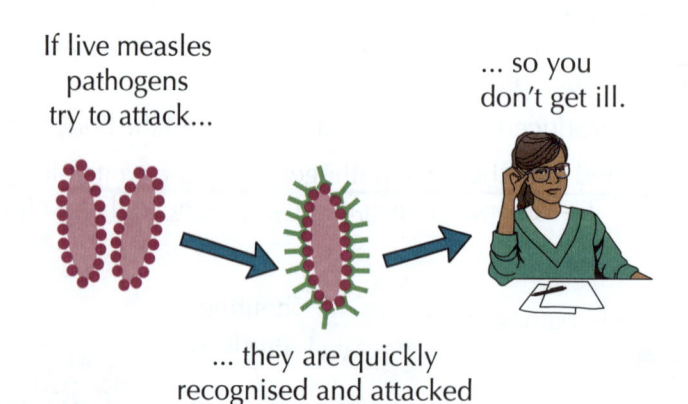

If live measles pathogens try to attack... they are quickly recognised and attacked by antibodies... ...so you don't get ill.

Practice exam questions are a lot like vaccinations...

We expose you to some harmless questions (the vaccine) that you learn how to recognise and answer, then when you're confronted with the real exam (the full strength pathogen), you've got the necessary knowledge (antibodies) to answer (kill) them. Gosh, you'd best get revising...

Q1　Basia is vaccinated against flu and Cassian isn't. They are both exposed to a flu virus. Cassian falls ill whereas Basia doesn't. Explain why. [2 marks]

Topic B3 — Infection and Response

Fighting Disease — Vaccination

*Having a whole range of **vaccinations** is pretty much standard now, so children today are **much less likely** to catch the kinds of diseases that they might have in the past. That doesn't mean that vaccination is without its problems though...*

There are **Pros** and **Cons** of **Vaccination**

Pros:

1) Vaccines have helped control lots of communicable diseases that were once common in the UK (e.g. polio, measles, whooping cough, rubella, mumps, tetanus...).

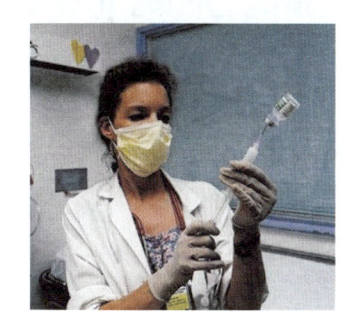

> Because of vaccinations, smallpox no longer occurs at all, and polio infections have fallen by 99%.

2) Big outbreaks of disease — called epidemics — can be prevented if a large percentage of the population is vaccinated. That way, even the people who aren't vaccinated are unlikely to catch the disease because there are fewer people able to pass it on. But if a significant number of people aren't vaccinated, the disease can spread quickly through them and lots of people will be ill at the same time.

Cons:

1) Vaccines don't always work — sometimes they don't give you immunity.

2) You can sometimes have a bad reaction to a vaccine (e.g. swelling, or maybe something more serious like a fever or seizures). But bad reactions are very rare.

Prevention is better than cure...

Deciding whether to have a vaccination means balancing risks — the risk of catching the disease if you don't have a vaccine, against the risk of having a bad reaction if you do. As always, you need to look at the evidence. For example, if you get measles (the disease), there's about a 1 in 15 chance that you'll get complications (e.g. pneumonia) — and about 1 in 500 people who get measles actually die. However, the number of people who have a problem with the vaccine is more like 1 in 1 000 000.

Topic B3 — Infection and Response

Fighting Disease — Drugs

You've probably had to take some sort of **medicine** if you've been ill, e.g. cough remedies, painkillers. And you're about to find out why it's important to only take **antibiotics** when you really need them.

Some Drugs Just Relieve Symptoms — Others Cure the Problem

1) Painkillers (e.g. aspirin) are drugs that relieve pain. However, they don't actually tackle the cause of the disease or kill pathogens, they just help to reduce the symptoms.
2) Other drugs do a similar kind of thing — reduce the symptoms without tackling the underlying cause. For example, lots of "cold remedies" don't actually cure colds.
3) Antibiotics (e.g. penicillin) work differently — they actually kill (or prevent the growth of) the bacteria causing the problem without killing your own body cells. Different antibiotics kill different types of bacteria, so it's important to be treated with the right one.
4) But antibiotics don't destroy viruses (e.g. flu or cold viruses). Viruses reproduce using your own body cells, which makes it very difficult to develop drugs that destroy just the virus without killing the body's cells.
5) The use of antibiotics has greatly reduced the number of deaths from communicable diseases caused by bacteria.

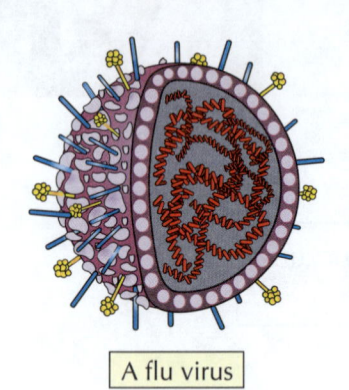

A flu virus

Bacteria Can Become Resistant to Antibiotics

1) Bacteria can mutate — sometimes the mutations cause them to be resistant to (not killed by) an antibiotic.
2) If you have an infection, some of the bacteria might be resistant to antibiotics.
3) This means that when you treat the infection, only the non-resistant strains of bacteria will be killed.
4) The individual resistant bacteria will survive and reproduce, and the population of the resistant strain will increase. This is an example of natural selection (see page 139).
5) This resistant strain could cause a serious infection that can't be treated by antibiotics. E.g. MRSA (methicillin-resistant *Staphylococcus aureus*) causes serious wound infections and is resistant to the powerful antibiotic methicillin.
6) To slow down the rate of development of resistant strains, it's important for doctors to avoid over-prescribing antibiotics. So you won't get them for a sore throat, only for something more serious.
7) It's also important that you finish the whole course of antibiotics and don't just stop once you feel better.

Antibiotic resistance is inevitable...

Antibiotic resistance is scary. Bacteria reproduce quickly, and so are pretty fast at evolving to deal with threats (e.g. antibiotics). If we were back in the situation where we had no way to treat bacterial infections, it'd be a bit of a nightmare. So do your bit, and finish your courses of antibiotics.

Topic B3 — Infection and Response

Fighting Disease — Drugs

*New drugs against diseases don't just appear out of nowhere. There's a **very lengthy process** which a new drug has to go through before it can be used in **humans** (more on that on the next page). **First of all**, though, a new drug has to be **discovered** — this is where plants and microorganisms come in...*

Many Drugs Originally Came From Plants

1) Plants produce a variety of chemicals to defend themselves against pests and pathogens.

2) Some of these chemicals can be used as drugs to treat human diseases or relieve symptoms.

3) A lot of our current medicines were discovered by studying plants used in traditional cures. For example:

> 1) Aspirin is used as a painkiller and to lower fever. It was developed from a chemical found in willow.
> 2) Digitalis is used to treat heart conditions. It was developed from a chemical found in foxgloves.

4) Some drugs were extracted from microorganisms. For example:

> 1) Alexander Fleming was clearing out some Petri dishes containing bacteria.
> 2) He noticed that one of the dishes of bacteria also had mould on it and the area around the mould was free of the bacteria.
> 3) He found that the mould (called *Penicillium notatum*) on the Petri dish was producing a substance that killed the bacteria — this substance was penicillin.

5) These days, drugs are made on a large scale in the pharmaceutical industry — they're synthesised by chemists in labs.

6) However, the process still might start with a chemical extracted from a plant.

Good old mould — saving lives since 1928...

Drug development is a big industry. A lot of money and time goes into developing new and better drugs, but it can all start with something as humble as a plant or a microorganism.

Topic B3 — Infection and Response

Developing Drugs

*New drugs are constantly being developed. But before they can be given to the general public, they have to go through a thorough **testing** procedure. This is what usually happens...*

There are **Three Main Stages** in Drug Testing

1) In preclinical testing, drugs are tested on human cells and tissues in the lab.

> However, you can't use human cells and tissues to test drugs that affect whole or multiple body systems, e.g. testing a drug for blood pressure must be done on a whole animal because it has an intact circulatory system.

2) The next step in preclinical testing is to test the drug on live animals.

> 1) This is to test efficacy (whether the drug works and produces the effect you're looking for), to find out about its toxicity (how harmful it is) and to find the best dosage (the concentration that should be given, and how often it should be given).
> 2) The law in Britain states that any new drug must be tested on two different live mammals. Some people think it's cruel to test on animals, but others believe this is the safest way to make sure a drug isn't dangerous before it's given to humans.

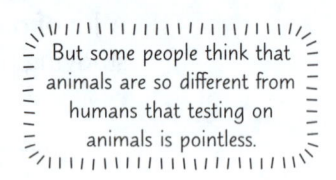

But some people think that animals are so different from humans that testing on animals is pointless.

3) If the drug passes the tests on animals then it's tested on human volunteers in a clinical trial.

> 1) First, the drug is tested on healthy volunteers. This is to make sure that it doesn't have any harmful side effects when the body is working normally. At the start of the trial, a very low dose of the drug is given and this is gradually increased.
> 2) If the results of the tests on healthy volunteers are good, the drugs can be tested on people suffering from the illness. The optimum dose is found — this is the dose of drug that is the most effective and has few side effects.
> 3) To test how well the drug works, patients are randomly put into two groups. One is given the new drug, the other is given a placebo (a substance that's like the drug being tested but doesn't do anything). This is so the doctor can see the actual difference the drug makes — it allows for the placebo effect (when the patient expects the treatment to work and so feels better, even though the treatment isn't doing anything).
> 4) Clinical trials are blind — the patient in the study doesn't know whether they're getting the drug or the placebo. In fact, they're often double-blind — neither the patient nor the doctor knows until all the results have been gathered. This is so the doctors monitoring the patients and analysing the results aren't subconsciously influenced by their knowledge.
> 5) The results of drug testing and drug trials aren't published until they've been through peer review. This helps to prevent false claims.

Peer review is when other scientists check that the work is valid and has been carried out rigorously — see page 2.

The placebo effect doesn't work with revision...

... you can't just expect to get a good mark and then magically get it. I know, I know, there's a lot of information to take in on this page, but just read it through slowly. There's nothing too tricky here — it's just a case of going over it again and again until you've got it all firmly lodged in your memory.

Topic B3 — Infection and Response

Warm-Up & Exam Questions

It's easy to think you've learnt everything in the section until you try the Warm-Up Questions.
Don't panic if there's a bit you've forgotten, just go back over that bit until it's firmly fixed in your brain.

Warm-Up Questions

1) How is the skin adapted to defend against the entry of pathogens?
2) What is the role of the immune system?
3) From what organism was the drug digitalis sourced originally?
4) What is meant by the efficacy of a drug?
5) What is a placebo?
6) Why are placebos used in drug trials?

Exam Questions

1   There are many different lines of defence in the human body that help to prevent pathogens from entering the blood. *(Grade 4-6)*

1.1   What is the role of the hairs and mucus in the nose?

[1 mark]

1.2   How do the cilia in the trachea and bronchi help to defend the body?

[1 mark]

1.3   What does the stomach produce to kill pathogens?

[1 mark]

2   A scientist is carrying out a clinical trial. *(Grade 6-7)*

2.1   What is a drug tested on in a clinical trial? Tick **one** box.

☐ human cells
☐ human volunteers
☐ live animals
☐ human tissue

[1 mark]

2.2   The clinical trial is double blind. Explain what this means.

[2 marks]

2.3   Apart from the toxicity of the drug, give **two** other factors that scientists research during drug testing.

[2 marks]

2.4   The results from drug testing are assessed by peer review. Explain what this means and why it is done.

[2 marks]

Topic B3 — Infection and Response

Exam Questions

3 White blood cells play an important role in defence against pathogens, including the production of antibodies and antitoxins.

3.1 Apart from producing antibodies and antitoxins, give **one** other method that white blood cells use to defend the body against pathogens.

[1 mark]

3.2 Explain why the production of antibodies is specific to a certain disease.

[1 mark]

4 The development of antibiotics has helped to save many lives.
However, the overuse of antibiotics may be a threat to global health in the future.
Penicillin is an example of an antibiotic.

4.1 Name the organism that penicillin originates from.

[1 mark]

4.2 Explain why the overuse of antibiotics may be a threat to global health in the future.

[2 marks]

4.3 Infection with rhinovirus causes the common cold.
Explain why antibiotics such as penicillin are not used to treat a cold.

[1 mark]

5 Rubella is a communicable viral disease.

The rubella virus is spread in droplets through the air when an infected person coughs, sneezes or talks. The virus causes several symptoms including fever and painful joints. Fortunately, the spread of the disease can be reduced by vaccination.

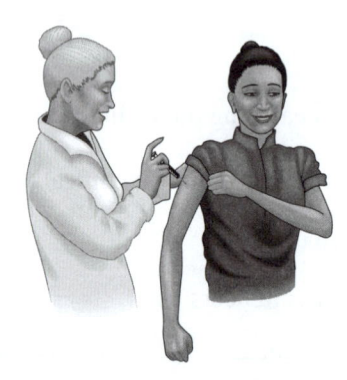

5.1 Suggest a drug that patients with rubella may be given to relieve their symptoms.

[1 mark]

5.2 Explain why it might be difficult to develop a drug which destroys rubella in the body.

[2 marks]

5.3* Explain how being vaccinated against rubella can prevent a person from catching the disease and suggest why vaccinating a large proportion of the population reduces the risk of someone who hasn't been vaccinated from catching rubella.

[6 marks]

5.4 Suggest **one** reason why some individuals may choose not to receive a vaccination against a disease.

[1 mark]

Topic B3 — Infection and Response

Topic B4 — Bioenergetics

Photosynthesis

*First, **photosynthesis equations**. Then onto how plants use **glucose**...*

Photosynthesis Produces Glucose Using Light

1) Photosynthesis uses energy to change carbon dioxide and water into glucose and oxygen.
2) It takes place in chloroplasts in green plant cells — they contain pigments like chlorophyll that absorb light.
3) Energy is transferred to the chloroplasts from the environment by light.
4) Photosynthesis is endothermic — this means energy is transferred from the environment in the process.
5) The word equation for photosynthesis is:

$$\text{carbon dioxide} + \text{water} \xrightarrow{\text{light}} \text{glucose} + \text{oxygen}$$

6) Here's the symbol equation too:

$$6CO_2 + 6H_2O \xrightarrow{\text{light}} C_6H_{12}O_6 + 6O_2$$

Plants Use Glucose in Five Main Ways...

1) For respiration — This transfers energy from glucose (see p.98) which enables the plants to convert the rest of the glucose into various other useful substances.

2) Making cellulose — Glucose is converted into cellulose for making strong plant cell walls (see p.18).

3) Making amino acids — Glucose is combined with nitrate ions (absorbed from the soil) to make amino acids, which are then made into proteins.

4) Stored as oils or fats — Glucose is turned into lipids (fats and oils) for storing in seeds.

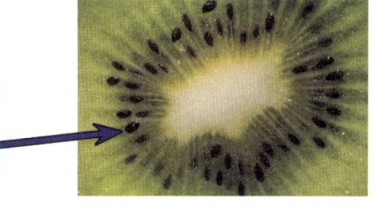

5) Stored as starch — Glucose is turned into starch and stored in roots, stems and leaves, ready for use when photosynthesis isn't happening, like in the winter. Starch is insoluble, which makes it much better for storing than glucose — a cell with lots of glucose in would draw in loads of water and swell up.

'Photo' means light and 'synthesis' means putting together...

...so photosynthesis means 'putting together using light'. And of course the thing being put together is glucose. Well, I guess that's one way of remembering it... (Maybe just learn the word equation instead.)

Topic B4 — Bioenergetics

The Rate of Photosynthesis

*The rate of photosynthesis is affected by the intensity of **light**, the concentration of **CO_2**, and the **temperature**. Plants also need **water** for photosynthesis, but when a plant is so short of water that it becomes the **limiting factor** in photosynthesis, it's already in such **trouble** that this is the least of its worries.*

Limiting Factors Affect the Rate of Photosynthesis

1) Any of these three factors can become the limiting factor — this just means that it's stopping photosynthesis from happening any faster.
2) These factors have a combined effect on the rate of photosynthesis, but which factor is limiting at a particular time depends on the environmental conditions:

   - at night it's pretty obvious that light is the limiting factor,
   - in winter it's often the temperature,
   - if it's warm enough and bright enough, the amount of CO_2 is usually limiting.

3) Chlorophyll can also be a limiting factor of photosynthesis.

   The amount of chlorophyll in a plant can be affected by disease (e.g. infection with the tobacco mosaic virus) or environmental stress, such as a lack of nutrients. These factors can cause chloroplasts to become damaged or to not make enough chlorophyll. This means the rate of photosynthesis is reduced because they can't absorb as much light.

Not Enough Light Slows Down the Rate of Photosynthesis

1) Light provides the energy needed for photosynthesis.
2) As the light level is raised, the rate of photosynthesis increases steadily — but only up to a certain point.
3) Beyond that, it won't make any difference — as light intensity increases, the rate will no longer increase. This is because it'll be either the temperature or the CO_2 level which is now the limiting factor, not light.

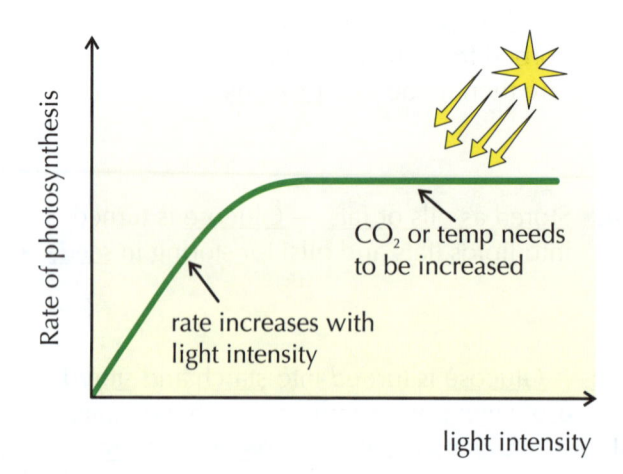

4) In the lab, you can change the light intensity by moving a lamp closer to or further away from your plant (see page 93 for this experiment).
5) But if you just plot the rate of photosynthesis against "distance of lamp from the plant", you get a weird-shaped graph. To get a graph like the one above you either need to measure the light intensity at the plant using a light meter or do a bit of nifty maths with your results.

The Rate of Photosynthesis

Too Little Carbon Dioxide Also Slows it Down

CO_2 is one of the raw materials needed for photosynthesis.

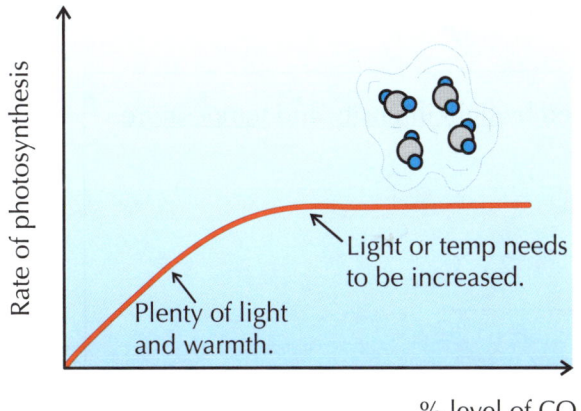

1) As with light intensity, the amount of CO_2 will only increase the rate of photosynthesis up to a point.
2) After this, the graph flattens out — as the amount of CO_2 increases, the rate no longer increases. This shows that CO_2 is no longer the limiting factor.
3) As long as light and CO_2 are in plentiful supply then the factor limiting photosynthesis must be temperature.

The Temperature has to be Just Right

Temperature affects the rate of photosynthesis because it affects the enzymes involved.

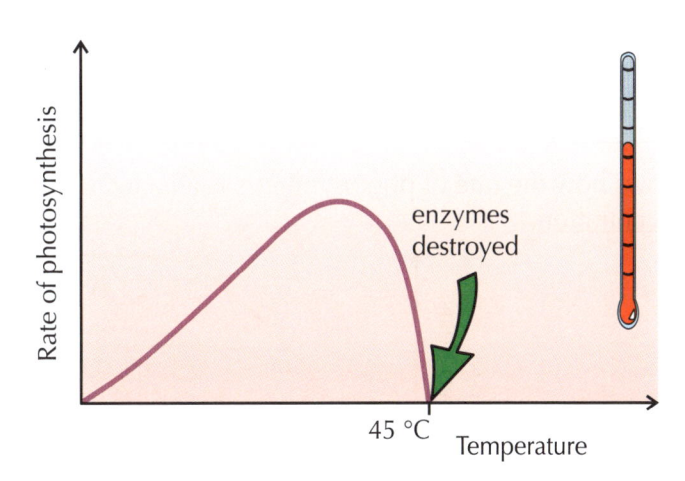

1) Usually, if the temperature is the limiting factor it's because it's too low — the enzymes needed for photosynthesis work more slowly at low temperatures.
2) But if the plant gets too hot, the enzymes it needs for photosynthesis and its other reactions will be damaged.
3) This happens at about 45 °C (which is pretty hot for outdoors, although greenhouses can get that hot if you're not careful).

Graphs, graphs and more graphs...

It's really vital that you've got your head around limiting factors, particularly the graphs. I say this because on the next page you're going to have to tackle graphs that have more than one limiting factor — so there's no point moving on until you're completely happy with dealing with just one on its own first.

Topic B4 — Bioenergetics

The Rate of Photosynthesis

*Now that you know all about **limiting factors**, it's time to take it to the next level...*

One Graph May Show the Effect of Many Limiting Factors

You could get a graph that shows more than one limiting factor on the rate of photosynthesis, for example:

The graph shows how the rate of photosynthesis is affected by light intensity and temperature.

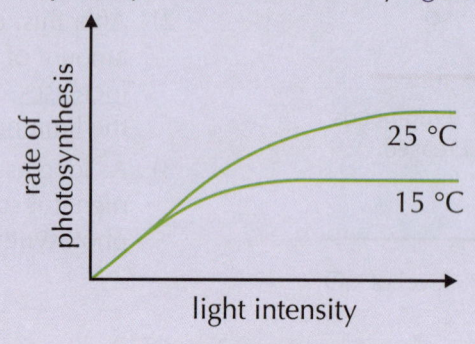

[Graph: rate of photosynthesis vs light intensity, showing two curves — 25 °C (higher) and 15 °C (lower)]

1) At the start, both of the lines show that as the light intensity increases, the rate of photosynthesis increases steadily.

2) But the lines level off when light is no longer the limiting factor. The line at 25 °C levels off at a higher point than the one at 15 °C, showing that temperature must have been a limiting factor at 15 °C.

The graph shows how the rate of photosynthesis is affected by light intensity and CO_2 concentration.

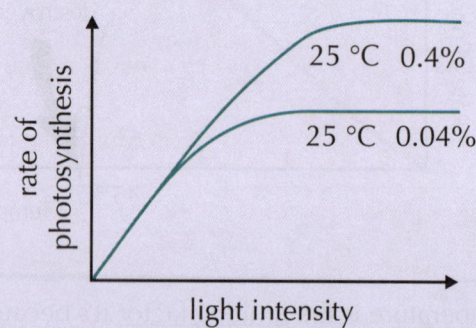

[Graph: rate of photosynthesis vs light intensity, showing two curves — 25 °C 0.4% (higher) and 25 °C 0.04% (lower)]

1) Again, both the lines level off when light is no longer the limiting factor.

2) The line at the higher CO_2 concentration of 0.4% levels off at a higher point than the one at 0.04%. This means CO_2 concentration must have been a limiting factor at 0.04% CO_2. The limiting factor here isn't temperature because it's the same for both lines (25 °C).

Make sure you know how to read from graphs

EXAM TIP — In the exam, you might have to describe what's going on in a graph of limiting factors. Don't panic — just look at the graph carefully, making sure you pay attention to the axes, as well as any additional labels, to see how the factors shown are affecting the rate of photosynthesis.

Topic B4 — Bioenergetics

Measuring the Rate of Photosynthesis

*It's practical time again. This one lets you see how changing **light intensity** affects the **rate of photosynthesis**.*

Oxygen Production Shows the Rate of Photosynthesis   PRACTICAL

Canadian pondweed can be used to measure the effect of light intensity on the rate of photosynthesis. The rate at which the pondweed produces oxygen corresponds to the rate at which it's photosynthesising — the faster the rate of oxygen production, the faster the rate of photosynthesis.

Here's how the experiment works:

1) A source of white light is placed at a specific distance from the pondweed.

2) The pondweed is left to photosynthesise for a set amount of time.
   As it photosynthesises, the oxygen released will collect in the capillary tube.

3) At the end of the experiment, the syringe is used to draw the gas bubble in the tube up alongside a ruler and the length of the gas bubble is measured. This is proportional to the volume of O_2 produced.

4) For this experiment, any variables that could affect the results should be controlled, e.g. the temperature and time the pondweed is left to photosynthesise.

5) The experiment is repeated twice with the light source at the same distance and the mean volume of O_2 produced is calculated.

6) Then the whole experiment is repeated with the light source at different distances from the pondweed.

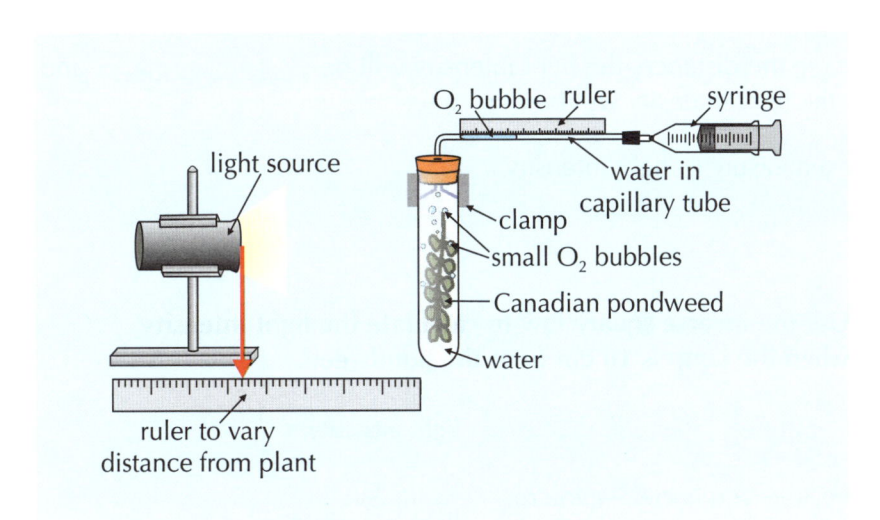

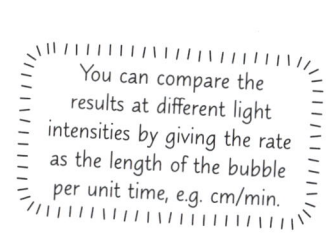

You can compare the results at different light intensities by giving the rate as the length of the bubble per unit time, e.g. cm/min.

The apparatus above can be altered to measure the effect of temperature or CO_2 on photosynthesis.
For example:

1) The test tube of pondweed can be put into a water bath at a set temperature, or a measured amount of sodium hydrogencarbonate can be dissolved in the water (which gives off CO_2).

2) The experiment can then be repeated with different temperatures of water / concentrations of sodium hydrogencarbonate.

Canadian pondweed is not native to the UK, so it must be disposed of carefully after the experiment — it shouldn't be released into the environment.

Topic B4 — Bioenergetics

Measuring the Rate of Photosynthesis

This page is all about the inverse square law. It can be a bit tricky to get your head around, so focus...

The Inverse Square Law Links Light Intensity and Distance

1) In the experiment on the previous page, when the lamp is moved away from the pondweed, the amount of light that reaches the pondweed decreases.

2) You can say that as the distance increases, the light intensity decreases. In other words, distance and light intensity are inversely proportional to each other.

3) However, it's not quite as simple as that. It turns out that light intensity decreases in proportion to the square of the distance. This is called the inverse square law and is written out like this:

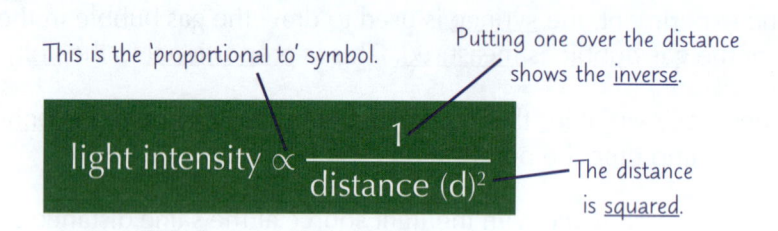

$$\text{light intensity} \propto \frac{1}{\text{distance (d)}^2}$$

- This is the 'proportional to' symbol.
- Putting one over the distance shows the inverse.
- The distance is squared.

4) The inverse square law means that if you halve the distance, the light intensity will be four times greater and if you divide the distance by three, the light intensity will be nine times greater.

5) Likewise, if you double the distance, the light intensity will be four times smaller and if you treble the distance, the light intensity will be nine times smaller.

6) You can use $1/d^2$ as a measure of light intensity.

EXAMPLE

Use the inverse square law to calculate the light intensity when the lamp is 10 cm from the pondweed.

1) Use the formula $\frac{1}{d^2}$.

   $\text{light intensity} = \frac{1}{d^2}$

2) Fill in the values you know — you're given the distance, so put that in.

   $\text{light intensity} = \frac{1}{10^2}$

3) Calculate the answer.

   $= 0.01$ a.u.

'a.u.' stands for 'arbitrary units'.

As one thing goes up, the other goes down...

That's what inverse proportion is all about. So here, as distance decreases, light intensity increases.

Q1 According to the inverse square law, describe what happens to the light intensity when the distance between a plant and its light source is doubled. [1 mark]

Q2 A plant is moved from 15 cm away from its light source to 5 cm away from its light source. Using the inverse square law, show that the light intensity becomes nine times greater. [3 marks]

Topic B4 — Bioenergetics

Ideal Conditions for Photosynthesis

*Growing plants outdoors can be **very difficult**, especially on a **large scale** — it's almost impossible to control the weather and other conditions. But there's a way around that...*

You can Artificially Create the Ideal Conditions for Farming

1) The most common way to artificially create the ideal environment for plants is to grow them in a greenhouse.

2) Greenhouses help to trap the Sun's heat, and make sure that the temperature doesn't become limiting. In winter a farmer or gardener might use a heater as well to keep the temperature at the ideal level. In summer it could get too hot, so they might use shades and ventilation to cool things down.

3) Light is always needed for photosynthesis, so commercial farmers often supply artificial light after the Sun goes down to give their plants more quality photosynthesis time.

Greenhouses are used to grow plants, including food crops, flowers and tobacco plants.

4) Farmers and gardeners can also increase the level of carbon dioxide in the greenhouse. A fairly common way is to use a paraffin heater to heat the greenhouse. As the paraffin burns, it makes carbon dioxide as a by-product.

5) Keeping plants enclosed in a greenhouse also makes it easier to keep them free from pests and diseases. The farmer can add fertilisers to the soil as well, to provide all the minerals needed for healthy growth.

6) Sorting all this out costs money — but if the farmer can keep the conditions just right for photosynthesis, the plants will grow much faster and a decent crop can be harvested much more often, which can then be sold. It's important that a farmer supplies just the right amount of heat, light, etc. — enough to make the plants grow well, but not more than the plants need, as this would just be wasting money.

Greenhouses control the growing environment

Farmers use greenhouses to make sure crops get the right amount of carbon dioxide, light and heat. They can alter the conditions using paraffin heaters, artificial light and ventilation. This ensures nothing becomes a limiting factor for photosynthesis, which means a good crop is produced.

Topic B4 — Bioenergetics

Warm-Up & Exam Questions

Time for a break in the topic and some questions. Do them now, whilst all that learning is fresh in your mind. Using that knowledge will help you to remember it all, and that's what this game is all about.

Warm-Up Questions

1) What does the chemical symbol $C_6H_{12}O_6$ represent?
2) What is meant by a limiting factor for the rate of photosynthesis?
3) Explain why the rate of photosynthesis decreases if the temperature is too high.
4) What could you measure to show the rate of photosynthesis?
5) Write down the inverse square law for light intensity.
6) Why might a farmer want to increase the rate of photosynthesis in her greenhouse of tomatoes?

Exam Questions

1 Photosynthesis produces glucose using light. *(Grade 4-6)*

1.1 Complete the word equation for photosynthesis.

carbon dioxide + ... $\xrightarrow{\text{light}}$ glucose + ...

[2 marks]

1.2 Plants use some of the glucose they produce to make a substance which strengthens their cell walls. Which of the following strengthens cells walls?
Tick **one** box.

☐ cellulose   ☐ oils   ☐ starch   ☐ fats

[1 mark]

1.3 Give **two** other ways that plants use the glucose they produce in photosynthesis.

[2 marks]

PRACTICAL

2 A student did an experiment to see how the rate of photosynthesis depends on light intensity. **Figure 1** shows some of her apparatus. *(Grade 4-6)*

2.1 How can the student measure the rate of photosynthesis?

[1 mark]

2.2 State the dependent variable and the independent variable in this experiment.

[2 marks]

2.3 State **one** factor that should be kept constant during this experiment.

[1 mark]

Figure 1: gas bubbles, LIGHT SOURCE, pond plant

Topic B4 — Bioenergetics

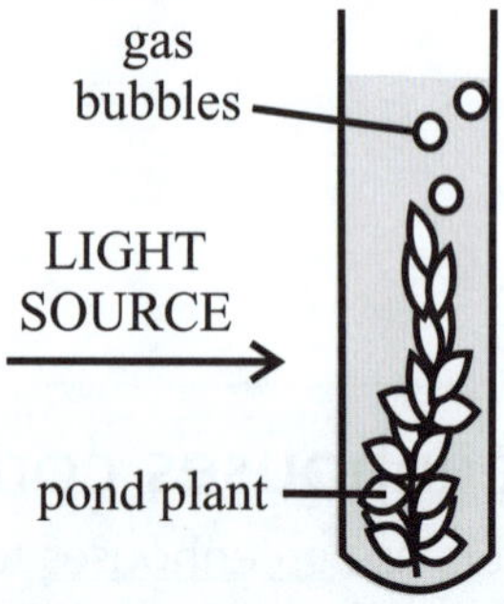

Exam Questions

3 A student investigated the effect of different concentrations of carbon dioxide on the rate of photosynthesis of his Swiss cheese plant. The results are shown in **Figure 2**. *(Grade 6-7)*

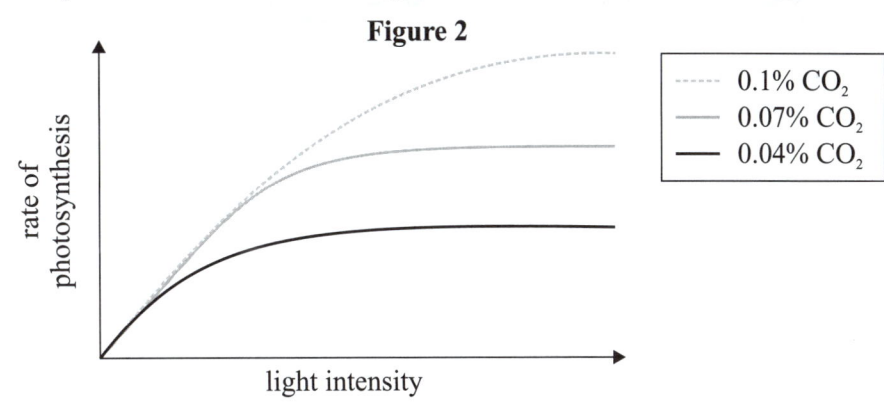

Figure 2

- - - - 0.1% CO_2
―― 0.07% CO_2
━━ 0.04% CO_2

(rate of photosynthesis vs light intensity)

3.1 Describe the effect that increasing the concentration of CO_2 has on the rate of photosynthesis as light intensity increases.

[2 marks]

3.2 Explain why all the lines on the graph level off eventually.

[1 mark]

4 **Figure 3** shows a variegated leaf. It is partly green and partly white. Chlorophyll is present in the green parts of the leaf but not the white parts. *(Grade 6-7)*

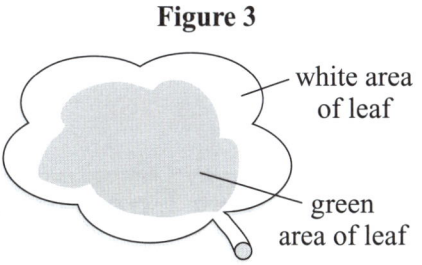

Figure 3 (white area of leaf, green area of leaf)

A student did an experiment in which part of the leaf was covered with black paper, as shown in **Figure 4**. The leaf was then exposed to light for four hours and was then tested for starch.

Figure 4 (black paper, hole in paper)

4.1 Complete **Figure 4** by shading in the part(s) of the leaf that you would expect to contain **starch**.

[1 mark]

4.2 Explain your answer to **4.1**.

[2 marks]

5 A student is investigating the effect of light intensity on the rate of photosynthesis by placing a lamp at various distances from a plant and measuring the rate of photosynthesis. Use the inverse square law to calculate the light intensity when the lamp is 7.5 cm from the plant. Give your answer in arbitrary units (a.u.) to 2 significant figures. *(Grade 7-9)*

[2 marks]

Topic B4 — Bioenergetics

Respiration

*You need **energy** to keep your body going. Energy comes from **food**, and it's **transferred** by **respiration**.*

Respiration is **NOT** "Breathing In and Out"

Respiration involves many reactions. These are really important reactions, as respiration transfers the energy that the cell needs to do just about everything — this energy is used for all living processes.

1) Respiration is not breathing in and breathing out, as you might think.

2) Respiration is the process of transferring energy from the breakdown of glucose (sugar) — and it goes on in every cell in your body continuously.

3) It happens in plants too. All living things respire.
   It's how they transfer energy from their food to their cells.

> RESPIRATION is the process of TRANSFERRING ENERGY FROM GLUCOSE, which goes on IN EVERY CELL.

4) Respiration is exothermic — it transfers energy to the environment.

Respiration **Transfers Energy** for All Kinds of Things

Here are three examples of how organisms use the energy transferred by respiration:

1) To build up larger molecules from smaller ones (like proteins from amino acids).

2) In animals it's used to allow the muscles to contract (so they can move about).

3) In mammals and birds the energy is used to keep their body temperature steady in colder surroundings. (Unlike other animals, mammals and birds keep their bodies constantly warm.)

Respiration releases energy from glucose

So... respiration is a pretty important thing. Cyanide is a really nasty toxin that stops respiration by stopping enzymes involved in the process from working — so it's pretty poisonous (it can kill you). Your brain, heart and liver are affected first because they have the highest energy demands... nice.

Topic B4 — Bioenergetics

Metabolism

*Metabolism is going on **all of the time**. Right now. And now. Even now. Okay, you get the picture. Time to read all about it.*

Metabolism is ALL the Chemical Reactions in an Organism

1) In a cell there are lots of chemical reactions happening all the time, which are controlled by enzymes.

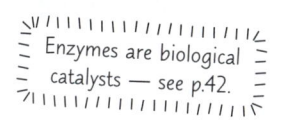

   Enzymes are biological catalysts — see p.42.

2) Many of these reactions are linked together to form bigger reactions:

   reactant —enzyme→ product —enzyme→ product —enzyme→ product

3) In some of these reactions, larger molecules are made from smaller ones. For example:

   > 1) Lots of small glucose molecules are joined together in reactions to form starch (a storage molecule in plant cells), glycogen (a storage molecule in animal cells) and cellulose (a component of plant cell walls).

   > 2) Lipid molecules are each made from one molecule of glycerol and three fatty acids.

   > 3) Glucose is combined with nitrate ions to make amino acids, which are then made into proteins.

4) In other reactions, larger molecules are broken down into smaller ones. For example:

   > 1) Glucose is broken down in respiration. Respiration transfers energy to power all the reactions in the body that make molecules.

   > 2) Excess protein is broken down in a reaction to produce urea. Urea is then excreted in urine.

5) The sum (total) of all of the reactions that happen in a cell or the body is called its metabolism.

It's still going on now

Enzymes are key to metabolism, so if you need a reminder about them, now is a good time to head back to page 42. Even if you are happy with enzymes, don't move on just yet — check you've taken in everything on this page before you flip over to continue on through the world of respiration. It's all important stuff.

Topic B4 — Bioenergetics

Aerobic and Anaerobic Respiration

*There are **two types** of **respiration** — aerobic and anaerobic.*

Aerobic Respiration Needs Plenty of Oxygen

1) Aerobic respiration is respiration using oxygen.
   It's the most efficient way to transfer energy from glucose.
2) Aerobic respiration goes on all the time in plants and animals.
3) Most of the reactions in aerobic respiration happen inside mitochondria (see page 17).
4) Here are the word and symbol equations for aerobic respiration:

$$\text{glucose} + \text{oxygen} \longrightarrow \text{carbon dioxide} + \text{water}$$

$$C_6H_{12}O_6 + 6O_2 \longrightarrow 6CO_2 + 6H_2O$$

Anaerobic Respiration is Used if There's Not Enough Oxygen

When you do vigorous exercise and your body can't supply enough oxygen to your muscles, they start doing anaerobic respiration as well as aerobic respiration.

1) "Anaerobic" just means "without oxygen". It's the incomplete breakdown of glucose, making lactic acid.
2) Here's the word equation for anaerobic respiration in muscle cells:

$$\text{glucose} \longrightarrow \text{lactic acid}$$

3) Anaerobic respiration does not transfer nearly as much energy as aerobic respiration. This is because glucose isn't fully oxidised (because it doesn't combine with oxygen).
4) So, anaerobic respiration is only useful in emergencies, e.g. during exercise when it allows you to keep on using your muscles for a while longer.

Anaerobic Respiration in Plants and Yeast is Slightly Different

1) Plants and yeast cells can respire without oxygen too, but they produce ethanol (alcohol) and carbon dioxide instead of lactic acid.
2) Here's the word equation for anaerobic respiration in plants and yeast cells:

Yeast are single-celled organisms.

$$\text{glucose} \longrightarrow \text{ethanol} + \text{carbon dioxide}$$

3) Anaerobic respiration in yeast cells is called fermentation.
4) In the food and drinks industry, fermentation by yeast is of great value because it's used to make bread and alcoholic drinks, e.g. beer and wine.
5) In bread-making, it's the carbon dioxide from fermentation that makes bread rise.
6) In beer and wine-making, it's the fermentation process that produces alcohol.

Exercise

*When you **exercise**, your body responds in a number of helpful ways...*

When You Exercise You Respire More

1) Muscles need energy from respiration to contract. When you exercise, some of your muscles contract more frequently than normal so you need more energy. This energy comes from increased respiration.
2) The increase in respiration in your cells means you need to get more oxygen into them.
3) Your breathing rate and breath volume increase to get more oxygen into the blood, and your heart rate increases to get this oxygenated blood around the body faster. This removes CO_2 more quickly at the same time.
4) When you do really vigorous exercise (like sprinting) your body can't supply oxygen to your muscles quickly enough, so they start respiring anaerobically (see the previous page).
5) This is NOT the best way to transfer energy from glucose because lactic acid builds up in the muscles, which gets painful.
6) Long periods of exercise also cause muscle fatigue — the muscles get tired and then stop contracting efficiently.

Remember, lactic acid is formed from the incomplete oxidation of glucose.

Anaerobic Respiration Leads to an Oxygen Debt

1) After resorting to anaerobic respiration, when you stop exercising you'll have an "oxygen debt".
2) An oxygen debt is the amount of extra oxygen your body needs to react with the build up of lactic acid and remove it from the cells. Oxygen reacts with the lactic acid to form harmless CO_2 and water.
3) In other words you have to "repay" the oxygen that you didn't get to your muscles in time, because your lungs, heart and blood couldn't keep up with the demand earlier on.
4) This means you have to keep breathing hard for a while after you stop, to get more oxygen into your blood, which is transported to the muscle cells.
5) The pulse and breathing rate stay high whilst there are high levels of lactic acid and CO_2.
6) Your body also has another way of coping with the high level of lactic acid — the blood that enters your muscles transports the lactic acid to the liver. In the liver, the lactic acid is converted back to glucose.

You Can Investigate The Effect of Exercise on The Body

1) You can measure breathing rate by counting breaths, and heart rate by taking the pulse.
2) To take the pulse, you put two fingers on the inside of your wrist or your neck and count the number of pulses in 1 minute.
3) E.g. you could take your pulse after:

   - sitting down for 5 minutes,
   - then after 5 minutes of gentle walking,
   - then again after 5 minutes of slow jogging,
   - then again after running for 5 minutes.

   You could then plot your results in a bar chart.

4) Your pulse rate will increase the more intense the exercise is, as your body needs to get more oxygen to the muscles and take more carbon dioxide away from the muscles.
5) To reduce the effect of any random errors on your results, do it as a group and plot the average pulse rate for each exercise.

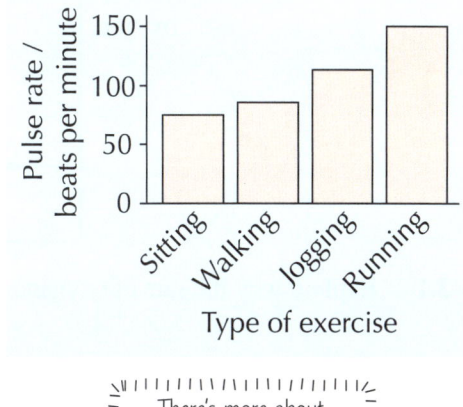

There's more about random error on page 8.

Very vigorous exercise = anaerobic respiration = oxygen debt

Q1 Look at the graph above. Predict which type of exercise would lead to the highest concentration of lactic acid in the blood after 10 minutes. Explain your answer. [4 marks]

Topic B4 — Bioenergetics

Warm-Up & Exam Questions

You know the drill by now — work your way through the Warm-Up questions, then the Exam Questions.

Warm-Up Questions

1) Give two examples of how animals use the energy transferred by respiration.
2) What is metabolism?
3) What are the reactants of aerobic respiration?
4) What is the process of anaerobic respiration in yeast called?
5) State three changes that take place in the body during vigorous exercise.

Exam Questions

1   Respiration is a process carried out by all living cells. *Grade 4-6*
    It can take place aerobically or anaerobically.

1.1   Give **two** differences between aerobic and anaerobic respiration.

[2 marks]

1.2   Write the word equation for aerobic respiration.

[2 marks]

2   In the human body, respiration may be aerobic or anaerobic at different times. *Grade 6-7*

2.1   Write down the word equation for anaerobic respiration in humans.

[1 mark]

2.2   Explain why the body uses anaerobic respiration during vigorous exercise.

[2 marks]

3   **Figure 1** shows the rate of oxygen use by a person before, during and after a period of exercise. *Grade 6-7*

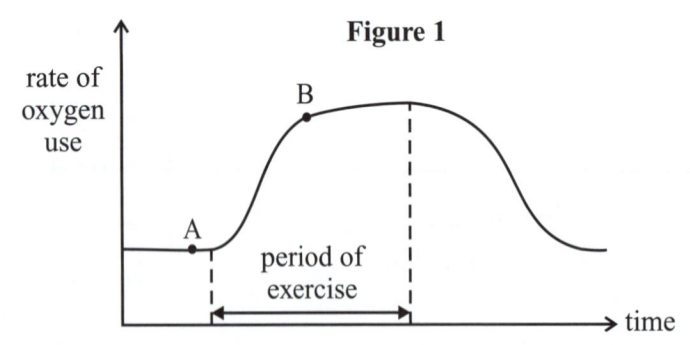

Figure 1

(Graph showing rate of oxygen use vs time, with point A before the period of exercise and point B during the period of exercise.)

3.1   Explain why the rate of oxygen consumption is higher at **B** than at **A**.

[2 marks]

3.2   Suggest why oxygen use remains high, even after the period of exercise ends.

[1 mark]

4   The hormone glucagon is secreted by the pancreas. It stimulates the conversion of glycogen to glucose in the liver. Suggest why the blood glucagon level increases during vigorous exercise. *Grade 7-9*

[2 marks]

Topic B4 — Bioenergetics

Revision Summary for Topics B1-4

Well, that's Topics B1-4 done. Now there's only one way to find out whether you've learnt anything.
- Try these questions and tick off each one when you get it right.
- When you're completely happy with a topic, tick it off.

For even more practice, try the Retrieval Quizzes for Topics B1-4 — just scan the QR codes!

Topic B1 — Cell Biology (p.17-37) ☐

1) What three things do plant cells have that animal cells don't?
2) How have electron microscopes increased our understanding of subcellular structures?
3) Why do cells differentiate?
4) Draw a diagram of a nerve cell. Why is it this shape?
5) What is mitosis used for by multicellular organisms?
6) What type of molecules move by osmosis?
7) Give the two main differences between active transport and diffusion.
8) Explain how leaves are adapted to maximise the amount of carbon dioxide that gets to their cells.

Topic B2 — Organisation (p.40-72) ☐

9) Give an example of a human organ system.
10) What does it mean when an enzyme has been 'denatured'?
11) List the three places where amylase is made in the human body.
12) Name the solution that you would use to test for the presence of lipids in a food sample.
13) Explain why the circulatory system in humans is described as a 'double circulatory system'.
14) How are arteries adapted to carry blood away from the heart?
15) What is the function of plasma?
16) Give a factor other than disease that can affect health.
17) Give an example of where different types of disease might interact in the body.
18) Give one risk factor for Type 2 diabetes.
19) What is the function of phloem?
20) How could you measure the rate of transpiration in a plant?

Topic B3 — Infection and Response (p.75-86) ☐

21) How do viruses cause cell damage?
22) How can destroying vectors help to prevent the spread of disease?
23) What is injected into the body during a vaccination?
24) How does antibiotic resistance arise in a population of bacteria?
25) What two things are drugs tested on in preclinical testing?

Topic B4 — Bioenergetics (p.89-101) ☐

26) Where in a plant cell does photosynthesis take place?
27) Name the products of photosynthesis.
28) In the inverse square law, how are light intensity and distance linked?
29) What process transfers energy to make new molecules in cells?
30) What is the word equation for anaerobic respiration in:
   a) muscle cells,
   b) yeast cells?

Topic B5 — Homeostasis and Response

Homeostasis

Homeostasis — a word that strikes fear into the heart of many a GCSE student. But it's really not that bad at all. This page is a brief **introduction** to the topic, so you need to **nail all of this** before you can move on.

Homeostasis — Maintaining a Stable Internal Environment

1) The conditions inside your body need to be kept steady, even when the external environment changes.

2) This is really important because your cells need the right conditions in order to function properly, including the right conditions for enzyme action (see p.43).

3) Homeostasis is all about the regulation of the conditions inside your body (and cells) to maintain a stable internal environment, in response to changes in both internal and external conditions.

4) You have loads of automatic control systems in your body that regulate your internal environment — these include both nervous and hormonal communication systems. For example, there are control systems that maintain your body temperature, your blood glucose level (see page 112) and your water content.

5) All your automatic control systems are made up of three main components which work together to maintain a steady condition — cells called receptors, coordination centres (including the brain, spinal cord and pancreas) and effectors.

Negative Feedback Counteracts Changes

Your automatic control systems keep your internal environment stable using a mechanism called negative feedback. When the level of something (e.g. water or temperature) gets too high or too low, your body uses negative feedback to bring it back to normal.

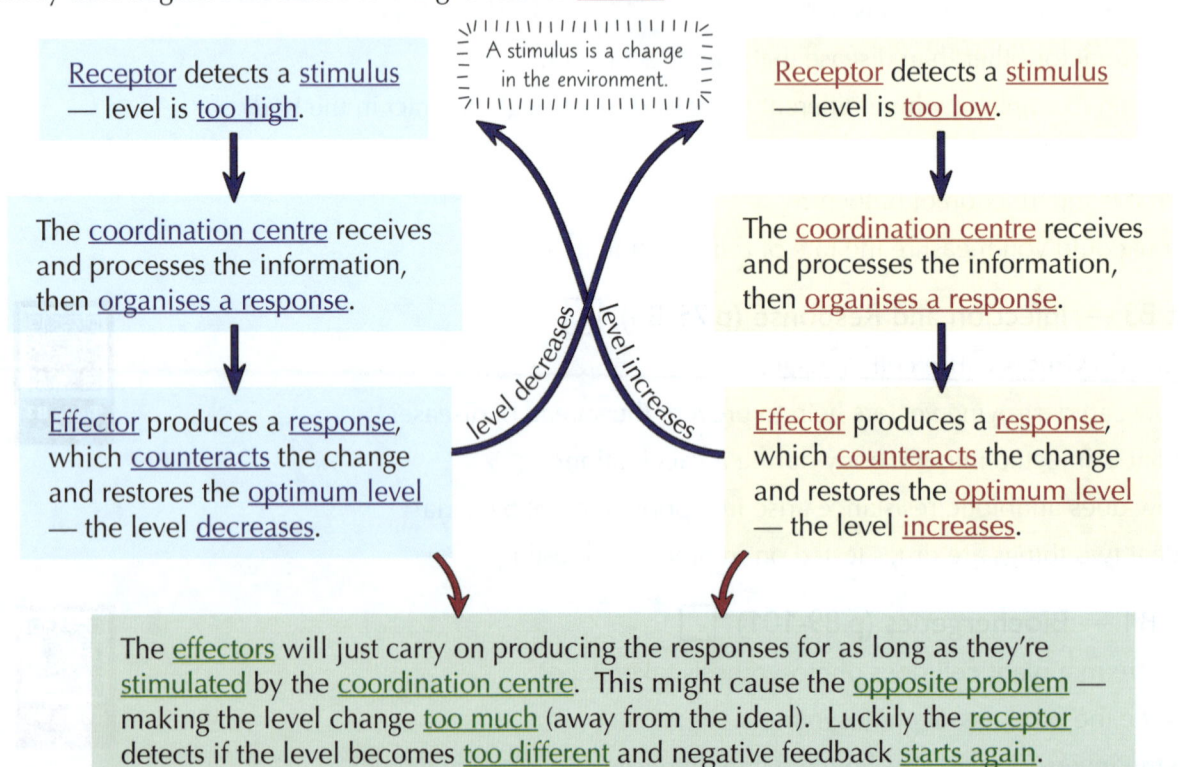

A stimulus is a change in the environment.

Left path (level too high):
- Receptor detects a stimulus — level is too high.
- The coordination centre receives and processes the information, then organises a response.
- Effector produces a response, which counteracts the change and restores the optimum level — the level decreases.

Right path (level too low):
- Receptor detects a stimulus — level is too low.
- The coordination centre receives and processes the information, then organises a response.
- Effector produces a response, which counteracts the change and restores the optimum level — the level increases.

The effectors will just carry on producing the responses for as long as they're stimulated by the coordination centre. This might cause the opposite problem — making the level change too much (away from the ideal). Luckily the receptor detects if the level becomes too different and negative feedback starts again.

This process happens without you thinking about it — it's all automatic.

The Nervous System

*The **nervous system** means that humans can **react to their surroundings** and **coordinate their behaviour**.*

The Nervous System Detects and Reacts to Stimuli

1) Organisms need to respond to stimuli (changes in the environment) in order to survive.
2) A single-celled organism can just respond to its environment, but the cells of multicellular organisms need to communicate with each other first.
3) So as multicellular organisms evolved, they developed nervous and hormonal communication systems.

The Nervous System is made up of Different Parts

1) Central Nervous System (CNS)
   In vertebrates (animals with backbones) this consists of the brain and spinal cord only. In mammals, the CNS is connected to the body by sensory neurones and motor neurones.

2) Sensory Neurones
   The neurones that carry information as electrical impulses from the receptors to the CNS.

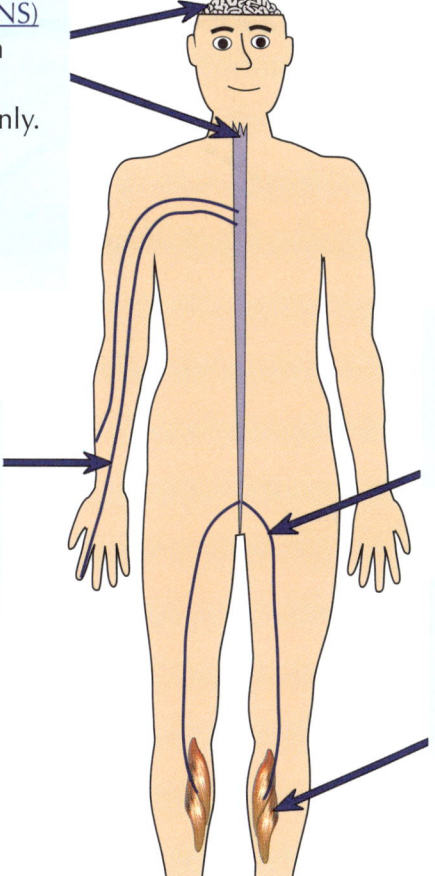

3) Motor Neurones
   The neurones that carry electrical impulses from the CNS to effectors.

4) Effectors
   All your muscles and glands, which respond to nervous impulses.

Receptors and Effectors can form part of Complex Organs

1) Receptors are the cells that detect stimuli.
2) There are many different types of receptors, such as taste receptors on the tongue and sound receptors in the ears.
3) Receptors can form part of larger, complex organs, e.g. the retina of the eye is covered in light receptor cells.
4) Effectors respond to nervous impulses and bring about a change.
5) Muscles and glands are known as effectors — they respond in different ways. Muscles contract in response to a nervous impulse, whereas glands secrete hormones.

The retina is the inner layer of tissue at the back of the eye.

Topic B5 — Homeostasis and Response

The Nervous System

The Central Nervous System (CNS) Coordinates the Response

The CNS is a coordination centre — it receives information from the receptors and then coordinates a response (decides what to do about it). The response is carried out by effectors.

For example, a small bird is eating some seed...
1) ...when, out of the corner of its eye, it spots a cat skulking towards it (this is the stimulus).
2) The receptors in the bird's eye are stimulated.
3) Sensory neurones carry the information from the receptors to the CNS.
4) The CNS decides what to do about it.
5) The CNS sends information to the muscles in the bird's wings (the effectors) along motor neurones.
6) The muscles contract and the bird flies away to safety.

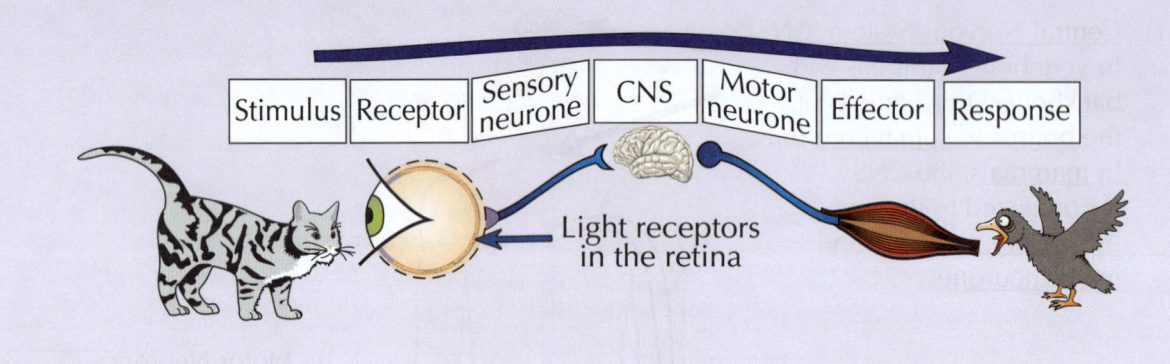

Stimulus → Receptor → Sensory neurone → CNS → Motor neurone → Effector → Response

Light receptors in the retina

Synapses Connect Neurones

1) The connection between two neurones is called a synapse.
2) The nerve signal is transferred by chemicals which diffuse (move) across the gap.
3) These chemicals then set off a new electrical signal in the next neurone.

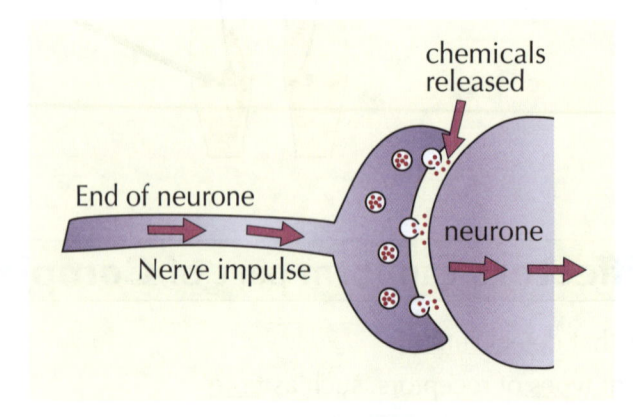

End of neurone — Nerve impulse — chemicals released — neurone

Don't let the thought of exams play on your nerves...

Don't forget that it's only large animals like mammals and birds that have complex nervous systems. Simple animals like jellyfish don't — everything they do is a reflex response (see next page).

Topic B5 — Homeostasis and Response

Reflexes

Neurones transmit information very quickly to and from the brain, and your brain quickly decides how to respond to a stimulus. But reflexes are even quicker...

Reflexes Help Prevent Injury

1) Reflexes are rapid, automatic responses to certain stimuli that don't involve the conscious part of the brain — they can reduce the chances of being injured.

   - For example, if someone shines a bright light in your eyes, your pupils automatically get smaller so that less light gets into the eye — this stops it getting damaged.

   - Or if you get a shock, your body releases the hormone adrenaline automatically — it doesn't wait for you to decide that you're shocked.

2) The passage of information in a reflex (from receptor to effector) is called a reflex arc.

The Reflex Arc Goes Through the Central Nervous System

1) The neurones in reflex arcs go through the spinal cord or through an unconscious part of the brain.

2) When a stimulus (e.g. a painful bee sting) is detected by receptors, impulses are sent along a sensory neurone to the CNS.

3) When the impulses reach a synapse between the sensory neurone and a relay neurone, they trigger chemicals to be released (see previous page). These chemicals cause impulses to be sent along the relay neurone.

4) When the impulses reach a synapse between the relay neurone and a motor neurone, the same thing happens. Chemicals are released and cause impulses to be sent along the motor neurone.

5) The impulses then travel along the motor neurone to the effector (in this example it's a muscle).

Relay neurones connect sensory neurones to motor neurones.

1. Bee stings finger.
2. Stimulation of pain receptors.
3. Impulses travel along a sensory neurone.
4. Impulses are passed along a relay neurone, via a synapse.
5. Impulses travel along a motor neurone, via a synapse.
6. When impulses reach muscle, it contracts.

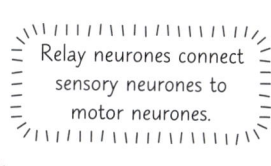

6) The muscle then contracts and moves your hand away from the bee.

7) Because you don't have to think about the response (which takes time) it's quicker than normal responses.

Don't get all twitchy — just learn it...

Reflexes bypass your conscious brain completely when a quick response is essential.

Q1   What is a reflex action? [1 mark]

Q2   A chef touches a hot pan. A reflex reaction causes him to immediately move his hand away.
   a) State the effector in this reflex reaction. [1 mark]
   b) Describe the pathway of the reflex from stimulus to effector. [4 marks]

Topic B5 — Homeostasis and Response

PRACTICAL: Investigating Reaction Time

*Reaction time is the time it takes to **respond to a stimulus** — it's often **less** than a **second**. It can be **affected** by factors such as **age**, **gender** or **drugs**.*

You Can Measure Reaction Time

Caffeine is a drug that can speed up a person's reaction time.
The effect of caffeine on reaction time can be measured like this...

1) The person being tested should sit with their arm resting on the edge of a table (this should stop them moving their arm up or down during the test).
2) Hold a ruler vertically between their thumb and forefinger. Make sure that the zero end of the ruler is level with their thumb and finger. Then let go without giving any warning.
3) The person being tested should try to catch the ruler as quickly as they can — as soon as they see it fall.
4) Reaction time is measured by the number on the ruler where it's caught — the further down it's caught (i.e. the higher the number), the slower their reaction time.
5) Repeat the test several times then calculate the mean distance that the ruler fell.
6) The person being tested should then have a caffeinated drink (e.g. 300 ml of cola). After ten minutes, repeat steps 1 to 5.

With a little bit of maths, it's possible to work out the reaction time in seconds using the mean distance.

7) You need to control any variables to make sure that this is a fair test.

> For example, you should use the same person to catch the ruler each time, and that person should always use the same hand to catch the ruler. Also, the ruler should always be dropped from the same height, and you should make sure that the person being tested has not had any caffeine (or anything else that may affect their reaction time) before the start of the experiment.

8) Too much caffeine can cause unpleasant side-effects, so the person being tested should avoid drinking any more caffeine for the rest of the day after the experiment is completed.

Reaction Time Can Be Measured Using a Computer

1) Simple computer tests can also be used to measure reaction time.

> For example, the person being tested has to click the mouse (or press a key) as soon as they see a stimulus on the screen, e.g. a box change colour.

2) Computers can give a more precise reaction time because they remove the possibility of human error from the measurement.
3) As the computer can record reaction time in milliseconds, it can also give a more accurate measurement.
4) Using a computer can also remove the possibility that the person can predict when to respond — using the ruler test, the catcher may learn to anticipate the drop by reading the tester's body language.

As with any practical, you need to control the variables

Q1 Some students investigated the effect of an energy drink on reaction time. They measured their reaction times using a computer test. They had to click the mouse when the screen changed from red to green. Each student repeated the test five times before having an energy drink, and five times afterwards.
 a) The results for one of the students before having the energy drink were as follows:
  242 ms, 256 ms, 253 ms, 249 ms, 235 ms. Calculate the mean reaction time. [2 marks]
 b) Suggest two variables that the students needed to control during their investigation. [2 marks]

Topic B5 — Homeostasis and Response

Warm-Up & Exam Questions

Welcome to some questions. There are quite a few of them, but that's because they're pretty important...

Warm-Up Questions

1) What is homeostasis?
2) State three things that are controlled by homeostasis in the human body.
3) What name is given to the connection between two neurones?
4) Name the three types of neurone in a reflex arc.
5) State one factor that affects human reaction time.

Exam Questions

PRACTICAL

1   A student is taking part in an experiment to test reaction times. Every time a red triangle appears on the computer screen in front of her, she has to click the mouse. *Grade 4-6*

1.1   Suggest what the stimulus, receptors and effectors are in this experiment.

[3 marks]

1.2   The student took the test three times. Her reaction time in test 1 was 328 ms. Her reaction time in test 2 was 346 ms. Her mean reaction time was 343 ms. Calculate her reaction time for test 3.

[2 marks]

2   Young babies have several reflexes not usually present in adults. For example, if an object is placed in the palm of a newborn baby's hand, the baby will move their fingers to grasp the object. The reflex arc for this reflex is shown in **Figure 1**. *Grade 6-7*

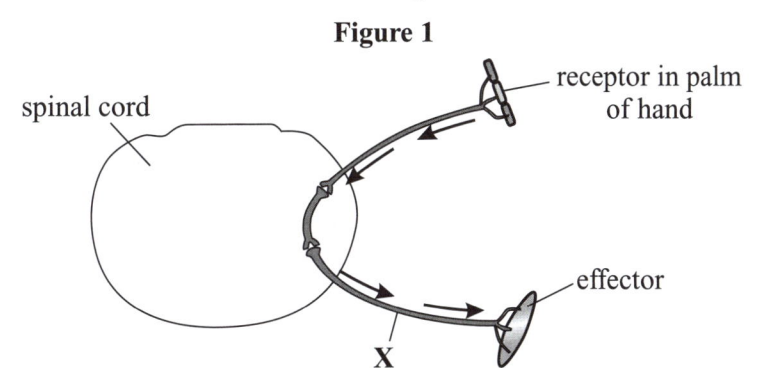

Figure 1

(diagram showing spinal cord, receptor in palm of hand, effector, and structure labelled X)

2.1   Name the structure labelled **X** on **Figure 1**.

[1 mark]

2.2   State the type of effector in this response and describe its action.

[2 marks]

2.3   Explain how an electrical impulse in one neurone is able to pass to the next neurone.

[2 marks]

2.4   If an object is placed in the palm of a baby over 6 months old, it can choose whether it wants to grasp hold of the object. Describe **one** way in which the pathway of nervous impulses involved in grasping an object differs between a newborn baby and a baby older than 6 months.

[1 mark]

Topic B5 — Homeostasis and Response

The Endocrine System

The other way to send information around the body (apart from along nerves) is by using **hormones**.

Hormones Are Chemical Messengers Sent in the Blood

1) Hormones are chemical molecules released directly into the blood.
2) They are carried in the blood to other parts of the body, but only affect particular cells in particular organs (called target organs).
3) Hormones control things in organs and cells that need constant adjustment.
4) Hormones are produced in (and secreted by) various glands, called endocrine glands. These glands make up your endocrine system.
5) Hormones tend to have relatively long-lasting effects.

Endocrine Glands Are Found in Different Places in The Body

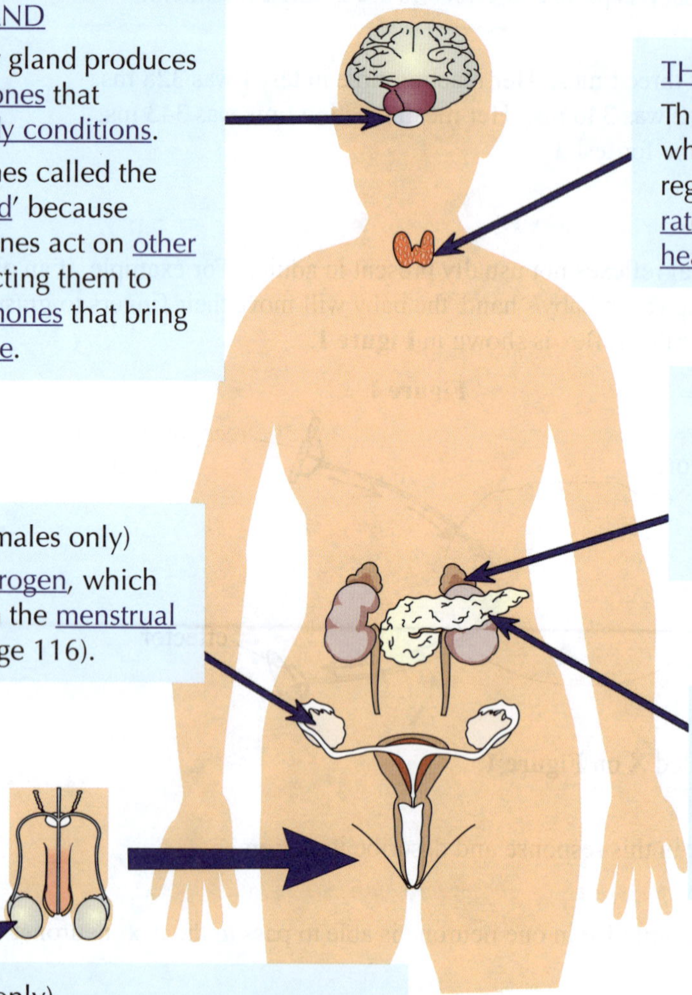

PITUITARY GLAND
1) The pituitary gland produces many hormones that regulate body conditions.
2) It is sometimes called the 'master gland' because these hormones act on other glands, directing them to release hormones that bring about change.

THYROID
This produces thyroxine, which is involved in regulating things like the rate of metabolism, heart rate and temperature.

ADRENAL GLAND
This produces adrenaline, which is used to prepare the body for a 'fight or flight' response (see page 120).

OVARIES (females only)
Produce oestrogen, which is involved in the menstrual cycle (see page 116).

PANCREAS
This produces insulin, which is used to regulate the blood glucose level (see page 112).

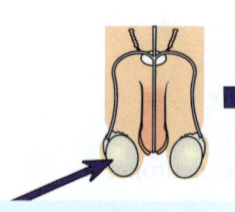

TESTES (males only)
Produce testosterone, which controls puberty and sperm production in males (see page 115).

Topic B5 — Homeostasis and Response

Comparing Nerves and Hormones

*Now you know that there are **two** ways information can be sent round the body — via the **nervous** or **hormonal** systems — here's a recap of the differences between them...*

Hormones and Nerves Carry Messages in Different Ways

Hormones and nerves do similar jobs — they both carry information and instructions around the body. But there are some important differences between them:

Nerves

1) Very FAST action.

2) Act for a very SHORT TIME.

3) Act on a very PRECISE AREA.

Hormones

1) SLOWER action.

2) Act for a LONG TIME.

3) Act in a more GENERAL way.

If you're not sure whether a response is nervous or hormonal, have a think about the speed of the reaction and how long it lasts.

If the Response is Really Quick, It's Probably Nervous

Some information needs to be passed to effectors really quickly (e.g. pain signals, or information from your eyes telling you about the lion heading your way), so it's no good using hormones to carry the message — they're too slow.

If a Response Lasts For a Long Time, It's Probably Hormonal

For example, when you get a shock, a hormone called adrenaline is released into the body (causing the fight-or-flight response, where your body is hyped up ready for action). You can tell it's a hormonal response (even though it kicks in pretty quickly) because you feel a bit wobbly for a while afterwards.

Nerves, hormones — no wonder revision makes me tense...

Hormones control various organs and cells in the body, though they tend to control things that aren't immediately life-threatening (so things like sexual development, blood sugar level, water content, etc.).

Topic B5 — Homeostasis and Response

Controlling Blood Glucose

*You should remember from page 104 that **homeostasis** is all about maintaining a stable internal environment. **Blood glucose** is controlled as part of homeostasis — **insulin** and **glucagon** are the two **hormones** involved.*

Insulin and Glucagon Control Blood Glucose Level

1) Eating foods containing carbohydrate puts glucose (a type of sugar) into the blood from the gut.
2) The normal metabolism of cells removes glucose from the blood.
3) Vigorous exercise removes much more glucose from the blood.
4) Excess glucose can be stored as glycogen in the liver and in the muscles.
5) The level of glucose in the blood must be kept steady. Changes are monitored and controlled by the pancreas, using the hormones insulin and glucagon, in a negative feedback cycle:

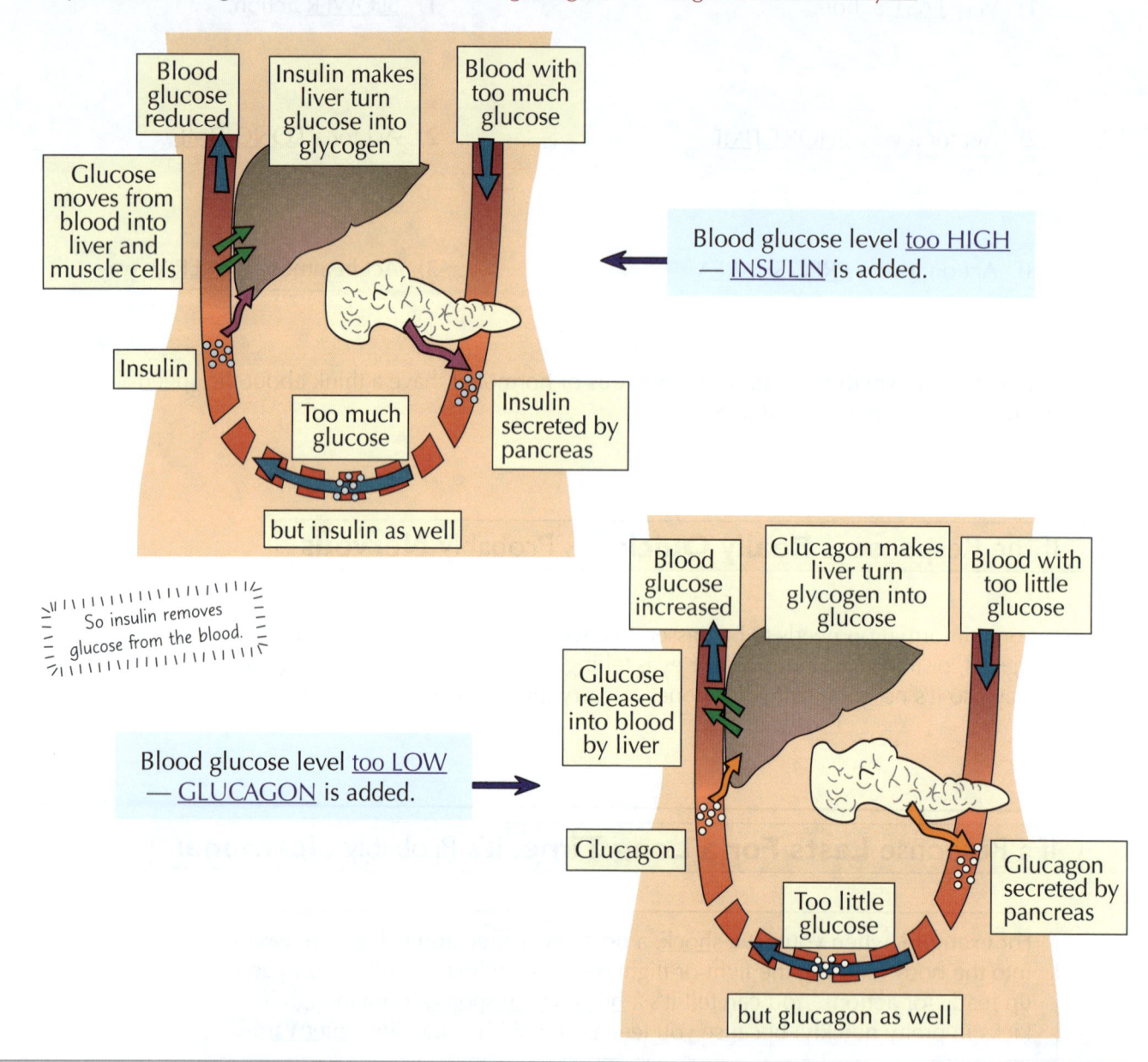

Blood glucose level too HIGH — INSULIN is added.

- Blood with too much glucose
- Insulin makes liver turn glucose into glycogen
- Blood glucose reduced
- Glucose moves from blood into liver and muscle cells
- Insulin
- Too much glucose
- Insulin secreted by pancreas
- but insulin as well

So insulin removes glucose from the blood.

Blood glucose level too LOW — GLUCAGON is added.

- Blood with too little glucose
- Glucagon makes liver turn glycogen into glucose
- Blood glucose increased
- Glucose released into blood by liver
- Glucagon
- Too little glucose
- Glucagon secreted by pancreas
- but glucagon as well

And people used to think the pancreas was just a cushion... (true)

This stuff can seem a bit confusing at first, but if you learn those two diagrams, it should get a bit easier.

Q1 The graph shows the relative secretion rates of insulin and glucagon as the blood glucose level increases. Which curve represents glucagon? Explain your answer. **[2 marks]**

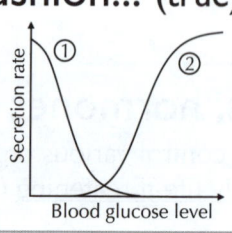

Topic B5 — Homeostasis and Response

Diabetes

Sometimes, homeostasis goes wrong. **Diabetes** *is an example of this.*

With Diabetes, You Can't Control Your Blood Sugar Level

Diabetes is a condition that affects your ability to control your blood sugar level. There are two types:

Type 1 Diabetes — Little or No Insulin is Made

1) Type 1 diabetes is where the pancreas produces little or no insulin.

2) This means a person's blood glucose level can rise to a level that can kill them.

3) People with Type 1 diabetes need insulin therapy — this usually involves several injections of insulin throughout the day, most likely at mealtimes. This makes sure that glucose is removed from the blood quickly once the food has been digested, stopping the level getting too high. It's a very effective treatment.

4) The amount of insulin that needs to be injected depends on the person's diet and how active they are.

5) As well as insulin therapy, people with Type 1 diabetes need to think about limiting the intake of food rich in simple carbohydrates, e.g. sugars (which cause the blood glucose to rise rapidly) and taking regular exercise (which helps to remove excess glucose from the blood).

Type 2 Diabetes — Insulin Resistance

1) Type 2 diabetes is where a person becomes resistant to their own insulin (they still produce insulin, but their body's cells don't respond properly to the hormone).

2) This can also cause a person's blood sugar level to rise to a dangerous level.

3) Being overweight can increase your chance of developing Type 2 diabetes, as obesity is a major risk factor in the development of the disease.

4) Type 2 diabetes can be controlled by eating a carbohydrate-controlled diet and getting regular exercise.

EXAM TIP

Be prepared to interpret graphs in the exam

You could be asked to interpret a graph showing the effects of insulin on the blood sugar levels of people with and without diabetes. Don't panic — just study the graph carefully (including the axes labels) so you know exactly what it's showing you. Then apply your blood sugar knowledge.

Topic B5 — Homeostasis and Response

Warm-Up & Exam Questions

Right then, another lot of pages down. Now there's just the small matter of answering some questions...

Warm-Up Questions

1) How do hormones travel to their target organs?
2) Name five endocrine glands found in the male human body.
3) What does insulin do?
4) What is Type 2 diabetes?

Exam Questions

1   **Figure 1** shows how the blood glucose level is regulated in humans. *Grade 6-7*

Figure 1

Organ A secretes insulin → Organ B stores glucose → blood glucose falls → Organ A secretes glucagon → Organ B releases glucose → blood glucose rises → (back to Organ A secretes insulin)

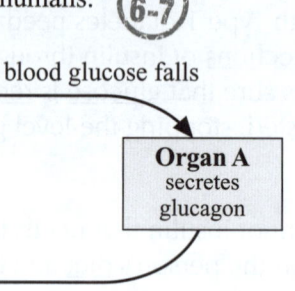

1.1   Identify organs A and B in **Figure 1**.

[2 marks]

1.2   Apart from organ B releasing glucose, suggest **one** reason why the blood glucose level could rise.

[1 mark]

1.3   With reference to **Figure 1**, explain what goes wrong with the regulation of blood glucose level in people with Type 1 diabetes.

[3 marks]

1.4   Describe what the hormone glucagon does.

[1 mark]

2   Hypopituitarism is a condition in which the pituitary gland stops secreting one or more of the pituitary hormones, or doesn't secrete enough of these hormones. People with hypopituitarism may experience tiredness and weight gain. They may also feel the cold more. These symptoms are all linked to low thyroid hormone levels. *Grade 7-9*

Suggest and explain why someone with hypopituitarism may experience these symptoms.

[3 marks]

3   Glycogen synthase is an enzyme which helps to convert glucose into glycogen in the body. *Grade 7-9*

3.1   Glycogen synthase is present in the liver.
Give **one** other location in the body where glycogen synthase is also likely to be present.

[1 mark]

3.2   Some people do not have enough functioning glycogen synthase in their liver.
When these people eat, their blood sugar level can become extremely high. Suggest why.

[3 marks]

Topic B5 — Homeostasis and Response

Puberty and the Menstrual Cycle

The monthly **release of an egg** from a woman's ovaries is part of the **menstrual cycle**.

Hormones Promote Sexual Characteristics at Puberty

At puberty, your body starts releasing sex hormones that trigger off secondary sexual characteristics (such as the development of facial hair in men and breasts in women) and cause eggs to mature in women.

- In men, the main reproductive hormone is testosterone. It's produced by the testes and stimulates sperm production.
- In women, the main reproductive hormone is oestrogen. It's produced by the ovaries. As well as bringing about physical changes, oestrogen is also involved in the menstrual cycle.

The Menstrual Cycle Has Four Stages

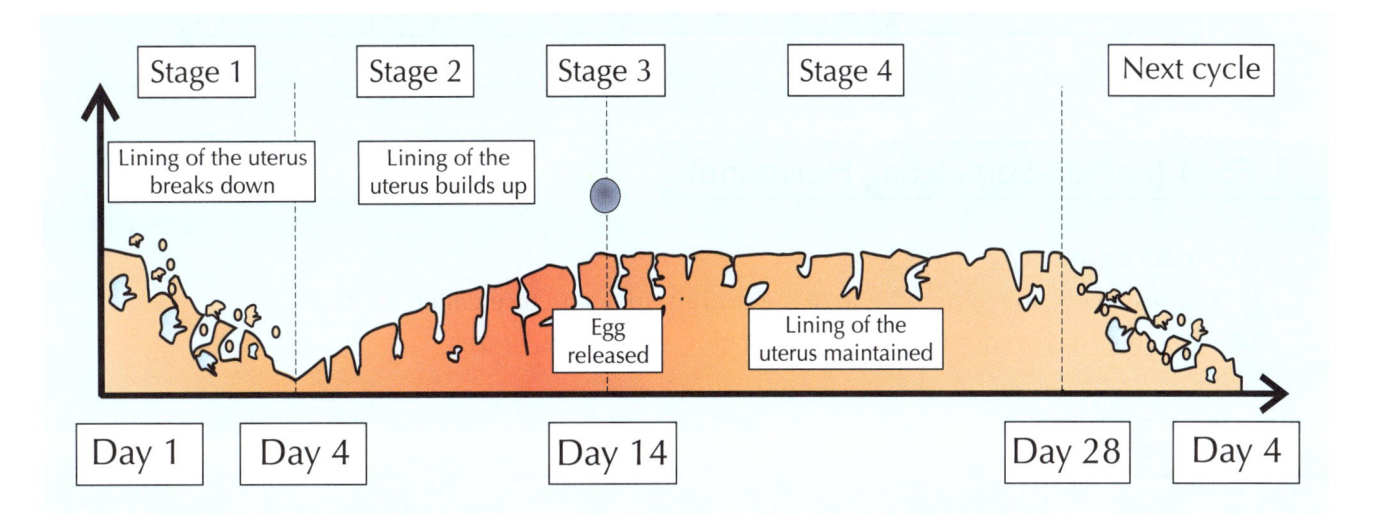

Stage 1

Day 1 — menstruation starts. The uterus lining breaks down for about four days.

Stage 2

The uterus lining builds up again, from day 4 to day 14, into a thick spongy layer full of blood vessels, ready to receive a fertilised egg.

Stage 3

An egg develops and is released from the ovary at day 14 — this is called ovulation.

Stage 4

The wall is then maintained for about 14 days until day 28. If no fertilised egg has landed on the uterus wall by day 28, the spongy lining starts to break down and the whole cycle starts again.

Topic B5 — Homeostasis and Response

Puberty and the Menstrual Cycle

*There's **more than one** hormone involved in the menstrual cycle...*

The Menstrual Cycle is Controlled by Four Hormones

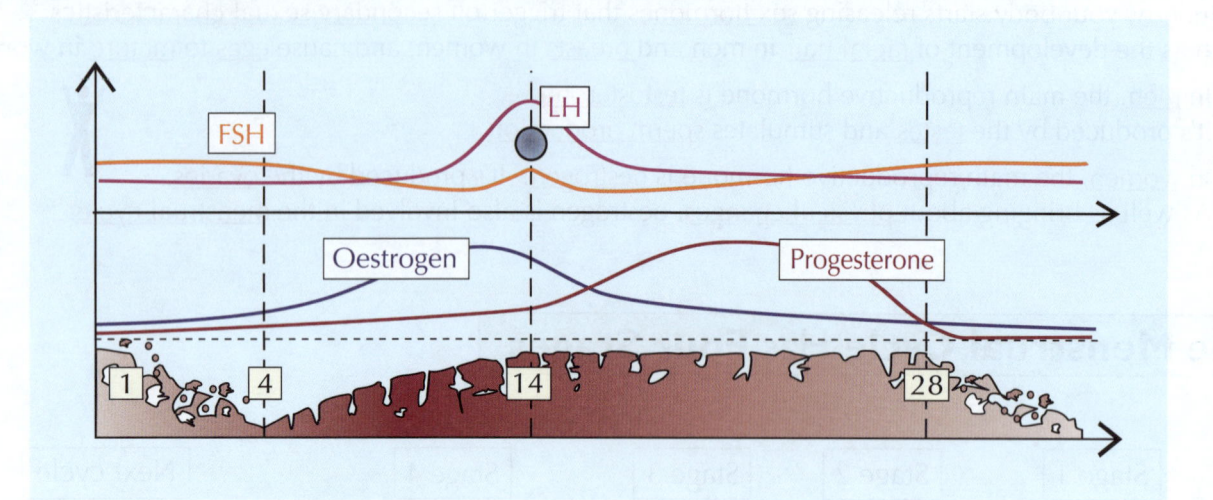

1. FSH (Follicle-Stimulating Hormone)

1) Produced in the pituitary gland.
2) Causes an egg to mature in one of the ovaries, in a structure called a follicle.
3) Stimulates the ovaries to produce oestrogen.

2. Oestrogen

1) Produced in the ovaries.
2) Causes the lining of the uterus to grow.
3) Stimulates the release of LH (which causes the release of an egg) and inhibits release of FSH.

3. LH (Luteinising Hormone)

1) Produced by the pituitary gland.
2) Stimulates the release of an egg at day 14 (ovulation).

4. Progesterone

1) Produced in the ovaries by the remains of the follicle after ovulation.
2) Maintains the lining of the uterus during the second half of the cycle. When the level of progesterone falls, the lining breaks down.
3) Inhibits the release of LH and FSH.

Examiners love a good menstrual cycle graph...

Learn this page until you know what hormone does what and understand the graph above.

Topic B5 — Homeostasis and Response

Controlling Fertility

Pregnancy can happen if sperm reaches the ovulated egg. *Contraception* tries to *stop* this happening.

Hormones Can Be Used to Reduce Fertility

1) Oestrogen can be used to prevent the release of an egg — so it can be used as a method of contraception.

2) This may seem kind of strange (since naturally oestrogen helps stimulate the release of eggs). But if oestrogen is taken every day to keep the level of it permanently high, it inhibits the production of FSH, and after a while egg development and production stop and stay stopped.

3) Progesterone also reduces fertility, e.g. by stimulating the production of thick mucus which prevents any sperm getting through and reaching an egg.

Oestrogen and Progesterone Can Be Taken in a Pill

1) The pill is an oral contraceptive containing oestrogen and progesterone (known as the combined oral contraceptive pill).

2) It's over 99% effective at preventing pregnancy, but it can cause side effects like headaches and nausea and it doesn't protect against sexually transmitted diseases.

There's also a progesterone-only pill — it has fewer side effects than the pill, and is just as effective.

Other Contraceptives Also Contain Hormones

Here are some examples:

1) The contraceptive patch contains oestrogen and progesterone (the same as the combined pill). It's a small (5 cm × 5 cm) patch that's stuck to the skin. Each patch lasts one week.

2) The contraceptive implant is inserted under the skin of the arm. It releases a continuous amount of progesterone, which stops the ovaries releasing eggs, makes it hard for sperm to swim to the egg, and stops any fertilised egg implanting in the uterus. An implant can last for three years.

3) The contraceptive injection also contains progesterone. Each dose lasts 2 to 3 months.

4) An intrauterine device (IUD) is a T-shaped device that is inserted into the uterus to kill sperm and prevent implantation of a fertilised egg. There are two main types — plastic IUDs that release progesterone and copper IUDs that prevent the sperm surviving in the uterus.

So oestrogen and progesterone can be used to prevent pregnancy...

As you probably already know, hormonal contraceptives are not the only contraceptives you can use. You'll find out about non-hormonal methods on the next page — but get this lot learnt first.

Topic B5 — Homeostasis and Response

Controlling Fertility

*Not everyone wants to avoid getting pregnant — **hormones** can also be used to **increase fertility**. First up though, a bit on **non-hormonal methods** of **contraception**...*

Barriers Stop Egg and Sperm Meeting

1) Non-hormonal forms of contraception are designed to stop the sperm from getting to the egg.
2) Condoms are worn over the penis during intercourse to prevent the sperm entering the vagina. There are also female condoms that are worn inside the vagina. Condoms are the only form of contraception that will protect against sexually transmitted diseases.
3) A diaphragm is a shallow plastic cup that fits over the cervix (the entrance to the uterus) to form a barrier. It has to be used with spermicide (a substance that disables or kills the sperm).
4) Spermicide can be used alone as a form of contraception, but it is not as effective (only about 70-80%).

There are Other Ways to Avoid Pregnancy

1) Sterilisation — this involves cutting or tying the fallopian tubes (which connect the ovaries to the uterus) in a female, or the sperm duct (the tube between the testes and penis) in a male. This is a permanent procedure. However, there is a very small chance that the tubes can rejoin.
2) 'Natural methods' — Pregnancy may be avoided by finding out when in the menstrual cycle the woman is most fertile and avoiding sexual intercourse on those days. It's popular with people who think that hormonal and barrier methods are unnatural, but it's not very effective.
3) Abstinence — The only way to be completely sure that sperm and egg don't meet is to not have intercourse.

Hormones Can Be Used to Increase Fertility

1) Some women have levels of FSH (follicle-stimulating hormone) that are too low to cause their eggs to mature. This means that no eggs are released and the women can't get pregnant.
2) The hormones FSH and LH can be given to women as a fertility drug to stimulate ovulation.
3) The use of hormones to increase fertility has one big pro:

> It helps a lot of women to get pregnant when previously they couldn't... pretty obvious.

4) There are some cons though:

> 1) It doesn't always work — some women may have to do it many times, which can be expensive.
> 2) Too many eggs could be stimulated, resulting in unexpected multiple pregnancies (twins, triplets, etc.).

The winner of best contraceptive ever — just not doing it...

You might be asked to evaluate the different hormonal and non-hormonal methods of contraception in your exam. If you do, make sure you weigh up and write about both the pros and the cons of each method.

Topic B5 — Homeostasis and Response

Controlling Fertility

If the use of FSH and LH alone can't help a woman to get pregnant, IVF may be considered...

IVF Can Also Help Couples to Have Children

If a woman cannot get pregnant using medication, she may chose to try IVF ("*in vitro* fertilisation").

1) IVF involves collecting eggs from the woman's ovaries and fertilising them in a lab using the man's sperm.
2) IVF treatment can also involve a technique called Intra-Cytoplasmic Sperm Injection (ICSI), where the sperm is injected directly into an egg. It's useful if the man has a very low sperm count.
3) The fertilised eggs are then grown into embryos in a laboratory incubator.
4) Once the embryos are tiny balls of cells, one or two of them are transferred to the woman's uterus to improve the chance of pregnancy.
5) FSH and LH are given before egg collection to stimulate several eggs to mature (so more than one egg can be collected).
6) IVF has a pretty obvious benefit:

    Fertility treatment can give an infertile couple a child.

7) But there are also downsides to IVF:

    1) Multiple births can happen if more than one embryo grows into a baby — these are risky for the mother and babies (there's a higher risk of miscarriage, stillbirth...).
    2) The success rate of IVF is low — the average success rate in the UK is about 26%. This makes the process incredibly stressful and often upsetting, especially if it ends in multiple failures.
    3) As well as being emotionally stressful, the process is also physically stressful for the woman. Some women have a strong reaction to the hormones — e.g. abdominal pain, vomiting, dehydration.

Advances in Technology Have Improved IVF

1) Advances in microscope techniques have helped to improve the techniques (and therefore the success rate) of IVF.
2) Specialised micro-tools have been developed to use on the eggs and sperm under the microscope. They're also used to remove single cells from the embryo for genetic testing (to check that it is healthy — see page 134).
3) More recently, the development of time-lapse imaging (using a microscope and camera built into the incubator) means that the growth of the embryos can be continuously monitored to help identify those that are more likely to result in a successful pregnancy.

Some People Are Against IVF

1) The process of IVF often results in unused embryos that are eventually destroyed. Because of this, some people think it is unethical because each embryo is a potential human life.
2) The genetic testing of embryos before implantation also raises ethical issues as some people think it could lead to the selection of preferred characteristics, such as gender or eye colour.

Topic B5 — Homeostasis and Response

Adrenaline and Thyroxine

You've met a lot of human hormones so far, but **two more** won't hurt...

Adrenaline Prepares You for "Fight or Flight"

1) Adrenaline is a hormone released by the adrenal glands, which are just above the kidneys (see p.110).

2) Adrenaline is released in response to stressful or scary situations — your brain detects fear or stress and sends nervous impulses to the adrenal glands, which respond by secreting adrenaline.

3) It gets the body ready for 'fight or flight' by triggering mechanisms that increase the supply of oxygen and glucose to cells in the brain and muscles. E.g. adrenaline increases heart rate.

Hormone Release can be Affected by Negative Feedback

Your body can control the levels of hormones (and other substances) in the blood using negative feedback systems. When the body detects that the level of a substance has gone above or below the normal level, it triggers a response to bring the level back to normal again. Here's an example of just that:

Thyroxine Regulates Metabolism

1) Thyroxine is a hormone released by the thyroid gland, which is in the neck (see p.110).

2) It plays an important role in regulating the basal metabolic rate — the speed at which chemical reactions in the body occur while the body is at rest. Thyroxine is also important for loads of processes in the body, such as stimulating protein synthesis for growth and development.

3) Thyroxine is released in response to thyroid stimulating hormone (TSH), which is released from the pituitary gland.

4) A negative feedback system keeps the amount of thyroxine in the blood at the right level — when the level of thyroxine in the blood is higher than normal, the secretion of TSH from the pituitary gland is inhibited (stopped). This reduces the amount of thyroxine released from the thyroid gland, so the level in the blood falls back towards normal.

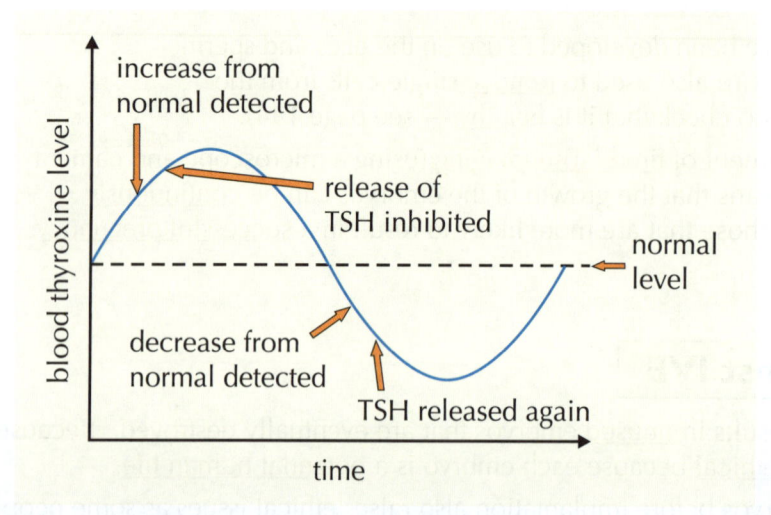

Thyroxine is made in the thyroid gland from iodine and amino acids.

Topic B5 — Homeostasis and Response

Warm-Up & Exam Questions

If these questions don't get your adrenaline pumping, I don't know what will. Better get started...

Warm-Up Questions

1) Name the hormone that stimulates an egg to mature in the ovary.
2) Name three forms of contraception that reduce fertility using progesterone, not oestrogen.
3) Give one drawback to using hormones to increase fertility.
4) What is the role of FSH and LH during IVF?
5) Name the gland that releases thyroxine.

Exam Questions

1   The menstrual cycle is controlled by several different hormones. *(Grade 4-6)*

1.1   What effect does oestrogen have on the release of FSH?

[1 mark]

1.2   Which hormone is responsible for maintaining the uterus lining?

[1 mark]

1.3   On what day of the menstrual cycle is the egg released?

[1 mark]

2   The combined oral contraceptive pill contains oestrogen and progesterone. *(Grade 6-7)*

2.1   Explain how taking oestrogen can prevent pregnancy.

[2 marks]

2.2   Progesterone can prevent pregnancy by preventing ovulation.
Explain **one** other way in which taking progesterone can prevent pregnancy.

[2 marks]

The combined pill is taken once a day in a '21 day pill, 7 day no pill' cycle. One of the problems with the combined pill is that women may forget to take it on the days they are supposed to.

2.3   Suggest an alternative method of hormonal contraception that may be more suitable for a woman who is worried about remembering to take the combined pill. Explain your choice.

[2 marks]

2.4   A couple in their late 30s who have already had three children are looking for a more permanent method of contraception. Suggest **one** method of contraception that may be suitable for them.

[1 mark]

3   A dog suddenly runs towards a cat across the street, which frightens the cat. *(Grade 7-9)*

Explain what would happen to the cat's heart rate when it sees the dog and explain why this response is beneficial.

[5 marks]

Topic B5 — Homeostasis and Response

Topic B6 — Inheritance, Variation and Evolution

DNA

The first step in understanding **genetics** is getting to grips with **DNA**.

Chromosomes Are Really Long Molecules of DNA

1) DNA stands for deoxyribonucleic acid. It's the chemical that all of the genetic material in a cell is made up from.

2) It contains coded information — basically all the instructions to put an organism together and make it work.

3) So it's what's in your DNA that determines what inherited characteristics you have.

4) DNA is found in the nucleus of animal and plant cells, in really long structures called chromosomes.

5) Chromosomes normally come in pairs.

6) DNA is a polymer. It's made up of two strands coiled together in the shape of a double helix.

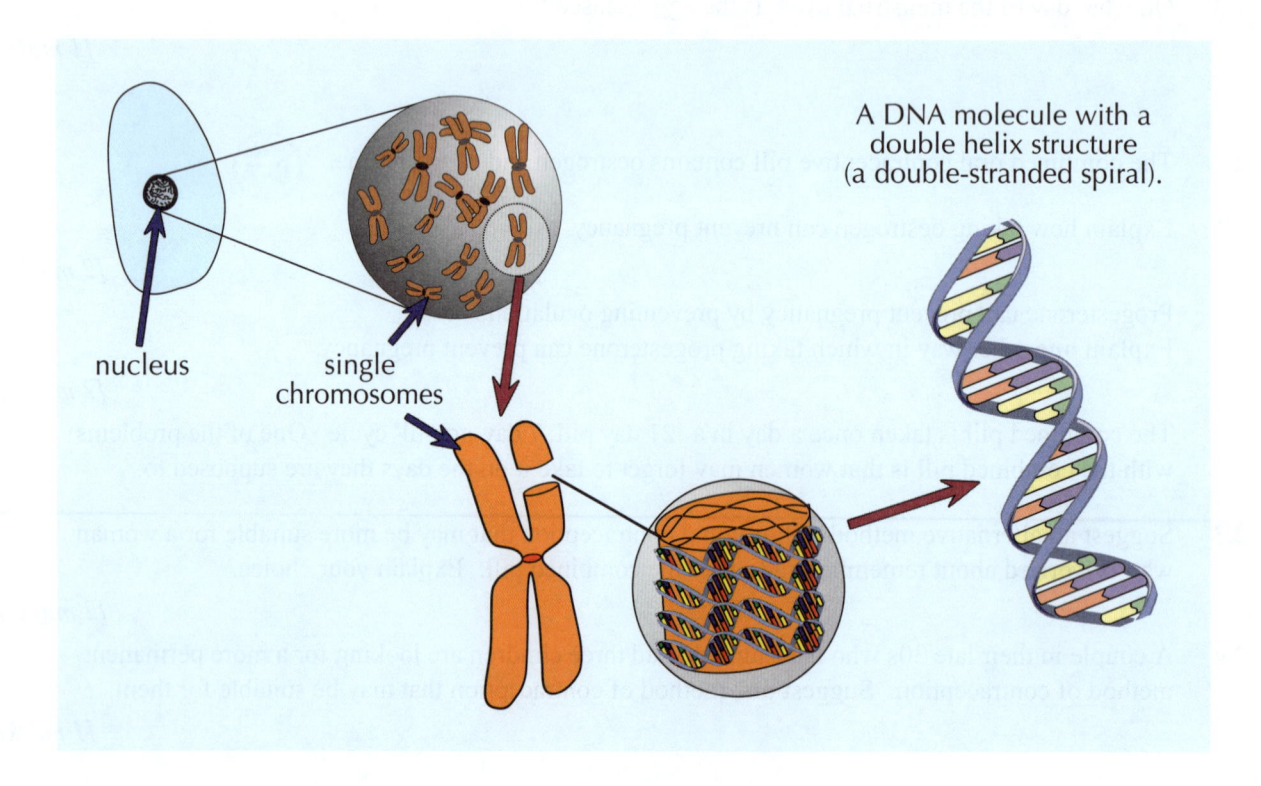

A DNA molecule with a double helix structure (a double-stranded spiral).

nucleus   single chromosomes

Every living organism has DNA

Remember, DNA contains all the instructions to 'build' an organism. The instructions are different for each type of organism on Earth (otherwise all living things would be the same). There's a lot more about DNA and chromosomes coming up in this topic so make sure you understand this page before you move on.

Topic B6 — Inheritance, Variation and Evolution

DNA

DNA determines what **characteristics** an organism has — it's a **very important** molecule.
It's not surprising then that scientists are **super keen** on understanding more about it.

A **Gene** Codes for a **Specific Protein**

1) A gene is a small section of DNA found on a chromosome.
2) Each gene codes for (tells the cells to make) a particular sequence of amino acids which are put together to make a specific protein.
3) Only 20 amino acids are used, but they make up thousands of different proteins.
4) Genes simply tell cells in what order to put the amino acids together.
5) DNA also determines what proteins the cell produces, e.g. haemoglobin, keratin.
6) That in turn determines what type of cell it is, e.g. red blood cell, skin cell.

Every Organism Has a **Genome**

1) Genome is just the fancy term for the entire set of genetic material in an organism.
2) Scientists have worked out the complete human genome.
3) Understanding the human genome is a really important tool for science and medicine for many reasons.

   1) It allows scientists to identify genes in the genome that are linked to different types of disease.

   2) Knowing which genes are linked to inherited diseases could help us to understand them better and could help us to develop effective treatments for them.

   3) Scientists can look at genomes to trace the migration of certain populations of people around the world. All modern humans are descended from a common ancestor who lived in Africa, but humans can now be found all over the planet. The human genome is mostly identical in all individuals, but as different populations of people migrated away from Africa, they gradually developed tiny differences in their genomes. By investigating these differences, scientists can work out when new populations split off in a different direction and what route they took.

Your genes make you different from everyone else

Working out the human genome was a massive project — it involved scientists from many different parts of the world and took more than ten years to complete. Still, if scientists can use the information to help us understand more about diseases and how to fight them, then I reckon it was well worth all the effort.

Topic B6 — Inheritance, Variation and Evolution

Reproduction

*Reproduction is important for all species. It can happen in **two** different ways...*

Sexual Reproduction Produces Genetically Different Cells

1) Sexual reproduction is where genetic information from two organisms (a father and a mother) is combined to produce offspring which are genetically different to either parent.
2) In sexual reproduction, the mother and father produce gametes (sex cells) by meiosis (see next page) — e.g. egg and sperm cells in animals.
3) In humans, each gamete contains 23 chromosomes — half the number of chromosomes in a normal cell. (Instead of having two of each chromosome, a gamete has just one of each.)
4) The egg (from the mother) and the sperm cell (from the father) then fuse together (fertilisation) to form a cell with the full number of chromosomes (half from the father, half from the mother).

> SEXUAL REPRODUCTION involves the fusion of male and female gametes. Because there are TWO parents, the offspring contain a mixture of their parents' genes.

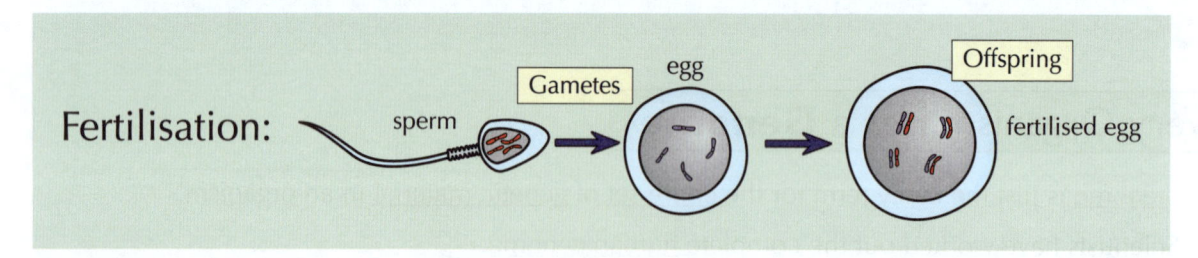

Fertilisation: sperm → Gametes egg → Offspring fertilised egg

5) This is why the offspring inherits features from both parents — it's received a mixture of chromosomes from its mum and its dad (and it's the chromosomes that decide how you turn out).
6) This mixture of genetic information produces variation in the offspring.
7) Flowering plants can reproduce in this way too. They also have egg cells, but their version of sperm is known as pollen.

Asexual Reproduction Produces Genetically Identical Cells

1) In asexual reproduction there's only one parent so the offspring are genetically identical to that parent.
2) Asexual reproduction happens by mitosis — an ordinary cell makes a new cell by dividing in two (see page 27).
3) The new cell has exactly the same genetic information (i.e. genes) as the parent cell — it's called a clone.

> In ASEXUAL REPRODUCTION there's only ONE parent. There's no fusion of gametes, no mixing of chromosomes and no genetic variation between parent and offspring. The offspring are genetically identical to the parent — they're clones.

4) Bacteria, some plants and some animals reproduce asexually.

You might need to reproduce these facts in the exam...

The main messages on this page are that: 1) sexual reproduction needs two parents and forms cells that are genetically different to the parents, so there's lots of genetic variation. And 2) asexual reproduction needs just one parent to make genetically identical cells, so there's no genetic variation in the offspring.

Topic B6 — Inheritance, Variation and Evolution

Meiosis

*If you're wondering how gametes end up with **half** the number of **chromosomes** of a normal cell, read on...*

Gametes Are Produced by Meiosis

1) As you know from the previous page, gametes only have one copy of each chromosome, so that when gamete fusion takes place, you get the right amount of chromosomes again (two copies of each).
2) To make gametes which only have half the original number of chromosomes, cells divide by meiosis. This process involves two cell divisions. In humans, it only happens in the reproductive organs (the ovaries in females and testes in males).

Meiosis Produces Cells Which Have Half the Normal Number of Chromosomes

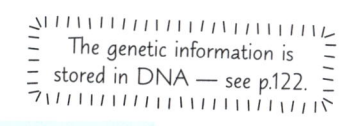

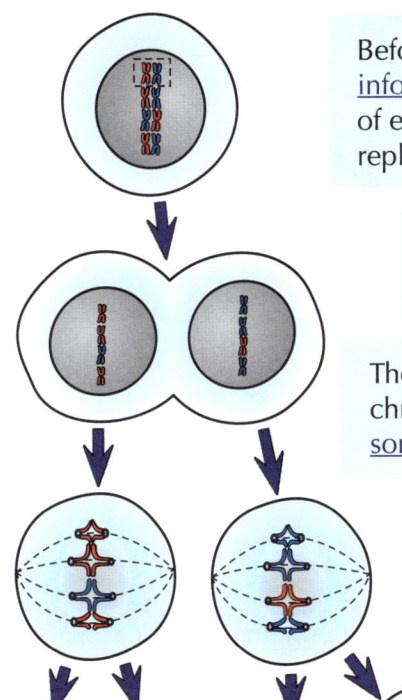

The genetic information is stored in DNA — see p.122.

Before the cell starts to divide, it duplicates its genetic information, forming two armed chromosomes — one arm of each chromosome is an exact copy of the other arm. After replication, the chromosomes arrange themselves into pairs.

In the first division in meiosis the chromosome pairs line up in the centre of the cell.

The pairs are then pulled apart so each new cell only has one copy of each chromosome. Some of the father's chromosomes (shown in blue) and some of the mother's chromosomes (shown in red) go into each new cell.

In the second division, the chromosomes line up again in the centre of the cell. The arms of the chromosomes are pulled apart.

You get four gametes, each with only a single set of chromosomes in it. Each of the gametes is genetically different from the others because the chromosomes all get shuffled up during meiosis and each gamete only gets half of them, at random.

The Cell Produced by Gamete Fusion Replicates Itself

1) After two gametes have fused during fertilisation, the resulting new cell divides by mitosis to make a copy of itself.
2) Mitosis repeats many times to produce lots of new cells in an embryo.
3) As the embryo develops, these cells then start to differentiate (see page 23) into the different types of specialised cell that make up a whole organism.

There's loads on mitosis on page 28.

Now that I have your undivided attention...

Remember, in humans, meiosis only occurs in reproductive organs.

Q1   Human body cells contain 46 chromosomes each. The graph on the right shows how the mass of DNA per cell changed as some cells divided by meiosis in a human ovary. How many chromosomes were present in each cell when they reached stage 6? [1 mark]

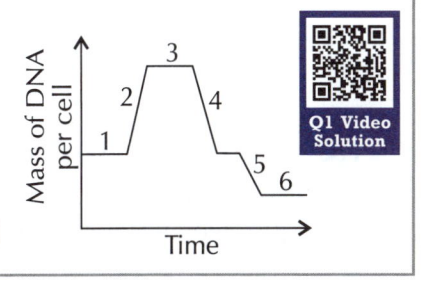

Topic B6 — Inheritance, Variation and Evolution

X and Y Chromosomes

*Now for a couple of **very important** little chromosomes...*

Your **Chromosomes** Control Whether You're **Male** or **Female**

1) There are 23 pairs of chromosomes in every human body cell (see page 27).
2) Of these, 22 are matched pairs of chromosomes that just control characteristics.
3) The 23rd pair are labelled XX or XY.
4) They're the two chromosomes that decide your sex — whether you turn out male or female.

Males have an X and a Y chromosome: XY
The Y chromosome causes male characteristics.

Females have two X chromosomes: XX
The XX combination allows
female characteristics to develop.

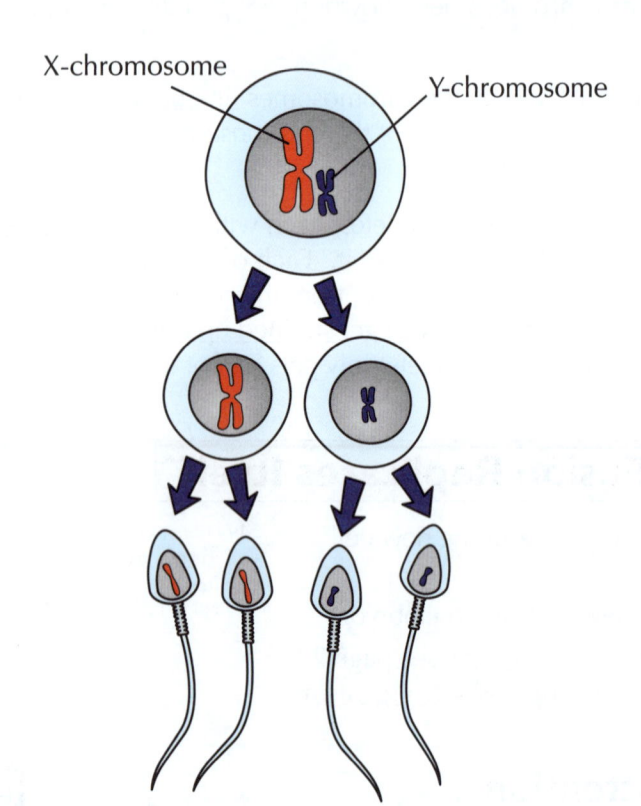

When making sperm, the X and Y chromosomes are drawn apart in the first division in meiosis. There's a 50% chance each sperm cell gets an X chromosome and a 50% chance it gets a Y chromosome.

A similar thing happens when making eggs. But the original cell has two X-chromosomes, so all the eggs have one X-chromosome.

The Y chromosome is physically smaller than the X chromosome

It's possible for people to have one X and two Y chromosomes, or even three X chromosomes, in their cells. But you just need to remember that XX gives female characteristics and XY gives male characteristics.

Topic B6 — Inheritance, Variation and Evolution

X and Y Chromosomes

You can work out the **probability** of offspring being male or female by using a **genetic diagram**.

Genetic Diagrams Show the Possible Combinations of Gametes

1) To find the probability of getting a boy or a girl, you can draw a genetic diagram.

2) Genetic diagrams are just models that are used to show all the possible genetic outcomes when you cross together different genes or chromosomes.

3) Put the possible gametes (eggs or sperm) from one parent down the side, and those from the other parent along the top.

4) Then in each middle square you fill in the letters from the top and side that line up with that square. The pairs of letters in the middle show the possible combinations of the gametes.

5) There are two XX results and two XY results, so there's the same probability of getting a boy or a girl.

6) Don't forget that this 50:50 ratio is only a probability at each pregnancy.

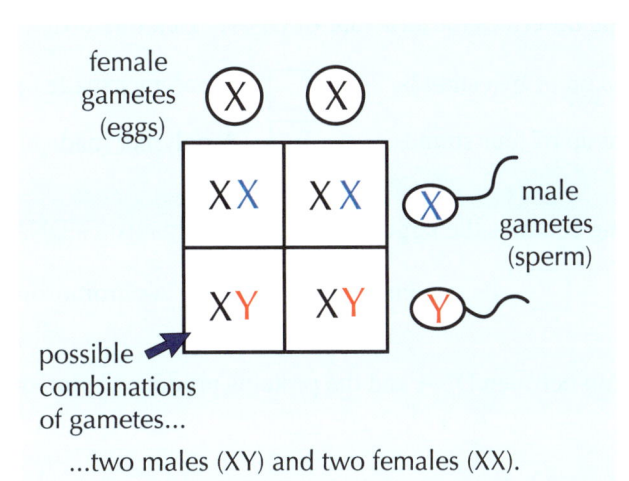

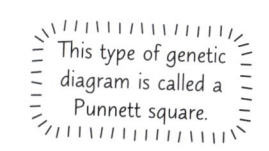

This type of genetic diagram is called a Punnett square.

...two males (XY) and two females (XX).

There's More Than One Type of Genetic Diagram

The other type of genetic diagram looks a bit more complicated, but it shows exactly the same thing.

1) At the top are the parents.

2) The middle circles show the possible gametes that are formed. One gamete from the female combines with one gamete from the male (during fertilisation).

3) The criss-cross lines show all the possible ways the X and Y chromosomes could combine. The possible combinations of the offspring are shown in the bottom circles.

4) Remember, only one of these possibilities would actually happen for any one offspring.

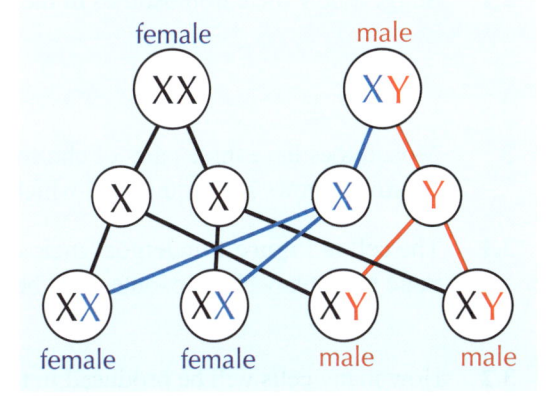

These diagrams aren't as scary as they look...

Most genetic diagrams you'll see in exams concentrate on a gene, instead of a chromosome. But the principle's the same. Don't worry — there are loads of other examples on pages 130-133.

Topic B6 — Inheritance, Variation and Evolution

Warm-Up & Exam Questions

It's time to see how much you picked up about meiosis, reproduction and sex chromosomes...

Warm-Up Questions

1) What is a gene?
2) Suggest why there is variation in the offspring of sexual reproduction.
3) How many cell divisions take place in meiosis?
4) What combination of sex chromosomes do human females have?

Exam Questions

1 An organism's genetic material is made up of a chemical called DNA. *(Grade 4-6)*

1.1 Which of the following describes the structure of DNA? Tick **one** box.

☐ A protein made up of two strands.   ☐ A polymer made up of two strands.

☐ A protein made up of four strands. ☐ A polymer made up of four strands.

[1 mark]

1.2 Which of the following contains the largest amount of an organism's DNA? Tick **one** box.

☐ A gene   ☐ Its genome   ☐ A chromosome

[1 mark]

1.3 Explain the relationship between DNA and the proteins produced by an organism.

[3 marks]

2 Some species of worm can produce offspring through a process called fragmentation. In this process, fragments of the parent's body break off and undergo cell division by mitosis to develop into mature, complete organisms. *(Grade 4-6)*

2.1 What term is used to describe this form of reproduction?

[1 mark]

2.2 Suggest how the chromosomes in the offspring will compare to those of the parent worm.

[1 mark]

3 Mosquitoes have three pairs of chromosomes in their body cells. **Figure 1** shows a mosquito cell which is about to divide by meiosis. *(Grade 6-7)*

Figure 1

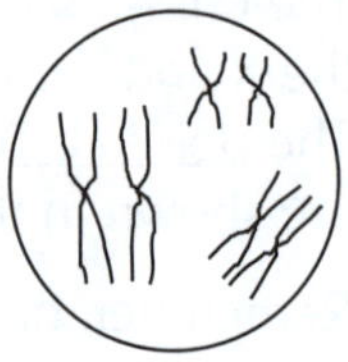

3.1 The cell in **Figure 1** undergoes meiosis. State how many chromosomes will be present in each new cell produced.

[1 mark]

3.2 How many cells will be produced in total when the cell in **Figure 1** undergoes meiosis?

[1 mark]

3.3 Explain how the processes of meiosis and fertilisation lead to genetic variation in the mosquito's offspring.

[3 marks]

Topic B6 — Inheritance, Variation and Evolution

Genetic Diagrams

*For those of you expecting to see a **diagram** or two on a page called 'Genetic Diagrams', prepare to be disappointed. You need to understand a bit more about what genetic diagrams **show** to start with...*

Some Characteristics are Controlled by Single Genes

1) What genes you inherit control what characteristics you develop.

2) Different genes control different characteristics. Some characteristics are controlled by a single gene, e.g. mouse fur colour and red-green colour blindness in humans.

3) However, most characteristics are controlled by several genes interacting.

4) All genes exist in different versions called alleles (which are represented by letters in genetic diagrams).

5) You have two versions (alleles) of every gene in your body — one on each chromosome in a pair.

6) If an organism has two alleles for a particular gene that are the same, then it's homozygous for that trait. If its two alleles for a particular gene are different, then it's heterozygous.

7) If the two alleles are different, only one can determine what characteristic is present. The allele for the characteristic that's shown is called the dominant allele (use a capital letter for dominant alleles — e.g. 'C'). The other one is called recessive (and you show these with small letters — e.g. 'c').

8) For an organism to display a recessive characteristic, both its alleles must be recessive (e.g. cc). But to display a dominant characteristic the organism can be either CC or Cc, because the dominant allele overrules the recessive one if the plant/animal/other organism is heterozygous.

9) Your genotype is the combination of alleles you have. Your alleles work at a molecular level to determine what characteristics you have — your phenotype.

There are lots of fancy words to learn on this page...

EXAM TIP Make sure you fully understand what all the different terms on this page mean (i.e. genes, alleles, homozygous, heterozygous, dominant, recessive, genotype and phenotype). You'll feel much more comfortable going into the exam knowing that these words aren't going to trip you up.

Topic B6 — Inheritance, Variation and Evolution

Genetic Diagrams

Genetic Diagrams Show the **Possible Alleles** of **Offspring**

Suppose you start breeding hamsters with superpowers. The allele which causes hamsters to have superpowers is recessive ("b"), whilst normal (boring) behaviour is due to a dominant allele ("B").

1) A superpowered hamster must have the genotype bb. But a normal hamster could be BB or Bb.

2) Here's what happens if you breed from two homozygous hamsters:

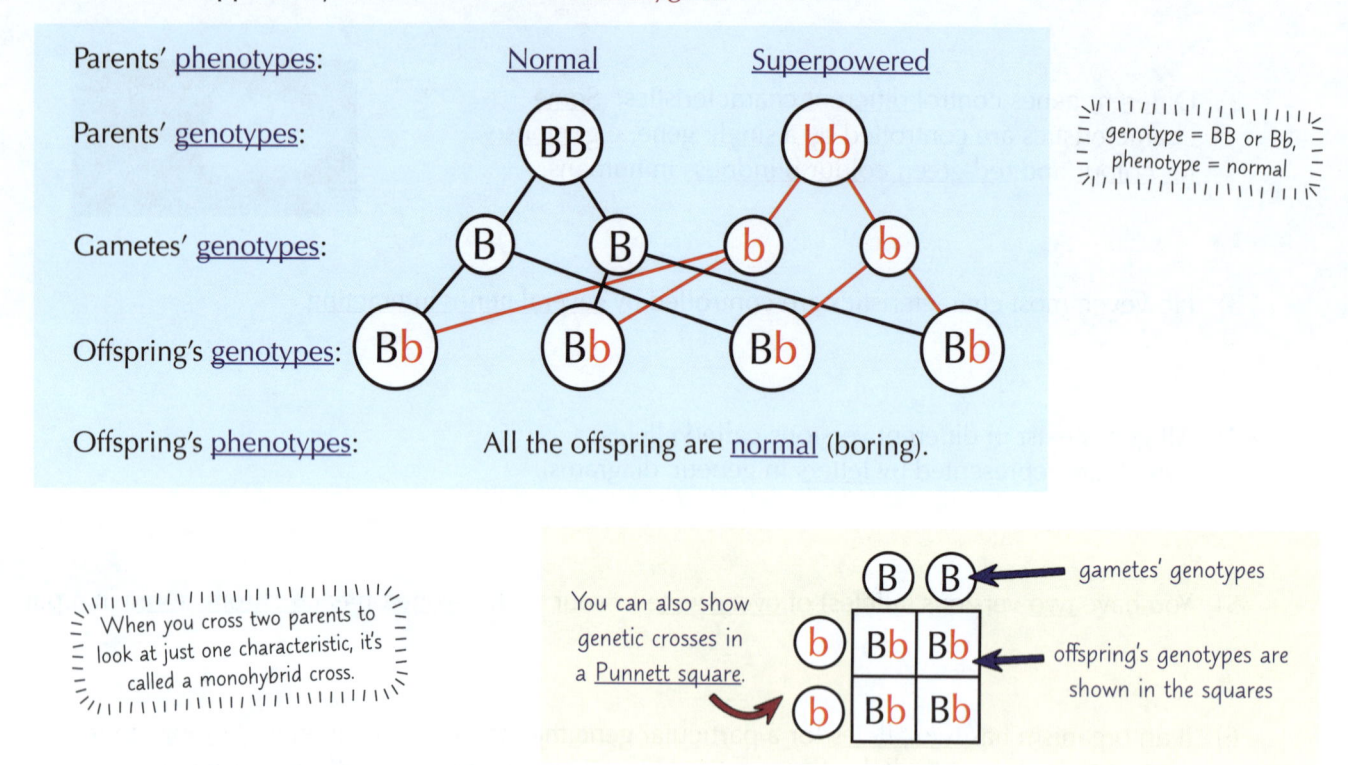

Parents' phenotypes: Normal   Superpowered

Parents' genotypes: BB   bb

Gametes' genotypes: B B b b

Offspring's genotypes: Bb Bb Bb Bb

Offspring's phenotypes: All the offspring are normal (boring).

genotype = BB or Bb, phenotype = normal

When you cross two parents to look at just one characteristic, it's called a monohybrid cross.

You can also show genetic crosses in a Punnett square.

	B	B
b	Bb	Bb
b	Bb	Bb

← gametes' genotypes
← offspring's genotypes are shown in the squares

3) If two of these offspring now breed, you'll get the next generation:

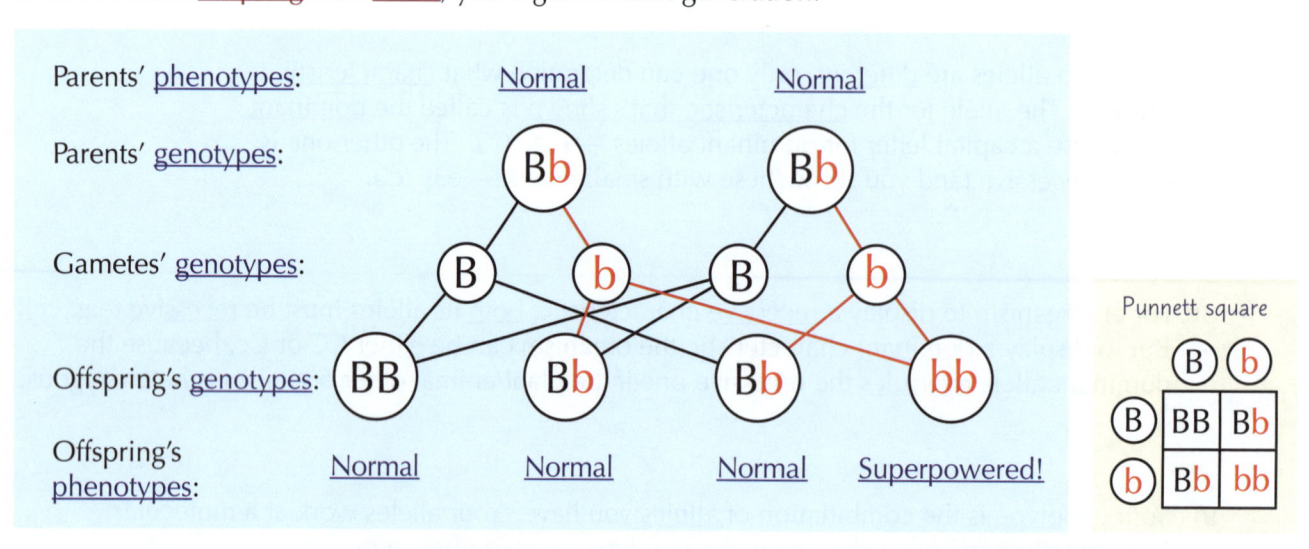

Parents' phenotypes: Normal   Normal

Parents' genotypes: Bb   Bb

Gametes' genotypes: B b B b

Offspring's genotypes: BB Bb Bb bb

Offspring's phenotypes: Normal Normal Normal Superpowered!

Punnett square

	B	b
B	BB	Bb
b	Bb	bb

4) That's a 3:1 ratio of normal to superpowered offspring in this generation (a 1 in 4 or 25% probability of superpowers).

But remember — genetic diagrams only tell you probabilities. They don't say definitely what'll happen.

Genetic diagrams aren't that scary — you just need to practise them...

You should know how to produce and interpret both of these types of genetic diagram before exam day.

Topic B6 — Inheritance, Variation and Evolution

More Genetic Diagrams

*In the exam, you could be asked to **predict** and **explain** the outcomes of crosses between individuals for each possible combination of dominant and recessive alleles of a gene. You should be able to draw a genetic diagram and work it out — but it'll be easier if you've seen them all before. So here are some more examples.*

All the Offspring are Normal

Let's take another look at the superpowered hamster example from page 130:

In this cross, a homozygous dominant hamster (BB) is crossed with a homozygous recessive hamster (bb). All the offspring are normal (boring).

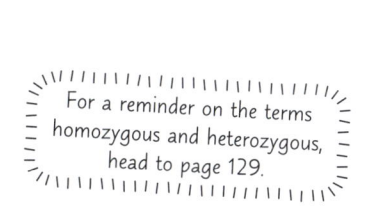

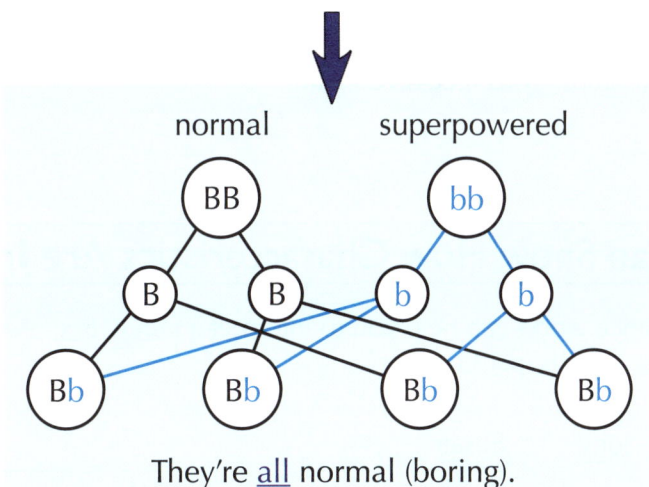

For a reminder on the terms homozygous and heterozygous, head to page 129.

normal   superpowered

BB   bb

B   B   b   b

Bb   Bb   Bb   Bb

They're all normal (boring).

But, if you crossed a homozygous dominant hamster (BB) with a heterozygous hamster (Bb), you would also get all normal (boring) offspring.

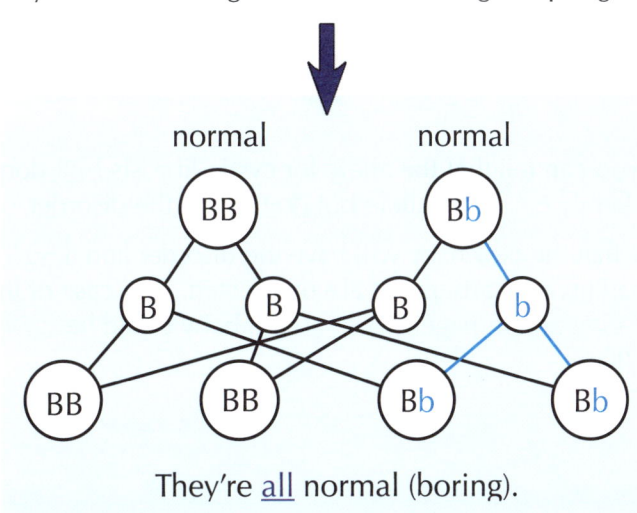

normal   normal

BB   Bb

B   B   B   b

BB   BB   Bb   Bb

They're all normal (boring).

To find out which it was you'd have to breed the offspring together and see what kind of ratio you got that time — then you'd have a good idea. If it was 3:1, it's likely that you originally had BB and bb.

Topic B6 — Inheritance, Variation and Evolution

More Genetic Diagrams

*One more example of a genetic cross diagram coming up on this page. Then a little bit about another type of genetic diagram called a **family tree**...*

There's a 1:1 Ratio in the Offspring

1) A cat with long hair was bred with another cat with short hair.
2) The long hair is caused by a dominant allele 'H', and the short hair by a recessive allele 'h'.
3) The cats had 8 kittens — 4 with long hair and 4 with short hair.
4) This is a 1:1 ratio — it's what you'd expect when a parent with only one dominant allele (heterozygous — Hh) is crossed with a parent with two recessive alleles (homozygous recessive — hh).

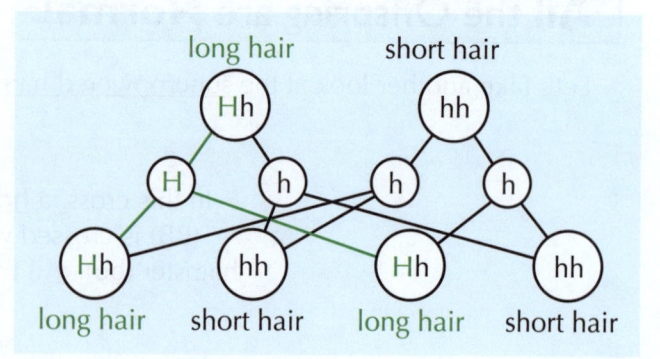

Family Trees Can Show How Characteristics Are Inherited

1) Knowing how inheritance works can help you to interpret a family tree — this is one for cystic fibrosis (p.133).

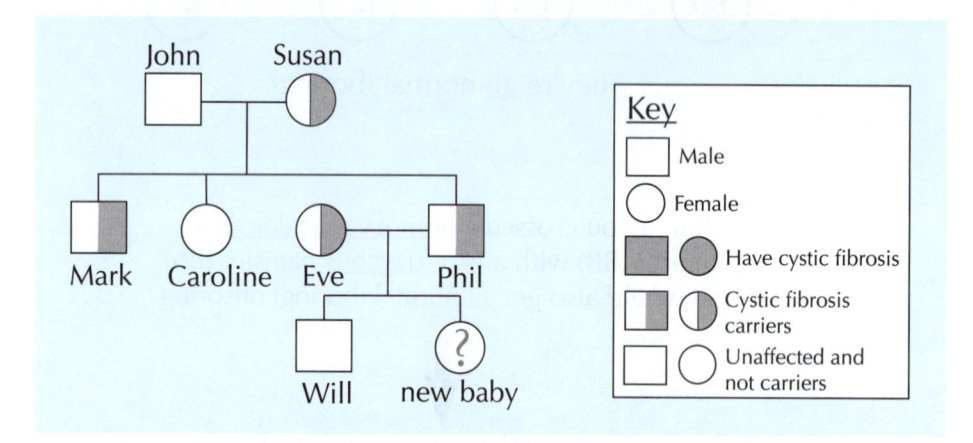

2) From the family tree, you can tell that the allele for cystic fibrosis isn't dominant because plenty of the family carry the allele but don't have the disorder.

3) There is a 25% chance that the new baby will have the disorder and a 50% chance that it will be a carrier, as both of its parents are carriers but are unaffected. The case of the new baby is just the same as in the genetic diagram on page 133 — so the baby could be unaffected (FF), a carrier (Ff) or have cystic fibrosis (ff).

It's enough to make you go cross-eyed...

Now, here's a fascinating practice question about peas...

Q1 Round peas are caused by the dominant allele, R. The allele for wrinkly peas, r, is recessive. Using a Punnett square, predict the ratio of plants with round peas to plants with wrinkly peas for a cross between a heterozygous pea plant and a pea plant that is homozygous recessive. [3 marks]

Topic B6 — Inheritance, Variation and Evolution

Inherited Disorders

*Some disorders can be **inherited** from your parents. Many of these can be **screened** for in embryos.*

Cystic Fibrosis is Caused by a Recessive Allele

Cystic fibrosis is a genetic disorder of the cell membranes. It results in the body producing a lot of thick sticky mucus in the air passages and in the pancreas.

1) The allele which causes cystic fibrosis is a recessive allele, 'f', carried by about 1 person in 25.
2) Because it's recessive, people with only one copy of the allele won't have the disorder — they're known as carriers.
3) For a child to have the disorder, both parents must be either carriers or have the disorder themselves.
4) As the diagram shows, there's a 1 in 4 chance of a child having the disorder if both parents are carriers.

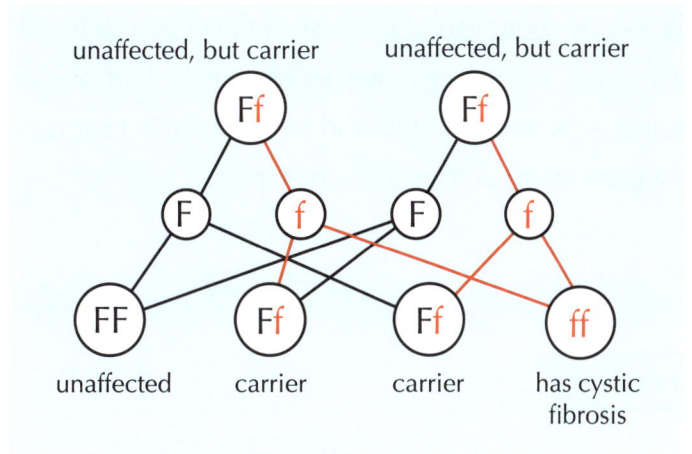

unaffected, but carrier — Ff   unaffected, but carrier — Ff

F   f   F   f

FF   Ff   Ff   ff
unaffected   carrier   carrier   has cystic
                                       fibrosis

Polydactyly is Caused by a Dominant Allele

Polydactyly is a genetic disorder where a baby's born with extra fingers or toes. It doesn't usually cause any other problems so isn't life-threatening.

1) The disorder is caused by a dominant allele, 'D', and so can be inherited if just one parent carries the defective allele.
2) The parent that has the defective allele will have the condition too since the allele is dominant.
3) As the genetic diagram shows, there's a 50% chance of a child having the disorder if one parent has one D allele.

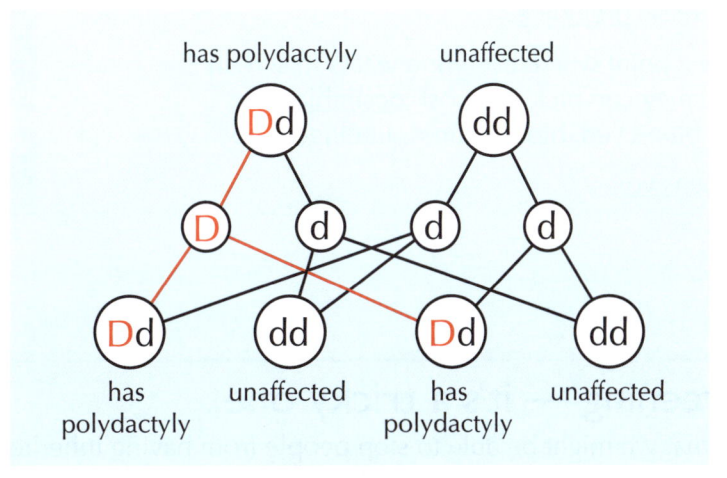

has polydactyly — Dd   unaffected — dd

D   d   d   d

Dd   dd   Dd   dd
has   unaffected has   unaffected
polydactyly   polydactyly

Topic B6 — Inheritance, Variation and Evolution

Inherited Disorders

Embryos Can Be Screened for Genetic Disorders

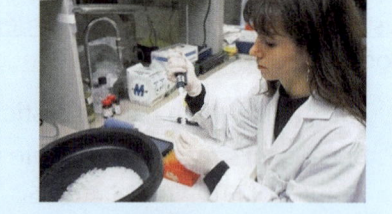

1) During *in vitro* fertilisation (IVF), embryos are fertilised in a laboratory, and then implanted into the mother's womb.
2) Before being implanted, it's possible to remove a cell from each embryo and analyse its genes.
3) Many genetic disorders can be detected in this way, such as cystic fibrosis.
4) It's also possible to get DNA from an embryo in the womb and test that for disorders.
5) There are lots of ethical, social and economic concerns surrounding embryo screening.
6) Embryonic screening is quite controversial because of the decisions it can lead to.
7) For embryos produced by IVF — after screening, embryos with 'bad' alleles would be destroyed.
8) For embryos in the womb — screening could lead to the decision to terminate the pregnancy.
9) Here are some more arguments for and against screening:

For Embryonic Screening

1) It will help to stop people suffering.
2) Treating disorders costs the Government (and the taxpayers) a lot of money.
3) There are laws to stop it going too far. At the moment parents cannot even select the sex of their baby (unless it's for health reasons).

Against Embryonic Screening

1) It implies that people with genetic problems are 'undesirable' — this could increase prejudice.
2) There may come a point where everyone wants to screen their embryos so they can pick the most 'desirable' one, e.g. they want a blue-eyed, blond-haired, intelligent boy.
3) Screening is expensive.

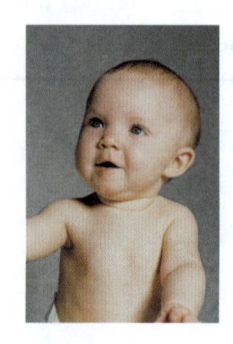

Embryo screening — it's a tricky one...
It's great to think that we might be able to stop people from having inherited disorders that cause suffering, but there are many concerns to think about too. Try writing a balanced argument for and against embryo screening — it's good practice.

Topic B6 — Inheritance, Variation and Evolution

Warm-Up & Exam Questions

There's no better preparation for exam questions than doing... err... practice exam questions. Hang on, what's this I see...

Warm-Up Questions

1) What are alleles?
2) What does genotype mean?
3) Why won't someone heterozygous for the cystic fibrosis allele have the disorder?
4) What is polydactyly?
5) Outline what embryo screening involves.

Exam Questions

1 Cystic fibrosis is a genetic disorder caused by recessive alleles. *Grade 4-6*

F = the normal allele   **f** = the faulty allele that leads to cystic fibrosis

Figure 1 is an incomplete Punnett square showing the possible inheritance of cystic fibrosis from one couple.

Figure 1

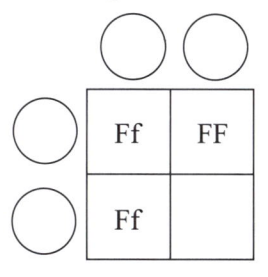

	Ff	FF
	Ff	

1.1 Complete the Punnett square to show the missing offspring's genotype and the genotypes of the gametes.

[2 marks]

1.2 What proportion of the possible offspring are homozygous?

[1 mark]

1.3 State the phenotypes of the parents.

[2 marks]

2 Fruit flies usually have red eyes. However, there are a small number of white-eyed fruit flies. Having white eyes is a recessive characteristic. *Grade 6-7*

Two fruit flies with red eyes have the heterozygous genotype for this characteristic. They are crossed to produce offspring.

2.1 Draw a genetic diagram to show the possible phenotypes of the offspring.
Use **R** to represent the dominant allele and **r** to represent the recessive allele.

[3 marks]

2.2 State the probability that one of the fruit flies' offspring will have white eyes.

[1 mark]

Topic B6 — Inheritance, Variation and Evolution

Exam Questions

3 Polydactyly is a genetic disorder transmitted by the dominant allele **D**.
The corresponding recessive allele is **d**.
Figure 2 shows the family pedigree of a family with a history of polydactyly.

Figure 2

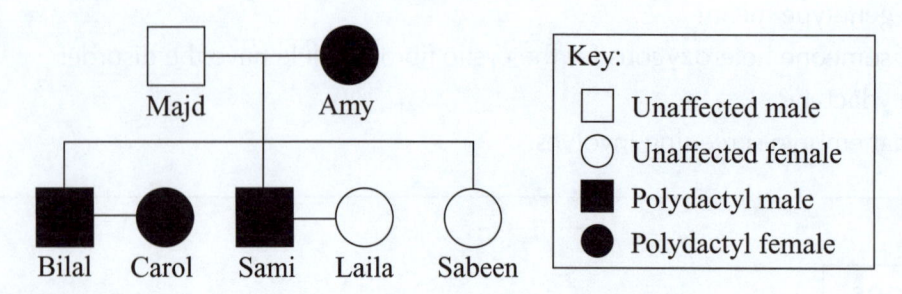

Majd — Amy
Children: Bilal, Carol, Sami, Laila, Sabeen

Key:
☐ Unaffected male
○ Unaffected female
■ Polydactyl male
● Polydactyl female

Using the information given above, state what Amy's genotype must be.
Explain your answer.

[2 marks]

4 Colour blindness in humans is caused by a recessive allele located on the X chromosome.
It is more common in men because men carry only one X chromosome.

A man who is colour blind has a child with a woman who does not have the recessive allele.

4.1 Draw a genetic diagram to show the possible sex of the offspring.

[3 marks]

4.2 The child is a boy. Explain why the boy will not be colour blind.

[1 mark]

4.3 State the probability that a daughter of this couple would be colour blind.

[1 mark]

5 Albinism is a condition characterised by the lack of pigment in the hair and skin.
It is caused by the recessive allele **a**. The dominant allele **A** results in normal pigmentation.

5.1 State the possible genotypes of a rabbit that shows no symptoms of albinism.

[1 mark]

A rabbit with albinism mated with a rabbit that showed no symptoms of the condition.
56% of the offspring had albinism.

5.2 Deduce the genotypes of the parent rabbits and the possible genotypes of their offspring.
Use a genetic diagram to explain your answer.

[3 marks]

5.3 From your genetic diagram, what percentage of offspring are likely to have albinism?

[1 mark]

5.4 Explain why the percentage of offspring which were born with albinism was not the same as that suggested by your genetic diagram.

[1 mark]

Topic B6 — Inheritance, Variation and Evolution

Variation

*You'll probably have noticed that not all people are **identical**. There are reasons for this.*

Organisms of the Same Species Have Differences

1) Different species look... well... different — my dog definitely doesn't look like a daisy.
2) But even organisms of the same species will usually look at least slightly different — e.g. in a room full of people you'll see different colour hair, individually shaped noses, a variety of heights, etc.
3) These differences are called the variation within a species.
4) Variation can be huge within a population.
5) There are two types of variation — genetic variation and environmental variation.

Different Genes Cause Genetic Variation

1) Variation can be genetic — this means it's caused by differences in genotype.
2) Genotype is all of the genes and alleles that an organism has.
3) An organism's genotype affects its phenotype — the characteristics that it displays.
4) An organism's genes are inherited (passed down) from its parents (see page 124).

Characteristics are also Influenced by the Environment

1) It's not only genotype that can affect an organism's phenotype — interactions with its environment (conditions in which it lives) can also influence phenotype.
2) For example:

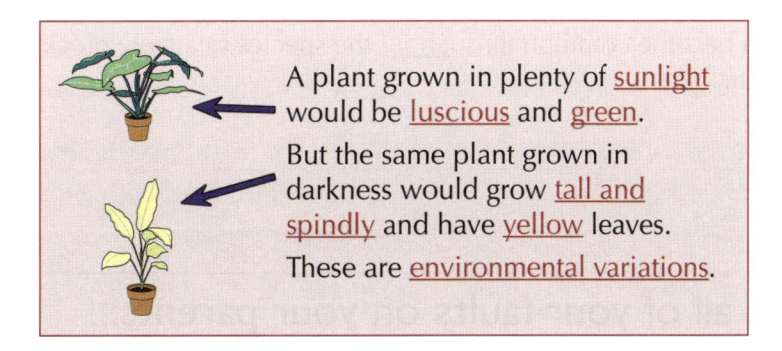

A plant grown in plenty of sunlight would be luscious and green.
But the same plant grown in darkness would grow tall and spindly and have yellow leaves.
These are environmental variations.

Topic B6 — Inheritance, Variation and Evolution

Variation

Most Characteristics are Due to Genes AND the Environment

1) Most variation in phenotype is determined by a mixture of genetic and environmental factors.
2) For example, the maximum height that an animal or plant could grow to is determined by its genes. But whether it actually grows that tall depends on its environment (e.g. how much food it gets).

Mutations are Changes to the Genome

1) Occasionally, a gene may mutate. A mutation is a rare, random change in an organism's DNA that can be inherited. Mutations occur continuously.

   Alleles (see page 129) are genetic variants.

2) Mutations mean that the gene is altered, which produces a genetic variant (a different form of the gene).
3) As the gene codes for the sequence of amino acids that make up a protein, gene mutations sometimes lead to changes in the protein that it codes for.
4) Most genetic variants have very little or no effect on the protein the gene codes for. Some will change it to such a small extent that its function is unaffected. This means that most mutations have no effect on an organism's phenotype.
5) Some variants have a small influence on the organism's phenotype — they alter the individual's characteristics but only slightly. For example:

   > Some characteristics, e.g. eye colour, are controlled by more than one gene. A mutation in one of the genes may change the eye colour a bit, but the difference might not be huge.

6) Very occasionally, variants can have such a dramatic effect that they determine phenotype. For example:

   > The genetic disorder, cystic fibrosis, is caused by a mutation that has a huge effect on phenotype. The gene codes for a protein that controls the movement of salt and water into and out of cells. However, the protein produced by the mutated gene doesn't work properly. This leads to excess mucus production in the lungs and digestive system, which can make it difficult to breathe and to digest food.

7) If the environment changes, and the new phenotype makes an individual more suited to the new environment, it can become common throughout the species relatively quickly by natural selection — see the next page.

You can't blame all of your faults on your parents...

Although the genes that you inherit from your parents are really important at determining what characteristics you have, the conditions in which you live usually play a role too.

Topic B6 — Inheritance, Variation and Evolution

Evolution

*Evolution is very important. Without it we wouldn't have the great **variety of life** we have on Earth today.*

> THEORY OF EVOLUTION: All of today's species have evolved from simple life forms that first started to develop over three billion years ago.

Only the Fittest Survive

Charles Darwin came up with a really important theory about evolution, called evolution by natural selection.

1) Darwin knew that organisms in a species show wide variation in their characteristics (phenotypic variation). He also knew that organisms have to compete for limited resources in an ecosystem.

2) Darwin concluded that the organisms with the most suitable characteristics for the environment would be more successful competitors and would be more likely to survive. This idea is called the 'survival of the fittest'.

3) The successful organisms that survive are more likely to reproduce and pass on the genes for the characteristics that made them successful to their offspring.

4) The organisms that are less well adapted would be less likely to survive and reproduce, so they are less likely to pass on their genes to the next generation.

5) Over time, beneficial characteristics become more common in the population and the species changes — it evolves.

New Discoveries Have Helped to Develop the Theory

1) Darwin's theory wasn't perfect. Because the relevant scientific knowledge wasn't available at the time, he couldn't give a good explanation for why new characteristics appeared or exactly how individual organisms passed on beneficial adaptations to their offspring.

2) However, the discovery of genetics supported Darwin's idea — it provided an explanation of how organisms born with beneficial characteristics can pass them on (i.e. via their genes) and showed that it is genetic variants (see page 138) that give rise to phenotypes that are suited to the environment.

3) Other evidence was also found by looking at fossils of different ages (the fossil record) — this allows you to see how changes in organisms developed slowly over time.

4) The relatively recent discovery of how bacteria are able to evolve to become resistant to antibiotics also further supports evolution by natural selection.

5) The theory of evolution by natural selection is now widely accepted.

Natural selection — the fittest pass on their genes...

Natural selection's all about the organisms with the best characteristics surviving to pass on their genes so that the whole species ends up adapted to its environment.

Q1 The sugary nectar in some orchid flowers is found at the end of a long tube behind the flower. There are moth species with long tongues that can reach the nectar. Explain how natural selection could have led to the moths developing long tongues. [4 marks]

Topic B6 — Inheritance, Variation and Evolution

Evolution

*Species need to **continue evolving** in order to **survive**. Sometimes this evolution creates a whole **new species**, but if a species can't evolve fast enough it might **die out** completely.*

The Development of a New Species is Called Speciation

1) Over a long period of time, the phenotype of organisms can change so much because of natural selection that a completely new species is formed. This is called speciation.
2) Speciation happens when populations of the same species change enough to become reproductively isolated — this means that they can't interbreed to produce fertile offspring.

Extinction is When No Individuals of a Species Remain

The fossil record contains many species that don't exist any more — these species are said to be extinct. Species become extinct for these reasons:

1) The environment changes too quickly (e.g. destruction of habitat).

2) A new predator kills them all (e.g. humans hunting them).

3) A new disease kills them all.

4) They can't compete with another (new) species for food.

5) A catastrophic event happens that kills them all (e.g. a volcanic eruption or a collision with an asteroid).

Example — Dodos

1) Dodos are now extinct.
2) Humans not only hunted them, but introduced other animals which ate all their eggs, and we destroyed the forest where they lived — they really didn't stand a chance...

Evolution's happening all the time...

Many species evolve so slowly that there are no significant changes in them within our lifetime. However, some species (e.g. bacteria) reproduce really quickly, so we're able to watch evolution in action.

Topic B6 — Inheritance, Variation and Evolution

Warm-Up & Exam Questions

You need to test your knowledge with a few Warm-Up Questions, followed by some Exam Questions...

Warm-Up Questions

1) Explain what is meant by environmental variation.
2) According to the theory of evolution, what have all of today's species evolved from?
3) Give three factors that can lead to a species becoming extinct.

Exam Questions

1   Helen and Stephanie are identical twins. *(Grade 4-6)*
    This means they have identical DNA.

1.1 Helen weighs 7 kg more than Stephanie.
    Explain whether this is due to genes, environmental factors or both.

    [2 marks]

1.2 Stephanie has a birthmark on her shoulder. Helen doesn't.
    State whether birthmarks are caused by genes and explain your answer.

    [1 mark]

2   Genetic variation in a population arises partly due to mutations. *(Grade 6-7)*

2.1 Explain what is meant by genetic variation.

    [1 mark]

2.2 Explain how mutations can increase variation in a species.

    [3 marks]

2.3 Some mutations are neutral, having no effect on an organism, but some do have an impact.
    Suggest how some mutations may be beneficial.

    [2 marks]

3* **Figure 1** shows a type of stingray. The stingray's appearance mimics a flat rock. *(Grade 7-9)*
    It spends most of its time on a rocky sea bed.

Figure 1

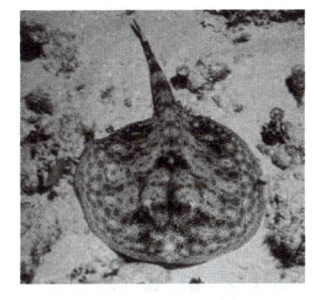

Describe and explain how the stingray might have evolved to look like this.

[4 marks]

Topic B6 — Inheritance, Variation and Evolution

Selective Breeding

'*Selective breeding*' sounds like it has the potential to be a tricky topic, but it's actually dead simple. You take the **best** plants or animals and breed them together to get the best possible **offspring**. That's it.

Selective Breeding is Very Simple

Selective breeding is when humans artificially select the plants or animals that are going to breed so that the genes for particular characteristics remain in the population. Organisms are selectively bred to develop features that are useful or attractive, for example:

- Animals that produce more meat or milk.
- Crops with disease resistance.
- Dogs with a good, gentle temperament.
- Decorative plants with big or unusual flowers.

This is the basic process involved in selective breeding:

1) From your existing stock, select the ones which have the characteristics you're after.
2) Breed them with each other.
3) Select the best of the offspring, and breed them together.
4) Continue this process over several generations, and the desirable trait gets stronger and stronger. Eventually, all the offspring will have the characteristic.

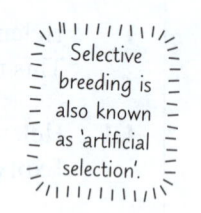

Selective breeding is also known as 'artificial selection'.

In agriculture (farming), selective breeding can be used to improve yields. E.g. to improve meat yields, a farmer could breed together the cows and bulls with the best characteristics for producing meat, e.g. large size. After doing this for several generations the farmer would get cows with a very high meat yield.

Selective breeding is nothing new — people have been doing it for thousands of years. It's how we ended up with edible crops from wild plants and how we got domesticated animals like cows and dogs.

The Main Drawback is a Reduction in the Gene Pool

1) The main problem with selective breeding is that it reduces the gene pool — the number of different alleles (forms of a gene) in a population. This is because the farmer keeps breeding from the "best" animals or plants — which are all closely related. This is known as inbreeding.
2) Inbreeding can cause health problems because there's more chance of the organisms inheriting harmful genetic defects when the gene pool is limited. Some dog breeds are particularly susceptible to certain defects because of inbreeding — e.g. pugs often have breathing problems.
3) There can also be serious problems if a new disease appears, because there's not much variation in the population. All the stock are closely related to each other, so if one of them is going to be killed by a new disease, the others are also likely to succumb to it.

Selective Breeding → Reduction in the number of different alleles (forms of a gene) → Less chance of any resistant alleles being present in the population

---

Selective breeding is just breeding the best to get the best...

Different breeds of dog came from selective breeding. E.g., somebody thought 'I like this small, yappy wolf — I'll breed it with this other one'. After thousands of generations, we got poodles.

Q1 Explain how you could selectively breed for floppy ears in rabbits. [4 marks]
Q2 What potential issues can selective breeding cause? [3 marks]

Topic B6 — Inheritance, Variation and Evolution

Genetic Engineering

*Genetic engineering is a relatively new area of science (well, it began in the 1970s). We've already put the technology to **good use** and it has many more **exciting possibilities** too...*

Genetic Engineering Transfers Genes Between Organisms

The basic idea of genetic engineering is to transfer a gene responsible for a desirable characteristic from one organism's genome into another organism, so that it also has the desired characteristic.

1) A useful gene is isolated (cut) from one organism's genome using enzymes and is inserted into a vector.

2) The vector is usually a virus or a bacterial plasmid (a fancy piece of circular DNA found in bacterial cells), depending on the type of organism that the gene is being transferred to.

3) When the vector is introduced to the target organism, the useful gene is inserted into its cell(s).

4) Scientists use this method to do all sorts of things. For example:

   1) Bacteria have been genetically modified to produce human insulin that can be used to treat diabetes.

   2) Genetically modified (GM) crops have had their genes modified, e.g. to improve the size and quality of their fruit, or make them resistant to disease, insects and herbicides (chemicals used to kill weeds).

   3) Sheep have been genetically engineered to produce substances, like drugs, in their milk that can be used to treat human diseases.

   4) Scientists are researching genetic modification treatments for inherited diseases caused by faulty genes, e.g. by inserting working genes into people with the disease. This is called gene therapy.

5) In some cases, the transfer of the gene is carried out when the organism receiving the gene is at an early stage of development (e.g. egg or embryo). This means that the organism develops with the characteristic coded for by the gene.

Genetic engineering has huge potential benefits...

Scientists are creating all sorts of weird and wonderful creatures with their genetic engineering sets. E.g. they have made cats that glow in the dark thanks to a gene taken from a jellyfish. But of course they don't just do it for fun — they're usually aiming to make organisms that benefit humans in some way.

Topic B6 — Inheritance, Variation and Evolution

Genetic Engineering

*On the face of it, **genetic engineering** is great.*
*But like most other things, there are **benefits** and **risks** that you need to consider.*

Genetic Engineering is a Controversial Topic

1) Genetic engineering is an exciting new area of science, which has the potential for solving many of our problems (e.g. treating diseases, more efficient food production etc.) but not everyone thinks it's a great idea.

2) There are worries about the long-term effects of genetic engineering — that changing an organism's genes might accidentally create unplanned problems, which could get passed on to future generations.

There Are Pros and Cons of GM Crops

Pros:

1) On the plus side, the characteristics chosen for GM crops can increase the yield, making more food.
2) People living in developing nations often lack nutrients in their diets. GM crops could be engineered to contain the nutrient that's missing. For example, 'golden rice' is a GM rice crop that contains beta-carotene — lack of this substance causes blindness.
3) GM crops are already being grown in some places, often without any problems.

Cons:

1) Some people say that growing GM crops will affect the number of wild flowers (and so the population of insects) that live in and around the crops — reducing farmland biodiversity.
2) Not everyone is convinced that GM crops are safe and some people are concerned that we might not fully understand the effects of eating them on human health. E.g. people are worried they may develop allergies to the food — although there's probably no more risk for this than for eating usual foods.
3) A big concern is that transplanted genes may get out into the natural environment. For example, the herbicide resistance gene may be picked up by weeds, creating a new 'superweed' variety.

If only there was a gene to make revision easier...

At the end of the day, it's down to the Government to weigh up all the evidence for the pros and cons before making a decision on how this scientific knowledge is used. All that the scientists can do is make sure the Government has all the information that it needs to make the decision.

Topic B6 — Inheritance, Variation and Evolution

Warm-Up & Exam Questions

By doing these Warm-Up Questions, you'll soon find out if you've got the basic facts straight.

Warm-Up Questions

1) Why might a plant nursery use selective breeding?
2) Explain why selective breeding can make some breeds more likely to inherit genetic defects.
3) Name one useful product that humans have genetically modified bacteria to produce.

Exam Questions

1 Organisms can be genetically modified.
This means an organism's genes can be altered to alter its characteristics.

Grade 4-6

1.1 Give **one** function of the enzymes used in genetic engineering.

[1 mark]

1.2 Suggest **one** useful way that plants can be genetically modified.

[1 mark]

1.3 Some people think that it is wrong to genetically modify crop plants.
Give **two** different objections that people might have.

[2 marks]

2 The characteristics of two varieties of wheat plants are shown in **Table 1**.

Grade 6-7

Table 1

Variety	Grain yield	Resistance to bad weather
Tall stems	High	Low
Dwarf stems	Low	High

Describe how selective breeding could be used to create a wheat plant with a high grain yield and high resistance to bad weather.

[3 marks]

3 **Figure 1** shows the milk yield for a population of cows over three generations. The peak of each curve shows the average milk yield per generation.

Grade 6-7

3.1 Do you think that selective breeding is likely to have been used with these cows? Explain your answer.

[1 mark]

3.2 Calculate the percentage increase in the average milk yield per year per cow between generation 1 and generation 3.

[2 marks]

Figure 1

Key:
Generation 1
Generation 2
Generation 3

x-axis: Milk yield (litres produced per year per cow)
y-axis: Number of cows

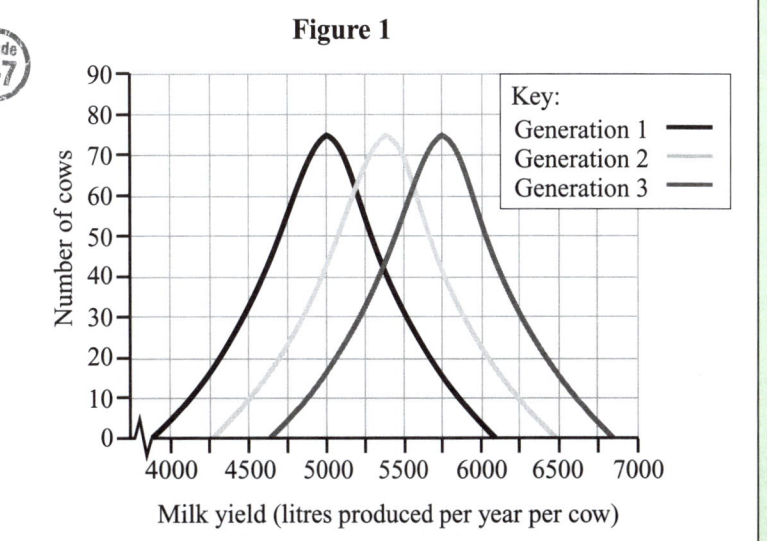

Topic B6 — Inheritance, Variation and Evolution

Fossils

*Fossils are great. If they're **well-preserved**, you can see what oldy-worldy creatures **looked** like. They also show how living things have **evolved**. Although we're not sure how life started in the first place...*

Fossils are the Remains of Plants and Animals

Fossils are the remains of organisms from many thousands of years ago, which are found in rocks. They provide the evidence that organisms lived ages ago. Fossils can tell us a lot about how much or how little organisms have changed (evolved) over time. Fossils form in rocks in one of three ways:

1) From gradual replacement by minerals

1) Things like teeth, shells, bones etc., which don't decay easily, can last a long time when buried.
2) They're eventually replaced by minerals as they decay, forming a rock-like substance shaped like the original hard part.
3) The surrounding sediments also turn to rock, but the fossil stays distinct inside the rock and eventually someone digs it up.

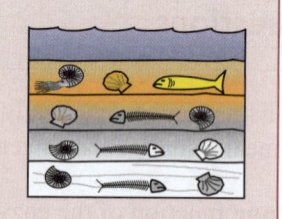

Most fossils happen this way.

2) From casts and impressions

1) Sometimes, fossils are formed when an organism is buried in a soft material like clay. The clay later hardens around it and the organism decays, leaving a cast of itself. An animal's burrow or a plant's roots (rootlet traces) can be preserved as casts.
2) Things like footprints can also be pressed into these materials when soft, leaving an impression when it hardens.

3) From preservation in places where no decay happens

1) In amber (a clear yellow 'stone' made from fossilised resin) and tar pits there's no oxygen or moisture so decay microbes can't survive.
2) In glaciers it's too cold for the decay microbes to work.
3) Peat bogs are too acidic for decay microbes.

A fully preserved man they named 'Pete Marsh' was found in a bog.

But No One Knows How Life Began

Fossils show how much or how little different organisms have changed (evolved) as life has developed on Earth over millions of years. But where did the first living thing come from...

1) There are various hypotheses suggesting how life first came into being, but no one really knows.
2) Maybe the first life forms came into existence in a primordial swamp (or under the sea) here on Earth. Maybe simple organic molecules were brought to Earth on comets — these could have then become more complex organic molecules, and eventually very simple life forms.
3) These hypotheses can't be supported or disproved because there's a lack of good, valid evidence:
   - Many early forms of life were soft-bodied, and soft tissue tends to decay away completely — so the fossil record is incomplete.
   - Fossils that did form millions of years ago may have been destroyed by geological activity, e.g. the movement of tectonic plates may have crushed fossils already formed in the rock.

Don't get bogged down by all this information...

It's a bit mind-boggling really how fossils can still exist even millions of years after the organism died. They really are fascinating things, and scientists have learned a whole lot from studying them in detail.

Topic B6 — Inheritance, Variation and Evolution

Antibiotic-Resistant Bacteria

*The discovery of **antibiotics** was a huge benefit to medicine — but they might **not** be a **permanent solution**.*

Bacteria can Evolve and Become Antibiotic-Resistant

1) Like all organisms, bacteria sometimes develop random mutations (changes) in their DNA. These can lead to changes in the bacteria's characteristics, e.g. being less affected by a particular antibiotic. This can lead to antibiotic-resistant strains forming as the gene for antibiotic resistance becomes more common in the population.

2) To make matters worse, because bacteria are so rapid at reproducing, they can evolve quite quickly.

3) For the bacterium, the ability to resist antibiotics is a big advantage. It's better able to survive, even in a host who's being treated to get rid of the infection, and so it lives for longer and reproduces many more times. This increases the population size of the antibiotic-resistant strain.

4) Antibiotic-resistant strains are a problem for people who become infected with these bacteria because they aren't immune to the new strain and there is no effective treatment. This means that the infection easily spreads between people. Sometimes drug companies can come up with a new antibiotic that's effective, but 'superbugs' that are resistant to most known antibiotics are becoming more common.

5) MRSA is a relatively common 'superbug' that's really hard to get rid of. It often affects people in hospitals and can be fatal if it enters their bloodstream.

The gene for antibiotic resistance becomes more common in the population because of natural selection — see page 139 for more.

Antibiotic Resistance is Becoming More Common

1) For the last few decades, we've been able to deal with bacterial infections pretty easily using antibiotics. The death rate from infectious bacterial diseases (e.g. pneumonia) has fallen dramatically.

2) But the problem of antibiotic resistance is getting worse — partly because of the overuse and inappropriate use of antibiotics, e.g. doctors prescribing them for non-serious conditions or infections caused by viruses.

Antibiotics don't kill viruses — see p.84.

3) The more often antibiotics are used, the bigger the problem of antibiotic resistance becomes, so it's important that doctors only prescribe antibiotics when they really need to:

> It's not that antibiotics actually cause resistance — they create a situation where naturally resistant bacteria have an advantage and so increase in numbers.

4) It's also important that you take all the antibiotics a doctor prescribes for you:

> Taking the full course makes sure that all the bacteria are destroyed, which means that there are none left to mutate and develop into antibiotic-resistant strains.

5) In farming, antibiotics can be given to animals to prevent them becoming ill and to make them grow faster. This can lead to the development of antibiotic-resistant bacteria in the animals which can then spread to humans, e.g. during meat preparation and consumption. Increasing concern about the overuse of antibiotics in agriculture has led to some countries restricting their use.

6) The increase in antibiotic resistance has encouraged drug companies to work on developing new antibiotics that are effective against the resistant strains. Unfortunately, the rate of development is slow, which means we're unlikely to be able to keep up with the demand for new drugs as more antibiotic-resistant strains develop and spread. It's also a very costly process.

Topic B6 — Inheritance, Variation and Evolution

Classification

*It seems to be a basic human urge to want to **classify** things — that's the case in **biology** anyway...*

Classification is Organising Living Organisms into Groups

1) Traditionally, organisms have been classified according to a system first proposed in the 1700's by Carl Linnaeus, which groups living things according to their characteristics and the structures that make them up.
2) In this system (known as the Linnaean system), living things are first divided into kingdoms (e.g. the plant kingdom).
3) The kingdoms are then subdivided into smaller and smaller groups — phylum, class, order, family, genus, species.

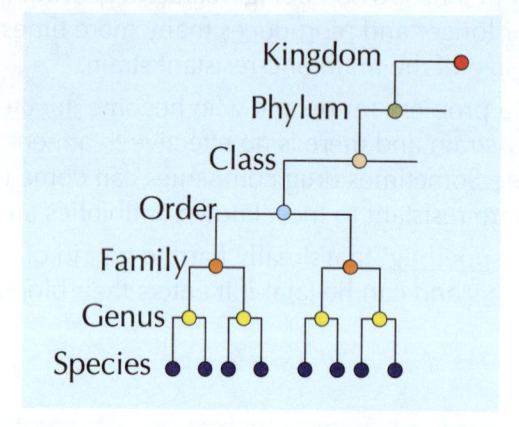

Classification Systems Change Over Time

1) As knowledge of the biochemical processes taking place inside organisms developed and microscopes improved (which allowed us to find out more about the internal structures of organisms), scientists put forward new models of classification.
2) In 1990, Carl Woese proposed the three-domain system. Using evidence gathered from new chemical analysis techniques such as RNA sequence analysis, he found that in some cases, species thought to be closely related in traditional classification systems are in fact not as closely related as first thought.
3) In the three-domain system, organisms are first of all split into three large groups called domains:

   1) ARCHAEA — Organisms in this domain are primitive bacteria. They're often found in extreme places such as hot springs and salt lakes.

   2) BACTERIA — This domain contains true bacteria like *E. coli* and *Staphylococcus*. Although they often look similar to Archaea, there are lots of biochemical differences between them.

   3) EUKARYOTA — This domain includes a broad range of organisms including fungi (page 76), plants, animals and protists (page 76).

4) These are then subdivided into smaller groups — kingdom, phylum, class, order, family, genus, species.

Topic B6 — Inheritance, Variation and Evolution

Classification

*A bit of a **Latin** lesson for you now. And a diagram of a **funny looking tree**.*

Organisms Are **Named** According to the **Binomial System**

1) In the binomial system, every organism is given its own two-part Latin name.

2) The first part refers to the genus that the organism belongs to. This gives you information on the organism's ancestry. The second part refers to the species. E.g. humans are known as *Homo sapiens*. '*Homo*' is the genus and '*sapiens*' is the species.

3) The binomial system is used worldwide and means that scientists in different countries or who speak different languages all refer to a particular species by the same name — avoiding potential confusion.

Evolutionary Trees Show **Evolutionary Relationships**

1) Evolutionary trees show how scientists think different species are related to each other.

2) They show common ancestors and relationships between species. The more recent the common ancestor, the more closely related the two species — and the more characteristics they're likely to share.

3) Scientists analyse lots of different types of data to work out evolutionary relationships. For living organisms, they use the current classification data (e.g. DNA analysis and structural similarities). For extinct species, they use information from the fossil record (see page 140).

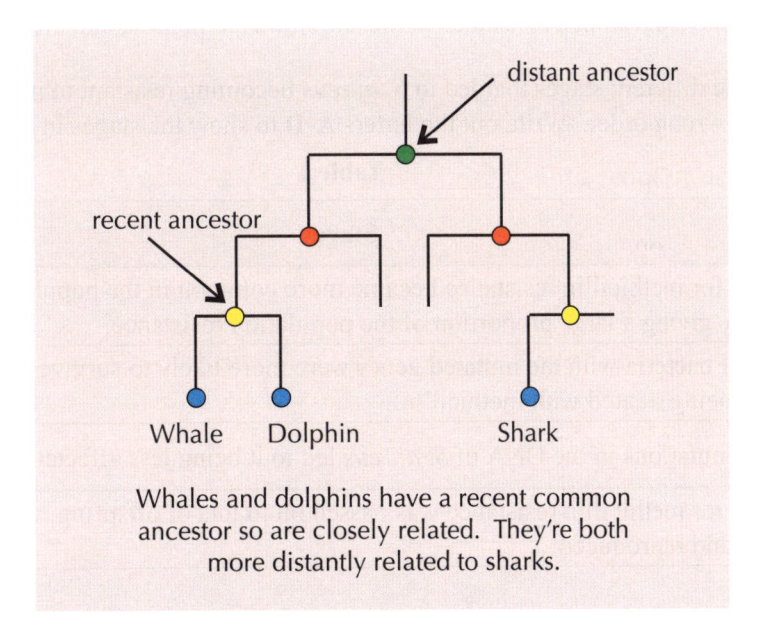

Whales and dolphins have a recent common ancestor so are closely related. They're both more distantly related to sharks.

Binomial system — uh oh, sounds like maths...

In the binomial system the genus comes first, then the species. Sometimes, the genus in a binomial name is abbreviated to a capital letter with a full stop after it.

Q1 The evolutionary tree on the right shows the relationship between four species, A-D.
Which two species shown in the tree are the most closely related? [1 mark]

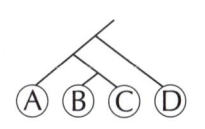

Topic B6 — Inheritance, Variation and Evolution

Warm-Up & Exam Questions

The end of the topic is in sight now — just a few more questions to check you've been paying attention.

Warm-Up Questions

1) Suggest what makes low-oxygen environments suitable for the formation of fossils.
2) Suggest a situation where antibiotics could be prescribed inappropriately.
3) Explain why it's important that people take the full course of antibiotics they are prescribed.
4) What species does the Eurasian beaver, *Castor fiber*, belong to?

Exam Questions

1 **Figure 1** shows a section of an evolutionary tree.

1.1 Which species is the most recent common ancestor of Species **F** and Species **G**?

[1 mark]

1.2 Would you expect Species **D** to look similar to Species **E**? Give a reason for your answer.

[1 mark]

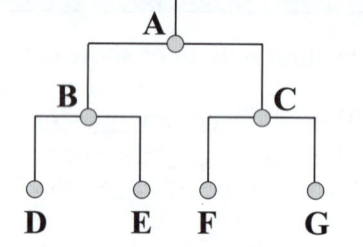

2 *Staphylococcus aureus* (*S. aureus*) is a common bacterium that is found on the skin and mucous membranes. It can cause serious illness in people with weakened immune systems. Some strains of the bacterium have developed resistance to the antibiotic methicillin, and are known as MRSA.

2.1 **Table 1** shows the different stages that led to *S. aureus* becoming resistant to methicillin. The stages are shown in the wrong order. Write out the letters **A-D** to show the stages in the correct order.

Table 1

	Stage
A	The gene for methicillin resistance became more common in the population over time, eventually giving a large proportion of the population resistance.
B	Individual bacteria with the mutated genes were more likely to survive and reproduce in a host being treated with methicillin.
C	Random mutations in the DNA of *S. aureus* led to it being less affected by methicillin.
D	The gene for methicillin resistance was passed on to lots of offspring, which also survived and reproduced.

[2 marks]

2.2 Suggest why MRSA is a more serious problem in hospitals than in wider society.

[2 marks]

2.3 Explain why antibiotic resistance in bacteria is a concern for humans.

[1 mark]

2.4 Suggest why the National Health Service (NHS) is trying to reduce the use of antibiotics.

[3 marks]

Topic B6 — Inheritance, Variation and Evolution

Topic B7 — Ecology

Competition

Ecology is all about **organisms** and the **environment** they live in, and how the two **interact**. Simple.

First Learn Some Words to Help You Understand Ecology...

This topic will make a lot more sense if you become familiar with these terms first:

1) Habitat — the place where an organism lives.
2) Population — all the organisms of one species living in a habitat.
3) Community — the populations of different species living in a habitat.
4) Abiotic factors — non-living factors of the environment, e.g. temperature.
5) Biotic factors — living factors of the environment, e.g. food.
6) Ecosystem — the interaction of a community of living organisms (biotic) with the non-living (abiotic) parts of their environment.

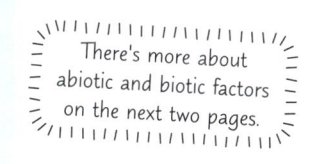

There's more about abiotic and biotic factors on the next two pages.

Organisms Compete for Resources to Survive

Organisms need things from their environment and from other organisms in order to survive and reproduce:

1) Plants need light and space, as well as water and mineral ions (nutrients) from the soil.
2) Animals need space (territory), food, water and mates.

Organisms compete with other species (and members of their own species) for the same resources.

Any Change in Any Environment can Have Knock-on Effects

1) In a community, each species depends on other species for things such as food, shelter, pollination and seed dispersal — this is called interdependence.
2) The interdependence of all the living things in an ecosystem means that any major change in the ecosystem (such as one species being removed) can have far-reaching effects.
3) The diagram on the right shows part of a food web (a diagram of what eats what) from a stream.
4) Stonefly larvae are particularly sensitive to pollution. Suppose pollution killed them in this stream. The table below shows some of the effects this might have on some of the other organisms in the food web.

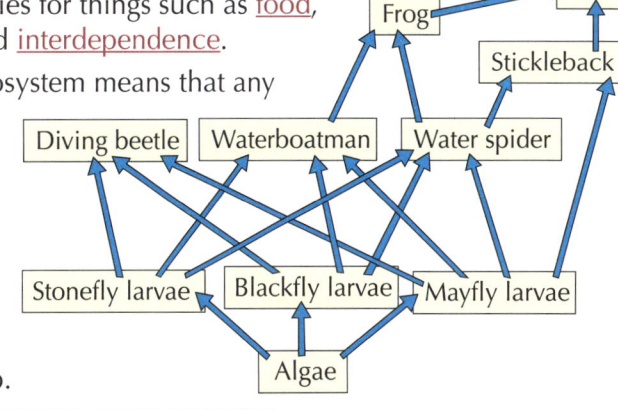

Organism	Effect of loss of stonefly larvae	Effect on population
Blackfly larvae	Less competition for algae	Increase
	More likely to be eaten by predators	Decrease
Water spider	Less food	Decrease
Stickleback	Less food (if water spider or mayfly larvae numbers decrease)	Decrease

Remember that food webs are very complex and that these effects are difficult to predict accurately.

5) In some communities, all the species and environmental factors are in balance so that the population sizes are roughly constant (they may go up and down in cycles — see p.155). These are called stable communities. Stable communities include tropical rainforests and ancient oak woodlands.

Survival — the prize for being a winner

Q1 Give three things plants compete for in an ecosystem. [3 marks]

Q2 Using the food web above, suggest what might happen to the frog population if the stickleback population decreased. [2 marks]

Abiotic and Biotic Factors

*The environment in which organisms live **changes** all the time. The things that change are either **abiotic** (non-living) or **biotic** (living) factors. These can have a big **effect** on a community...*

Abiotic Factors Can Vary in an Ecosystem...

Abiotic factors are non-living factors. For example:

1) Moisture level
2) Light intensity
3) Temperature
4) Carbon dioxide level (for plants)
5) Wind intensity and direction
6) Oxygen level (for aquatic animals)
7) Soil pH and mineral content

Light intensity can vary within an ecosystem because of shading caused by, e.g. tree cover.

Different organisms are adapted (see page 154) to different abiotic conditions.

Changes in Abiotic Factors Can Affect Populations

1) A change in the environment could be an increase or decrease in an abiotic factor, e.g. an increase in temperature. These changes can affect the sizes of populations in a community.

2) This means they can also affect the population sizes of other organisms that depend on them (see previous page).

3) For example, animals depend on plants for food, so a decrease in a plant population could affect the animal species in a community.

4) Here are two examples of changes in abiotic factors which may affect plant populations:

- A decrease in light intensity, temperature or level of carbon dioxide could decrease the rate of photosynthesis in a plant species (see p.90-91).
- This could affect plant growth and cause a decrease in the population size.

- A decrease in the mineral content of the soil (e.g. a lack of nitrates) could cause nutrient deficiencies.
- This could also affect plant growth and cause a decrease in the population size.

A = not, biotic = living, so abiotic means non-living

Some human activities can affect the abiotic factors of ecosystems, see pages 164, 167 and 168 for more. As you can see from this page, this can affect some organisms directly and other organisms indirectly.

Topic B7 — Ecology

Abiotic and Biotic Factors

*The previous page shows how abiotic factors can affect the **populations** in an ecosystem, but changes in **biotic factors** can also have big consequences. This page has a few examples to show you how.*

Biotic Factors Can Also Vary in an Ecosystem

Biotic factors are living factors.
Here are some examples of biotic factors that might affect organisms in an ecosystem:

1) New predators arriving
2) Competition — one species may outcompete another so that numbers are too low to breed
3) New pathogens
4) Availability of food

Changes in Biotic Factors Can have Knock-On Effects

1) A change in the environment could be the introduction of a new biotic factor, e.g. a new predator or pathogen.

2) These changes can affect the sizes of populations in a community, which can have knock-on effects because of interdependence (see page 151). Here are a few examples:

> A new predator could cause a decrease in the prey population. There's more about predator-prey populations on p.155.

> Red and grey squirrels live in the same habitat and eat the same food. Grey squirrels outcompete the red squirrels — so the population of red squirrels is decreasing.

> 1) The following graph shows the effect of a new pathogen on Species A.
> 2) The population size of Species A was increasing up until 1985, when it decreased rapidly until 1990 — suggesting that 1985 was the year that the new pathogen arrived.
> 3) The population started to rise again after 1990.

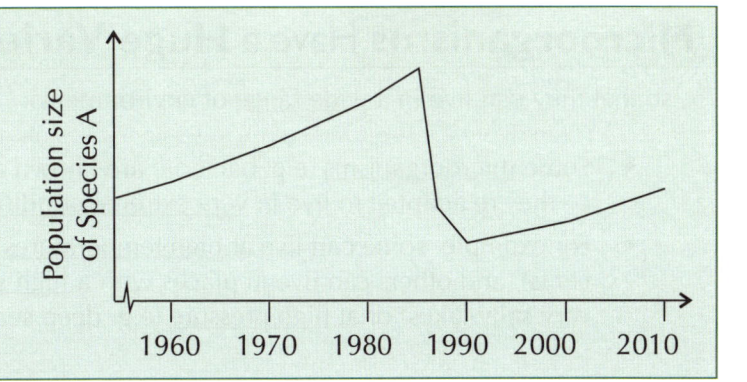

Changing biotic factors — it's like dominoes...

REVISION TIP: Learn the list of factors here, as well as on the previous page. I reckon this is a prime time for shutting the book, scribbling them all down and then checking how you did.

Topic B7 — Ecology

Adaptations

*Life exists in so many **different environments** because the **organisms** that live in them have **adapted** to them.*

Adaptations Allow Organisms to Survive

Organisms, including microorganisms, are adapted to live in different environmental conditions. The features or characteristics that allow them to do this are called adaptations. Adaptations can be:

1. Structural

These are features of an organism's body structure — such as shape or colour. For example:

Arctic animals like the Arctic fox have white fur so they're camouflaged against the snow. This helps them avoid predators and sneak up on prey.	Animals that live in cold places (like whales) have a thick layer of blubber (fat) and a low surface area to volume ratio to help them retain heat.	Animals that live in hot places (like camels) have a thin layer of fat and a large surface area to volume ratio to help them lose heat.

2. Behavioural

These are ways that organisms behave. Many species (e.g. swallows) migrate to warmer climates during the winter to avoid the problems of living in cold conditions.

3. Functional

These are things that go on inside an organism's body that can be related to processes like reproduction and metabolism (all the chemical reactions happening in the body). For example:

Desert animals conserve water by producing very little sweat and small amounts of concentrated urine.	Brown bears hibernate over winter. They lower their metabolism, which conserves energy, so they don't have to hunt when there's not much food about.

Microorganisms Have a Huge Variety of Adaptations...

...so that they can live in a wide range of environments:

- Some microorganisms (e.g. bacteria) are known as extremophiles — they're adapted to live in very extreme conditions.
- For example, some can live at high temperatures (e.g. in super hot volcanic vents), and others can live in places with a high salt concentration (e.g. very salty lakes) or at high pressure (e.g. deep sea vents).

Organisms can adapt to life in the most extreme environments

Q1 The diagram on the right shows a penguin. Penguins live in the cold, icy environment of the Antarctic. They swim in the sea to hunt for fish to eat. Some penguins also huddle together in large groups to keep warm.
  a) What type of adaptation is being described when penguins 'huddle together'? [1 mark]
  b) Explain one structural adaptation a penguin has to its environment. [2 marks]

Topic B7 — Ecology

Food Chains

*You might remember **food webs** from page 151. Well, **food chains** are a similar idea — except that you only really show one part of a food web in a food chain. Read on to find out more...*

Food Chains Show What's Eaten by What in an Ecosystem

1) Food chains always start with a producer.
   Producers make (produce) their own food using energy from the Sun.
2) Producers are usually green plants or algae — they make glucose by photosynthesis (see page 89).
3) When a green plant produces glucose, some of it is used to make other biological molecules in the plant.
4) These biological molecules are the plant's biomass — the mass of living material.
5) Biomass can be thought of as energy stored in a plant.
6) Energy is transferred through living organisms in an ecosystem when organisms eat other organisms.
7) Producers are eaten by primary consumers. Primary consumers are then eaten by secondary consumers and secondary consumers are eaten by tertiary consumers. Here's an example of a food chain:

Producers → Primary consumers → Secondary consumer

5000 dandelions... feed... 100 rabbits... which feed... 1 fox.

Consumers are organisms that eat other organisms. 'Primary' means 'first', so primary consumers are the first consumers in a food chain. Secondary consumers are second and tertiary consumers are third.

Populations of Prey and Predators Go in Cycles

Consumers that hunt and kill other animals are called predators, and their prey are what they eat. In a stable community containing prey and predators (as most of them do of course):

1) The population of any species is usually limited by the amount of food available.
2) If the population of the prey increases, then so will the population of the predators.
3) However as the population of predators increases, the number of prey will decrease.

For more about a stable community see page 151.

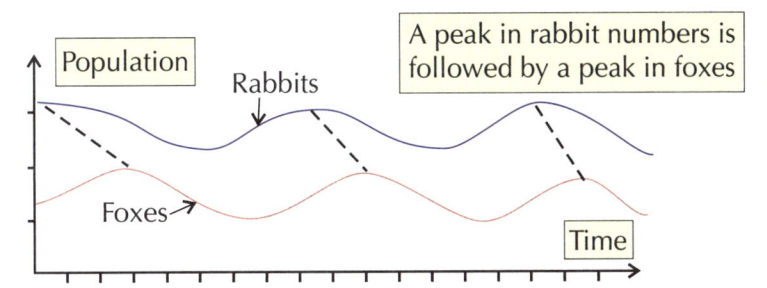

A peak in rabbit numbers is followed by a peak in foxes

- E.g. more grass means more rabbits.
- More rabbits means more foxes.
- But more foxes means fewer rabbits.
- Eventually fewer rabbits will mean fewer foxes again.
- This up and down pattern continues...

4) Predator-prey cycles are always out of phase with each other. This is because it takes a while for one population to respond to changes in the other population.

E.g. when the number of rabbits goes up, the number of foxes doesn't increase immediately because it takes time for them to reproduce.

A food chain shows part of a food web

Q1 Look at the following food chain for a particular area: grass → grasshopper → rat → snake
   a) Name the producer in the food chain. [1 mark]
   b) How many consumers are there in the food chain? [1 mark]
   c) Name the primary consumer in the food chain. [1 mark]
   d) All the rats in the area are killed.
      Explain two effects that this could have on the food chain. [4 marks]

Topic B7 — Ecology

Warm-Up & Exam Questions

This ecology topic's a long one — so make sure you've really got these first few pages stuck in your head before moving on and learning the rest. These questions should help you out.

Warm-Up Questions

1) What is the correct scientific term for all the different species in a habitat?
2) What is an ecosystem?
3) Give four examples of abiotic factors that could affect a land-based plant species.
4) What is meant by a structural adaptation?
5) What is meant by a producer in a food chain?

Exam Questions

1 **Figure 1** shows a food chain for a particular area:

Figure 1

algae → shrimp → sea turtle → tiger shark

1.1 What term is used to describe the tiger shark in **Figure 1**? Tick **one** box.

☐ producer ☐ primary consumer ☐ secondary consumer ☐ tertiary consumer

[1 mark]

1.2 Explain the importance of the algae in **Figure 1**.

[2 marks]

2 The Harris's antelope squirrel lives in hot deserts in parts of the USA and Mexico. It has grey fur, small ears and does not sweat. It has sharp claws which enable it to dig burrows, in which it lives. Above ground, during the hottest parts of the day it often holds its large tail over its head, or lies in the shade with its limbs spread out wide.

2.1 Give **one** functional adaptation the Harris's antelope squirrel has to its environment.

[1 mark]

2.2 Explain **one** behavioural adaptation the Harris's antelope squirrel has to its environment.

[2 marks]

3 Cutthroat trout are present in lakes in Yellowstone National Park. In the last few decades, lake trout have been introduced to the lakes. However, lake trout have emerged as predators of the cutthroat trout.

3.1 Explain how the introduction of the lake trout might cause the population sizes of both species of fish to fluctuate over time.

[5 marks]

3.2 Give **two** other biotic factors that could affect the size of the cutthroat trout population.

[2 marks]

Topic B7 — Ecology

Using Quadrats   **PRACTICAL**

*This is where the **fun** starts. Studying **ecology** gives you the chance to **rummage around** in bushes, get your hands **dirty** and look at some **real organisms**, living in the **wild**.*

Environmental Variation Affects the Distribution of Organisms

1) As you know from page 151, a habitat is the place where an organism lives, e.g. a playing field.
2) The distribution of an organism is where an organism is found, e.g. in a part of the playing field.
3) Where an organism is found is affected by environmental factors (see pages 152-153). An organism might be more common in one area than another due to differences in environmental factors between the two areas. For example, in the playing field, you might find that daisies are more common in the open than under trees, because there's more light available in the open.
4) There are a couple of ways to study the distribution of an organism. You can:
   - measure how common an organism is in two sample areas (e.g. using quadrats) and compare them.
   - study how the distribution changes across an area, e.g. by placing quadrats along a transect (p.158). Both of these methods give quantitative data (numbers) about the distribution.

Use Quadrats to Study The Distribution of Small Organisms

A quadrat is a square frame enclosing a known area, e.g. 1 m². To compare how common an organism is in two sample areas (e.g. shady and sunny spots in that playing field) just follow these simple steps:

1) Place a 1 m² quadrat on the ground at a random point within the first sample area. E.g. divide the area into a grid and use a random number generator to pick coordinates.
2) Count all the organisms within the quadrat.
3) Repeat steps 1 and 2 as many times as you can.
4) Work out the mean number of organisms per quadrat within the first sample area.

A quadrat

EXAMPLE **Fatima counted the number of daisies in 7 quadrats within her first sample area and recorded the following results: 18, 20, 22, 23, 23, 23, 25.**

Here the MEAN is: $\frac{\text{TOTAL number of organisms}}{\text{NUMBER of quadrats}} = \frac{154}{7} = 22$ daisies per quadrat

5) Repeat steps 1 to 4 in the second sample area.
6) Finally compare the two means. E.g. you might find 2 daisies per m² in the shade, and 22 daisies per m² (lots more) in the open field.

You Can Also Work Out the Population Size of an Organism in One Area

EXAMPLE **Students used quadrats, each with an area of 0.5 m², to randomly sample daisies on an open field. The students found a mean of 10.5 daisies per quadrat. The field had an area of 800 m². Estimate the population of daisies on the field.**

1) Work out the mean number of organisms per m².
   $1 \div 0.5 = 2$
   $2 \times 10.5 = 21$ daisies per m²

2) Then multiply the mean by the total area (in m²) of the habitat.
   $800 \times 21 = 16\ 800$ daisies on the open field

The population size of an organism is sometimes called its abundance.

If your quadrat has an area of 1 m², the mean number of organisms per m² is just the same as the mean number per quadrat.

Don't try to study elephants using a quadrat

Q1 A 1200 m² field was randomly sampled for buttercups using a quadrat with an area of 0.25 m². A mean of 0.75 buttercups were found per quadrat. Estimate the total population of buttercups. [2 marks]

Topic B7 — Ecology

PRACTICAL

Using Transects

*So, now you think you've learnt **all about** distribution. Well **hold on** — there's more **ecology fun** to be had.*

Use Transects to Study The Distribution of Organisms

You can use lines called transects to help find out how organisms (like plants) are distributed across an area — e.g. if an organism becomes more or less common as you move from a hedge towards the middle of a field. Here's what to do:

1) Mark out a line in the area you want to study using a tape measure.

2) Then collect data along the line.

3) You can do this by just counting all the organisms you're interested in that touch the line.

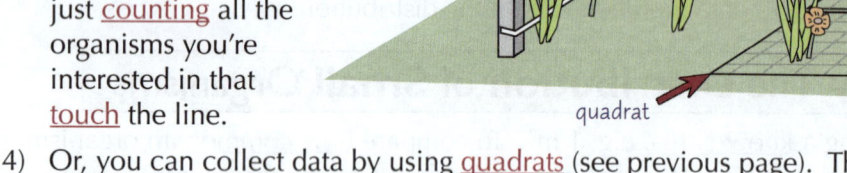

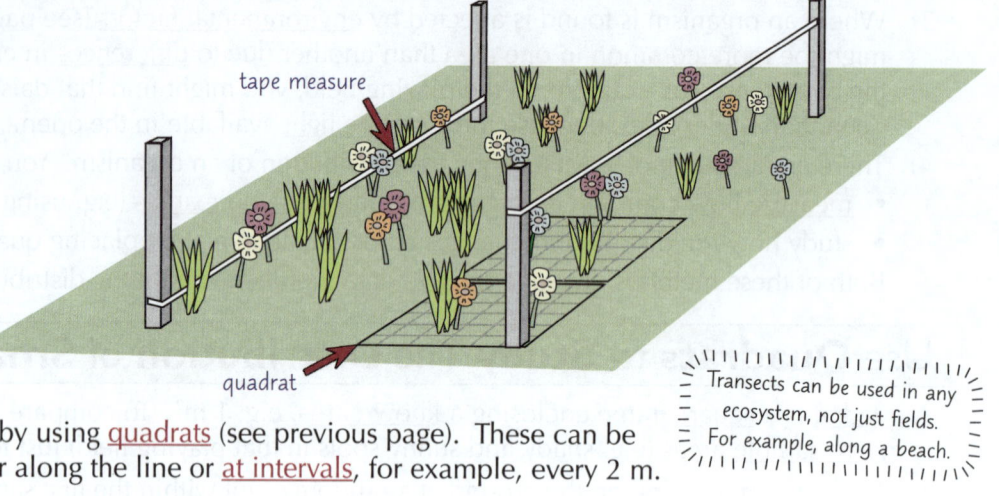

4) Or, you can collect data by using quadrats (see previous page). These can be placed next to each other along the line or at intervals, for example, every 2 m.

Transects can be used in any ecosystem, not just fields. For example, along a beach.

You Can Estimate the Percentage Cover of a Quadrat

If it's difficult to count all the individual organisms in the quadrat (e.g. if they're grass) you can calculate the percentage cover. This means estimating the percentage area of the quadrat covered by a particular type of organism, e.g. by counting the number of little squares covered by the organisms.

EXAMPLE

Some students were measuring the distribution of organisms from one corner of a school playing field to another, using quadrats placed at regular intervals along a transect. Below is a picture of one of the quadrats. Calculate the percentage cover of each organism, A and B.

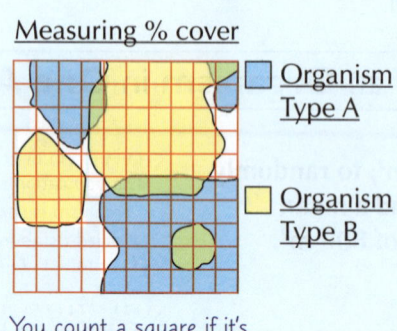

Measuring % cover

☐ Organism Type A
☐ Organism Type B

You count a square if it's more than half covered.

1) Count the number of squares covered by organism A.

2) Make this into a percentage — divide the number of squares covered by the organism by the total number of squares in the quadrat (100), then multiply the result by 100.

3) Do the same for organism B.

Type A = 42 squares

(42/100) × 100
= 0.42 × 100 = **42%**

Type B = 47 squares

(47/100) × 100
= 0.47 × 100 = **47%**

PRACTICAL TIP

You don't need fancy kit to study the distribution of organisms

So if you want to measure the distribution of a organism across an area, you could use a transect. You can use them alone or along with quadrats. Using percentage cover instead of number of organisms is a good way of studying the distribution of plants, as there may be too many to count.

Topic B7 — Ecology

The Water Cycle

The **amount** of water on Earth is pretty much **constant** — but **where** it is changes.
Water moves between **rivers**, **lakes**, **oceans** and the **atmosphere** in what's known as the **water cycle**.

The Water Cycle Means Water is Endlessly Recycled

The water here on planet Earth is constantly recycled.
There are four key steps you should understand:

1) Energy from the Sun makes water evaporate from the land and sea, turning it into water vapour. Water also evaporates from plants — this is known as transpiration (see p.70).

2) The warm water vapour is carried upwards (as warm air rises). When it gets higher up it cools and condenses to form clouds.

3) Water falls from the clouds as precipitation (usually rain, but sometimes snow or hail) onto land, where it provides fresh water for plants and animals.

As warm water vapour rises it cools down and forms clouds.

4) It then drains into the sea, before the whole process starts again.

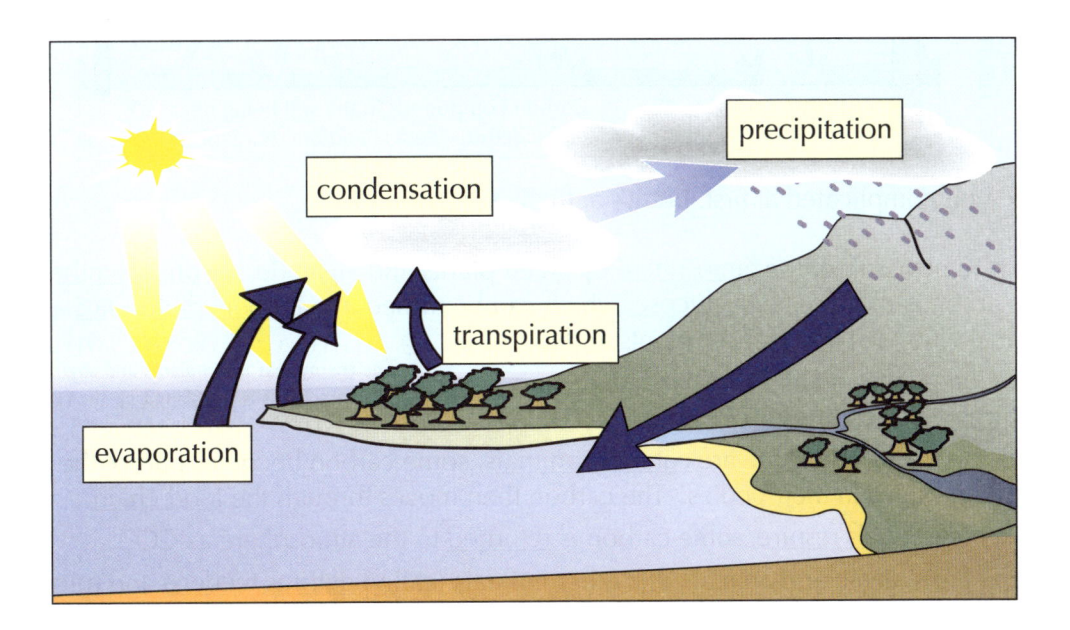

Evaporation, transpiration, condensation, precipitation

The water cycle is really easy — there are four main stages and they're all pretty straightforward. So there's absolutely no excuse not to learn it inside out. The most important thing to remember is that it's a cycle — a continuous process with no beginning or end. Water that falls to the ground as rain (or any other kind of precipitation for that matter) will eventually end up back in the clouds again.

Topic B7 — Ecology

The Carbon Cycle

Recycling may be a buzz word for us but it's old school for nature. All the **nutrients** in our environment are constantly being **recycled** — there's a nice balance between what **goes in** and what **goes out** again.

Elements are Cycled Back to the Start of the Food Chain by Decay

1) Living things are made of materials they take from the world around them. E.g. plants turn elements like carbon, oxygen, hydrogen and nitrogen from the soil and the air into the complex compounds (carbohydrates, proteins and fats) that make up living organisms. These get passed up the food chain.
2) These materials are returned to the environment in waste products, or when the organisms die and decay.
3) Materials decay because they're broken down (digested) by microorganisms. This happens faster in warm, moist, aerobic (oxygen rich) conditions because microorganisms are more active in these conditions.
4) Decay puts the stuff that plants need to grow (e.g. mineral ions) back into the soil.
5) In a stable community, the materials that are taken out of the soil and used by plants etc. are balanced by those that are put back in. There's a constant cycle happening.

The Constant Cycling of Carbon is called the Carbon Cycle

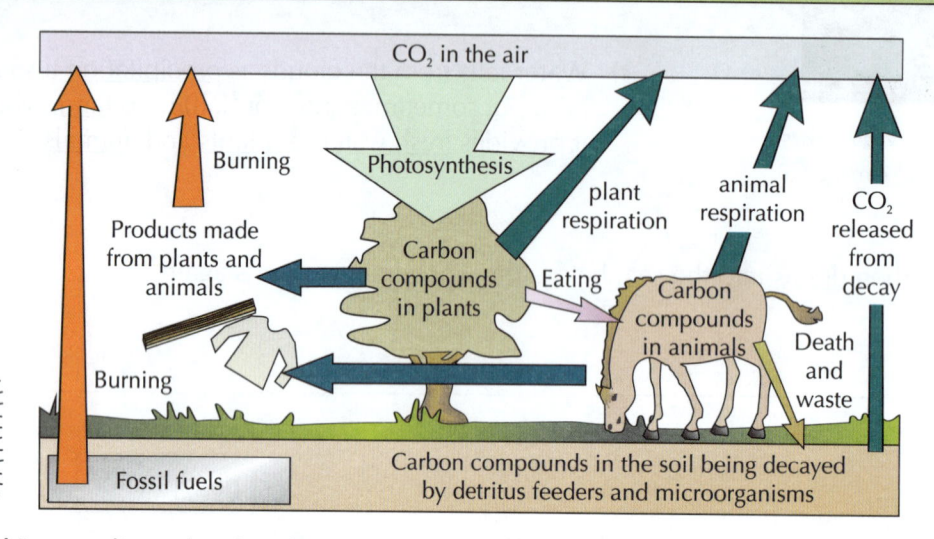

That can look a bit complicated at first, but it's actually pretty simple:

1) CO_2 is removed from the atmosphere by green plants and algae during photosynthesis. The carbon is used to make glucose, which can be turned into carbohydrates, fats and proteins that make up the bodies of the plants and algae.
2) When the plants and algae respire, some carbon is returned to the atmosphere as CO_2.

The energy that green plants and algae get from photosynthesis is transferred up the food chain.

3) When the plants and algae are eaten by animals, some carbon becomes part of the fats and proteins in their bodies. The carbon then moves through the food chain.
4) When the animals respire, some carbon is returned to the atmosphere as CO_2.
5) When plants, algae and animals die, other animals (called detritus feeders) and microorganisms feed on their remains. When these organisms respire, CO_2 is returned to the atmosphere.
6) Animals also produce waste that is broken down by detritus feeders and microorganisms.
7) The combustion (burning) of wood and fossil fuels also releases CO_2 back into the air.
8) So the carbon (and energy) is constantly being cycled — from the air, through food chains (via plants, algae and animals, and detritus feeders and microorganisms) and eventually back out into the air again.

Topic B7 — Ecology

Warm-Up & Exam Questions

You can't just stare at these pages and expect all of the information to go in. Especially the practical pages with the maths examples. Do these questions to see how well you really know the stuff.

Warm-Up Questions

1) What is a transect?
2) A student counted the number of daises in five quadrats and recorded the following results: 14, 11, 11, 12, 12. What is the mean number of daises per quadrat?
3) What is the role of microorganisms in the carbon cycle?
4) How is the carbon in fossil fuels returned to the atmosphere?

Exam Questions

1   Figure 1 shows a simplified version of the carbon cycle. *Grade 4-6*

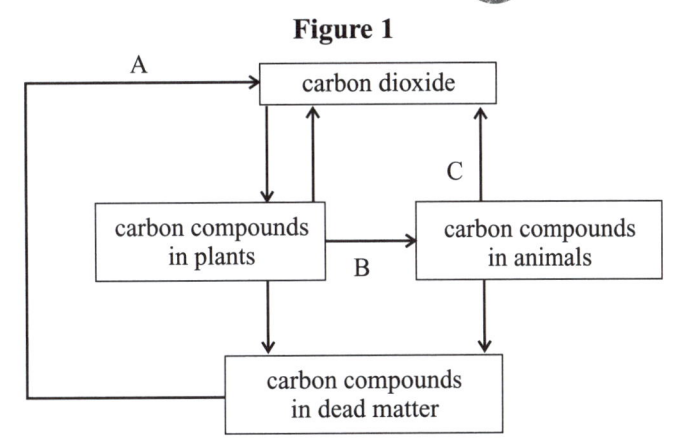

Figure 1

[Diagram: carbon dioxide box at top; arrow A from "carbon compounds in dead matter" up to carbon dioxide; arrows from carbon dioxide down to "carbon compounds in plants"; arrow B from "carbon compounds in plants" to "carbon compounds in animals"; arrow C from "carbon compounds in animals" up to carbon dioxide; arrows down from plants and animals to "carbon compounds in dead matter"]

1.1   Name the process that is occurring at stage **B**.
[1 mark]

1.2   Name the process that is occurring at stage **C**.
[1 mark]

1.3   Explain how carbon is released from dead matter in the soil (stage **A**).
[2 marks]

1.4   Name the only process in the carbon cycle that removes carbon dioxide from the air.
[1 mark]

2   The water cycle describes the constant movement of water molecules on the Earth. *Grade 6-7*

2.1   In the water cycle, how does water move from plants into the air?
[1 mark]

2.2   Describe the shortest route a water molecule could take through the water cycle to get from an ocean to a garden pond.
[4 marks]

Topic B7 — Ecology

Exam Questions

PRACTICAL

3 Some students investigated the distribution of poppies across a field next to a wood. A sketch of the area is shown in **Figure 2**.

Grade 6-7

Figure 2

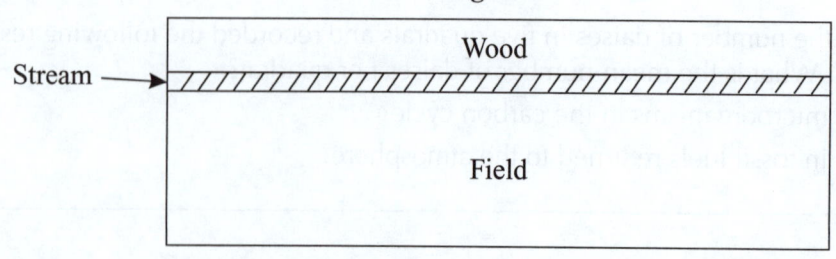

Stream → Wood

Field

The students' results are shown in **Table 1**.

Table 1

Number of poppies per m²	5	9	14	19	26
Distance from wood (m)	2	4	6	8	10

3.1 Describe how the students could have used quadrats to obtain the results in **Table 1**.

[3 marks]

3.2 Describe the trend in the results in **Table 1**.

[1 mark]

3.3 The students suggest that a change in light intensity across the field may affect the distribution of the poppies. Give **two** additional factors which may also affect the distribution of the poppies.

[2 marks]

The students decided to investigate the distribution of two grass species in the field as well. **Figure 3** shows a sketch that the students made of the two grass species in one of their quadrats.

Figure 3

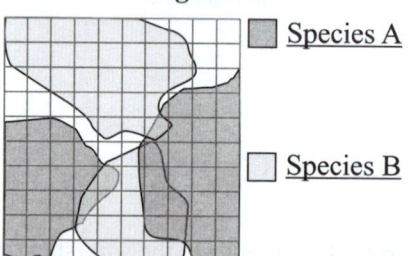

■ Species A

□ Species B

3.4 Use **Figure 3** to estimate the percentage cover of species A and species B in the quadrat.

[2 marks]

3.5 Give **one** reason why the students may have decided to estimate the percentage cover of the two grasses.

[1 mark]

4* An area of woodland is cleared to build a house. The tree trunks are taken away to be dried and used in furniture making. The smaller tree branches are used for firewood. The green plants are piled up at the edge of the building site.

Grade 7-9

Describe how carbon stored in the vegetation that has been cleared could be returned to the atmosphere.

[6 marks]

Topic B7 — Ecology

Biodiversity and Waste Management

*Unfortunately, human activity can **negatively affect** the **planet** and its **variety of life**.*

Earth's **Biodiversity** is Important

> Biodiversity is the variety of different species of organisms on Earth, or within an ecosystem.

1) High biodiversity is important. It makes sure that ecosystems (see p.151) are stable because different species depend on each other for things like shelter and food. Different species can also help to maintain the right physical environment for each other (e.g. the acidity of the soil).

2) For the human species to survive, it's important that a good level of biodiversity is maintained.

3) Lots of human actions, including waste production (see the next page) and deforestation (see p.168), as well as global warming (see p.165) are reducing biodiversity. However, it's only recently that we've started taking measures to stop this from continuing.

There are Over **Seven Billion People** in the World

1) The population of the world is currently rising very quickly, and it's not slowing down — look at the graph...

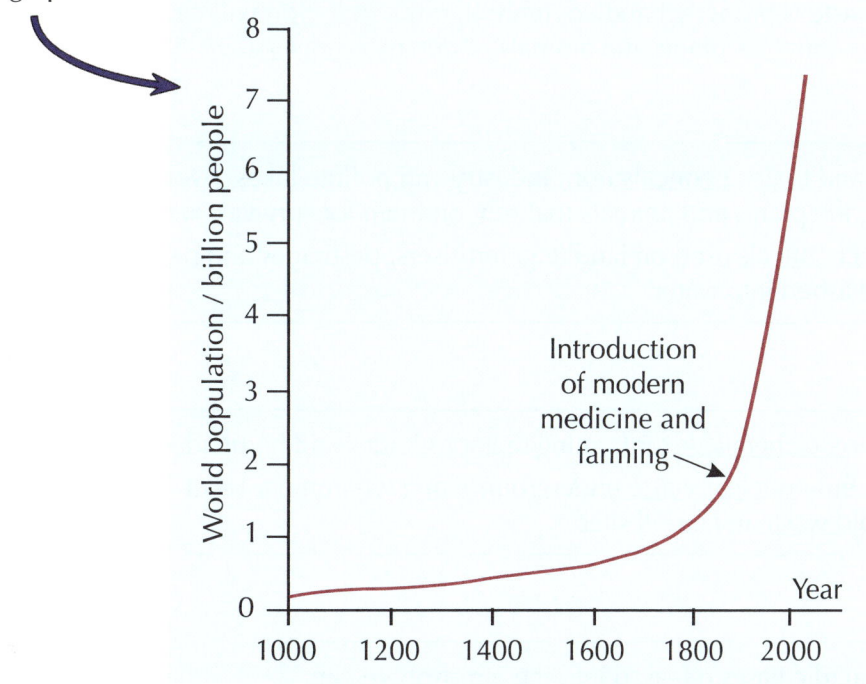

Introduction of modern medicine and farming

2) This is mostly due to modern medicine and farming methods, which have reduced the number of people dying from disease and hunger.

3) This is great for all of us humans, but it means we're having a bigger effect on the environment we live in.

Topic B7 — Ecology

Biodiversity and Waste Management

We're Making Increasing Demands on the Environment

When the Earth's population was much smaller, the effects of human activity were usually small and local. Nowadays though, our actions can have a far more widespread effect.

1) Our increasing population puts pressure on the environment, as we take the resources we need to survive.

2) But people around the world are also demanding a higher standard of living (and so demand luxuries to make life more comfortable — cars, computers, etc.). So we use more raw materials (e.g. oil to make plastics), but we also use more energy for the manufacturing processes. This all means we're taking more and more resources from the environment more and more quickly.

3) Unfortunately, many raw materials are being used up quicker than they're being replaced. So if we carry on like we are, one day we're going to run out.

We're Also Producing More Waste

As we make more and more things we produce more and more waste, including waste chemicals. And unless this waste is properly handled, more harmful pollution will be caused. Pollution affects water, land and air and kills plants and animals, reducing biodiversity.

Water
- Sewage and toxic chemicals from industry can pollute lakes, rivers and oceans, affecting the plants and animals that rely on them for survival (including humans).
- And the chemicals used on land (e.g. fertilisers, pesticides and herbicides) can be washed into water.

Land
- We use toxic chemicals for farming (e.g. pesticides and herbicides).
- We also bury nuclear waste underground, and we dump a lot of household waste in landfill sites.

Air
Smoke and acidic gases released into the atmosphere can pollute the air, e.g. sulfur dioxide can cause acid rain.

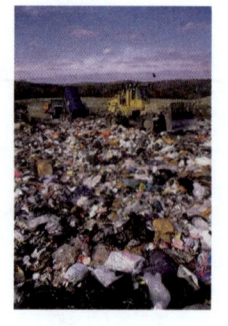

More people, more mess, less space, fewer resources...

...you might call it a recipe for disaster. As you can see, there's a lot of work for us to do in improving our waste management and also finding ways to deal with a growing human population.

Topic B7 — Ecology

Global Warming

*You might remember the **carbon cycle** from p.160. Well, carbon dioxide has an important role in keeping the Earth **warm enough** for life. It's not so good when there's **too much** of it in the atmosphere though...*

Carbon Dioxide and Methane Trap Energy from the Sun

1) The temperature of the Earth is a balance between the energy it gets from the Sun and the energy it radiates back out into space.

2) Gases in the atmosphere naturally act like an insulating layer. They absorb most of the energy that would normally be radiated out into space, and re-radiate it in all directions (including back towards the Earth). This increases the temperature of the planet.

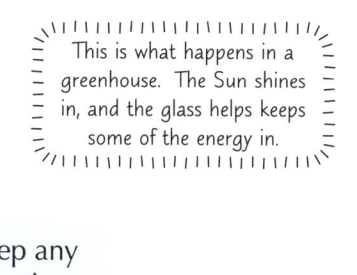

This is what happens in a greenhouse. The Sun shines in, and the glass helps keeps some of the energy in.

3) If this didn't happen, then at night there'd be nothing to keep any energy in, and we'd quickly get very cold indeed. But recently we've started to worry that this effect is getting a bit out of hand.

4) There are several different gases in the atmosphere which help keep the energy in. They're called "greenhouse gases", and the main ones whose levels we worry about are carbon dioxide (CO_2) and methane — because the levels of these two gases are rising quite sharply.

5) The Earth is gradually heating up because of the increasing levels of greenhouse gases — this is global warming. Global warming is a type of climate change and causes other types of climate change, e.g. changing rainfall patterns.

Topic B7 — Ecology

Global Warming

*The Earth is getting **warmer**. Climate scientists are now trying to work out what the **effects** of global warming might be — sadly, it's not as simple as everyone having nicer summers.*

The Consequences of Global Warming Could be Pretty Serious

There are several reasons to be worried about global warming. Here are a few:

Sea levels rising

1) Higher temperatures cause seawater to expand and ice to melt, causing the sea level to rise.
2) It has risen a little bit over the last 100 years.
3) If it keeps rising it'll be bad news for people and animals living in low-lying places.
4) It will lead to flooding, resulting in the loss of habitats (where organisms live).

Changes in species distribution

1) The distribution of many wild animal and plant species may change as temperatures increase and the amount of rainfall changes in different areas.
2) Some species may become more widely distributed, e.g. species that need warmer temperatures may spread further as the conditions they thrive in exist over a wider area.
3) Other species may become less widely distributed, e.g. species that need cooler temperatures may have smaller ranges as the conditions they thrive in exist over a smaller area.

Changes in migration patterns

There could be changes in migration patterns, e.g. some birds may migrate further north, as more northern areas are getting warmer.

Reduction in biodiversity

Biodiversity (see p.163) could be reduced if some species are unable to survive a change in the climate, so become extinct.

We need to act fast, before the worst effects of climate change

Global warming is rarely out of the news. Most scientists accept that it's happening and that human activity has caused most of the recent warming, based on the evidence that has so far been collected. However, they don't know exactly what the effects will be and scientists will have to collect more data before these questions can really be answered.

Topic B7 — Ecology

Deforestation and Land Use

Trees and *peat bogs* trap carbon dioxide and *lock it up*. The problems start when it *escapes*...

Humans Use **Lots of Land** for **Lots of Purposes**

1) We use land for things like building, quarrying, farming and dumping waste.
2) This means that there's less land available for other organisms.
3) Sometimes, the way we use land has a bad effect on the environment — for example, if it requires deforestation (see next page) or the destruction of habitats like peat bogs and other areas of peat (see below).

Destroying Peat Bogs Adds **More CO₂** to the Atmosphere

1) Bogs are areas of land that are acidic and waterlogged. Plants that live in bogs don't fully decay when they die, because there's not enough oxygen. The partly-rotted plants gradually build up to form peat.

2) So the carbon in the plants is stored in the peat instead of being released into the atmosphere.

3) However, peat bogs are often drained so that the area can be used as farmland, or the peat is cut up and dried to use as fuel. It's also sold to gardeners as compost. Peat is being used faster than it forms.

4) When peat is drained, it comes into more contact with air and some microorganisms start to decompose it.

5) When these microorganisms respire, they use oxygen and release carbon dioxide, contributing to global warming (see page 165). Carbon dioxide is also released when peat is burned as a fuel.

6) Destroying the bogs also destroys (or reduces the area of) the habitats of some of the animals, plants and microorganisms that live there, so reduces biodiversity.

We need to use land, but we also need a healthy environment

We can't really avoid using land — we've got to if we want to e.g. grow enough food or build enough houses for people. The human population is increasing so it's likely that we'll use even more land in the future — we'll have to find a way to manage land use to reduce the negative effects on the environment.

Topic B7 — Ecology

Deforestation and Land Use

Many parts of the world have **already** been radically changed by deforestation — for example, much of the **UK** used to be covered in forests. Deforestation can be **bad news** for several reasons.

Deforestation Means Chopping Down Trees

1) Deforestation is the cutting down of forests.
2) This causes big problems when it's done on a large-scale, such as cutting down rainforests in tropical areas.
3) It's done for various reasons, including:

- To clear land for farming (e.g. cattle or rice crops) to provide more food.
- To grow crops from which biofuels based on ethanol can be produced.

Deforestation Can Cause Many Problems

Less carbon dioxide taken in

- Cutting down loads of trees means that the amount of carbon dioxide removed from the atmosphere during photosynthesis is reduced.
- Trees 'lock up' some of the carbon that they absorb during photosynthesis in their wood, which can remove it from the atmosphere for hundreds of years. Removing trees means that less is locked up.

More CO_2 in the atmosphere causes global warming (see page 165), which leads to climate change.

More carbon dioxide in the atmosphere

- Carbon dioxide is released when trees are burnt to clear land. (Carbon in wood doesn't contribute to atmospheric pollution until it's released by burning.)
- Microorganisms feeding on bits of dead wood release carbon dioxide as a waste product of respiration.

Less biodiversity

- Biodiversity (p.163) is the variety of different species — the more species, the greater the biodiversity.
- Habitats like forests can contain a huge number of different species of plants and animals, so when they are destroyed there is a danger of many species becoming extinct — biodiversity is reduced.

EXAM TIP — **Not a very cheerful page, I know...**
Make sure you can link together all the information on pages 165-168 — for example, how deforestation and peat burning can contribute to global warming, and how this might affect biodiversity. In the exam, you might get an extended response question that requires you to draw on several different areas of knowledge like this.

Topic B7 — Ecology

Maintaining Ecosystems and Biodiversity

*It's really important that biodiversity is **maintained** as damage to ecosystems or populations of species can be **hard to undo**. This page is about some of the different **methods** that can be used to maintain biodiversity.*

There are Programmes to Protect Ecosystems and Biodiversity

1) It's important that biodiversity is maintained at a high enough level to make sure that ecosystems are stable (see page 151).
2) In some areas, programmes have been set up by concerned citizens and scientists to minimise damage by human activities (see page 164) to ecosystems and biodiversity. Here are a few examples:

1. Breeding Programmes

1) Breeding programmes have been set up to help prevent endangered species from becoming extinct.
2) These are where animals are bred in captivity to make sure the species survives if it dies out in the wild.
3) Individuals can sometimes be released into the wild to boost or re-establish a population.

Pandas are an endangered species. Many efforts have been made to breed pandas in captivity.

2. Habitat Protection

1) Programmes to protect and regenerate rare habitats like mangroves, heathland and coral reefs have been started. Protecting these habitats helps to protect the species that live there — preserving the ecosystem and biodiversity in the area.
2) There are programmes to reintroduce hedgerows and field margins around fields on farms where only a single type of crop is grown. Field margins are areas of land around the edges of fields where wild flowers and grasses are left to grow. Hedgerows and field margins provide a habitat for a wider variety of organisms than could survive in a single crop habitat.

3. Preventing Global Warming

1) Some governments have introduced regulations and programmes to reduce the level of deforestation taking place and the amount of carbon dioxide being released into the atmosphere by businesses.
2) This could reduce the increase of global warming (see page 165).

4. Reducing Waste

1) People are encouraged to recycle to reduce the amount of waste that gets dumped in landfill sites.
2) This could reduce the amount of land taken over for landfill, leaving ecosystems in place.

Topic B7 — Ecology

Maintaining Ecosystems and Biodiversity

Conflicting Pressures Affect How Biodiversity is Maintained

Sadly for noble biodiversity warriors, maintaining biodiversity isn't as simple as you would hope. There are lots of conflicting pressures that have to be taken into account. For example:

1. The Costs of Programmes

1) Protecting biodiversity costs money.
2) For example, governments sometimes pay farmers a subsidy to reintroduce hedgerows and field margins to their land.
3) It can also cost money to keep a watch on whether the programmes and regulations designed to maintain biodiversity are being followed.
4) There can be conflict between protecting biodiversity and saving money — money may be prioritised for other things.

2. The Effect on the Local Economy

1) Protecting biodiversity may come at a cost to local people's livelihoods.
2) For example, reducing the amount of deforestation is great for biodiversity, but the people who were previously employed in the tree-felling industry could be left unemployed.
3) This could affect the local economy if people move away with their family to find work.

3. Protecting Food Security

1) There can be conflict between protecting biodiversity and protecting our food security.
2) Sometimes certain organisms are seen as pests by farmers (e.g. locusts and foxes) and are killed to protect crops and livestock so that more food can be produced.
3) As a result, however, the food chain and biodiversity can be affected.

4. The Development of Society

1) Development is important, but it can affect the environment.
2) Many people want to protect biodiversity in the face of development, but sometimes land is in such high demand that previously untouched land with high biodiversity has to be used for development.
3) For example, for housing developments on the edges of towns, or for new agricultural land in developing countries.

So we should do what we can — within some limits

Like many situations in ecology, maintaining biodiversity isn't black and white. There are lots of factors to take into account before decisions on the best way to go forward can be made.

Warm-Up & Exam Questions

I hope you've got all of that important information in your head. There's a lot to remember here, so have a flick back when you're doing these questions in case you've forgotten any little details.

Warm-Up Questions

1) What is meant by the term 'biodiversity'?
2) Give two greenhouse gases.
3) How are populations of endangered species preserved by breeding programmes?
4) Explain how biodiversity can be increased in areas that farm single crops.

Exam Questions

1 Humans are producing increasing amounts of waste.
This has negative consequences for biodiversity and the environment. *(Grade 4-6)*

1.1 Give **two** types of waste that pollute the air.
[2 marks]

1.2 Describe **one** way in which waste produced by humans pollutes water.
[1 mark]

1.3 Give **two** reasons why humans are producing increasingly more waste.
[2 marks]

2 Global warming may lead to a decline in biodiversity in the future. *(Grade 6-7)*

2.1 Apart from a decline in biodiversity, suggest **two** possible biological consequences of global warming.
[2 marks]

2.2 Describe **two** measures being used by some governments in order to reduce global warming.
[2 marks]

3 Peat bogs can be drained, so that the peat can be cut up and used as a source of fuel. *(Grade 6-7)*

3.1 Explain why draining peat bogs and using the peat as a fuel can contribute to global warming.
[4 marks]

3.2 Apart from contributing to global warming, explain **one** negative consequence of destroying peat bogs.
[2 marks]

4 Wetlands are areas of land in which the soil is saturated with water. In New Zealand, the area of freshwater wetlands has decreased by a huge amount, largely due to human activities, such as draining the wetlands for building or farming. New Zealand now has conservation schemes in place which protect many of the remaining wetlands. *(Grade 7-9)*

4.1 In terms of biodiversity, suggest why it's important for humans that New Zealand and other countries in the world protect their wetlands.
[3 marks]

4.2 Suggest **two** reasons why people in New Zealand may be against schemes which protect its wetlands.
[2 marks]

Topic B7 — Ecology

Revision Summary for Topics B5-7

That's Topics B5-7 done. I bet you're in the mood for a list of revision questions now. You're in luck.
- Try these questions and tick off each one when you get it right.
- When you're completely happy with a topic, tick it off.

For even more practice, try the Retrieval Quizzes for Topics B5-7 — just scan the QR codes!

Topic B5 — Homeostasis and Response (p.104-120) ☐

1) What is a stimulus?
2) What makes up the central nervous system and what does it do?
3) What is the purpose of a reflex action?
4) What is a hormone?
5) Give two differences between nervous and hormonal responses.
6) What is the difference between how Type 1 and Type 2 diabetes are usually controlled?
7) Draw a timeline of the 28 day menstrual cycle. Label the four stages of the cycle and label when the egg is released.
8) Briefly describe how IVF is carried out.

Topic B6 — Inheritance, Variation and Evolution (p.122-149) ☐

9) What do genes code for?
10) Which type of reproduction produces genetically identical cells?
11) State the type of cell division used to make gametes in humans.
12) What does it mean if someone is heterozygous for a gene?
13) What is the chance of a child being born with polydactyly if one parent has a single dominant allele for the gene that controls it?
14) Give two arguments for and two arguments against screening embryos for genetic disorders.
15) What is variation?
16) Explain how beneficial characteristics can become more common in a population over time.
17) What is selective breeding?
18) What is genetic engineering?
19) Name the groups that organisms are classified into in the Linnaean system.
20) Who proposed the 'three-domain system' of classification in 1990?

Topic B7 — Ecology (p.151-170) ☐

21) Define 'habitat'.
22) Explain what is meant by a 'stable community'.
23) What are biotic and abiotic factors?
24) What happens to the population size of a predator if its prey becomes more common in an ecosystem?
25) Suggest why you might use a transect when investigating the distribution of organisms.
26) Describe the four main stages involved in the water cycle.
27) Explain the role of photosynthesis in the carbon cycle.
28) Suggest why it's important to have high biodiversity in an ecosystem.
29) Give an example of how global warming could reduce biodiversity.
30) How can recycling programmes help to protect ecosystems?

Topic C1 — Atomic Structure and the Periodic Table

Atoms

All substances are made of **atoms**. They're really **tiny** — too small to see, even with your microscope. Atoms are so tiny that a **50p piece** contains about 77 400 000 000 000 000 000 000 of them.

Atoms Contain Protons, Neutrons and Electrons

Atoms have a radius of about 0.1 nanometres (that's 1×10^{-10} m). There are a few different (and equally useful) modern models of the atom — but chemists tend to like the model below best.

A nanometre (nm) is one billionth of a metre. Shown in standard form, that's 1×10^{-9} m. Standard form is used for showing really large or really small numbers.

The Nucleus

1) It's in the middle of the atom.
2) It contains protons and neutrons.
3) The nucleus has a radius of around 1×10^{-14} m (that's around 1/10 000 of the radius of an atom).
4) It has a positive charge because of the protons.
5) Almost the whole mass of the atom is concentrated in the nucleus.

The Electrons

1) Move around the nucleus in electron shells.
2) They're negatively charged and tiny, but they cover a lot of space.
3) The volume of their orbits determines the size of the atom.
4) Electrons have virtually no mass.

Particle	Relative Mass	Relative Charge
Proton	1	+1
Neutron	1	0
Electron	Very small	−1

Protons are heavy and positively charged. Neutrons are heavy and neutral. Electrons are tiny and negatively charged.

Number of Protons Equals Number of Electrons

1) Atoms are neutral — they have no charge overall (unlike ions).
2) This is because they have the same number of protons as electrons.
3) The charge on the electrons is the same size as the charge on the protons, but opposite — so the charges cancel out.
4) In an ion, the number of protons doesn't equal the number of electrons. This means it has an overall charge. For example, an ion with a 2− charge, has two more electrons than protons.

An ion is an atom or group of atoms that has lost or gained electrons.

Atomic Number and Mass Number Describe an Atom

1) The nuclear symbol of an atom tells you its atomic (proton) number and mass number.
2) The atomic number tells you how many protons there are.
3) The mass number tells you the total number of protons and neutrons in the atom.
4) To get the number of neutrons, just subtract the atomic number from the mass number.

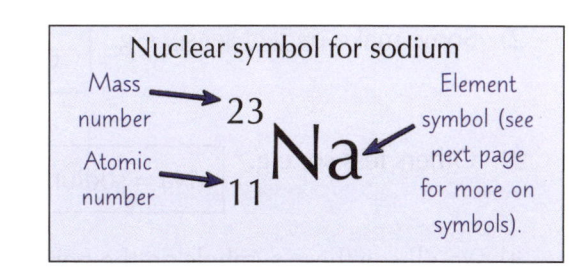

Nuclear symbol for sodium

Mass number → 23
Atomic number → 11
Na
Element symbol (see next page for more on symbols).

Atoms make up pretty much everything

If you get to grips with this stuff then you'll have a better chance understanding the rest of chemistry.

Q1 An atom of gallium has an atomic number of 31 and a mass number of 70. Give the number of electrons, protons and neutrons in the atom. [3 marks]

Elements

*An **element** is a substance made up of atoms that all have the **same** number of **protons** in their nucleus.*

Elements Consist of Atoms With the Same Atomic Number

Atoms can have different numbers of protons, neutrons and electrons. It's the number of protons in the nucleus that decides what type of atom it is.

> For example, an atom with one proton in its nucleus is hydrogen and an atom with two protons is helium.

If a substance only contains atoms with the same number of protons it's called an element.

So all the atoms of a particular element (e.g. nitrogen) have the same number of protons and different elements have atoms with different numbers of protons.

There are about 100 different elements. Each element consists of only one type of atom — see diagram below.

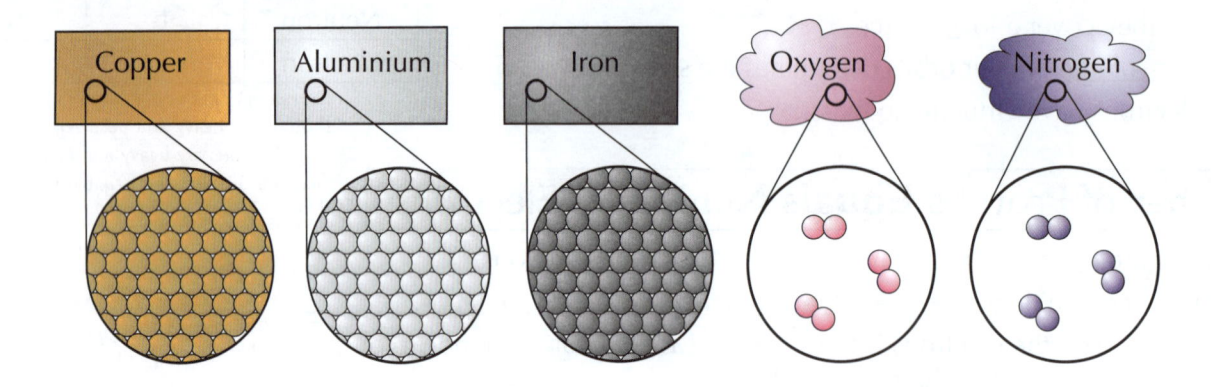

Copper   Aluminium   Iron   Oxygen   Nitrogen

Atoms Can be Represented by Symbols

1) Atoms of each element can be represented by a one or two letter symbol — it's a type of shorthand that saves you the bother of having to write the full name of the element.
2) Some make perfect sense, e.g.
   C = carbon   O = oxygen   Mg = magnesium
3) Others less so, e.g.
   Na = sodium   Fe = iron   Pb = lead

Most of these odd symbols actually come from the Latin names of the elements.

4) You'll see these symbols on the periodic table (see page 192).

All atoms in an element have the same number of protons

Atoms and elements — make sure you know what they are and the differences between them. You don't need to learn all the symbols as you can use a periodic table but it's handy to know the common ones.

Topic C1 — Atomic Structure and the Periodic Table

Isotopes

*What's inside different atoms of the **same element** can vary. Read on to find out how...*

Isotopes are the Same Except for Extra Neutrons

1) Isotopes are defined as:

> Different forms of the same element, which have the
> SAME number of PROTONS but a DIFFERENT number of NEUTRONS.

2) So isotopes have the same atomic number but different mass numbers.

3) A very popular example of a pair of isotopes are carbon-12 and carbon-13.

Carbon-12
- 6 PROTONS
- 6 ELECTRONS
- 6 NEUTRONS

$^{12}_{6}C$

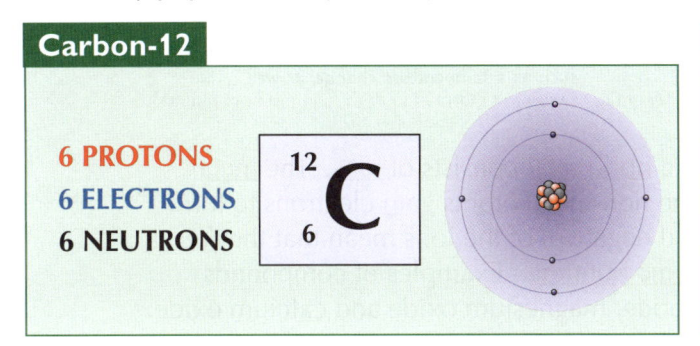

Carbon-13
- 6 PROTONS
- 6 ELECTRONS
- 7 NEUTRONS

$^{13}_{6}C$

4) Because many elements can exist as a number of different isotopes, relative atomic mass (A_r) is used instead of mass number when referring to the element as a whole.

> Relative atomic mass is an average mass taking into account the different masses and abundances (amounts) of all the isotopes that make up the element.

5) You can use this formula to work out the relative atomic mass of an element:

$$\text{relative atomic mass } (A_r) = \frac{\text{sum of (isotope abundance} \times \text{isotope mass number)}}{\text{sum of abundances of all the isotopes}}$$

EXAMPLE Copper has two stable isotopes. Cu-63 has an abundance of 69.2% and Cu-65 has an abundance of 30.8%. Calculate the relative atomic mass of copper to 1 decimal place.

$$\text{Relative atomic mass} = \frac{(69.2 \times 63) + (30.8 \times 65)}{69.2 + 30.8} = \frac{4359.6 + 2002}{100} = \frac{6361.6}{100} = 63.616 = 63.6$$

Isotopes of an element will have different numbers of neutrons

Make sure you understand and know how to use the formula to find the A_r of an element.

Q1 A substance consists of atoms which all have the same number of protons and electrons but different numbers of neutrons. Explain why this substance is an element. [1 mark]

Q2 Silicon, Si, has three stable isotopes. Si-28 has an abundance of 92.2%, Si-29 has an abundance of 4.7% and Si-30 has an abundance of 3.1%. Calculate silicon's relative atomic mass to 1 decimal place. [2 marks]

Topic C1 — Atomic Structure and the Periodic Table

Compounds

*It would be great if we only had to deal with elements. But unluckily for you, elements can mix and match to make lots of new substances called **compounds**. And this makes things a little bit more complicated...*

Atoms Join Together to Make Compounds

1) When elements react, atoms combine with other atoms to form compounds.

2) Compounds are substances formed from two or more elements, the atoms of each are in fixed proportions throughout the compound and they're held together by chemical bonds.

3) Making bonds involves atoms giving away, taking or sharing electrons. Only the electrons are involved — the nuclei of the atoms aren't affected at all when a bond is made.

4) It's usually difficult to separate the original elements of a compound out again — a chemical reaction is needed to do this.

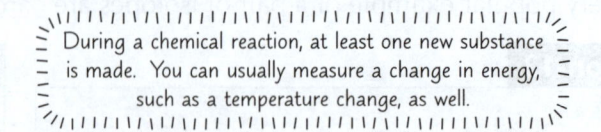

   During a chemical reaction, at least one new substance is made. You can usually measure a change in energy, such as a temperature change, as well.

5) A compound which is formed from a metal and a non-metal consists of ions. The metal atoms lose electrons to form positive ions and the non-metal atoms gain electrons to form negative ions. The opposite charges (positive and negative) of the ions mean that they're strongly attracted to each other. This is called ionic bonding. Examples of compounds which are bonded ionically include sodium chloride, magnesium oxide and calcium oxide.

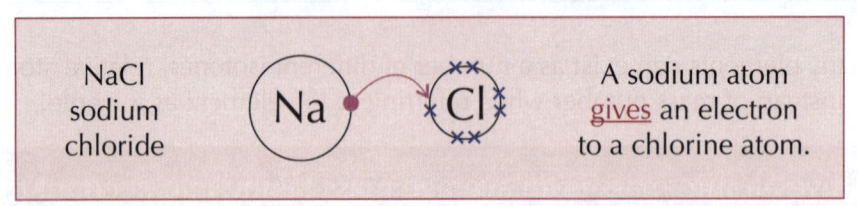

   NaCl
   sodium
   chloride

   A sodium atom gives an electron to a chlorine atom.

6) A compound formed from non-metals consists of molecules. Each atom shares an electron with another atom — this is called covalent bonding. Examples of compounds that are bonded covalently include hydrogen chloride gas, carbon monoxide, and water.

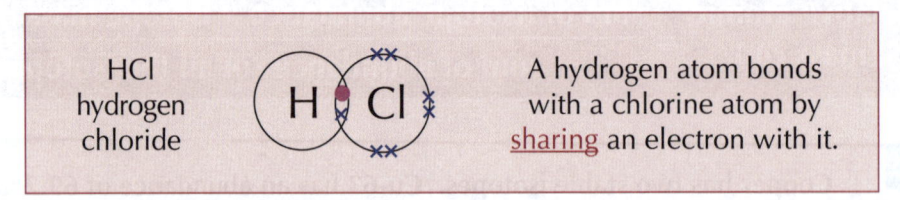

   HCl
   hydrogen
   chloride

   A hydrogen atom bonds with a chlorine atom by sharing an electron with it.

7) The properties of a compound are usually totally different from the properties of the original elements.

   For example, if iron (a lustrous magnetic metal) and sulfur (a nice yellow powder) react, the compound formed (iron sulfide) is a dull grey solid lump, and doesn't behave anything like either iron or sulfur.

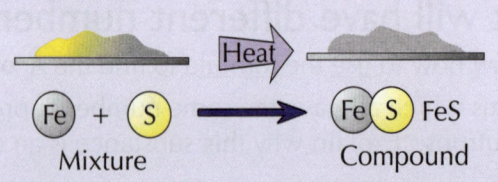

   Fe + S →(Heat) FeS
   Mixture   Compound

Topic C1 — Atomic Structure and the Periodic Table

Formulas and Equations

Formulas and *equations* are used to show what is happening to substances involved in **chemical reactions**. They tell us what **atoms** are involved and how the substances change during a reaction.

A Formula Shows What Atoms are in a Compound

Just as elements can be represented by symbols, compounds can be represented by formulas. The formulas are made up of elemental symbols in the same proportions that the elements can be found in the compound.

1) For example, carbon dioxide, CO_2, is a compound formed from a chemical reaction between carbon and oxygen. It contains 1 carbon atom and 2 oxygen atoms.

2) Here's another example: the formula of sulfuric acid is H_2SO_4. So, each molecule contains 2 hydrogen atoms, 1 sulfur atom and 4 oxygen atoms.

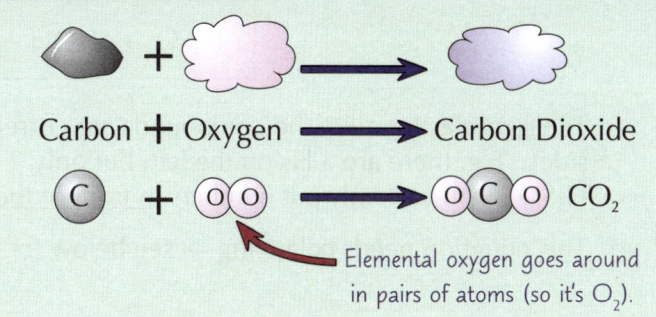

3) There might be brackets in a formula, e.g. calcium hydroxide is $Ca(OH)_2$. The little number outside the bracket applies to everything inside the brackets. So in $Ca(OH)_2$ there's 1 calcium atom, 2 oxygen atoms and 2 hydrogen atoms.

Carbon + Oxygen → Carbon Dioxide

C + O O → O C O CO_2

Elemental oxygen goes around in pairs of atoms (so it's O_2).

Here are some examples of formulas which might come in handy:

1) Carbon dioxide — CO_2
2) Ammonia — NH_3
3) Water — H_2O
4) Sodium chloride — NaCl
5) Carbon monoxide — CO
6) Hydrochloric acid — HCl
7) Calcium chloride — $CaCl_2$
8) Sodium carbonate — Na_2CO_3
9) Sulfuric acid — H_2SO_4

Chemical Changes are Shown Using Chemical Equations

One way to show a chemical reaction is to write a word equation. It's not as quick as using chemical symbols and you can't tell straight away what's happened to each of the atoms, but it's dead easy.

Here's an example — you're told that methane burns in oxygen giving carbon dioxide and water:

methane + oxygen → carbon dioxide + water

The molecules on the left-hand side of the equation are called the reactants (because they react with each other).

The molecules on the right-hand side are called the products (because they've been produced from the reactants).

Symbol Equations Show the Atoms on Both Sides

Chemical changes can be shown in a kind of shorthand using symbol equations. Symbol equations just show the symbols or formulas of the reactants and products...

You'll have spotted that there's a '2' in front of the Mg and the MgO. The reason for this is explained on the next page.

magnesium + oxygen → magnesium oxide
$2Mg + O_2$ → $2MgO$

Formulas show us which elements make up a compound

There'll be a lot of different molecules popping up throughout this book. Have a look through and when you find one you don't know, use its formula to work out what elements it contains.

Q1   How many atoms are in one particle of Na_2CO_3? [1 mark]

Q2   A compound has the formula $Al_2(SO_4)_3$. Name the elements and state how many atoms of each element are represented in its formula. [1 mark]

Topic C1 — Atomic Structure and the Periodic Table

Formulas and Equations

Symbol Equations Need to be Balanced

1) There must always be the same number of atoms on both sides — they can't just disappear.
2) You balance the equation by putting numbers in front of the formulas where needed.
3) Take this equation for reacting sulfuric acid (H_2SO_4) with sodium hydroxide (NaOH) to get sodium sulfate (Na_2SO_4) and water (H_2O):

$$H_2SO_4 + NaOH \rightarrow Na_2SO_4 + H_2O$$

The formulas for all of the compounds are correct but the numbers of some atoms don't match up on both sides. E.g. there are 3 Hs on the left, but only 2 on the right. You can't change formulas like H_2SO_4 to H_2SO_5. You can only put numbers in front of them.

4) This equation needs balancing — see below for how to do this.

Here's how to Balance an Equation

The more you practise, the quicker you get, but all you do is this:

1) Find an element that doesn't balance and pencil in a number to try and sort it out.
2) See where it gets you. It may create another imbalance, but if so, pencil in another number and see where that gets you.
3) Carry on chasing unbalanced elements and it'll sort itself out pretty quickly.

EXAMPLE

In the equation above you soon notice we're short of H atoms on the RHS (Right-Hand Side).

1) The only thing you can do about that is make it $2H_2O$ instead of just H_2O:

$$H_2SO_4 + NaOH \rightarrow Na_2SO_4 + 2H_2O$$

2) But that now causes too many H atoms and O atoms on the RHS, so to balance that up you could try putting 2NaOH on the LHS (Left-Hand Side):

$$H_2SO_4 + 2NaOH \rightarrow Na_2SO_4 + 2H_2O$$

3) And suddenly there it is! Everything balances. And you'll notice the Na just sorted itself out.

Getting good at balancing equations takes patience and practice

Remember, a number in front of a formula applies to the entire formula — so, $3Na_2SO_4$ means three lots of Na_2SO_4. The little numbers within or at the end of a formula only apply to the atom or brackets immediately before. So the 4 in Na_2SO_4 means there are 4 Os, but there's just 1 S, not 4.

Q1 Balance the equation: $Fe + Cl_2 \rightarrow FeCl_3$ [1 mark]

Q2 Hydrogen and oxygen molecules are formed in a reaction where water splits apart.
For this reaction: a) State the word equation. b) Give a balanced symbol equation. [3 marks]

Topic C1 — Atomic Structure and the Periodic Table

Warm-Up & Exam Questions

So, you reckon you know your elements from your compounds?... Have a go at these questions and see how you do. If you get stuck on something just flick back and give it another read through.

Warm-Up Questions

1) What does the mass number tell you about an atom?
2) What is the definition of an element?
3) Describe what a compound is.
4) What does a compound formed from a metal and a non-metal consist of?
5) Balance this equation for the reaction of glucose ($C_6H_{12}O_6$) and oxygen:
   $C_6H_{12}O_6 + O_2 \rightarrow CO_2 + H_2O$

Exam Questions

1 This question is about atomic structure. *Grade 4-6*

1.1 Use your knowledge to complete **Table 1**.

Table 1

Name of particle	Relative charge
Proton	....
Neutron	....

[2 marks]

1.2 Where are protons and neutrons found in an atom?

[1 mark]

1.3 An atom has 8 electrons. How many protons does the atom have?

[1 mark]

1.4 What is the relative mass of a proton?

[1 mark]

2 **Table 2** gives some information about nitrogen. *Grade 4-6*

Table 2

Element	Number of protons	Mass number
nitrogen	7	14

2.1 How many neutrons does nitrogen have?

[1 mark]

2.2 Describe how the information in **Table 2** can be used to work out the atomic number of nitrogen.

[1 mark]

2.3 What is the chemical symbol for nitrogen?

[1 mark]

Topic C1 — Atomic Structure and the Periodic Table

Exam Questions

3 Methane (CH$_4$) burns in oxygen to make carbon dioxide and water. *Grade 6-7*

3.1 State the names of the reactants in this reaction.
[1 mark]

3.2 State the names of the products in this reaction.
[1 mark]

3.3 Which molecule involved in the reaction is composed of only one element.
[1 mark]

3.4 Complete and balance the symbol equation for the reaction below.

.........CH$_4$ + ... → ....CO$_2$ + ...H$_2$O

[2 marks]

4 Sulfuric acid reacts with ammonia to form ammonium sulfate, (NH$_4$)$_2$SO$_4$. *Grade 6-7*

4.1 Complete and balance the symbol equation below.

.... + ... → (NH$_4$)$_2$SO$_4$

[3 marks]

4.2 In the balanced equation, how many atoms are there in the reactants?
[1 mark]

4.3 How many hydrogen atoms are present in ammonium sulfate?
[1 mark]

5 Carbon has several isotopes. These include carbon-12 and carbon-13. Details about the carbon-13 isotope are shown below. *Grade 7-9*

$$^{13}_{6}C$$

5.1 Explain what an isotope is.
[3 marks]

5.2 Give the number of protons, neutrons and electrons that carbon-13 contains.
[3 marks]

5.3 Details of element **X** are shown below.

$$^{13}_{7}X$$

Explain how you can tell that element **X** is not an isotope of carbon.
[1 mark]

5.4 There are two isotopes of element **X**. One isotope has a mass number of 13 and a percentage abundance of 79%. The other isotope has a mass number of 14 and a percentage abundance of 21%. Use this information to calculate the relative atomic mass of element **X**. Give your answer to 1 d.p.
[4 marks]

Topic C1 — Atomic Structure and the Periodic Table

Mixtures

Mixtures are exactly what they sound like, two or more **elements** or **compounds** mixed together.

Mixtures are Easily Separated — Not Like Compounds

1) Unlike in a compound, there's no chemical bond between the different parts of a mixture.

2) The parts of a mixture can be either elements or compounds, and they can be separated out by physical methods such as filtration (p. 183), crystallisation (p.183), simple distillation (p.185), fractional distillation (p.186) and chromatography (see next page).

A physical method is one that doesn't involve a chemical reaction, so doesn't form any new substances.

Air is a mixture of gases, mainly nitrogen, oxygen, carbon dioxide and argon. The gases can all be separated out fairly easily.

Crude oil is a mixture of different length hydrocarbon molecules.

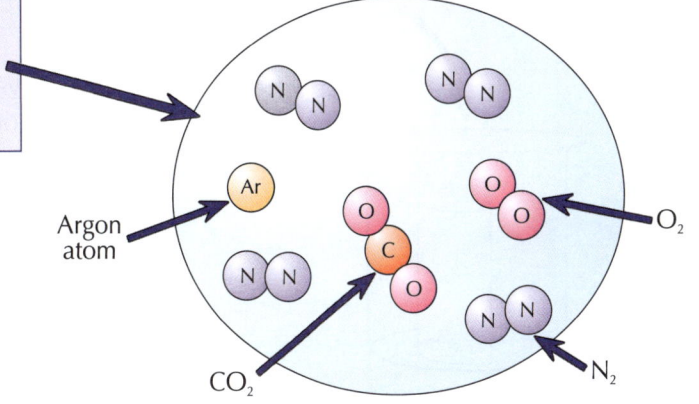

3) The properties of a mixture are just a mixture of the properties of the separate parts — the chemical properties of a substance aren't affected by it being part of a mixture.

For example, a mixture of iron powder and sulfur powder will show the properties of both iron and sulfur. It will contain grey magnetic bits of iron and bright yellow bits of sulfur.

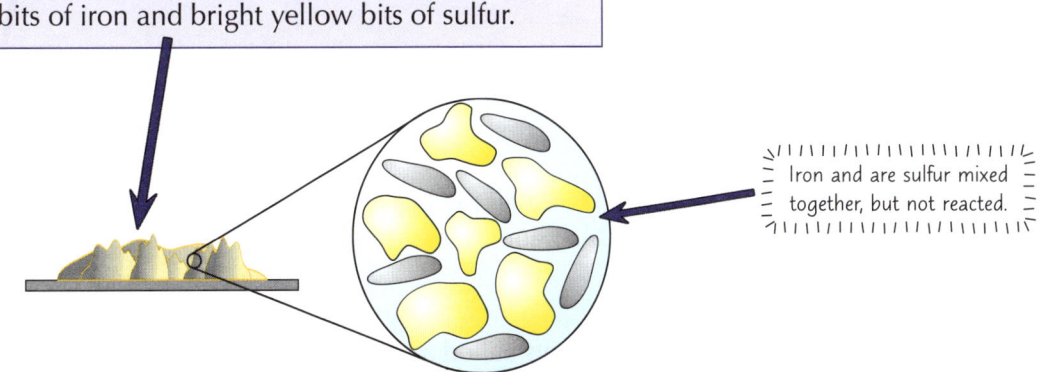

Iron and are sulfur mixed together, but not reacted.

Mixtures can be separated without a chemical reaction

Remember that the different parts of mixtures aren't chemically combined, this means their chemical properties remain unchanged and the compounds or elements can be separated by physical methods.

Topic C1 — Atomic Structure and the Periodic Table

Chromatography

Paper chromatography is a really useful technique to separate compounds out of a mixture.

You Need to Know How to Do Paper Chromatography

One method of separating substances in a mixture is through chromatography. This technique can be used to separate different dyes in an ink. Here's how you can do it:

1) Draw a line near the bottom of a sheet of filter paper. (Use a pencil to do this — pencil marks are insoluble and won't dissolve in the solvent.)

2) Add a spot of the ink to the line and place the sheet in a beaker of solvent, e.g. water.

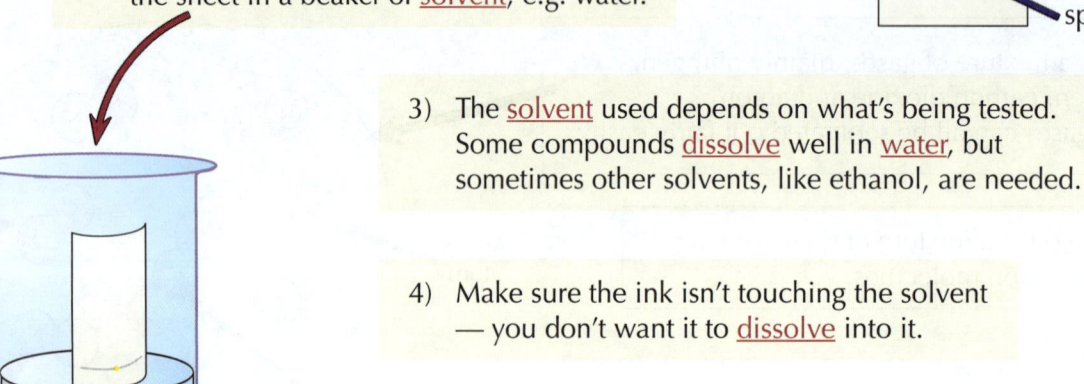

3) The solvent used depends on what's being tested. Some compounds dissolve well in water, but sometimes other solvents, like ethanol, are needed.

4) Make sure the ink isn't touching the solvent — you don't want it to dissolve into it.

5) Place a lid on top of the container to stop the solvent evaporating.

6) The solvent seeps up the paper, carrying the ink with it.

The point the solvent has reached as it moves up the paper is the solvent front.

7) Each different dye in the ink will move up the paper at a different rate so the dyes will separate out. Each dye will form a spot in a different place — 1 spot per dye in the ink.

8) If any of the dyes in the ink are insoluble (won't dissolve) in the solvent you've used, they'll stay on the baseline.

9) When the solvent has nearly reached the top of the paper, take the paper out of the beaker and leave it to dry.

10) The end result is a pattern of spots called a chromatogram.

A chromatogram

Chromatography separates the different dyes in inks

PRACTICAL TIP: Make sure you use a pencil to draw your baseline on the sheet of paper for your chromatogram. If you use a pen, all the components of the ink in the pen will get separated, along with the substance you're analysing, which will make your results very confusing.

Topic C1 — Atomic Structure and the Periodic Table

Filtration and Crystallisation **PRACTICAL**

*Filtration and crystallisation are **methods** of **separating mixtures**. Chemists use these techniques all the time to separate **solids** from **liquids**, so it's worth making sure you know how to do them.*

Filtration Separates Insoluble Solids from Liquids

1) Filtration can be used if your product is an insoluble solid that needs to be separated from a liquid reaction mixture.
2) It can be used in purification as well. For example, solid impurities in the reaction mixture can be separated out using filtration.

   Insoluble means the solid can't be dissolved in the liquid.

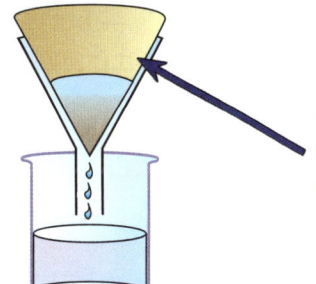

Filter paper folded into a cone shape — the solid is left in the filter paper.

Two Ways to Separate Soluble Solids from Solutions

If a solid can be dissolved it's described as being soluble. There are two methods you can use to separate a soluble salt from a solution — evaporation and crystallisation.

Evaporation

1) Pour the solution into an evaporating dish.

2) Slowly heat the solution. The solvent will evaporate and the solution will get more concentrated. Eventually, crystals will start to form.

3) Keep heating the evaporating dish until all you have left are dry crystals.

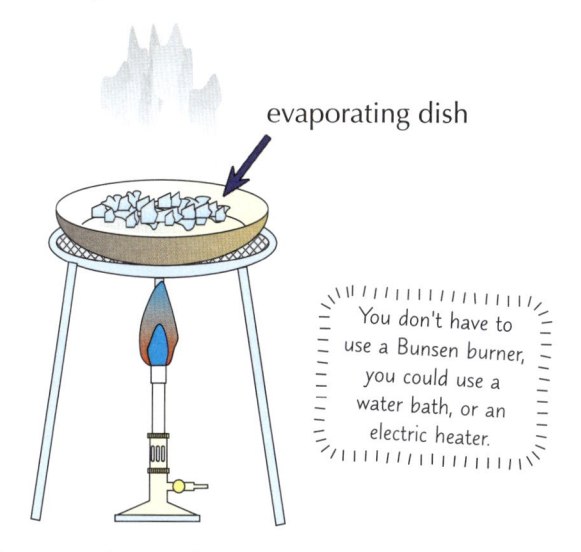

evaporating dish

You don't have to use a Bunsen burner, you could use a water bath, or an electric heater.

Evaporation is a really quick way of separating a soluble salt from a solution, but you can only use it if the salt doesn't decompose (break down) when its heated. Otherwise, you'll have to use crystallisation.

Crystallisation

1) Pour the solution into an evaporating dish and gently heat the solution. Some of the solvent will evaporate and the solution will get more concentrated.
2) Once some of the solvent has evaporated, or when you see crystals start to form (the point of crystallisation), remove the dish from the heat and leave the solution to cool.
3) The salt should start to form crystals as it becomes insoluble in the cold, highly concentrated solution.
4) Filter the crystals out of the solution, and leave them in a warm place to dry. You could also use a drying oven or a desiccator.

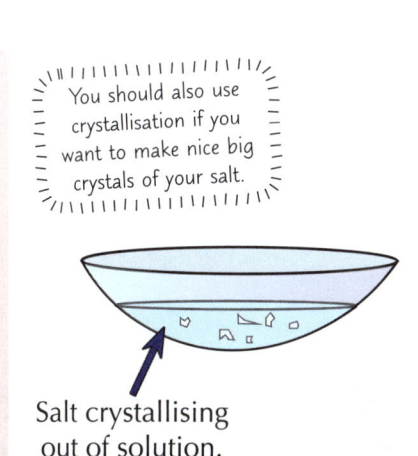

You should also use crystallisation if you want to make nice big crystals of your salt.

Salt crystallising out of solution.

Topic C1 — Atomic Structure and the Periodic Table

PRACTICAL: Filtration and Crystallisation

*Here's how you can put filtration and crystallisation to **good use**. Separating rock salt...*

Filtration and Crystallisation can be Used to Separate Rock Salt

1) Rock salt is simply a mixture of salt and sand (they spread it on the roads in winter).
2) Salt and sand are both compounds — but salt dissolves in water and sand doesn't. This vital difference in their physical properties gives a great way to separate them. Here's what to do...

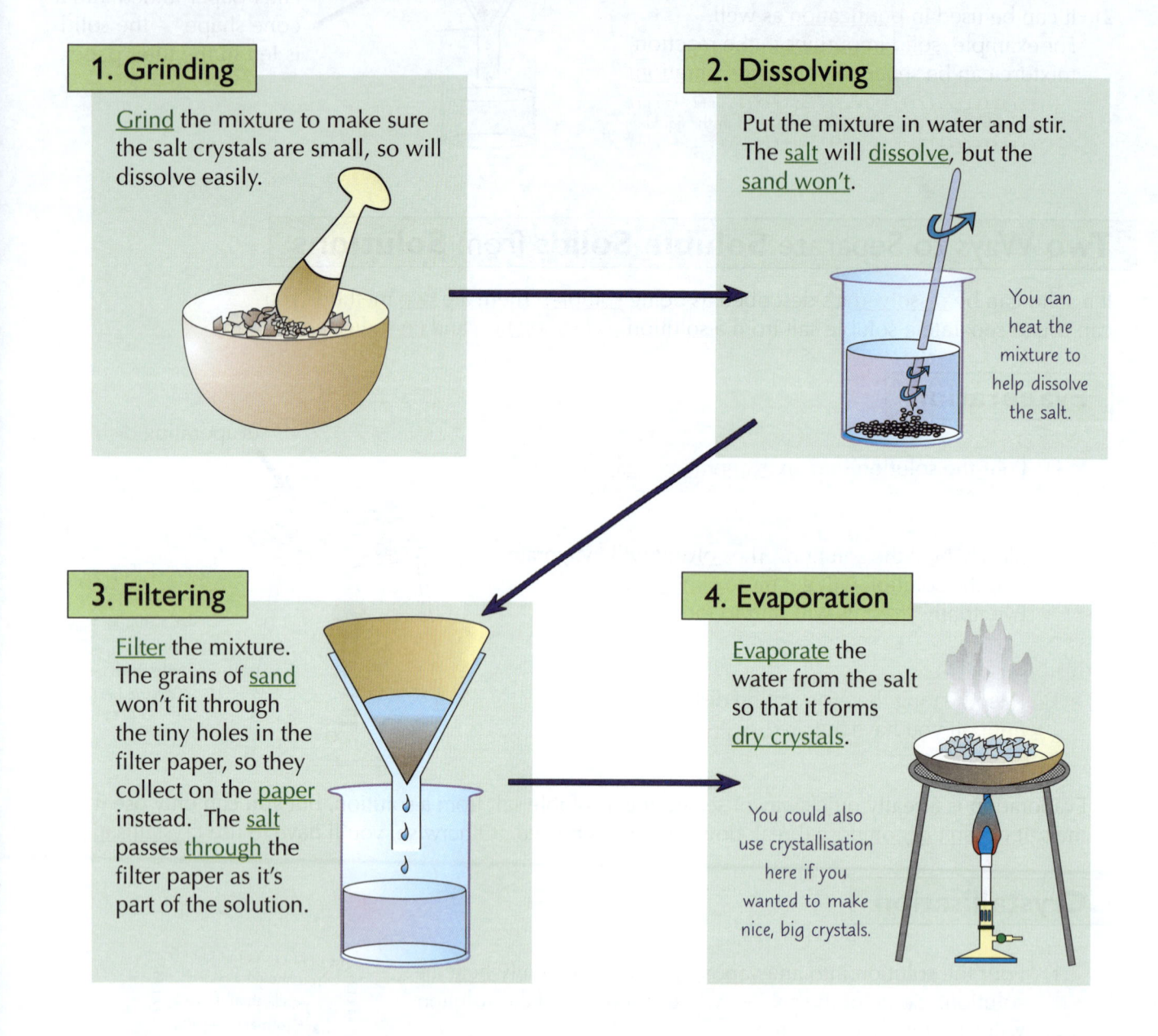

1. Grinding
Grind the mixture to make sure the salt crystals are small, so will dissolve easily.

2. Dissolving
Put the mixture in water and stir. The salt will dissolve, but the sand won't.

You can heat the mixture to help dissolve the salt.

3. Filtering
Filter the mixture. The grains of sand won't fit through the tiny holes in the filter paper, so they collect on the paper instead. The salt passes through the filter paper as it's part of the solution.

4. Evaporation
Evaporate the water from the salt so that it forms dry crystals.

You could also use crystallisation here if you wanted to make nice, big crystals.

REVISION TIP

Separating rock salt requires filtration and evaporation
You may be asked how to separate another type of mixture containing insoluble and soluble solids — just apply the same method and think through what is happening in each stage.

Topic C1 — Atomic Structure and the Periodic Table

Distillation

PRACTICAL

*Distillation is used to separate mixtures which contain **liquids**. This first page looks at **simple** distillation.*

Simple Distillation is Used to Separate Out Solutions

1) <u>Simple distillation</u> is used for separating out a <u>liquid</u> from a <u>solution</u>.

2) The solution is <u>heated</u>. The part of the solution that has the lowest boiling point <u>evaporates</u> first.

3) The <u>vapour</u> is then <u>cooled</u>, <u>condenses</u> (turns back into a liquid) and is <u>collected</u>.

4) The rest of the <u>solution</u> is left behind in the flask.

You can use simple distillation to get <u>pure water</u> from <u>seawater</u>. The <u>water</u> evaporates and is condensed and collected. Eventually you'll end up with just the <u>salt</u> left in the flask.

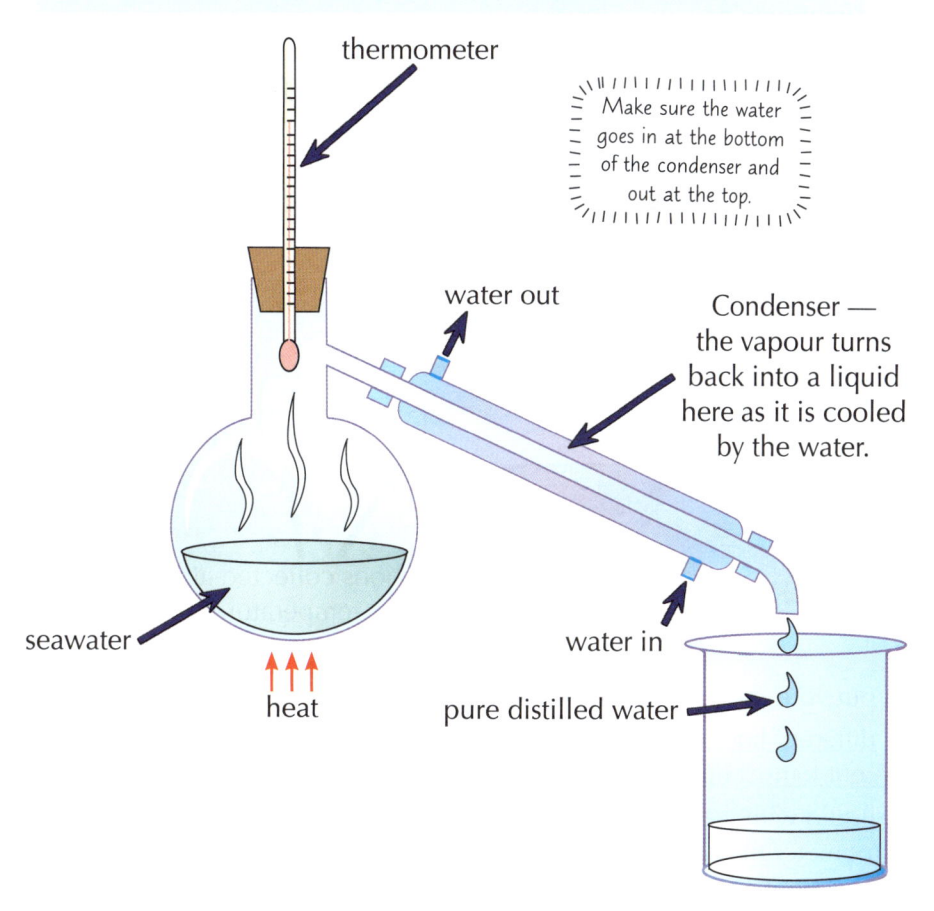

Make sure the water goes in at the bottom of the condenser and out at the top.

thermometer

water out

Condenser — the vapour turns back into a liquid here as it is cooled by the water.

seawater

heat

water in

pure distilled water

5) The <u>problem</u> with simple distillation is that you can only use it to separate things with <u>very different</u> boiling points — if the temperature goes higher than the boiling point of the substance with the higher boiling point, they will <u>mix</u> again.

6) If you have a <u>mixture of liquids</u> with <u>similar boiling points</u> you need another method to separate them — like fractional distillation (see next page).

Heating → Evaporating → Cooling → Condensing

You might have used <u>distilled water</u> in chemistry experiments. Because it's been distilled, there <u>aren't</u> any <u>impurities</u> in it (like ions, see page 202) that might interfere with experimental results. Clever stuff.

Topic C1 — Atomic Structure and the Periodic Table

Distillation

*Another type of distillation is **fractional distillation**. This is more complicated to carry out than simple distillation but it can separate out **mixtures of liquids** even if their **boiling points** are close together.*

Fractional Distillation is Used to Separate a Mixture of Liquids

Here is a lab demonstration that can be used to model the fractional distillation of crude oil at a refinery.

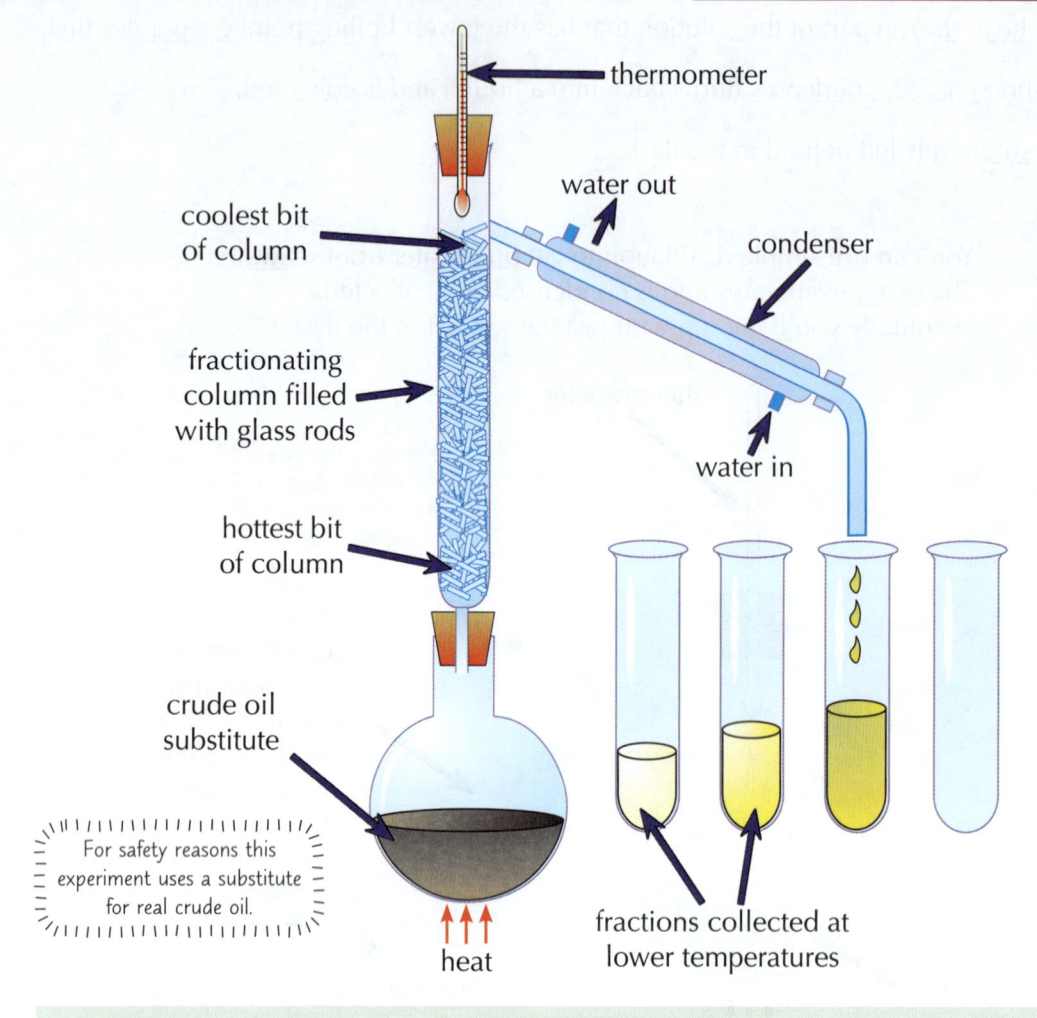

- thermometer
- coolest bit of column
- water out
- condenser
- fractionating column filled with glass rods
- water in
- hottest bit of column
- crude oil substitute
- For safety reasons this experiment uses a substitute for real crude oil.
- heat
- fractions collected at lower temperatures

1) You put your mixture in a flask and stick a fractionating column on top. Then you heat it.
2) The different liquids will all have different boiling points — so they will evaporate at different temperatures.
3) The liquid with the lowest boiling point evaporates first. When the temperature on the thermometer matches the boiling point of this liquid, it will reach the top of the column.
4) Liquids with higher boiling points might also start to evaporate. But the column is cooler towards the top. So they will only get part of the way up before condensing and running back down towards the flask.
5) When the first liquid has been collected, you raise the temperature until the next one reaches the top.

Fractional distillation is used in the lab and industry

You've made it to the end of the pages on separation techniques, so make sure you understand what each of the methods can be used to separate and the apparatus set up for each technique.

Q1 Propan-1-ol, methanol and ethanol have boiling points of 97 °C, 65 °C and 78 °C respectively. A student uses fractional distillation to separate a mixture of these compounds. State which liquid will be collected in the second fraction and explain why. [2 marks]

Topic C1 — Atomic Structure and the Periodic Table

Warm-Up & Exam Questions — PRACTICAL

So the last few pages have all been about mixtures and how to separate them. Here are some questions to get stuck into and make sure you know your filtration from your distillation...

Warm-Up Questions

1) What is the definition of a mixture?
2) Name a separation technique that could be used to separate a soluble solid from a solution.
3) Which technique could you use to separate a mixture of liquids with similar boiling points?

Exam Questions

1 A forensic scientist is using paper chromatography to compare different inks which contain a mixture of dyes. He draws a pencil line near the bottom of a sheet of filter paper and adds a spot of each of the different inks to the line with a gap between each spot. *(Grade 4-6)*

1.1 Describe the next step that's required to carry out paper chromatography.
[1 mark]

1.2 Why is pencil used to make the line on the filter paper?
[1 mark]

2 Lawn sand is a mixture of insoluble sharp sand and soluble ammonium sulfate fertiliser. *(Grade 6-7)*

2.1 Describe how you would obtain pure, dry samples of the two components of lawn sand in the lab.
[3 marks]

2.2 A student separated 51.4 g of lawn sand into sharp sand and ammonium sulfate. After separation, the total mass of the two products was 52.6 g. Suggest a reason for the difference in mass.
[1 mark]

3 Table 1 gives the boiling points of three liquids. *(Grade 6-7)*

3.1 State why simple distillation cannot be used to separate water from a solution of water and methanoic acid.
[1 mark]

Table 1

Liquid	Boiling point (°C)
Methanoic acid	101
Propanone	56
Water	100

3.2 The apparatus in **Figure 1** was used to separate a mixture of propanone and water.
Complete the table using the options below.

no liquid   water   propanone   both liquids

Temperature on thermometer	Contents of the flask	Contents of the beaker
30 °C	....	....
65 °C	....	....
110 °C	....	....

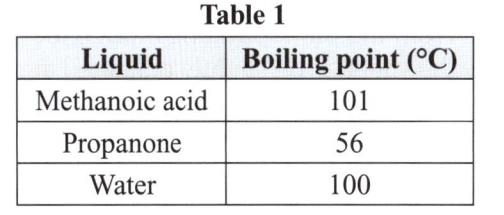

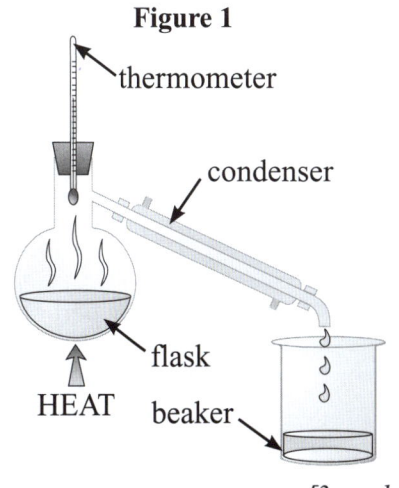

Figure 1 (thermometer, condenser, flask, HEAT, beaker)

[3 marks]

Topic C1 — Atomic Structure and the Periodic Table

The History of the Atom

*You may have thought you were done with the **atom** after page 173. Unfortunately, you don't get away that easily. The next couple of pages are all about how **scientists** came to understand the atom as we do today.*

The Theory of Atomic Structure Has Changed Over Time

1) At the start of the 19th century John Dalton described atoms as solid spheres, and said that different spheres made up the different elements.

2) In 1897 J J Thomson concluded from his experiments that atoms weren't solid spheres. His measurements of charge and mass showed that an atom must contain even smaller, negatively charged particles — electrons.

3) The 'solid sphere' idea of atomic structure had to be changed. The new theory was known as the 'plum pudding model'.

4) The plum pudding model showed the atom as a ball of positive charge with electrons stuck in it.

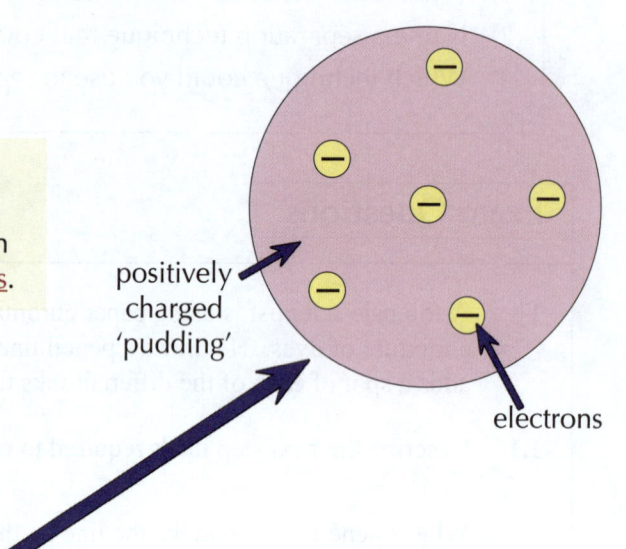

Rutherford Showed that the Plum Pudding Model Was Wrong

1) In 1909 Ernest Rutherford and his student Ernest Marsden conducted the famous alpha particle scattering experiments. They fired positively charged alpha particles at an extremely thin sheet of gold.

2) From the plum pudding model, they were expecting the particles to pass straight through the sheet or be slightly deflected at most. This was because the positive charge of each atom was thought to be very spread out through the 'pudding' of the atom. But, whilst most of the particles did go straight through the gold sheet, some were deflected more than expected, and a small number were deflected backwards. So the plum pudding model couldn't be right.

3) Rutherford came up with an idea to explain this new evidence — the nuclear model of the atom. In this, there's a tiny, positively charged nucleus at the centre, where most of the mass is concentrated. A 'cloud' of negative electrons surrounds this nucleus — so most of the atom is empty space. When alpha particles came near the concentrated, positive charge of the nucleus, they were deflected. If they were fired directly at the nucleus, they were deflected backwards. Otherwise, they passed through the empty space.

A few particles are deflected backwards by the nucleus.

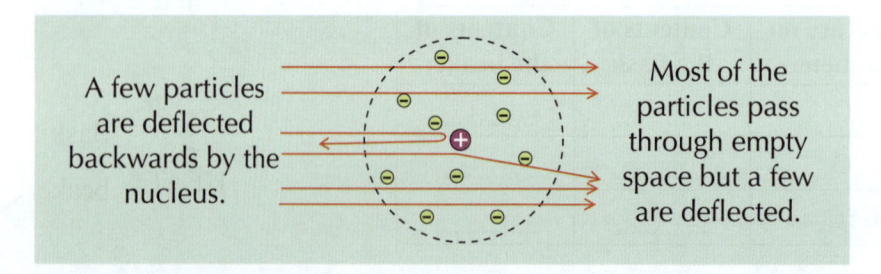

Most of the particles pass through empty space but a few are deflected.

Topic C1 — Atomic Structure and the Periodic Table

The History of the Atom

Bohr's **Nuclear Model** Explains a Lot

1) Scientists realised that electrons in a 'cloud' around the nucleus of an atom, as Rutherford described, would be attracted to the nucleus, causing the atom to collapse.

2) Niels Bohr's nuclear model of the atom suggested that all the electrons were contained in shells.

3) Bohr proposed that electrons orbit the nucleus in fixed shells and aren't anywhere in between. Each shell is a fixed distance from the nucleus.

4) Bohr's theory of atomic structure was supported by many experiments and it helped to explain lots of other scientists' observations at the time.

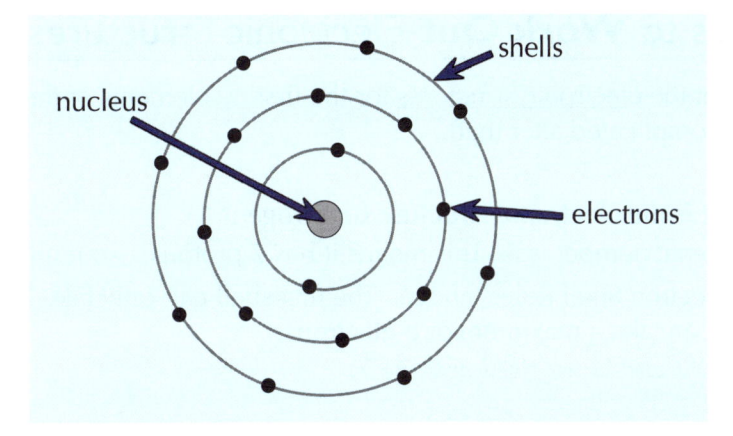

Further Experiments Showed the **Existence** of **Protons**

1) Further experimentation by Rutherford and others gave the conclusion that the nucleus could be divided into smaller particles, each of which has the same charge as a hydrogen nucleus.

2) About 20 years after scientists had accepted that atoms have nuclei, James Chadwick carried out an experiment which provided evidence for neutral particles in the nucleus. These became known as neutrons. The discovery of neutrons resulted in a model of the atom which was pretty close to the modern day accepted version, known as the nuclear model (see page 173).

Our understanding of what an atom looks like has changed

Our understanding of the atom has gone through many stages thanks to other people's work being built upon with new evidence and new predictions made. A fine example of the scientific method.

Topic C1 — Atomic Structure and the Periodic Table

Electronic Structure

The fact that electrons occupy 'shells' around the nucleus is what causes the whole of chemistry. Remember that, and watch how it applies to each bit of it.

Electron Shell Rules:

1) Electrons always occupy shells (sometimes called energy levels).
2) The lowest energy levels are always filled first — these are the ones closest to the nucleus.
3) Only a certain number of electrons are allowed in each shell:

   1st shell: 2   2nd shell: 8   3rd shell: 8

4) Atoms are much happier when they have full electron shells — like the noble gases in Group 0.
5) In most atoms, the outer shell is not full and this makes the atom want to react to fill it.

Electron configurations can be shown as diagrams like this...

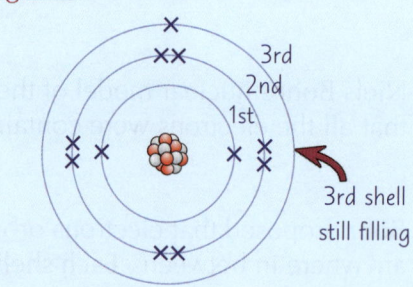

...or as numbers like this: 2, 8, 1
Both of the configurations above are for sodium.

Follow the Rules to Work Out Electronic Structures

You can easily work out the electronic structures for the first 20 elements of the periodic table (things get a bit more complicated after that).

EXAMPLE   What is the electronic structure of nitrogen?
1) Nitrogen's atomic number is 7. This means it has 7 protons... so it must have 7 electrons.
2) Follow the 'Electron Shell Rules' above. The first shell can only take 2 electrons and the second shell can take a maximum of 8 electrons.
So the electronic structure for nitrogen must be 2, 5.

EXAMPLE   What is the electronic structure of magnesium?
1) Magnesium's atomic number is 12. This means it has 12 protons... so it must have 12 electrons.
2) Follow the 'Electron Shell Rules' above. The first shell can only take 2 electrons and the second shell can take a maximum of 8 electrons, so the third shell must also be partially filled.
So the electronic structure for magnesium must be 2, 8, 2.

Here are some more examples of electronic structures:

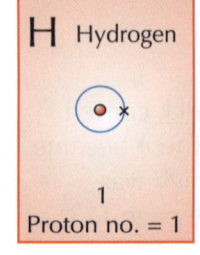

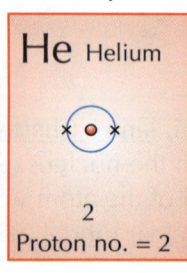

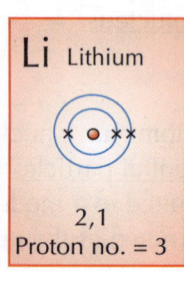

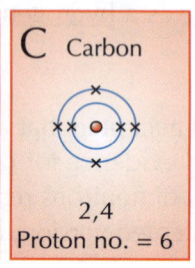

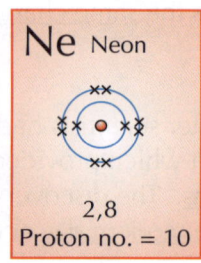

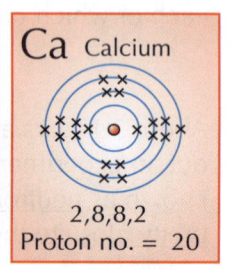

H Hydrogen	He Helium	Li Lithium	C Carbon	Ne Neon	Ca Calcium
1	2	2,1	2,4	2,8	2,8,8,2
Proton no. = 1	Proton no. = 2	Proton no. = 3	Proton no. = 6	Proton no. = 10	Proton no. = 20

Electron shells — one of the most important ideas in chemistry

It's really important to learn the rules for filling electron shells — make sure you practise.

Q1 Give the electronic structure of aluminium (atomic number = 13). [1 mark]
Q2 Give the electronic structure of argon (atomic number = 18). [1 mark]

Topic C1 — Atomic Structure and the Periodic Table

Development of the Periodic Table

We haven't always known as much about chemistry as we do now. Early chemists looked to try and understand **patterns** in the elements' properties to get a bit of understanding.

In the Early 1800s Elements Were Arranged By Atomic Weight

Until quite recently, there were two obvious ways to categorise elements:

1) Their physical and chemical properties   2) Their atomic weight

1) Remember, scientists had no idea of atomic structure or of protons, neutrons or electrons, so there was no such thing as atomic number to them.
(It was only in the 20th century after protons and electrons were discovered that it was realised the elements were best arranged in order of atomic number.)

2) Back then, the only thing they could measure was atomic weight, and so the known elements were arranged in order of atomic weight. When this was done, a periodic pattern was noticed in the properties of the elements. This is where the name 'periodic table' comes from...

3) Early periodic tables were not complete and some elements were placed in the wrong group. This is because elements were placed in the order of atomic weight and did not take into account their properties.

Dmitri Mendeleev Left Gaps and Predicted New Elements

1) In 1869, Dmitri Mendeleev overcame some of the problems of early periodic tables by taking 50 known elements and arranging them into his Table of Elements — with various gaps as shown.

Mendeleev's Table of the Elements

```
H
Li  Be                                          B  C  N  O  F
Na Mg                                           Al Si P  S  Cl
K  Ca *  Ti V  Cr Mn Fe Co Ni Cu Zn *  *  As Se Br
Rb Sr Y  Zr Nb Mo *  Ru Rh Pd Ag Cd In Sn Sb Te I
Cs Ba *  *  Ta W  *  Os Ir Pt Au Hg Tl Pb Bi
```

2) Mendeleev put the elements mainly in order of atomic weight but did switch that order if the properties meant it should be changed. An example of this can been seen with Te and I — iodine actually has a smaller atomic weight but is placed after tellurium as it has similar properties to the elements in that group.

3) Gaps were left in the table to make sure that elements with similar properties stayed in the same groups. Some of these gaps indicated the existence of undiscovered elements and allowed Mendeleev to predict what their properties might be. When they were found and they fitted the pattern it helped confirm Mendeleev's ideas. For example, Mendeleev made really good predictions about the chemical and physical properties of an element he called ekasilicon, which we know today as germanium.

> The discovery of isotopes (see page 175) in the early 20th century confirmed that Mendeleev was correct to not place elements in a strict order of atomic weight but to also take account of their properties. Isotopes of the same element have different masses but have the same chemical properties so occupy the same position on the periodic table.

By leaving gaps in the table Mendeleev had the right idea

Make sure you can describe what Mendeleev did to overcome problems with early periodic tables.

Topic C1 — Atomic Structure and the Periodic Table

The Modern Periodic Table

*Chemists were getting pretty close to producing something that you might **recognise** as a periodic table. The big breakthrough came when the **structure** of the **atom** was understood a bit better.*

The Periodic Table Helps you to See Patterns in Properties

1) There are 100ish elements, which all materials are made of.
2) In the periodic table the elements are laid out in order of increasing atomic (proton) number. Arranging the elements like this means there are repeating patterns in the properties of the elements (the properties are said to occur periodically, hence the name periodic table).
3) If it wasn't for the periodic table organising everything, you'd have a hard job remembering all those properties.
4) It's a handy tool for working out which elements are metals and which are non-metals. Metals are found to the left and non-metals to the right.

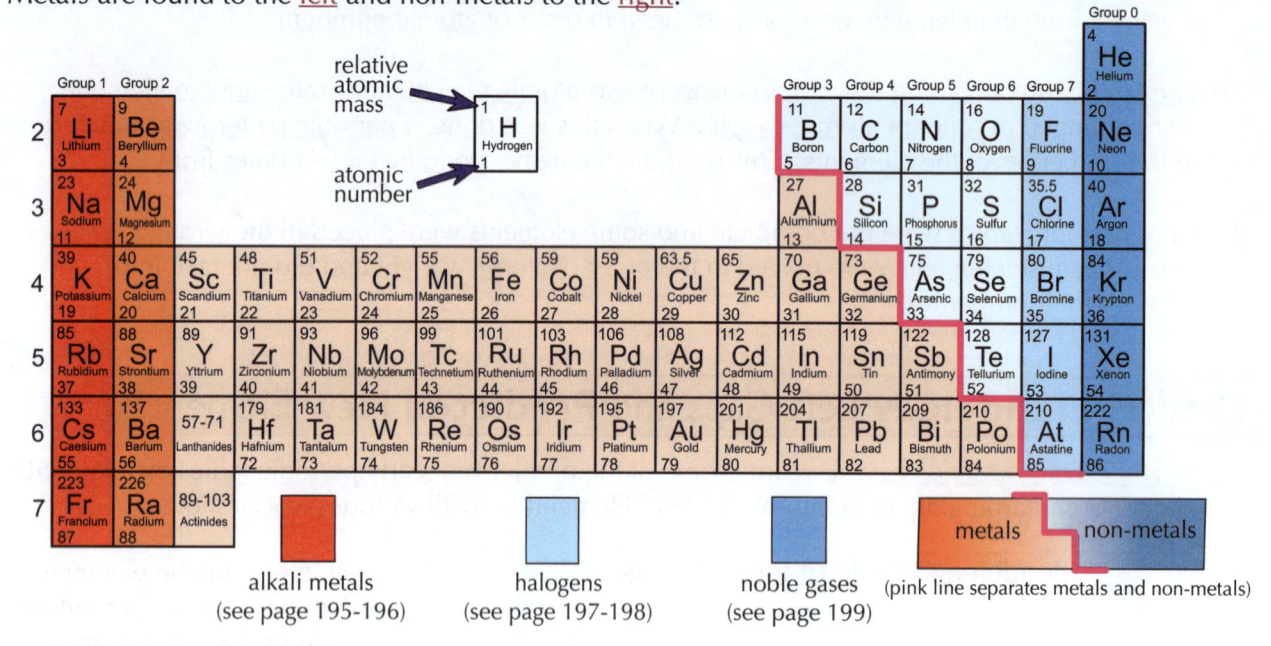

alkali metals (see page 195-196)   halogens (see page 197-198)   noble gases (see page 199)   (pink line separates metals and non-metals)

5) Elements with similar properties form columns.
6) These vertical columns are called groups.
7) The group number tells you how many electrons there are in the outer shell. For example, Group 1 elements all have one electron in their outer shell and Group 7 all have seven electrons in their outer shell. The exception to the rule is Group 0, for example helium has two electrons in its outer shell. This is useful as the way atoms react depends upon the number of electrons in their outer shell. So all elements in the same group are likely to react in a similar way.
8) If you know the properties of one element, you can predict properties of other elements in that group — and in the exam, you might be asked to do this. For example the Group 1 elements are Li, Na, K, Rb, Cs and Fr. They're all metals and they react in a similar way (see pages 191-196).
9) You can also make predictions about trends in reactivity. E.g. in Group 1, the elements react more vigorously as you go down the group. And in Group 7, reactivity decreases as you go down the group.
10) The rows are called periods. Each new period represents another full shell of electrons.

The modern periodic table is vital for understanding chemistry

This is a good example of how science progresses. A scientist has a basically good (though incomplete) hypothesis (see page 2), other scientists question it and bring more evidence to the table. The hypothesis may be modified or even scrapped to take account of available evidence. Only when all of the available evidence supports a hypothesis will it be accepted.

Topic C1 — Atomic Structure and the Periodic Table

Warm-Up & Exam Questions

The last few pages have been tough with lots of information to learn. Luckily, here are some questions to get your head around to help you test your understanding.

Warm-Up Questions

1) Describe J J Thomson's model of the atom.
2) How many electrons can be held in the following:
   a) the first shell of an atom?
   b) the second shell of an atom?
3) What discovery supported Mendeleev's decision not to place elements in order of atomic weight?

Exam Questions

1 Sodium has an atomic number of 11. *(Grade 4-6)*

1.1 Complete the dot and cross diagram to show the electron configuration of sodium.

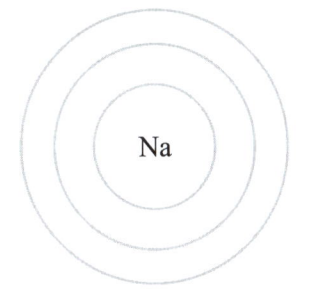

(Na)

[1 mark]

1.2 Sodium is in Group 1.
Name another element that would have the same number of outer shell electrons.

[1 mark]

1.3 How many electrons does sodium need to lose so that it has a full outer shell?

[1 mark]

2 The periodic table contains all the known elements arranged in order. *(Grade 6-7)*

2.1 How were elements generally ordered in early periodic tables?

[1 mark]

2.2 How are the elements arranged in the modern periodic table?

[1 mark]

2.3 If two elements are in the same group of the periodic table what will they have in common? Explain your answer.

[1 mark]

3* Describe how the theory of atomic structure has changed throughout history. *(Grade 7-9)*

[6 marks]

Topic C1 — Atomic Structure and the Periodic Table

Metals and Non-Metals

*Metals are used for all sorts of things so they're **really important** in modern life.*

Most Elements are Metals

1) Metals are elements which can form positive ions when they react.
2) They're towards the bottom and to the left of the periodic table.
3) Most elements in the periodic table are metals.
4) Non-metals are at the far right and top of the periodic table.
5) Non-metals don't generally form positive ions when they react.

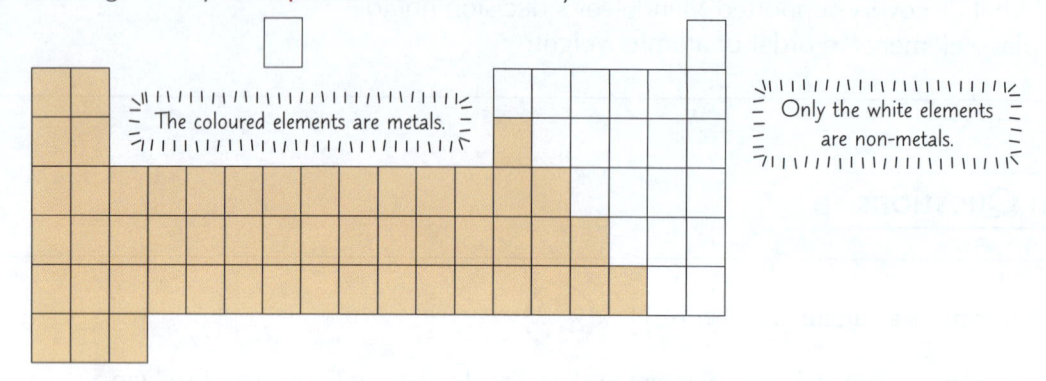

The coloured elements are metals.

Only the white elements are non-metals.

The Electronic Structure of Atoms Affects How They Will React

1) Atoms generally react to form a full outer shell. They do this via losing, gaining or sharing electrons.
2) Metals to the left of the periodic table don't have many electrons to remove and metals towards the bottom of the periodic table have outer electrons which are a long way from the nucleus so feel a weaker attraction. Both these effects mean that not much energy is needed to remove the electrons so it's feasible for the elements to react to form positive ions with a full outer shell.
3) For non-metals, forming positive ions is much more difficult. This is because they are either to the right of the periodic table — where they have lots of electrons to remove to get a full outer shell, or towards the top — where the outer electrons are close to the nucleus so feel a strong attraction. It's far more feasible for them to either share or gain electrons to get a full outer shell.

Metals and Non-Metals Have Different Physical Properties

1) All metals have metallic bonding which causes them to have similar basic physical properties.

   - They're strong (hard to break), but can be bent or hammered into different shapes (malleable).
   - They're great at conducting heat and electricity.
   - They have high boiling and melting points.

2) As non-metals don't have metallic bonding, they don't tend to exhibit the same properties as metals. They tend to be dull looking, more brittle, aren't always solids at room temperature, don't generally conduct electricity and often have a lower density.

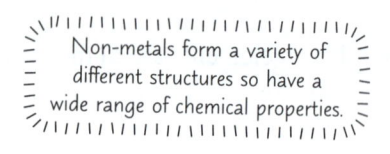

Non-metals form a variety of different structures so have a wide range of chemical properties.

Metals have quite different properties from non-metals

So, all metals can conduct electricity and heat and be bent into shape, whereas mainly non-metals can't.

Topic C1 — Atomic Structure and the Periodic Table

Group 1 Elements

*Group 1 elements are known as the **alkali metals** — these are silvery solids that have to be stored in oil (and handled with forceps) as they're very reactive.*

The Group 1 Elements are Reactive, Soft Metals

1) The alkali metals are lithium, sodium, potassium, rubidium, caesium and francium.
2) The alkali metals are all soft and have low density. The first three in the group are less dense than water.
3) They all have one electron in their outer shell. This makes them very reactive and gives them similar properties.

Trends of Alkali Metals:

The trends for the alkali metals as you go down Group 1 include:

1) Increasing reactivity — the outer electron is more easily lost as the attraction between the nucleus and electron decreases, because the electron is further away from the nucleus the further down the group you go.
2) Lower melting and boiling points.
3) Higher relative atomic mass.

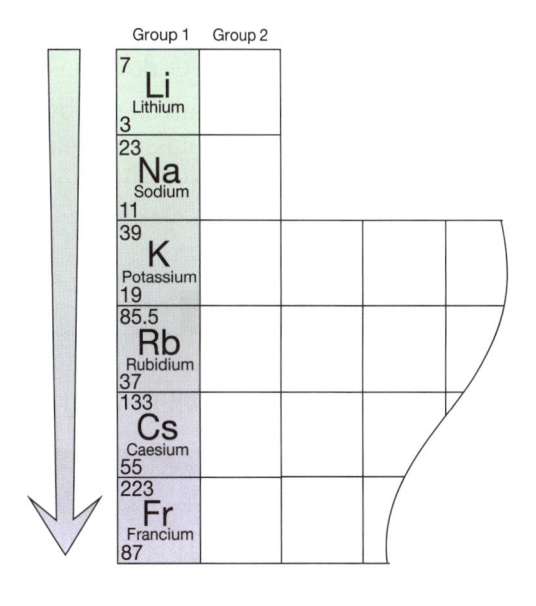

Alkali Metals Form Ionic Compounds with Non-Metals

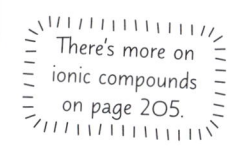

There's more on ionic compounds on page 205.

1) The Group 1 elements don't need much energy to lose their one outer electron to form a full outer shell, so they readily form 1+ ions.
2) It's so easy for them to lose their outer electron that they only ever react form ionic compounds. These compounds are usually white solids that dissolve in water to form colourless solutions.

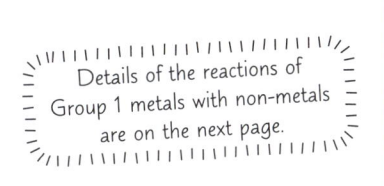

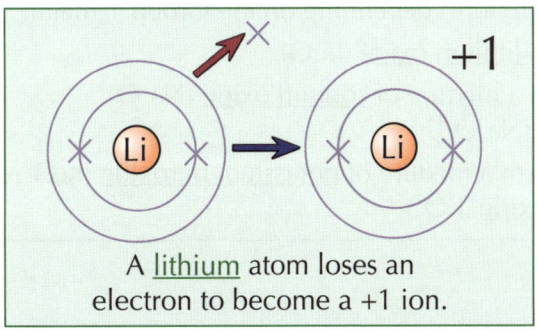

Details of the reactions of Group 1 metals with non-metals are on the next page.

A lithium atom loses an electron to become a +1 ion.

The properties of Group 1 metals change as you go down the group

In the exam you might be given a trend and then asked to predict properties of other Group 1 metals. For example, the reactivity of Group 1 metals increases as you go down the group, so you know that potassium will react more vigorously than sodium.

Topic C1 — Atomic Structure and the Periodic Table

Group 1 Elements

You met **Group 1 metals** on the previous page, so now it's time to learn about some of their **reactions**...

Reactions of Alkali Metals with Non-Metals:

Reaction with water

1) When Group 1 metals are put in water, they react vigorously to produce hydrogen gas and metal hydroxides — compounds that dissolve in water to produce alkaline solutions.

$$2Na_{(s)} + 2H_2O_{(l)} \rightarrow 2NaOH_{(aq)} + H_{2(g)}$$
sodium + water → sodium hydroxide + hydrogen

All the Group 1 metals react with water in a similar way.

2) The more reactive (lower down in the group) an alkali metal is, the more violent the reaction.
3) The amount of energy given out by the reaction increases down the group — the reaction with potassium releases enough energy to ignite hydrogen.

Reaction with chlorine

1) Group 1 metals react vigorously when heated in chlorine gas to form white metal chloride salts.

$$2Na_{(s)} + Cl_{2(g)} \rightarrow 2NaCl_{(s)}$$
sodium + chlorine → sodium chloride

2) As you go down the group, reactivity increases so the reaction with chlorine gets more vigorous.

Reaction with oxygen

The Group 1 metals can react with oxygen to form a metal oxide. Different types of oxide will form depending on the Group 1 metal:

- Lithium reacts to form lithium oxide (Li_2O).
- Sodium reacts to form a mixture of sodium oxide (Na_2O) and sodium peroxide (Na_2O_2).
- Potassium reacts to form a mixture of potassium peroxide (K_2O_2) and potassium superoxide (KO_2).

The reactions with oxygen are why Group 1 metals tarnish in the air — the metal reacts with oxygen in the air to form a dull metal oxide layer.

So now you know why they are called alkali metals...

...because they react with water to give alkaline solutions. Make sure you also know how they react with chlorine and oxygen. Memorise a couple of example equations for these reactions.

Q1 Write a word equation for the reaction between lithium and water. [1 mark]

Topic C1 — Atomic Structure and the Periodic Table

Group 7 Elements

*The **Group 7** elements are known as the halogens. Similarly to the **alkali metals**, halogens also show trends down the group. However, these trends are a bit different...*

The Halogens are All Non-Metals with Coloured Vapours

- Fluorine is a very reactive, poisonous yellow gas.
- Chlorine is a fairly reactive, poisonous dense green gas.
- Bromine is a dense, poisonous, red-brown volatile liquid.
- Iodine is a dark grey crystalline solid or a purple vapour.
- They all exist as molecules which are pairs of atoms.

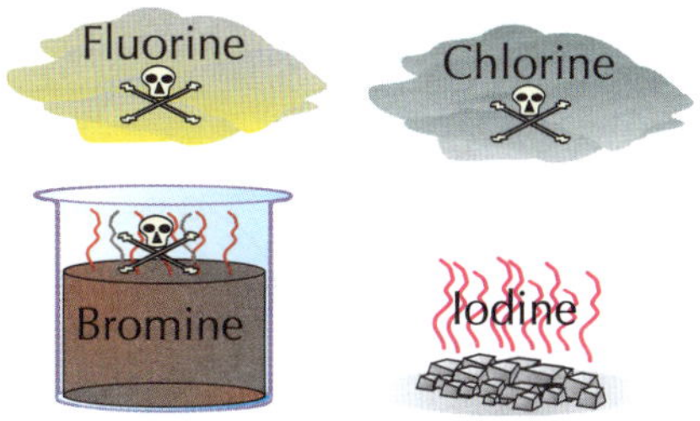

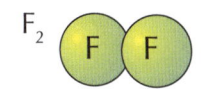

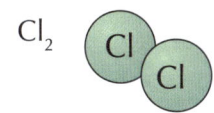

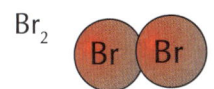

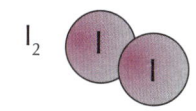

F_2 Cl_2 Br_2 I_2

Learn These Trends:

As you go down Group 7, the halogens:

1) become less reactive — it's harder to gain an extra electron, because the outer shell's further from the nucleus.
2) have higher melting and boiling points.
3) have higher relative atomic masses.

All the Group 7 elements react in similar ways. This is because they all have seven electrons in their outer shell.

You can use these trends to predict properties of halogens. For example, you know that iodine will have a higher boiling point than chlorine as it's further down the group in the periodic table.

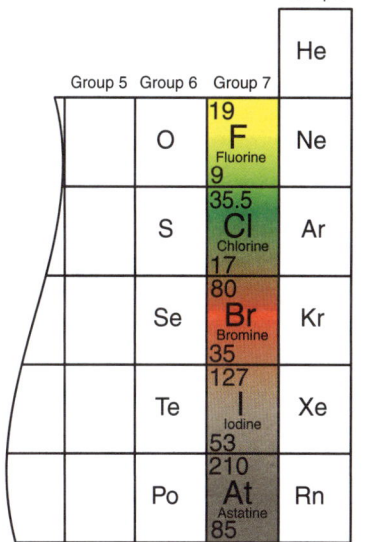

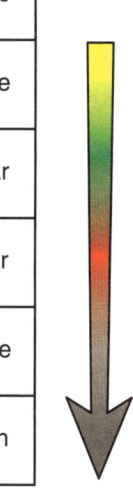

Halogens can Form Molecular Compounds

Halogen atoms can share electrons via covalent bonding (see page 208) with other non-metals so as to achieve a full outer shell. For example HCl, PCl_5, HF and CCl_4 contain covalent bonds. The compounds that form when halogens react with non-metals all have simple molecular structures.

Halogens all exist as molecules with two atoms

Just like alkali metals, you may be asked to predict the properties of a halogen from a given trend down the group. Make sure you understand why their electronic structure means halogens react in similar ways.

Topic C1 — Atomic Structure and the Periodic Table

Group 7 Elements

Halogens Form **Ionic Bonds** with **Metals**

1) The halogens form <u>1– ions</u> called <u>halides</u> (F⁻, Cl⁻, Br⁻ and I⁻) when they bond with <u>metals</u>, for example Na⁺Cl⁻ or Fe³⁺Br⁻₃.
2) The compounds that form have <u>ionic structures</u>.
3) The diagram shows the bonding in sodium chloride, NaCl.

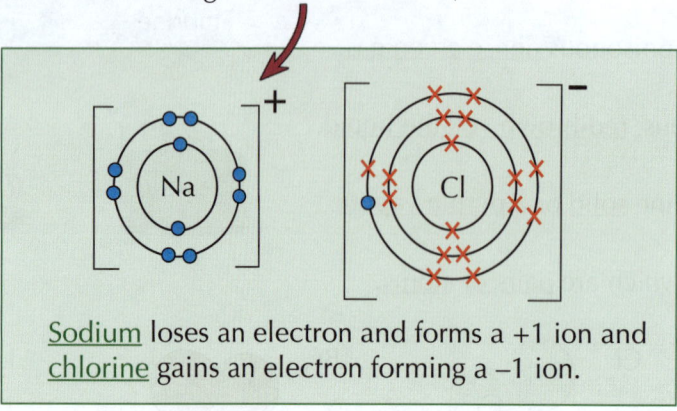

<u>Sodium</u> loses an electron and forms a +1 ion and <u>chlorine</u> gains an electron forming a –1 ion.

More Reactive Halogens Will **Displace** Less Reactive Ones

A <u>displacement reaction</u> can occur between a more reactive halogen and the salt of a less reactive one.

For example, <u>chlorine</u> can displace <u>bromine</u> and <u>iodine</u> from an aqueous <u>solution</u> of its salt (a <u>bromide</u> or <u>iodide</u>). <u>Bromine</u> will also displace <u>iodine</u> because of the <u>trend</u> in <u>reactivity</u>.

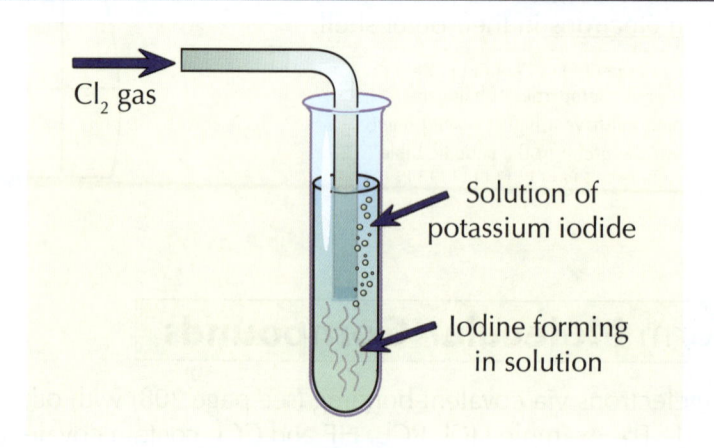

$$Cl_{2\,(g)} + 2KI_{(aq)} \rightarrow I_{2\,(aq)} + 2KCl_{(aq)}$$
Pale Green — Brown

$$Cl_{2\,(g)} + 2KBr_{(aq)} \rightarrow Br_{2\,(aq)} + 2KCl_{(aq)}$$
Pale Green — Orange

Cl₂ gas — Solution of potassium iodide — Iodine forming in solution

Halogens all have different reactivities

You don't have to be a mind-reader to be able to guess the kind of thing they could ask you about <u>halogens</u> in the exam. Something about <u>displacement reactions</u> seems very possible — will iodine displace bromine from some compound or other, for instance. Make sure you learn the <u>trends</u> too.

Q1 Give the balanced symbol equation for the displacement reaction between bromine and sodium iodide. [1 mark]

Topic C1 — Atomic Structure and the Periodic Table

Group 0 Elements

*The **noble gases don't react** with very much and you can't even see them — makes them, a bit **dull** really.*

Group 0 Elements are All Inert, Colourless Gases

1) Group 0 elements are called the noble gases and include the elements helium, neon and argon (plus a few others).
2) They all have eight electrons in their outer energy level, apart from helium which has two, giving them a full outer-shell. As their outer shell is energetically stable they don't need to give up or gain electrons to become more stable. This means they are more or less inert — they don't react with much at all.

   Helium only has electrons in the first shell, which only needs 2 to be filled.
3) They exist as monatomic gases — single atoms not bonded to each other.
4) All elements in Group 0 are colourless gases at room temperature.
5) As the noble gases are inert they're non-flammable — they won't set on fire.

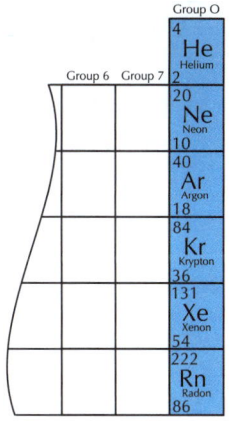

There are Patterns in the Properties of the Noble Gases

1) The boiling points of the noble gases increase as you move down the group along with increasing relative atomic mass.
2) The increase in boiling point is due to an increase in the number of electrons in each atom leading to greater intermolecular forces between them which need to be overcome. There's more on intermolecular forces for small molecules on page 210.
3) In the exam you may be given the boiling point of one noble gas and asked to estimate the value for another one. So make sure you know the pattern.

Noble Gas
helium
neon
argon
krypton
xenon
radon

Increasing boiling point ↓

EXAMPLE
Neon is a gas at 25°C. Predict what state helium is at this temperature.

Helium has a lower boiling than neon as it is further up the group.
So, helium must also be a gas at 25°C.

EXAMPLE
Radon and krypton have boiling points of −62 °C and −153 °C respectively. Predict the boiling point of xenon.

Xenon comes in between radon and krypton in the group so you can predict that its boiling point would be halfway between their boiling points: (−153) + (−62) = −215
−215 ÷ 2 = −107.5 ≈ −108°C

So, xenon should have a boiling point of about −108 °C

The actual boiling point of xenon is −108 °C — just as predicted.

Just like other groups of elements, the noble gases follow patterns...

Although they're unreactive and hard to see, they're actually pretty useful. It took a while to discover them, but we now know all about them, including the trend in their boiling points.

Topic C1 — Atomic Structure and the Periodic Table

Warm-Up & Exam Questions

These questions are all about the groups of the periodic table that you need to know about. Treat the exam questions like the real thing — don't look back through the book until you've finished.

Warm-Up Questions

1) What kind of ions do metals form?
2) Give three physical properties of most metals.
3) Which product is formed when lithium reacts with oxygen?
4) Do halide ions have a positive or a negative charge?
5) In which group of the periodic table are the noble gases?

Exam Questions

1 Table 1 shows some of the physical properties of four of the halogens. *Grade 4-6*

Table 1

Halogen	Properties			
	Atomic number	Colour	Physical state at room temperature	Reactivity
Fluorine	9	yellow	gas	....
Chlorine	17	green	gas	....
Bromine	35	red-brown	liquid	....
Iodine	53	dark grey	solid	....

1.1 Table 1 has a column for reactivity. Write an **X** in the row of the halogen with the **highest** reactivity and a **Y** in the row of the halogen with the **lowest** reactivity.

[2 marks]

1.2 Which halogen in **Table 1** has the highest melting point?

[1 mark]

2 Figure 1 shows the periodic table. *Grade 4-6*

2.1 Element **X** is found in the first column of the periodic table. What name is given to the elements found in this part of the table?

[1 mark]

2.2 Element **Y** does not conduct electricity. Predict whether element **Y** will be found to the left or the right of line **A** in **Figure 1**. Explain your answer.

[2 marks]

Topic C1 — Atomic Structure and the Periodic Table

Exam Questions

3 Chlorine is a Group 7 element.
Its electron arrangement is shown in the diagram below.

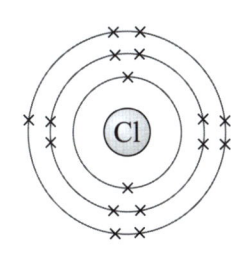

Grade 6-7

3.1 Chlorine is very reactive and forms compounds with metals.
What type of bonds form between chlorine and metals?

[1 mark]

When chlorine is bubbled through potassium iodide solution a reaction occurs.
The equation below shows the reaction.

$$Cl_{2(g)} + 2KI_{(aq)} \rightarrow I_{2(aq)} + 2KCl_{(aq)}$$

3.2 State what type of reaction this is.

[1 mark]

3.3 Which is the less reactive halogen in this reaction? Explain your answer.

[2 marks]

3.4 Chlorine gas can also react with potassium bromide.
Using your knowledge of Group 7 elements predict the products of this reaction and their states.
Give an explanation for you answer.

[4 marks]

3.5 None of the elements in Group 0 will react with potassium iodide or potassium bromide.
Using your knowledge of the electronic structure of the Group 0 elements,
explain why no reaction occurs.

[2 marks]

4 Group 1 elements are metals.
They include lithium, sodium and potassium.

Grade 6-7

4.1 Explain why the Group 1 elements react vigorously with water.

[1 mark]

4.2 The Group 1 elements all react with water at a different rate. Explain why this is.

[3 marks]

4.3 Give the two products formed when potassium reacts with water.

[2 marks]

4.4 During these reactions a solution is formed.
Is this solution acidic, neutral or alkaline?

[1 marks]

Topic C1 — Atomic Structure and the Periodic Table

Topic C2 — Bonding, Structure and Properties of Matter

Ions

Ions crop up all over the place in chemistry. You're gonna have to be able to explain **how** they form and predict the **charges** of simple ions formed by elements in Groups 1, 2, 6 and 7.

Ions are Made When Electrons are Transferred

1) <u>Ions</u> are <u>charged</u> particles — they can be <u>single atoms</u> (e.g. Cl⁻) or <u>groups of atoms</u> (e.g. NO₃⁻).

2) When <u>atoms</u> lose or gain electrons to form ions, all they're trying to do is get a <u>full outer shell</u> like a <u>noble gas</u> (also called a "<u>stable electronic structure</u>"). Atoms with full outer shells are very <u>stable</u>.

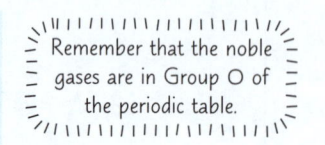

   Remember that the noble gases are in Group 0 of the periodic table.

3) When <u>metals</u> form ions, they <u>lose</u> electrons from their <u>outer shell</u> to form <u>positive ions</u>.

4) When <u>non-metals</u> form ions, they <u>gain</u> electrons into their <u>outer shell</u> to form <u>negative ions</u>.

5) The <u>number</u> of electrons lost or gained is the same as the <u>charge</u> on the ion. E.g. If 2 electrons are <u>lost</u> the charge is 2+. If 3 electrons are <u>gained</u> the charge is 3–.

Ionic Bonding — Transfer of Electrons

1) When a <u>metal</u> and a <u>non-metal</u> react together, the <u>metal atom loses</u> electrons to form a <u>positively charged ion</u> and the <u>non-metal gains these electrons</u> to form a <u>negatively charged ion</u>.

2) These oppositely charged ions are <u>strongly attracted</u> to one another by <u>electrostatic forces</u>. This attraction is called an <u>ionic bond</u>.

3) The diagram below shows the formation of an <u>ionic bond</u> between sodium and chlorine to form the ionic compound <u>sodium chloride</u>.

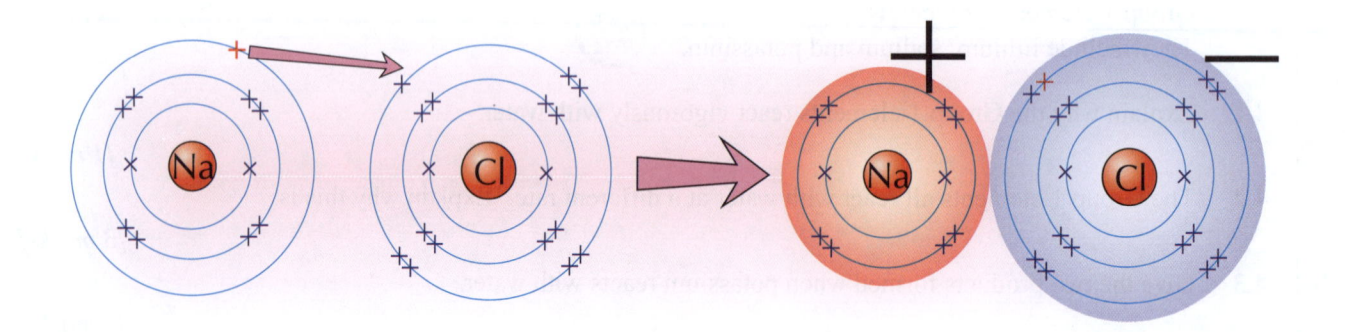

Metals and non-metals form ionic bonds

Some atoms <u>gain</u> electrons and some atoms <u>lose</u> electrons. An ionic bond is just the <u>attraction</u> between the electrostatic charges of the newly formed ions.

Q1   Explain why simple ions often have noble gas electronic structures.   [2 marks]

Ions

*You don't need to remember what elements form which ions — the **periodic table** is here to help you...*

Groups **1 & 2** and **6 & 7** are the Most Likely to Form **Ions**

1) The elements that <u>most readily</u> form ions are those in <u>Groups 1, 2, 6 and 7</u>.
2) <u>Group 1 and 2 elements</u> are <u>metals</u> and they <u>lose</u> electrons to form <u>positive ions</u> (<u>cations</u>).
3) <u>Group 6 and 7 elements</u> are <u>non-metals</u>. They <u>gain</u> electrons to form <u>negative ions</u> (<u>anions</u>).
4) Elements in the same <u>group</u> all have the same number of <u>outer electrons</u>. So they have to <u>lose or gain</u> the same number to get a full outer shell. And this means that they form ions with the <u>same charges</u>.

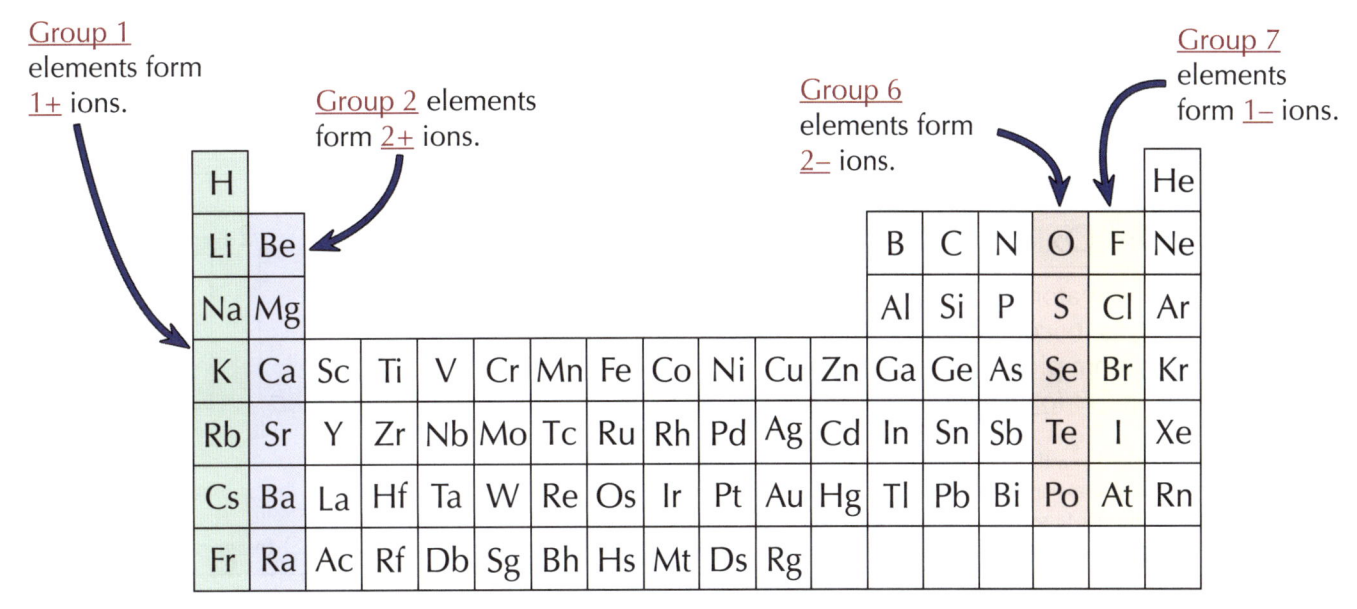

<u>Group 1</u> elements form <u>1+</u> ions.

<u>Group 2</u> elements form <u>2+</u> ions.

<u>Group 6</u> elements form <u>2−</u> ions.

<u>Group 7</u> elements form <u>1−</u> ions.

H																	He
Li	Be											B	C	N	O	F	Ne
Na	Mg											Al	Si	P	S	Cl	Ar
K	Ca	Sc	Ti	V	Cr	Mn	Fe	Co	Ni	Cu	Zn	Ga	Ge	As	Se	Br	Kr
Rb	Sr	Y	Zr	Nb	Mo	Tc	Ru	Rh	Pd	Ag	Cd	In	Sn	Sb	Te	I	Xe
Cs	Ba	La	Hf	Ta	W	Re	Os	Ir	Pt	Au	Hg	Tl	Pb	Bi	Po	At	Rn
Fr	Ra	Ac	Rf	Db	Sg	Bh	Hs	Mt	Ds	Rg							

Have a look back at page 190 for how to work out electronic structures.

A <u>sodium</u> atom (Na) is in <u>Group 1</u> so it <u>loses</u> 1 electron to form a sodium ion (Na$^+$) with the same electronic structure as <u>neon</u>: Na → Na$^+$ + e$^−$.

A <u>magnesium</u> atom (Mg) is in <u>Group 2</u> so it <u>loses</u> 2 electrons to form a magnesium ion (Mg^{2+}) with the same electronic structure as <u>neon</u>: Mg → Mg^{2+} + 2e$^−$.

A <u>chlorine</u> atom (Cl) is in <u>Group 7</u> so it <u>gains</u> 1 electron to form a chloride ion (Cl$^−$) with the same electronic structure as <u>argon</u>: Cl + e$^−$ → Cl$^−$.

An <u>oxygen</u> atom (O) is in <u>Group 6</u> so it <u>gains</u> 2 electrons to form an oxide ion (O$^{2−}$) with the same electronic structure as <u>neon</u>: O + 2e$^−$ → O$^{2−}$.

Topic C2 — Bonding, Structure and Properties of Matter

Ions

Dot and Cross Diagrams Show How Ionic Bonds are Formed

Dot and cross diagrams show the arrangement of electrons in an atom or ion. Each electron is represented by a dot or a cross. So these diagrams can show which atom the electrons in an ion originally came from.

Sodium Chloride (NaCl)

The sodium atom gives up its outer electron, becoming an Na⁺ ion. The chlorine atom picks up the electron, becoming a Cl⁻ (chloride) ion.

Here, the dots represent the Na electrons and the crosses represent the Cl electrons (all electrons are really identical, but this is a good way of following their movement).

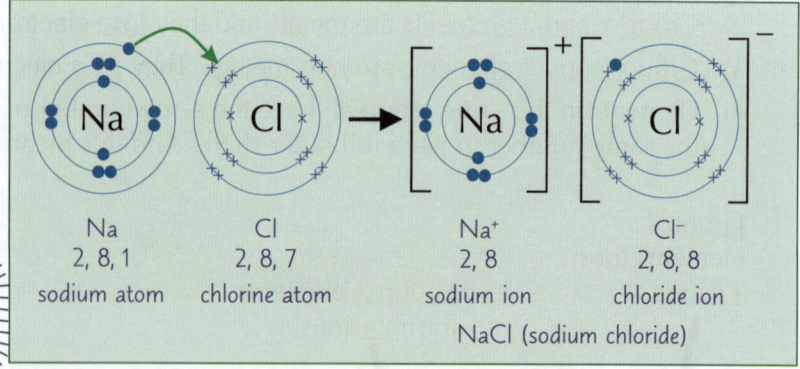

Na — 2, 8, 1 — sodium atom
Cl — 2, 8, 7 — chlorine atom
Na⁺ — 2, 8 — sodium ion
Cl⁻ — 2, 8, 8 — chloride ion
NaCl (sodium chloride)

Magnesium Oxide (MgO)

The magnesium atom gives up its two outer electrons, becoming an Mg²⁺ ion. The oxygen atom picks up the electrons, becoming an O²⁻ (oxide) ion.

Here we've only shown the outer shells of electrons on the dot and cross diagram — it makes it much simpler to see what's going on.

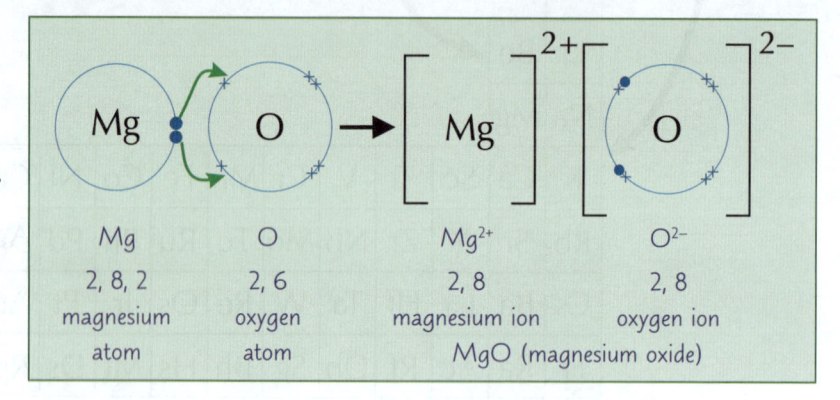

Mg — 2, 8, 2 — magnesium atom
O — 2, 6 — oxygen atom
Mg²⁺ — 2, 8 — magnesium ion
O²⁻ — 2, 8 — oxygen ion
MgO (magnesium oxide)

Magnesium Chloride (MgCl₂)

The magnesium atom gives up its two outer electrons, becoming an Mg²⁺ ion.
The two chlorine atoms pick up one electron each, becoming two Cl⁻ (chloride) ions.

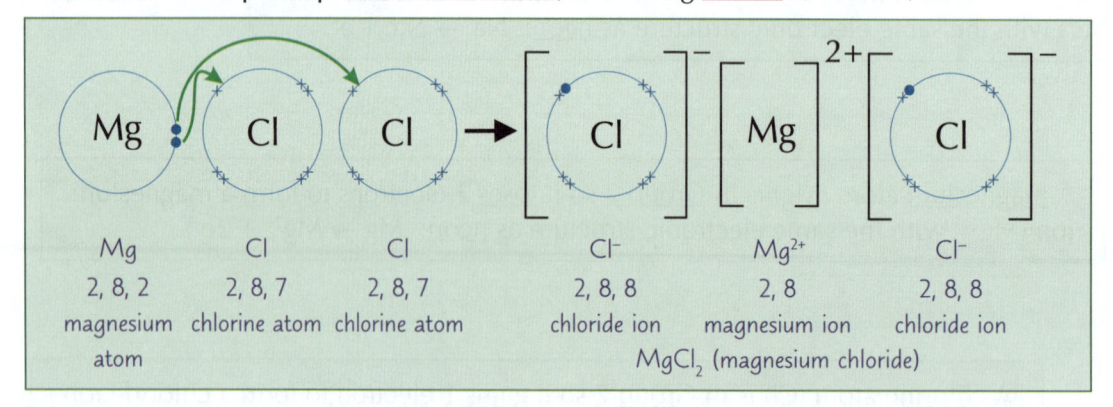

Mg — 2, 8, 2 — magnesium atom
Cl — 2, 8, 7 — chlorine atom
Cl — 2, 8, 7 — chlorine atom
Cl⁻ — 2, 8, 8 — chloride ion
Mg²⁺ — 2, 8 — magnesium ion
Cl⁻ — 2, 8, 8 — chloride ion
MgCl₂ (magnesium chloride)

Dot and cross diagrams are useful for showing how ionic compounds are formed, but they don't show the structure of the compound, the size of the ions or how they're arranged.

Show the electronic structure of ions with square brackets

Whether or not you're able to reproduce the drawings on this page all comes down to how well you've understood ionic bonding. (So if you're struggling, try reading the previous few pages again.)

Q1 Describe what is represented on a dot and cross diagram by an arrow pointing from an electron shell of one atom to an electron shell of another atom. [1 mark]

Q2 Draw a dot and cross diagram to show how potassium (a Group 1 metal) and bromine (a Group 7 non-metal) form potassium bromide (KBr). [3 marks]

Topic C2 — Bonding, Structure and Properties of Matter

Ionic Compounds

*An **ionic compound** is any compound that only contains **ionic bonds**...*

Ionic Compounds Have A Regular Lattice Structure

1) Ionic compounds have a structure called a giant ionic lattice.
2) The ions form a closely packed regular lattice arrangement and there are very strong electrostatic forces of attraction between oppositely charged ions, in all directions in the lattice.

The electrostatic attraction between the oppositely charged ions is ionic bonding.

A single crystal of sodium chloride (table salt) is one giant ionic lattice. The Na^+ and Cl^- ions are held together in a regular lattice. The lattice can be represented in different ways...

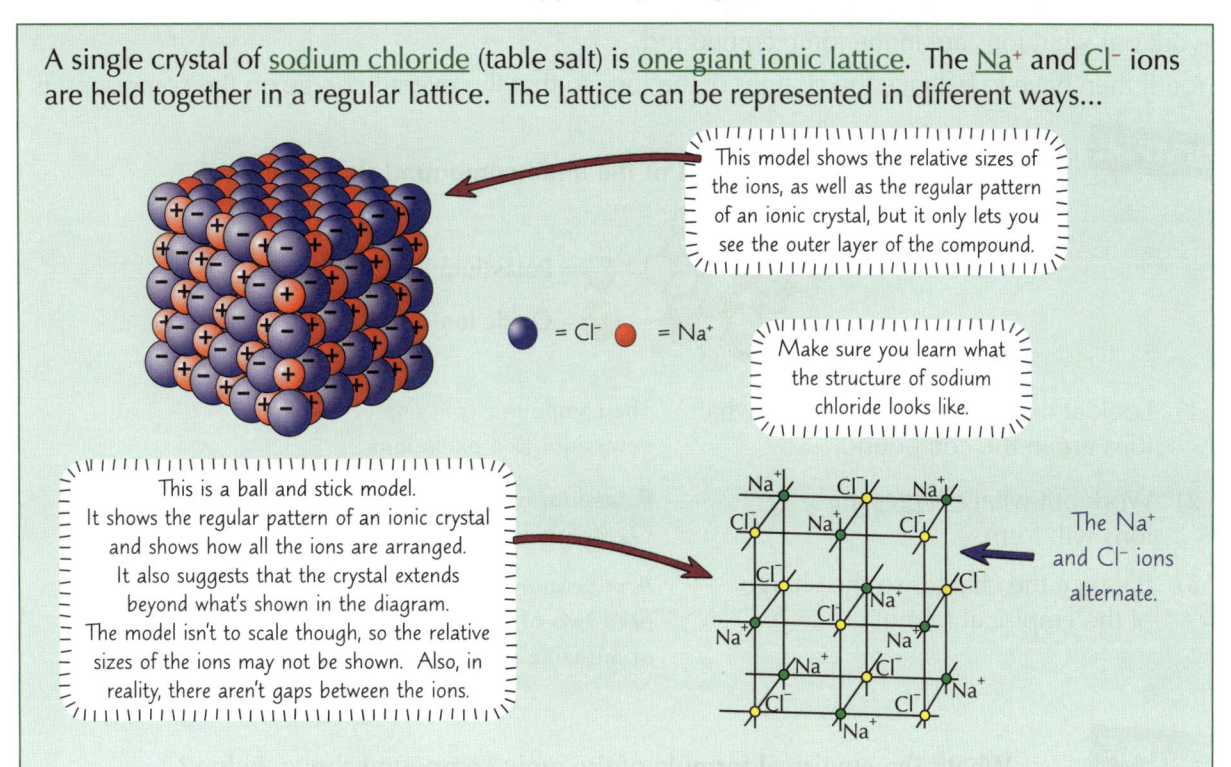

This model shows the relative sizes of the ions, as well as the regular pattern of an ionic crystal, but it only lets you see the outer layer of the compound.

● = Cl^- ● = Na^+

Make sure you learn what the structure of sodium chloride looks like.

This is a ball and stick model. It shows the regular pattern of an ionic crystal and shows how all the ions are arranged. It also suggests that the crystal extends beyond what's shown in the diagram. The model isn't to scale though, so the relative sizes of the ions may not be shown. Also, in reality, there aren't gaps between the ions.

The Na^+ and Cl^- ions alternate.

Ionic Compounds All Have Similar Properties

1) They all have high melting points and high boiling points due to the many strong bonds between the ions. It takes lots of energy to overcome this attraction.
2) When they're solid, the ions are held in place, so the compounds can't conduct electricity.
3) When ionic compounds melt, the ions are free to move and they'll carry electric charge.
4) Some ionic compounds also dissolve easily in water. The ions separate and are all free to move in the solution, so they'll carry electric charge.

Dissolved in water

Melted

Topic C2 — Bonding, Structure and Properties of Matter

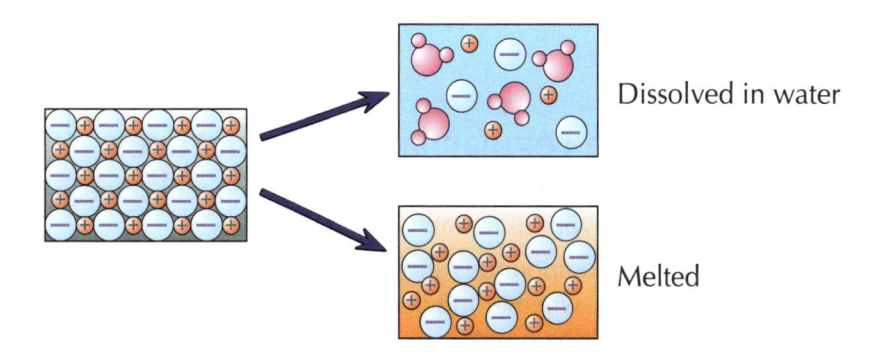

Ionic Compounds

Look at Charges to Find the Formula of an Ionic Compound

1) You might have to work out the empirical formula of an ionic compound from a diagram of the compound.
2) If it's a dot and cross diagram, count up how many atoms there are of each element. Write this down to give you the empirical formula.
3) If you're given a 3D diagram of the ionic lattice, use it to work out what ions are in the ionic compound.
4) You'll then have to balance the charges of the ions so that the overall charge on the compound is zero.

EXAMPLE What's the empirical formula of the ionic compound shown below?

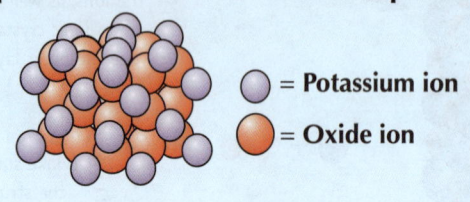

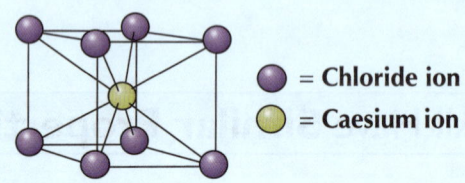

◯ = Potassium ion
🟠 = Oxide ion

1) Look at the diagram to work out what ions are in the compound.
   The compound contains potassium and oxide ions.
2) Work out what charges the ions will form.
   Potassium is in Group 1 so forms 1+ ions. Oxygen is in Group 6 so forms 2− ions.
3) Balance the charges so the charge of the empirical formula is zero.
   A potassium ion only has a 1+ charge, so you'll need two of them to balance out the 2− charge of an oxide ion. The empirical formula is K_2O.

EXAMPLE What's the empirical formula of the ionic compound shown below?

● = Chloride ion
● = Caesium ion

1) Look at the diagram to work out what ions are in the compound.
   The compound contains caesium ions and chloride ions.
2) Work out what charges the ions will form.
   Caesium is in Group 1 so forms 1+ ions. Chlorine is in Group 7 so forms 1− ions.
3) Balance the charges so the charge of the empirical formula is zero.
   A caesium ion has a 1+ charge, so you only need one to balance out the 1− charge of the chloride ion. The empirical formula is CsCl.

Ionic compounds have regular lattice structures

As long as you can find the charge of the ions in an ionic compound, you can work out the empirical formula. Try practising with different ionic compounds.

● = sulfide ion
● = magnesium ion

Q1 The structure of an ionic compound is shown on the right.
   a) Predict, with reasoning, whether the compound has a high or a low melting point. [2 marks]
   b) Explain why the compound can conduct electricity when molten. [1 mark]
   c) Use the diagram to find the empirical formula of the compound. [3 marks]

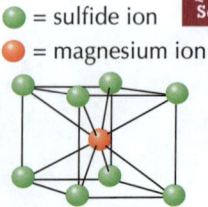

Topic C2 — Bonding, Structure and Properties of Matter

Warm-Up & Exam Questions

Congratulations you got to the end of the pages on ions — time to make sure you know them back to front...

Warm-Up Questions

1) What is an ion?
2) What is the charge on a ion formed from a Group 2 element?
3) What is the charge on a ion formed from a Group 7 element?
4) Sodium chloride has a giant ionic structure. Does it have a high or a low boiling point?
5) Why do some ionic compounds conduct electricity when dissolved in water?
6) What is the formula of the compound containing Al^{3+} and OH^- ions only?

Exam Questions

1 **Figure 1** shows the electronic structures of sodium and fluorine.

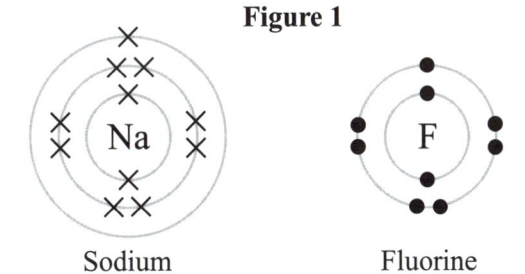

Grade 4-6

Figure 1

Sodium   Fluorine

1.1 Describe what will happen when sodium and fluorine react, in terms of electrons.

[2 marks]

1.2 When sodium and fluorine react they form an ionic compound.
Describe the structure of an ionic compound

[3 marks]

2 When lithium reacts with oxygen it forms the ionic compound Li_2O.

Grade 6-7

2.1 Name the compound formed.

[1 mark]

2.2 Complete **Figure 2** below using arrows to show how the electrons are transferred when Li_2O is formed. Show the electron arrangements and the charges on the ions formed.

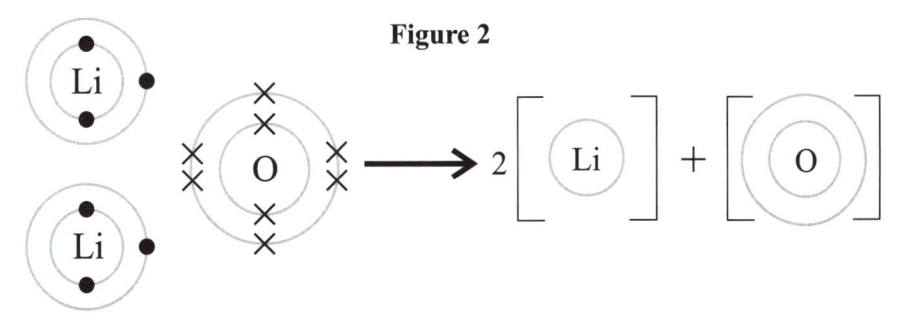

Figure 2

[3 marks]

2.3 Explain why Li_2O conducts electricity when molten.

[2 marks]

2.4 Lithium forms an ionic compound with chlorine.
What is the formula of this compound? Explain why this is.

[2 marks]

Topic C2 — Bonding, Structure and Properties of Matter

Covalent Bonding

*Some elements bond ionically (see page 202) but others form strong **covalent** bonds. This is where atoms **share** electrons with each other so that they've got full outer shells.*

Covalent Bonds — Sharing Electrons

1) When non-metal atoms bond together, they share pairs of electrons to make covalent bonds.
2) The positively charged nuclei of the bonded atoms are attracted to the shared pair of electrons by electrostatic forces, making covalent bonds very strong.
3) Atoms only share electrons in their outer shells (highest energy levels).
4) Each single covalent bond provides one extra shared electron for each atom.
5) Each atom involved generally makes enough covalent bonds to fill up its outer shell. Having a full outer shell gives them the electronic structure of a noble gas, which is very stable.
6) Covalent bonding happens in compounds of non-metals (e.g. H_2O) and in non-metal elements (e.g. Cl_2).

There are Different Ways of Drawing Covalent Bonds

1) You can use dot and cross diagrams to show the bonding in covalent compounds.
2) Electrons drawn in the overlap between the outer orbitals of two atoms are shared between those atoms.
3) Dot and cross diagrams are useful for showing which atoms the electrons in a covalent bond come from, but they don't show the relative sizes of the atoms, or how the atoms are arranged in space.
4) The displayed formula of ammonia (NH_3) shows the covalent bonds as single lines between atoms.
5) This is a great way of showing how atoms are connected in large molecules. However, they don't show the 3D structure of the molecule, or which atoms the electrons in the covalent bond have come from.
6) The 3D model of ammonia shows the atoms, the covalent bonds and their arrangement in space next to each other. But 3D models can quickly get confusing for large molecules where there are lots of atoms to include. They don't show where the electrons in the bonds have come from, either.
7) You can find the molecular formula of a simple molecular compound from any of these diagrams by counting up how many atoms of each element there are.

Nitrogen has five outer electrons...

...so it needs to form three covalent bonds to make up the extra three electrons needed.

You don't have to draw the orbitals in dot and cross diagrams. The important thing is that you get all the dots and crosses in the right places.

A molecular formula shows you how many atoms of each element are in a molecule.

EXAMPLE

A diagram of the molecule ethane is shown on the right. Use the diagram to find the molecular formula of ethane.

In the diagram, there are two carbon atoms and six hydrogen atoms. So the molecular formula is C_2H_6.

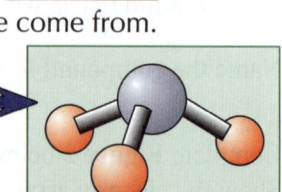

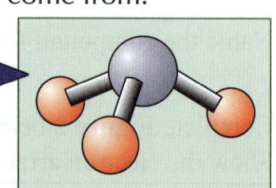

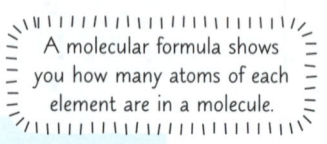

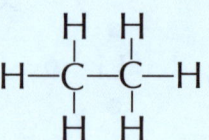

Covalent bonds involve the sharing of a pair of electrons

There are dot and cross diagrams for more covalent molecules on the next two pages, but make sure you can draw the different diagrams that are used to show the bonding in ammonia first.

Q1 Draw a dot and cross diagram to show the bonding in a molecule of ammonia (NH_3). [2 marks]

Topic C2 — Bonding, Structure and Properties of Matter

Covalent Bonding

Learn Some Examples of Simple Molecular Substances

Simple molecular substances are made up of molecules containing a few atoms joined together by covalent bonds. Here are some common examples that you should know...

Hydrogen, H₂

Hydrogen atoms have just one electron. They only need one more to complete the first shell...

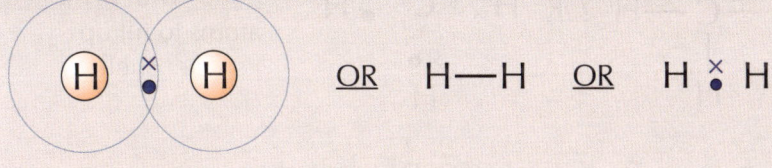

...so they often form single covalent bonds, either with other hydrogen atoms or with other elements, to achieve this.

Chlorine, Cl₂

Each chlorine atom needs just one more electron to complete the outer shell...

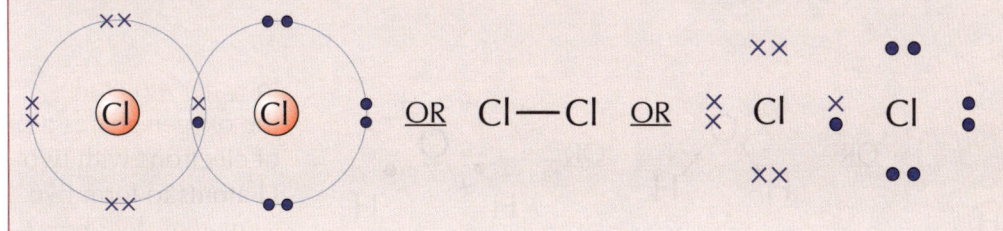

...so two chlorine atoms can share one pair of electrons and form a single covalent bond.

Oxygen, O₂

Each oxygen atom needs two more electrons to complete its outer shell...

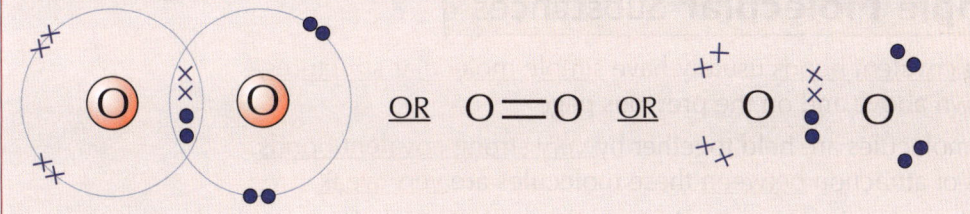

...so in oxygen gas two oxygen atoms share two pairs of electrons with each other making a double covalent bond.

Nitrogen, N₂

A nitrogen atom needs three more electrons to complete its outer shell...

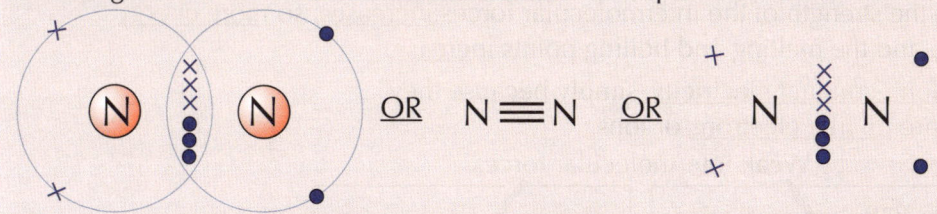

...so two nitrogen atoms share three pairs of electrons to fill their outer shells. This creates a triple bond.

Hydrogen chloride, HCl

This is very similar to H₂ and Cl₂...

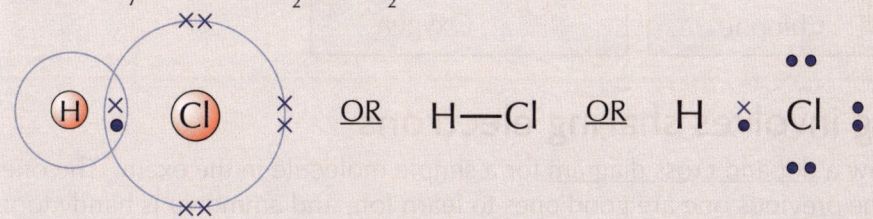

...again, both atoms only need one more electron to complete their outer shells.

Topic C2 — Bonding, Structure and Properties of Matter

Covalent Bonding

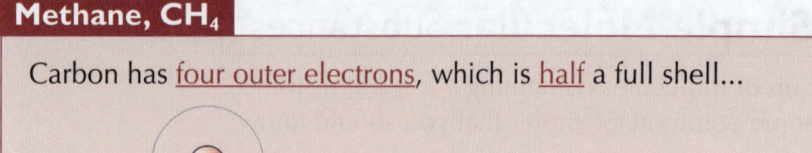

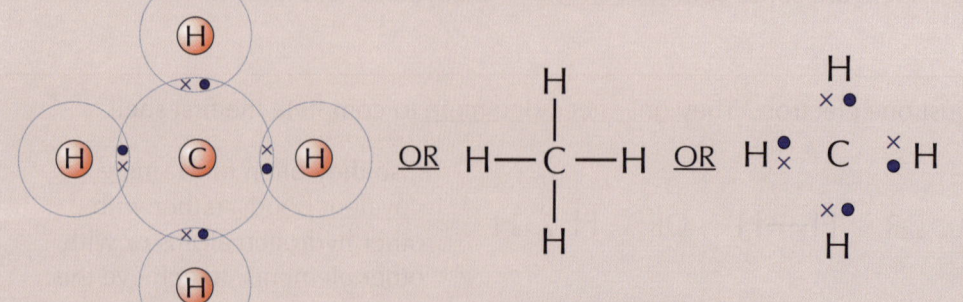

Methane, CH₄

Carbon has four outer electrons, which is half a full shell...

It can form four covalent bonds with hydrogen atoms to fill up its outer shell.

Make sure you can also draw the dot and cross diagram of ammonia, NH₃, which is on page 208.

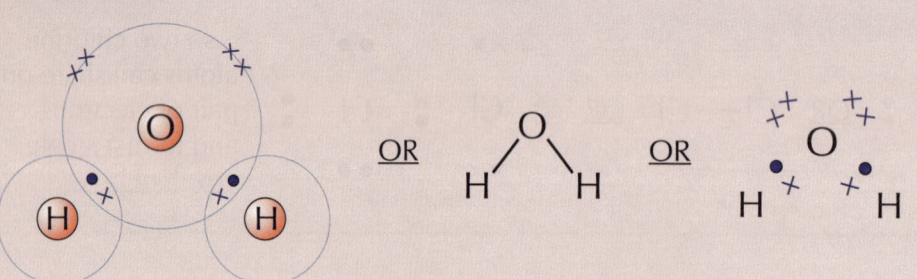

Water, H₂O

In water molecules, the oxygen shares a pair of electrons with two H atoms to form two single covalent bonds.

Properties of Simple Molecular Substances

1) Substances containing covalent bonds usually have simple molecular structures, like the examples shown above and on the previous page.
2) The atoms within the molecules are held together by very strong covalent bonds. By contrast, the forces of attraction between these molecules are very weak.
3) To melt or boil a simple molecular compound, you only need to break these feeble intermolecular forces and not the covalent bonds. So the melting and boiling points are very low, because the molecules are easily parted from each other.
4) Most molecular substances are gases or liquids at room temperature.
5) As molecules get bigger, the strength of the intermolecular forces increases, so more energy is needed to break them, and the melting and boiling points increase.
6) Molecular compounds don't conduct electricity, simply because they aren't charged, so there are no free electrons or ions.

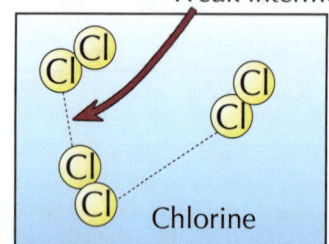

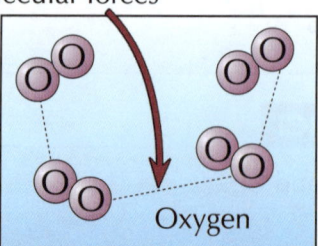

Weak intermolecular forces

Chlorine

Oxygen

Covalent bonding involves sharing electrons

EXAM TIP You might be asked to draw a dot and cross diagram for a simple molecule in the exam. The ones shown on this page and the previous one are good ones to learn (oh, and ammonia is handy too).

Topic C2 — Bonding, Structure and Properties of Matter

Warm-Up & Exam Questions

The questions on this page are all about covalent bonding. Go through them and if you have any problems, make sure you look back at the relevant pages again until you've got to grips with it.

Warm-Up Questions

1) What is a covalent bond?
2) How many covalent bonds does a molecule of nitrogen have?
3) In which states are most simple molecular substances at room temperature?
4) Which forces are stronger in simple molecular substances — covalent bonds or intermolecular forces?
5) What forces need to be overcome to boil a simple molecular compound?

Exam Questions

1 Methane is a covalently bonded molecule with the formula CH_4. *(Grade 4-6)*

Complete the dot and cross diagram for the methane molecule.
Show only the outer electrons.

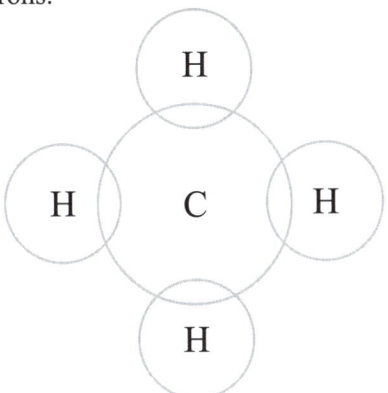

[2 marks]

2 Dot and cross diagrams can be used to show the position of electrons in covalent molecules. *(Grade 4-6)*

2.1 Draw a dot and cross diagram for oxygen (O_2). Only show the outer electrons.

[2 marks]

2.2 Nitrogen is in Group 5 of the periodic table.
How many bonds does it need to make to gain a full outer shell?

[1 mark]

3 Hydrogen chloride is a simple molecular substance. *(Grade 6-7)*

3.1 Explain why hydrogen chloride has poor electrical conductivity.

[1 mark]

3.2 Explain how the atoms are held together in a molecule of hydrogen chloride.

[2 marks]

3.3 A molecule of hydrogen chloride has a stronger bond than a molecule of chlorine (Cl_2).
However, hydrogen chloride boils at −85 °C, whereas chlorine boils at −34 °C.
Suggest and explain why chlorine has a higher boiling point than hydrogen chloride.

[3 marks]

Topic C2 — Bonding, Structure and Properties of Matter

Polymers

*Most polymers are held together with **covalent bonds**. However, these molecules are a bit different to the simple covalent compounds you have already met...*

Polymers Are Long Chains of Repeating Units

1) In a polymer, lots of small units are linked together to form a long molecule that has repeating sections. All the atoms in a polymer are joined by strong covalent bonds.

Instead of drawing out a whole long polymer molecule (which can contain thousands or even millions of atoms), you can draw the shortest repeating section, called the repeating unit, like this:

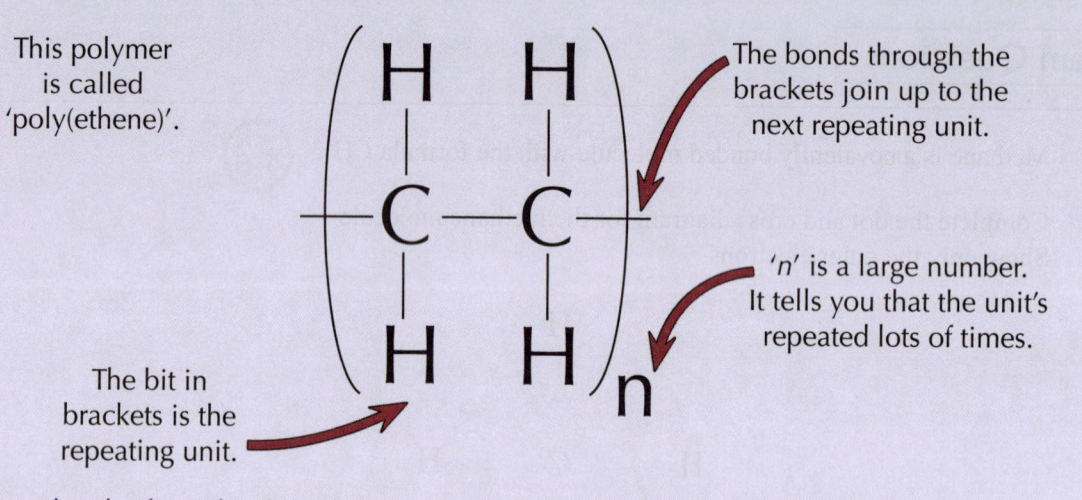

This polymer is called 'poly(ethene)'.

The bit in brackets is the repeating unit.

The bonds through the brackets join up to the next repeating unit.

'n' is a large number. It tells you that the unit's repeated lots of times.

To find the molecular formula of a polymer, write down the molecular formula of the repeating unit in brackets, and put an 'n' outside. So for poly(ethene), the molecular formula of the polymer is $(C_2H_4)_n$.

2) The intermolecular forces between polymer molecules are larger than between simple covalent molecules, so more energy is needed to break them. This means most polymers are solid at room temperature.

3) The intermolecular forces are still weaker than ionic or covalent bonds, so they generally have lower boiling points than ionic or giant molecular compounds.

Polymers are very large molecules

Make sure you can work out a polymer's molecular formula. To do this you need to be comfortable with what the repeating unit of a polymer is.

Q1 The repeating unit of poly(chloroethene) is shown on the right. What's the molecular formula of poly(chloroethene)? [1 mark]

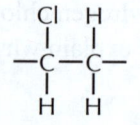

Topic C2 — Bonding, Structure and Properties of Matter

Giant Covalent Structures

Polymers and simple molecular substances aren't the only compounds held together by covalent bonds. Giant covalent structures are too — some are found in nature, while others can be made in a lab.

Giant Covalent Structures Are Macromolecules

1) In giant covalent structures, all the atoms are bonded to each other by strong covalent bonds.
2) They have very high melting and boiling points as lots of energy is needed to break the covalent bonds between the atoms.
3) They don't contain charged particles, so they don't conduct electricity — not even when molten (except for a few weird exceptions such as graphite, see next page).
4) The main examples are diamond and graphite, which are both made from carbon atoms only, and silicon dioxide (silica).

Diamond

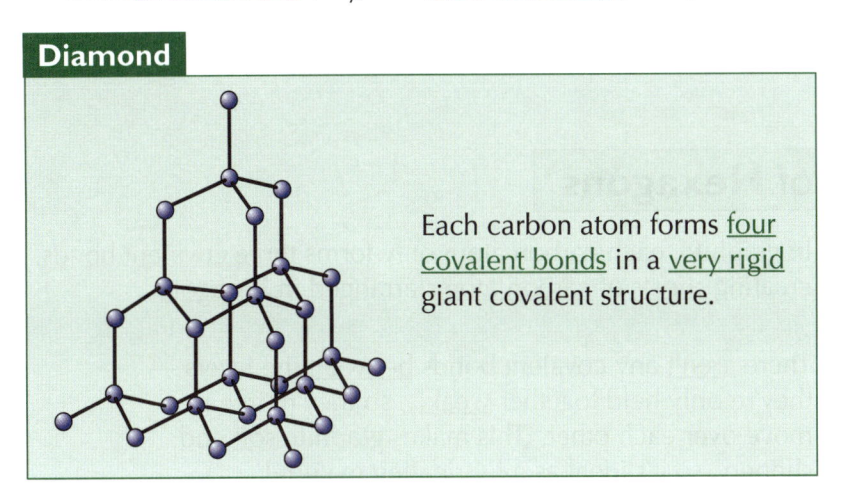

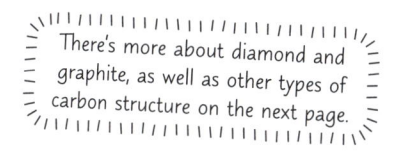

Each carbon atom forms four covalent bonds in a very rigid giant covalent structure.

There's more about diamond and graphite, as well as other types of carbon structure on the next page.

Graphite

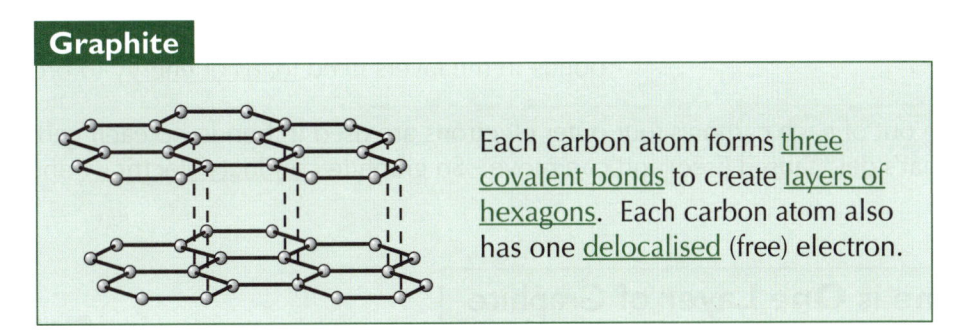

Each carbon atom forms three covalent bonds to create layers of hexagons. Each carbon atom also has one delocalised (free) electron.

Silicon dioxide

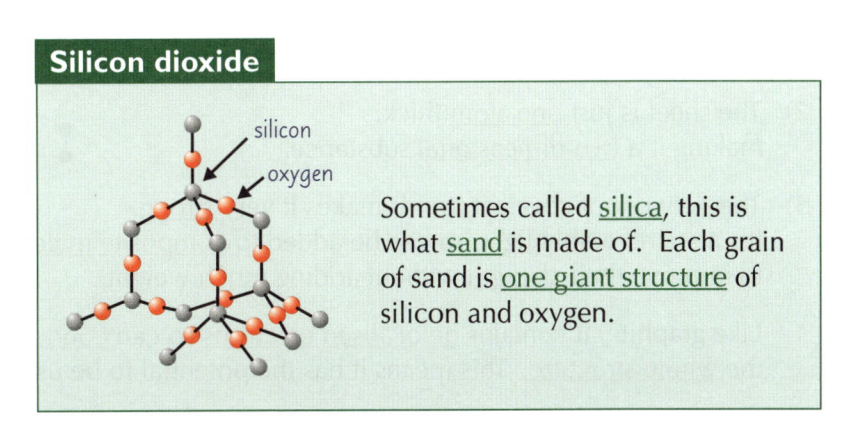

Sometimes called silica, this is what sand is made of. Each grain of sand is one giant structure of silicon and oxygen.

Giant covalent structures have high melting and boiling points

To melt or boil a giant covalent structure, you have to break very strong covalent bonds. The high melting and boiling points of diamond, graphite and silicon are caused by the strength of their covalent bonds.

Topic C2 — Bonding, Structure and Properties of Matter

Allotropes of Carbon

Allotropes are just different **structural forms** of the **same element** in the **same physical state**, e.g. they're all solids. Carbon has quite a few allotropes with lots of different properties.

Diamond is Very Hard

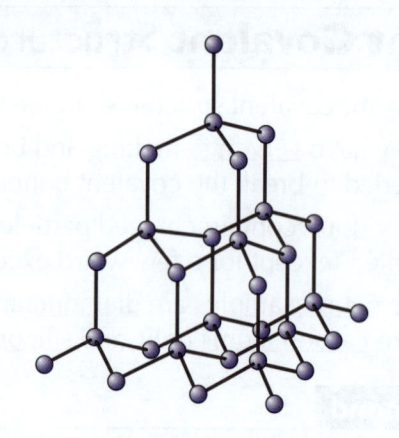

1) Diamond has a giant covalent structure, made up of carbon atoms that each form four covalent bonds. This makes diamond really hard.

2) Those strong covalent bonds take a lot of energy to break and give diamond a very high melting point.

3) It doesn't conduct electricity because it has no free electrons or ions.

Graphite Contains Sheets of Hexagons

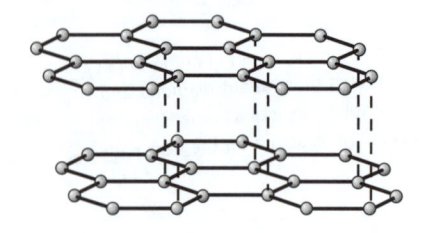

1) In graphite, each carbon atom only forms three covalent bonds, creating sheets of carbon atoms arranged in hexagons.

2) There aren't any covalent bonds between the layers — they're only held together weakly, so they're free to move over each other. This makes graphite soft and slippery, so it's ideal as a lubricating material.

3) Graphite's got a high melting point — the covalent bonds in the layers need loads of energy to break.

4) Only three out of each carbon's four outer electrons are used in bonds, so each carbon atom has one electron that's delocalised (free) and can move. So graphite conducts electricity and thermal energy.

Graphene is One Layer of Graphite

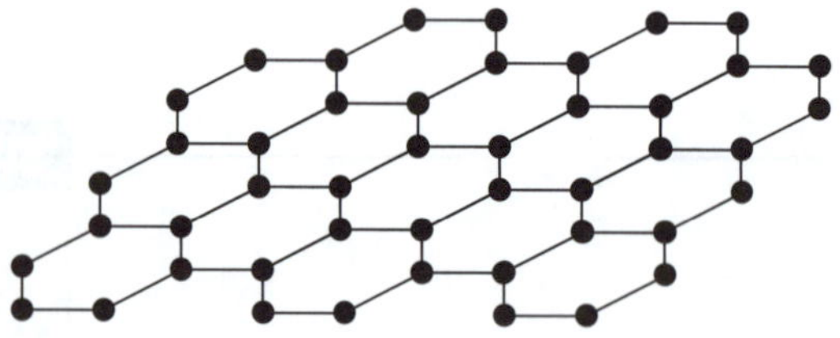

1) Graphene is a sheet of carbon atoms joined together in hexagons.

2) The sheet is just one atom thick, making it a two-dimensional substance.

3) The network of covalent bonds makes it very strong. It's also incredibly light, so can be added to composite materials to improve their strength without adding much weight.

4) Like graphite, it contains delocalised electrons so can conduct electricity through the whole structure. This means it has the potential to be used in electronics.

Diamond, graphite and graphene contain exactly the same atoms
The different substances on this page are made purely from carbon — there's no difference at all in their atoms. The difference in properties is all down to the way the atoms are held together.

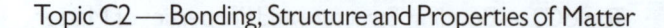

Topic C2 — Bonding, Structure and Properties of Matter

Allotropes of Carbon

Diamond, *graphite*, and *graphene* aren't the only allotropes of carbon.
In fact, we are discovering and making new allotropes of carbon all the time.

Fullerenes Form Spheres and Tubes

1) Fullerenes are molecules of carbon, shaped like closed tubes or hollow balls.

2) They're mainly made up of carbon atoms arranged in hexagons, but can also contain pentagons (rings of five carbon atoms) or heptagons (rings of seven carbon atoms).

Buckminsterfullerene was the first fullerene to be discovered. It's got the molecular formula C_{60} and forms a hollow sphere containing 20 hexagons and 12 pentagons.

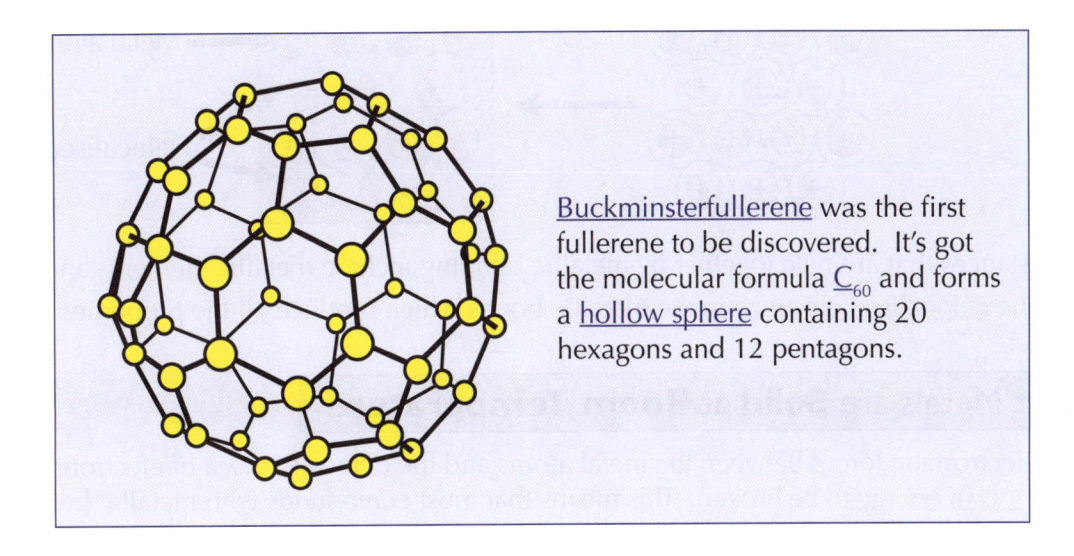

3) Fullerenes can be used to 'cage' other molecules. The fullerene structure forms around another atom or molecule, which is then trapped inside. This could be used to deliver a drug into the body.

4) Fullerenes have a huge surface area, so they could help make great industrial catalysts — individual catalyst molecules could be attached to the fullerenes (the bigger the surface area the better).

Catalysts speed up the rates of chemical reactions without being used up themselves (see p.255).

5) Fullerenes also make great lubricants.

1) Fullerenes can form nanotubes — tiny carbon cylinders.
2) The ratio between the length and the diameter of nanotubes is very high.
3) Nanotubes can conduct both electricity and thermal energy (heat).
4) They also have a high tensile strength (they don't break when they're stretched).
5) Technology that uses very small particles such as nanotubes is called nanotechnology. Nanotubes can be used in electronics or to strengthen materials without adding much weight, such as in tennis racket frames.

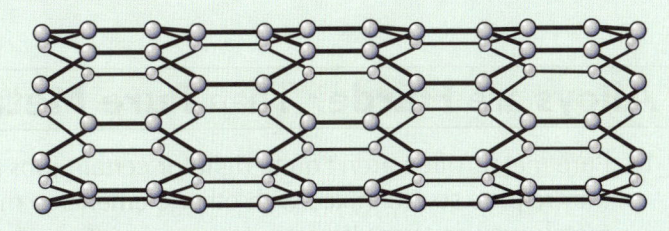

Fullerenes are really useful materials

REVISION TIP Before you move on, make sure you can explain the properties of the allotropes of carbon. While you are at it, don't forget to learn the potential uses of fullerenes that are mentioned on this page.

Topic C2 — Bonding, Structure and Properties of Matter

Metallic Bonding

Ever wondered what gives a metal its properties? Most of it comes down to bonding...

Metallic Bonding Involves Delocalised Electrons

1) Metals also consist of a giant structure.
2) The electrons in the outer shell of the metal atoms are delocalised (free to move around). There are strong forces of electrostatic attraction between the positive metal ions and the shared negative electrons.
3) These forces of attraction hold the atoms together in a regular structure and are known as metallic bonding. Metallic bonding is very strong.

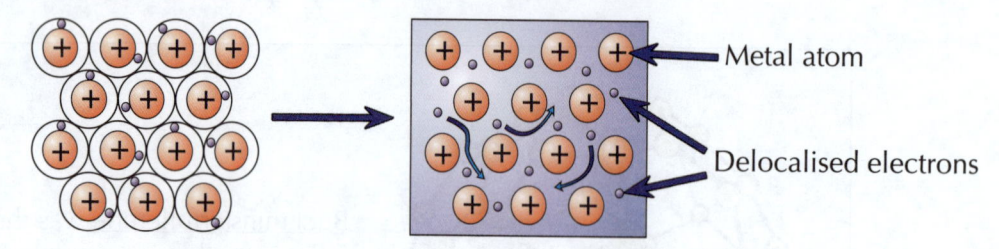

4) Substances that are held together by metallic bonding include metallic elements and alloys (see below).
5) It's the delocalised electrons in the metallic bonds which produce all the properties of metals...

Most Metals are Solid at Room Temperature

The electrostatic forces between the metal atoms and the delocalised sea of electrons are very strong, so need lots of energy to be broken. This means that most compounds with metallic bonds have very high melting and boiling points, so they're generally solid at room temperature.

Metals are Good Conductors of Electricity and Heat

The delocalised electrons carry electrical charge and thermal (heat) energy through the whole structure, so metals are good conductors of electricity and heat.

Most Metals are Malleable

The layers of atoms in a metal can slide over each other, making metals malleable — this means that they can be bent or hammered or rolled into flat sheets.

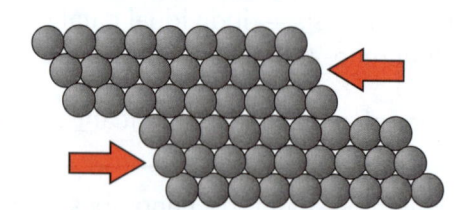

Alloys are Harder Than Pure Metals

1) Pure metals often aren't quite right for certain jobs — they're often too soft when they're pure so are mixed with other elements to make them harder. Most of the metals we use everyday are alloys — a mixture of two or more metals or a metal and another element. Alloys are harder and so more useful than pure metals.
2) Different elements have different sized atoms. So when another element is mixed with a pure metal, the new metal atoms will distort the layers of metal atoms, making it more difficult for them to slide over each other. This makes alloys harder than pure metals.

Metallic bonding is what makes metals, well... metals

You should understand what metallic bonding is, and be able to relate how it causes metals to have the properties they do. Also, don't forget to learn the differences between alloys and pure metals.

Topic C2 — Bonding, Structure and Properties of Matter

Warm-Up & Exam Questions

Lots of information to learn on the previous few pages — here are some questions to test yourself on.

Warm-Up Questions

1) How are the repeating units in a polymer bonded together?
2) At room temperature, what state are most polymers in?
3) Describe the differences in the hardness and electrical conductivity of diamond and graphite.
4) Which fullerene was the first to be discovered?
5) Explain why most metals are malleable.

Exam Questions

1 Silicon carbide has a giant covalent structure and is a solid at room temperature. *(Grade 4-6)*

1.1 Explain, in terms of its bonding and structure, why silicon carbide has a high melting point.

[2 marks]

1.2 Give **one** other example of a substance with a giant covalent structure.

[1 mark]

2 Graphite, diamond and fullerenes are entirely made from carbon but have different properties. *(Grade 6-7)*

2.1 Why does the structure of graphite make it a useful lubricant?

[2 marks]

2.2 Using your knowledge of the structure of diamond, suggest why it is useful as a cutting tool.

[2 marks]

2.3 Suggest **one** possible use for fullerenes.

[1 mark]

2.4 Explain why graphite is able to conduct electricity.

[1 mark]

3 **Figure 1** shows the arrangement of atoms in pure iron. *(Grade 6-7)*

Figure 1

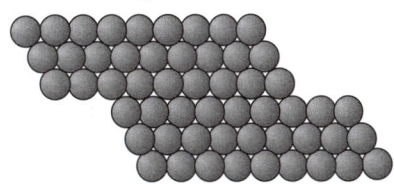

3.1 Steel is an alloy of iron and carbon.
Sketch a similar diagram to show the arrangement of atoms in steel.

[2 marks]

3.2 Steel is harder than iron. Explain why.

[3 marks]

Topic C2 — Bonding, Structure and Properties of Matter

States of Matter

You can explain quite a bit of stuff in **chemistry** if you can get your head round this lot.

The **Three States of Matter** — Solid, Liquid and Gas

Materials come in three different forms — solid, liquid and gas. These are the three states of matter. Which state something is at a certain temperature (solid, liquid or gas) depends on how strong the forces of attraction are between the particles of the material. How strong the forces are depends on THREE THINGS:

1) the material (the structure of the substance and the type of bonds holding the particles together),
2) the temperature,
3) the pressure.

The particles could be atoms, ions or molecules.

You can use a model called particle theory to explain how the particles in a material behave in each of the three states of matter by considering each particle as a small, solid, inelastic sphere.

Solids

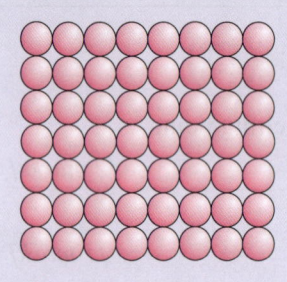

1) In solids, there are strong forces of attraction between particles, which holds them close together in fixed positions to form a very regular lattice arrangement.
2) The particles don't move from their positions, so all solids keep a definite shape and volume, and don't flow like liquids.
3) The particles vibrate about their positions — the hotter the solid becomes, the more they vibrate (causing solids to expand slightly when heated).

Liquids

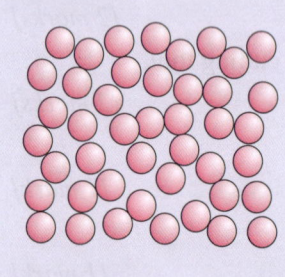

1) In liquids, there's a weak force of attraction between the particles. They're randomly arranged and free to move past each other, but they tend to stick closely together.
2) Liquids have a definite volume but don't keep a definite shape, and will flow to fill the bottom of a container.
3) The particles are constantly moving with random motion. The hotter the liquid gets, the faster they move. This causes liquids to expand slightly when heated.

Gases

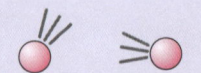

1) In gases, the force of attraction between the particles is very weak — they're free to move and are far apart. The particles in gases travel in straight lines.
2) Gases don't keep a definite shape or volume and will always fill any container.
3) The particles move constantly with random motion. The hotter the gas gets, the faster they move. Gases either expand when heated, or their pressure increases.

Particle theory is a great model for explaining the three states of matter, but it isn't perfect. In reality, the particles aren't solid or inelastic and they aren't spheres — they're atoms, ions or molecules. Also, the model doesn't show the forces between the particles, so there's no way of knowing how strong they are.

Topic C2 — Bonding, Structure and Properties of Matter

States of Matter

Substances Can Change from One State to Another

Physical changes don't change the particles — just their arrangement or their energy.

1) When a solid is heated, its particles gain more energy.

2) This makes the particles vibrate more, which weakens the forces that hold the solid together.

3) At a certain temperature, called the melting point the particles have enough energy to break free from their positions. This is called MELTING and the solid turns into a liquid.

4) When a liquid is heated, again the particles get even more energy.

5) This energy makes the particles move faster, which weakens and breaks the bonds holding the liquid together.

6) At a certain temperature, called the boiling point, the particles have enough energy to break their bonds. This is BOILING (or evaporating). The liquid becomes a gas.

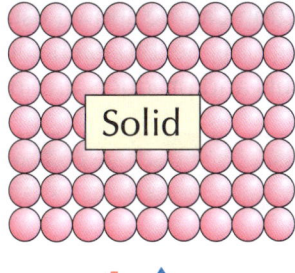

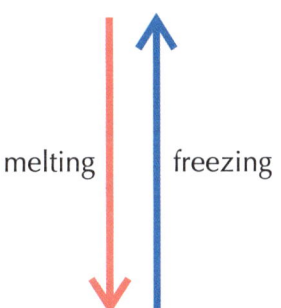

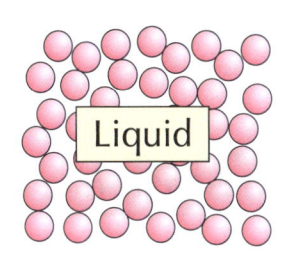

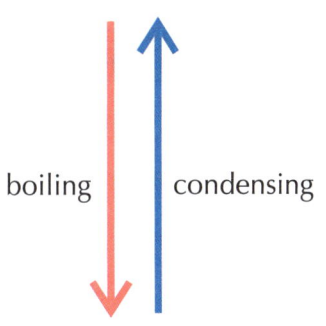

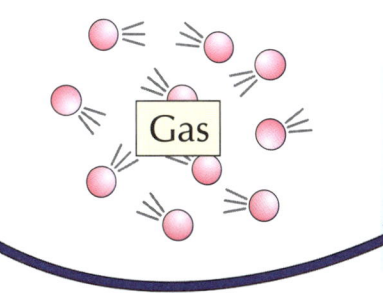

Solid — melting / freezing — **Liquid** — boiling / condensing — **Gas**

12) At the melting point, so many bonds have formed between the particles that they're held in place. The liquid becomes a solid. This is FREEZING.

11) There's not enough energy to overcome the attraction between the particles, so more bonds form between them.

10) When a liquid cools, the particles have less energy, so move around less.

9) At the boiling point, so many bonds have formed between the gas particles that the gas becomes a liquid. This is called CONDENSING.

8) Bonds form between the particles.

7) As a gas cools, the particles no longer have enough energy to overcome the forces of attraction between them.

So, the amount of energy needed for a substance to change state depends on how strong the forces between particles are. The stronger the forces, the more energy is needed to break them, and so the higher the melting and boiling points of the substance.

Topic C2 — Bonding, Structure and Properties of Matter

States of Matter

*The state a substance is in can be really important in working out **how it will react**. This page is all about how chemists show what the **state** of a substance is and how they **predict** what state a substance will be in.*

State Symbols Tell You the State of a Substance in an Equation

You saw on page 177 how a chemical reaction can be shown using a word equation or symbol equation. Symbol equations can also include state symbols next to each substance — they tell you what physical state the reactants and products are in:

(s) — solid   (l) — liquid   (g) — gas   (aq) — aqueous

'Aqueous' means 'dissolved in water'.

Here are a couple of examples:

Aqueous hydrogen chloride reacts with solid calcium carbonate to form aqueous calcium chloride, liquid water and carbon dioxide gas:

$$2HCl_{(aq)} + CaCO_{3(s)} \rightarrow CaCl_{2(aq)} + H_2O_{(l)} + CO_{2(g)}$$

Chlorine gas reacts with aqueous potassium iodide to form aqueous potassium chloride and solid iodine:

$$Cl_{2(g)} + 2KI_{(aq)} \rightarrow 2KCl_{(aq)} + I_{2(s)}$$

You Might Need to Predict the State of a Substance

1) You might be asked to predict what state a substance is in at a certain temperature.
2) If the temperature's below the melting point of substance, it'll be a solid. If it's above the boiling point, it'll be a gas. If it's in between the two points, then it's a liquid.

EXAMPLE
Which of the molecular substances in the table is a liquid at room temperature (25 °C)?

	Melting point	Boiling point
oxygen	−219 °C	−183 °C
nitrogen	−210 °C	−196 °C
bromine	−7 °C	59 °C

Oxygen and nitrogen have boiling points below 25 °C, so will both be gases at room temperature. So the answer's bromine. It melts at −7 °C and boils at 59 °C. So, it'll be a liquid at room temperature.

The bulk properties such as the melting point of a material depend on how lots of atoms interact together. An atom on its own doesn't have these properties.

Physical changes are reversible

Make sure you can describe what happens to particles, and the forces between them, as a substance is heated and cooled. Don't forget to learn the technical terms for each state change.

Q1 Ethanol melts at −114 °C and boils at 78 °C. Predict the state that ethanol is in at:
   a) −150 °C   b) 0 °C   c) 25 °C   d) 100 °C   [4 marks]

Topic C2 — Bonding, Structure and Properties of Matter

Warm-Up & Exam Questions

Reckon you know all there is to know about this section? Have a go at these questions and see how you get on. If you get stuck on something — just flick back and give it another read through.

Warm-Up Questions

1) What three factors are the strength of the forces between particles dependent on?
2) What state of matter has a fixed lattice arrangement?
3) Is the strength of the attraction between particles of a gas strong or weak?
4) What happens to the particles in a gas when it is heated?
5) Describe what happens when a gas condenses.
6) Write down how you would show that sodium ions (Na⁺) are in solution in a symbol equation.

Exam Questions

1.1 **Figure 1** shows a vessel in a distillery. The walls of the vessel are solid copper.

Grade 4-6

Figure 1

Complete the sentences about solids using words from the box.
Each word may be used once, more than once or not at all.

| weak | move | colder | hotter | random |
| strong | expand | heavier | dissolve | regular |

In solids, there are .... forces of attraction between particles,

which hold them in fixed positions in a .... arrangement.

The particles don't .... from their positions, so solids keep their shape.

The .... the solid becomes, the more the particles in the solid vibrate.

[4 marks]

1.2 Inside the vessel, liquid ethanol is turned into ethanol gas.
Describe the changes in arrangement, movement and energy of the
particles when the liquid ethanol is heated to become a gas.

[2 marks]

2 This question is on states of matter. *Grade 6-7*

2.1 Using particle theory, explain why gases fill their containers.

[2 marks]

2.2 Using particle theory, explain why liquids flow.

[2 marks]

2.3 Chlorine has a melting point of −101.5 °C and a boiling point of −34 °C.
Predict what state chlorine will be in at −29 °C.

[1 mark]

Topic C2 — Bonding, Structure and Properties of Matter

Topic C3 — Quantitative Chemistry

Relative Formula Mass

*Calculating **relative formula mass** is straight forward enough, but things can get a bit more confusing when you start working out the **percentage compositions** of compounds.*

Compounds Have a Relative Formula Mass, M_r

If you have a compound like $MgCl_2$ then it has a relative formula mass, M_r, which is the relative atomic masses of all the atoms in the molecular formula added together.

You can find the relative atomic mass (A_r) of an element from the periodic table — it's the same as its mass number. See page 159 for more.

EXAMPLE **Find the relative formula mass of $MgCl_2$.**

1) Look up the relative atomic masses of all the elements in the compound on the periodic table. (In the exams, you might be given the A_r you need in the question.)
   A_r of Mg = 24 and the A_r of Cl = 35.5.
2) Add up all the relative atomic masses of the atoms in the compound.
   Mg + (2 × Cl) = 24 + (2 × 35.5) = 95   So M_r of $MgCl_2$ = **95**

There are two chlorine atoms in $MgCl_2$, so the relative atomic mass of chlorine needs to be multiplied by 2.

You Can Calculate the % Mass of an Element in a Compound

This is actually dead easy — so long as you've learnt this formula:

$$\text{Percentage mass of an element in a compound} = \frac{A_r \times \text{number of atoms of that element}}{M_r \text{ of the compound}} \times 100$$

EXAMPLE **Find the percentage mass of sodium in sodium carbonate, Na_2CO_3.**

A_r of sodium = 23, A_r of carbon = 12, A_r of oxygen = 16
M_r of Na_2CO_3 = (2 × 23) + 12 + (3 × 16) = 106

Percentage mass of sodium = $\frac{A_r \times \text{number of atoms of that element}}{M_r \text{ of the compound}} \times 100 = \frac{23 \times 2}{106} \times 100 = \mathbf{43\%}$

You might also come across more complicated questions where you need to work out the percentage mass.

EXAMPLE

A mixture contains 20% iron ions by mass. What mass of iron chloride ($FeCl_2$) would you need to provide the iron ions in 50 g of the mixture? A_r of Fe = 56, A_r of Cl = 35.5.

1) Find the mass of iron in the mixture.
   The mixture contains 20% iron by mass, so in 50 g there will be $50 \times \frac{20}{100} = 10$ g of iron.

2) Calculate the percentage mass of iron in iron chloride.
   Percentage mass of iron = $\frac{A_r \times \text{number of atoms of iron}}{M_r \text{ of iron chloride}} \times 100 = \frac{56}{56 + (2 \times 35.5)} \times 100 = 44.09...\%$

3) Calculate the mass of iron chloride that contains 10 g of iron.
   Iron chloride contains 44.09% iron by mass, so there will be 10 g of iron in $10 \div \frac{44.09...}{100} = 23$ g
   So you need **23 g** of iron chloride to provide the iron in 50 g of the mixture.

Relative formula mass — add up all the relative atomic masses

The best way to get to grips with all this stuff is by practising. Have a go at these questions...

Q1   Calculate the relative formula mass (M_r) of: a) H_2O b) LiOH   c) H_2SO_4 **[3 marks]**

Q2   Calculate the percentage composition by mass of potassium in potassium hydroxide (KOH).   **[2 marks]**

Q2 Video Solution

Topic C3 — Quantitative Chemistry

The Mole and Mass

The mole can be pretty confusing. I think it's the word that puts people off. It's difficult to see the relevance of the word "mole" to anything but a small burrowing animal.

"The Mole" is Simply the Name Given to an Amount of a Substance

1) Just like "a million" is this many: 1 000 000; or "a billion" is this many: 1 000 000 000, so "the Avogadro constant" is this many: 602 000 000 000 000 000 000 000 or 6.02×10^{23}. And that's all it is. Just a number.

2) One mole of any substance is just an amount of that substance that contains an Avogadro number of particles — so 6.02×10^{23} particles. The particles could be atoms, molecules, ions or electrons.

The symbol for the unit 'moles' is 'mol'.

3) So why is such a long number like the Avogadro constant used? The answer is that the mass of that number of atoms or molecules of any substance is exactly the same number of grams as the relative atomic mass (A_r) or relative formula mass (M_r) of the element or compound.

4) In other words, one mole of atoms or molecules of any substance will have a mass in grams equal to the relative formula mass (A_r or M_r) for that substance. Here are some examples:

> Carbon has an A_r of 12.
> So one mole of carbon weighs exactly 12 g.

> Nitrogen gas, N_2, has an M_r of 28 (2 × 14).
> So one mole of N_2 weighs exactly 28 g.

> Carbon dioxide, CO_2, has an M_r of 44 (12 + [2 × 16]).
> So one mole of CO_2 weighs exactly 44 g.

5) This means that 12 g of carbon, or 28 g of nitrogen, or 44 g of carbon dioxide, all contain the same number of particles, namely one mole or 6.02×10^{23} atoms or molecules.

Topic C3 — Quantitative Chemistry

The Mole and Mass

So you now you know what a mole is, you probably want to know how to work out the number of moles in a given mass of a substance, right? Well you're in luck...

Nice Formula to Find the Number of Moles in a Given Mass:

$$\text{Number of moles} = \frac{\text{mass in g (of an element or compound)}}{M_r \text{ (of the element or compound)}}$$

EXAMPLE How many moles are there in 66 g of carbon dioxide (CO_2)?
1) Calculate the M_r of carbon dioxide. M_r of CO_2 = 12 + (16 × 2) = 44
2) Use the formula above to find out how many moles there are.   No. of moles = Mass (g) ÷ M_r = 66 ÷ 44 = **1.5 mol**

You can rearrange the equation above using this handy formula triangle. You could use it to find the mass of a known number of moles of a substance, or to find the M_r of a substance from a known mass and number of moles. Just cover up the thing you want to find with your finger and write down what's left showing.

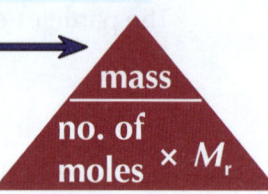

$$\frac{\text{mass}}{\text{no. of moles} \times M_r}$$

EXAMPLE What mass of carbon is there in 4 moles of carbon dioxide?
There are 4 moles of carbon in 4 moles of CO_2.
Cover up 'mass' in the formula triangle. That leaves you with 'no. of moles × M_r'.
So the mass of 4 moles of carbon = 4 × 12 = **48 g**

In a Chemical Reaction, Mass is Always Conserved

1) During a chemical reaction no atoms are destroyed and no atoms are created.
2) This means there are the same number and types of atoms on each side of a reaction equation.
3) Because of this, no mass is lost or gained — we say that mass is conserved during a reaction. For example:

$$2Li + F_2 \rightarrow 2LiF$$

In this reaction, there are 2 lithium atoms and 2 fluorine atoms on each side of the equation.

4) By adding up the relative formula masses of the substances on each side of a balanced symbol equation, you can see that mass is conserved. The total M_r of all the reactants equals the total M_r of the products.

EXAMPLE
Show that mass is conserved in this reaction: $2Li + F_2 \rightarrow 2LiF$.
1) Add up the relative formula masses on the left-hand side of the equation.
   $2 \times M_r(Li) + 2 \times M_r(F) = (2 \times 7) + (2 \times 19) = 14 + 38 = 52$
2) Add up the relative formula masses on the right-hand side of the equation.
   $2 \times M_r(LiF) = 2 \times (7 + 19) = 2 \times 26 = 52$
   The total M_r on the left hand side of the equation is equal to the total M_r on the right hand side, so mass is conserved.

There's more about balanced symbol equations on p.178.

The M_r of the reactants will always equal the M_r of the products

Q1 Calculate the number of moles in 90 g of water (H_2O). $A_r(O) = 16$, $A_r(H) = 1$.   [2 marks]

Q2 Calculate the mass of 0.20 mol of potassium bromide (KBr). $A_r(K) = 39$, $A_r(Br) = 80$. [2 marks]

Topic C3 — Quantitative Chemistry

The Mole and Mass

If the Mass Seems to Change, There's Usually a Gas Involved

In some experiments, you might observe a change of mass of an unsealed reaction vessel during a reaction. There are usually two explanations for this:

Explanation 1:

1) If the mass increases, it's probably because one of the reactants is a gas that's found in air (e.g. oxygen) and all the products are solids, liquids or aqueous.

2) Before the reaction, the gas is floating around in the air. It's there, but it's not contained in the reaction vessel, so you can't account for its mass.

3) When the gas reacts to form part of the product, it becomes contained inside the reaction vessel — so the total mass of the stuff inside the reaction vessel increases.

> For example, when a metal reacts with oxygen in an unsealed container, the mass of the container increases. The mass of the metal oxide produced equals the total mass of the metal and the oxygen that reacted from the air.
> $$metal_{(s)} + oxygen_{(g)} \rightarrow metal\ oxide_{(s)}$$

Explanation 2:

1) If the mass decreases, it's probably because one or more of the products are gases and all the reactants are solids, liquids or aqueous.

2) Before the reaction, all the reactants are contained in the reaction vessel.

3) If the vessel isn't enclosed, then any gases can escape from the reaction vessel as they're formed. They're no longer contained in the reaction vessel, so you can't account for their mass — the total mass of the stuff inside the reaction vessel decreases.

> For example, when a metal carbonate thermally decomposes to form a metal oxide and carbon dioxide gas, the mass of the reaction vessel will decrease if it isn't sealed. But in reality, the mass of the metal oxide and the carbon dioxide produced will equal the mass of the metal carbonate that decomposed.
> $$metal\ carbonate_{(s)} \rightarrow metal\ oxide_{(s)} + carbon\ dioxide_{(g)}$$

Remember from the particle model on page 218 that a gas will expand to fill any container it's in. So if the reaction vessel isn't sealed, any gas formed expands out from the vessel, and escapes into the air around.

Mass is ALWAYS conserved

There is quite a bit to take in on these pages, but it's all really important in everything you do in chemistry. Make sure you learn the equation on the previous page — it'll crop up again later.

Q1 Show that mass is conserved in the reaction: $H_2SO_{4(aq)} + 2NaOH_{(aq)} \rightarrow Na_2SO_{4(aq)} + 2H_2O_{(l)}$
$A_r(H) = 1$, $A_r(O) = 16$, $A_r(Na) = 23$, $A_r(S) = 32$ [5 marks]

Topic C3 — Quantitative Chemistry

Warm-Up & Exam Questions

If you feel like you need some practice with relative masses and mole calculations, then you're in luck. Here's a nice bunch of questions for you to have a go at.

Warm-Up Questions

1) What name is given to the sum of the relative atomic masses of the atoms in a molecule?
2) What is the name given to the particular number of particles equal to one mole of a substance?
3) Write down the definition of a mole.
4) What is the mass of one mole of iron?
5) What is the mass of one mole of oxygen gas?

Exam Questions

1 Boron can form a number of covalent compounds.
Use the A_r values B = 11, O = 16, F = 19 and H = 1 to calculate the relative formula masses of these boron compounds: *(Grade 4-6)*

1.1 BF_3

[1 mark]

1.2 $B(OH)_3$

[1 mark]

2 A student was asked to calculate the number of moles and the masses of different compounds she would be using in her lab practical. *(Grade 4-6)*
State the formula used to work out the number of moles from the mass of a compound.

[1 mark]

3 A teacher has a 140 g sample of potassium hydroxide (KOH). *(Grade 6-7)*
Calculate, in grams, how much more KOH the teacher needs to have a 4 mole sample.

[3 marks]

4 A scientist burnt 300 g of metal **X** in an unsealed beaker. She then weighed the contents of the beaker and found that it now weighed 500 g. *(Grade 6-7)*
All of the metal **X** reacted to form a single product, a metal oxide.

4.1 Explain why the mass increased during the reaction.

[1 mark]

4.2 Analysis of the metal oxide shows that it contains 40% oxygen by mass.
What is the percentage mass of metal **X** in the oxide?

[1 mark]

4.3 The scientist plans to use the metal oxide as part of a mixture.
The final mixture contains 24% metal **X** by mass, which all comes from the metal oxide.
What mass of the metal oxide was used to make 8.0 g of the mixture?

[2 marks]

Topic C3 — Quantitative Chemistry

The Mole and Equations

*Remember the '**number of moles = mass ÷ M$_r$**' equation from page 224? This is where it comes into its own.*

The Numbers in Chemical Equations Mean Different Things

Remember those balanced equations back on page 178? Well, the big numbers in front of the chemical formulas of the reactants and products tell you how many moles of each substance takes part or is formed during the reaction. For example:

$$Mg_{(s)} + 2HCl_{(aq)} \rightarrow MgCl_{2(aq)} + H_{2(g)}$$

In this reaction, 1 mole of magnesium and 2 moles of hydrochloric acid react together to form 1 mole of magnesium chloride and 1 mole of hydrogen gas.

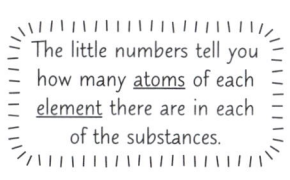

The little numbers tell you how many atoms of each element there are in each of the substances.

You Can Balance Equations Using Reacting Masses

If you know the masses of the reactants and products that took part in a reaction, you can work out the balanced symbol equation for the reaction. Here are the steps you should take:

1) Divide the mass of each substance by its relative formula mass to find the number of moles.
2) Divide the number of moles of each substance by the smallest number of moles in the reaction.
3) If any of the numbers aren't whole numbers, multiply all the numbers by the same amount so that they all become whole numbers.
4) Write the balanced symbol equation for the reaction by putting these numbers in front of the chemical formulas.

EXAMPLE

8.1 g of zinc oxide (ZnO) reacts completely with 0.60 g of carbon to form 2.2 g of carbon dioxide and 6.5 g of zinc. Write a balanced symbol equation for this reaction. $A_r(C) = 12$, $A_r(O) = 16$, $A_r(Zn) = 65$.

1) Work out M_r for each of the substances in the reaction:
   ZnO: 65 + 16 = 81   C: 12   CO$_2$: 12 + (2 × 16) = 44   Zn: 65

2) Divide the mass of each substance by its M_r to calculate how many moles of each substance reacted or were produced:

   ZnO: $\frac{8.1}{81}$ = 0.10 mol   C: $\frac{0.60}{12}$ = 0.050 mol

   CO$_2$: $\frac{2.2}{44}$ = 0.050 mol   Zn: $\frac{6.5}{65}$ = 0.10

3) Divide by the smallest number of moles, which is 0.050:

   ZnO: $\frac{0.10}{0.050}$ = 2.0   C: $\frac{0.050}{0.050}$ = 1.0

   CO$_2$: $\frac{0.050}{0.050}$ = 1.0   Zn: $\frac{0.10}{0.050}$ = 2.0

   These numbers give the ratio of the amounts of each substance in the reaction equation.

4) The numbers are all whole numbers, so you can write out the balanced symbol equation straight away:

$$2ZnO + C \rightarrow CO_2 + 2Zn$$

Practise, Practise, Practise

Make sure that there's the same number of atoms of each element on both sides of your equation.

Q1 84 g of N$_2$ reacts completely with 18 g of H$_2$ to produce 102 g of NH$_3$.
    $M_r(N_2) = 28$, $M_r(H_2) = 2$, $M_r(NH_3) = 17$.
    a) Calculate how many moles of each substance reacted or was produced. [3 marks]
    b) Use your answer to part a) to write a balanced symbol equation for this reaction. [2 marks]

Topic C3 — Quantitative Chemistry

Concentration and Limiting Reactants

*Reactions don't go on forever — it depends how much stuff is in the reaction flask (the **concentration**). If one reactant gets **used up** in a reaction before the rest, then the reaction will **stop**. That reactant's called **limiting**.*

Concentration is a Measure of How Crowded Things Are

1) Lots of reactions in chemistry take place between substances that are dissolved in a solution. The amount of a substance (e.g. the mass or the number of moles) in a certain volume of a solution is called its concentration.
2) The more solute (the substance that's dissolved) there is in a given volume, the more concentrated the solution.
3) One way to measure the concentration of a solution is by calculating the mass of a substance in a given volume of solution. The units will be units of mass/units of volume. Here's how to calculate the concentration of a solution in g/dm³:

$$\text{concentration} = \frac{\text{mass of solute}}{\text{volume of solvent}}$$

in g/dm³ — concentration; in g — mass of solute; in dm³ — volume of solvent

EXAMPLE
What's the concentration, in g/dm³, of a solution of sodium chloride where 30 g of sodium chloride is dissolved in 0.2 dm³ of water?

concentration = $\frac{30}{0.2}$ = 150 g/dm³

1 dm³ = 1000 cm³

4) You can calculate the mass of a solute in solution by rearranging the formula above to: mass = conc. × volume.

Reactions Stop When One Reactant is Used Up

When some magnesium carbonate (MgCO₃) is placed into a beaker of hydrochloric acid, you can tell a reaction is taking place because you see lots of bubbles of gas being given off. After a while, the amount of fizzing slows down and the reaction eventually stops...

1) The reaction stops when all of one of the reactants is used up. Any other reactants are in excess. They're usually added in excess to make sure that the other reactant is used up.
2) The reactant that's used up in a reaction is called the limiting reactant (because it limits the amount of product that's formed).
3) The amount of product formed is directly proportional to the amount of limiting reactant. For example, if you halve the amount of limiting reactant, the amount of product formed will also halve. If you double the amount of limiting reactant, the amount of product will double (as long as it is still the limiting reactant).
4) This is because if you add more reactant there will be more reactant particles to take part in the reaction, which means more product particles.

Moles, mass, volume, concentration — don't get them confused

Don't forget to learn the equation for finding the concentration of a solution and how to rearrange it.

Q1 Calculate the concentration, in g/dm³, of a solution that contains 0.6 g of salt in 15 cm³ of solvent. [2 marks]

Q1 Video Solution

Topic C3 — Quantitative Chemistry

Concentration and Limiting Reactants

The Amount of Product Depends on the Limiting Reactant

You can calculate the mass of a product formed in a reaction by using the mass of the limiting reactant and the balanced reaction equation.

1) Write out the balanced equation.

2) Work out relative formula masses (M_r) of the reactant and product you want.

3) Find out how many moles there are of the substance you know the mass of.

4) Use the balanced equation to work out how many moles there'll be of the other substance. In this case, that's how many moles of product will be made of this many moles of reactant.

5) Use the number of moles to calculate the mass.

Here's an Example Mass Calculation:

EXAMPLE Calculate the mass of aluminium oxide formed when 135 g of aluminium is burned in air.

1) Write out the balanced equation: $4Al + 3O_2 \rightarrow 2Al_2O_3$

2) Calculate the relative formula masses: Al: 27 Al_2O_3: (2 × 27) + (3 × 16) = 102 — You don't have to find M_r of oxygen because it's in excess.

3) Calculate the number of moles of aluminium in 135 g: Moles = $\frac{mass}{M_r} = \frac{135}{27} = 5$

4) Look at the ratio of moles in the equation: 4 moles of Al react to produce 2 moles of Al_2O_3 — half the number of moles are produced. So 5 moles of Al will react to produce 2.5 moles of Al_2O_3.

   If the question asked for the number of moles of aluminium oxide formed, you'd stop here.

5) Calculate the mass of 2.5 moles of aluminium oxide: mass = moles × M_r = 2.5 × 102 = **255 g**

The mass of product (in this case aluminium oxide) is called the yield of a reaction. Masses you calculate in this way are called theoretical yields. In practice you never get 100% of the yield, so the amount of product you get will be less than you calculated.

When the limiting reactant is used up, the reaction will stop

The key thing here is that the amount of product depends on the reactant which gets used up first.

Q1 The balanced equation for the reaction between chlorine and potassium bromide is:
$$Cl_2 + 2KBr \rightarrow Br_2 + 2KCl$$
Calculate the mass of potassium chloride produced when 23.8 g of potassium bromide reacts in an excess of chlorine. A_r(K) = 39, A_r(Br) = 80, A_r(Cl) = 35.5. [4 marks]

Topic C3 — Quantitative Chemistry

Warm-Up & Exam Questions

Think you know everything there is to about moles, limiting reactants and the volumes of gases? Time to put that to the test with some questions...

Warm-Up Questions

1) What do the numbers in front of the reactants and products in a balanced chemical equation stand for?
2) State why you might want to make sure one reactant is in excess when carrying out a chemical reaction.
3) What is meant by concentration?
4) In a reaction, what happens to the amount of product formed if the limiting reactant is halved?

Exam Questions

1   3.5 g of Li reacts completely with 4 g of O_2 to produce 7.5 g of Li_2O. *Grade 6-7*
$A_r(Li) = 7$, $M_r(O_2) = 32$, $M_r(Li_2O) = 30$.

1.1   Calculate how many moles of each substance reacted or was produced.

[2 marks]

1.2   Use your answer to part **1.1** to write a balanced symbol equation for this reaction.

[2 marks]

2   Sulfuric acid reacts with sodium hydrogen carbonate to produce aqueous sodium sulfate, water and carbon dioxide. The balanced equation for this reaction is: *Grade 6-7*

$$H_2SO_{4(aq)} + 2NaHCO_{3(s)} \rightarrow Na_2SO_{4(aq)} + 2H_2O_{(l)} + 2CO_{2(g)}$$

2.1   A student reacted 6.0 g of solid $NaHCO_3$ with an excess of sulfuric acid. Calculate the theoretical yield of Na_2SO_4 for this reaction.

[5 marks]

2.2   Sodium hydrogen carbonate is the limiting reactant in the example in **2.1**. Describe what is meant by the limiting reactant.

[1 mark]

3   A solution contains 24.5 g of solute in 160 cm^3 of solvent. *Grade 7-9*

3.1   Calculate the concentration of the solution. Give your answer to 3 significant figures.

[3 marks]

3.2   A student needs to have 200 cm^3 of the same solution at a concentration of 75 g/dm^3. How many grams of solute should she add to the solvent?

[2 marks]

3.3   At 25 °C the solubility of the solute is 56 kg per 100 dm^3. Calculate the minimum volume in dm^3 (at 25 °C) needed to dissolve 640 g of the solute. Give your answer to 3 significant figures.

[4 marks]

Topic C3 — Quantitative Chemistry

Topic C4 — Chemical Changes

Acids and Bases

Acids and *bases* crop up everywhere in chemistry — so here's the lowdown on the basics of pH...

The pH Scale Goes From 0 to 14

1) The pH scale is a measure of how acidic or alkaline a solution is.
2) The lower the pH of a solution, the more acidic it is.
   The higher the pH of a solution, the more alkaline it is.
3) A neutral substance (e.g. pure water) has pH 7.

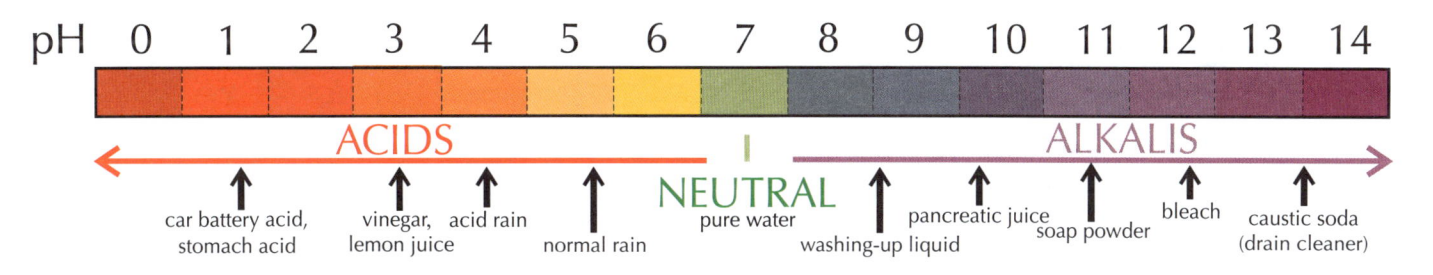

pH 0 1 2 3 4 5 6 7 8 9 10 11 12 13 14

← ACIDS | ALKALIS →
NEUTRAL

- car battery acid, stomach acid
- vinegar, lemon juice
- acid rain
- normal rain
- pure water
- washing-up liquid
- pancreatic juice
- soap powder
- bleach
- caustic soda (drain cleaner)

You Can Measure the pH of a Solution

1) An indicator is a dye that changes colour depending on whether it's above or below a certain pH. Some indicators contain a mixture of dyes that means they gradually change colour over a broad range of pH. These are called wide range indicators and they're useful for estimating the pH of a solution. For example, universal indicator gives the colours shown above.
2) A pH probe attached to a pH meter can also be used to measure pH electronically. The probe is placed in the solution you are measuring and the pH is given on a digital display as a numerical value, meaning it's more accurate than an indicator.

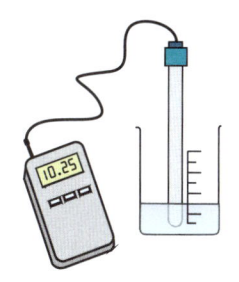

Acids and Bases Neutralise Each Other

1) An acid is a substance that forms an aqueous solution with a pH of less than 7. Acids form H^+ ions in water.
2) A base is any substance that will react with an acid to form a salt.
3) An alkali is a base that dissolves in water to form a solution with a pH greater than 7. Alkalis form OH^- ions in water.

The reaction between acids and bases is called neutralisation:

$$acid + base \rightarrow salt + water$$

Neutralisation between acids and alkalis can be seen in terms of H^+ and OH^- ions like this:

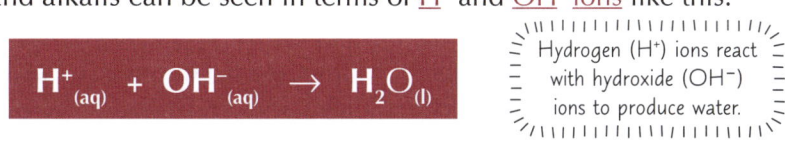

$$H^+_{(aq)} + OH^-_{(aq)} \rightarrow H_2O_{(l)}$$

Hydrogen (H^+) ions react with hydroxide (OH^-) ions to produce water.

When an acid neutralises a base (or vice versa), the products are neutral, i.e. they have a pH of 7. An indicator can be used to show that a neutralisation reaction is over.

Interesting fact — your skin is slightly acidic (pH 5.5)

When you mix an acid with an alkali, hydrogen ions from the acid react with hydroxide ions from the alkali to make water. The leftover bits of the acid and alkali make a salt.

Topic C4 — Chemical Changes

Strong Acids, Weak Acids and their Reactions

*Right, it's time for **strong acids** versus **weak acids**. Brace yourself, it's not the simplest bit of chemistry ever...*

Acids **Produce Protons** in **Water**

An H^+ ion is just a proton.

The thing about acids is that they ionise in aqueous solution — they produce hydrogen ions, H^+.
For example:

$$HCl \rightarrow H^+ + Cl^-$$
$$HNO_3 \rightarrow H^+ + NO_3^-$$

These acids don't produce hydrogen ions until they meet water. So, for example, hydrogen chloride gas isn't acidic.

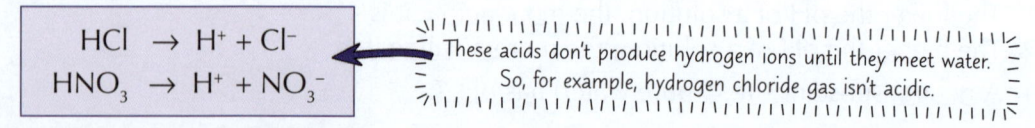

Acids Can be **Strong** or **Weak**

1) Strong acids (e.g. sulfuric, hydrochloric and nitric acids) ionise completely in water. All the acid particles dissociate to release H^+ ions.

$$\text{Strong acid: } HCl \longrightarrow H^+ + Cl^-$$

2) Weak acids (e.g. ethanoic, citric and carbonic acids) do not fully ionise in solution. Only a small proportion of acid particles dissociate to release H^+ ions.

3) The ionisation of a weak acid is a reversible reaction, which sets up an equilibrium between the undissociated and dissociated acid. Since only a few of the acid particles release H^+ ions, the position of equilibrium lies well to the left.

$$\text{Weak acid: } CH_3COOH \rightleftharpoons H^+ + CH_3COO^-$$

For more on equilibria turn to p.263.

4) The pH of an acid or alkali is a measure of the concentration of H^+ ions in the solution.

5) For every decrease of 1 on the pH scale, the concentration of H^+ ions increases by a factor of 10. So, an acid that has a pH of 4 has 10 times the concentration of H^+ ions of an acid that has a pH of 5. For a decrease of 2 on the pH scale, the concentration of H^+ ions increases by a factor of 100. The general rule for this is:

$$\text{Factor } H^+ \text{ ion concentration changes by} = 10^{-X}$$

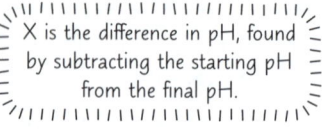

X is the difference in pH, found by subtracting the starting pH from the final pH.

EXAMPLE

During an experiment, the pH of a solution fell from pH 7 to pH 4. By what factor had the hydrogen ion concentration of the solution changed?

Difference in pH = final pH − starting pH = 4 − 7 = −3.
Factor that H^+ ion concentration changed by = $10^{-(-3)} = 10^3$ (or 1000)

If the pH of the solution increases, the answer will be a decimal. For example if the pH of a solution increases by 1, the H^+ ion concentration changes by a factor of 10^{-1} = 0.1. (This is the same as saying that the H^+ concentration has decreased by a factor of 10.)

6) The pH of a strong acid is always lower than the pH of a weaker acid if they have the same concentration.

Strong acids ionise completely, but weak acids don't

Calculating the factor that hydrogen ion concentration changes by as pH changes can be a bit tricky. The best way to get to grips with it is just to get lots of practice at using the formula.

Q1 Name a strong acid. [1 mark]

Q2 A student added strong acid to a weakly acidic solution of pH 6. The pH of the new solution was found to be pH 3. By how many times did the concentration of H^+ increase? [1 mark]

Q2 Video Solution

Topic C4 — Chemical Changes

Strong Acids, Weak Acids and their Reactions

Don't Confuse **Strong** Acids with **Concentrated** Acids

1) Acid strength (i.e. strong or weak) tells you what proportion of the acid molecules ionise in water.

2) The concentration of an acid is different. Concentration measures how much acid there is in a certain volume of water. Concentration is basically how watered down your acid is.

Concentration describes the total number of dissolved acid molecules — not the number of molecules that are ionised to produce hydrogen ions at any given moment.

3) The larger the amount of acid there is in a certain volume of liquid, the more concentrated the acid is.

4) So you can have a dilute (not very concentrated) but strong acid, or a concentrated but weak acid.

5) pH will decrease with increasing acid concentration regardless of whether it's a strong or weak acid.

Metal **Oxides** and Metal **Hydroxides** are **Bases**

1) Some metal oxides and metal hydroxides dissolve in water. These soluble compounds are alkalis. As you saw on page 231, alkalis react with acids in neutralisation reactions.

2) Even bases that won't dissolve in water will still take part in neutralisation reactions with acids.

3) So, all metal oxides and metal hydroxides react with acids to form a salt and water.

$$\text{Acid + Metal Oxide} \rightarrow \text{Salt + Water}$$

$$\text{Acid + Metal Hydroxide} \rightarrow \text{Salt + Water}$$

The **Combination** of Metal and Acid Decides the **Salt**

This isn't exactly exciting, but it's pretty important, so try and get the hang of it:

hydrochloric acid	+	copper oxide	→	copper chloride	+	water
2HCl	+	CuO	→	CuCl$_2$	+	H$_2$O
hydrochloric acid	+	sodium hydroxide	→	sodium chloride	+	water
HCl	+	NaOH	→	NaCl	+	H$_2$O

sulfuric acid	+	zinc oxide	→	zinc sulfate	+	water
H$_2$SO$_4$	+	ZnO	→	ZnSO$_4$	+	H$_2$O
sulfuric acid	+	calcium hydroxide	→	calcium sulfate	+	water
H$_2$SO$_4$	+	Ca(OH)$_2$	→	CaSO$_4$	+	2H$_2$O

To work out the formula of an ionic compound, you need to balance the charges of the positive and negative ions so the compound is neutral. For more on formulas of ionic compounds, see p.206.

nitric acid	+	magnesium oxide	→	magnesium nitrate	+	water
2HNO$_3$	+	MgO	→	Mg(NO$_3$)$_2$	+	H$_2$O
nitric acid	+	potassium hydroxide	→	potassium nitrate	+	water
HNO$_3$	+	KOH	→	KNO$_3$	+	H$_2$O

Topic C4 — Chemical Changes

Strong Acids, Weak Acids and their Reactions

Acids and Metal Carbonates Produce Carbon Dioxide

Metal carbonates are also bases. They will react with acids to produce a salt, water and carbon dioxide.

Acid + Metal Carbonate → Salt + Water + Carbon Dioxide

Here are a few examples of acid and metal carbonate reactions:

hydrochloric acid	+	sodium carbonate	→	sodium chloride	+	water	+	carbon dioxide
$2HCl$	+	Na_2CO_3	→	$2NaCl$	+	H_2O	+	CO_2
sulfuric acid	+	calcium carbonate	→	calcium sulfate	+	water	+	carbon dioxide
H_2SO_4	+	$CaCO_3$	→	$CaSO_4$	+	H_2O	+	CO_2

You can Make Soluble Salts Using an Insoluble Base   **PRACTICAL**

1) You need to pick the right acid, plus an insoluble base such as an insoluble hydroxide, metal oxide or carbonate.

   You can also make some salts by reacting a metal with an acid (see page 237 for more).

   For example, if you want to make copper chloride, you could mix hydrochloric acid and copper oxide: $CuO_{(s)} + 2HCl_{(aq)} → CuCl_{2\,(aq)} + H_2O_{(l)}$

2) Gently warm the dilute acid using a Bunsen burner, then turn off the Bunsen burner.

3) Add the insoluble base to the acid a bit at a time until no more reacts (i.e. the base is in excess). You'll know when all the acid has been neutralised because, even after stirring, the excess solid will just sink to the bottom of the flask.

4) Then filter out the excess solid to get the salt solution (see p.183).

5) To get pure, solid crystals of the salt, gently heat the solution using a water bath or an electric heater to evaporate some of the water (to make it more concentrated) and then stop heating it and leave the solution to cool. Crystals of the salt should form, which can be filtered out of the solution and then dried. This is called crystallisation (see p.183).

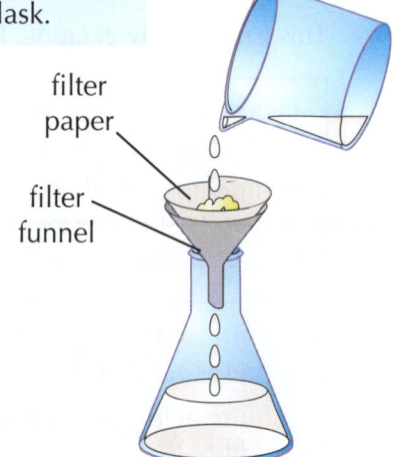

Quite a few reactions to learn here...

...but it's not so bad really, because they're all acid + base → salt + water (and sometimes carbon dioxide). You could also be asked to describe how you would make a pure, dry sample of a given soluble salt, so make sure you know the method and a suitable acid and base to use.

Q1 Calcium carbonate is added to hydrochloric acid. Write the word equation and the balanced symbol equation for the reaction that occurs.   [3 marks]

Topic C4 — Chemical Changes

Warm-Up & Exam Questions

So you think you know everything there is to know about acids? Time to put yourself to the test.

Warm-Up Questions

1) What range of values can pH take?
2) What term is used to describe a solution with a pH of 7?
3) What's the difference between a strong acid and a weak acid?
4) If the pH of the solution rises from 2 to 5, what factor has the hydrogen ion concentration of the solution changed by?
5) Name the two substances formed when nitric acid reacts with copper hydroxide.

Exam Questions

1 A student had a sample of acid in a test tube. He gradually added some alkali to the acid. *(Grade 4-6)*

1.1 Name the type of ion that acids produce in aqueous solutions.

[1 mark]

1.2 What type of reaction took place in the student's experiment? Tick **one** box.

☐ thermal decomposition ☐ redox

☐ neutralisation ☐ combustion

[1 mark]

2 All metal hydroxides are bases. They can react with acids to form a salt and water. *(Grade 6-7)*

2.1 Sodium hydroxide is a soluble base. What name is given to bases that dissolve in water?

[1 mark]

2.2 Complete and balance the symbol equation given below for the reaction of nitric acid with magnesium hydroxide.

$$2HNO_3 + Mg(OH)_2 \rightarrow \text{.................} + \text{.................}$$

[2 marks]

PRACTICAL

3 Silver nitrate is a soluble salt. It can be made by adding an excess of insoluble silver carbonate to nitric acid until no further reaction occurs. *(Grade 6-7)*

Figure 1

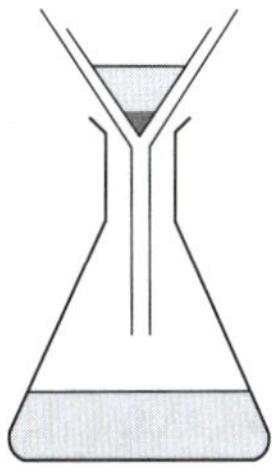

3.1 Give **one** observation that would indicate that the reaction is complete.

[1 mark]

3.2 Once the reaction is complete, the excess silver carbonate can be separated from the silver nitrate solution using the apparatus shown in **Figure 1**. What is this method of separation called?

[1 mark]

3.3 Describe how you could produce solid silver nitrate from silver nitrate solution.

[3 marks]

Topic C4 — Chemical Changes

Metals and their Reactivity

Metals can be placed in order of reactivity. This can be really useful for predicting their reactions.

The Reactivity Series — How Well a Metal Reacts

1) The reactivity series lists metals in order of their reactivity towards other substances.

2) For metals, their reactivity is determined by how easily they lose electrons — forming positive ions. The higher up the reactivity series a metal is, the more easily it will form positive ions.

3) When metals react with water or acid, they lose electrons and form positive ions. So, the higher a metal is in the reactivity series, the more easily it reacts with water or acid.

4) If you compare the relative reactivity of different metals with either an acid or water and put them in order from the most reactive to the least reactive, the order you get is the reactivity series.

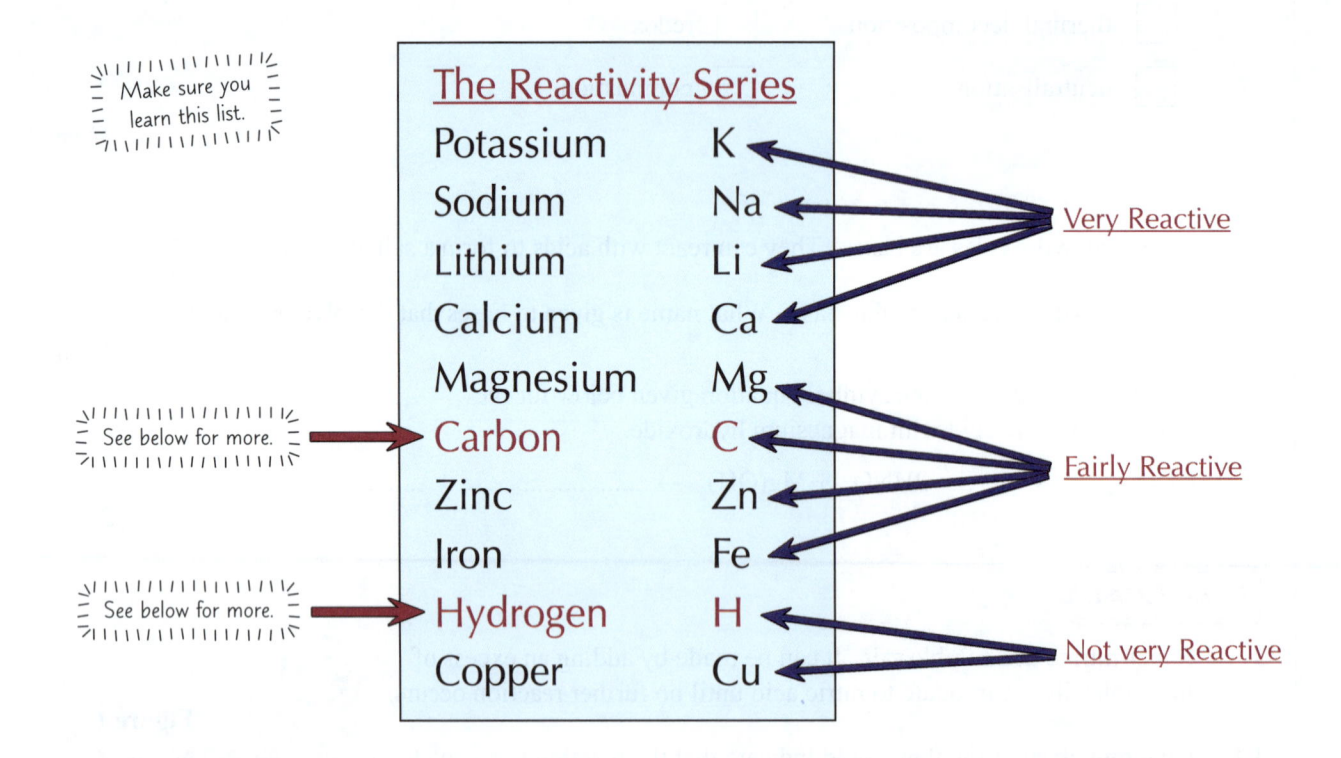

Make sure you learn this list.

The Reactivity Series

Potassium	K	← Very Reactive
Sodium	Na	
Lithium	Li	
Calcium	Ca	
Magnesium	Mg	
Carbon	C	← Fairly Reactive
Zinc	Zn	
Iron	Fe	
Hydrogen	H	
Copper	Cu	← Not very Reactive

See below for more. → Carbon

See below for more. → Hydrogen

Carbon and Hydrogen

Carbon and hydrogen are non-metals, but they're often included in the reactivity series, because this gives you information about how metals will react with them:

- Metals that are less reactive than carbon can be extracted from their ores by reduction with carbon (see p.238). Metals that are more reactive than carbon cannot be extracted in this way.
- Metals that are more reactive than hydrogen (above it in the reactivity series) will react with acids. Metals less reactive than hydrogen will not react with acids.

Topic C4 — Chemical Changes

Metals and their Reactivity

How Metals React With Acids Tells You About Their Reactivity

Some metals react with acids to produce a salt and hydrogen gas.

$$\text{Acid} + \text{Metal} \rightarrow \text{Salt} + \text{Hydrogen}$$

Hydrochloric acid will react to form chloride salts and sulfuric acid will react to form sulfate salts.

1) The speed of reaction is indicated by the rate at which the bubbles of hydrogen are given off.

2) The more reactive the metal, the faster the reaction will go. Very reactive metals like potassium, sodium, lithium and calcium react explosively, but less reactive metals such as magnesium, zinc and iron react less violently. In general, copper won't react with cold, dilute acids.

Magnesium reacts vigorously with cold dilute acids like $HCl_{(aq)}$ and $H_2SO_{4(aq)}$ and produces loads of bubbles.

Both zinc and iron react fairly slowly with dilute acids, but more strongly if you heat them up.

magnesium

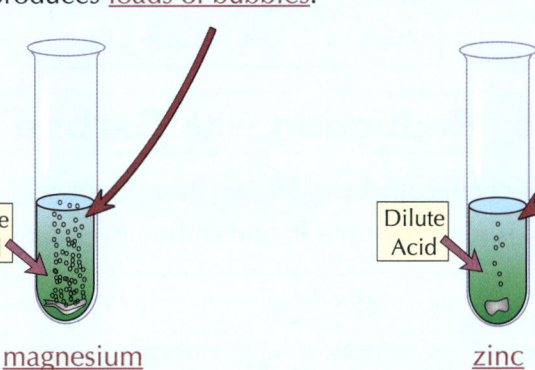

$Mg_{(s)} + 2HCl_{(aq)} \rightarrow MgCl_{2(aq)} + H_{2(g)}$

$Mg_{(s)} + H_2SO_{4(aq)} \rightarrow MgSO_{4(aq)} + H_{2(g)}$

zinc

$Zn_{(s)} + 2HCl_{(aq)} \rightarrow ZnCl_{2(aq)} + H_{2(g)}$

$Zn_{(s)} + H_2SO_{4(aq)} \rightarrow ZnSO_{4(aq)} + H_{2(g)}$

iron

$Fe_{(s)} + 2HCl_{(aq)} \rightarrow FeCl_{2(aq)} + H_{2(g)}$

$Fe_{(s)} + H_2SO_{4(aq)} \rightarrow FeSO_{4(aq)} + H_{2(g)}$

You can use the burning splint test (see page 274) to confirm that hydrogen is formed in these reactions.

Metals Also React with Water

The reactions of metals with water also show the reactivity of metals.

$$\text{Metal} + \text{Water} \rightarrow \text{Metal Hydroxide} + \text{Hydrogen}$$

For example, calcium: $Ca_{(s)} + 2H_2O_{(l)} \rightarrow Ca(OH)_{2(aq)} + H_{2(g)}$

You can see more on the reactions of Group 1 metals with water on page 196.

1) The metals potassium, sodium, lithium and calcium will all react with water.

2) Less reactive metals like zinc, iron and copper won't react with water.

Metals at the top of the reactivity series are highly reactive

You can use the results of experiments like these to work out an order of reactivity for the metals that you used. Just remember, the more vigorous the reaction, the more reactive the metal.

Q1 Give the balanced equation, including state symbols, for the reaction of sodium and water. [3 marks]

Topic C4 — Chemical Changes

Metals and their Reactivity

Metals Often Have to be Separated from their Oxides

1) Most metals aren't found in the earth in their pure form. They tend to be fairly reactive, so they're usually found as compounds and have to be extracted before they can be used.
2) Lots of common metals, like iron and aluminium, react with oxygen to form their oxides, which are found in the ground. This process is an example of oxidation. These oxides are often the ores that the metals need to be extracted from.
3) A reaction that separates a metal from its oxide is called a reduction reaction.

An ore is a type of rock that contains metal compounds.

Formation of Metal Ore:

Oxidation = Gain of Oxygen

For example, magnesium can be oxidised to make magnesium oxide.
$$2Mg + O_2 \rightarrow 2MgO$$

Extraction of Metal:

Reduction = Loss of Oxygen

For example, copper oxide can be reduced to copper.
$$2CuO + C \rightarrow 2Cu + CO_2$$

Some Metals can be Extracted by Reduction with Carbon

1) Some metals can be extracted from their ores chemically by reduction using carbon.
2) In this reaction, the ore is reduced as oxygen is removed from it, and carbon gains oxygen so is oxidised.

For example:

$$2Fe_2O_3 + 3C \rightarrow 4Fe + 3CO_2$$
iron(III) oxide + carbon → iron + carbon dioxide

3) As you saw on p.236, the position of the metal in the reactivity series determines whether it can be extracted by reduction with carbon.

- Metals higher than carbon in the reactivity series have to be extracted using electrolysis, which is expensive. — Extracted by using electrolysis.
- Metals below carbon in the reactivity series can be extracted by reduction using carbon. For example, iron oxide is reduced in a blast furnace to make iron. This is because carbon can only take the oxygen away from metals which are less reactive than carbon itself is. — Extracted by reduction with carbon.

The Reactivity Series

Potassium	K	more reactive
Sodium	Na	
Lithium	Li	
Calcium	Ca	
Magnesium	Mg	
CARBON	**C**	
Zinc	Zn	
Iron	Fe	
Hydrogen	H	
Copper	Cu	less reactive

A few metals are so unreactive that they are found in the earth as the metal itself. For example, gold is mined as its elemental form.

Carbon can't reduce the metals above it in the reactivity series

Make sure you understand the difference between reduction and oxidation and make sure that you can spot which substance has been reduced and which substance has been oxidised in a reaction.

Q1 Write a balanced equation for the reduction of lead oxide, PbO, by carbon, C. [2 marks]

Q2 A mining company tried to extract calcium from its ore by reduction with carbon. The process did not work. Explain why. [1 mark]

Topic C4 — Chemical Changes

Redox Reactions

*Reduction and oxidation **doesn't** just mean the loss or gain of oxygen — it can also refer to **electron** transfer.*

If Electrons are Transferred, it's a Redox Reaction

Oxidation can mean the addition of oxygen (or a reaction with it), and reduction can be the removal of oxygen. But you can also define oxidation and reduction in terms of electrons:

> A loss of electrons is called oxidation.

> A gain of electrons is called reduction.

Make sure you learn these definitions.

A handy way to remember this is using the mnemonic OIL RIG:

> Oxidation Is Loss, Reduction Is Gain   (of electrons)

REDuction and OXidation happen at the same time — hence the name "REDOX".

Some Examples of Redox Reactions:

Metals reacting with acids

1) All reactions of metals with acids (see page 237) are redox reactions.
2) For example, the reaction of iron with dilute sulfuric acid is a redox reaction.
3) The iron atoms lose electrons to become iron(II) ions — they are oxidised by the hydrogen ions.
   $$Fe \rightarrow Fe^{2+} + 2e^-$$
4) The hydrogen ions gain electrons to become hydrogen atoms — they are reduced by the iron atoms.
   $$2H^+ + 2e^- \rightarrow H_2$$
5) The ionic equation (see page 240) for the redox reaction is: $Fe + 2H^+ \rightarrow Fe^{2+} + H_2$

Ionic equations only show the things that are actually reacting — the sulfate ions from the acid aren't shown here, because nothing happens to them.

Halogen Displacement Reactions

1) A more reactive halogen can displace a less reactive halogen from a salt solution (see page 198).
2) For example, chlorine can displace bromine from potassium bromide solution.
3) The chlorine atoms gain electrons to become chloride ions — they are reduced by the bromide ions.
   $$Cl_2 + 2e^- \rightarrow 2Cl^-$$
4) The bromide ions lose electrons to become bromine atoms — they are oxidised by the chlorine atoms.
   $$2Br^- \rightarrow Br_2 + 2e^-$$
5) The ionic equation for this redox reaction is: $Cl_2 + 2Br^- \rightarrow 2Cl^- + Br_2$

Same here — the ionic equation doesn't show the potassium ions from the potassium bromide, because nothing happens to them.

Remember OIL RIG — 'Oxidation Is Loss, Reduction Is Gain'

OIL RIG is a pretty handy way of reminding yourself about what goes on during a redox reaction. Make sure that you don't forget that redox reactions are all about the transfer of electrons.

Topic C4 — Chemical Changes

Redox Reactions

Metal Displacement Reactions are Redox Reactions

1) If you put a reactive metal into the solution of a dissolved metal compound, the reactive metal will replace the less reactive metal in the compound (see the reactivity series on page 236).
2) This type of reaction is another example of a displacement reaction.
3) Here's the rule to remember:

> A MORE REACTIVE metal will displace a LESS REACTIVE metal from its compound.

For example, if you put iron in a solution of copper sulfate ($CuSO_4$) the more reactive iron will "kick out" the less reactive copper from the solution. You end up with iron sulfate solution ($FeSO_4$) and copper metal:

$$\text{iron + copper sulfate} \rightarrow \text{iron sulfate + copper}$$
$$Fe_{(s)} + CuSO_{4(aq)} \rightarrow FeSO_{4(aq)} + Cu_{(s)}$$

In this reaction the iron loses 2 electrons to become a 2+ ion — it's oxidised.

$$Fe \rightarrow Fe^{2+} + 2e^-$$

The copper ion gains these 2 electrons to become a copper atom — it's reduced.

$$Cu^{2+} + 2e^- \rightarrow Cu$$

This reaction is used in industry to produce pure copper from copper salt solutions and cheap scrap iron.

4) In metal displacement reactions it's always the metal ion that gains electrons and is reduced. The metal atom always loses electrons and is oxidised.
5) In the exam you could be asked to write word or symbol equations for metal displacement reactions.

Ionic Equations Show Just the Useful Bits of Reactions

1) In an ionic equation only the particles that react and the products they form are shown. For example:

$$Mg_{(s)} + Zn^{2+}_{(aq)} \rightarrow Mg^{2+}_{(aq)} + Zn_{(s)}$$

2) This just shows the displacement of zinc ions by magnesium metal. Here's what the full equation of the above reaction would be if you'd started off with magnesium metal and zinc chloride solution:

$$Mg_{(s)} + ZnCl_{2(aq)} \rightarrow MgCl_{2(aq)} + Zn_{(s)}$$

3) If you write out the equation so you can see all the ions, you'll see that the chloride ions don't change in the reaction — they're spectator ions.

$$Mg_{(s)} + Zn^{2+}_{(aq)} + 2Cl^-_{(aq)} \rightarrow Mg^{2+}_{(aq)} + 2Cl^-_{(aq)} + Zn_{(s)}$$

4) You don't include spectator ions in the ionic equation, so to get from this to the ionic equation, you cross out the chloride ions.
5) The ionic equation just concentrates on the substances which are oxidised or reduced.

A displacement reaction is a type of redox reaction

Try writing some ionic equations now — write the ionic equation for the reaction between zinc and iron chloride ($FeCl_2$). What's being oxidised? What's being reduced?

Q1 The equation for the reaction of zinc and iron sulfate is: $Zn_{(s)} + FeSO_{4(aq)} \rightarrow ZnSO_{4(aq)} + Fe_{(s)}$
 a) Write an ionic equation for the reaction. [1 mark]
 b) State which species is being reduced and which is being oxidised. [2 marks]

Q1 Video Solution

Topic C4 — Chemical Changes

Warm-Up & Exam Questions

Hoping to test your knowledge with some testing chemistry questions? You're in luck...

Warm-Up Questions

1) What determines the reactivity of a metal?
2) Magnesium is reacted with dilute hydrochloric acid. Give the name of the salt formed.
3) Which two substances are formed when a metal reacts with water?
4) This equation shows how zinc reacts with copper chloride: $Zn_{(s)} + CuCl_{2(aq)} \rightarrow ZnCl_{2(aq)} + Cu_{(s)}$
   a) Write an ionic equation for this reaction.
   b) State which species in this reaction is being oxidised.

Exam Questions

1 **Figure 1** shows part of the reactivity series of metals. Hydrogen has also been included in this reactivity series. *Grade 4-6*

Figure 1

Potassium	K
Sodium	Na
Calcium	Ca
Magnesium	Mg
Zinc	Zn
Iron	Fe
HYDROGEN	H
Copper	Cu

1.1 Name **one** metal from **Figure 1** that is more reactive than magnesium.

[1 mark]

1.2 Name **one** metal from **Figure 1** which would not react with acids at all.

[1 mark]

1.3 A student places a small piece of zinc into dilute acid. The mixture produces bubbles of hydrogen gas fairly slowly. Use this information to predict what would happen if the student repeated the experiment using iron.

[2 marks]

2 Iron can be extracted by the reduction of iron(III) oxide (Fe_2O_3) with carbon (C), to produce iron and carbon dioxide. *Grade 6-7*

2.1 Write a balanced symbol equation for this reaction.

[2 marks]

2.2 Explain why the iron(III) oxide is described as being reduced during this reaction.

[1 mark]

3 A student adds a piece of copper to some iron sulfate solution and a piece of iron to some copper sulfate solution. **Figure 2** shows what the test tubes looked like just after he added the metals. Predict what he will observe in both tubes, **A** and **B**, after 2 hours. Explain your answer. *Grade 7-9*

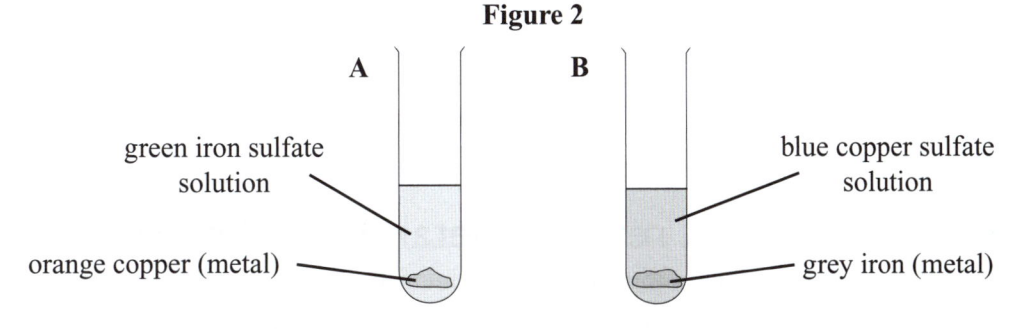

Figure 2

A: green iron sulfate solution, orange copper (metal)

B: blue copper sulfate solution, grey iron (metal)

[6 marks]

Topic C4 — Chemical Changes

Electrolysis

You need to know the ins and outs of how **electrolysis** works. So buckle up, here we go...

Electrolysis Means 'Splitting Up with Electricity'

1) During electrolysis, an electric current is passed through an electrolyte. The electrolyte is a molten or dissolved ionic compound (it must be molten or dissolved so that the ions are free to move).

2) The ions move towards the electrodes, where they react, and the compound decomposes.

3) The positive ions in the electrolyte will move towards the cathode (−ve electrode) and gain electrons (they are reduced).

4) The negative ions in the electrolyte will move towards the anode (+ve electrode) and lose electrons (they are oxidised).

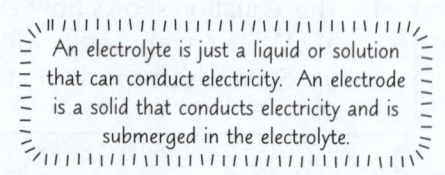

An electrolyte is just a liquid or solution that can conduct electricity. An electrode is a solid that conducts electricity and is submerged in the electrolyte.

5) This creates a flow of charge through the electrolyte as ions travel to the electrodes.

6) As ions gain or lose electrons, they form the uncharged element and are discharged from the electrolyte.

Electrolysis of Molten Ionic Solids Forms Elements

1) An ionic solid can't be electrolysed because the ions are in fixed positions and can't move.

2) Molten ionic compounds can be electrolysed because the ions can move freely and conduct electricity.

3) Molten ionic compounds are always broken up into their elements. A good example of this is the electrolysis of molten lead bromide:

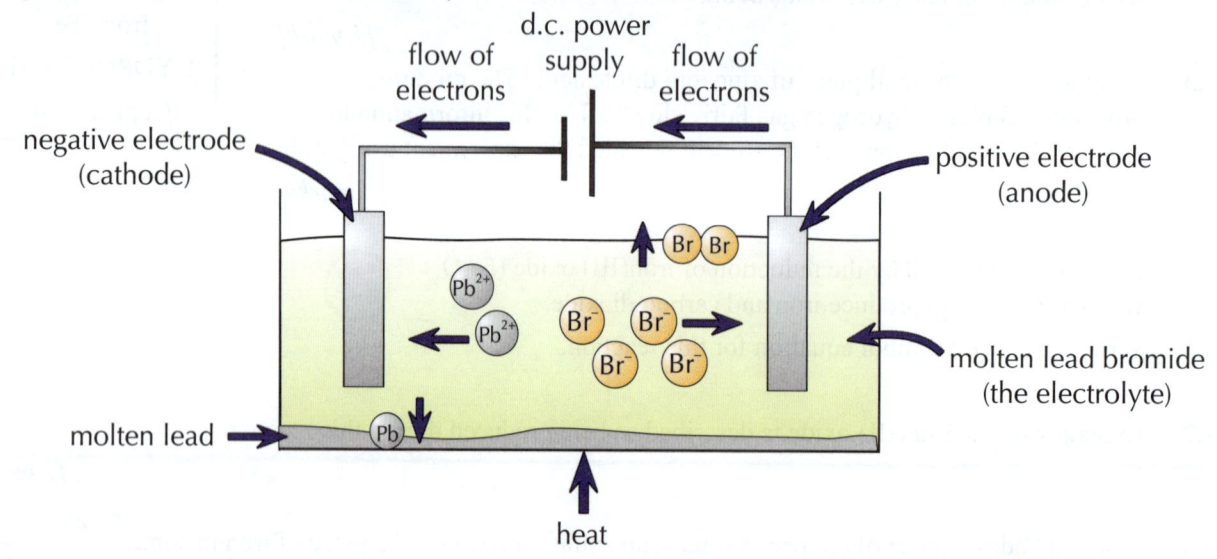

4) The electrodes should be made of an inert material, so they don't react with the electrolyte.

5) Positive metal ions are reduced to the element at the cathode:
$$Pb^{2+} + 2e^- \rightarrow Pb$$

6) Negative non-metal ions are oxidised to the element at the anode:
$$2Br^- \rightarrow Br_2 + 2e^-$$

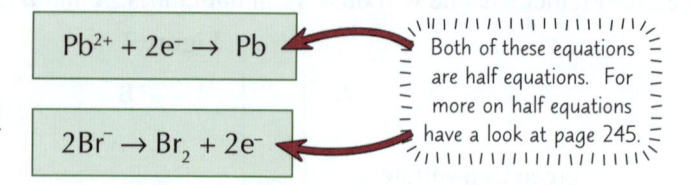

Both of these equations are half equations. For more on half equations have a look at page 245.

Electrolysis is used to extract reactive metals from their ores

It might be jolly useful for your exams to learn the products of electrolysis of molten lead bromide...

Q1   A student carries out electrolysis on molten calcium chloride. What is produced at:
a) the anode?   b) the cathode?   [2 marks]

Topic C4 — Chemical Changes

Electrolysis

Metals can be Extracted From Their Ores Using Electrolysis

If a metal is too reactive to be reduced with carbon (page 238) or reacts with carbon, then electrolysis can be used to extract it. Extracting metals via this method is very expensive as lots of energy is required to melt the ore and produce the required current. For example:

1) Aluminium is extracted from the ore bauxite by electrolysis. Bauxite contains aluminium oxide, Al_2O_3.

2) Aluminium oxide has a very high melting temperature so it's mixed with cryolite to lower the melting point.

Cryolite is an aluminium based compound with a lower melting point than aluminium oxide.

3) The molten mixture contains free ions — so it'll conduct electricity.

4) The positive Al^{3+} ions are attracted to the negative electrode where they each pick up three electrons and turn into neutral aluminium atoms. These then sink to the bottom of the electrolysis tank.

5) The negative O^{2-} ions are attracted to the positive electrode where they each lose two electrons. The neutral oxygen atoms will then combine to form O_2 molecules.

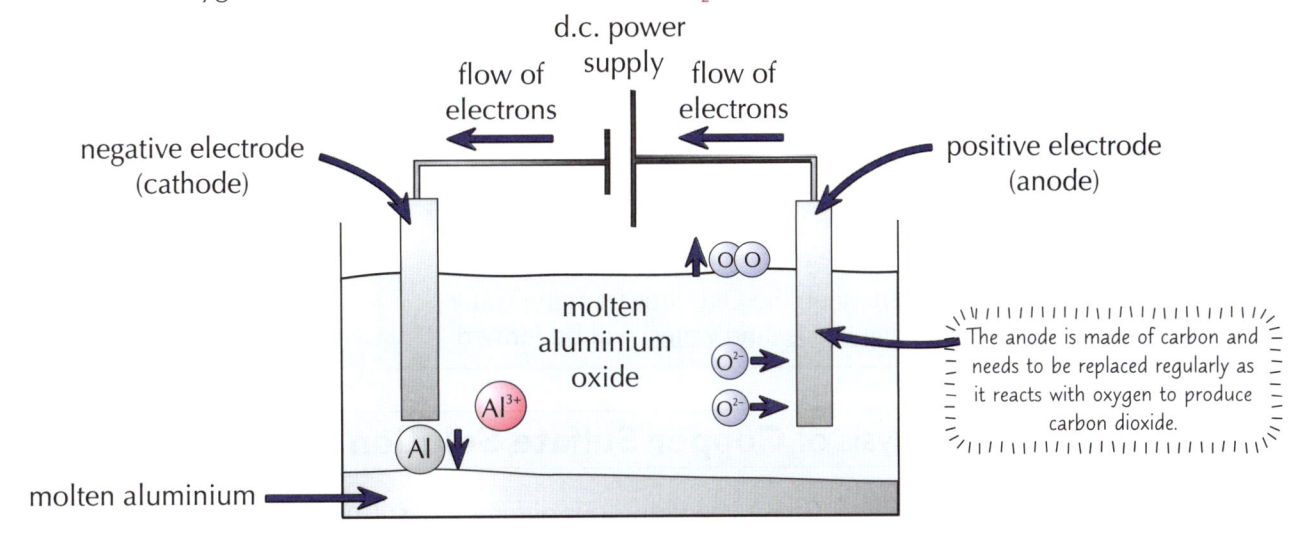

The anode is made of carbon and needs to be replaced regularly as it reacts with oxygen to produce carbon dioxide.

At the Negative Electrode:

1) Metals form positive ions, so they're attracted to the negative electrode.
2) So aluminium is produced at the negative electrode:

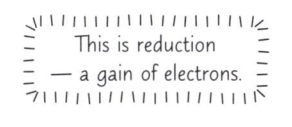

$$Al^{3+} + 3e^- \rightarrow Al$$

This is reduction — a gain of electrons.

At the Positive Electrode:

1) Non-metals form negative ions, so they're attracted to the positive electrode.
2) So oxygen is produced at the positive electrode:

$$2O^{2-} \rightarrow O_2 + 4e^-$$

This is oxidation — a loss of electrons.

Overall Equation:

aluminium oxide → aluminium + oxygen
$$2Al_2O_{3(l)} \rightarrow 4Al_{(l)} + 3O_{2(g)}$$

Topic C4 — Chemical Changes

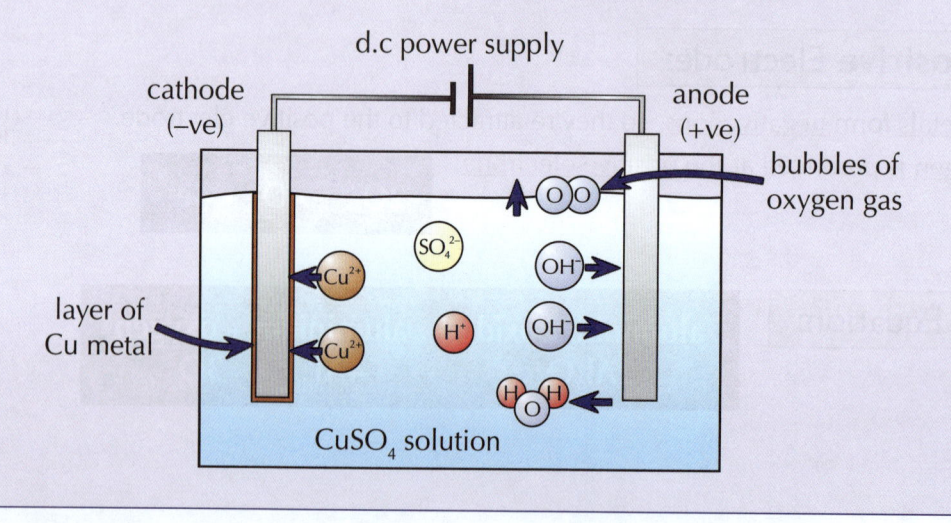

Electrolysis of Aqueous Solutions

When carrying out **electrolysis** on an **aqueous solution** you have to factor in the ions in **water**.

It May be Easier to Discharge Ions from Water than the Solute

1) In aqueous solutions, as well as the ions from the ionic compound, there will be hydrogen ions (H⁺) and hydroxide ions (OH⁻) from the water: $H_2O_{(l)} \rightleftharpoons H^+_{(aq)} + OH^-_{(aq)}$

2) Which ions are discharged at the electrodes when the solution is electrolysed will depend on the relative reactivity of all the ions in the solution.

Cathode

- At the cathode, if H⁺ ions and metal ions are present, hydrogen gas will be produced if the metal ions form an elemental metal that is more reactive than hydrogen (e.g. sodium ions).
- If the metal ions form an elemental metal that is less reactive than hydrogen (e.g. copper ions), a solid layer of the pure metal will be produced instead, which will coat the cathode.

Anode

At the anode, if OH⁻ and halide ions (Cl⁻, Br⁻, I⁻) are present, molecules of chlorine, bromine or iodine will be formed.

If no halide ions are present, then the OH⁻ ions from the water will be discharged and oxygen gas (and water) will be formed.

Example 1: Electrolysis of Copper Sulfate Solution

A solution of copper(II) sulfate ($CuSO_4$) contains four different ions: Cu^{2+}, SO_4^{2-}, H^+ and OH^-.

Copper metal is less reactive than hydrogen, so at the cathode copper metal is produced and coats the electrode:

$$Cu^{2+} + 2e^- \rightarrow Cu$$

There aren't any halide ions present, so at the anode oxygen and water are produced: The oxygen can be seen as bubbles.

$$4OH^- \rightarrow O_2 + 2H_2O + 4e^-$$

Topic C4 — Chemical Changes

Electrolysis of Aqueous Solutions

Example 2: Electrolysis of **Sodium Chloride Solution**

A solution of sodium chloride (NaCl) contains four different ions: Na^+, Cl^-, OH^- and H^+.

Sodium metal is more reactive than hydrogen. So at the cathode, hydrogen gas is produced.

$$2H^+ + 2e^- \rightarrow H_2$$

Chloride ions are present in the solution. So at the anode chlorine gas is produced.

$$2Cl^- \rightarrow Cl_2 + 2e^-$$

You can do an electrolysis experiment in the lab using a set-up like the one on page 410. Once the experiment is finished you can test any gaseous products to work out what has been produced at the electrodes:

- Chlorine bleaches damp litmus paper, turning it white.
- Hydrogen makes a "squeaky pop" with a lighted splint.
- Oxygen will relight a glowing splint.

For more on tests for gases, turn to page 274.

The Half Equations — Make Sure the Electrons Balance

1) Half equations show the reactions at the electrodes (they show ions or atoms gaining or losing electrons).
2) You can combine the half equations for the reactions at both electrodes to get the ionic equation for the overall reaction. The important thing to remember when you combine half equations is that the number of electrons shown in each half equation must be the same.

> For the electrolysis of aqueous sodium chloride solution the half equations are:
> Negative Electrode: $2H^+ + 2e^- \rightarrow H_2$
> Positive Electrode: $2Cl^- \rightarrow Cl_2 + 2e^-$ (or $2Cl^- - 2e^- \rightarrow Cl_2$)
> You can combine these to get the ionic equation: $2H^+ + 2Cl^- \rightarrow H_2 + Cl_2$

The electrons on each side of the half equations balance, so they cancel out in the full ionic equation.

Remember, if there are no halide ions in an aqueous solution, OH^- ions are discharged at the positive electrode. The half equation for this is: $4OH^- \rightarrow O_2 + 2H_2O + 4e^-$ (or $4OH^- - 4e^- \rightarrow O_2 + 2H_2O$)

Remember — all aqueous solutions contain OH^- and H^+ ions

This electrolysis business is a bit confusing — you need to take it slow and make sure you get it.

Q1 An aqueous solution of copper bromide, $CuBr_2$, is electrolysed using inert electrodes.
State what is produced at: a) the anode, b) the cathode. [2 marks]

Topic C4 — Chemical Changes

Warm-Up & Exam Questions

Time to test your mettle. Try and get through the following questions. If there's anything you're not quite sure about, have a look at the pages again until you can answer the questions without batting an eyelid.

Warm-Up Questions

1) At which electrode are metals deposited during electrolysis?
2) What products are made when molten zinc chloride is electrolysed?
3) During the electrolysis of molten aluminium oxide are the aluminium ions being reduced or oxidised?
4) What is formed at the cathode during the electrolysis of an aqueous solution of potassium hydroxide?

Exam Questions

1   Aluminium is extracted by electrolysis of molten aluminium oxide (Al_2O_3). *Grade 6-7*

1.1   The aluminium oxide is dissolved in molten cryolite. State why.

[1 mark]

1.2   Complete the half equation below for the reaction that occurs at the negative electrode.

$$............ + 3e^- \rightarrow ....$$

[1 mark]

1.3   Complete the half equation below for the reaction that occurs at the positive electrode.

$$............ \rightarrow .... + 4e^-$$

[1 mark]

1.4   The positive electrode is made of carbon. Explain why it will need to be replaced over time.

[2 marks]

2   When sodium solution chloride is electrolysed, a gas is produced at each electrode. *Grade 6-7*

2.1   Name the gas produced at the negative electrode.

[1 mark]

2.2   Give the half equation for the reaction at the negative electrode.

[1 mark]

2.3   Name the gas produced at the positive electrode.

[1 mark]

2.4   Give the half equation for the reaction at the positive electrode.

[1 mark]

2.5   Explain why sodium hydroxide is left in solution at the end of the reaction.

[2 marks]

2.6   If copper chloride solution is electrolysed, copper metal is produced at the negative electrode, instead of the gas named in **2.1**. Explain why.

[1 mark]

Topic C4 — Chemical Changes

Topic C5 — Energy Changes

Exothermic and Endothermic Reactions

*Whenever chemical reactions occur, there are changes in **energy**. This means that when chemicals get together, things either **heat up** or **cool down**. I'll give you a heads up — this page is a good 'un.*

Energy is Moved Around in Chemical Reactions

1) Chemicals store a certain amount of energy — and different chemicals store different amounts.
2) If the products of a reaction store more energy than the original reactants, then they must have taken in the difference in energy between the products and reactants from the surroundings during the reaction.
3) But if they store less, then the excess energy was transferred to the surroundings during the reaction.
4) The overall amount of energy doesn't change. This is because energy is conserved in reactions — it can't be created or destroyed, only moved around. This means the amount of energy in the universe always stays the same.

In an Exothermic Reaction, Heat is Given Out

> An exothermic reaction is one which transfers energy to the surroundings, usually by heating. This is shown by a rise in temperature.

1) The best example of an exothermic reaction is burning fuels — also called combustion. This gives out a lot of energy — it's very exothermic.
2) Neutralisation reactions (acid + alkali) are also exothermic.
3) Many oxidation reactions are exothermic. For example, adding sodium to water releases energy, so it must be exothermic — see page 196. The reaction releases energy and the sodium moves about on the surface of the water as it is oxidised.
4) Exothermic reactions have lots of everyday uses. For example:

> - Some hand warmers use the exothermic oxidation of iron in air (with a salt solution catalyst) to release energy.
> - Self heating cans of hot chocolate and coffee also rely on exothermic reactions between chemicals in their bases.

In an Endothermic Reaction, Heat is Taken In

> An endothermic reaction is one which takes in energy from the surroundings. This is shown by a fall in temperature.

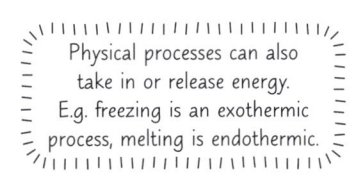

Physical processes can also take in or release energy. E.g. freezing is an exothermic process, melting is endothermic.

1) Endothermic reactions are much less common than exothermic reactions, but they include:
   - The reaction between citric acid and sodium hydrogencarbonate.
   - Thermal decomposition — e.g. heating calcium carbonate causes it to decompose into calcium oxide (also called quicklime) and carbon dioxide:

   Calcium carbonate → $CaCO_{3(s)}$ (+ HEAT) → $CO_{2(g)}$ + $CaO_{(s)}$ ← Quicklime

2) Endothermic reactions also have everyday uses. For example:

> Endothermic reactions are used in some sports injury packs — the chemical reaction allows the pack to become instantly cooler without having to put it in the freezer.

Exothermic and Endothermic Reactions

*Sometimes it's **not enough** to just know if a reaction is **endothermic** or **exothermic**. You may also need to know **how much** energy is absorbed or released — you can do experiments to find this out. Fun, fun, fun...*

Energy Transfer can be Measured — PRACTICAL

1) You can measure the amount of energy released by a chemical reaction (in solution) by taking the temperature of the reagents (making sure they're the same), mixing them in a polystyrene cup and measuring the temperature of the solution at the end of the reaction (see diagram below).

2) The biggest problem with energy measurements is the amount of energy lost to the surroundings.

3) You can reduce it a bit by putting the polystyrene cup into a beaker of cotton wool to give more insulation, and putting a lid on the cup to reduce energy lost by evaporation.

4) This method works for neutralisation reactions or reactions between metals and acids, or carbonates and acids.

5) You can also use this method to investigate what effect different variables have on the amount of energy transferred — e.g. the mass or concentration of the reactants used.

Here's how you could test the effect of acid concentration on the energy released in a neutralisation reaction between hydrochloric acid (HCl) and sodium hydroxide (NaOH):

1) Put 25 cm³ of 0.25 mol/dm³ of hydrochloric acid and sodium hydroxide in separate beakers.

2) Place the beakers in a water bath set to 25 °C until they are both at the same temperature (25 °C).

3) Add the HCl followed by the NaOH to a polystyrene cup with a lid — as in the diagram.

4) Take the temperature of the mixture every 30 seconds, and record the highest temperature.

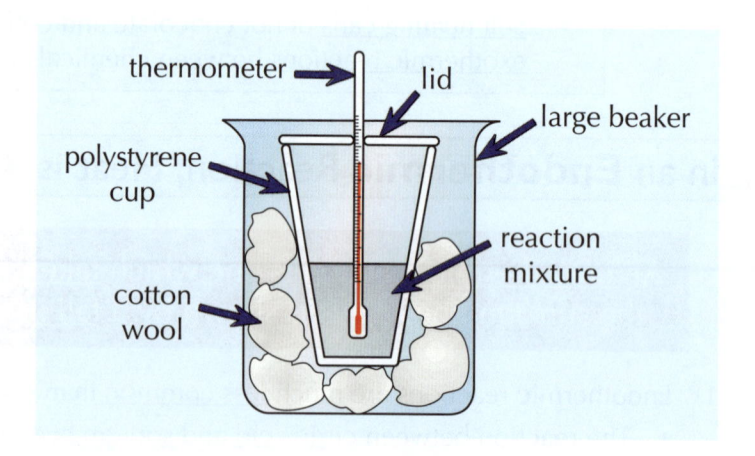

5) Repeat steps 1-4 using 0.5 mol/dm³ and then 1 mol/dm³ of hydrochloric acid.

To get a reasonably accurate reading, insulate your reaction

The experiment on this page is an example of a neutralisation reaction, which is an exothermic reaction. Remember, in an exothermic reaction the particles transfer energy to their surroundings. This means that the particles themselves lose energy, but the reaction mixture gets warmer.

Topic C5 — Energy Changes

Bond Energies

*So you know that chemical reactions can take in or release energy — this page is about what **causes** these energy changes. Hint — it's all to do with **making** and **breaking** chemical bonds.*

Energy Must Always be Supplied to Break Bonds

1) During a chemical reaction, old bonds are broken and new bonds are formed.
2) Energy must be supplied to break existing bonds — so bond breaking is an endothermic process.
3) Energy is released when new bonds are formed — so bond formation is an exothermic process.

There's more on energy transfer on page 247.

BOND BREAKING — ENDOTHERMIC

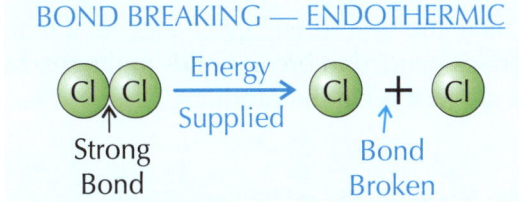

Cl–Cl (Strong Bond) → Energy Supplied → Cl + Cl (Bond Broken)

BOND FORMING — EXOTHERMIC

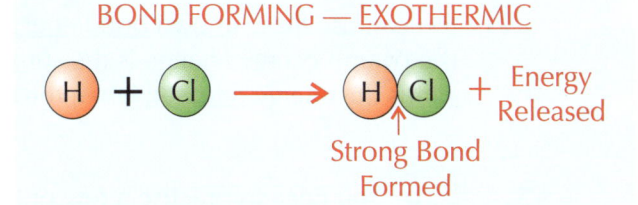

H + Cl → H–Cl (Strong Bond Formed) + Energy Released

4) In exothermic reactions the energy released by forming bonds is greater than the energy used to break them. In endothermic reactions the energy used to break bonds is greater than the energy released by forming them.

Reaction Profiles Show Energy Changes

Reaction profiles are sometimes called energy level diagrams.

Reaction profiles are diagrams that show the relative energies of the reactants and products in a reaction, and how the energy changes over the course of the reaction.

1) This reaction profile shows an exothermic reaction — the products are at a lower energy than the reactants. The difference in height represents the overall energy change in the reaction (the energy given out) per mole.
2) The initial rise in the line represents the energy needed to break the old bonds and start the reaction. This is the activation energy (E_a).
3) The activation energy is the minimum amount of energy the reactants need to collide with each other and react.
4) The greater the activation energy, the more energy needed to start the reaction — this has to be supplied, e.g. by heating the reaction mixture.

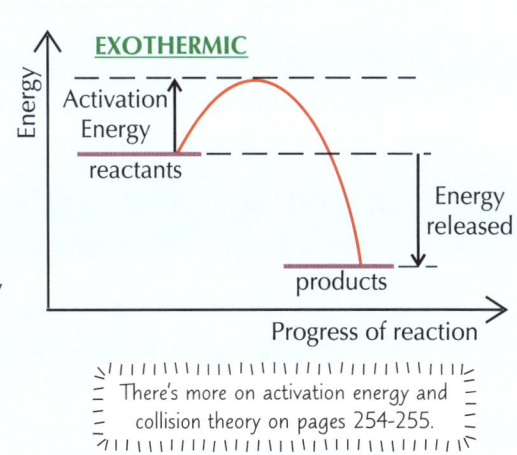

EXOTHERMIC — graph showing Energy vs Progress of reaction, with Activation Energy from reactants to peak, and Energy released from reactants level down to products level.

There's more on activation energy and collision theory on pages 254-255.

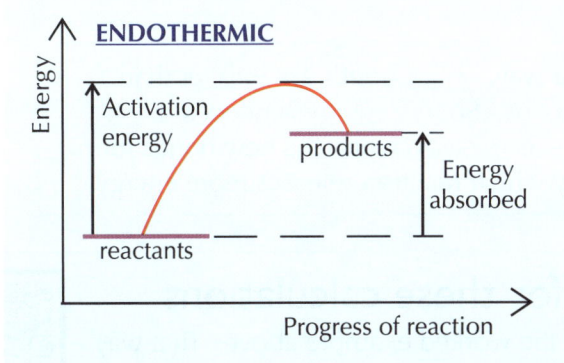

ENDOTHERMIC — graph showing Energy vs Progress of reaction, with Activation energy from reactants to peak, products at higher level than reactants, Energy absorbed marked.

5) This reaction profile shows an endothermic reaction because the products are at a higher energy than the reactants.

6) The difference in height represents the overall energy change during the reaction (the energy taken in) per mole.

Breaking bonds requires energy, forming bonds releases energy

Q1 Here is the equation for the combustion of methane in air: $CH_{4(g)} + 2O_{2(g)} \rightarrow CO_{2(g)} + 2H_2O_{(g)}$
    Draw a reaction profile for this reaction. [3 marks]

Topic C5 — Energy Changes

Bond Energies

*You need to be able to **work out** the energy change for a particular reaction. Here's a nice little **example**, complete with explanation, to get you started.*

Bond Energy **Calculations** Need to be **Practised**

1) <u>Every</u> chemical bond has a particular <u>bond energy</u> associated with it. This <u>bond energy</u> varies slightly depending on what <u>compound</u> the bond occurs in.

2) You can use these <u>known bond energies</u> to calculate the <u>overall energy change</u> for a reaction. The overall energy change is the <u>sum</u> of the energies <u>needed</u> to break bonds in the reactants <u>minus</u> the energy <u>released</u> when the new bonds are formed in the products.

3) You need to <u>practise</u> a few of these, but the basic idea is really very simple...

EXAMPLE

Using the bond energies given below, calculate the energy change for the reaction between H_2 and Cl_2 forming HCl:

H — H + Cl — Cl → 2H — Cl
H_2 + Cl_2 → 2HCl

The bond energies you need are:
- H—H: +436 kJ/mol
- Cl—Cl: +242 kJ/mol
- H—Cl: +431 kJ/mol

1) Find the <u>energy required</u> to break the original bonds:
   (1 × H–H) + (1 × Cl–Cl) = 436 kJ/mol + 242 kJ/mol = 678 kJ/mol

2) Find the <u>energy released</u> by forming the new bonds.
   2 × H–Cl = 2 × 431 kJ/mol = 862 kJ/mol

3) Find the <u>overall energy change</u> for the reaction using this equation:
   Overall energy change = energy required to break bonds − energy released by forming bonds
   = 678 kJ/mol − 862 kJ/mol = **−184 kJ/mol**

You <u>can't compare</u> the overall energy changes of reactions unless you know the <u>numerical differences</u> in the bond energies.

Chlorine and bromine react with hydrogen in a similar way. <u>Br–Br</u> bonds are <u>weaker</u> than Cl–Cl bonds and <u>H–Br</u> bonds are <u>weaker</u> than H–Cl bonds. So <u>less energy</u> is needed to <u>break</u> the bonds in the reaction with bromine, but <u>less energy</u> is <u>released</u> when the new bonds form. So unless you know the <u>exact difference</u>, you can't say which reaction releases more energy.

You need a balanced chemical equation for these calculations

It's helpful to <u>lay out</u> the information the way that is shown in the worked example above. That way you won't get all your bond energies mixed up and you'll be able to clearly see what you have do.

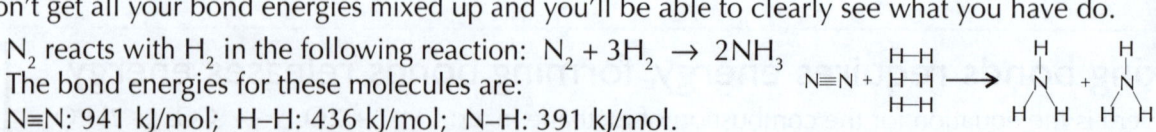

Q1 N_2 reacts with H_2 in the following reaction: $N_2 + 3H_2 \rightarrow 2NH_3$
The bond energies for these molecules are:
N≡N: 941 kJ/mol; H–H: 436 kJ/mol; N–H: 391 kJ/mol.
Calculate the overall energy change for this reaction. [3 marks]

Topic C5 — Energy Changes

Warm-Up & Exam Questions

Funny diagrams, bond energy calculations, a practical — there's a lot to get your head around in just a few pages here. Here are some questions so that you can check how you're getting on.

Warm-Up Questions

1) What is an exothermic reaction?
2) What is an endothermic reaction?
3) Is energy released when bonds are formed or when bonds are broken?
4) What is meant by the activation energy of a reaction?

Exam Questions

1   The diagrams in **Figure 1** represent the energy changes in four different chemical reactions. *(Grade 4-6)*

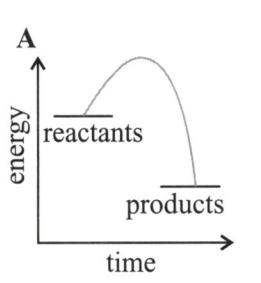

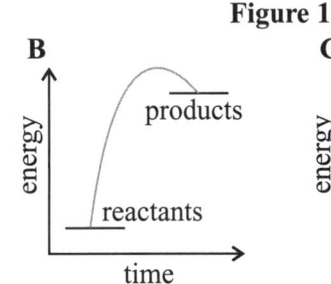

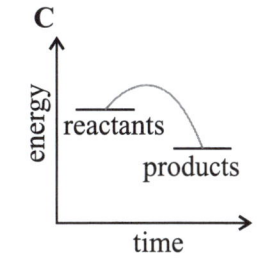

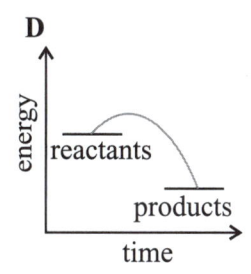

Figure 1

A: reactants (high) → products (low)
B: reactants (low) → products (high)
C: reactants (high) → products (low)
D: reactants (high) → products (low)

Write the letter of **one** diagram, **A**, **B**, **C** or **D**, which illustrates an endothermic reaction.

[1 mark]

PRACTICAL

2   A student places two beakers of ethanoic acid and dilute potassium hydroxide into a water bath until they are both 25 °C. He adds the ethanoic acid and then the potassium hydroxide to a polystyrene cup. After 1 minute the temperature of the mixture is 28.5 °C. *(Grade 6-7)*

2.1   Is this reaction endothermic or exothermic? Explain your answer.

[2 marks]

2.2   The student put a lid on the polystyrene cup during the experiment. Suggest why this was done.

[1 mark]

3   When methane burns in air it produces carbon dioxide and water, as shown in **Figure 2**. The bond energies for each bond in the molecules involved are shown in **Figure 3**. *(Grade 7-9)*

Figure 2

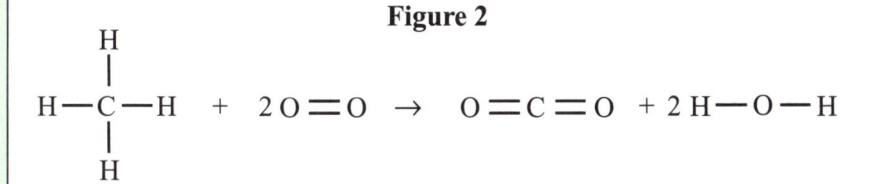

H–CH₂–H with extra H (methane structure) + 2 O=O → O=C=O + 2 H–O–H

Figure 3

	Bond energies (kJ/mol):
C – H	414
O = O	494
C = O	800
O – H	459

3.1   Which **two** types of bond are broken during the reaction shown in **Figure 2**?

[1 mark]

3.2   Calculate the overall energy change for the reaction shown in **Figure 2**.

[3 marks]

Topic C5 — Energy Changes

Revision Summary for Topics C1-5

That wraps up Topics C1-5 — time to find out how much you really know.
- Try these questions and tick off each one when you get it right.
- When you're completely happy with a topic, tick it off.

For even more practice, try the Retrieval Quizzes for Topics C1-5 — just scan the QR codes!

Topic C1 — Atomic Structure and the Periodic Table (p.173-199) ☐

1) Sketch an atom. Label the nucleus and the electrons.
2) How similar are the properties of a compound to the elements that it's made from?
3) What is the difference between a compound and a mixture?
4) Describe how different substances are separated by fractional distillation.
5) What did Bohr's nuclear model of the atom suggest?
6) Give the electronic structure of the following elements as numbers:
   a) helium   b) carbon   c) sodium
7) State three trends in Group 1 elements as you go down the group.
8) What is the charge of the ions that halogens form when they react with metals?

Topic C2 — Bonding, Structure and Properties of Matter (p.202-220) ☐

9) Describe how an ionic bond forms.
10) Sketch dot and cross diagrams to show the formation of:
    a) sodium chloride   b) magnesium oxide   c) magnesium chloride
11) Describe how covalent bonds form.
12) Describe the structure of a polymer.
13) Explain why metals have the following properties:
    a) good conduction of heat and electricity
    b) solid at room temperature
14) Name the three states of matter.

Topic C3 — Quantitative Chemistry (p.222-229) ☐

15) How do you calculate the percentage mass of an element in a compound?
16) What is the formula that relates the number of moles of a substance to its mass and M_r?
17) Give the equation for working out the concentration of a solution in g/dm^3.

Topic C4 — Chemical Changes (p.231-245) ☐

18) Give the general word equation for the reaction between an acid and a base.
19) Write a balanced equation for the reaction between hydrochloric acid and sodium carbonate.
20) What is the general word equation for the reaction of a metal with an acid?
21) In terms of electrons, give the definition of oxidation.
22) During the manufacture of aluminium from bauxite, which electrode is aluminium formed at?

Topic C5 — Energy Changes (p.247-250) ☐

23) Name two different types of chemical reaction which are exothermic.
24) Give an everyday example of an endothermic reaction.
25) Which part of an energy level diagram shows the activation energy?

Topics C1-5 — Revision Summary

Topic C6 — The Rate and Extent of Chemical Change

Rates of Reaction

*Rates of reaction are pretty **important**. In the **chemical industry**, the **faster** you make **chemicals**, the **faster** you make **money**.*

Reactions Can Go at All Sorts of Different Rates

1) The rate of a chemical reaction is how fast the reactants are changed into products.
2) One of the slowest is the rusting of iron (it's not slow enough though — what about my little Mini).
3) Other slow reactions include chemical weathering — like acid rain damage to limestone buildings.
4) An example of a moderate speed reaction would be the metal magnesium reacting with an acid to produce a gentle stream of bubbles.
5) Burning is a fast reaction, but explosions are even faster and release a lot of gas. Explosive reactions are all over in a fraction of a second.

You Need to Understand Graphs for the Rate of Reaction

1) You can find the speed of a reaction by recording the amount of product formed, or the amount of reactant used up over time (see page 256).
2) The steeper the line on the graph, the faster the rate of reaction. Over time the line becomes less steep as the reactants are used up.
3) The quickest reactions have the steepest lines and become flat in the least time.
4) The plot below uses the amount of product formed over time to show how the speed of a particular reaction varies under different conditions.

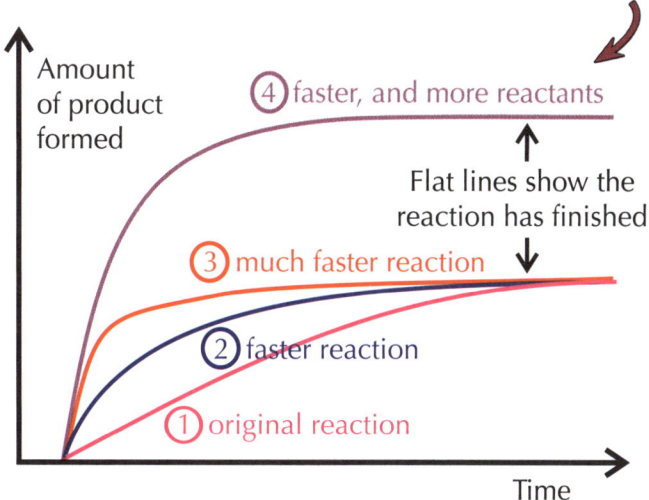

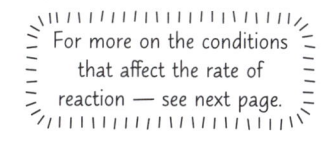

For more on the conditions that affect the rate of reaction — see next page.

Graph axes: Amount of product formed vs Time
- ④ faster, and more reactants
- ③ much faster reaction
- ② faster reaction
- ① original reaction

Flat lines show the reaction has finished

- Graph 1 represents the original reaction.
- Graphs 2 and 3 represent the reaction taking place quicker, but with the same initial amounts of reactants. The slopes of the graphs are steeper than for graph 1.
- Graphs 1, 2 and 3 all converge at the same level, showing that they all produce the same amount of product although they take different times to produce it.
- Graph 4 shows more product and a faster reaction. This can only happen if more reactant(s) are added at the start.

Factors Affecting Rates of Reaction

*I'd ask you to **guess** what these two pages are about, but the **title** pretty much says it all really. Read on...*

Particles Must **Collide** with **Enough Energy** in Order to **React**

1) Reaction rates are explained perfectly by collision theory. The rate of a chemical reaction depends on:

   - The collision frequency of reacting particles (how often they collide). The more collisions there are the faster the reaction is. E.g. doubling the frequency of collisions doubles the rate.
   - The energy transferred during a collision. Particles have to collide with enough energy for the collision to be successful.

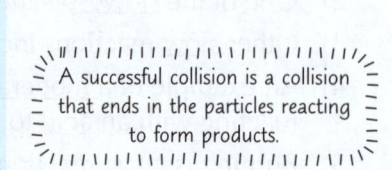

   A successful collision is a collision that ends in the particles reacting to form products.

2) You might remember from page 249 that the minimum amount of energy that particles need to react is called the activation energy. Particles need this much energy to break the bonds in the reactants and start the reaction.

3) Factors that increase the number of collisions (so that a greater proportion of reacting particles collide) or the amount of energy particles collide with will increase the rate of the reaction.

The **Rate of Reaction** Depends on **Four Things**

1) Temperature.
2) The concentration of a solution or the pressure of gas.
3) Surface area — this changes depending on the size of the lumps of a solid.
4) The presence of a catalyst.

More Collisions Increases the **Rate of Reaction**

All four methods of increasing the rate of a reaction can be explained in terms of increasing the number of successful collisions between the reacting particles:

Increasing the **Temperature** Increases the Rate

1) When the temperature is increased, the particles all move faster.
2) If they're moving faster, they're going to collide more frequently.
3) Also the faster they move the more energy they have, so more of the collisions will have enough energy to make the reaction happen.

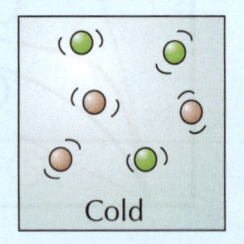

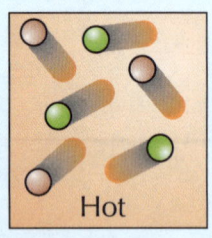

Cold   Hot

Increasing the **Concentration** or **Pressure** Increases the Rate

1) If a solution is made more concentrated, it means there are more particles knocking about in the same volume of water (or other solvent).
2) Similarly, when the pressure of a gas is increased, it means that the same number of particles occupies a smaller space.
3) This makes collisions between the reactant particles more frequent.

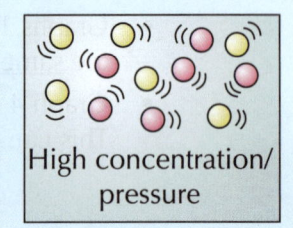

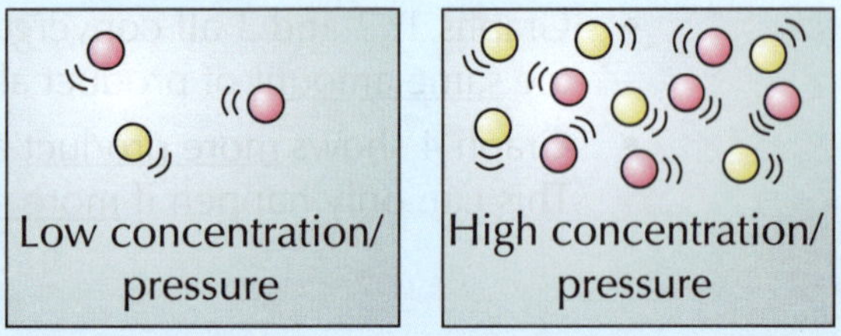

Low concentration/pressure   High concentration/pressure

Topic C6 — The Rate and Extent of Chemical Change

Factors Affecting Rates of Reaction

Increasing the **Surface Area** Increases the Rate

1) If one of the reactants is a solid, then breaking it up into smaller pieces will increase its surface area to volume ratio.
2) This means that for the same volume of the solid, the particles around it will have more area to work on — so there will be collisions more frequently.

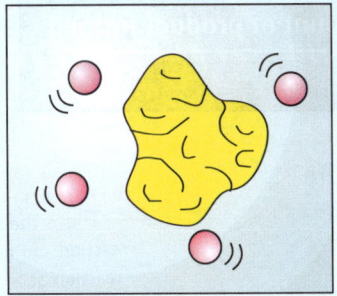

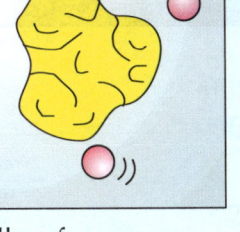

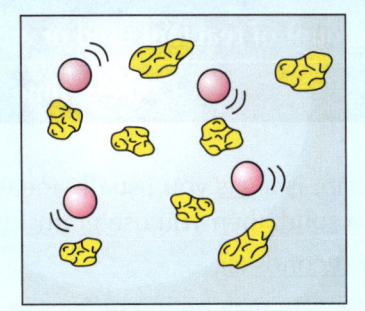

Small surface area

Big surface area

Using a **Catalyst** Increases the Rate

1) A catalyst is a substance that speeds up a reaction, without being used up in the reaction itself. This means it's not part of the overall reaction equation.
2) Different catalysts are needed for different reactions, but they all work by decreasing the activation energy needed for the reaction to occur. They do this by providing an alternative reaction pathway with a lower activation energy.

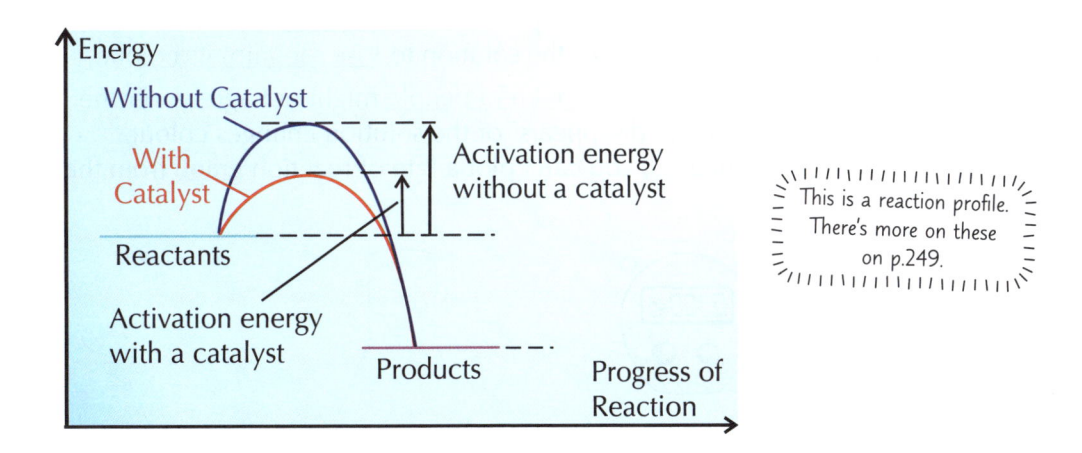

This is a reaction profile. There's more on these on p.249.

3) Enzymes are biological catalysts — they catalyse reactions in living things.

It's easier to learn stuff when you know the reasons for it

Once you've learnt everything off these two pages, the rates of reaction stuff should start making a lot more sense to you. The concept's fairly simple — the more often particles bump into each other, and the harder they hit when they do, the faster the reaction happens.

Topic C6 — The Rate and Extent of Chemical Change

PRACTICAL — Measuring Rates of Reaction

*All this talk about rates of reactions is fine and dandy, but it's no good if you can't **measure** it.*

You can Calculate the Rate of Reaction from Experimental Results

1) The rate of a reaction can be observed either by how quickly the reactants are used up or how quickly the products are formed:

$$\text{Rate of Reaction} = \frac{\text{Amount of reactant used or amount of product formed}}{\text{Time}}$$

2) When the product or reactant is a gas you usually measure the amount in cm^3. If it's a solid, then you use grams (g).
3) Time is often measured in seconds (s).
4) This means that the units for rate may be in cm^3/s or in g/s.
5) You can also measure the amount of product or reactant in moles — so the units of rate could also be mol/s.
6) There are three different ways of measuring the rate of a reaction:

This is the mean rate of reaction. To find the rate of a reaction at a particular time, you'll need to plot a graph and find the gradient at that time (see page 260).

1) Precipitation and Colour Change

1) You can record the visual change in a reaction if the initial solution is transparent and the product is a precipitate which clouds the solution (it becomes opaque).
2) You can observe a mark through the solution and measure how long it takes for it to disappear — the faster the mark disappears, the quicker the reaction.
3) If the reactants are coloured and the products are colourless (or vice versa), you can time how long it takes for the solution to lose (or gain) its colour.
4) The results are very subjective — different people might not agree over the exact point when the mark 'disappears' or the solution changes colour. Also, if you use this method, you can't plot a rate of reaction graph from the results.

A posh way of saying that the cloudiness of a solution changes is to say that its 'turbidity' changes.

PRACTICAL TIP — Make sure you use a method appropriate to your experiment

The method shown on this page only works if there's a really obvious change in the solution. If there's only a small change in colour, it might not be possible to observe and time the change.

Topic C6 — The Rate and Extent of Chemical Change

Measuring Rates of Reaction **PRACTICAL**

2) Change in Mass (Usually Gas Given Off)

1) Measuring the speed of a reaction that produces a gas can be carried out using a mass balance.
2) As the gas is released, the mass disappearing is measured on the balance.
3) The quicker the reading on the balance drops, the faster the reaction.
4) If you take measurements at regular intervals, you can plot a rate of reaction graph and find the rate quite easily (see page 260 for more).
5) This is the most accurate of the three methods described because the mass balance is very accurate. But it has the disadvantage of releasing the gas straight into the room.

Putting cotton wool in the top of the flask lets the gas escape but stops the acid spitting out.

3) The Volume of Gas Given Off

1) This involves the use of a gas syringe to measure the volume of gas given off.
2) The more gas given off during a given time interval, the faster the reaction.
3) Gas syringes usually give volumes accurate to the nearest cm³, so they're quite accurate. You can take measurements at regular intervals and plot a rate of reaction graph using this method too. You have to be quite careful though — if the reaction is too vigorous, you can easily blow the plunger out of the end of the syringe.

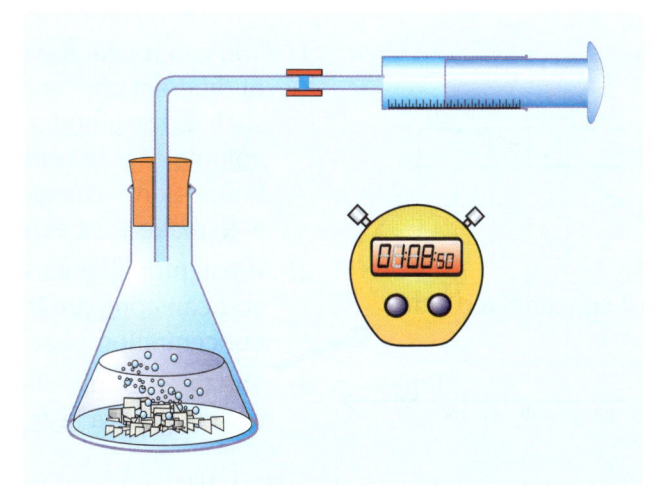

Each of these three methods has pros and cons

PRACTICAL TIP The mass balance method is only accurate as long as the flask isn't too hot, otherwise the loss in mass that you see might be partly due to evaporation of liquid as well as being due to the loss of gas formed during the reaction. The first method (on the previous page) is subjective so it isn't very accurate, but if you're not producing a gas you can't use either of the other two.

Topic C6 — The Rate and Extent of Chemical Change

PRACTICAL: Rate Experiments

*This page shows how you can use the method on the previous page in a **real investigation**. Get your safety goggles on and let's go...*

Magnesium and HCl React to Produce H_2 Gas

1) Start by adding a set volume of dilute hydrochloric acid to a conical flask.
2) Now add some magnesium ribbon to the acid and quickly attach an empty gas syringe to the flask.
3) Start the stopwatch. Take readings of the volume of gas in the gas syringe at regular intervals.

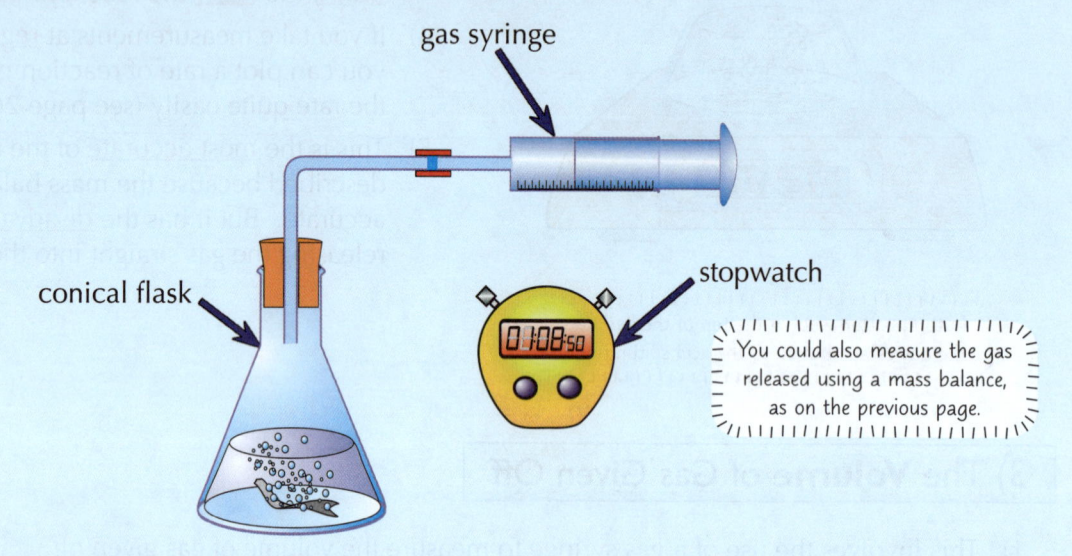

You could also measure the gas released using a mass balance, as on the previous page.

4) Plot the results in a table.
5) Now you can plot a graph with time on the x-axis and volume of gas produced on the y-axis.

You Can Investigate the Effect of Using Different Acid Concentrations

You can use the method above to investigate the effect of acid concentration on the rate of reaction:

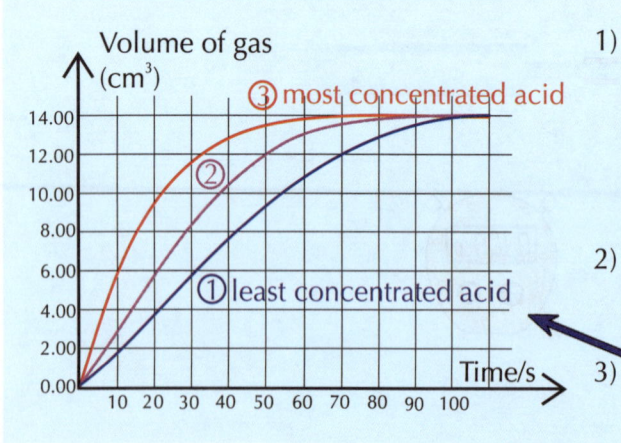

1) You can repeat the experiment above with a number of different concentrations of acid. Variables such as the amount of magnesium ribbon and the volume of acid used should be kept the same each time — only change the acid's concentration. This is to make your experiment a fair test — see p.6.
2) If you plot all your results on the same graph, you can compare them to see how the concentration of acid affects the rate of reaction.
3) The three graphs show that a higher concentration of acid gives a faster rate of reaction.

The hypothesis for this experiment could be something like 'As the concentration of acid increases, the rate of reaction will increase.'

Don't forget about any safety precautions you need to take

MATHS TIP — The graph above shows how to compare rates of reactions when using different concentrations of acid, but if you want to calculate a numerical value for the rate you need to use a calculation. Take a look at p.260 for how to find the rate of reaction from a graph.

Topic C6 — The Rate and Extent of Chemical Change

Rate Experiments

PRACTICAL

*Here's how to use the method that you saw on page 256. It's a bit **less accurate** than using a mass balance, but you need to know how to do it in case you want to investigate a reaction that **doesn't produce a gas**.*

Sodium Thiosulfate and HCl Produce a Cloudy Precipitate

1) These two chemicals are both clear solutions. They react together to form a yellow precipitate of sulfur.
2) Start by adding a set volume of dilute sodium thiosulfate to a conical flask.
3) Place the flask on a piece of paper with a black cross drawn on it.
4) Add some dilute HCl to the flask and start the stopwatch.
5) Now watch the black cross disappear through the cloudy sulfur and time how long it takes to go.

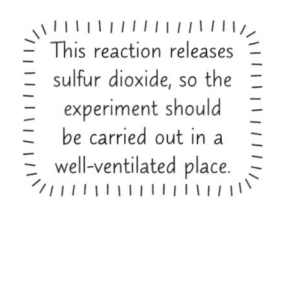

This reaction releases sulfur dioxide, so the experiment should be carried out in a well-ventilated place.

The hypothesis for this experiment could be something like 'As the concentration of acid increases, the solution will go cloudy more quickly.'

You Can Investigate How the Concentration of Acid Affects the Rate

1) The reaction can be repeated with solutions of either reactant at different concentrations. (Only change the concentration of one reactant at a time though.) The depth of the liquid must be kept the same each time.
2) These results show the effect of increasing the concentration of HCl on the rate of reaction, when added to an excess of sodium thiosulfate.

Concentration of HCl (g/dm³)	20	35	50	65	80
Time taken for mark to disappear (s)	193	184	178	171	164

3) The higher the concentration, the quicker the reaction and therefore the less time it takes for the mark to disappear.
4) One sad thing about this reaction is that it doesn't give a set of graphs. Well I think it's sad. All you get is a set of readings of how long it took till the mark disappeared for each concentration. Boring.

Although you could draw a graph of concentration against 1/time which will give you an approximate rate.

Make sure you can clearly see the cross through the flask at the start

Makes sure you learn both the methods on these two pages for investigating rate, but don't forget that other methods (e.g. the one using a balance that you saw earlier in the topic) can also be used. It's not just the effect of concentration you can investigate with these experiments, either — you can also use them to see how other factors (such as temperature, surface area or the presence of a catalyst) affect rate.

Topic C6 — The Rate and Extent of Chemical Change

Finding Reaction Rates from Graphs

You might remember a bit about how to interpret graphs on reaction rate from page 253 — well this page shows you how to use them to calculate rates.

You can Calculate the Mean Reaction Rate from a Graph

1) Remember, a rate of reaction graph shows the amount of product formed or amount of reactant used up on the y-axis and time on the x-axis.
2) So to find the mean rate for the whole reaction, you just work out the overall change in the y-value and then divide this by the total time taken for the reaction.
3) You can also use the graph to find the mean rate of reaction between any two points in time:

EXAMPLE

The graph shows the volume of gas released by a reaction, measured at regular intervals. Find the mean rate of reaction between 20 s and 40 s.

Mean rate of reaction = change in y ÷ change in x
= (19 cm³ − 15 cm³) ÷ 20 s
= 0.2 cm³/s

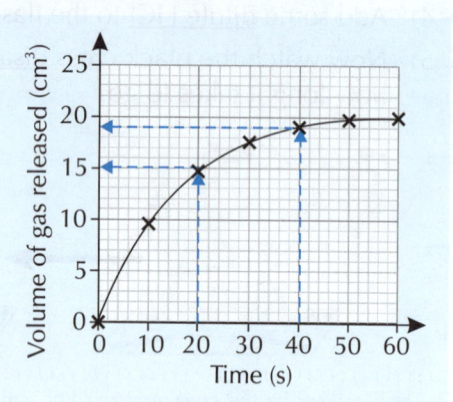

If you're asked to find the mean rate of reaction for the whole reaction, remember that the reaction finishes as soon as the line on the graph goes flat.

Draw a Tangent to Find the Reaction Rate at a Particular Point

If you want to find the rate of the reaction at a particular point in time, you need to find the gradient (slope) of the curve at that point. The easiest way to do this is to draw a tangent to the curve — a straight line that touches the curve at one point and doesn't cross it. You then work out the gradient of the tangent. It's simpler than it sounds, honest...

EXAMPLE

The graph below shows the mass of reactant used up measured at regular intervals during a chemical reaction. What is the rate of reaction at 3 minutes?

1) Position a ruler on the graph at the point where you want to know the rate — here it's 3 minutes.
2) Adjust the ruler until the space between the ruler and the curve is equal on both sides of the point.
3) Draw a line along the ruler to make the tangent. Extend the line right across the graph. 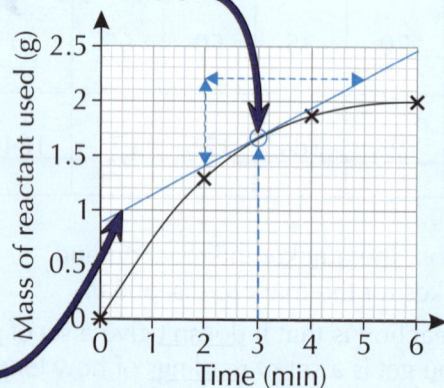
4) Pick two points on the line that are easy to read. Use them to calculate the gradient of the tangent in order to find the rate:

gradient = change in y ÷ change in x
= (2.2 − 1.4) ÷ (5.0 − 2.0)
= 0.8 ÷ 3.0
= 0.27

So, the rate of reaction at 3 minutes was **0.27 g/min**.

You can use a tangent to a curve to find out the gradient

Q1 Magnesium powder was added to a conical flask containing dilute H_2SO_4. H_2 was produced and collected in a gas syringe. The volume of gas released was recorded at 10 second intervals in the following table:

Time (s)	10	20	30	40	50	60
Volume of H_2 (cm³)	18	28	34	38	40	41

a) Plot these results on a graph and draw a line of best fit. [3 marks]
b) Find the rate of the reaction at time = 25 s. [4 marks]

Topic C6 — The Rate and Extent of Chemical Change

Warm-Up & Exam Questions — PRACTICAL

It's easy to think that you've understood something when you've just read through it. These questions should test whether you really understand the previous chunk of pages, and get you set for the next bit.

Warm-Up Questions

1) Give an example of a reaction that happens very slowly, and one that is very fast.
2) According to collision theory, what must happen in order for two particles to react?
3) Why does increasing the concentration of solutions increase the rate of a reaction?
4) What units of rate would be used for a reaction where the change in mass of a reaction vessel (measured in grams) has been recorded over time (measured in seconds)?
5) Describe how you could measure the rate of a precipitation reaction.

Exam Questions

1 **Figure 1** shows one method of measuring the rate of a reaction which produces a gas. *(Grade 4-6)*

Figure 1

(diagram showing a conical flask connected to apparatus labelled X)

1.1 What piece of apparatus necessary for measuring the rate of this reaction, is missing from **Figure 1**?
[1 mark]

1.2 Name of the piece of apparatus in **Figure 1** labelled **X**.
[1 mark]

1.3 Describe **one** other method of measuring the rate of a reaction which produces a gas.
[2 marks]

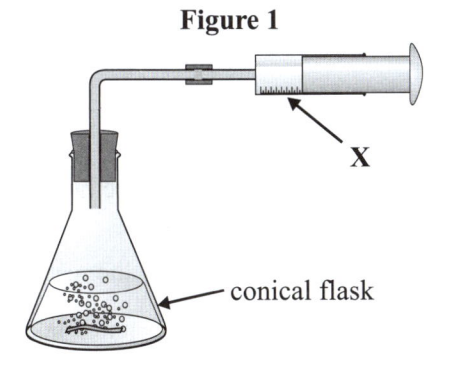

2 Set volumes of sodium thiosulfate and hydrochloric acid were reacted at different temperatures. The time taken for a black cross to be obscured by the sulfur precipitate was measured at each temperature. The results are shown in **Table 1**. *(Grade 6-7)*

Table 1

Temperature (°C)	Time (s)
55	6
36	11
24	17
16	27
9	40
5	51

2.1 Give **two** variables that should be kept constant in this experiment.
[2 marks]

2.2 Plot the results on a graph (with time on the *x*-axis) and draw a line of best fit.
[4 marks]

2.3 Describe the relationship illustrated by your graph.
[1 mark]

2.4 Describe how the results would change if the experiment was repeated with a **lower** concentration of sodium thiosulfate.
[1 mark]

2.5 Explain how using a lower reactant concentration affects the rate of a reaction.
[3 marks]

2.6 Suggest how you could assess if the results of the experiment are repeatable.
[2 marks]

Topic C6 — The Rate and Extent of Chemical Change

PRACTICAL Exam Questions

3 A teacher demonstrated an experiment to investigate the effect of temperature on the rate of a reaction. The teacher added dilute hydrochloric acid at 20 °C to marble chips and measured the volume of gas produced at regular time intervals. The teacher then repeated the experiment at 30 °C using the same mass of marble chips of the same size. The results are shown in **Figure 2**. *(Grade 6-7)*

Figure 2

Volume of gas (cm³) vs *Time (s)* — curve A above curve B, both levelling off at the same plateau.

3.1 On **Figure 2**, which curve, **A** or **B**, shows the result of the experiment at 30 °C?
[1 mark]

3.2 Sketch the curve you would expect if you repeated the experiment at 25 °C onto **Figure 2**. Label it **C**.
[1 mark]

3.3 The teacher made sure that the same volume and concentration of acid was used in each repeat. Explain why these variables needed to be controlled.
[1 mark]

3.4 Does **Figure 2** suggest that the teacher successfully controlled these variables? Explain your answer.
[1 mark]

3.5 Which of the following methods could also be used to measure the rate of this reaction? Tick **one** box.

- Measuring how quickly the reaction loses mass. ☐
- Timing how long the reaction takes to go cloudy. ☐
- Timing how long the reaction takes to start. ☐

[1 mark]

4 Calcium carbonate powder was added to a conical flask containing dilute HCl. CO_2 was produced and collected in a gas syringe. The volume of gas released was recorded at 10 second intervals in **Table 2**: *(Grade 6-7)*

Table 2

Time (s)	0	10	20	30	40	50	60
Volume of CO_2 (cm³)	0	24	32	36	38	39	40

4.1 Calculate the mean rate of reaction between 0 and 60 seconds.
[2 marks]

4.2 Plot these results on a graph and draw a line of best fit.
[4 marks]

4.3 Find the rate of the reaction 25 seconds after starting the experiment.
[4 marks]

5* Hydrogen gas and ethene gas react to form ethane. Nickel can be used as a catalyst for this reaction. *(Grade 7-9)*

Using your knowledge of collision theory, explain how the rate of this reaction can be increased.
[6 marks]

Topic C6 — The Rate and Extent of Chemical Change

Reversible Reactions

*Some reactions can go **backwards**. Honestly, that's all you need...*

Reversible Reactions Will Reach Equilibrium

This equation shows a reversible reaction — the products (C and D) can react to form the reactants (A and B) again:

$$A + B \rightleftharpoons C + D$$

The '$\rightleftharpoons$' shows the reaction goes both ways.

1) As the reactants react, their concentrations fall — so the forward reaction will slow down (see page 254). But as more and more products are made and their concentrations rise, the backward reaction will speed up.
2) After a while the forward reaction will be going at exactly the same rate as the backward one — the system is at equilibrium.
3) At equilibrium, both reactions are still happening, but there's no overall effect (it's a dynamic equilibrium). This means the concentrations of reactants and products have reached a balance and won't change.
4) Equilibrium is only reached if the reversible reaction takes place in a 'closed system'. A closed system just means that none of the reactants or products can escape and nothing else can get in.

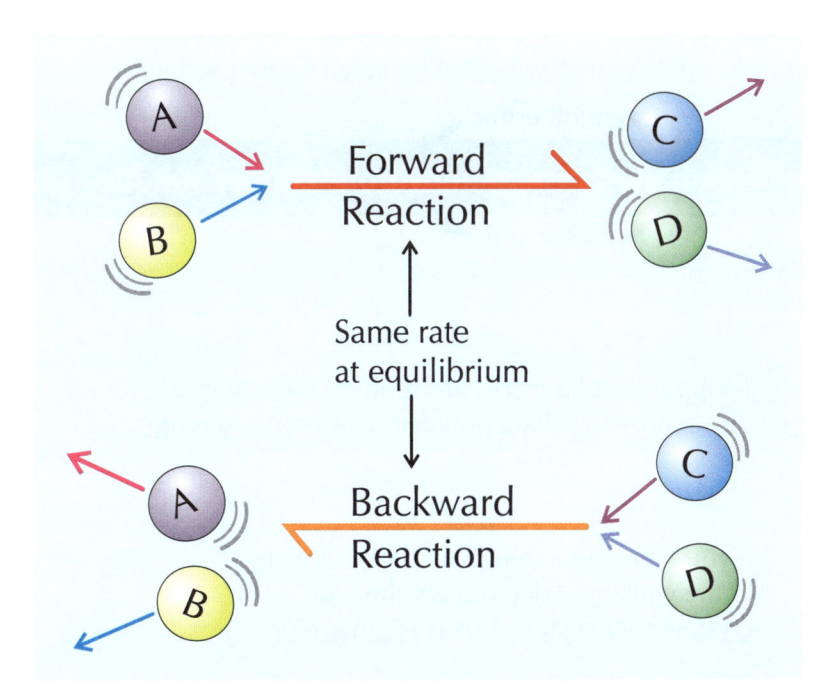

Dynamic equilibrium — lots of activity, but not to any great effect

The idea of dynamic equilibrium is something that you need to get to grips with, as things will get more complicated on the next couple of pages. Have another read and make sure you've got the basics sorted.

Topic C6 — The Rate and Extent of Chemical Change

Reversible Reactions

*In a reversible reaction, both the forward and the reverse reactions are happening **at the same time**. Certain conditions can be **more favourable** to one reaction than the other, making it happen faster.*

The **Position of Equilibrium** Can be on the **Right** or the **Left**

1) When a reaction's at equilibrium it doesn't mean the amounts of reactants and products are equal.
2) If the equilibrium lies to the right, the concentration of products is greater than that of the reactants.
3) If the equilibrium lies to the left, the concentration of reactants is greater than that of the products.
4) The position of equilibrium depends on the following conditions (as well as the reaction itself):

   1) the temperature,
   2) the pressure (this only affects equilibria involving gases),
   3) the concentration of the reactants and products.

E.g. ammonium chloride ⇌ ammonia + hydrogen chloride
Heating this reaction moves the equilibrium to the right (more ammonia and hydrogen chloride) and cooling it moves it to the left (more ammonium chloride).

The next page tells you why these things affect equilibrium position.

Reversible Reactions Can Be Endothermic and Exothermic

1) In reversible reactions, if the reaction is endothermic in one direction, it will be exothermic in the other.
2) The energy transferred from the surroundings by the endothermic reaction is equal to the energy transferred to the surroundings during the exothermic reaction.
3) A good example is the thermal decomposition of hydrated copper sulfate:

See page 247 for more on endothermic and exothermic reactions.

endothermic
hydrated copper sulfate ⇌ anhydrous copper sulfate + water
exothermic

'Anhydrous' just means 'without water', and 'hydrated' means 'with water'.

If you heat blue hydrated copper(II) sulfate crystals, it drives the water off and leaves white anhydrous copper(II) sulfate powder. This is endothermic.

If you then add a couple of drops of water to the white powder you get the blue crystals back again. This is exothermic.

> **REVISION TIP**
>
> ### More of the products = equilibrium lies to the right
> This whole energy transfer thing is a fairly simple idea — don't be put off by the long words. Remember, "exo-" = external, "-thermic" = heat, so an exothermic reaction is one that gives out heat. And "endo-" = erm... the other one. OK, there's no easy way to remember that one. Tough.

Topic C6 — The Rate and Extent of Chemical Change

Le Chatelier's Principle

*Reversible reactions don't like being messed around — so if you change something, the system will **respond** to undo the change.*

Reversible Reactions Try to Counteract Changes...

1) Le Chatelier's Principle is the idea that if you change the conditions of a reversible reaction at equilibrium, the system will try to counteract that change.
2) It can be used to predict the effect of any changes you make to a reaction system.

...Such as Changes to the Temperature...

1) All reactions are exothermic in one direction and endothermic in the other (see previous page).
2) If you decrease the temperature, the equilibrium will move in the exothermic direction to produce more heat. This means you'll get more products for the exothermic reaction and fewer products for the endothermic reaction.
3) If you raise the temperature, the equilibrium will move in the endothermic direction to try and decrease it. You'll now get more products for the endothermic reaction and fewer products for the exothermic reaction.

$N_2 + 3H_2 \rightleftharpoons 2NH_3$
Here the forward reaction is exothermic — a decrease in temperature moves equilibrium to the right (more NH_3).

...Pressure...

1) Changing the pressure only affects an equilibrium involving gases.
2) If you increase the pressure, the equilibrium tries to reduce it — it moves in the direction where there are fewer molecules of gas.
3) If you decrease the pressure, the equilibrium tries to increase it — it moves in the direction where there are more molecules of gas.
4) You can use the balanced symbol equation for a reaction to see which side has more molecules of gas.

$N_2 + 3H_2 \rightleftharpoons 2NH_3$
There are 4 moles on the left (1 of N_2 and 3 of H_2) but only 2 on the right. So, if you increase the pressure, the equilibrium shifts to the right (more NH_3).

...or Concentration

1) If you change the concentration of either the reactants or the products, the system will no longer be at equilibrium.
2) So the system responds to bring itself back to equilibrium again.
3) If you increase the concentration of the reactants the system tries to decrease it by making more products.
4) If you decrease the concentration of products the system tries to increase it again by reducing the amount of reactants.

$N_2 + 3H_2 \rightleftharpoons 2NH_3$
If more N_2 or H_2 is added, the forward reaction increases to produce more NH_3.

So, you do one thing, and the reaction does the other...

The best way to get your head around all this is to practise it. So find a reversible reaction, and then think about how changing each condition will affect the position of equilibrium.

Q1 For each of the following reactions, state the effect of an increase in pressure on the amount of products at equilibrium.
  a) $CO_{2(g)} + H_2O_{(l)} \rightleftharpoons H_2CO_{3(aq)}$ [1 mark]
  b) $NH_4Cl_{(s)} \rightleftharpoons NH3_{(g)} + HCl_{(g)}$ [1 mark]
  c) $2CO_{(g)} + O_{2(g)} \rightleftharpoons 2CO_{2(g)}$ [1 mark]

Topic C6 — The Rate and Extent of Chemical Change

Warm-Up & Exam Questions

Not long now till this section's over, but first there are some questions for you to tackle.

Warm-Up Questions

1) What can you say about forward and backward reaction rates at equilibrium?
2) For a reversible reaction, what is the effect on equilibrium of removing some of the reactants from the reaction mixture?
3) For the reaction, $N_{2(g)} + O_{2(g)} \rightleftharpoons 2NO_{(g)}$, what would be the effect on the equilibrium of changing the gas pressure?

Exam Questions

1 In the reaction below, substances A and B react to form substances C and D. *(Grade 4-6)*

$$2A + B \rightleftharpoons 2C + D$$

1.1 What can you deduce about this reaction from the symbol $\rightleftharpoons$?

[1 mark]

1.2 What is meant by the term **dynamic equilibrium**?

[1 mark]

2 This question is about how pressure affects the position of equilibrium. *(Grade 6-7)*

Reaction 1: $N_2O_{4(g)} \rightleftharpoons 2NO_{2(g)}$

Reaction 2: $ClNO_{2(g)} + NO_{(g)} \rightleftharpoons NO_{2(g)} + ClNO_{(g)}$

2.1 For Reaction 1, explain the effect of an **increase** in pressure on the amount of products at equilibrium.

[2 marks]

2.2 For Reaction 2, explain the effect of a **decrease** in pressure on the amount of products at equilibrium.

[2 marks]

3 When calcium carbonate is heated to a high temperature in a closed system, an equilibrium is reached: *(Grade 6-7)*

$$CaCO_{3(s)} \rightleftharpoons CaO_{(s)} + CO_{2(g)}$$

The forward reaction is endothermic.

3.1 Does the reverse reaction take in or give out energy? Explain your answer.

[2 marks]

3.2 Explain why changing the temperature of a reversible reaction always affects the position of the equilibrium.

[2 marks]

3.3 For the reaction shown above, describe what would happen to the equilibrium position if the temperature was raised.

[1 mark]

Topic C6 — The Rate and Extent of Chemical Change

Topic C7 — Organic Chemistry

Hydrocarbons

*Organic chemistry is about compounds that contain **carbon**. **Hydrocarbons** are the simplest organic compounds. As you're about to discover, their **properties** are affected by their **structure**.*

Hydrocarbons Only Contain Hydrogen and Carbon Atoms

1) A hydrocarbon is any compound that is formed from carbon and hydrogen atoms only.

2) So $C_{10}H_{22}$ (decane, an alkane) is a hydrocarbon, but $CH_3COOC_3H_7$ (an ester) is not — it contains oxygen.

Alkanes Have All C–C Single Bonds

1) Alkanes are the simplest type of hydrocarbon you can get. Their general formula is:

$$C_nH_{2n+2}$$

2) The alkanes are a homologous series — a group of organic compounds that react in a similar way.

3) Alkanes are saturated compounds — each carbon atom forms four single covalent bonds.

4) The first four alkanes are methane, ethane, propane and butane.

A drawing showing all the atoms and bonds in a molecule is called a displayed formula.

Methane
Formula: CH_4

Ethane
Formula: C_2H_6

Propane
Formula: C_3H_8

Butane
Formula: C_4H_{10}

Hydrocarbons only contain hydrogen and carbon

REVISION TIP: To help remember the names of the first four alkanes just remember: **M**ice **E**at **P**eanut **B**utter. Practise drawing the structures and get to grips with their formulas using the general formula.

Hydrocarbons

Hydrocarbon **Properties Change** as the Chain Gets **Longer**

As the length of the carbon chain changes, the properties of the hydrocarbon change:

1) The shorter the carbon chain, the more runny the hydrocarbon is — that is, the less viscous (gloopy) it is.

2) The shorter the carbon chain, the more volatile the hydrocarbon is. "More volatile" means it turns into a gas at a lower temperature. So, the shorter the carbon chain, the lower the temperature at which that hydrocarbon vaporises or condenses — and the lower its boiling point.

3) Also, the shorter the carbon chain, the more flammable (easier to ignite) the hydrocarbon is.

The properties of hydrocarbons affect how they're used for fuels. E.g. short chain hydrocarbons with lower boiling points are used as 'bottled gases' — stored under pressure as liquids in bottles.

Complete Combustion Occurs When There's Plenty of **Oxygen**

1) The complete combustion of any hydrocarbon in oxygen releases lots of energy. The only waste products are carbon dioxide and water vapour.

$$\text{hydrocarbon} + \text{oxygen} \rightarrow \text{carbon dioxide} + \text{water} \quad (+ \text{energy})$$

2) During combustion, both carbon and hydrogen from the hydrocarbon are oxidised. Oxidation can be defined as the gain of oxygen.

3) Hydrocarbons are used as fuels due to the amount of energy released when they combust completely.

4) You need to be able to give a balanced symbol equation for the complete combustion of a simple hydrocarbon fuel when you're given its molecular formula. It's pretty easy — here's an example:

EXAMPLE Write a balanced equation for the complete combustion of methane (CH_4).

1) On the left hand side, there's one carbon atom, so only one molecule of CO_2 is needed to balance this.

$$CH_4 + ?O_2 \rightarrow CO_2 + ?H_2O$$

2) On the left hand side, there are four hydrogen atoms, so two water molecules are needed to balance them.

$$CH_4 + ?O_2 \rightarrow CO_2 + 2H_2O$$

3) There are four oxygen atoms on the right hand side of the equation. Two oxygen molecules are needed on the left to balance them.

$$CH_4 + 2O_2 \rightarrow CO_2 + 2H_2O$$

Alkanes are useful fuels as they release energy when burnt

The chain lengths of hydrocarbons have a big effect on their properties and how useful they are.

Q1 Write a balanced symbol equation for the complete combustion of ethane, C_2H_6. [2 marks]

Q2 Robyn has two alkanes, C_5H_{12} and $C_{10}H_{22}$. Compare the following properties of the alkanes:
a) viscosity b) boiling point c) flammability [3 marks]

Topic C7 — Organic Chemistry

Fractional Distillation

Crude oil can be used to make loads of useful things, such as fuels. But you can't just put crude oil in your car. First, the different hydrocarbons have to be separated. That's where **fractional distillation** comes in.

Crude Oil is Made Over a Long Period of Time

1) Crude oil is a fossil fuel. It's formed from the remains of plants and animals, mainly plankton, that died millions of years ago and were buried in mud. Over millions of years, with high temperature and pressure, the remains turn to crude oil, which can be drilled up from the rocks where it's found.
2) Fossil fuels like coal, oil and gas are called non-renewable fuels as they take so long to make that they're being used up much faster than they're being formed. They're finite resources (see p.286) — one day they'll run out.

Fractional Distillation is Used to Separate Hydrocarbon Fractions

1) Crude oil is a mixture of lots of different hydrocarbons, most of which are alkanes.
2) The different compounds in crude oil are separated by fractional distillation.

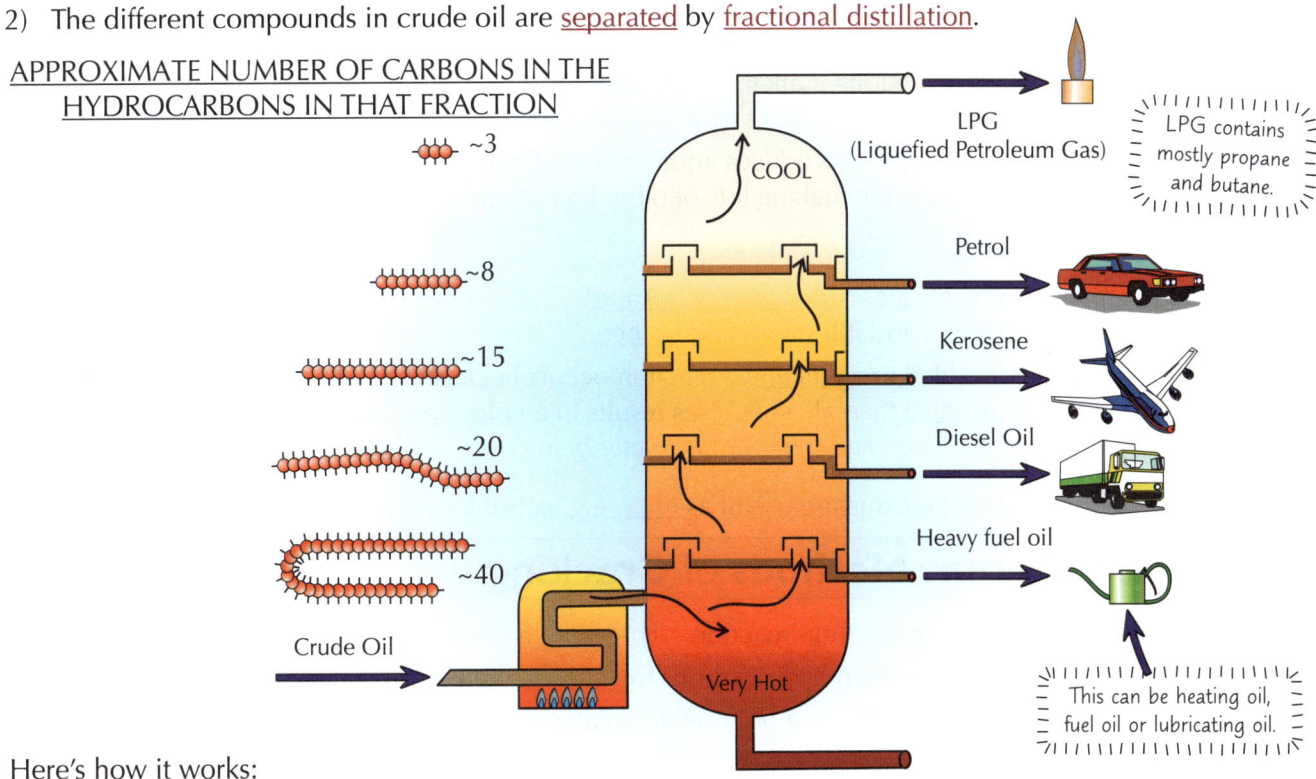

APPROXIMATE NUMBER OF CARBONS IN THE HYDROCARBONS IN THAT FRACTION

~3 — LPG (Liquefied Petroleum Gas) — *LPG contains mostly propane and butane.*

~8 — Petrol

~15 — Kerosene

~20 — Diesel Oil

~40 — Heavy fuel oil — *This can be heating oil, fuel oil or lubricating oil.*

Here's how it works:

- The oil is heated until most of it has turned into gas. The gases enter a fractionating column (and the liquid bit is drained off).
- In the column there's a temperature gradient (it's hot at the bottom and gets cooler as you go up).
- The longer hydrocarbons have high boiling points. They condense back into liquids and drain out of the column early on, when they're near the bottom. The shorter hydrocarbons have lower boiling points. They condense and drain out much later on, near to the top of the column where it's cooler.
- You end up with the crude oil mixture separated out into different fractions. Each fraction contains a mixture of hydrocarbons that all contain a similar number of carbon atoms, so have similar boiling points.

Fractional distillation separates crude oil into useful compounds

Q1 Petrol drains further up a fractionating column than diesel.
Use the diagram of the fractionating column to explain why the boiling point of petrol is lower than that of diesel. [2 marks]

Topic C7 — Organic Chemistry

Uses and Cracking of Crude Oil

*Crude oil has fuelled **modern civilisation** — it would be a very different world if we hadn't discovered oil.*

Crude Oil has Various Uses Important in Modern Life

1) Oil provides the fuel for most modern transport — cars, trains, planes, the lot. Diesel oil, kerosene, heavy fuel oil and LPG (liquid petroleum gas) all come from crude oil.
2) The petrochemical industry uses some of the hydrocarbons from crude oil as a feedstock to make new compounds for use in things like polymers, solvents, lubricants, and detergents.
3) All the products you get from crude oil are examples of organic compounds (compounds containing carbon atoms). The reason you get such a large variety of products is because carbon atoms can bond together to form different groups called homologous series. These groups contain similar compounds with many properties in common.

Cracking Means Splitting Up Long-Chain Hydrocarbons

1) Short-chain hydrocarbons are flammable so make good fuels and are in high demand. However, long-chain hydrocarbons form thick gloopy liquids like tar which aren't all that useful.
2) As a result of this a lot of the longer alkane molecules produced from fractional distillation are turned into smaller, more useful ones by a process called cracking.
3) As well as alkanes, cracking also produces another type of hydrocarbon called alkenes. Alkenes are used as a starting material when making lots of other compounds and can be used to make polymers.

Bromine water can be used to test for alkenes.
1) When orange bromine water is added to an alkane, no reaction will happen and it'll stay bright orange.
2) If bromine water is added to an alkene a reaction occurs because alkenes are more reactive than alkanes. This results in a colourless compound being produced and the bromine water being decolourised.

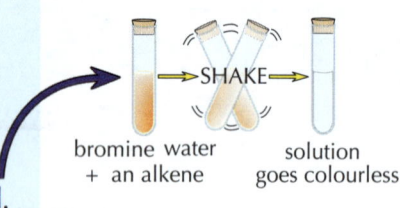

4) Some of the products of cracking are useful as fuels, e.g. petrol for cars and paraffin for jet fuel.

There are Different Methods of Cracking

1) Cracking is a thermal decomposition reaction — breaking molecules down by heating them.
2) The first step is to heat long-chain hydrocarbons to vaporise them (turn them into a gas).
3) Then the vapour can be passed over a hot powdered aluminium oxide catalyst.
4) The long-chain molecules split apart on the surface of the specks of catalyst — this is catalytic cracking.
5) You can also crack hydrocarbons if you vaporise them, mix them with steam and then heat them to a very high temperature. This is known as steam cracking.

Make sure that, when writing equations for cracking, there are the same number of carbon and hydrogen atoms on both sides of the equation.

You need to be able to balance chemical equations for cracking. For example:

Long-chain hydrocarbon molecule → Shorter alkane molecule + alkene

E.g. decane (ten C atoms) → octane (eight C atoms) + ethene (two C atoms)
(too much of this in crude oil) (useful for petrol) (for making plastics)

Cracking breaks long-chain hydrocarbons into shorter ones

Q1 Pentane, C_5H_{12}, can be cracked into ethene and one other hydrocarbon. Give the balanced symbol equation for the cracking reaction. [1 mark]

Topic C7 — Organic Chemistry

Warm-Up & Exam Questions

Hydrocarbons contain only hydrogen and carbon atoms. This page contains only Warm-Up and Exam Questions. Time to get thinking.

Warm-Up Questions

1) Name the first four alkanes.
2) What kind of bonds are present in alkanes?
3) Why are alkanes often used as fuels?
4) Suggest a use of crude oil fractions that modern society depends on.
5) What sort of hydrocarbon molecules are cracked?

Exam Questions

1 Which alkane is shown below? *Grade 4-6*
Tick **one** box.

$$\begin{array}{c} H\ \ H \\ |\ \ \ | \\ H-C-C-H \\ |\ \ \ | \\ H\ \ H \end{array}$$

butane ☐   propane ☐   ethane ☐   methane ☐

[1 mark]

2 Alkanes are a homologous series of hydrocarbons made up of chains of carbon atoms surrounded by hydrogen atoms. *Grade 4-6*

Pentane is an alkane with the formula C_5H_{12}.

2.1 State the name of the alkane that comes before pentane in the homologous series.

[1 mark]

2.2 State the formula of the alkane that comes before pentane in the homologous series.

[1 mark]

2.3 Suggest **two** materials produced from hydrocarbons by the petrochemical industry.

[2 marks]

3 Draw **one** line from each property of hydrocarbons to its trend with changing molecular size. *Grade 4-6*

Property	Trend
Flammability	Increases as the molecules get bigger
Viscosity	
Boiling point	Decreases as the molecules get bigger

[3 marks]

Topic C7 — Organic Chemistry

Exam Questions

4 Crude oil can be separated into a number of different compounds in a fractional distillation column. **Figure 1** shows a fractional distillation column. *Grade 6-7*

Figure 1

FRACTIONS: A, B, C, D, E, F

Crude oil enters at X.

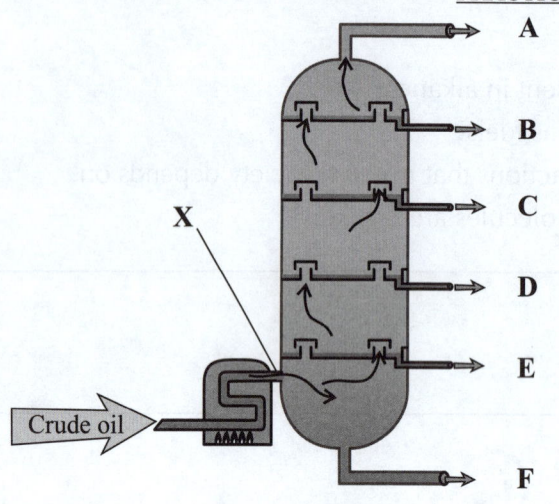

4.1 Which letter, **A-F**, represents the fraction with the longest hydrocarbon molecules?

[1 mark]

4.2 Which letter, **A-F**, represents the fraction with the lowest boiling point?

[1 mark]

4.3 Gaseous crude oil enters near the bottom of the fractional distillation column (point **X** in **Figure 1**). Explain why different fractions exit the column at different points and how this relates to their structure.

[3 marks]

5 Alkanes burn in excess oxygen by complete combustion. *Grade 6-7*

5.1 What two products are made by the complete combustion of an alkane?

[2 marks]

5.2 Complete the equation below for the complete combustion of propane (C_3H_8):

$$C_3H_8 + \ldots O_2 \rightarrow \ldots\ldots + \ldots\ldots$$

[2 marks]

5.3 Carbon and hydrogen atoms gain oxygen during the combustion of hydrocarbons. What type of reaction is this?

[1 mark]

6 Cracking is a process used to break longer chain molecules in crude oil down to shorter ones. *Grade 7-9*

6.1 Why is cracking an important process in the petrochemical industry?

[1 mark]

6.2 Octane (C_8H_{18}) can be cracked to form two products, ethane and propene (C_3H_6). Complete the equation below for this reaction:

$$C_8H_{18} \rightarrow \ldots\ldots + \ldots C_3H_6$$

[2 marks]

6.3 Describe the **two** methods used by the petrochemical industry for cracking hydrocarbons.

[4 marks]

Topic C7 — Organic Chemistry

Topic C8 — Chemical Analysis

Purity and Formulations

*Substances are often not **100% pure** — they might have **other stuff** that you can't see mixed in with them. The purity of a substance might need to be **checked**, before, say, a drug is made from it.*

Purity is Defined Differently in Chemistry to Everyday

1) Usually when you refer to a substance as being pure you mean that nothing has been added to it, so it's in its natural state. For example, pure milk or beeswax.
2) In chemistry, a pure substance is something that only contains one compound or element throughout — not mixed with anything else.

The Boiling or Melting Point Tells You How Pure a Substance Is

1) A chemically pure substance will melt or boil at a specific temperature.
2) You can test the purity of a sample by measuring its melting or boiling point and comparing it with the melting or boiling point of the pure substance (which you can find in a data book).
3) The closer your measured value is to the actual melting or boiling point, the purer your sample is.
4) Impurities in your sample will lower the melting point and increase the melting range of your substance.
5) Impurities in your sample will also increase the boiling point and may result in your sample boiling over a range of temperatures.

Formulations are Mixtures with Exact Amounts of Components

1) Formulations are useful mixtures with a precise purpose that are made by following a 'formula' (a recipe). Each component in a formulation is present in a measured quantity, and contributes to the properties of the formulation so that it meets its required function.

Take a look at p.181 for more on mixtures.

> For example, paints are formulations composed of:
>
> Pigment — gives the paint colour (for example titanium oxide is used as a pigment in white paints).
>
> Solvent — used to dissolve the other components and alter the viscosity (runniness).
>
> Binder (resin) — forms a film that holds the pigment in place after it's been painted on.
>
> Additives — added to further change the physical and chemical properties of the paint.
>
> Depending on the purpose of the paint, the chemicals used and their amounts will be changed so the paint produced is right for the job.

2) Formulations are really important in the pharmaceutical industry. For example, by altering the formulation of a pill, chemists can make sure it delivers the drug to the correct part of the body at the right concentration, that it's consumable and has a long enough shelf life.
3) In everyday life, formulations can be found in cleaning products, fuels, cosmetics, fertilisers, metal alloys (see p.216) and even food and drink.
4) When you buy a product, you might find that it has information about its composition on the packaging. For example, the ratio or percentage of each component. This tells you the product's a formulation. It also lets you choose a formulation with the right composition for your particular use.

Make sure you can use data to identify pure and impure substances...

Knowing how pure a product is can be vital in industries such as pharmaceuticals and the food industry. Extra stuff in it by mistake could change the properties of the product, and even make it dangerous.

Topic C8 — Chemical Analysis

Testing for Gases

PRACTICAL

*Ahh... tests, glorious tests. Luckily, these aren't the kind of tests you have to **revise** for, but you should probably revise these tests for your exam — it's **swings** and **roundabouts** really...*

There are Tests for Four Common Gases

1) Chlorine

Chlorine bleaches damp litmus paper, turning it white. (If you use blue litmus paper it may turn red for a moment first though — that's because a solution of chlorine is acidic.)

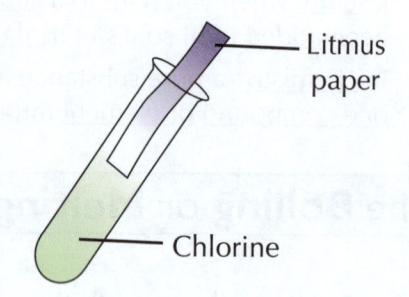

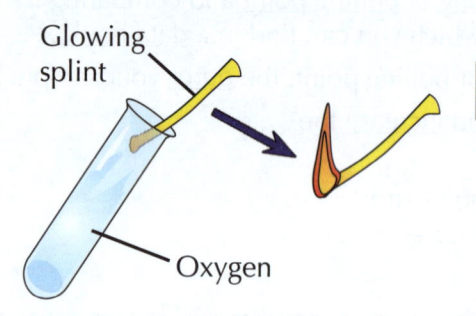

Litmus paper
Chlorine

2) Oxygen

Glowing splint
Oxygen

If you put a glowing splint inside a test tube containing oxygen, the oxygen will relight the glowing splint.

3) Carbon Dioxide

Bubbling carbon dioxide through (or shaking carbon dioxide with) an aqueous solution of calcium hydroxide (known as limewater) causes the solution to turn cloudy.

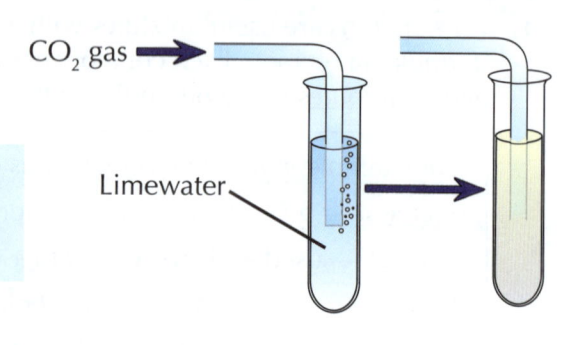

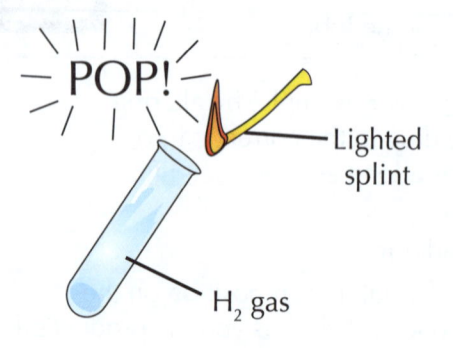

CO_2 gas
Limewater

4) Hydrogen

POP!
Lighted splint
H_2 gas

If you hold a burning splint at the open end of a test tube containing hydrogen, you'll get a "squeaky pop". (The noise comes from the hydrogen burning quickly in the oxygen in the air to form water.)

These are all really useful tests to know...

The method you use to collect a gas will depend on whether it's lighter or heavier than air. If it's heavier (like chlorine), you have the test tube the right way up and the gas will sink to the bottom. If it's lighter (like hydrogen), you have the test tube upside-down and the gas will rise to fill it.

Topic C8 — Chemical Analysis

Paper Chromatography

PRACTICAL

You met chromatography on page 182. Now it's time to see **how it works**.

Chromatography uses Two Phases

Chromatography is an analytical method used to separate the substances in a mixture. You can also use information from a chromatography experiment to help identify the substances that you have separated. There are different types of chromatography, but they all have two 'phases':

A mobile phase — where the molecules can move. This is always a liquid or a gas.
A stationary phase — where the molecules can't move. This can be a solid or a really thick liquid.

1) During a chromatography experiment, the substances in the sample constantly move between the mobile and the stationary phases — an equilibrium is formed between the two phases.
2) The mobile phase moves through the stationary phase, and anything dissolved in the mobile phase moves with it.
3) How quickly a chemical moves depends on how it's 'distributed' between the two phases — whether it spends more time in the mobile phase or the stationary phase.
4) The chemicals that spend more time in the mobile phase than the stationary phase will move further through the stationary phase.
5) The components in a mixture will normally separate through the stationary phase, so long as all the components spend different amounts of time in the mobile phase.
6) The separated components form spots. The number of spots formed may change in different solvents as the distribution of the chemical will change depending on the solvent.
7) A pure substance will only ever form one spot in any solvent, since there is only one substance in the sample.

Paper Chromatography

In paper chromatography the stationary phase is the chromatography paper (often filter paper) and the mobile phase is the solvent (e.g. ethanol or water).

The amount of time the molecules spend in each phase depends on two things:

- How soluble they are in the solvent.
- How attracted they are to the paper.

Molecules with a higher solubility in the solvent, and which are less attracted to the paper, will spend more time in the mobile phase — and they'll be carried further up the paper.

The method for carrying out paper chromatography is on page 182.

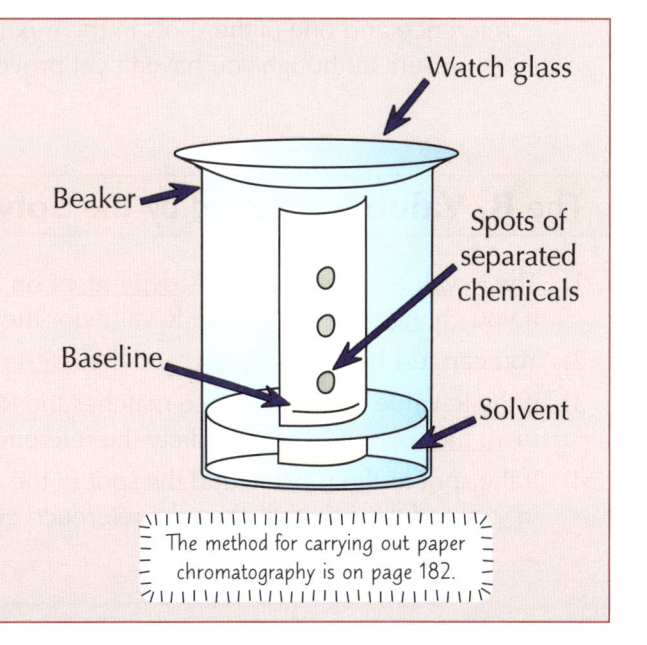

Chromatography revision — it's a phase you have to get through...

Chromatography works because each of the chemicals in a mixture spends different amounts of time dissolved in the mobile phase and stuck to the stationary phase. It's great — all you need is some paper and a bit of solvent. There's more about using it to identify chemicals coming up on the next page.

Topic C8 — Chemical Analysis

PRACTICAL: Paper Chromatography

*Now that you know a bit of the **theory** behind how paper chromatography works, here's how you can use a **chromatogram** to analyse a particular substance and find out **what's in it**.*

You can Calculate the R_f Value for Each Chemical

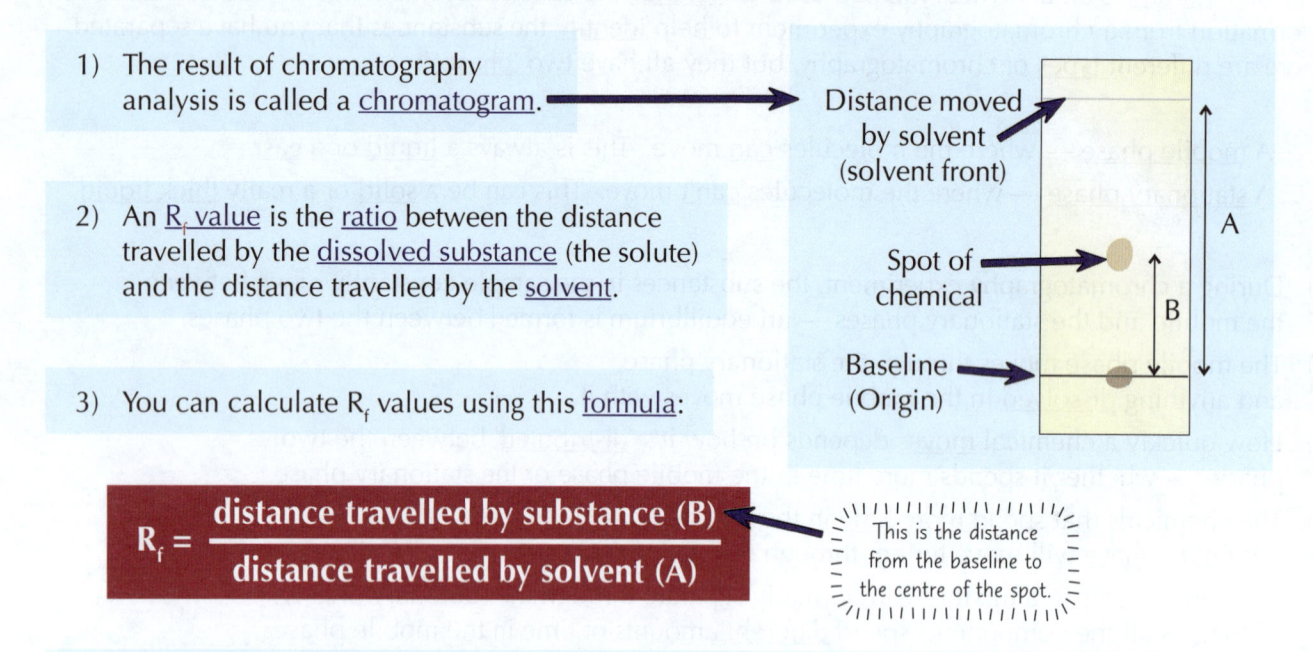

1) The result of chromatography analysis is called a chromatogram. → Distance moved by solvent (solvent front)

2) An R_f value is the ratio between the distance travelled by the dissolved substance (the solute) and the distance travelled by the solvent.

3) You can calculate R_f values using this formula:

$$R_f = \frac{\text{distance travelled by substance (B)}}{\text{distance travelled by solvent (A)}}$$

This is the distance from the baseline to the centre of the spot.

4) The further through the stationary phase a substance moves, the larger the R_f value.

5) Chromatography is often carried out to see if a certain substance is present in a mixture. To do this, you run a pure sample of that substance (a reference) alongside the unknown mixture. If the R_f values of the reference and one of the spots in the mixture match, the substance may be present (although you haven't yet proved they're the same).

The R_f Value is Affected by the Solvent

1) The R_f value of a substance is dependent on the solvent you use — if you change the solvent the R_f value for the substance will change.
2) You can test both the mixture and the reference in a number of different solvents.
3) If the R_f value of the reference matches the R_f value of one of the spots in the mixture in all the solvents, then it's likely the reference compound is present in the mixture.
4) If the spot in the mixture and the spot in the reference only have the same R_f value in some of the solvents, then the reference compound isn't present in the mixture.

You need to learn the formula for R_f

Sometimes, when you're doing paper chromatography, you'll end up with a spot left sitting on the baseline, even after your solvent has run all the way up the paper. Any substance that remains on the baseline is insoluble in that solvent — you could try to identify it by using a different solvent.

Q1 A spot on a chromatogram moved 6.3 cm from the baseline. The solvent front moved 8.4 cm. Calculate the R_f value. [1 mark]

Topic C8 — Chemical Analysis

Warm-Up & Exam Questions

Look, a chromatography question — those things are fun. Get your investigative hat on and get stuck in...

Warm-Up Questions

1) What is meant by a pure substance in chemistry?
2) What effect will impurities in a substance have on its boiling point?
3) Give an example of a formulation used in everyday life.
4) What effect does chromatography have on a mixture?

Exam Questions

PRACTICAL

1 Electrolysis of water gives hydrogen gas and oxygen gas. *Grade 4-6*

1.1 Describe how you could identify hydrogen gas using a simple laboratory test.

[2 marks]

1.2 Describe how you could identify oxygen gas using a simple laboratory test.

[2 marks]

PRACTICAL

2 A scientist used chromatography to analyse the composition of five food colourings. Four of the colourings were unknown (**A – D**). The other was sunrise yellow. The results are shown in **Figure 1**. *Grade 6-7*

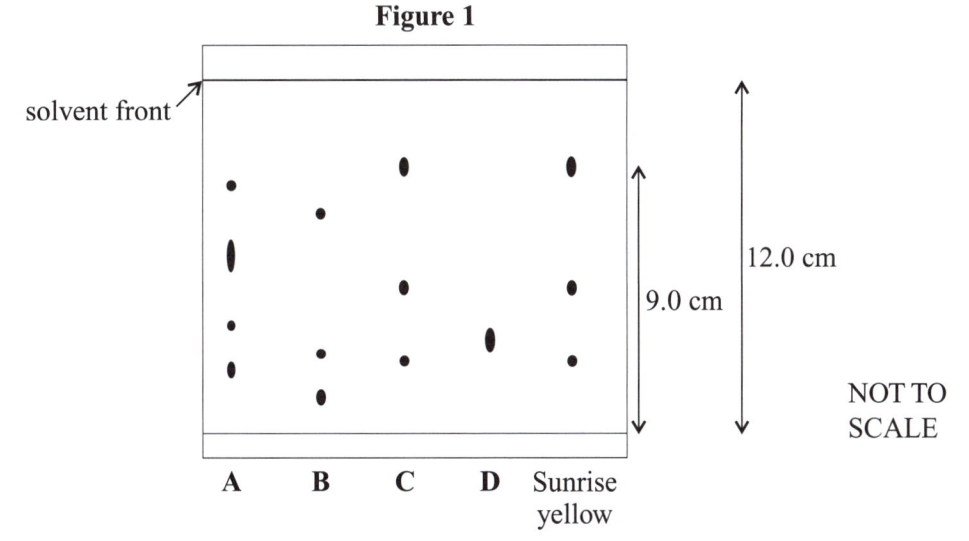

Figure 1

(chromatogram showing spots for A, B, C, D, Sunrise yellow; solvent front at 12.0 cm, with 9.0 cm marked; NOT TO SCALE)

2.1 Which food colouring is most likely to be a pure compound?

[1 mark]

2.2 Which food colouring definitely contains at least four different compounds?

[1 mark]

2.3 Which of the food colourings, **A-D**, could be the same as sunrise yellow?

[1 mark]

2.4 Calculate the R_f value for the spot of chemical in sunrise yellow which is furthest up the chromatogram.

[2 marks]

Topic C8 — Chemical Analysis

The Evolution of the Atmosphere

*Theories for how the Earth's atmosphere **evolved** have changed a lot over the years — it's hard to gather evidence from such a **long time period** and from **so long ago** (4.6 billion years). Here is one idea we've got:*

Phase 1 — Volcanoes Gave Out Gases

1) The first billion years of Earth's history were pretty explosive — the surface was covered in volcanoes that erupted and released lots of gases.

2) We think this was how the early atmosphere was formed.

3) The early atmosphere was probably mostly made up of carbon dioxide, with virtually no oxygen. This is quite like the atmospheres of Mars and Venus today.

4) Volcanic activity also released nitrogen, which built up in the atmosphere over time, as well as water vapour and small amounts of methane and ammonia.

Phase 2 — Oceans, Algae and Green Plants Absorbed CO_2

1) When the water vapour in the atmosphere condensed, it formed the oceans.

2) Lots of carbon dioxide was removed from the early atmosphere as it dissolved in the oceans. This dissolved carbon dioxide then went through a series of reactions to form carbonate precipitates that formed sediments on the seabed.

3) Later, marine animals evolved. Their shells and skeletons contained some of these carbonates from the oceans.

4) Green plants and algae evolved and absorbed some of the carbon dioxide so that they could carry out photosynthesis (see next page).

Before volcanic activity, the Earth didn't even have an atmosphere

One way scientists can get information about what Earth's atmosphere was like in the past is from Antarctic ice cores. Each year a layer of ice forms with tiny bubbles of air trapped in it. The deeper you go in the ice, the older the air. So analysing bubbles from different layers shows you how the atmosphere has changed.

Topic C9 — Chemistry of the Atmosphere

The Evolution of the Atmosphere

Some Carbon Became Trapped in Fossil Fuels and Rocks

Some of the carbon that organisms took in from the atmosphere and oceans became locked up in rocks and fossil fuels after the organisms died.

1) When plants, plankton and marine animals die, they fall to the seabed and get buried by layers of sediment.

2) Over millions of years, they become compressed and form sedimentary rocks, oil and gas — trapping the carbon within them (helping to keep it out of the atmosphere).

3) Things like coal, crude oil and natural gas that are made by this process are called 'fossil fuels'.

4) Crude oil and natural gas are formed from deposits of plankton. These fossil fuels form reservoirs under the seabed when they get trapped in rocks.

5) Coal is a sedimentary rock made from thick plant deposits.

6) Limestone is also a sedimentary rock. It's mostly made of calcium carbonate deposits from the shells and skeletons of marine organisms.

The shells of marine organisms like this one are made of calcium carbonate. They form deposits on the seabed when the organism dies.

Phase 3 — Green Plants and Algae Produced Oxygen

1) As well as absorbing the carbon dioxide in the atmosphere, green plants and algae produced oxygen by photosynthesis — this is when plants use light to convert carbon dioxide and water into sugars:

$$\text{carbon dioxide} + \text{water} \xrightarrow{\text{light}} \text{glucose} + \text{oxygen}$$
$$6CO_2 + 6H_2O \rightarrow C_6H_{12}O_6 + 6O_2$$

2) Algae evolved first — about 2.7 billion years ago.

3) Then over the next billion years or so, green plants also evolved.

4) As oxygen levels built up in the atmosphere over time, more complex life (like animals) could evolve.

5) Eventually, about 200 million years ago, the atmosphere reached a composition similar to how it is today:
  - approximately 80% nitrogen,
  - approximately 20% oxygen,
  - small amounts of other gases (each making up less than 1% of the atmosphere), mainly carbon dioxide, noble gases and water vapour.

Not too much CO_2 and enough O_2 — just right for complex life

Another way that scientists can work out what the atmosphere was like billions of years ago is to look at the chemical composition of rocks. They can also look for the appearance of different organisms in the fossil record (including plants and algae) to try to work out what might have caused the changes they see.

Topic C9 — Chemistry of the Atmosphere

Climate Change and Greenhouse Gases

*Greenhouse gases are important, but can also cause **problems** — it's all about keeping a delicate **balance**.*

Carbon Dioxide is a Greenhouse Gas

1) Greenhouse gases like carbon dioxide, methane and water vapour act like an insulating layer in the Earth's atmosphere — this, amongst other factors, allows the Earth to be warm enough to support life.

2) All particles absorb certain frequencies of radiation. Greenhouse gases don't absorb the incoming short wavelength radiation from the Sun — but they do absorb the long wavelength radiation that gets reflected back off the Earth.

3) Then they re-radiate it in all directions — including back towards the Earth.

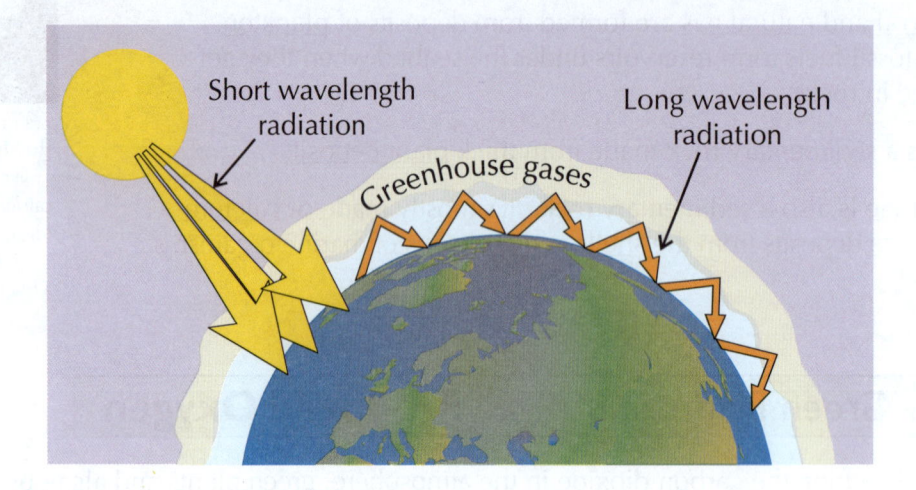

4) The long wave radiation is thermal radiation, so it results in warming of the surface of the Earth. This is the greenhouse effect.

5) Some forms of human activity affect the amount of greenhouse gases in the atmosphere. For example:

> - Deforestation — fewer trees means less CO_2 is removed from the atmosphere via photosynthesis.
>
> - Burning fossil fuels — carbon that was 'locked up' in these fuels is released as CO_2.
>
> - Agriculture — more farm animals produce more methane through their digestive processes.
>
> - Creating waste — more landfill sites and more waste from agriculture means more CO_2 and methane released by decomposition of waste.

Greenhouse gases aren't all bad — we need them to survive

Without greenhouse gases our planet would be incredibly cold — the greenhouse effect warms the Earth enough for it to support living things. Without it we wouldn't be here. But the overall balance of gases in the atmosphere matters, as you're about to find out...

Q1 Describe the greenhouse effect and how it affects global temperature. [4 marks]

Topic C9 — Chemistry of the Atmosphere

Climate Change and Greenhouse Gases

Increasing Carbon Dioxide is Linked to Climate Change

1) The Earth's temperature does vary naturally.

2) But recently, the average temperature of the Earth's surface has been increasing by amounts that are greater than we would expect to see naturally. Most scientists agree that the extra carbon dioxide from human activity is causing this increase, and that increasing global temperature will lead to climate change.

3) Evidence for this has been peer-reviewed (see page 2) — so you know that this information is reliable.

4) Unfortunately, it's hard to fully understand the Earth's climate — this is because it's so complex, and there are so many variables, that it's very hard to make a model that isn't oversimplified.

5) This has led to speculation about the link between carbon dioxide and climate change, particularly in the media (where stories may be biased, or only some of the information given).

Climate Change Could Have Dangerous Consequences

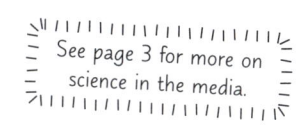

See page 3 for more on science in the media.

The Earth's climate is complex, but it's still important to make predictions about the consequences of climate change so that policy-makers can make decisions now. For example:

1) An increase in global temperature could lead to polar ice caps melting — causing a rise in sea levels, increased flooding in coastal areas and coastal erosion.

2) Changes in rainfall patterns (the amount, timing and distribution) may cause some regions to get too much or too little water. This, along with changes in temperature, may affect the ability of certain regions to produce food.

3) The frequency and severity of storms may also increase.

4) Changes in temperature and the amount of water available in a habitat may affect wild species, leading to differences in their distribution.

People can get quite hot under the collar talking about all this...

That's because climate change could have a massive impact on many people's lives across the world. It's really important that we understand what causes it, as well as how to prevent any damaging consequences.

Topic C9 — Chemistry of the Atmosphere

Carbon Footprints

*It's generally accepted that greenhouse gas emissions from **human activities** are causing **climate change**. Knowing what causes the **biggest** emissions of carbon dioxide could help us focus our efforts to **reduce** them.*

Carbon Footprints are Tricky to Measure

1) Carbon footprints are basically a measure of the amount of carbon dioxide and other greenhouse gases released over the full life cycle of something.

2) That something could be a service (e.g. the school bus), an event (e.g. the Olympics), a product (e.g. a toastie maker) — almost anything.

3) Measuring the total carbon footprint of something can be very hard, though — or even impossible.

4) That's because there are so many different factors to consider — for example, you would have to count the emissions released as a result of manufacturing all the parts of your toastie maker and in making it, not to mention the emissions produced when you actually use it and finally dispose of it.

5) Still, a rough calculation can give a good idea of what the worst emitters are, so that people can avoid them in the future.

There are Ways of Reducing Carbon Footprints

You can't always measure a carbon footprint exactly, but there are always ways to reduce it. Anything that reduces the amount of greenhouse gases (e.g. carbon dioxide or methane) given out by a process will also reduce its carbon footprint. Here are some things that can be done:

1) Renewable energy sources or nuclear energy could be used instead of fossil fuels.

2) Using more efficient processes could conserve energy and cut waste. Lots of waste decomposes to release methane, so this will reduce methane emissions.

3) Governments could tax companies or individuals based on the amount of greenhouse gases they emit — e.g. taxing cars based on the amount of carbon dioxide they emit over a set distance could mean that people choose to buy cars that are more fuel-efficient and so less polluting.

4) Governments can also put a cap on emissions of all greenhouse gases that companies make — then sell licences for emissions up to that cap.

5) There's also technology that captures the CO_2 produced by burning fossil fuels before it's released into the atmosphere — it can then be stored deep underground in cracks in the rock, such as old oil wells.

Topic C9 — Chemistry of the Atmosphere

Carbon Footprints

But Making Reductions is Still Difficult

1) It's easy enough saying that we should cut emissions, but actually doing it — that's a different story.

2) For a start, there's still a lot of work to be done on alternative technologies that result in lower CO_2 emissions. For example:

- Carbon capture and storage (see previous page) is a relatively new idea. At the moment the technology is still at the developmental stage.
- Many renewable energy technologies, e.g. solar panels, are still quite expensive. More development should make them cheaper, so they can be used more widely.

3) A lot of governments are also worried that making changes to reduce carbon dioxide emissions could have an impact on the economic growth of their countries — which could be bad for people's well-being. This is particularly important for countries that are still developing.

Forests take in carbon dioxide and burning trees releases carbon dioxide. So preventing deforestation can help to cut a country's carbon footprint.

4) Because not everyone is on board, it's hard to make international agreements to reduce emissions. Most countries don't want to sacrifice their economic development if they think that others won't do the same.

5) It's not just governments, though — individuals (particularly those in developed countries) need to make changes to their lifestyles. For example:

An individual can reduce their personal carbon footprint by:
- choosing to cycle or walk instead of using a car,
- reducing how much they use air travel,
- doing anything that saves energy at home (e.g. turning heating down).

6) But it might be hard to get people to make changes if they don't want to and if there isn't enough education provided about why the changes are necessary and how to make them.

Lifestyle changes can be tough, but they might be essential in future

You need to be able to describe how carbon footprints could be reduced — don't forget that governments, as well as individuals, can take actions to reduce carbon emissions. Make sure that you can also give reasons why it can be hard to get countries and people to take actions to reduce their carbon footprints.

Topic C9 — Chemistry of the Atmosphere

Air Pollution

*Increasing carbon dioxide is causing climate change. But CO_2 isn't the only gas released when fossil fuels burn — you also get other nasty gases, like **oxides of nitrogen**, **sulfur dioxide** and **carbon monoxide**.*

Combustion of Fossil Fuels Releases Gases and Particles

1) Fossil fuels, such as crude oil and coal, contain hydrocarbons. During combustion, the carbon and hydrogen in these compounds are oxidised, so that carbon dioxide and water vapour are released back into the atmosphere.

   Hydrocarbons are compounds that only contain hydrogen and carbon (see p.267).

2) When there's plenty of oxygen, all the fuel burns — this is called complete combustion.

3) If there's not enough oxygen, some of the fuel doesn't burn — this is called incomplete combustion. Under these conditions, solid particles (called particulates), made up of soot (carbon) and unburned hydrocarbons, are released and carbon monoxide can be produced as well as carbon dioxide.

4) Particulates in the air can cause all sorts of problems:

   - If particulates are inhaled, they can get stuck in the lungs and cause damage. This can then lead to respiratory problems.
   - They're bad for the environment too. Particulates (and the clouds they help to produce), reflect sunlight back into space. This means that less light reaches the Earth, causing global dimming.

5) It's not just particulates from incomplete combustion that cause problems. Carbon monoxide is pretty nasty too.

   - Carbon monoxide (CO) is really dangerous because it can stop your blood from doing its job of carrying oxygen around the body.
   - It does this by binding to the haemoglobin in your blood that normally carries O_2 — so less oxygen is able to be transported round your body.
   - A lack of oxygen in the blood can lead to fainting, a coma or even death.
   - Carbon monoxide doesn't have any colour or smell, so it's very hard to detect. This makes it even more dangerous.

Sulfur Dioxide and Oxides of Nitrogen Can be Released

1) Sulfur dioxide (SO_2) is released during the combustion of fossil fuels, such as coal, that contain sulfur impurities — the sulfur in the fuel becomes oxidised.

2) Nitrogen oxides are created from a reaction between the nitrogen and oxygen in the air, caused by the heat of burning. (This can happen in the internal combustion engines of cars.)

3) When these gases mix with water in clouds they form dilute sulfuric acid or dilute nitric acid. This then falls as acid rain.

4) Acid rain kills plants and damages buildings and statues. It also makes metal corrode.

5) Not only that, but sulfur dioxide and nitrogen oxides can also be bad for human health — they cause respiratory problems if they're breathed in.

You can test for sulfur impurities in a fuel by bubbling the gases from combustion through universal indicator solution. If the fuel contains sulfur, the gases will contain SO_2, which will form sulfuric acid and turn the universal indicator red.

Fossil fuels are bad news — but we depend on them for many things...

...so a big reduction in their use is likely to be hard to achieve. Make sure you know the different pollutants that are given out when fuels burn, as well as the differences between complete and incomplete combustion.

Topic C9 — Chemistry of the Atmosphere

Warm-Up & Exam Questions

There's lots of important information in this section, from the Earth's atmosphere to climate change and pollution. Answer these questions to see what you can remember and what you need to go over again.

Warm-Up Questions

1) Where do scientists think the gases that made up Earth's early atmosphere came from?
2) Give an example of a sedimentary rock.
3) Give an example of a fossil fuel.
4) Suggest one way that an individual could reduce their personal carbon footprint.
5) Name two potential pollutants that could be released as a result of incomplete combustion of hydrocarbons, that wouldn't be released as a result of complete combustion.

Exam Questions

1   Use words from the box to complete the sentences below.   *Grade 4-6*

| oxygen | carbon | carbon dioxide | photosynthesis | respiration |

Once green plants had evolved, they thrived in Earth's early atmosphere which was rich in

.... These plants also produced .... by the process of ....

Some of the .... from dead plants eventually became 'locked up' in fossil fuels.

[4 marks]

2   Burning fossil fuels can produce pollutants like carbon dioxide, sulfur dioxide and particulate matter.   *Grade 6-7*

2.1   Describe how sulfur dioxide can cause acid rain.

[2 marks]

2.2   Give **one** environmental problem caused by acid rain.

[1 mark]

2.3   Explain how burning fossil fuels can lead to global dimming.

[3 marks]

2.4   Carbon dioxide is a greenhouse gas. Describe how the greenhouse effect is responsible for warming the surface of the Earth.

[4 marks]

3   Many people believe that it is necessary for individuals to reduce their carbon footprints in order to prevent climate change from happening in the future.   *Grade 7-9*

3.1   Define the term 'carbon footprint'.

[1 mark]

3.2* Describe some of the effects that an increase in global temperature could have on the environment. Explain the impact these effects may have on humans.

[6 marks]

Topic C9 — Chemistry of the Atmosphere

Topic C10 — Using Resources

Finite and Renewable Resources

*There are lots of different resources that humans use to provide **energy** for things like **heating** or **travelling**, as well as for **building materials** and **food**. Unfortunately, some of these resources will **run out** one day.*

Natural Resources Come From the Earth, Sea and Air

1) Natural resources form without human input. They include anything that comes from the earth, sea or air. For example, cotton for clothing or oil for fuel.
2) Some of these natural products can be replaced by synthetic products or improved upon by man-made processes. For example, rubber is a natural product that can be extracted from the sap of a tree, however man-made polymers have now been made which can replace rubber in uses such as tyres.
3) Agriculture provides conditions where natural resources can be enhanced for our needs. E.g. the development of fertilisers have meant we can produce a high yield of crops.

Some Natural Resources will Run Out

1) Renewable resources reform at a similar rate to, or faster than, we use them.
2) For example, timber is a renewable resource as trees can be planted following a harvest and only take a few years to regrow. Other examples of renewable resources include fresh water and food.
3) Finite (non-renewable) resources, aren't formed quickly enough to be considered replaceable.
4) Finite resources include fossil fuels and nuclear fuels such as uranium and plutonium. Minerals and metals found in ores in the earth are also non-renewable materials.
5) After they've been extracted, many finite resources undergo man-made processes to provide fuels and materials necessary for modern life. E.g. crude oil can undergo fractional distillation (see p.269) to produce products such as petrol, and metal ores can be reduced to produce pure metals (see p.238).

Tables, Charts and Graphs Give You an Insight Into Different Resources

You may be asked to interpret information about resources in the exam.

EXAMPLE

The table below shows information for two resources, coal and timber. Identify which resource is which.

The time it takes for Resource 1 to reform is 10^5 times shorter than Resource 2 suggesting it is a renewable resource. Resource 1 also has a much lower energy density than Resource 2, so is more likely to be timber than coal.

Resource 1 is timber and Resource 2 is coal.

	Energy Density (MJ/m^3)	Time it takes to form
Resource 1	7 600-11 400	10 years
Resource 2	23 000-26 000	10^6 years

10^6 is a shorthand way of showing 1 000 000. This is because $10^6 = 10 \times 10 \times 10 \times 10 \times 10 \times 10 = 1 000 000$.

Extracting Finite Resources has Risks

1) Many modern materials are made from raw, finite resources, e.g. most plastics and building materials.
2) People have to balance the social, economic and environmental effects of extracting finite resources.

For example, mining metal ores is good because useful products can be made. It also provides local people with jobs and brings money into the area. However, mining ores is bad for the environment as it uses loads of energy, scars the landscape, produces lots of waste and destroys habitats.

Natural resources can be either renewable or finite
Before you move on, make sure you learn a few examples of finite and renewable resources.

Topic C10 — Using Resources

Sustainability

*Many materials used in the modern world are **limited**. Scientists are constantly trying to find new and improved ways to extract and use natural resources **more sustainably**.*

Chemistry is **Improving Sustainability**

1) Sustainable development is an approach to development that takes account of the needs of present society while not damaging the lives of future generations.

2) As you saw on the previous page, not all resources are renewable so it's unsustainable to keep using them.

3) As well as using resources, extracting resources can be unsustainable due to the amount of energy used and waste produced. Processing the resources into useful materials, such as glass or bricks, can be unsustainable too as the processes often use energy that's made from finite resources.

4) If people reduce how much they use of a finite resource, that resource is more likely to last longer. Reducing usage of these resources will also reduce the use of anything needed to produce them.

5) We can't stop using finite resources altogether, but chemists can develop and adapt processes that use lower amounts of finite resources and reduce damage to the environment. For example, chemists have developed catalysts that reduce the amount of energy required for certain industrial processes.

Copper-Rich Ores are in **Short Supply**

1) Copper is a finite resource — the supply of copper-rich ores is limited.
2) One way to improve its sustainability is by extracting it from low-grade ores (ores without much copper in). Scientists are looking into new ways of doing this:

Bioleaching

Bacteria are used to convert copper compounds in the ore into soluble copper compounds, separating out the copper from the ore in the process. The leachate (the solution produced by the process) contains copper ions, which can be extracted, e.g. by electrolysis (see p.242) or displacement (see p.240) with a more reactive metal, e.g. scrap iron.

These methods can be used to extract other metals too.

Phytomining

Phytomining involves growing plants in soil that contains copper. The plants can't use or get rid of the copper so it gradually builds up in the leaves. The plants can be harvested, dried and burned in a furnace. The ash contains soluble copper compounds from which copper can be extracted by electrolysis or displacement using scrap iron.

3) Traditional methods of copper mining are pretty damaging to the environment (see next page). These new methods of extraction have a much smaller impact, but the disadvantage is that they're slow.

The extraction of resources can be unsustainable

If we keep using finite resources at the rate that we currently are, one day they will run out. We need to find alternatives for finite resources, but in the meantime we can use methods to make them last as long as possible. For example, bioleaching and phytomining are a way of making reserves of metal ores last longer.

Topic C10 — Using Resources

Recycling

*Once an object made from a finite resource is worn out, it's usually **more sustainable** to **recycle** it than to use new raw materials to replace it. Read on to find out why...*

Recycling Metals is Important

1) Mining and extracting metals takes lots of energy, most of which comes from burning fossil fuels.

2) Recycling metals often uses much less energy than is needed to mine and extract new metal, conserves the finite amount of each metal in the earth and cuts down on the amount of waste getting sent to landfill.

> Recycling is a way to reduce our need for copper-rich ores.

3) Metals are usually recycled by melting them and then casting them into the shape of the new product.

4) Depending on what the metal will be used for after recycling, the amount of separation required for recyclable metals can change. For example:

> Waste steel and iron can be kept together as they can be both added to iron in a blast furnace to reduce the amount of iron ore required.

> A blast furnace is used to extract iron from its ore at a high temperature using carbon.

Glass can Also be Recycled

Glass recycling can help sustainability by reducing the amount of energy needed to make new glass products, and also the amount of waste created when used glass is thrown away.

1) Glass bottles can often be reused without reshaping.

2) Other forms of glass can't be reused so they're recycled instead. Usually the glass is separated by colour and chemical composition before being recycled.

3) The glass is crushed and then melted to be reshaped for use in glass products such as bottles or jars. It might also be used for a different purpose such as insulating glass wool for wall insulation in homes.

REVISION TIP

Recycling is key to sustainability — it's useful in lots of ways...
Remember that recycling doesn't just reduce the use of raw materials, it reduces the amount of energy used, the amount of damage to the environment and the amount of waste produced.

Topic C10 — Using Resources

Life Cycle Assessments

*If a company wants to manufacture a new product, they carry out a **life cycle assessment (LCA)**.*

Life Cycle Assessments Show Total Environmental Costs

1) A life cycle assessment (LCA) looks at every stage of a product's life to assess the impact it would have on the environment.
2) Here are the different stages that need to be considered:

1) Getting the Raw Materials

1) Extracting raw materials needed for a product can damage the local environment, for example, mining metals. Extraction can also result in pollution due to the amount of energy needed.
2) Raw materials often need to be processed to extract the desired materials and this often needs large amounts of energy. For example, extracting metals from ores or fractional distillation of crude oil.

2) Manufacturing and Packaging

1) Manufacturing products and their packaging can use a lot of energy resources and can also cause a lot of pollution. For example, harmful fumes such as carbon monoxide or hydrogen chloride.
2) You also need to think about any waste products and how to dispose of them. The chemical reactions used to make compounds from their raw materials can produce waste products. Some waste can be turned into other useful chemicals, reducing the amount that ends up polluting the environment.

4) Product Disposal

1) Products are often disposed of in landfill sites. This takes up space and pollutes land and water. E.g. paint may wash off a product in landfill and pollute a river.
2) Energy is used to transport waste to landfill, which causes pollutants to be released into the atmosphere.
3) Products might be incinerated (burnt), which causes air pollution.

3) Using the Product

1) The use of a product can damage the environment. For example, burning fuels releases greenhouse gases and other harmful substances. Fertilisers can leach into streams and rivers causing damage to ecosystems.
2) How long a product is used for or how many uses it gets is also a factor — products that need lots of energy to produce but are used for ages may mean less waste in the long run.

LCAs look at the environmental impact of a product's entire life

Doing a life cycle assessment for a product can be a very time consuming and expensive process, as there is so much to take account of. Some things can only be predicted, for example, how a consumer will use a product. Get to grips with each stage and what factors have to be taken into account at every step.

Topic C10 — Using Resources

Life Cycle Assessments

You Can **Compare** Life Cycle Assessments for **Plastic** and **Paper Bags**

The table below shows how you might carry out a LCA of plastic and paper bags.

Life Cycle Assessment Stage	Plastic Bag	Paper Bag
Raw Materials	Crude oil	Timber
Manufacturing and Packaging	The compounds needed to make the plastic are extracted from crude oil by fractional distillation, followed by cracking and then polymerisation. Waste is reduced as the other fractions of crude oil have other uses.	Pulped timber is processed using lots of energy. Lots of waste is made.
Using the Product	Can be reused. Can be used for other things as well as shopping, for example bin liners.	Usually only used once.
Product Disposal	Recyclable but not biodegradable and will take up space in landfill and pollute land.	Biodegradable, non-toxic and can be recycled.

Life cycle assessments have shown that even though plastic bags aren't biodegradable, they take less energy to make and have a longer lifespan than paper bags, so may be less harmful to the environment.

There are **Problems** with **Life Cycle Assessments**

1) The use of energy, some natural resources and the amount of certain types of waste produced by a product over it's lifetime can be easily quantified. But the effect of some pollutants is harder to give a numerical value to. E.g. it's difficult to apply a value to the negative visual effects of plastic bags in the environment compared to paper ones.

2) So, producing an LCA is not an objective method as it takes into account the values of the person carrying out the assessment. This means LCAs can be biased.

3) Selective LCAs, which only show some of the impacts of a product on the environment, can also be biased as they can be written to deliberately support the claims of a company in order to give them positive advertising.

LCAs aren't all they are cracked up to be...

EXAM TIP: In the exam, you may have to analyse LCAs comparing different products and come to a conclusion about which product is the most environmentally friendly. But don't forget that not all environmental impacts can be measured in an LCA. Also, the opinions of the assessors have an effect on the result of the assessment and the results can be misused to suit an organisations aims.

Topic C10 — Using Resources

Warm-Up & Exam Questions

That's some more revision done and dusted and now it's time to test yourself on how much you've taken in. Have a go at the questions on this page to see if you need to revisit some topics.

Warm-Up Questions

1) Give an example of a natural resource which has been replaced by a man-made alternative.
2) What is sustainable development?
3) Give three positive effects of recycling metals.
4) What are the four stages that need to be considered to conduct a life cycle assessment?

Exam Questions

1 Natural resources are formed without human input and are used for construction, fuel and food. *Grade 4-6*

1.1 What is a finite natural resource?
Tick **one** box.

☐ A natural resource that can never be remade.
☐ A natural resource that will never run out.
☐ A natural resource that doesn't renew itself quickly enough to be considered replaceable.
☐ A natural resource that can only be used in certain conditions.

[1 mark]

1.2 Aluminium is used to make soft drink cans. Extracting aluminium is a very energy intensive process. Suggest **two** ways that the use of soft drink cans can be made more sustainable.

[2 marks]

2 Copper needs to be extracted from its ore before it can be used. *Grade 6-7*

2.1 Explain why scientists have developed ways of extracting copper from low-grade ores.

[1 mark]

2.2 Copper can be extracted from low-grade ores by a process called bioleaching.
Explain how the process works.

[2 marks]

2.3 Give **one** advantage of using processes such as bioleaching rather than traditional mining.

[1 marks]

2.4 Give **one** disadvantage of using processes such as bioleaching rather than traditional mining.

[1 mark]

3 A life cycle assessment looks at the environmental impact of a product over its lifetime. *Grade 6-7*

3.1 Describe why it can be difficult to give a complete assessment of a product over its entire life cycle.

[1 mark]

3.2 A company carried out a LCA on one of their products but didn't take into account its disposal. However, an independent LCA found the disposal of the product to have the greatest environmental impact of any part of the product's life cycle.
Suggest why the LCA performed by the company didn't include details of the disposal of the product.

[2 marks]

Topic C10 — Using Resources

Potable Water and Water Treatment

*We all need safe drinking water. The **way** that water's made safe depends on **local conditions**.*

Potable Water is Water You Can Drink

1) Potable water is water that's been treated or is naturally safe for humans to drink — it's essential for life.
2) Chemists wouldn't call it pure, though. Pure water only contains H$_2$O molecules whereas potable water can contain lots of other dissolved substances.
3) The important thing is that the levels of dissolved salts aren't too high, that it has a pH between 6.5 and 8.5 and also that there aren't any nasties (like bacteria or other microbes) swimming around in it.

How Potable Water is Produced Depends on Where You Are

1) Rainwater is a type of fresh water. Fresh water is water that doesn't have much dissolved in it.
2) When it rains, water can either collect as surface water (in lakes, rivers and reservoirs) or as groundwater (in rocks called aquifers that trap water underground).
3) In the UK, the source of fresh water used depends on location. Surface water tends to dry up first, so in warm areas, e.g. the south-east, most of the domestic water supply comes from groundwater.
4) Even though it only has low levels of dissolved substances, water from these fresh water sources still needs to be treated to make it safe before it can be used. This process includes:

Filtration — a wire mesh screens out large twigs etc, and then gravel and sand beds filter out any other solid bits.

— mesh
— sand and gravel filtration
— sterilisation

Sterilisation — the water is sterilised to kill any harmful bacteria or microbes. This can be done by bubbling chlorine gas through it or by using ozone or ultraviolet light.

Chemicals can also be added to the water supply, such as fluoride (which is good for teeth). This is controversial, because people aren't given any choice over whether they consume them or not.

5) In some very dry countries, e.g. Kuwait, there's not enough surface or groundwater and instead sea water must be treated by desalination to provide potable water. In these countries distillation (see next page) can be used to desalinate sea water.
6) Sea water can also be treated by processes that use membranes — like reverse osmosis. The salty water is passed through a membrane that only allows water molecules to pass through. Ions and larger molecules are trapped by the membrane so separated from the water.
7) Both distillation and reverse osmosis need loads of energy, so they're really expensive and not practical for producing large quantities of fresh water.

Water must be treated before it can be drunk safely

Distilling salty water could be useful if you end up stranded on a desert island. And for your exams.

Q1   Describe the steps used to treat fresh water to make it potable.   [2 marks]

Topic C10 — Using Resources

Potable Water and Water Treatment

You can Test and Distil Water in the Lab — PRACTICAL

1) First, test the pH of the water using a pH meter. If the pH is too high or too low, you'll need to neutralise it by adding acid (if the pH is high) or alkali (if the pH is low). Use a pH meter to tell you when the solution is between 6.5 and 8.5.

2) To distil the water, pour the salty water into a distillation apparatus, like the one on p.185. Heat the flask from below. The water will boil and form steam, leaving any dissolved salts in the flask. The steam will condense back to liquid water in the condenser and can be collected as it runs out.

3) Retest the pH of the water with a pH meter to check that it's between pH 6.5 and 8.5.

4) You can tell whether there were salts in the water by looking to see whether there are any crystals in the round bottomed flask once the water's been distilled.

Waste Water Comes from Lots of Different Sources

1) We use water for lots of things at home — like having a bath, going to the toilet, doing the washing-up, etc. When you flush this water down the drain, it goes into the sewers and towards sewage treatment plants.

2) Agricultural systems also produce a lot of waste water including nutrient run-off from fields and slurry from animal farms.

3) Sewage from domestic or agricultural sources has to be treated to remove any organic matter and harmful microbes before it can be put back into fresh water sources like rivers or lakes. Otherwise it would make them very polluted and would pose health risks.

4) Industrial processes also produce a lot of waste water that has to be collected and treated.

5) As well as organic matter, industrial waste water can also contain harmful chemicals — so it has to undergo additional stages of treatment before it is safe to release it into the environment.

The water that comes out of our taps has been treated

Location is a really important factor in determining how water is treated. For example, in the UK, there is a lot of fresh water available so this is filtered and then sterilised. However, in very dry countries a more expensive process may have to be used, such as the distillation or reverse osmosis of sea water.

Topic C10 — Using Resources

Potable Water and Water Treatment

*It may not be glamorous but dealing with waste water is vital to stop us **polluting** our environment.*

Sewage Treatment Happens in Several Stages

Some of the processes involved in treating waste water at sewage treatment plants include:

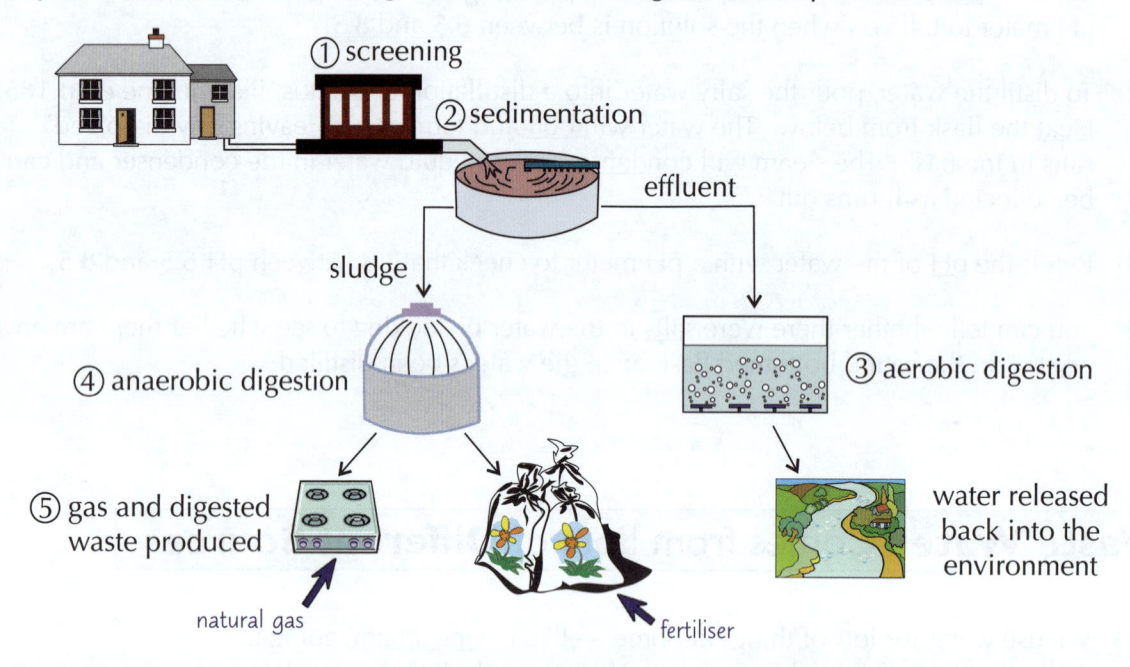

① screening
② sedimentation
③ aerobic digestion
④ anaerobic digestion
⑤ gas and digested waste produced → natural gas, fertiliser

effluent → aerobic digestion → water released back into the environment
sludge → anaerobic digestion

1) Before being treated, the sewage is screened — this involves removing any large bits of material (like twigs or plastic bags) as well as any grit.

2) Then it's allowed to stand in a settlement tank and undergoes sedimentation — the heavier suspended solids sink to the bottom to produce sludge while the lighter effluent floats on the top.

   Aerobic just means with oxygen, whereas anaerobic means without oxygen.

3) The effluent in the settlement tank is removed and treated by biological aerobic digestion. This is when air is pumped through the water to encourage aerobic bacteria to break down any organic matter — including other microbes in the water.

4) The sludge from the bottom of the settlement tank is also removed and transferred into large tanks. Here it gets broken down by bacteria in a process called anaerobic digestion.

5) Anaerobic digestion breaks down the organic matter in the sludge, releasing methane gas in the process. The methane gas can be used as an energy source and the remaining digested waste can be used as a fertiliser.

6) For waste water containing toxic substances, additional stages of treatment may involve adding chemicals (e.g. to precipitate metals), UV radiation or using membranes.

Sewage treatment requires more processes than treating fresh water but uses less energy than the desalination of salt water, so could be used as an alternative in areas where there's not much fresh water. For example, Singapore is treating waste water and recycling it back into drinking supplies. However, some people don't like the idea of drinking water that used to be sewage.

Waste water can be recycled to produce potable water

To learn the stages of water treatment, cover the diagram, write out each step and then check it.

Q1 Name and describe the first two stages of waste water treatment at a sewage treatment plant. [2 marks]

Topic C10 — Using Resources

Warm-Up & Exam Questions

Now you know all there is to possibly know about water it's time to test yourself with some questions.

Warm-Up Questions

1) Describe two features of potable water that make it safe for drinking.
2) What is the first step in treating fresh water?
3) In addition to organic matter, what else may have to be removed from industrial waste water?
4) What is produced following the sedimentation stage of water treatment?

Exam Questions

1 Figure 1 shows how water in some parts of the UK is treated during the production of potable water. *(Grade 6-7)*

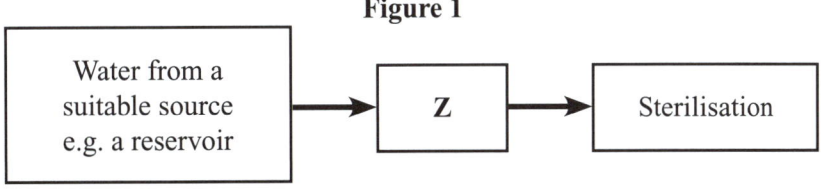

Figure 1

Water from a suitable source e.g. a reservoir → Z → Sterilisation

1.1 Describe the difference between potable water and pure water.

[1 mark]

1.2 Describe what happens during stage **Z** in **Figure 1**.

[2 marks]

1.3 Suggest **three** agents that could be used during the sterilisation stage of the process.

[3 marks]

2 Waste water from human activities must undergo treatment before being released into the environment. The stages of sewage treatment include screening, sedimentation, anaerobic digestion and aerobic digestion. *(Grade 6-7)*

2.1 State the stage at which large pieces of material, such as twigs, are removed.

[1 mark]

2.2 During sedimentation, effluent is produced. Describe what happens during the next step in the treatment of effluent following sedimentation.

[2 marks]

2.3 In areas where fresh water is limited, treated waste water and sea water can be used as drinking water. Describe two disadvantages of using these processes compared to the treatment of fresh water.

[2 marks]

PRACTICAL

3 In some dry countries potable water is produced by the distillation of salt water. A student carries out distillation of salt water in the lab. *(Grade 6-7)*

3.1 Describe **two** tests which can be used to determine whether or not the distilled water contains any sodium or chloride ions.

[4 marks]

3.2 Suggest a further test that would need to be carried out before the water could be considered potable.

[1 mark]

Topic C10 — Using Resources

Revision Summary for Topics C6-10

That wraps up Topics C6-10 — time to see how you do with these questions.
- Try these questions and tick off each one when you get it right.
- When you're completely happy with a topic, tick it off.

For even more practice, try the Retrieval Quizzes for Topics C6-10 — just scan the QR codes!

Topic C6 — The Rate and Extent of Chemical Change (p.253-265)

1) On a rate of reaction graph, what does a steep line show?
2) What are the four factors that affect the rate of a reaction?
3) How does a catalyst increase the rate of a reaction?
4) State the equation that could be used to calculate the mean rate of a reaction.
5) Give three possible units for the rate of a chemical reaction.
6) What is a tangent?
7) How would you use a tangent to find the gradient of a curve at a particular point?
8) Which one of the following statements is true?
    a) In a reaction at equilibrium, there is the same amount of products as reactants.
    b) If the forward reaction in a reversible reaction is exothermic, then the reverse reaction is endothermic.
    c) If the equilibrium of a system lies to the right, then the concentration of products is less than the concentration of reactants.

Topic C7 — Organic Chemistry (p.267-270)

9) What is the general word equation for the complete combustion of a hydrocarbon?
10) How is crude oil formed?
11) Cracking is a thermal decomposition reaction. Explain what this means.

Topic C8 — Chemical Analysis (p.273-276)

12) Describe how you could test the purity of a sample of a chemical.
13) Describe the test for carbon dioxide.
14) Draw and label a diagram of the set-up you would use to carry out a paper chromatography experiment.

Topic C9 — Chemistry of the Atmosphere (p.278-284)

15) Describe how limestone was formed from organisms millions of years ago.
16) State the approximate composition of the atmosphere today.
17) Explain how the greenhouse effect keeps the Earth warm.
18) Explain why it can be difficult to persuade countries to reduce their carbon dioxide emissions.
19) Describe how the following air pollutants are produced:
    a) particulates, b) carbon monoxide, c) sulfur dioxide, d) nitrogen oxides.

Topic C10 — Using Resources (p.286-294)

20) Give two examples of renewable resources.
21) Describe how metals are usually recycled.
22) Describe what life cycle assessments (LCAs) do.
23) Name a process that can be used to make seawater safe to drink.
24) Why is it important to treat waste water before releasing it into the environment?

Topic P1 — Energy

Energy Stores

*Energy is **never used up**. Instead it's just **transferred** between different **energy stores** and different objects...*

Energy is Transferred Between Stores

When energy is transferred to an object, the energy is stored in one of the object's energy stores. The energy stores you need to know are:

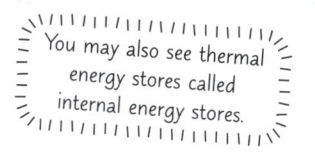

You may also see thermal energy stores called internal energy stores.

1) Thermal energy stores.
2) Kinetic energy stores.
3) Gravitational potential energy stores.
4) Elastic potential energy stores.
5) Chemical energy stores.
6) Magnetic energy stores.
7) Electrostatic energy stores.
8) Nuclear energy stores.

Energy is transferred mechanically (by a force doing work), electrically (work done by moving charges), by heating (see below) or by radiation (e.g. light, p.388, or sound).

There's more on doing work on the next page.

When a System Changes, Energy is Transferred

1) A system is just a fancy word for a single object (e.g. the air in a piston) or a group of objects (e.g. two colliding vehicles) that you're interested in.

2) When a system changes, energy is transferred. It can be transferred into or away from the system, between different objects in the system or between different types of energy stores (e.g. from the kinetic energy store of an object to its thermal energy store).

3) Closed systems are systems where neither matter nor energy can enter or leave. The net change in the total energy of a closed system is always zero.

Energy can be Transferred by Heating

1) Take the example of boiling water in a kettle — you can think of the water as the system. Energy is transferred to the water (from the kettle's heating element) by heating, into the water's thermal energy store (causing the temperature of the water to rise).

2) You could also think of the kettle's heating element and the water together as a two-object system. Energy is transferred electrically to the thermal energy store of the kettle's heating element, which transfers energy by heating to the water's thermal energy store.

No matter what store it's in, it's all energy...

EXAM TIP
In the exam, make sure you refer to energy in terms of the store it's in. For example, if you're describing energy in a hot object, say it 'has energy in its thermal energy store'.

Work Done

*On the previous page, you saw how energy can be **transferred** between **energy stores** by **heating**. Well, that was just the start... This page is all about how energy is transferred when **work is done**.*

Energy can be Transferred by Doing Work

1) Work done is just another way of saying energy transferred — they're the same thing.
2) Work can be done when current flows (work is done against resistance in a circuit, see page 317) or by a force moving an object (there's more on this on page 356). Here are a few examples:

The initial force exerted by a person to throw a ball upwards does work. It causes an energy transfer from the chemical energy store of the person's arm to the kinetic energy store of the ball and arm.

an upwards force is exerted on the ball

The friction between a car's brakes and its wheels does work as the car slows down. It causes an energy transfer from the wheels' kinetic energy stores to the thermal energy store of the surroundings.

frictional forces cause a transfer of energy

In a collision between a car and a stationary object, the normal contact force between the car and the object does work. It causes energy to be transferred from the car's kinetic energy store to other energy stores, e.g. the elastic potential and thermal energy stores of the object and the car body. Some energy might also be transferred away by sound waves.

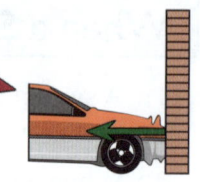

normal contact force causes a transfer of energy to the car

Falling Objects Also Transfer Energy

1) When something, e.g. a ball, is dropped from a height, it's accelerated by gravity. The gravitational force does work.
2) As it falls, energy from the object's gravitational potential energy (g.p.e) store is transferred to its kinetic energy store.
3) For a falling object when there's no air resistance:

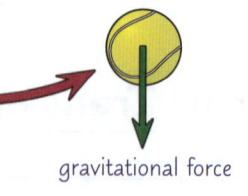

gravitational force

> Energy lost from the g.p.e. store = Energy gained in the kinetic energy store

4) In real life, air resistance (p.368) acts against all falling objects — it causes some energy to be transferred to other energy stores, e.g. the thermal energy stores of the object and surroundings.

Energy is transferred between the different stores of objects...

Energy stores pop up everywhere in physics. You need to be able to describe how energy is transferred, and which stores it gets transferred between, for any scenario.

Q1 Describe the energy transfers that occur when the wind causes a windmill to spin. [3 marks]

Topic P1 — Energy

Kinetic and Potential Energy Stores

*Now you've got your head around **energy stores**, it's time to see how you can calculate the amount of energy in **three** of the most common ones — **kinetic**, **gravitational potential** and **elastic potential** energy stores.*

Movement Means Energy in an Object's Kinetic Energy Store

1) Anything that is moving has energy in its kinetic energy store. Energy is transferred to this store when an object speeds up and is transferred away from this store when an object slows down.

2) The energy in the kinetic energy store depends on the object's mass and speed. The greater its mass and the faster it's going, the more energy there will be in its kinetic energy store.

3) There's a slightly tricky formula for it, so you have to concentrate a little bit harder for this one.

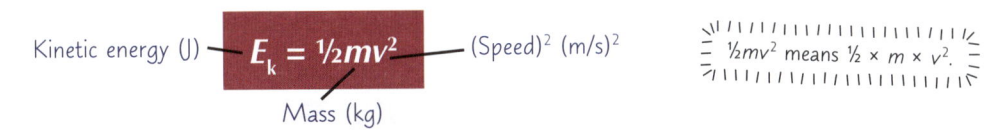

Kinetic energy (J) — $E_k = \frac{1}{2}mv^2$ — (Speed)² (m/s)²
Mass (kg)

$\frac{1}{2}mv^2$ means $\frac{1}{2} \times m \times v^2$.

EXAMPLE A car of mass 2500 kg is travelling at 20 m/s. Calculate the energy in its kinetic energy store.

$E_k = \frac{1}{2}mv^2 = \frac{1}{2} \times 2500 \times 20^2 =$ **500 000 J**

Raised Objects Store Energy in Gravitational Potential Energy Stores

1) Lifting an object in a gravitational field (page 354) requires work. This causes a transfer of energy to the gravitational potential energy (g.p.e.) store of the raised object. The higher the object is lifted, the more energy is transferred to this store.

2) The amount of energy in a gravitational potential energy store depends on the object's mass, its height and the strength of the gravitational field the object is in.

3) You can use this equation to find the change in energy in an object's gravitational potential energy store for a change in height, h.

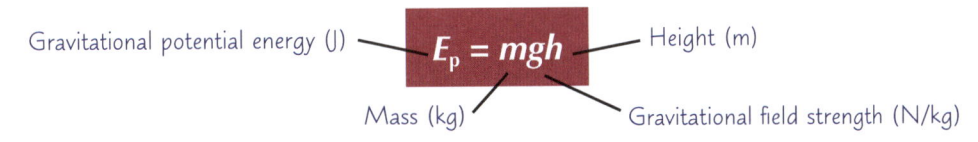

Gravitational potential energy (J) — $E_p = mgh$ — Height (m)
Mass (kg)   Gravitational field strength (N/kg)

Stretching can Transfer Energy to Elastic Potential Energy Stores

Stretching or squashing an object can transfer energy to its elastic potential energy store. So long as the limit of proportionality has not been exceeded (page 360) energy in the elastic potential energy store of a stretched spring can be found using:

Spring constant (N/m)
Elastic potential energy (J) — $E_e = \frac{1}{2}ke^2$ — Extension (m)

Greater height = more energy in gravitational potential stores...

Make sure you know what all the variables are in the equations above, and the units they're in.

Q1 A 2.0 kg object is dropped from a height of 10 m.
Calculate the speed of the object after it has fallen 5.0 m, assuming there is no air resistance.
Give your answer to 2 significant figures. $g = 9.8$ N/kg. **[5 marks]**

Topic P1 — Energy

Specific Heat Capacity

Specific heat capacity is really just a sciencey way of saying **how hard** it is to **heat** something up...

Different Materials Have Different Specific Heat Capacities

1) More energy needs to be transferred to the thermal energy store of some materials to increase their temperature than others.
2) For example:

> You need 4200 J to warm 1 kg of water by 1 °C, but only 139 J to warm 1 kg of mercury by 1 °C.

3) Materials that need to gain lots of energy in their thermal energy stores to warm up also transfer loads of energy when they cool down again. They can 'store' a lot of energy.
4) The measure of how much energy a substance can store is called its specific heat capacity.

> Specific heat capacity is the amount of energy needed to raise the temperature of 1 kg of a substance by 1 °C.

There's a Helpful Formula Involving Specific Heat Capacity

Below is the equation that links energy transferred to specific heat capacity (the Δ's just mean "change in").

$$\Delta E = mc\Delta\theta$$

- Change in thermal energy (J)
- Mass (kg)
- Specific heat capacity (J/kg°C)
- Temperature change (°C)

EXAMPLE

How much energy is needed to heat 2.00 kg of water from 10 °C to 100 °C? The specific heat capacity of water is 4200 J/kg°C.

1) First find the change in temperature (Δθ) in °C.

$\Delta\theta = 100 - 10 = 90$ °C

2) Now substitute this value, along with the values for mass and specific heat capacity, into the formula.

$\Delta E = mc\Delta\theta$
$= 2.00 \times 4200 \times 90$
$= 756\,000$ J

If you're **not** working out the energy, you'll have to rearrange the equation, so a formula triangle will come in dead handy. To use them, cover up the thing you want to find and write down what's left showing.
You write the bits of the formula in the triangle like this:

$$\frac{\Delta E}{m \times c \times \Delta\theta}$$

The line through the centre of the triangle means divide.

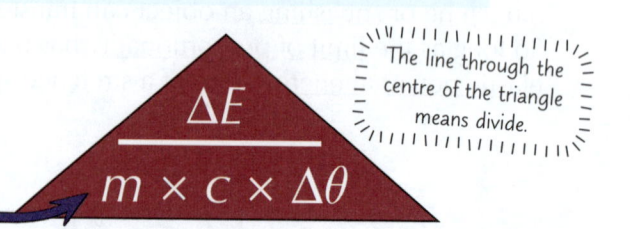

Some substances can store more energy than others...

Learn the definition of specific heat capacity and make sure you know how to use the formula above.

Q1 Find the final temperature of 5 kg of water, at an initial temperature of 5 °C, after 50 kJ of energy has been transferred to it. The specific heat capacity of water is 4200 J/kg°C. [3 marks]

Topic P1 — Energy

Investigating Specific Heat Capacity [PRACTICAL]

*This fun practical can be used to find out the **specific heat capacity** of a material.*

You Can Investigate Specific Heat Capacities

1) To investigate a solid material (e.g. copper), you'll need a block of the material with two holes in it (for the heater and thermometer to go into, see the image on the right).

2) Measure the mass of the block, then wrap it in an insulating layer (e.g. a thick layer of newspaper) to reduce the energy transferred from the block to the surroundings. Insert the thermometer and heater as shown on the right.

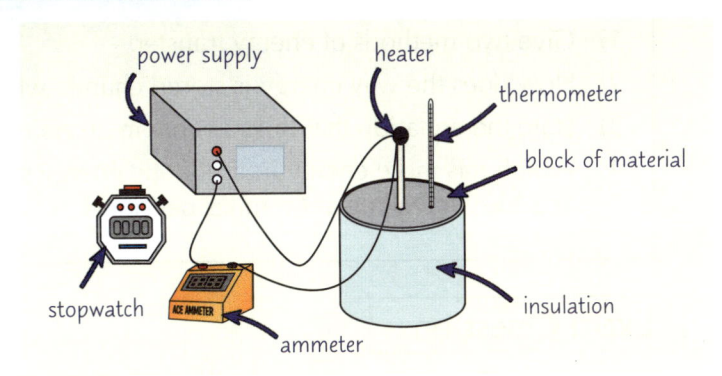

3) Measure the initial temperature of the block and set the potential difference, V, of the power supply to be 10 V. Turn on the power supply and start a stopwatch.

4) When you turn on the power, the current in the circuit (i.e. the moving charges) does work on the heater, transferring energy electrically from the power supply to the heater's thermal energy store. This energy is then transferred to the material's thermal energy store by heating, causing the material's temperature to increase.

5) As the block heats up, use the thermometer to measure its temperature e.g. every minute. Keep an eye on the ammeter — the current through the circuit, I, shouldn't change.

6) When you've collected enough readings (10 should do it), turn off the power supply.

7) Now you have to do some calculations to find the material's specific heat capacity:

- Using your measurement of the current and the potential difference of the power supply, you can calculate the power supplied to the heater, using $P = VI$ (p.330). You can use this to calculate how much energy, E, has been transferred to the heater at the time of each temperature reading using the formula $E = Pt$, where t is the time in seconds since the experiment began.

- If you assume all the energy supplied to the heater has been transferred to the block, you can plot a graph of energy transferred to the thermal energy store of the block against temperature. It should look something like this: ➡

   You may or may not get the curved bit at the beginning — don't worry about it.

- Find the gradient of the straight part of the graph. This is $\Delta\theta \div \Delta E$. You know from the equation on the last page that $\Delta E = mc\Delta\theta$. So the specific heat capacity of the material of the block is: $1 \div$ (gradient × the mass of the block).

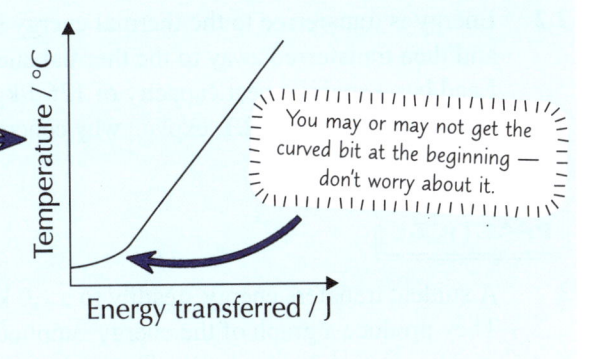

8) You can repeat this experiment with different materials to see how their specific heat capacities compare.

You can also investigate the specific heat capacity of liquids — just place the heater and thermometer in an insulated beaker filled with a known mass of the liquid.

Think about how you could improve your experiments...

PRACTICAL TIP If the hole in your material is bigger than your thermometer, you could put a small amount of water in the hole with the thermometer. This helps the thermometer to measure the temperature of the block more accurately, as water is a better thermal conductor than air (see page 304).

Topic P1 — Energy

Warm-Up & Exam Questions

These questions give you chance to use your knowledge about energy transfers and specific heat capacity.

Warm-Up Questions

1) Give two methods of energy transfer.
2) How does the way energy is stored change when someone throws a ball upwards?
3) State the equation that links energy in an object's kinetic energy store with mass and speed.
4) Which has more energy in its kinetic energy store: a person walking at 3 miles per hour, or a lorry travelling at 60 miles per hour?

Exam Questions

1 A motor lifts a load of mass 20 kg.
The load gains 137.2 J of energy in its gravitational potential energy store. *Grade 4-6*

1.1 State the equation that links gravitational potential energy, mass, gravitational field strength and height.
Use this equation to calculate the height through which the motor lifts the load.
Assume the gravitational field strength = 9.8 N/kg

[4 marks]

1.2 The motor releases the load and the load falls.
Ignoring air resistance, describe the changes in the way energy is stored that take place as the load falls.

[2 marks]

1.3 Describe how your answer to **1.2** would differ if air resistance was not ignored.

[1 mark]

2 36 000 J of energy is transferred to heat a 0.5 kg concrete block from 20 °C to 100 °C. *Grade 6-7*

2.1 Calculate the specific heat capacity of the concrete block.
Use the correct equation from the Physics Equation Sheet on page 542.

[4 marks]

2.2 Energy is transferred to the thermal energy store of an electric storage heater at night, and then transferred away to the thermal energy stores of the surroundings during the day.
Lead has a specific heat capacity of 126 J/kg°C.
Using your answer to **2.1**, explain why concrete blocks are used in storage heaters rather than lead blocks.

[2 marks]

PRACTICAL

3 A student transfers energy steadily to a 1.0 kg aluminium block.
They produce a graph of the energy supplied against the increase in temperature of the block, shown in **Figure 1**. *Grade 7-9*

Figure 1

3.1 Use **Figure 1** to find a value for the specific heat capacity of aluminium in J/kg°C. Use the correct equation from the Physics Equation Sheet on page 542.

[4 marks]

3.2 Would you expect the true value for the specific heat capacity of aluminium to be higher or lower than the value found in this experiment? Explain your answer.

[3 marks]

Topic P1 — Energy

Conservation of Energy and Power

*Repeat after me: **energy** is **NEVER** destroyed. Make sure you learn that fact, it's really important.*

You Need to Know the Conservation of Energy Principle

1) The conservation of energy principle is that energy is always conserved:

   > Energy can be transferred usefully, stored or dissipated, but can never be created or destroyed.

2) When energy is transferred between stores, not all of the energy is transferred usefully into the store that you want it to go to. Some energy is always dissipated when an energy transfer takes place.

3) Dissipated energy is sometimes called 'wasted energy' because the energy is being stored in a way that is not useful (usually energy has been transferred into thermal energy stores).

> A mobile phone is a system. When you use the phone, energy is usefully transferred from the chemical energy store of the battery in the phone. But some of this energy is dissipated in this transfer to the thermal energy store of the phone (you may have noticed your phone feels warm if you've been using it for a while).

4) You also need to be able to describe energy transfers for closed systems:

> A cold spoon is dropped into an insulated flask of hot soup, which is then sealed. You can assume that the flask is a perfect thermal insulator so the spoon and the soup form a closed system. Energy is transferred from the thermal energy store of the soup to the useless thermal energy store of the spoon (causing the soup to cool down slightly). Energy transfers have occurred within the system, but no energy has left the system — so the net change in energy is zero.

Power is the 'Rate of Doing Work' — i.e. How Much per Second

1) Power is the rate of energy transfer, or the rate of doing work.
2) Power is measured in watts. One watt = 1 joule of energy transferred per second.
3) You can calculate power using these equations:

   Power (W) — $P = \dfrac{E}{t}$ — Energy transferred (J) / Time (s)

   Power (W) — $P = \dfrac{W}{t}$ — Work done (J) / Time (s)

4) A powerful machine is not necessarily one which can exert a strong force (although it usually ends up that way). A powerful machine is one which transfers a lot of energy in a short space of time.

> Take two cars that are identical in every way apart from the power of their engines. Both cars race the same distance along a straight track to a finish line. The car with the more powerful engine will reach the finish line faster than the other car (it will transfer the same amount of energy but over less time).

Remember: energy cannot be created or destroyed...

When energy is wasted it's not destroyed — it just isn't stored usefully anymore.

Q1 A motor transfers 4.8 kJ of energy in 2 minutes. Calculate its power output. [3 marks]

Topic P1 — Energy

Conduction and Convection

It's time to meet two methods of energy transfer by **heating** — **conduction** and **convection**. Read on to find out how they **actually happen** and about the **energy transfers** that take place.

Conduction Occurs Mainly in Solids

> Conduction is the process where vibrating particles transfer energy to neighbouring particles.

1) Energy transferred to an object by heating is transferred to the thermal store of the object. This energy is shared across the kinetic energy stores of the particles in the object.

2) The particles in the part of the object being heated vibrate more and collide with each other. These collisions cause energy to be transferred between particles' kinetic energy stores. This is conduction.

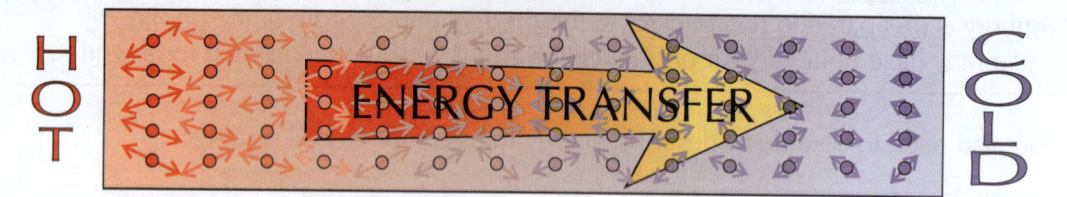

3) This process continues throughout the object until the energy is transferred to the other side of the object. It's then usually transferred to the thermal energy store of the surroundings (or anything else touching the object).

   Particles in liquids and gases are much more free to move around, which is why they usually transfer energy by convection instead of conduction.

4) Thermal conductivity is a measure of how quickly energy is transferred through a material in this way. Materials with a high thermal conductivity transfer energy between their particles quickly.

Convection Occurs Only in Liquids and Gases

> Convection is where energetic particles move away from hotter to cooler regions.

1) Convection can happen in gases and liquids. Energy is transferred by heating to the thermal store of the liquid or gas. As with conduction, this energy is shared across the kinetic energy stores of the gas or liquid's particles.

2) Unlike in solids, the particles in liquids and gases are able to move. When you heat a region of a gas or liquid, the particles move faster and the space between individual particles increases. This causes the density (p.335) of the region being heated to decrease.

3) Because liquids and gases can flow, the warmer and less dense region will rise above denser, cooler regions. So energetic particles move away from hotter to cooler regions — this is convection.

Some substances are better thermal conductors than others...

Denser materials (see page 335) are usually better conductors than less dense materials. It's easy to see why — particles that are right next to each other will pass energy between their kinetic energy stores far more effectively than particles that are far apart. For example, water is a much better thermal conductor than air.

Topic P1 — Energy

Reducing Unwanted Energy Transfers

*There are a few ways you can **reduce** the amount of energy scampering off to a **completely useless** store — **lubrication** and **thermal insulation** are the ones you need to know about. Read on to find out more...*

Lubrication Reduces Frictional Forces

1) Whenever something moves, there's usually at least one frictional force acting against it (p.368). This causes some energy in the system to be dissipated (p.303), e.g. air resistance can transfer energy from a falling object's kinetic energy store to its thermal energy store.

Streamlining reduces air resistance too, see p.368.

1) For objects that are being rubbed together, lubricants can be used to reduce the friction between the objects' surfaces when they move. Lubricants are usually liquids (like oil), so they can flow easily between objects and coat them.

Insulation Reduces the Rate of Energy Transfer by Heating

The last thing you want when you've made your house nice and toasty is for that energy to escape outside. There are a few things you can do to prevent energy losses through heating:

- Have thick walls that are made from a material with a low thermal conductivity. The thicker the walls and the lower their thermal conductivity, the slower the rate of energy transfer will be (so the building will cool more slowly).
- Use thermal insulation. Here are some examples:

1) Some houses have cavity walls, made up of an inner and an outer wall with an air gap in the middle. The air gap reduces the amount of energy transferred by conduction through the walls. Cavity wall insulation, where the cavity wall air gap is filled with a foam, can also reduce energy transfer by convection in the wall cavity.

2) Loft insulation can be laid out across the loft floor and ceiling. Fibreglass wool is often used which is a good insulator as it has pockets of trapped air. Loft insulation reduces energy loss by conduction and also helps prevent convection currents (a cycle where air particles are constantly being heated, rising, cooling and then sinking) from being created.

3) Double-glazed windows work in the same way as cavity walls — they have an air gap between two sheets of glass to prevent energy transfer by conduction through the windows.

4) Draught excluders around doors and windows reduce energy transfers by convection.

Reducing the difference between the temperature inside and outside the house will also reduce the rate of energy transfer.

Having a well-insulated house can reduce your heating bills...

When people talk of energy loss, it's not that the energy has disappeared. It still exists (see page 303), just not necessarily in the store we want. For example, in a car, you want the energy to transfer to the kinetic energy store of the wheels, and not to the thermal energy stores of the moving components.

Topic P1 — Energy

Efficiency

Devices have **energy transferred** to them, but only transfer **some** of that energy to **useful energy stores**. Wouldn't it be great if we could tell **how much** it **usefully transfers**? That's where **efficiency** comes in.

Most Energy Transfers Involve Some Waste Energy

1) Useful devices are only useful because they can transfer energy from one store to another.
2) As you'll probably have gathered by now, some of the input energy is usually wasted by being transferred to a useless energy store — usually a thermal energy store.
3) The less energy that is 'wasted' in this energy store, the more efficient the device is said to be.
4) You can improve the efficiency of energy transfers by insulating objects, lubricating them or making them more streamlined (see pages 305 and 368).
5) The efficiency for any energy transfer can be worked out using this equation:

$$\text{Efficiency} = \frac{\text{Useful output energy transfer}}{\text{Total input energy transfer}}$$

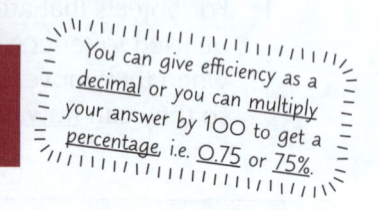

You can give efficiency as a decimal or you can multiply your answer by 100 to get a percentage, i.e. 0.75 or 75%.

6) You might not know the energy inputs and outputs of a device, but you can still calculate its efficiency as long as you know the power input and output:

$$\text{Efficiency} = \frac{\text{Useful power output}}{\text{Total power input}}$$

Useful Energy Output Isn't Usually Equal to Total Energy Input

1) For any given example you can talk about the types of energy being input and output, but remember — NO device is 100% efficient and the wasted energy is usually transferred to useless thermal energy stores.

2) Electric heaters are the exception to this. They're usually 100% efficient because all the energy in the electrostatic energy store is transferred to "useful" thermal energy stores.

3) Ultimately, all energy ends up transferred to thermal energy stores. For example, if you use an electric drill, its energy is transferred to lots of different energy stores, but quickly ends up all in thermal energy stores.

Higher efficiency means a lower proportion of wasted energy...

Make sure you can use and rearrange the equations for efficiency, then have a go at these questions.

Q1 A motor in a remote-controlled car transfers 300 J of energy into the car's energy stores. 225 J are transferred to the car's kinetic energy stores.
Calculate the efficiency of the motor. [2 marks]

Q2 A machine has a useful power output of 900 W and a total power input of 1200 W. In a given time, 72 kJ of energy is transferred to the machine.
Calculate the amount of energy usefully transferred by the machine in this time. [4 marks]

Topic P1 — Energy

Warm-Up & Exam Questions

Don't let your energy dissipate. These questions will let you see how efficient your revision has been.

Warm-Up Questions

1) State the principle of the conservation of energy.
2) What is power? State the units it is measured in.
3) Name two mechanisms in which energy is transferred by heating.
4) Give one way you could reduce the frictional forces in the hinge of an automatic door?
5) For a given material, how does its thermal conductivity affect the rate of energy transfer through it?
6) Why is the efficiency of an appliance always less than 100%?

Exam Questions

1 The motor of an electric scooter moves the scooter 10 metres along a flat, horizontal course in 20 seconds. During this time the motor does 1000 J of work. *(Grade 4-6)*

1.1 Write down the equation that links power, work done and time.
Use this equation to calculate the power of the motor.

[3 marks]

1.2 The moving parts of the scooter are lubricated. The scooter then completes the course in 18 seconds.
Explain, in terms of energy transfer, why the scooter completes the course in a faster time.

[2 marks]

1.3 The scooter's motor is replaced with a more powerful, but otherwise identical, motor.
It moves along the same 10 m course.
Describe how its performance will differ from before. Explain your answer.

[2 marks]

2 Torch A transfers 1200 J of energy per minute.
480 J of this is transferred away usefully as light, 690 J is transferred to useless thermal energy stores and 30 J is transferred away as sound. *(Grade 6-7)*

2.1 Write down the equation linking efficiency, useful output energy transfer and total input energy transfer.

[1 mark]

2.2 Calculate the efficiency of torch A.

[2 marks]

2.3 Torch B transfers 600 J of energy away usefully by light each minute.
Calculate the output power of torch B.

[2 marks]

2.4 Torch B has an efficiency of 0.55. Calculate input power of torch B.

[3 marks]

2.5 Each torch is powered by an identical battery. A student claims that the battery in torch B will go 'flat' quicker than in torch A because it transfers more energy away as light each minute.
Explain whether or not you agree with the student.

[2 marks]

Topic P1 — Energy

Energy Resources and their Uses

There are lots of **energy resources** available on Earth. They are either **renewable** or **non-renewable** resources.

Non-Renewable Energy Resources Will Run Out One Day

Non-renewable energy resources are fossil fuels and nuclear fuel (uranium and plutonium). Fossil fuels are natural resources that form underground over millions of years. They are typically burnt to provide energy. The three main fossil fuels are:

1) Coal
2) Oil
3) (Natural) Gas

- These will all 'run out' one day.
- They all do damage to the environment.
- But they are reliable.

Renewable Energy Resources Will Never Run Out

Renewable energy resources are:

1) The Sun (Solar)
2) Wind
3) Water waves
4) Hydro-electricity
5) Bio-fuel
6) Tides
7) Geothermal

- These will never run out — the energy can be 'renewed' as it is used.
- Most of them do damage the environment, but in less nasty ways than non-renewables.
- The trouble is they don't provide much energy and some of them are unreliable because they depend on the weather.

Energy Resources can be Used for Transport...

Transport is one of the most obvious places where fuel is used. Here are a few transportation methods that use either renewable or non-renewable energy resources:

Electricity can also be used to power vehicles, (e.g. trains and some cars). It can be generated using renewable or non-renewable energy resources (p.309-313).

NON-RENEWABLE ENERGY RESOURCES
- Petrol and diesel powered vehicles (including most cars) use fuel created from oil.
- Coal is used in some old-fashioned steam trains to boil water to produce steam.

RENEWABLE ENERGY RESOURCES
Vehicles that run on pure bio-fuels (p.312) or a mix of a bio-fuel and petrol or diesel (only the bio-fuel bit is renewable, though).

...And for Heating

Energy resources are also needed for heating things like your home.

NON-RENEWABLE ENERGY RESOURCES
- Natural gas is the most widely used fuel for heating homes in the UK. The gas is used to heat water, which is then pumped into radiators throughout the home.
- Coal is commonly burnt in fireplaces.
- Electric heaters (sometimes called storage heaters) which use electricity generated from non-renewable energy resources.

RENEWABLE ENERGY RESOURCES
- A geothermal (or ground source) heat pump uses geothermal energy resources (p.310) to heat buildings.
- Solar water heaters work by using the sun to heat water which is then pumped into radiators in the building.
- Burning bio-fuel or using electricity generated from renewable resources can also be used for heating.

Topic P1 — Energy

Wind and Solar Power

Renewable energy resources, like **wind** and **solar** resources, will not run out. They don't generate as much *electricity* as non-renewables though — if they did we'd all be using solar-powered toasters by now.

Wind Power — Lots of Little Wind Turbines

This involves putting lots of wind turbines (windmills) up in exposed places like on moors or round coasts.

1) Each turbine has a generator inside it — the rotating blades turn the generator and produce electricity.
2) There's no pollution (except for a bit when they're manufactured).
3) But they do spoil the view. You need about 1500 wind turbines to replace one coal-fired power station and 1500 of them cover a lot of ground — which would have a big effect on the scenery.
4) And they can be very noisy, which can be annoying for people living nearby.
5) There's also the problem of the turbines stopping when the wind stops or if the wind is too strong, and it's impossible to increase supply when there's extra demand (p.331). On average, wind turbines produce electricity 70-85% of the time.
6) The initial costs are quite high, but there are no fuel costs and minimal running costs.
7) There's no permanent damage to the landscape — if you remove the turbines, you remove the noise and the view returns to normal.

Solar Cells — Expensive but Not Much Environmental Damage

Solar cells generate electric currents directly from sunlight.

1) Solar cells are often the best source of energy to charge batteries in calculators and watches which don't use much electricity.
2) Solar power is often used in remote places where there's not much choice (e.g. the Australian outback) and to power electric road signs and satellites.
3) There's no pollution. (Although the factories do use quite a lot of energy and produce some pollution when they manufacture the cells.)
4) In sunny countries solar power is a very reliable source of energy — but only in the daytime. Solar power can still be cost-effective in cloudy countries like Britain though.
5) Like wind, you can't increase the power output when there is extra demand.
6) Initial costs are high but after that the energy is free and running costs almost nil.
7) Solar cells are usually used to generate electricity on a relatively small scale.

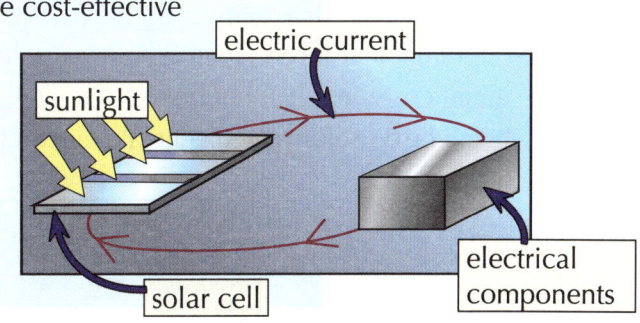

People love the idea of wind power — just not in their back yard...

It's easy to think that non-renewables are the answer to the world's energy problems. However, they have their downsides, and we definitely couldn't rely on them totally at present. Make sure you know the pros and cons for wind and solar power because there are more renewables coming up on the next page.

Topic P1 — Energy

Geothermal and Hydro-electric Power

*Here are some more examples of **renewable energy resources** — **geothermal** and **hydro-electric**. These ones are a bit more **reliable** than wind and solar — read on to find out why.*

Geothermal Power — Energy from Underground

Geothermal power uses energy from underground thermal energy stores.

1) This is only possible in volcanic areas where hot rocks lie quite near to the surface. The source of much of the energy is the slow decay of various radioactive elements, including uranium, deep inside the Earth.

2) This is actually brilliant free energy that's reliable with very few environmental problems.

3) Geothermal energy can be used to generate electricity, or to heat buildings directly.

4) The main drawbacks with geothermal energy are that there aren't very many suitable locations for power plants, and that the cost of building a power plant is often high compared to the amount of energy it produces.

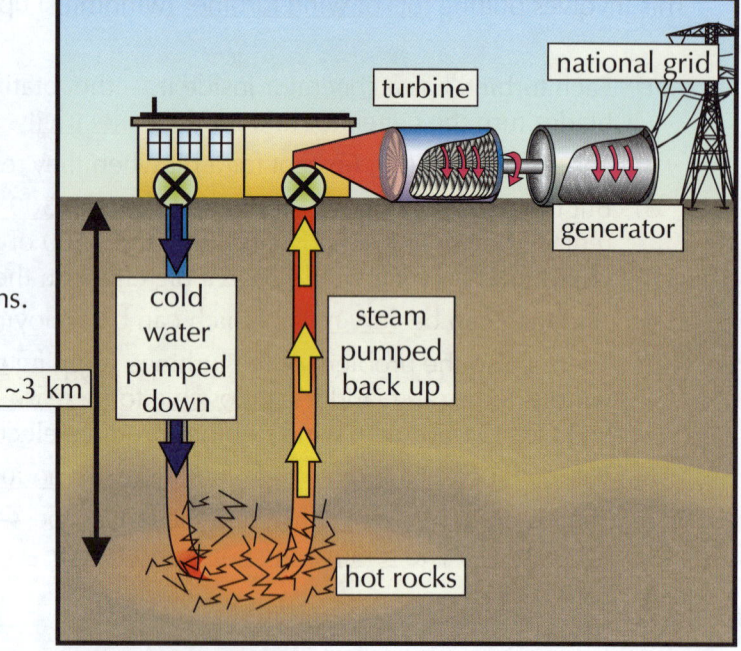

Hydro-electric Power Uses Falling Water

Hydro-electric power transfers energy from the kinetic store of falling water.

1) Hydro-electric power usually requires the flooding of a valley by building a big dam. Rainwater is caught and allowed out through turbines. There is no pollution (as such).

2) But there is a big impact on the environment due to the flooding of the valley (rotting vegetation releases methane and carbon dioxide) and possible loss of habitat for some species (sometimes the loss of whole villages). The reservoirs can also look very unsightly when they dry up. Putting hydroelectric power stations in remote valleys tends to reduce their impact on humans.

3) A big advantage is it can provide an immediate response to an increased demand for electricity.

4) There's no problem with reliability except in times of drought — but remember this is Great Britain we're talking about.

5) Initial costs are high, but there are no fuel costs and minimal running costs.

6) It can be a useful way to generate electricity on a small scale in remote areas.

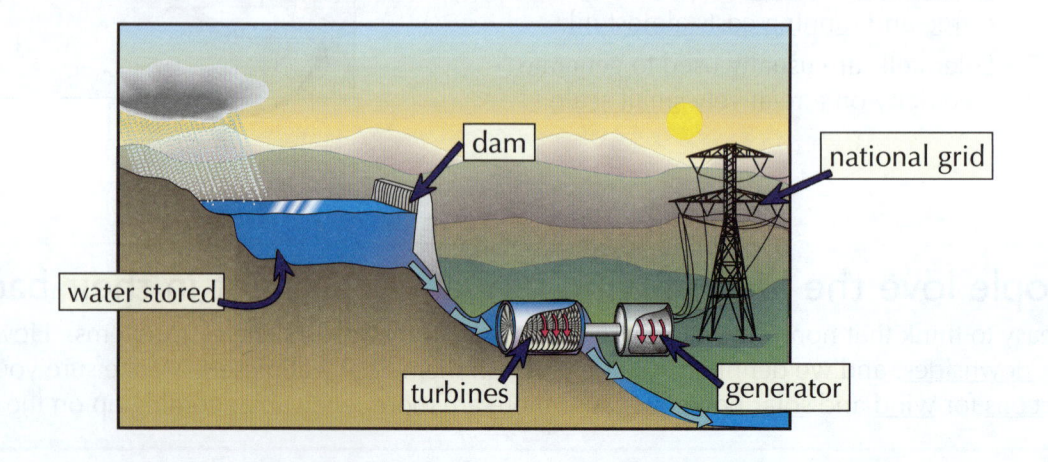

Topic P1 — Energy

Wave Power and Tidal Barrages

*Good ol' **water**. Not only can we drink it, we can also use it to **generate electricity**. It's easy to get confused between **wave** and **tidal** power as they both involve the seaside — but don't. They are completely different.*

Wave Power — Lots of Little Wave-Powered Turbines

1) You need lots of small wave-powered turbines located around the coast. Like with wind power (p.309) the moving turbines are connected to a generator.

2) There is no pollution. The main problems are disturbing the seabed and the habitats of marine animals, spoiling the view and being a hazard to boats.

3) They are fairly unreliable, since waves tend to die out when the wind drops.

4) Initial costs are high, but there are no fuel costs and minimal running costs. Wave power is never likely to provide energy on a large scale, but it can be very useful on small islands.

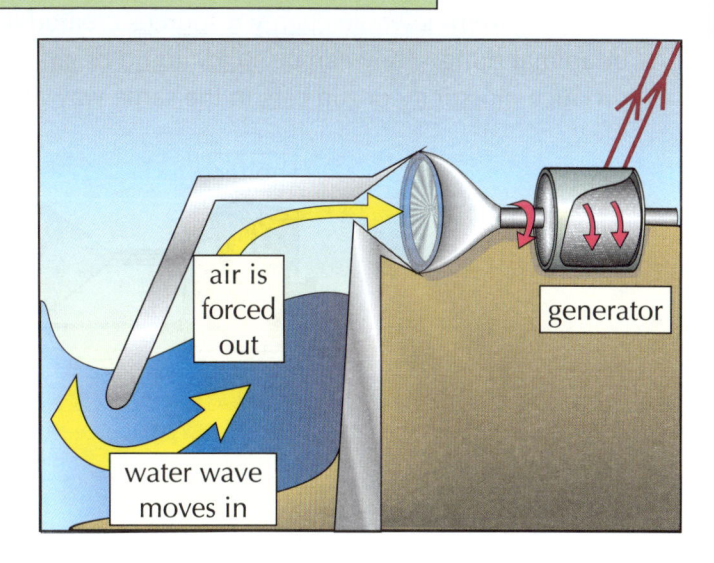

Tidal Barrages — Using the Sun and Moon's Gravity

1) Tides are used in lots of ways to generate electricity. The most common method is building a tidal barrage.

2) Tidal barrages are big dams built across river estuaries, with turbines in them. As the tide comes in it fills up the estuary. The water is then allowed out through turbines at a controlled speed.

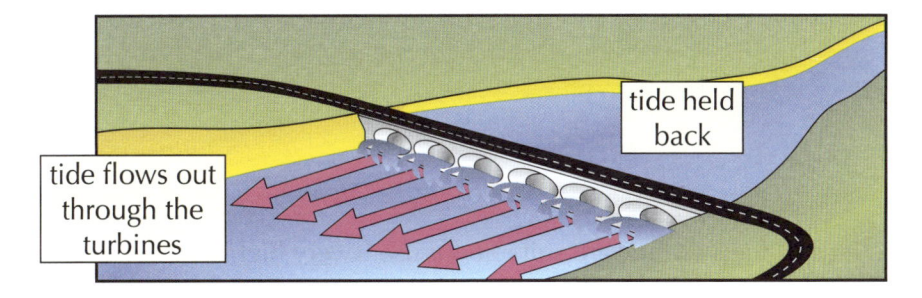

3) Tides are produced by the gravitational pull of the Sun and Moon.

4) There is no pollution. The main problems are preventing free access by boats, spoiling the view and altering the habitat of the wildlife, e.g. wading birds and sea creatures who live in the sand.

5) Tides are pretty reliable in the sense that they happen twice a day without fail, and always near to the predicted height. The only drawback is that the height of the tide is variable so lower (neap) tides will provide significantly less energy than the bigger (spring) tides. They also don't work when the water level is the same either side of the barrage — this happens four times a day because of the tides.

6) Initial costs are moderately high, but there are no fuel costs and minimal running costs. Even though it can only be used in some of the most suitable estuaries tidal power has the potential for generating a significant amount of energy.

Wave and tidal — power from the motion of the ocean...

The first large-scale tidal barrages started being built in the 1960s, so tidal power isn't a new thing. Wave power is still pretty experimental though. Make sure you know the differences in how they work.

Topic P1 — Energy

Bio-fuels

*And the **energy resources** just keep on coming. It's over soon, I promise. Just a few more to go.*

Bio-fuels are Made from Plants and Waste

Bio-fuels are renewable energy resources created from either plant products or animal dung. They can be solid, liquid or gas and can be burnt to produce electricity or run cars in the same way as fossil fuels.

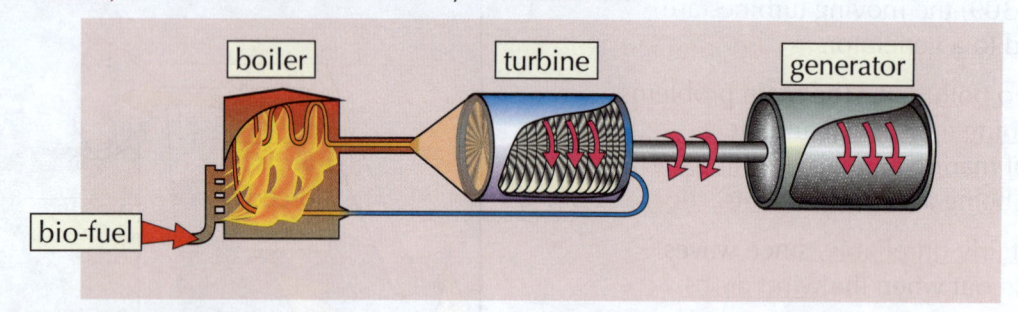

They have Pros...

1) They are supposedly carbon neutral, although there is some debate about this as it's only really true if you keep growing plants at the rate that you're burning things.

2) Bio-fuels are fairly reliable, as crops take a relatively short time to grow and different crops can be grown all year round. However, they cannot respond to immediate energy demands. To combat this, bio-fuels are continuously produced and stored for when they are needed.

... and Cons

1) The cost to refine bio-fuels so they are suitable for use is very high.

2) Some people worry that growing crops specifically for bio-fuels will mean there isn't enough space or water to meet the demands for crops that are grown for food.

3) In some regions, large areas of forest have been cleared to make room to grow bio-fuels, resulting in lots of species losing their natural habitats. The decay and burning of this vegetation also increases carbon dioxide (CO_2) and methane emissions.

REVISION TIP

In theory, bio-fuels are carbon neutral...

Stuff you've learnt in biology may help you get your head around this one. When plants grow, they absorb CO_2 from the atmosphere for photosynthesis, but when you burn bio-fuels, you release CO_2 into the atmosphere. A bio-fuel is 'carbon neutral' if the amount of CO_2 released by burning it is equal to the amount absorbed by the plants you grow to make the bio-fuel.

Non-Renewable Resources

*Renewable resources may sound like **great news** for the **environment**. But when it comes down to it, they **don't** currently meet all our needs so we still need those nasty, polluting **non-renewables**.*

Non-Renewables are Reliable...

1) Fossil fuels and nuclear energy are reliable. There's enough fossil and nuclear fuels to meet current demand, and they are extracted from the Earth at a fast enough rate that power plants always have fuel in stock. This means that the power plants can respond quickly to changes in demand (p.331).

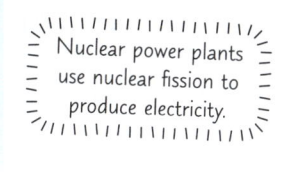

   Nuclear power plants use nuclear fission to produce electricity.

2) However, these fuels are slowly running out. If no new resources are found, some fossil fuel stocks may run out within a hundred years.

3) While the set-up costs of power plants can be quite high compared to some other energy resources, the running costs aren't that expensive. Combined with fairly low fuel extraction costs, using fossil fuels is a cost effective way to produce energy (which is why it's so popular).

...But Create Environmental Problems

1) Coal, oil and gas release carbon dioxide (CO_2) into the atmosphere when they're burned. All this CO_2 adds to the greenhouse effect, and contributes to global warming.
2) Burning coal and oil also releases sulfur dioxide, which causes acid rain — which can be harmful to trees and soils and can have far-reaching effects in ecosystems.
3) Acid rain can be reduced by taking the sulfur out before the fuel is burned, or cleaning up the emissions.
4) Views can be spoilt by fossil fuel power plants, and coal mining makes a mess of the landscape, especially "open-cast mining".
5) Oil spillages cause serious environmental problems, affecting mammals and birds that live in and around the sea. We try to avoid them, but they'll always happen.
6) Nuclear power is clean but the nuclear waste is very dangerous and difficult to dispose of.
7) Nuclear fuel (e.g. uranium or plutonium) is relatively cheap but the overall cost of nuclear power is high due to the cost of the power plant and final decommissioning.
8) Nuclear power always carries the risk of a major catastrophe like the Fukushima disaster in Japan.

Currently we Depend on Fossil Fuels

1) Over the 20th century, the electricity use of the UK hugely increased as the population grew and people began to use electricity for more and more things.
2) Since the beginning of the 21st century, electricity use in the UK has been decreasing (slowly), as we get better at making appliances more efficient (p.306) and become more careful with energy use at home.
3) Some of our electricity is produced using fossil fuels and from nuclear power.
4) Generating electricity isn't the only reason we burn fossil fuels — oil (diesel and petrol) is used to fuel cars, and gas is used to heat homes and cook food.

Topic P1 — Energy

Trends in Energy Resource Use

*Although we still rely on **non-renewables** for **a lot** of our energy needs at the moment, the balance is **shifting**.*

The Aim is to Increase Renewable Energy Use

We are trying to increase our use of renewable energy resources. This move towards renewable energy resources has been triggered by many things:

1) We now know that burning fossil fuels is very damaging to the environment (see last page). This makes many people want to use more renewable energy resources that affect the environment less.

2) People and governments are also becoming increasingly aware that non-renewables will run out one day. Many people think it's better to learn to get by without non-renewables before this happens.

3) Pressure from other countries and the public has meant that governments have begun to introduce targets for using renewable resources. This in turn puts pressure on energy providers to build new power plants that use renewable resources to make sure they do not lose business and money.

4) Car companies have also been affected by this change in attitude towards the environment. Electric cars and hybrids (cars powered by two fuels, e.g. petrol and electricity) are already on the market and their popularity is increasing.

It's Not That Straightforward Though

The use of renewables is limited by reliability, money and politics.

1) There's lots of scientific evidence supporting renewables, but although scientists can give advice, they don't have the power to make people, companies or governments change their behaviour.

2) Building new renewable power plants costs money, so some energy providers are reluctant to do this, especially when fossil fuels are so cost effective. The cost of switching to renewable power will have to be paid, either by customers in their bills, or through government and taxes. Some people don't want to or can't afford to pay, and there are arguments about whether it's ethical to make them.

3) Even if new power plants are built, there are arguments over where to put them. E.g. many people don't want to live next to a wind farm, causing protests. There are arguments over whether it's ethical to make people put up with wind farms built next to them when they may not agree with them.

4) Some energy resources like wind power are not as reliable as traditional fossil fuels, whilst others cannot increase their power output on demand. This would mean either having to use a combination of different power plants (which would be expensive) or researching ways to improve reliability.

5) Research on improving the reliability and cost of renewables takes time and money — it may be years before improvements are made, even with funding. Until then, we need non-renewable power.

6) Making personal changes can also be quite expensive. Hybrid cars are generally more expensive than equivalent petrol cars and things like solar panels for your home are still quite pricey. The cost of these things is slowly going down, but they are still not an option for many people.

Topic P1 — Energy

Warm-Up & Exam Questions

This is the last set of warm-up and exam questions on Topic P1. They're not *too* horrendous, I promise.

Warm-Up Questions

1) Name three non-renewable energy resources.
2) Give one advantage and one disadvantage associated with the reliability of renewable resources.
3) Describe one way that renewable energy resources can be used to power vehicles.
4) Give two ways in which using coal as an energy resource causes environmental problems.
5) Suggest two reasons why we can't just stop using fossil fuels immediately.

Exam Questions

1 The inhabitants of a remote island do not have the resources or expertise to build a nuclear power plant. They have no access to fossil fuels. *(Grade 4-6)*

1.1 The islanders have considered using wind, solar and hydro-electric power to generate electricity. Suggest **two** other renewable energy resources they could use.

[2 marks]

1.2 The islanders decide that hydro-electric power could reliably generate enough electricity for all their needs, but they are concerned about the environmental impact.
Give **one** environmental impact of using hydro-electric power to generate electricity.

[1 mark]

2 In the hydro-electric power station in **Figure 1**, water is held back behind a dam before being allowed to flow out through turbines. *(Grade 4-6)*

Figure 1

2.1 Describe the transfer between energy stores of the water which occurs during this process.

[2 marks]

2.2 The tides can also be used to generate electricity using tidal barrages.
Give **two** environmental advantages of generating electricity using tidal barrages.

[2 marks]

3 A family want to install solar panels on their roof. They have 10 m² of space on their roof for the solar panels. They use 32 500 000 J of energy per day. A 1 m² solar panel has an output of 200 W in good sunlight. *(Grade 6-7)*

3.1 Calculate the minimum number of 1 m² solar panels required to cover the family's daily energy use, assuming there are 5 hours of good sunlight in a day.

[5 marks]

3.2 Determine, using your answer from **3.1**, whether the family can install enough solar panels to provide all of the energy they use, assuming there are 5 hours of good sunlight every day.

[1 mark]

3.3 In reality, the number of hours of good sunlight in a day varies based on the weather and time of year. Discuss the reliability of energy from solar panels compared to from a local coal-fired power station.

[3 marks]

Topic P1 — Energy

Topic P2 — Electricity

Current and Circuit Symbols

*Isn't **electricity** great? Mind you it's pretty bad news if the **words** don't mean anything to you...*

Current is the flow of Electric Charge

1) Electric current is the flow of electric charge round the circuit. Current will only flow around a complete (closed) circuit if there's a potential difference. So a current can only flow if there's a source of potential difference. Unit of current: ampere, A.

2) In a single, closed loop (like the one on the right) the current has the same value everywhere in the circuit (see p.324).

3) Potential difference (or voltage) is the driving force that pushes the charge round. Unit of potential difference: volt, V.

4) Resistance is anything in the circuit which slows the flow down. Unit of resistance: ohm, Ω.

5) The current flowing through a component depends on the potential difference across it and the resistance of the component (see next page).

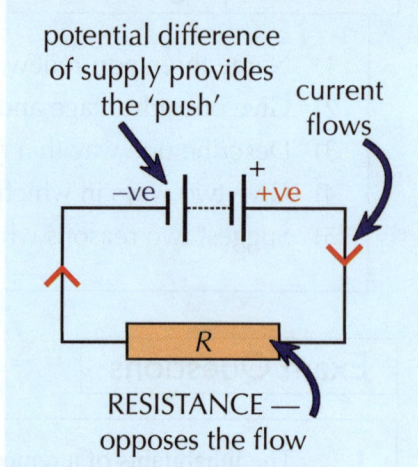

> The greater the resistance across a component, the smaller the current that flows through it (for a given potential difference across the component).

Total Charge Through a Circuit Depends on Current and Time

1) The size of the current is the rate of flow of charge. When current (*I*) flows past a point in a circuit for a length of time (*t*) then the charge (*Q*) that has passed is given by this formula:

Charge (C) = Current (A) × Time (s) $Q = It$

$$\frac{Q}{I \times t}$$

2) Current is measured in amperes (A), charge is measured in coulombs (C), time is measured in seconds (s).

3) More charge passes around the circuit when a bigger current flows.

Learn these Circuit Diagram Symbols

You need to be able to understand circuit diagrams and draw them using the correct symbols. Make sure all the wires in your circuit are straight lines and that the circuit is closed, i.e. you can follow a wire from one end of the power supply, through any components, to the other end of the supply (ignoring any switches).

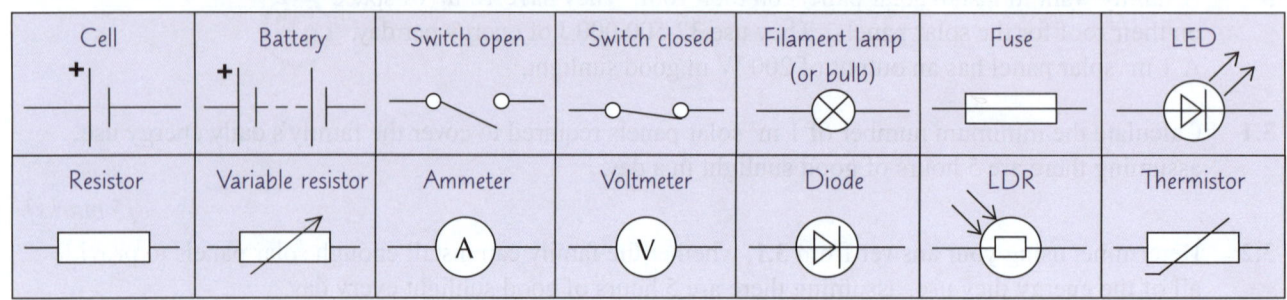

Cell	Battery	Switch open	Switch closed	Filament lamp (or bulb)	Fuse	LED
Resistor	Variable resistor	Ammeter	Voltmeter	Diode	LDR	Thermistor

A current will only flow in a closed circuit

Q1 A laptop charger passes a current of 8 A through a laptop battery. Calculate, in minutes, how long the charger needs to be connected to the battery for 28 800 C of charge to be transferred.   [4 marks]

Resistance

*Prepare yourself to meet one of the most **important equations** in electronics. It's all about **resistance**, **current** and **potential difference**... Now if that doesn't tempt you on to read this page, I don't know what will.*

There's a Formula Linking Potential Difference and Resistance

The formula linking potential difference, current and resistance is very useful (and pretty common):

You may see potential difference called voltage.

Potential difference (V) = Current (A) × Resistance (Ω) $V = IR$

EXAMPLE

Voltmeter V reads 6.0 V and resistor R is 4.0 Ω. What is the current through ammeter A?

1) Use the formula triangle for $V = I \times R$.
2) We need to find I, so the version we need is $I = V \div R$.
3) The answer is then:

$I = 6.0 \div 4.0 = 1.5$ A

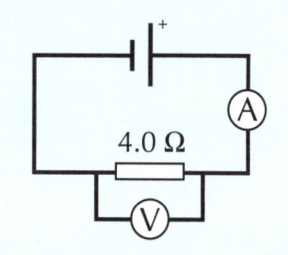

Use this formula triangle to rearrange the equation. Just cover up the thing you're trying to find, and what's left visible is the formula you're after.

Ohmic Conductors Have a Constant Resistance

For some components, as the current through them is changed, the resistance of the component changes as well.

1) The resistance of ohmic conductors (e.g. a wire or a resistor) doesn't change with the current. At a constant temperature, the current flowing through an ohmic conductor is directly proportional to the potential difference across it. (R is constant in $V = IR$.)

2) The resistance of some resistors and components does change, e.g. a filament lamp or a diode.

3) When an electrical charge flows through a filament lamp, it transfers some energy to the thermal energy store of the filament (p.297), which is designed to heat up. Resistance increases with temperature, so as the current increases, the filament lamp heats up more and the resistance increases.

4) For diodes, the resistance depends on the direction of the current. They will happily let current flow in one direction, but have a very high resistance if it is reversed.

Resistance can be temperamental when temperature changes...

In general, resistance increases with temperature (though there are exceptions, like thermistors — see p.321). So if the temperature is changing, the resistance of your component will be changing too.

Q1 An appliance is connected to a 230 V source.
Calculate the resistance of the appliance if a current of 5.0 A is flowing through it. [3 marks]

Topic P2 — Electricity

PRACTICAL: Investigating Resistance

Resistance can depend on a number of *factors*. Here's an *experiment* you can do to investigate one of them — how the resistance *varies* with the *length of the conductor*.

You Can Investigate the Factors Affecting Resistance

The resistance of a circuit can depend on a number of factors, like whether components are in series or parallel, p.326, or the length of wire used in the circuit. You can investigate the effect of wire length using the circuit below.

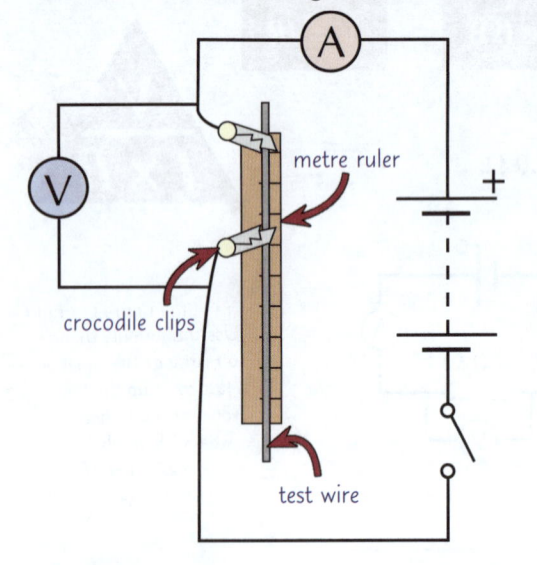

The Ammeter

1) Measures the current (in amps) flowing through the test wire.
2) The ammeter must always be placed in series with whatever you're investigating.

The Voltmeter

1) Measures the potential difference (or pd) across the test wire (in volts).
2) The voltmeter must always be placed in parallel around whatever you're investigating (p.325) — NOT around any other bit of the circuit, e.g. the battery.

See pages 323-325 for more on series and parallel circuits.

Method

1) Attach a crocodile clip to the wire level with 0 cm on the ruler.
2) Attach the second crocodile clip to the wire, e.g. 10 cm away from the first clip. Write down the length of the wire between the clips.
3) Close the switch, then record the current through the wire and the pd across it.
4) Open the switch, then move the second crocodile clip, e.g. another 10 cm, along the wire. Close the switch again, then record the new length, current and pd.
5) Repeat this for a number of different lengths of the test wire.
6) Use your measurements of current and pd to calculate the resistance for each length of wire, using $R = V \div I$ (from $V = IR$).
7) Plot a graph of resistance against wire length and draw a line of best fit.
8) Your graph should be a straight line through the origin, meaning resistance is directly proportional to length — the longer the wire, the greater the resistance.
9) If your graph doesn't go through the origin, it could be because the first clip isn't attached exactly at 0 cm, so all of your length readings are a bit out. This is a systematic error (p.8).

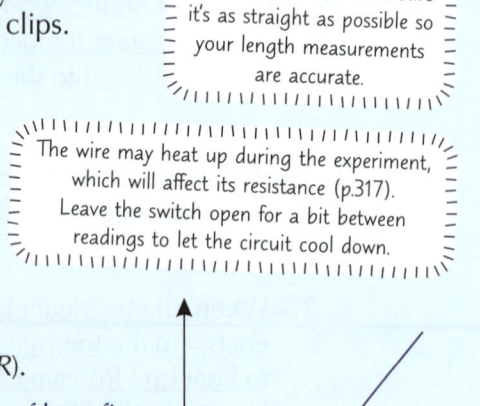

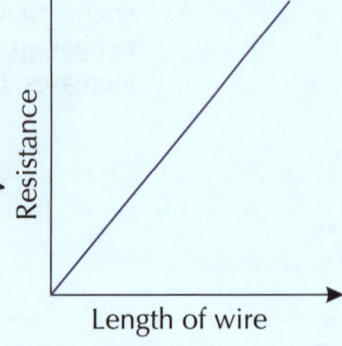

A thin wire will give you the best results. Make sure it's as straight as possible so your length measurements are accurate.

The wire may heat up during the experiment, which will affect its resistance (p.317). Leave the switch open for a bit between readings to let the circuit cool down.

Be careful with the temperature of the wire...

PRACTICAL TIP: If a large current flows through a wire, it can cause it to heat up (there's more on this on page 317). So use a low pd to stop it getting too hot and turn off the circuit between readings to let it cool.

Topic P2 — Electricity

I-V Characteristics — PRACTICAL

*You've met **ohmic conductors** already on page 317, but most circuit components **aren't** ohmic. You can see how circuit components behave by plotting an **I-V characteristic**.*

Three Very Important I-V Characteristics

1) The term 'I-V characteristic' refers to a graph which shows how the current (I) flowing through a component changes as the potential difference (V) across it is increased.
2) Linear components (e.g. an ohmic conductor) have an I-V characteristic that's a straight line.
3) Non-linear components (e.g. a filament lamp or a diode) have a curved I-V characteristic.

You can do this experiment to find a component's I-V characteristic:

Method

1) Set up the test circuit shown on the right.
2) Begin to vary the variable resistor. This alters the current flowing through the circuit and the potential difference across the component.
3) Take several pairs of readings from the ammeter and voltmeter to see how the potential difference across the component varies as the current changes. Repeat each reading twice more to get an average pd at each current.
4) Swap over the wires connected to the battery, so the direction of the current is reversed.
5) Plot a graph of current against voltage for the component.

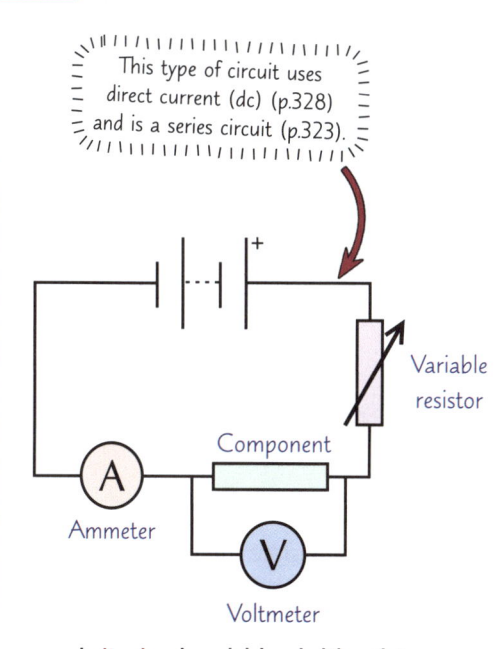

This type of circuit uses direct current (dc) (p.328) and is a series circuit (p.323).

The I-V characteristics you get for an ohmic conductor, filament lamp and diode should look like this:

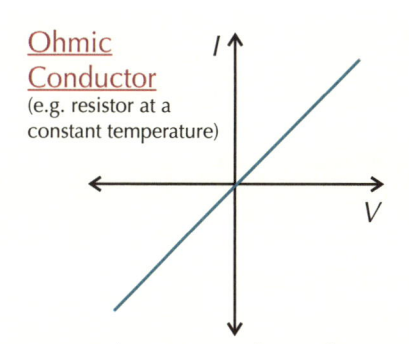

Ohmic Conductor (e.g. resistor at a constant temperature)

The current through an ohmic conductor (at a constant temperature) is directly proportional to potential difference, so you get a straight line.

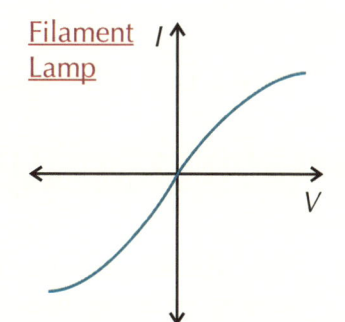

Filament Lamp

As the current increases, the temperature of the filament increases, so the resistance increases. This means less current can flow per unit pd, so the graph gets shallower — hence the curve.

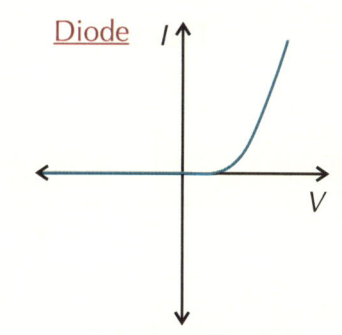

Diode

Current will only flow through a diode in one direction, as shown. The diode has very high resistance in the reverse direction.

Since $V = IR$, you can calculate the resistance at any point on the I-V characteristic by calculating $R = V \div I$.

You may be asked to interpret an I-V characteristic...

Make sure you take care when reading values off the graph. Pay close attention to the axes, and make sure you've converted all values to the correct units before you do any calculations.

Q1 Explain the shape of the filament lamp I-V characteristic above, for the quadrant where I and V are positive. [3 marks]

Topic P2 — Electricity

Warm-Up & Exam Questions

Phew — circuits aren't the easiest thing in the world, are they? Make sure you've understood the last few pages by trying these questions. If you get stuck, just go back and re-read the relevant page.

Warm-Up Questions

1) What are the units of resistance?
2) How does current through a component vary with resistance for a fixed potential difference?
3) Draw the symbol for a light-emitting diode (LED).
4) Give an example of an ohmic conductor.
5) How should a voltmeter be connected in a circuit to measure the pd across a component?
6) What is an *I-V* characteristic?

Exam Questions

1 **Figure 1** shows is a circuit diagram for a standard test circuit. When the switch is closed, the ammeter reads 0.30 A and the voltmeter reads 1.5 V. *(Grade 6-7)*

Figure 1

1.1 Calculate the resistance of the filament lamp.

[3 marks]

1.2 The switch is closed for 35 seconds. Calculate the total charge that flows through the filament lamp.

[2 marks]

1.3 The variable resistor is used to increase the resistance in the circuit. Describe how this will affect the current flowing through the circuit.

[1 mark]

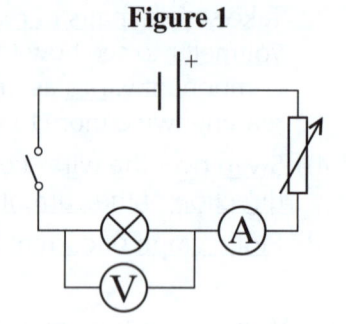

Figure 2

The resistance of a filament lamp changes with temperature.

1.4 On **Figure 2**, sketch the potential difference-current graph for a filament lamp.

[1 mark]

1.5 State what happens to the resistance of the filament lamp as the temperature of the filament increases.

[1 mark]

PRACTICAL

2 A student carried out an experiment using a standard test circuit where she varied the current and monitored what happened to the potential difference across a diode. **Figure 3** shows a graph of her results. *(Grade 6-7)*

Figure 3

2.1 State the dependent variable in this experiment.

[1 mark]

2.2 Explain why the graph in **Figure 3** shows zero current for negative pds.

[1 mark]

2.3 Calculate the resistance of the diode at the point marked A.

[4 marks]

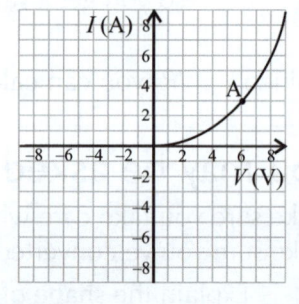

Topic P2 — Electricity

Circuit Devices

*You might consider yourself a bit of an expert in **circuit components** — you're enlightened about bulbs, you're switched on to switches... Just make sure you know these ones as well — they're a bit trickier.*

A Light-Dependent Resistor or "LDR"

1) An LDR is a resistor that is dependent on the intensity of light. In bright light, the resistance falls.
2) In darkness, the resistance is highest.
3) They have lots of applications including automatic night lights, outdoor lighting and burglar detectors.

This is the circuit symbol for a light-dependent resistor.

LDR — graph of Resistance in Ω vs Light Intensity (Dark → Light): resistance decreases as light intensity increases.

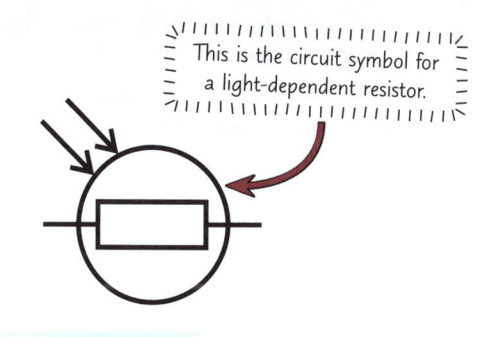

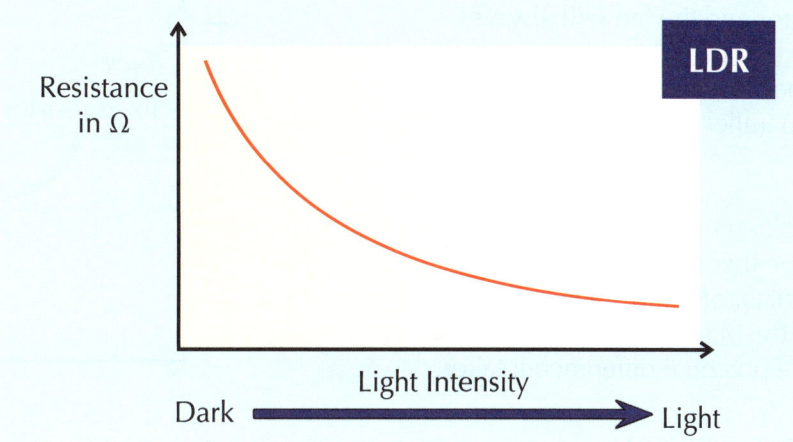

Thermistor Resistance Decreases as Temperature Increases

1) A thermistor is a temperature dependent resistor.
2) In hot conditions, the resistance drops.
3) In cool conditions, the resistance goes up.
4) Thermistors make useful temperature detectors, e.g. car engine temperature sensors and electronic thermostats.

This is the circuit symbol for a thermistor.

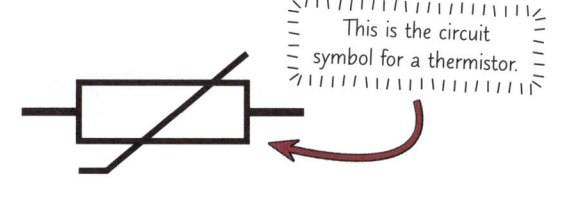

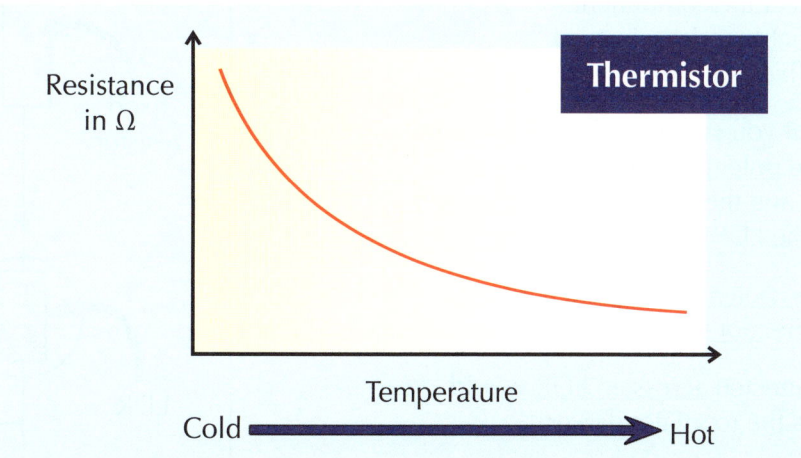

Thermistor — graph of Resistance in Ω vs Temperature (Cold → Hot): resistance decreases as temperature increases.

Thermistors and LDRs have many applications...

And they're not just limited to the examples on this page. Oh no. For example, LDRs are used in digital cameras to control how long the shutter should stay open for. If the light level is low, changes in the resistance cause the shutter to stay open for longer than if the light level was higher. How interesting.

Topic P2 — Electricity

Sensing Circuits

Now you've learnt about what **LDRs** and **thermistors** do, it's time to take a look at how they're put to use.

You Can Use LDRs and Thermistors in **Sensing Circuits**

Sensing circuits can be used to turn on or increase the power to components depending on the conditions that they are in.

1) The circuit on the right is a sensing circuit used to operate a fan in a room.

2) The fixed resistor and the fan will always have the same potential difference across them (because they're connected in parallel — see p.325).

3) The potential difference of the power supply is shared out between the thermistor and the loop made up of the fixed resistor and the fan according to their resistances — the bigger a component's resistance, the more of the potential difference it takes.

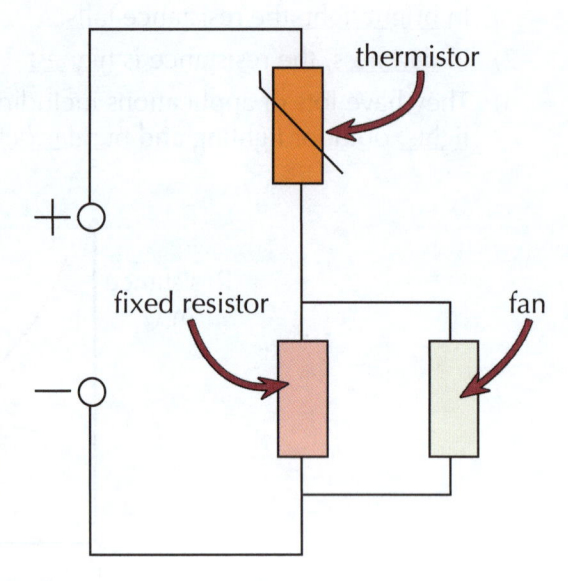

4) As the room gets hotter, the resistance of the thermistor decreases and it takes a smaller share of the potential difference from the power supply. So the potential difference across the fixed resistor and the fan rises, making the fan go faster.

You can Connect the **Component Across** the **Variable Resistor**

1) You can connect the component across the variable resistor instead of across the fixed resistor.

2) For example, if you connect a bulb in parallel to an LDR, the potential difference across both the LDR and the bulb will be high when it's dark and the LDR's resistance is high.

3) The greater the potential difference across a component, the more energy it gets.

4) So a bulb connected across an LDR would get brighter as the room got darker.

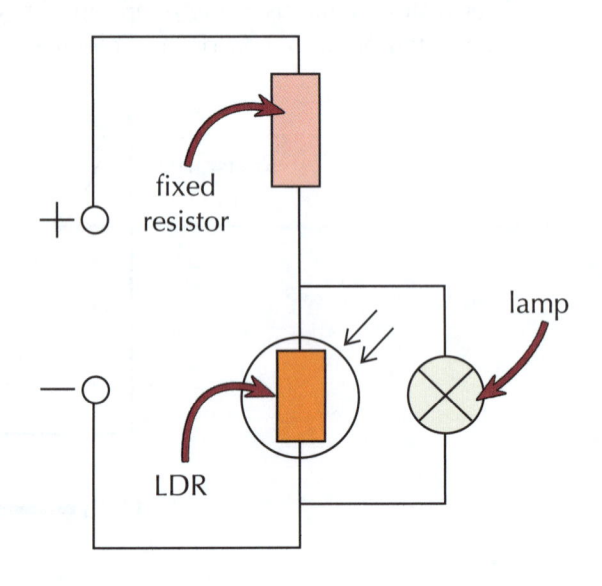

Sensing circuits react to changes in the surroundings...

Sensing circuits are a useful application of thermistors and LDRs, but they can be tricky to make sense of. They rely on the properties of series and parallel circuits — read on to learn all about them.

Topic P2 — Electricity

Series Circuits

*You need to be able to tell if components are connected in series or parallel **just by looking at circuit diagrams**. You also need to know the **rules** about what happens with both types. Read on to find out more.*

Series Circuits — All or Nothing

1) In series circuits, the different components are connected in a line, end to end, between the +ve and −ve of the power supply (except for voltmeters, which are always connected in parallel, but they don't count as part of the circuit).

2) If you remove or disconnect one component, the circuit is broken and they all stop. This is generally not very handy, and in practice very few things are connected in series.

3) You can use the following rules to design series circuits to measure quantities and test components (e.g. the test circuits on p.319 and p.326 and the sensing circuits on the last page).

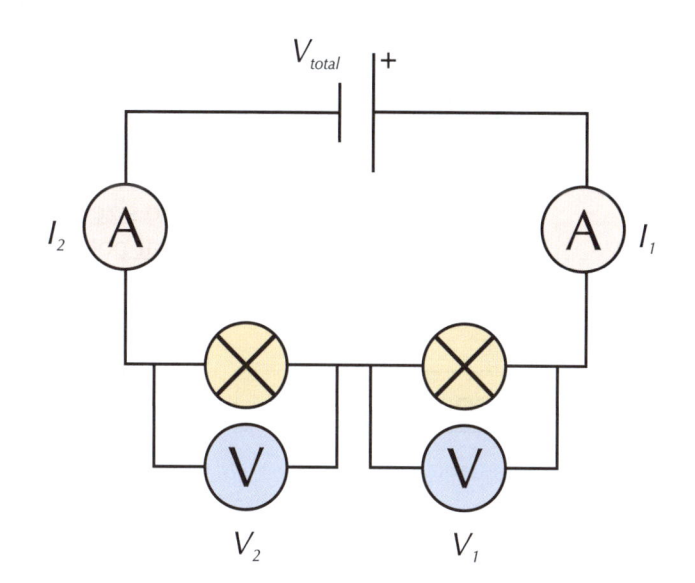

Cell Potential Differences Add Up

1) There is a bigger potential difference when more cells are in series, provided the cells are all connected the same way.

2) For example when two batteries of voltage 1.5 V are connected in series they supply a total of 3 V.

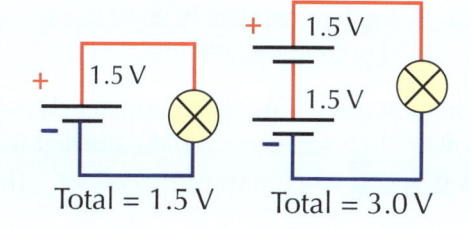

Total Potential Difference is Shared

In series circuits the total potential difference of the supply is shared between the various components. So the potential differences round a series circuit always add up to the source potential difference:

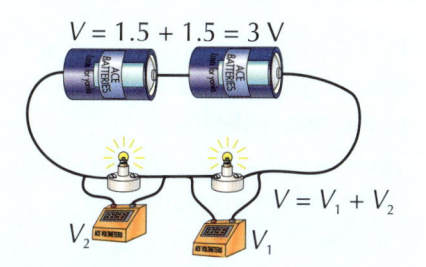

$$V_{total} = V_1 + V_2 + ...$$

There are two main types of circuit — series and parallel...

Remember, ammeters should always be connected in series, and voltmeters should always be connected in parallel. These components don't count towards how you define a circuit — you can have a parallel circuit (p.325) with ammeters connected in series, or a series circuit with voltmeters connected across components.

Topic P2 — Electricity

Series Circuits

We're not done with series circuits yet. Here's the low-down on current and resistance...

Current is the Same Everywhere

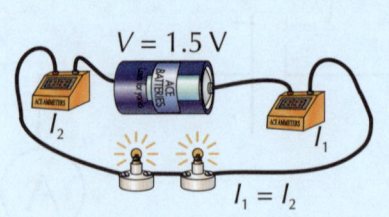

1) In series circuits the <u>same current</u> flows through <u>all components</u>, i.e:

$$I_1 = I_2 = ...$$

2) The <u>size</u> of the current is determined by the <u>total potential difference</u> of the cells and the <u>total resistance</u> of the circuit: i.e. $I = V \div R$.

Resistance Adds Up

1) In series circuits the <u>total resistance</u> of two components is just the <u>sum</u> of their resistances:

$$R_{total} = R_1 + R_2$$

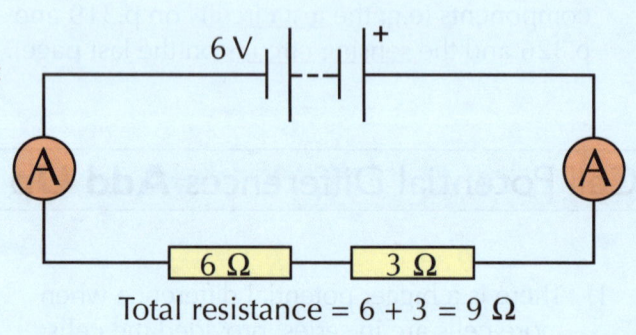

Total resistance = 6 + 3 = 9 Ω

2) This is because by <u>adding a resistor</u> in series, the two resistors have to <u>share</u> the total potential difference.

3) The potential difference across each resistor is <u>lower</u>, so the <u>current</u> through each resistor is also lower. In a series circuit, the current is the <u>same everywhere</u> so the total current in the circuit is <u>reduced</u> when a resistor is added. This means the total <u>resistance</u> of the circuit <u>increases</u>.

4) The <u>bigger</u> a component's <u>resistance</u>, the bigger its <u>share</u> of the <u>total potential difference</u>.

EXAMPLE

For the circuit diagram on the right, calculate the current passing through the circuit.

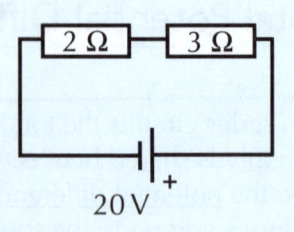

1) First find the <u>total resistance</u> by <u>adding together</u> the resistance of the two resistors.

$R_{total} = 2 + 3 = 5\ \Omega$

2) Then <u>rearrange</u> $V = IR$ and <u>substitute</u> in the values you have.

$I = V \div R$
$= 20 \div 5$
$= 4\ A$

Series circuits aren't used very much in the real world...

Since series circuits put <u>all</u> components on the <u>same loop of wire</u>, if one <u>component breaks</u>, it'll <u>break the circuit</u>, and all other components will <u>stop working</u> too.

Q1 A battery is connected in series with a 4 Ω resistor, a 5 Ω resistor and a 6 Ω resistor. A current of 0.6 A flows through the circuit. Calculate the potential difference of the battery. [3 marks]

Topic P2 — Electricity

Parallel Circuits

Parallel circuits can be a little bit trickier to wrap your head around, but they're much more *useful* than series circuits. Most electronics use a combination of series and parallel circuitry.

Parallel Circuits — Independence and Isolation

1) In parallel circuits, each component is separately connected to the +ve and –ve of the supply (except ammeters, which are always connected in series).

2) If you remove or disconnect one of them, it will hardly affect the others at all.

3) This is obviously how most things must be connected, for example in cars and in household electrics. You have to be able to switch everything on and off separately.

4) Everyday circuits often include a mixture of series and parallel parts.

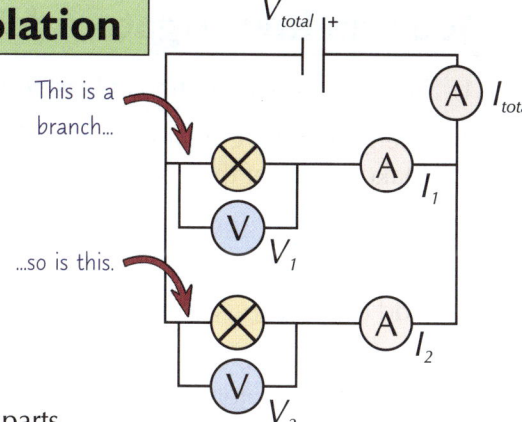

Potential Difference is the Same Across All Components

1) In parallel circuits all components get the full source pd, so the voltage is the same across all components: $V_1 = V_2 = V_3 = ...$

2) This means that identical bulbs connected in parallel will all be at the same brightness.

Current is Shared Between Branches

1) In parallel circuits the total current flowing around the circuit is equal to the total of all the currents through the separate components: $I_{total} = I_1 + I_2 + ...$

2) In a parallel circuit, there are junctions where the current either splits or rejoins. The total current going into a junction has to equal the total current leaving it.

3) If two identical components are connected in parallel then the same current will flow through each component.

Adding a Resistor in Parallel Reduces the Total Resistance

1) If you have two resistors in parallel, their total resistance is less than the resistance of the smallest of the two resistors.

2) This can be tough to get your head around, but think about it like this:

- In parallel, both resistors have the same potential difference across them as the source.
- This means the 'pushing force' making the current flow is the same as the source potential difference for each resistor that you add.
- But by adding another loop, the current has more than one direction to go in.
- This increases the total current that can flow around the circuit. Using $V = IR$, an increase in current means a decrease in the total resistance of the circuit.

The current flowing into a junction equals the current out

Q1 A circuit contains three resistors, each connected in parallel with a cell. Explain what happens to the total current and resistance in the circuit when one resistor is removed. [4 marks]

Topic P2 — Electricity

Circuits and Resistance

PRACTICAL

You saw on page 318 how the length of the wire used in a circuit affects its resistance. Now it's time to do an **experiment** to see how placing **resistors** in series or in parallel can affect the resistance of the **whole circuit**.

You Can Investigate Adding Resistors in Series...

1) First, you'll need to find at least four identical resistors.
2) Then build the circuit shown on the right using one of the resistors. Make a note of the potential difference of the battery (V). 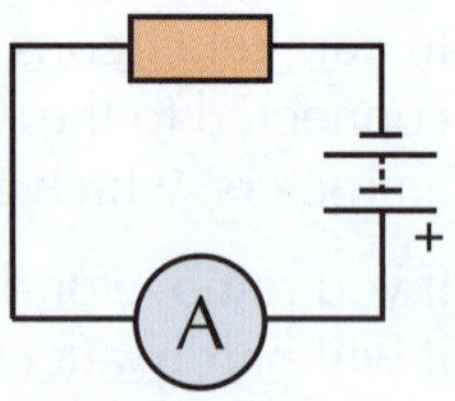
3) Measure the current through the circuit using the ammeter. Use this to calculate the resistance of the circuit using $R = V \div I$.
4) Add another resistor, in series with the first.
5) Again, measure the current through the circuit and use this and the potential difference of the battery to calculate the overall resistance of the circuit. 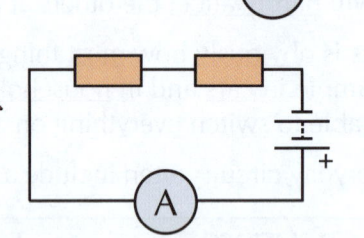
6) Repeat steps 4 and 5 until you've added all of your resistors.
7) Plot a graph of the number of resistors against the total resistance of the circuit (see below).

... or in Parallel

1) Using the same equipment as before (so the experiment is a fair test), build the same initial circuit.
2) Measure the total current through the circuit and calculate the resistance of the circuit using $R = V \div I$ (again, V is the potential difference of the battery).
3) Next, add another resistor, in parallel with the first. 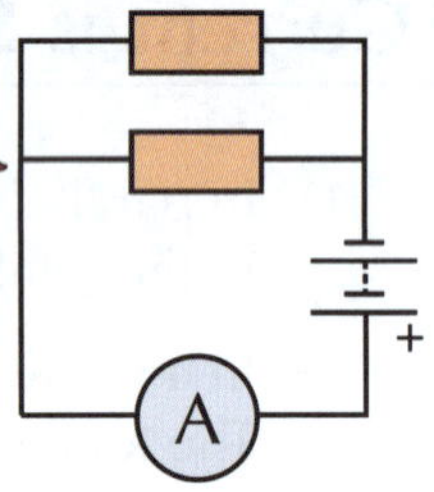
4) Measure the total current through the circuit and use this and the potential difference of the battery to calculate the overall resistance of the circuit.
5) Repeat steps 3 and 4 until you've added all of your resistors.
6) Plot a graph of the number of resistors in the circuit against the total resistance.

Your Results Should Match the Resistance Rules

1) You should find that adding resistors in series increases the total resistance of the circuit (adding a resistor decreases the total current through the circuit).
2) The more resistors you add, the larger the resistance of the whole circuit.

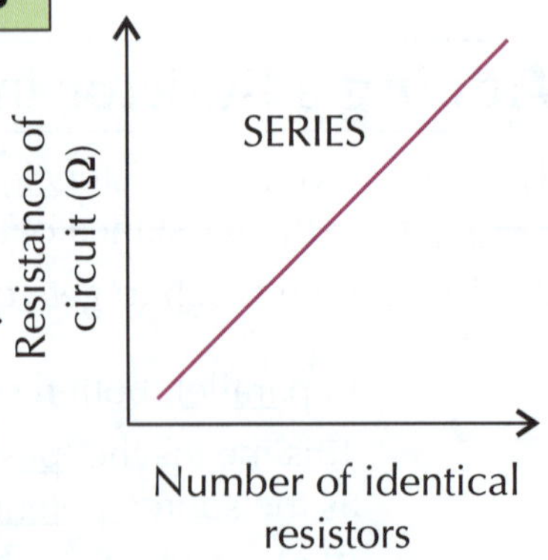

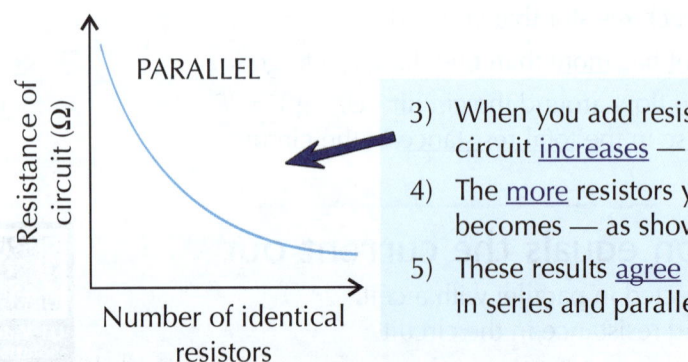

3) When you add resistors in parallel, the total current through the circuit increases — so the total resistance of the circuit has decreased.
4) The more resistors you add, the smaller the overall resistance becomes — as shown by the graph on the left.
5) These results agree with what you learnt about resistance in series and parallel circuits on pages 324 and 325.

Topic P2 — Electricity

Warm-Up & Exam Questions

Time to check and see what you can remember about those circuit devices, parallel and series circuits.

Warm-Up Questions

1) Give one use of a light-dependent resistor (LDR).
2) What happens to the resistance of a thermistor as its temperature increases?
3) Draw a circuit diagram of a sensing circuit where a bulb gets brighter with decreasing temperature.
4) Give one practical disadvantage of series circuits.
5) How do you work out the total resistance in a series circuit?
6) Which has the higher total resistance: two resistors in series, or the same two resistors in parallel?
7) Sketch a graph to show how the number of identical resistors connected together in parallel affects the total resistance in a circuit.

Exam Questions

1 Figure 1 shows a series circuit. *Grade 4-6*

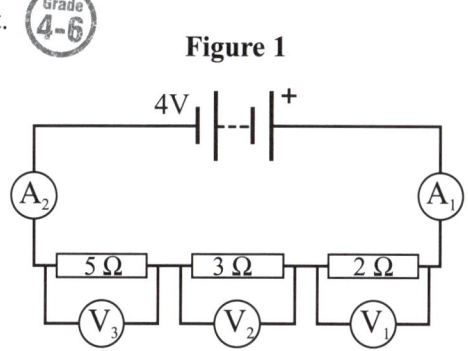

Figure 1

1.1 Calculate the total resistance in the circuit.

[2 marks]

1.2 The current through A_1 is 0.4 A.
What is the current through A_2? Explain your answer.

[2 marks]

1.3 V_1 reads 0.8 V and V_2 reads 1.2 V.
Calculate the reading on V_3.

[2 marks]

2 A parallel circuit is connected as shown in **Figure 2**. *Grade 7-9*

Figure 2

2.1 Give the reading on voltmeter V_1.

[1 mark]

2.2 Calculate the reading on ammeter A_1.

[3 marks]

2.3 Calculate the reading on ammeter A_2.

[2 marks]

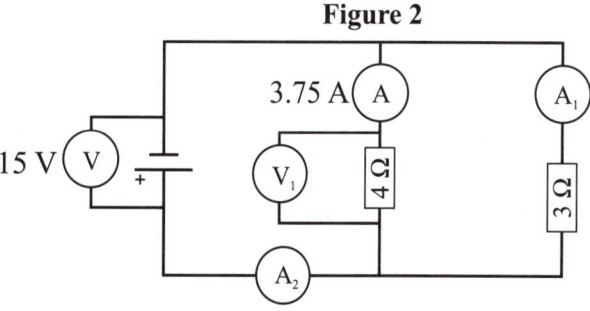

Topic P2 — Electricity

Electricity in the Home

Now you've learnt the basics of electrical circuits, it's time to see how electricity is used in everyday life.

Mains Supply is ac, Battery Supply is dc

1) There are two types of electricity supplies — alternating current (ac) and direct current (dc).
2) In ac supplies the current is constantly changing direction. Alternating currents are produced by alternating potential difference in which the positive and negative ends keep alternating.
3) The UK mains supply (the electricity in your home) is an ac supply at around 230 V.
4) The frequency of the ac mains supply is 50 cycles per second or 50 Hz (hertz).
5) By contrast, cells and batteries supply direct current (dc).
6) Direct current is a current that is always flowing in the same direction. It's created by a direct potential difference.

Most Cables Have Three Separate Wires

1) Most electrical appliances are connected to the mains supply by three-core cables. This means that they have three wires inside them, each with a core of copper and a coloured plastic coating.
2) The colour of the insulation on each cable shows its purpose.
3) The colours are always the same for every appliance. This is so that it is easy to tell the different wires apart.
4) You need to know the colour of each wire, what each of them is for and what their pd is.

LIVE WIRE — brown.
The live wire provides the alternating potential difference (at about 230 V) from the mains supply

NEUTRAL WIRE — blue.
The neutral wire completes the circuit — when the appliance is operating normally, current flows through the live and neutral wires. It is around 0 V.

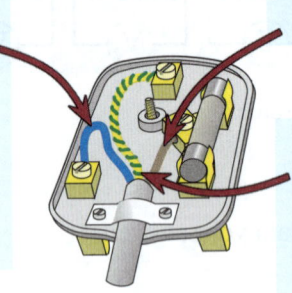

EARTH WIRE — green and yellow.
It is for protecting the wiring, and for safety — it stops the appliance casing from becoming live. It doesn't usually carry a current — only when there's a fault. It's also at 0 V.

Touching the Live Wire Gives You an Electric Shock

1) Your body (just like the earth) is at 0 V.
2) This means that if you touch the live wire, a large potential difference is produced across your body and a current flows through you.
3) This causes a large electric shock which could injure or even kill you.
4) Even if a plug socket or a light switch is turned off (i.e. the switch is open) there is still a danger of an electric shock. A current isn't flowing, but there is still a pd in the live wire. If you made contact with the live wire, your body would provide a link between the supply and the earth, so a current would flow through you.
5) Any connection between live and earth can be dangerous. If the link creates a low resistance path to earth, a huge current will flow, which could result in a fire.

Topic P2 — Electricity

Power of Electrical Appliances

You can think about **electrical circuits** in terms of **energy transfer** — the charge carriers take energy around the circuit. When they go through an electrical component energy is transferred to make the component work.

Energy is Transferred from Cells and Other Sources

1) You know from page 297 that a moving charge transfers energy. This is because the charge does work against the resistance of the circuit. (Work done is the same as energy transferred, p.298.)

2) Electrical appliances are designed to transfer energy to components in the circuit when a current flows.

Kettles transfer energy electrically from the mains ac supply to the thermal energy store of the heating element inside the kettle.	Energy is transferred electrically from the battery of a handheld fan to the kinetic energy store of the fan's motor.

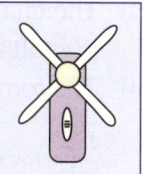

3) Of course, no appliance transfers all energy completely usefully. The higher the current, the more energy is transferred to the thermal energy stores of the components (and then the surroundings). You can calculate the efficiency of any electrical appliance — see p.306.

Energy Transferred Depends on the Power

1) The total energy transferred by an appliance depends on how long the appliance is on for and its power.
2) The power of an appliance is the energy that it transfers per second. So the more energy it transfers in a given time, the higher its power.
3) The amount of energy transferred by electrical work is given by:

Energy transferred (J) = Power (W) × Time (s) $E = Pt$

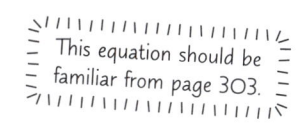

This equation should be familiar from page 303.

4) Appliances are often given a power rating — they're labelled with the maximum safe power that they can operate at. You can usually take this to be their maximum operating power.
5) The power rating tells you the maximum amount of energy transferred between stores per second when the appliance is in use.
6) This helps customers choose between models — the lower the power rating, the less electricity an appliance uses in a given time and so the cheaper it is to run.
7) But a higher power doesn't necessarily mean that it transfers more energy usefully. An appliance may be more powerful than another, but less efficient, meaning that it might still only transfer the same amount of energy (or even less) to useful stores (see p.306).

Power is the rate of energy transfer...

Get that equation for power hard-wired into your brain — you'll need it for the exams.

Q1   An appliance transfers 6000 J of energy in 30 seconds. Calculate its power. [2 marks]

Q2   Calculate the difference in the amount of energy transferred by a 250 W TV and a 375 W TV when they are both used for two hours. [4 marks]

More on Power

*As you've seen, the **power** of a device tells you how much **energy** it transfers **per second**. In electrical systems, there are a load of useful formulas you can use to calculate energy and power.*

Potential Difference is Energy Transferred per Charge Passed

1) When an electrical charge goes through a change in potential difference, energy is transferred.
2) Energy is supplied to the charge at the power source to 'raise' it through a potential.
3) The charge gives up this energy when it 'falls' through any potential drop in components elsewhere in the circuit.
4) The formula is really simple:

$$E = QV$$

Energy transferred (J) — Charge flow (C) — Potential difference (V)

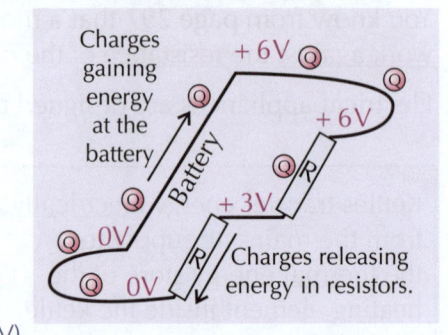

5) That means that a battery with a bigger pd will supply more energy to the circuit for every coulomb of charge which flows round it, because the charge is raised up "higher" at the start.

EXAMPLE
The motor in an electric toothbrush is attached to a 3 V battery. 140 C of charge passes through the circuit as it is used. Calculate the energy transferred.

$E = QV = 140 \times 3 = 420$ J

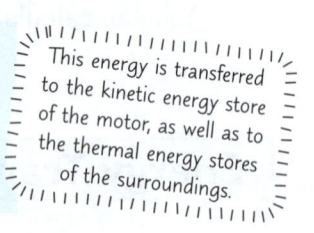

This energy is transferred to the kinetic energy store of the motor, as well as to the thermal energy stores of the surroundings.

Power Also Depends on Current and Potential Difference

1) As well as energy transferred in a given time, the power of an appliance can be found with:

Power (W) = Potential difference (V) × Current (A) $P = VI$

EXAMPLE
A 1.0 kW hair dryer is connected to a 230 V supply. Calculate the current through the hair dryer. Give your answer to two significant figures.

1) Rearrange the equation for current. $I = P \div V$
2) Make sure your units are correct. 1.0 kW = 1000 W
3) Then just stick in the numbers that you have. $I = 1000 \div 230 = 4.34... = 4.3$ A (to 2 s.f.)

2) You can also find the power if you don't know the potential difference. To do this, stick $V = IR$ from page 317 into $P = VI$, which gives you: $P = I^2R$ — Resistance (Ω)

Power is measured in watts, W — one W is equal to one J/s...

Remember, the power rating is the amount of energy transferred to an appliance per second.

Q1 Calculate the energy transferred from a 200 V source as 10 000 C of charge passes. [2 marks]

Q2 An appliance is connected to a 12 V source. A current of 4.0 A flows through it. Calculate the power of the appliance. [2 marks]

Q3 An appliance has a power of 2300 W and has a current of 10.0 A flowing through it. Calculate the resistance of the appliance. [3 marks]

Topic P2 — Electricity

The National Grid

The **national grid** is a giant web of wires that covers **the whole of Britain**, getting electricity from power stations to homes everywhere. Whoever you pay for your electricity, it's the national grid that gets it to you.

Electricity is Distributed via the National Grid

1) The national grid is a giant system of cables and transformers that covers the UK and connects power stations to consumers (anyone who is using electricity).

2) The national grid transfers electrical power from power stations anywhere on the grid (the supply) to anywhere else on the grid where it's needed (the demand) — e.g. homes and industry.

Electricity Production has to Meet Demand

1) Throughout the day, electricity usage (the demand) changes. Power stations have to produce enough electricity for everyone to have it when they need it.

2) They can predict when the most electricity will be used though. Demand increases when people get up in the morning, come home from school or work and when it starts to get dark or cold outside. Popular events like a sporting final being shown on TV could also cause a peak in demand.

3) Power stations often run at well below their maximum power output, so there's spare capacity to cope with a high demand, even if there's an unexpected shut-down of another station.

4) Lots of smaller power stations that can start up quickly are also kept in standby just in case.

Energy demands are ever increasing...

The national grid has been working since the 1930s and has gone through many changes and updates since then to meet increasing energy demands. Using energy-efficient appliances and switching unneeded lights off are some ways we might ensure that supply and demand stay in balance. It'll do wonders for your electricity bills too, as I'm sure your parents often remind you.

Topic P2 — Electricity

The National Grid

*To transfer electricity **efficiently**, the national grid makes use of some clever tech called **transformers**.*

The National Grid Uses a **High pd** and a **Low Current**

1) To transmit the huge amount of power needed, you need either a high potential difference or a high current (as $P = VI$, page 330).
2) The problem with a high current is that you lose loads of energy as the wires heat up and energy is transferred to the thermal energy store of the surroundings.
3) It's much cheaper to boost the pd up really high (to 400 000 V) and keep the current relatively low.
4) For a given power, increasing the pd decreases the current, which decreases the energy lost by heating the wires and the surroundings. This makes the national grid an efficient way of transferring energy.

Remember that power is the energy transferred in a given time, so a higher power means more energy transferred.

Potential Difference is Changed by a **Transformer**

1) To get the potential difference to 400 000 V to transmit power requires transformers as well as big pylons with huge insulators — but it's still cheaper.
2) The transformers have to step the potential difference up at one end, for efficient transmission, and then bring it back down to safe, usable levels at the other end.

3) The potential difference is increased ('stepped up') using a step-up transformer.
4) It's then reduced again ('stepped down') for domestic use using a step-down transformer.
5) Transformers are almost 100% efficient. So you can assume that the input power is equal to the output power. Using $P = VI$ from page 330, you can write this as:

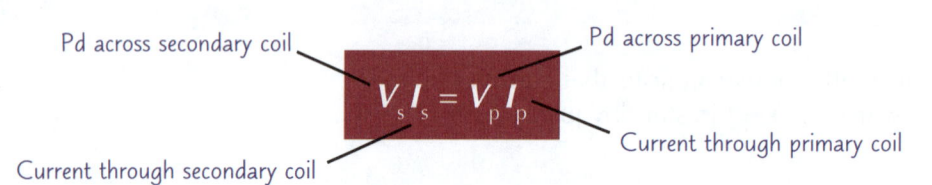

$$V_s I_s = V_p I_p$$

Pd across secondary coil — V_s
Current through secondary coil — I_s
Pd across primary coil — V_p
Current through primary coil — I_p

$V_s \times I_s$ is the power output at the secondary coil. $V_p \times I_p$ is the power input at the primary coil.

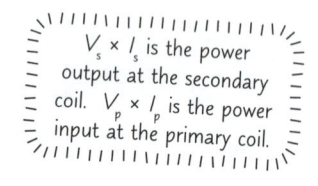

The national grid — it's a powerful thing...

The key to the efficiency of the national grid is the power equation, $P = VI$ (see page 330). Since power is proportional to both potential difference and current, if you have a constant power, but increase the potential difference using a transformer, the current must decrease. And vice versa.

Topic P2 — Electricity

Warm-Up & Exam Questions

Who knew there was so much to learn about electricity in the home and across the country?
See if it's switched on a lightbulb in your brain by trying out these questions.

Warm-Up Questions

1) Name the three wires in a three-core cable that connect electrical appliances to the mains supply.
2) What is the main energy transfer when electric current flows through an electric kettle?
3) What is the equation linking power, current and resistance?
4) What is the national grid?

Exam Questions

1 An electrical cable has become frayed so that the metal part of the live wire is exposed. Explain why you would get an electric shock if you touched it.

[3 marks]

2 **Table 1** shows the power and potential difference ratings for two kettles.

Table 1

	Power (kW)	Potential Difference (V)
Kettle A	2.8	230
Kettle B	3.0	230

2.1 State the equation linking power, potential difference and current.

[1 mark]

2.2 Calculate the current drawn from the mains supply by kettle A. State the correct unit.

[4 marks]

2.3 A student is deciding whether to buy kettle A or kettle B.
She wants to buy the kettle that boils water faster. Both kettles have an efficiency of 90%.
Suggest which kettle she should choose. Explain your answer.

[2 marks]

3 The national grid transmits electricity from power stations to homes and businesses all over the country.

3.1 Explain why the national grid uses step-up transformers.

[3 marks]

3.2 Electricity is passed through a step-down transformer. The potential difference across the primary coil is 4.00×10^5 V and the current through the primary coil is 2.00×10^3 A. The potential difference across the secondary coil is 2.75×10^5 V. Calculate the current in the secondary coil.

[3 marks]

4 A current of 0.5 A passes through a torch bulb. The torch is powered by a 3.0 V battery.

4.1 The torch is on for half an hour.
Calculate the amount of energy transferred from the battery in this time.

[4 marks]

4.2 Calculate how much charge passes through the torch in half an hour.

[3 marks]

Topic P2 — Electricity

Topic P3 — Particle Model of Matter

Particle Model

*The **particle model** is simpler than it sounds. It says that everything is made up of **lots of tiny particles** and describes how those particles behave in the three states of matter — **solids**, **liquids** and **gases**.*

The Particle Model can Explain the Three States of Matter

1) In the particle model, you can think of the particles that make up matter as tiny balls. You can explain the ways that matter behaves in terms of how these tiny balls move, and the forces between them.

2) The three states of matter are solid (e.g. ice), liquid (e.g. water) and gas (e.g. water vapour). The particles of a substance in each state are the same — only the arrangement and energy of the particles are different.

Solids

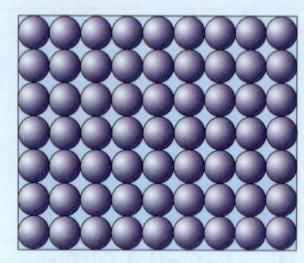

1) Strong forces of attraction hold the particles close together in a fixed, regular arrangement.
2) The particles don't have much energy so they can only vibrate about their fixed positions.
3) The density is generally highest in this state as the particles are closest together.

Liquids

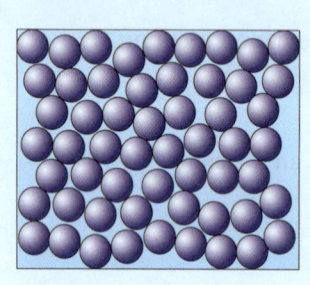

1) There are weaker forces of attraction between the particles.
2) The particles are close together, but can move past each other, and form irregular arrangements.
3) For any given substance, in the liquid state its particles will have more energy than in the solid state (but less energy than in the gas state).
4) They move in random directions at low speeds.
5) Liquids are generally less dense than solids.

Gases

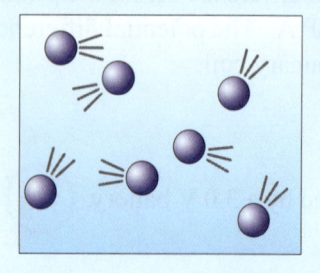

1) There are almost no forces of attraction between the particles.
2) For any given substance, in the gas state its particles will have more energy than in the solid state or the liquid state.
3) They are free to move, and travel in random directions and at high speeds.
4) Gases have low densities.

REVISION TIP

The higher their kinetic energy, the faster particles move...

Learn those diagrams above and make sure that you can describe the arrangement and movement of particles in solids, liquids and gases — it could earn you a few easy marks in the exam.

Density

Density tells you how much **mass** is packed into a given **volume** of space. You need to be able to work it out, as well as carry out **practicals** to work out the densities of different solids and liquids. Lucky you.

Density is a Measure of Compactness

Density is a measure of the 'compactness' of a substance. It relates the mass of a substance to how much space it takes up (i.e. it's a substance's mass per unit volume). The units of density are kg/m³ (the mass is in kg and the volume is in m³).

$$\text{Density (kg/m}^3\text{)} = \frac{\text{Mass (kg)}}{\text{Volume (m}^3\text{)}}$$

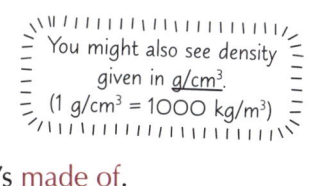

You might also see density given in g/cm³. (1 g/cm³ = 1000 kg/m³)

$$\frac{m}{\rho \times V}$$

1) The density of an object depends on what it's made of.
2) A dense material has its particles packed tightly together. The particles in a less dense material are more spread out — if you compressed the material, its particles would move closer together, and it would become more dense. (You wouldn't be changing its mass, but you would be decreasing its volume.)
3) This means that density varies between different states of matter (see previous page). Solids are generally denser than liquids, and gases are usually less dense than liquids.

You Need to be Able to Measure Density in Different Ways

To Find the Density of a Solid Object   PRACTICAL

1) Use a balance to measure its mass (see p.406).
2) For some solid shapes, you can find the volume using a formula. E.g. the volume of a cube is just width × height × length.
3) For a trickier shaped-solid, you can find its volume by submerging it in a eureka can filled with water. The water displaced by the object will be transferred to the measuring cylinder:
4) Record the volume of water in the measuring cylinder. This is the volume of the object.
5) Plug the object's mass and volume into the formula above to find its density.

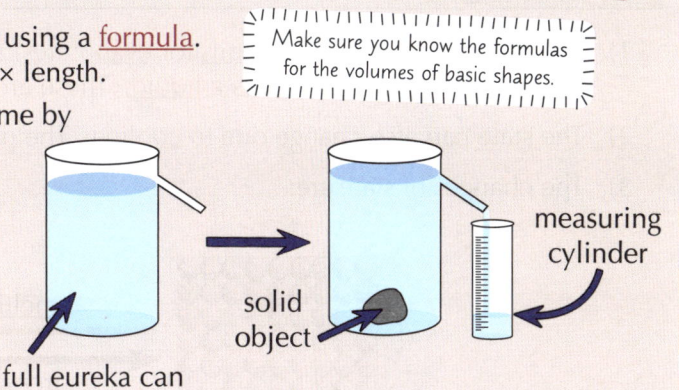

Make sure you know the formulas for the volumes of basic shapes.

To Find the Density of a Liquid   PRACTICAL

1) Place a measuring cylinder on a balance and zero the balance (see p.406).
2) Pour 10 ml of the liquid into the measuring cylinder and record the liquid's mass.
3) Pour another 10 ml into the measuring cylinder and record the total volume and mass. Repeat this process until the measuring cylinder is full.
4) For each measurement, use the formula to find the density. (Remember that 1 ml = 1 cm³.)
5) Finally, take an average of your calculated densities to get an accurate value for the density of the liquid.

Eureka cans help find the volume of irregularly shaped solids...

Remember — density is all about how tightly packed the particles in a substance are. Simple.

Q1 A 0.019 kg gemstone is placed into a full eureka can, causing 7.0 cm³ of water to be pushed out the spout into a measuring cylinder. Calculate the density of the gemstone in g/cm³. [3 marks]

Topic P3 — Particle Model of Matter

Internal Energy and Changes of State

*This page is all about heating things. Take a look at your **specific heat capacity** notes (p.300) before you start — you need to understand it and be able to be able to use $\Delta E = mc\Delta\theta$ for this topic too I'm afraid.*

Internal Energy is Stored by the Particles That Make Up a System

1) The particles in a system vibrate or move around — they have energy in their kinetic energy stores.

2) They also have energy in their potential energy stores due to their positions — don't worry about this.

3) The energy stored in a system is stored by its particles (atoms and molecules). The internal energy of a system is the total energy that its particles have in their kinetic and potential energy stores.

4) Heating the system transfers energy to its particles (they gain energy in their kinetic stores and move faster), increasing the internal energy.

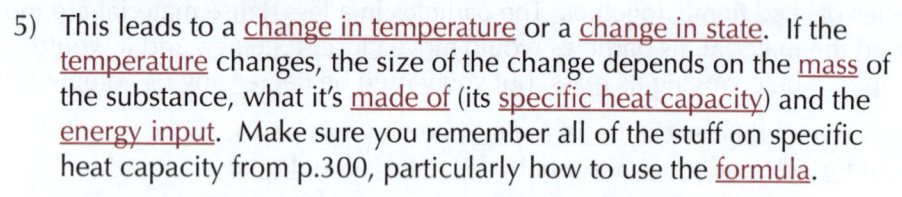

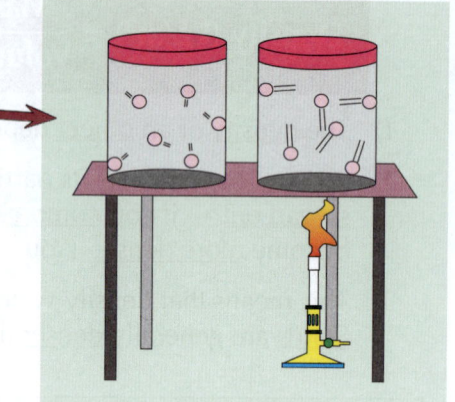

5) This leads to a change in temperature or a change in state. If the temperature changes, the size of the change depends on the mass of the substance, what it's made of (its specific heat capacity) and the energy input. Make sure you remember all of the stuff on specific heat capacity from p.300, particularly how to use the formula.

6) A change in state occurs if the substance is heated enough — the particles will have enough energy in their kinetic energy stores to break the bonds holding them together.

A Change of State Conserves Mass

1) When you heat a liquid, it boils (or evaporates) and becomes a gas. When you heat a solid, it melts and becomes a liquid. These are both changes of state.

2) The state can also change due to cooling. The particles lose energy and form bonds.

3) The changes of state are:

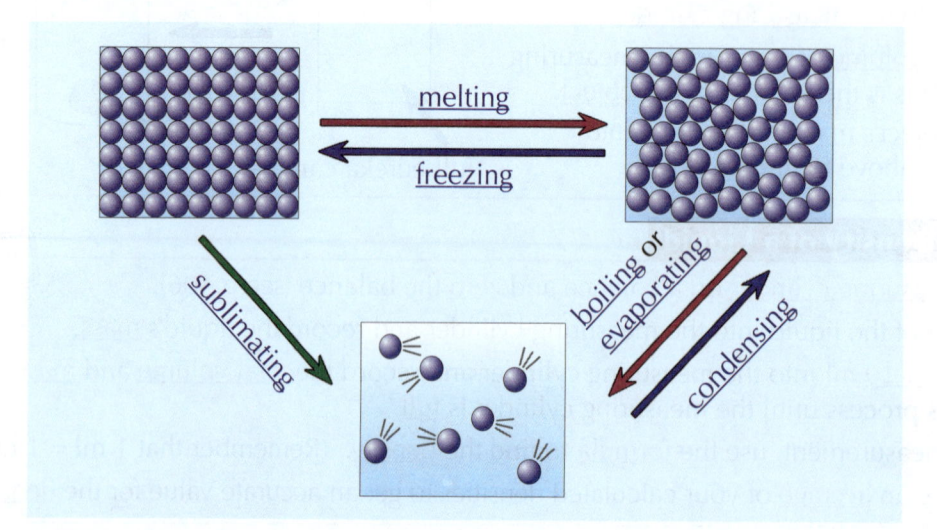

4) A change of state is a physical change (rather than a chemical change). This means you don't end up with a new substance — it's the same substance as you started with, just in a different form.

5) If you reverse a change of state (e.g. freeze a substance that has been melted), the substance will return to its original form and get back its original properties.

6) The number of particles doesn't change — they're just arranged differently. This means mass is conserved — none of it is lost when the substance changes state.

Topic P3 — Particle Model of Matter

Specific Latent Heat

*The **energy needed** to change the state of a substance is called **latent heat**. This is exciting stuff I tell you...*

A Change of State Requires Energy

When a substance is melting or boiling, you're still putting in energy and so increasing the internal energy, but the energy's used for breaking bonds between particles rather than raising the temperature. There are flat spots on the heating graph where energy is being transferred by heating but not being used to change the temperature.

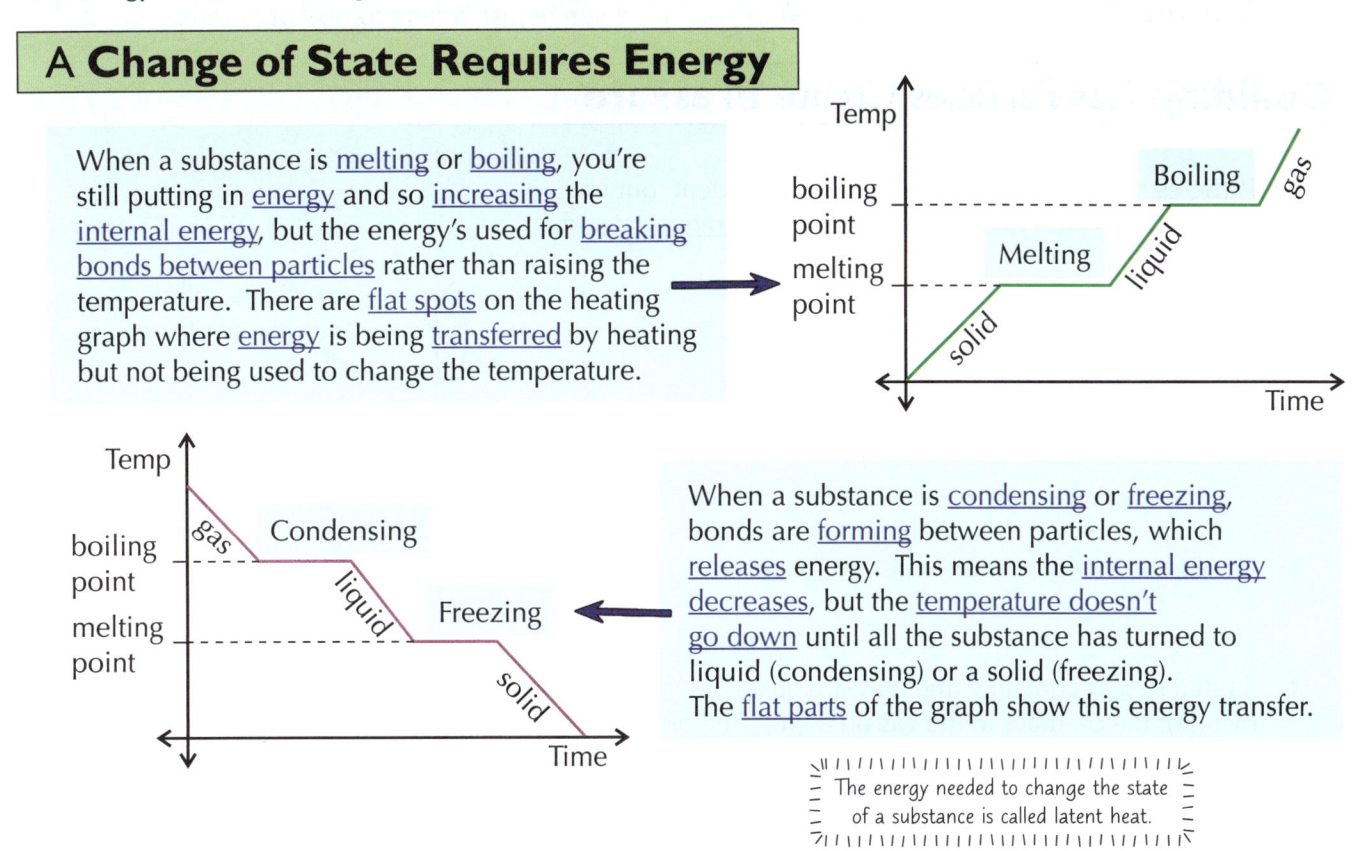

When a substance is condensing or freezing, bonds are forming between particles, which releases energy. This means the internal energy decreases, but the temperature doesn't go down until all the substance has turned to liquid (condensing) or a solid (freezing). The flat parts of the graph show this energy transfer.

The energy needed to change the state of a substance is called latent heat.

Specific Latent Heat is the Energy Needed to Change State

1) The specific latent heat (SLH) of a substance is the amount of energy needed to change 1 kg of it from one state to another without changing its temperature.
2) For cooling, specific latent heat is the energy released by a change in state.
3) Specific latent heat is different for different materials, and for changing between different states.
4) The specific latent heat for changing between a solid and a liquid (melting or freezing) is called the specific latent heat of fusion. The specific latent heat for changing between a liquid and a gas (evaporating, boiling or condensing) is called the specific latent heat of vaporisation.

There's a Formula for Specific Latent Heat

You can work out the energy needed (or released) when a substance of mass m changes state using this formula:

Energy (E) = Mass (m) × Specific Latent Heat (L)

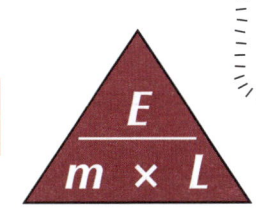

$$\frac{E}{m \times L}$$

Energy is given in joules (J), mass is in kg and SLH is in J/kg.

Don't get confused with specific heat capacity (p.300), which relates to a temperature rise of 1 °C. Specific latent heat is about changes of state where there's no temperature change.

Temperature doesn't change during a change of state...

When it comes to the specific latent heat of vaporisation and fusion, the formula's the same, but the process is different. Make sure you understand which process you're actually looking at.

Q1   The SLH of fusion for a particular substance is 120 000 J/kg. How much energy is needed to melt 250 g of the substance when it is already at its melting temperature?   [2 marks]

Topic P3 — Particle Model of Matter

Particle Motion in Gases

*The **particle model** helps explain how **temperature**, **pressure**, **volume** and **energy in kinetic stores** are all related. And this page is here to explain it all to you. I bet you're just itching to find out more...*

Colliding Gas Particles Create Pressure

1) Particles in gases (and liquids to a certain extent, but you don't need to worry about them) are free to move around.

2) As gas particles move about at high speeds, they bang into each other and whatever else happens to get in the way. When they collide with something, they exert a force on it.

3) Pressure is the force exerted per unit area.

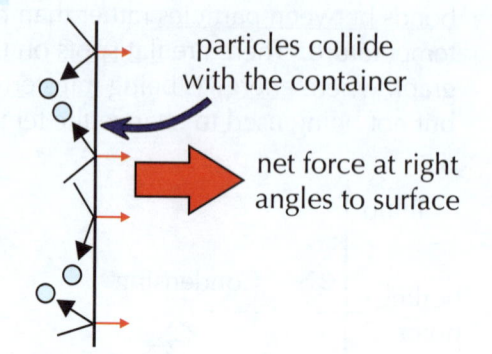

4) So in a sealed container, the outward gas pressure is the total force exerted by all of the particles in the gas on a unit area of the container walls.

Average Energy in Kinetic Stores is Related to Temperature

1) The particles in a gas are constantly moving with random directions and speeds. If you increase the temperature of a gas, you transfer energy into the kinetic energy stores of its particles (see page 297 for more on energy stores).

2) The temperature of a gas is related to the average energy in the kinetic energy stores of the particles in the gas. The higher the temperature, the higher the average energy.

3) So as you increase the temperature of a gas, the average speed of its particles increases. This is because the energy in the particles' kinetic energy stores is $½mv^2$ — p.299.

4) This means that, for a gas at a constant volume, increasing its temperature increases its pressure.

- As the particles are travelling quicker, it means that they hit the sides of the container more often in a given amount of time.
- Each particle also has a larger momentum (p.379) which means that they exert a larger force when they collide with the container.

These factors both increase the total force exerted on a unit area, and so increase the pressure.

Higher temperatures mean higher average energies in kinetic stores...

The particle model can be used to explain what happens when you change the temperature of a gas which is kept at a constant volume. Have a look back on page 334 for more about the particle model.

Topic P3 — Particle Model of Matter

Warm-Up & Exam Questions

Once you think you've got to grips with everything in this topic, all the way through from the particle model to that stuff about gases, it's time to test yourself with these questions. Let's see how you get on.

Warm-Up Questions

1) Describe the particles in a liquid in terms of their arrangement, energy and movement.
2) What is density a measure of?
3) How does cooling a system affect its internal energy?
4) What is the specific latent heat of vaporisation?
5) What are the units of specific latent heat?

Exam Questions

1 Substances can exist in different states of matter. *Grade 4-6*

1.1 Describe the arrangement and movement of the particles in a solid.

[2 marks]

If a substance is heated to a certain temperature it can change from a solid to a liquid.

1.2 Give the name of this process.

[1 mark]

1.3 If a liquid is heated to a certain temperature it starts to boil and become a gas.
Name the other process that causes a liquid to start to become a gas.

[1 mark]

PRACTICAL

2 A student has a collection of metal toy soldiers of different sizes made from the same metal. *Grade 6-7*

2.1 Which of the following statements about the toy soldiers is true? Tick **one** box.

☐ The masses and densities of each of the toy soldiers are the same.

☐ The masses of each of the toy soldiers are the same, but their densities may vary.

☐ The densities of each of the toy soldiers are the same, but their masses may vary.

☐ The densities and masses of each toy soldier may vary.

[1 mark]

The student wants to measure the density of one of the toy soldiers.
He has a eureka can, a measuring cylinder, a mass balance and some water.

2.2 State the **two** quantities the student must measure in order to calculate the density of the toy soldier.

[2 marks]

2.3* Describe the steps the student could take to find the density of the toy soldier using the equipment he has.

[6 marks]

Topic P3 — Particle Model of Matter

Exam Questions

3 The following question is about specific latent heat. *(Grade 6-7)*

3.1 What is the name given to the specific latent heat of a substance when it's changing between a solid and a liquid?

[1 mark]

3.2 The energy required to convert 40.8 g of liquid methanol to gaseous methanol is 47.7 J.
Calculate the specific latent heat of vaporisation of methanol.
Use the correct equation from the Physics Equation Sheet on page 542.
Give your answer in J/kg and to 3 significant figures.

[3 marks]

The energy used to change liquid methanol to gaseous methanol was supplied by heating the system.

3.3 How does the internal energy of the system change as the system is heated?
Explain your answer.

[2 marks]

3.4 Explain, using the particle model, what happens when methanol is heated so that it changes from a liquid to a gas.

[2 marks]

4 The movement of particles in a gas can be described using the particle model. *(Grade 6-7)*

4.1 Describe the particles in a gas using the particle model.
In your answer, you should refer to the arrangement, energy and movement of the particles.

[3 marks]

A scientist is calculating the density of a gas in a sealed, rigid container.

4.2 Use the particle model to explain how gas particles create pressure in a sealed container.

[2 marks]

4.3 State the equation that links density with mass and volume.

[1 mark]

4.4 A certain gas had a mass of 8.2 g and a volume of 6.69 cm^3.
Calculate the density of the gas.
Give your answer to an appropriate number of significant figures.

[4 marks]

The scientist heats the container.

4.5 What happens to the pressure of the gas within the container?
Explain your answer using the particle model.

[3 marks]

5 A student is doing an investigation into the masses of different materials of different densities.
A cube has edges of length 1.5 cm and a density of 3500 kg/m^3. *(Grade 7-9)*
Calculate the mass of the cube.

[5 marks]

Topic P3 — Particle Model of Matter

Topic P4 — Atomic Structure

Developing the Model of the Atom

*All this started with a Greek chap called Democritus in the 5th Century BC. He thought that **all matter**, whatever it was, was made up of **identical** lumps called "atomos". And that's as far as it got until the 1800s...*

The Plum Pudding Model was Replaced with the Nuclear Model

1) In 1804 John Dalton agreed with Democritus that matter was made up of tiny spheres ("atoms") that couldn't be broken up, but he reckoned that each element was made up of a different type of "atom".

2) Nearly 100 years later, J. J. Thomson discovered particles called electrons that could be removed from atoms. So Dalton's theory wasn't quite right (atoms could be broken up). Thomson suggested that atoms were spheres of positive charge with tiny negative electrons stuck in them like the fruit in a plum pudding — the plum pudding model.

3) That "plum pudding" theory didn't last though... In 1909, scientists in Rutherford's lab tried firing a beam of alpha particles (see p.344) at thin gold foil — this was the alpha scattering experiment. From the plum pudding model, they expected the particles to pass straight through the gold sheet, or only be slightly deflected.

4) But although most of the particles did go straight through the sheet, some were deflected more than expected, and a few were deflected back the way they had come — something the plum pudding model couldn't explain.

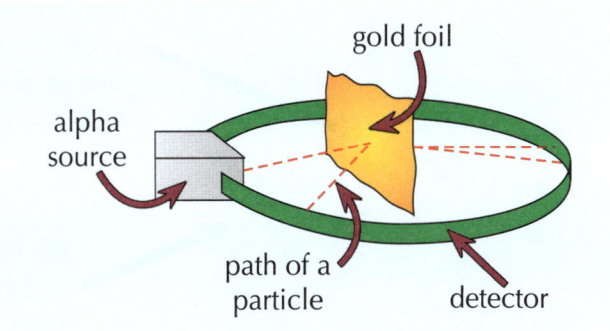

5) Because a few alpha particles were deflected back, the scientists realised that most of the mass of the atom was concentrated at the centre in a tiny nucleus. This nucleus must also have a positive charge, since it repelled the positive alpha particles.

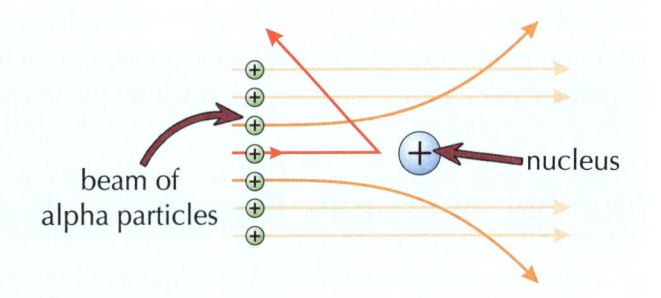

6) They also realised that because nearly all the alpha particles passed straight through, most of an atom is just empty space. This was the first nuclear model of the atom.

The gold foil experiment helped adapt the model of the atom...

WORKING SCIENTIFICALLY
Rutherford and his lab of scientists made a hypothesis, did an investigation and then analysed the data they got from it. By doing this, they showed that the plum pudding model of the atom must be wrong, so it was changed. This is a great example of the scientific method (see page 2) in action.

Developing the Model of the Atom

Rutherford and *Marsden's* model of the atom was a big leap forwards, but that's not the end of the story...

Bohr **Refined** Rutherford's **Nuclear Model** of the Atom

1) The nuclear model that resulted from the alpha particle scattering experiment was a positively charged nucleus surrounded by a cloud of negative electrons.

2) Niels Bohr said that electrons orbiting the nucleus do so at certain distances called energy levels. His theoretical calculations agreed with experimental data.

3) Evidence from further experiments changed the model to have a nucleus made up of a group of particles (protons) which all had the same positive charge that added up to the overall charge of the nucleus.

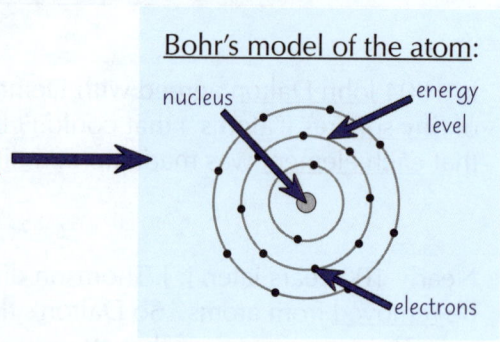

4) About 20 years after the idea of a nucleus was accepted, in 1932, James Chadwick proved the existence of the neutron, which explained the imbalance between the atomic and mass numbers (see next page).

Bohr's model of the atom: nucleus, energy level, electrons

Our **Current Model** of the Atom

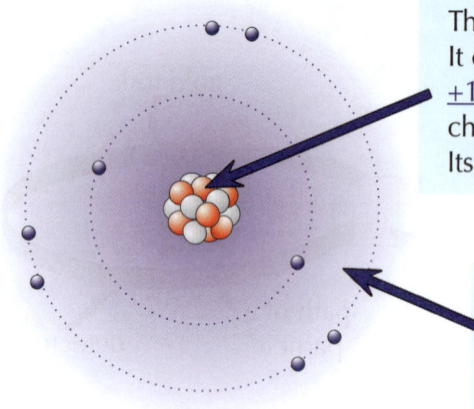

The nucleus is tiny but it makes up most of the mass of the atom. It contains protons (which are positively charged — they have a +1 relative charge) and neutrons (which are neutral, with a relative charge of 0) — which gives it an overall positive charge. Its radius is about 10 000 times smaller than the radius of the atom.

The rest of the atom is mostly empty space. Negative electrons (which have a relative charge of –1) whizz round the outside of the nucleus really fast. They give the atom its overall size — the radius of an atom is about 1×10^{-10} m.

We're currently pretty happy with this model, but there's no saying it won't change. Just like for the plum pudding model, new experiments sometimes mean we have to change or completely get rid of current models.

Number of Protons **Equals** Number of Electrons

1) In atoms, the number of protons = the number of electrons, as protons and electrons have an equal but opposite charge and atoms have no overall charge.

2) Electrons in energy levels can move within (or sometimes leave) the atom. If they gain energy by absorbing EM radiation (p.388) they move to a higher energy level, further from the nucleus. If they release EM radiation, they move to a lower energy level that is closer to the nucleus. If one or more outer electrons leaves the atom, the atom becomes a positively charged ion.

The model of the atom has developed over time...

Due to lots of scientists doing lots of experiments, we now have a better idea of what the atom's really like. We now know about the particles in atoms — protons, neutrons and electrons.

Topic P4 — Atomic Structure

Isotopes

Isotopes of an element look pretty similar, but watch out — they have **different numbers of neutrons**.

Atoms of the Same Element have the Same Number of Protons

1) All atoms of each element have a set number of protons (so each nucleus has a given positive charge). The number of protons in an atom is its atomic number.

2) The mass number of an atom (the mass of the nucleus) is the number of protons + the number of neutrons in its nucleus.

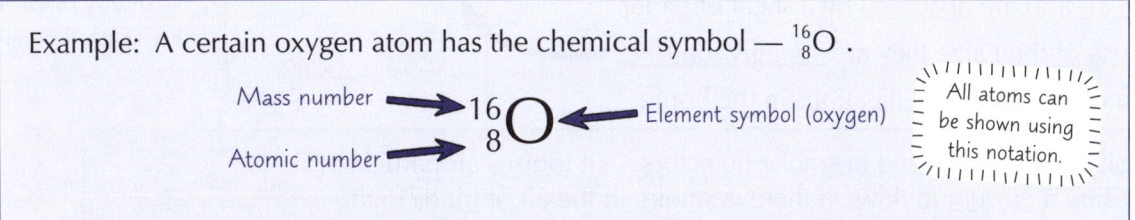

> Example: A certain oxygen atom has the chemical symbol — $^{16}_{8}O$.
>
> Mass number → 16
> Atomic number → 8 O ← Element symbol (oxygen)
>
> *All atoms can be shown using this notation.*
>
> - Oxygen has an atomic number of 8, this means all oxygen atoms have 8 protons.
> - This atom of oxygen has a mass number of 16.
>   Since it has 8 protons, it must have 16 − 8 = 8 neutrons.

Isotopes are Different Forms of the Same Element

1) Isotopes of an element are atoms with the same number of protons (the same atomic number, and so the same charge on the nucleus) but a different number of neutrons (a different mass number).

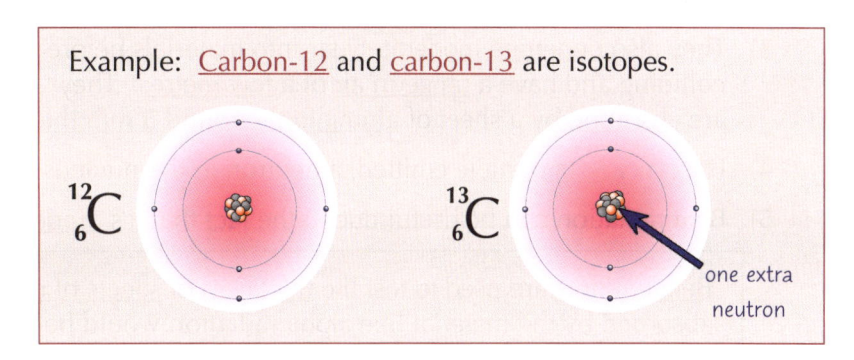

Example: Carbon-12 and carbon-13 are isotopes.

$^{12}_{6}C$ $^{13}_{6}C$ one extra neutron

2) All elements have different isotopes, but there are usually only one or two stable ones.

3) The other unstable isotopes tend to decay into other elements and give out radiation as they try to become more stable. This process is called radioactive decay.

4) Radioactive substances spit out one or more types of ionising radiation from their nucleus — the ones you need to know are alpha, beta and gamma radiation (see next page).

5) They can also release neutrons (n) when they decay.

6) Ionising radiation is radiation that knocks electrons off atoms, creating positive ions. The ionising power of a radiation source is how easily it can do this.

Topic P4 — Atomic Structure

Ionising Radiation

*There are three types of ionising radiation you need to know about — these are **alpha**, **beta** and **gamma**.*

Alpha Particles are Helium Nuclei

1) Alpha radiation is when an alpha particle (α) is emitted from the nucleus. An α-particle is two neutrons and two protons (like a helium nucleus).
2) They don't penetrate very far into materials and are stopped quickly — they can only travel a few cm in air and are absorbed by a sheet of paper.
3) Because of their size they are strongly ionising.
4) Alpha radiation has applications in the home:

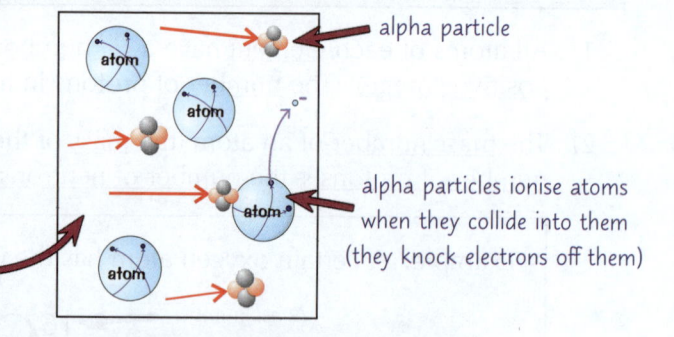

alpha particle

alpha particles ionise atoms when they collide into them (they knock electrons off them)

> Alpha radiation is used in smoke detectors — it ionises air particles, causing a current to flow. If there is smoke in the air, it binds to the ions — meaning the current stops and the alarm sounds.

Beta Particles are High-Speed Electrons

1) A beta particle (β) is simply a fast-moving electron released by the nucleus. Beta particles have virtually no mass and a charge of −1.
2) They are moderately ionising (see right).
3) They also penetrate moderately far into materials before colliding and have a range in air of a few metres. They are absorbed by a sheet of aluminium (around 5 mm thick).
4) For every beta particle emitted, a neutron in the nucleus has turned into a proton.
5) Beta radiation can be useful due to the fact that it's moderately penetrating:

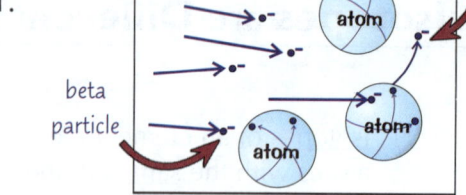

emitted electron

beta particle

> Beta emitters are used to test the thickness of sheets of metal, as the particles are not immediately absorbed by the material like alpha radiation would be and do not penetrate as far as gamma rays. Therefore, slight variations in thickness affect the amount of radiation passing through the sheet.

Gamma Rays are EM Waves with a Short Wavelength

1) Gamma rays (γ) are waves of electromagnetic radiation (p.388) released by the nucleus.
2) They penetrate far into materials without being stopped and will travel a long distance through air.
3) This means they are weakly ionising because they tend to pass through rather than collide with atoms. Eventually they hit something and do damage.
4) They can be absorbed by thick sheets of lead or metres of concrete.

Uses of gamma rays are on p.391.

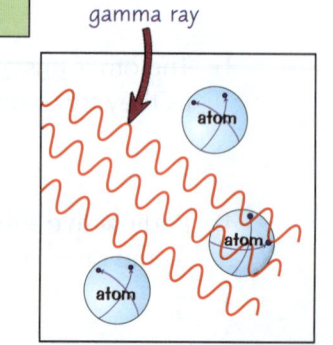

gamma ray

Alpha particles are more ionising than beta particles...

...and beta particles are more ionising than gamma rays. Make sure you get that memorised.

Q1 In order to sterilise medical equipment, radiation is directed at the equipment while it is sealed in packaging.
Explain whether alpha radiation would be suitable for this use.
[2 marks]

Q1 Video Solution

Topic P4 — Atomic Structure

Nuclear Equations

Nuclear equations show **radioactive decay** and once you get the hang of them they're **dead easy**. Get going.

Mass and Atomic Numbers Have to Balance

1) Nuclear equations are a way of showing radioactive decay by using element symbols (p.343). They're written in the form: atom before decay → atom(s) after decay + radiation emitted.

2) There is one golden rule to remember: the total mass and atomic numbers must be equal on both sides.

Alpha Decay Decreases the Charge and Mass of the Nucleus

1) Remember, alpha particles are made up of two protons and two neutrons. So when an atom emits an alpha particle, its atomic number reduces by 2 and its mass number reduces by 4.

2) A proton is positively charged and a neutron is neutral, so the charge of the nucleus decreases.

3) In nuclear equations, an alpha particle can be written as a helium nucleus: $^4_2$He.

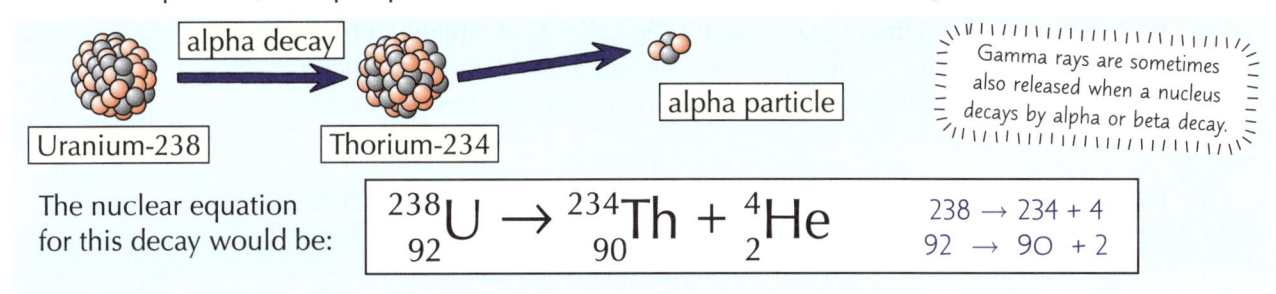

Gamma rays are sometimes also released when a nucleus decays by alpha or beta decay.

The nuclear equation for this decay would be:

$$^{238}_{92}U \rightarrow ^{234}_{90}Th + ^4_2He$$

238 → 234 + 4
92 → 90 + 2

Beta Decay Increases the Charge of the Nucleus

1) When beta decay occurs, a neutron in the nucleus turns into a proton and releases a fast-moving electron (the beta particle).

2) The number of protons in the nucleus has increased by 1. This increases the positive charge of the nucleus (the atomic number).

3) Because the nucleus has lost a neutron and gained a proton during beta decay, the mass of the nucleus doesn't change (protons and neutrons have the same mass).

4) A beta particle is written as $^0_{-1}$e in nuclear equations.

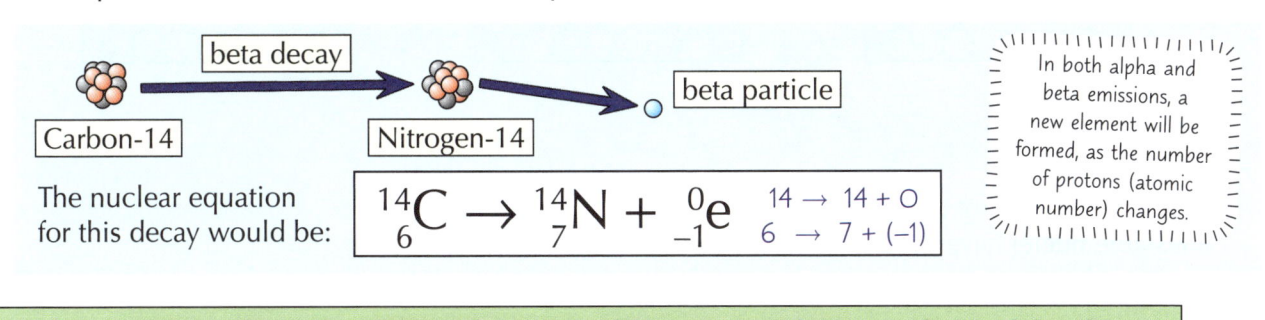

In both alpha and beta emissions, a new element will be formed, as the number of protons (atomic number) changes.

The nuclear equation for this decay would be:

$$^{14}_{6}C \rightarrow ^{14}_{7}N + ^0_{-1}e$$

14 → 14 + 0
6 → 7 + (−1)

Gamma Rays Don't Change the Charge or Mass of the Nucleus

1) Gamma rays are a way of getting rid of excess energy from a nucleus.

2) This means that there is no change to the atomic mass or atomic number of the atom.

3) In nuclear equations, gamma radiation is written as γ^0_0.

Mass and atomic numbers must balance in nuclear equations

Q1 What type of radiation is given off in this decay? $^8_3$Li → $^8_4$Be + radiation. [1 mark]

Q2 Write the nuclear equation for $^{219}_{86}$Rn decaying to polonium (Po) by emitting an alpha particle. [3 marks]

Topic P4 — Atomic Structure

Half-Life

*How quickly **unstable nuclei** decay is measured using **activity** and **half-life** — two very important terms.*

Radioactivity is a Totally Random Process

1) Radioactive substances give out radiation from the nuclei of their atoms — no matter what.

2) This radiation can be measured with a Geiger-Muller tube and counter, which records the count-rate — the number of radiation counts reaching it per second.

3) Radioactive decay is entirely random. So you can't predict exactly which nucleus in a sample will decay next, or when any one of them will decay.

4) But you can find out the time it takes for the amount of radiation emitted by a source to halve, this is known as the half-life. It can be used to make predictions about radioactive sources, even though their decays are random.

5) Half-life can be used to find the rate at which a source decays — its ACTIVITY. Activity is measured in becquerels, Bq (where 1 Bq is 1 decay per second).

The Radioactivity of a Source Decreases Over Time

1) Each time a radioactive nucleus decays to become a stable nucleus, the activity as a whole will decrease. (Older sources emit less radiation.)

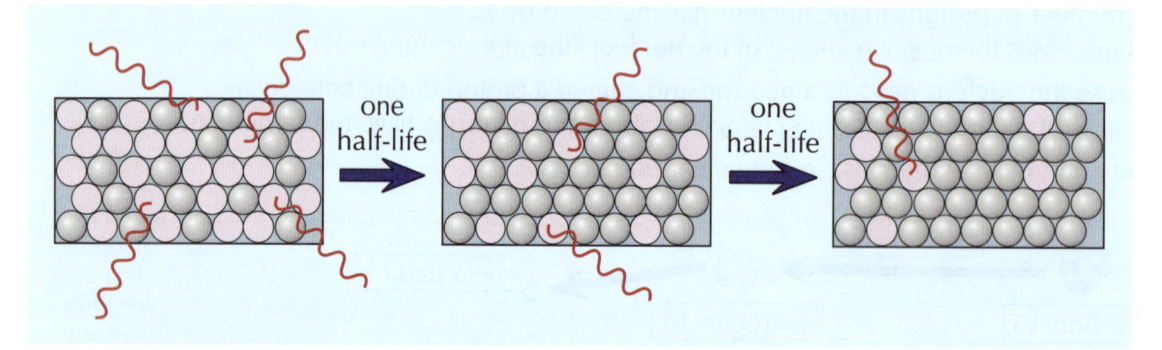

2) For some isotopes it takes just a few hours before nearly all the unstable nuclei have decayed, whilst others last for millions of years.

3) The problem with trying to measure this is that the activity never reaches zero, which is why we have to use the idea of half-life to measure how quickly the activity drops off.

The half-life is the time taken for the number of radioactive nuclei in an isotope to halve.

4) Half-life can also be described as the time taken for the activity, and so count-rate, to halve.

Different substances have different half-lives...

Some substances take a long time to decay, giving them a long half-life, while others decay in the blink of an eye. For example, neodymium-144 has a half-life of 2 million billion years, while helium-5 has a half-life of 7.6×10^{-22} seconds. That's 0.00000000000000000000076 seconds. Pretty speedy eh?

Topic P4 — Atomic Structure

Half-Life

You learnt all about what **half-life** is on the last page, but now it's time to find out how to **calculate** it. Fortunately, there's a pretty simple method you can use that involves an **activity-time graph**.

The Radioactivity of a Source Decreases Over Time

You might be asked to give the decline of activity or count-rate after a certain number of half-lives as a percentage of the original activity, like this:

EXAMPLE **The initial activity of a sample is 640 Bq. Calculate the final activity as a percentage of the initial activity after two half-lives.**

1) Find the activity after each half-life.

2) Now divide the final activity by the initial activity, then multiply by 100 to make it a percentage.

1 half-life: 640 ÷ 2 = 320
2 half-lives: 320 ÷ 2 = 160
(160 ÷ 640) × 100
= 0.25 × 100
= 25%

Always double check what the question is asking for — it may want a fraction, ratio or a percentage.

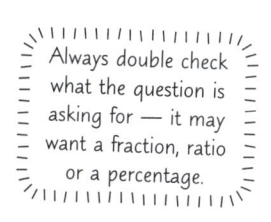

Finding the Half-Life of a Sample using a Graph

1) If you plot a graph of activity against time (taking into account background radiation), it will always be shaped like the one below.

2) The half-life is found from the graph by finding the time interval on the bottom axis corresponding to a halving of the activity on the vertical axis. Easy.

EXAMPLE **The activity of a sample of a radioactive material, X, is shown on the graph below. Calculate the half-life of material X.**

1) Read the initial activity off the graph. This is the activity when time = 0.

2) Divide the initial activity by 2 to find the value of half the initial activity.
   80 ÷ 2 = 40

3) Find this value on the y-axis and read along horizontally to the curve.

4) Then read down from the curve at this point to find the half-life.

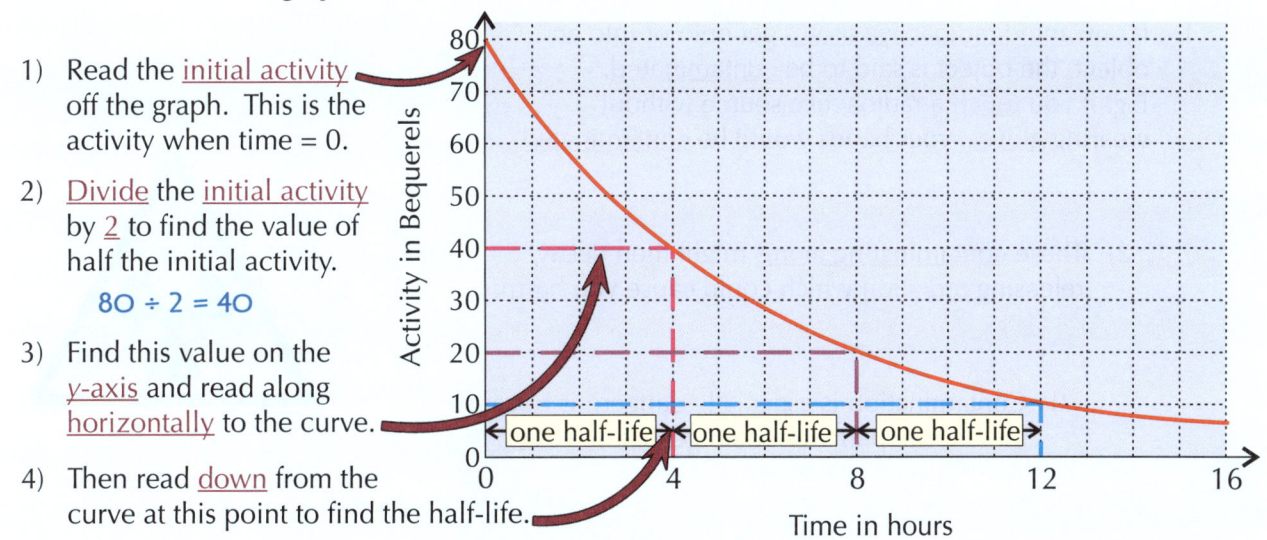

So the half-life of the sample is **4 hours**.

You can determine half-lives from graphs...

Make sure you can use graphs like the one above to work out half-lives. All you've got to do is read off the initial activity from the y-axis, then work out what half this activity would be by dividing by two. Then, just read off the time from the x-axis for this value, which is one half-life.

Q1 The initial count-rate of a sample is 40 cps. Show that the ratio of its final count rate to its initial count rate is 1:8 after three half-lives. [3 marks]

Topic P4 — Atomic Structure

Irradiation and Contamination

*There are two main things you need to be careful of when working with radiation — **exposure to radiation**, and **physical contact** with **radioactive substances**. It's dangerous stuff I tell you, so read with care...*

There are Risks to Using Radiation

Ionising radiation can enter living cells and ionise atoms within them. This can damage the cells (which can cause things like cancer) or kill them off completely. That's why it's important that you know the precautions to take when working with any sources of radiation.

Exposure to Radiation is called Irradiation

1) Objects near a radioactive source are irradiated by it. This simply means they're exposed to it (we're always being irradiated by background radiation sources).

2) Irradiating something does not make it radioactive.

3) Keeping sources in lead-lined boxes, standing behind barriers or being in a different room and using remote-controlled arms when working with radioactive sources are all ways of reducing irradiation.

Contamination is Radioactive Particles Getting onto Objects

1) If unwanted radioactive atoms get onto or into an object, the object is said to be contaminated. E.g. if you touch a radioactive source without wearing gloves, your hands would be contaminated.

2) These contaminating atoms might then decay, releasing radiation which could cause you harm.

3) Contamination is especially dangerous because radioactive particles could get inside your body.

4) Gloves and tongs should be used when handling sources, to avoid particles getting stuck to your skin or under your nails. Some industrial workers wear protective suits to stop them breathing in particles.

Safety precautions can help protect against hazards from radiation...

Radiation can be pretty dangerous stuff, so it's important to protect yourself when you're working with radioactive substances. Lead is often used to line storage boxes and in protective screens because it is very good at absorbing radiation, so it prevents a lot of the radiation from reaching what's on the other side.

Topic P4 — Atomic Structure

Irradiation and Contamination

Radioactive contamination and *irradiation* can both be pretty dangerous — but how dangerous they are depends on the **type of radiation** involved. Give this page a read to find out why.

Exposure to Some Sources can be More Harmful than to Others

Contamination or irradiation can cause different amounts of harm, based on the radiation type.

Irradiation

1) Outside the body, beta and gamma sources are the most dangerous. This is because beta and gamma can penetrate the body and get to delicate organs.

2) Alpha is less dangerous because it can't penetrate the skin and is easily blocked by a small air gap (p.344).

3) High levels of irradiation from all sources are dangerous, but especially from ones that emit beta and gamma.

Contamination

1) Inside the body, alpha sources are the most dangerous, because they do all their damage in a very localised area. So contamination, rather than irradiation, is the major concern when working with alpha sources.

2) Beta sources are less damaging inside the body, as radiation is absorbed over a wider area, and some passes out of the body altogether.

3) Gamma sources are the least dangerous inside the body, as they mostly pass straight out — they have the lowest ionising power, p.344.

Information About Radiation Should Be Communicated

The more we understand how different types of radiation affects our bodies, the better we can protect ourselves when using them. This is why it's so important that research about this is published. The data is peer-reviewed (see page 2) and can quickly become accepted, leading to many improvements in our use of radioactive sources.

Alpha sources are the most dangerous inside the body...

Alpha sources are the most ionising (see page 344), so if they get into the body, they can wreak havoc. Beta and gamma sources however are the most dangerous outside the body. This is because they are more penetrating than alpha sources (see page 344), so can get through the skin and cause damage to cells.

Topic P4 — Atomic Structure

Warm-Up & Exam Questions

Atoms may be tiny, but you could bag some big marks in your exams if you know them inside-out. Here are some questions to check just how great your understanding of atoms and radiation really is...

Warm-Up Questions

1) Describe our current, nuclear model of the atom.
2) Give the definition of the term 'isotope'.
3) Which are the most ionising — alpha particles or gamma rays?
4) Outline why beta emitters, rather than alpha or gamma emitters, are used to test the thickness of sheets of metal.
5) Name the type of nuclear radiation, the particles of which are electrons.
6) Name the type of nuclear radiation that is an electromagnetic wave.
7) What is the difference between radioactive contamination and irradiation?
8) Why is contamination by an alpha source more dangerous to humans than irradiation by an alpha source?

Exam Questions

1   Alpha, beta and gamma radiation sources were used to direct radiation at thin sheets of paper and aluminium. A detector was used to measure where radiation had passed through the sheets. The results are shown in **Figure 1**.

Figure 1

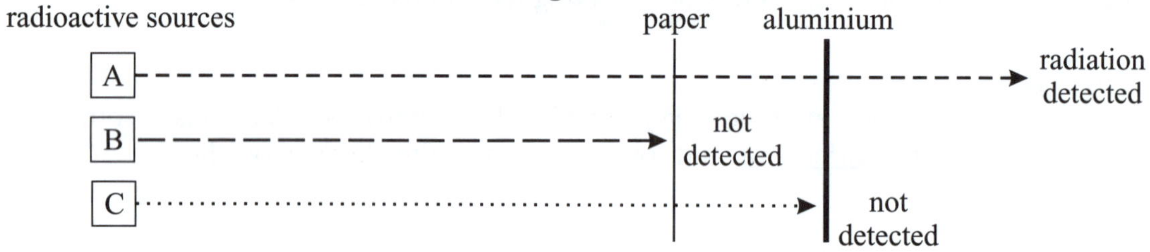

1.1   Name the type of radiation that source C emits. Explain your answer.

[2 marks]

1.2   Give **one** example of a detector that could have been used to detect the radiation.

[1 mark]

2   A sample of a highly ionising radioactive gas has a half-life of two minutes.

2.1   Define what is meant by the term 'half-life'.

[1 mark]

The sample contains a number of unstable nuclei.

2.2   Calculate the fraction of these nuclei that will be present after four minutes.

[2 marks]

Topic P4 — Atomic Structure

Exam Questions

3 A radioactive isotope sample has a half-life of 40 seconds. *Grade 6-7*
The initial activity of the sample is 8000 Bq.

3.1 Calculate the activity after 2 minutes. Give your answer in becquerels.
[2 marks]

3.2 After how many half-lives will the activity have fallen to 250 Bq?
[2 marks]

3.3 The radioactive source is left until its activity falls to 100 Bq.
Calculate the final activity as a percentage of the initial activity.
[2 marks]

4 Table 1 contains information about three atoms. *Grade 6-7*

Table 1

	Mass number	Atomic number
Atom A	32	17
Atom B	33	17
Atom C	32	16

4.1 Name the two types of particle that the nucleus of an atom contains.
[2 marks]

4.2 Define the term 'mass number' in the context of atoms.
[1 mark]

4.3 Which of the two atoms in Table 1 are isotopes of the same element? Explain your answer.
[2 marks]

5 Nuclear equations show what is produced when unstable nuclei decay. *Grade 7-9*

5.1 Draw a symbol that can be used to represent a beta particle in a nuclear equation.
[1 mark]

5.2 Describe what happens to the atomic number and the mass number
of an atom when it undergoes beta decay.
[2 marks]

5.3 Describe what happens to the atomic number and the mass number
of an atom when it undergoes gamma decay.
[2 marks]

5.4 Complete the nuclear equation, shown in Figure 2, which shows
a polonium isotope decaying by alpha emission.

Figure 2

$$\ldots_{84}Po \rightarrow {}^{205}_{\ldots}Pb + {}^{\ldots}_{\ldots}He$$

[3 marks]

Topic P4 — Atomic Structure

Revision Summary for Topics P1-4

Well, that's Topics P1-4 — time to see how much you've absorbed.
- Try these questions and tick off each one when you get it right.
- When you're completely happy with a topic, tick it off.

For even more practice, try the Retrieval Quizzes for Topics P1-4 — just scan the QR codes!

Topic P1 — Energy (p.297-314) ☐

1) Write down four energy stores.
2) Describe the energy transfers that occur when a car collides with a stationary object.
3) What is the definition of the specific heat capacity of a material?
4) Describe an experiment to find the specific heat capacity of a material.
5) Give two equations to calculate power.
6) How can you reduce unwanted energy transfers in a machine with moving components?
7) What is the efficiency of an energy transfer? Give the equation that relates efficiency to power.
8) What is the difference between renewable and non-renewable energy resources?
9) Describe how you can reduce the acid rain caused by burning coal and oil.
10) Explain why the UK plans to use more renewable energy resources in the future.

Topic P2 — Electricity (p.316-332) ☐

11) Define current and state an equation that links current, charge and time, with units for each.
12) Draw the circuit symbols for: a cell, a lamp, a diode, a fuse and an LDR.
13) What is the equation that links potential difference, current and resistance?
14) Explain how the resistance of an LDR varies with light intensity.
15) What happens to the resistance of a thermistor as it gets colder?
16) Explain why adding resistors in parallel decreases the total resistance of a circuit, but adding them in series increases the total resistance.
17) Describe an experiment that could be carried out to investigate how adding resistors in series and parallel affects the total resistance of a circuit.
18) What is the potential difference and the frequency of the UK mains supply?
19) State three equations that can be used to calculate electrical power.
20) What are the functions of step-up and step-down transformers?

Topic P3 — Particle Model of Matter (p.334-338) ☐

21) For each state of matter, describe the arrangement and movement of the particles.
22) Name the six changes of state.
23) A sample of gas is heated in a container with a fixed volume. What happens to the pressure of the gas as it is heated?

Topic P4 — Atomic Structure (p.341-349) ☐

24) Briefly describe how the model of an atom has changed over time.
25) What is the atomic number of an atom?
26) Name four things that may be emitted during radioactive decay.
27) What type of nuclear decay doesn't change the mass or charge of the nucleus?
28) Explain how you would find the half-life of a source, given a graph of its activity over time.
29) Define irradiation and contamination.

Topic P5 — Forces

Contact and Non-Contact Forces

*Just like sports, forces are either **contact** or **non-contact** and involve lots of **interaction**.*

Vectors Have Magnitude and Direction

1) Force is a vector quantity — vector quantities have a magnitude and a direction.
2) Lots of physical quantities are vector quantities:

   Vector quantities: force, velocity, displacement, acceleration, momentum, etc.

3) Some physical quantities only have magnitude and no direction. These are called scalar quantities:

   Scalar quantities: speed, distance, mass, temperature, time, etc.

4) Vectors are usually represented by an arrow — the length of the arrow shows the magnitude, and the direction of the arrow shows the direction of the quantity.

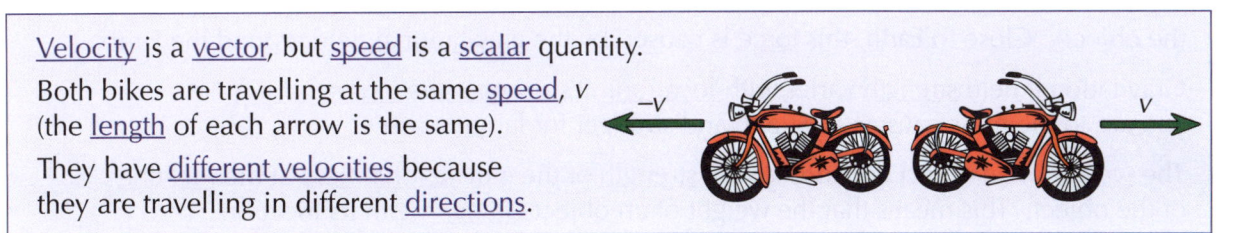

> Velocity is a vector, but speed is a scalar quantity.
> Both bikes are travelling at the same speed, v (the length of each arrow is the same).
> They have different velocities because they are travelling in different directions.

Forces Can be Contact or Non-Contact

1) A force is a push or a pull on an object that is caused by it interacting with something.
2) All forces are either contact or non-contact forces.
3) When two objects have to be touching for a force to act, that force is called a contact force.

   E.g. friction, air resistance, tension in ropes, normal contact force, etc.

4) If the objects do not need to be touching for the force to act, the force is a non-contact force.

   E.g. magnetic force, gravitational force, electrostatic force, etc.

5) When two objects interact, there is a force produced on both objects. An interaction pair is a pair of forces that are equal and opposite and act on two interacting objects. (This is basically Newton's Third Law — see p.372.)

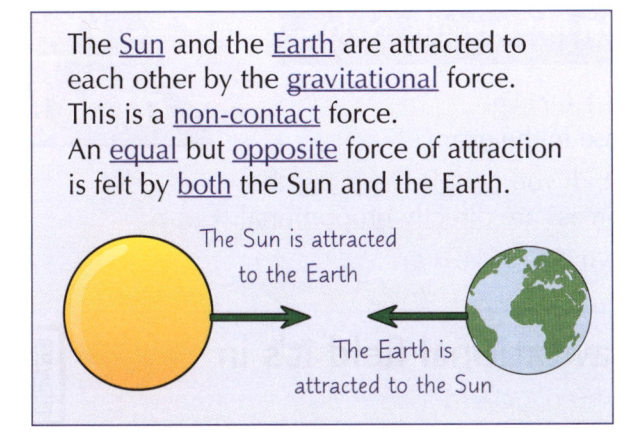

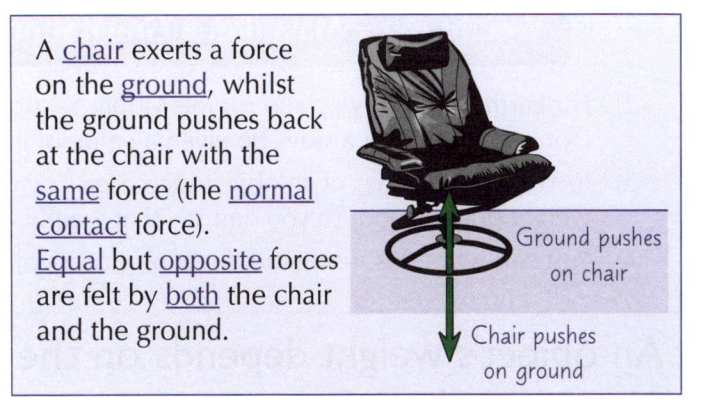

> The Sun and the Earth are attracted to each other by the gravitational force. This is a non-contact force. An equal but opposite force of attraction is felt by both the Sun and the Earth.
>
> The Sun is attracted to the Earth
> The Earth is attracted to the Sun

> A chair exerts a force on the ground, whilst the ground pushes back at the chair with the same force (the normal contact force). Equal but opposite forces are felt by both the chair and the ground.
>
> Ground pushes on chair
> Chair pushes on ground

Weight, Mass and Gravity

Gravity might seem like a rather **heavy** subject to tackle only a page into the topic, but you might end up finding it quite **attractive**. It's pretty important stuff, so make sure you understand it.

Gravitational Force is the Force of Attraction Between Masses

Gravity attracts all masses, but you only notice it when one of the masses is really really big, e.g. a planet. Anything near a planet or star is attracted to it very strongly.

This has two important effects:
1) On the surface of a planet, it makes all things fall towards the ground.
2) It gives everything a weight.

Weight and Mass are Not the Same

1) Mass is just the amount of 'stuff' in an object. For any given object this will have the same value anywhere in the universe.
2) Weight is the force acting on an object due to gravity (the pull of the gravitational force on the object). Close to Earth, this force is caused by the gravitational field around the Earth.
3) Gravitational field strength varies with location. It's stronger the closer you are to the mass causing the field, and stronger for larger masses.
4) The weight of an object depends on the strength of the gravitational field at the location of the object. This means that the weight of an object changes with its location.
5) For example, an object has the same mass whether it's on Earth or on the Moon — but its weight will be different. A 1 kg mass will weigh less on the Moon (about 1.6 N) than it does on Earth (about 9.8 N), simply because the gravitational field strength on the surface of the Moon is less.
6) Weight is a force measured in newtons. You can think of the force as acting from a single point on the object, called its centre of mass (a point at which you assume the whole mass is concentrated). For a uniform object (one that's the same density, p.335, throughout and is a regular shape), this will be at the centre of the object.
7) Weight is measured using a calibrated spring balance (or newtonmeter).
8) Mass is not a force. It's measured in kilograms with a mass balance (an old-fashioned pair of balancing scales).

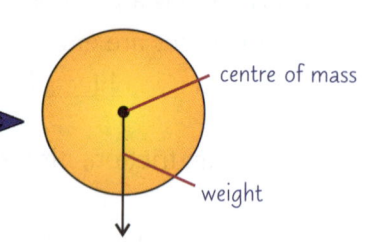

Mass and Weight are Directly Proportional

1) You can calculate the weight of an object if you know its mass (m) and the strength of the gravitational field that it is in (g):

> **Weight (N) = Mass (kg) × Gravitational Field Strength (N/kg)**

2) For Earth, $g \approx 9.8$ N/kg and for the Moon it's around 1.6 N/kg. Don't worry, you'll always be given a value of g to use in the exam.
3) Increasing the mass of an object increases its weight. If you double the mass, the weight doubles too, so you can say that weight and mass are directly proportional.
4) You can write this, using the direct proportionality symbol, as $W \propto m$.

An object's weight depends on the gravitational field it's in

Q1 Calculate the weight in newtons of a 5 kg mass:
 a) on Earth ($g \approx 9.8$ N/kg) b) on the Moon ($g \approx 1.6$ N/kg) [4 marks]

Resultant Forces

*When **multiple forces** act on an object, they can **add together** or **subtract** from each other until there's the equivalent of just **one** force acting in a **single direction**. This is the **resultant force**.*

Free Body Diagrams Show All the Forces Acting on an Object

1) You need to be able to describe all the forces acting on an isolated object or a system (p.297) — i.e. every force acting on the object or system but none of the forces the object or system exerts on the rest of the world.
2) For example, a skydiver's weight acts on her pulling her towards the ground and drag (air resistance) also acts on her, in the opposite direction to her motion.
3) This can be shown using a free body diagram like the ones below.
4) The sizes of the arrows show the relative magnitudes of the forces and the directions show the directions of the forces acting on the object.

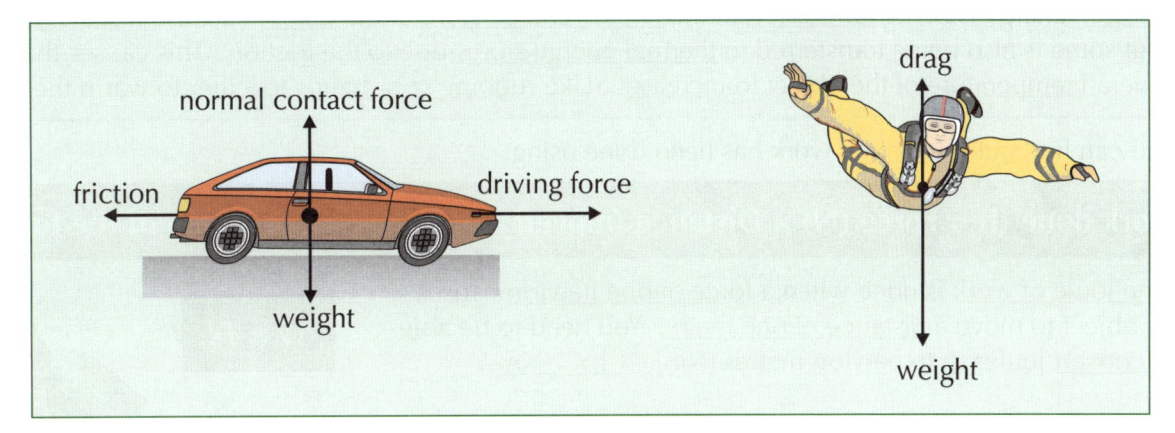

A Resultant Force is the Overall Force on a Point or Object

1) In most real situations there are at least two forces acting on an object along any direction.
2) If you have a number of forces acting at a single point, you can replace them with a single force (so long as the single force has the same effect as all the original forces together).
3) This single force is called the resultant force. For example, there is a downward resultant force acting on the skydiver above.
4) If the forces all act along the same line (they're all parallel), the overall effect is found by adding those going in the same direction and subtracting any going in the opposite direction.

EXAMPLE For the free body diagram shown on the right, calculate the resultant force acting on the van.

1) Consider the horizontal and vertical directions separately.
   Vertical: 1500 − 1500 = 0 N
   Horizontal: 1200 − 1000 N = 200 N
2) State the size and direction of the resultant force.
   The resultant force is 200 N to the left.

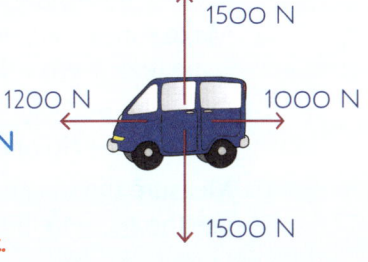

The resultant force — one force with the same result as many...

You'll most often encounter a resultant force as the difference between some kind of driving force and a resistive force, acting in opposite directions along the same line. For example, weight and air resistance for a falling object. But its not always so straightforward. Read on for some techniques for tackling them.

Topic P5 — Forces

Resultant Forces

If A Resultant Force Moves An Object, Work is Done

When a force moves an object through a distance, ENERGY IS TRANSFERRED and WORK IS DONE on the object.

1) To make something move (or keep it moving if there are frictional forces), a force must be applied.
2) The thing applying the force needs a source of energy (like fuel or food).
3) The force does 'work' to move the object and energy is transferred from one store to another (p.298).
4) Whether energy is transferred 'usefully' (e.g. lifting a load) or is 'wasted' (p.303) you can still say that 'work is done'. 'Work done' and 'energy transferred' are the same thing.

When you push something along a rough surface (like a carpet) you are doing work against frictional forces. Energy is being transferred to the kinetic energy store of the object because it starts moving, but some is also being transferred to thermal energy stores due to the friction. This causes the overall temperature of the object to increase. (Like rubbing your hands together to warm them up.)

5) You can find out how much work has been done using:

Work done (J) = Force (N) × Distance (moved along the line of action of the force) (m)

6) One joule of work is done when a force of one newton causes an object to move a distance of one metre. You need to be able to convert joules (J) to newton metres (Nm). 1 J = 1 Nm.

$W = Fs$

Use Scale Drawings to Find Resultant Forces

Working out resultant forces using scale diagrams isn't too tough. Here's what to do:

1) Draw all the forces acting on an object, to scale, 'tip-to-tail'.
2) Then draw a straight line from the start of the first force to the end of the last force — this is the resultant force.
3) Measure the length of the resultant force on the diagram to find the magnitude and the angle to find the direction of the force.

EXAMPLE A man is on an electric bicycle that has a driving force of 4 N north. However, the wind produces a force of 3 N east. Find the magnitude and direction of the resultant force.

1) Start by drawing a scale drawing of the forces acting.
2) Make sure you choose a sensible scale (e.g. 1 cm = 1 N).
3) Draw the resultant from the tail of the first arrow to the tip of the last arrow.
4) Measure the length of the resultant with a ruler and use the scale to find the force in N.
5) Use a protractor to measure the direction as a bearing.

A bearing is an angle measured clockwise from north, given as a 3 digit number, e.g. 10° = 010°.

1 cm = 1 N drawn to scale

Resultant force 5 cm = 5 N

Resultant force is 5 N on a bearing of 037°.

Work done is measured in joules, J — one J equals one Nm...

Although "work done" may sound like an odd phrase, all it means is "energy transferred".

Q1 A force of 20 N pushes an object 20 cm. Calculate the work done on the object. [3 marks]

Topic P5 — Forces

More on Forces

Scale diagrams are useful for more than just *calculating resultant forces*. You can also use them to check if forces are *balanced* and to *split* a force into *component parts*, as you're about to see...

An Object is in Equilibrium if the Forces on it are Balanced

1) If all of the forces acting on an object combine to give a resultant force of zero, the object is in equilibrium.
2) On a scale diagram, this means that the tip of the last force you draw should end where the tail of the first force you drew begins. E.g. for three forces, the scale diagram will form a triangle.

Make sure you draw the last force in the right direction. It's in the opposite direction to how you'd draw a resultant force.

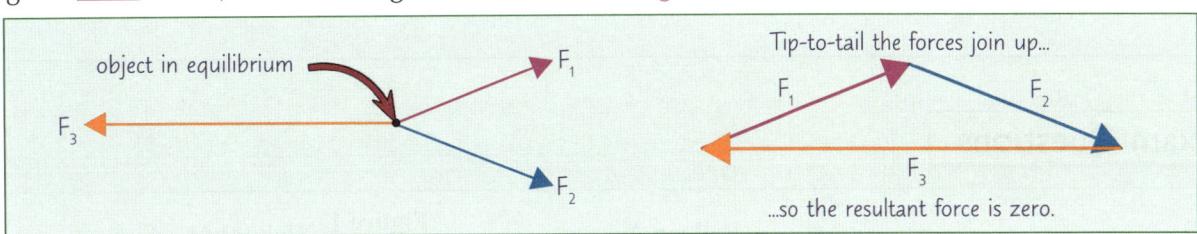

3) You might be given forces acting on an object and told to find a missing force, given that the object is in equilibrium. To do this, draw out the forces you do know (to scale and tip-to-tail), join the end of the last force to the start of the first force.
4) This line is the missing force so you can measure its size and direction.

You Can Split a Force into Components

1) Not all forces act horizontally or vertically — some act at awkward angles.
2) To make these easier to deal with, they can be split into two components at right angles to each other (usually horizontal and vertical).
3) Acting together, these components have the same effect as the single force.
4) You can resolve a force (split it into components) by drawing it on a scale grid.

EXAMPLE Use the grid below to resolve a 10 N force, acting at 53° above the horizontal, into horizontal and vertical components. Give your answers to 1 significant figure.

1) Begin by deciding on a scale for your grid. Here, we have 1 cm² squares, so an easy scale to work with would be if 1 cm = 1 N.
2) Next, draw your force to scale on the grid and at the right angle. Aim to have at least one end of the force arrow at the corner of a square on the grid.
3) Now draw a horizontal arrow from the bottom end of the force and a vertical arrow to the top end of the force to form a right angled triangle.
4) Measure the length of each arrow, and convert the lengths to N using your scale.

Diagrams not to scale.

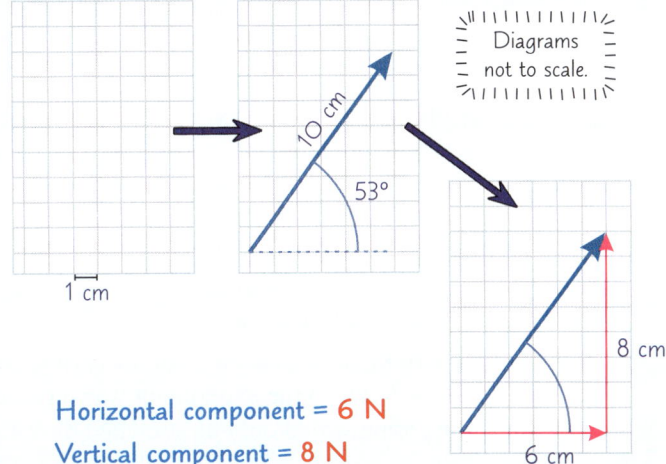

Horizontal component = 6 N
Vertical component = 8 N

With scale diagrams, you must keep things in proportion

Q1 An object in equilibrium is being acted on by three forces. The first force is 0.50 N acting south and the second force is 0.30 N acting on a bearing of 045°. Find the magnitude and bearing of the third force. **[3 marks]**

Topic P5 — Forces

Warm-Up & Exam Questions

Now you've learnt the basics of forces, it's time to act on your new knowledge.
Give these questions a whack and test how well you've forced those facts into your brain.

Warm-Up Questions

1) A tennis ball is dropped from a height.
   Name one contact force and one non-contact force that act on the ball as it falls.
2) Give an example of a vector quantity and a scalar quantity.
3) State the units of: a) gravitational field strength,   b) mass,   c) weight.
4) How can you tell if a set of forces are balanced using a scale diagram?

Exam Questions

1 Figure 1 shows two hot air balloons, labelled with the forces acting on them. *Grade 4-6*

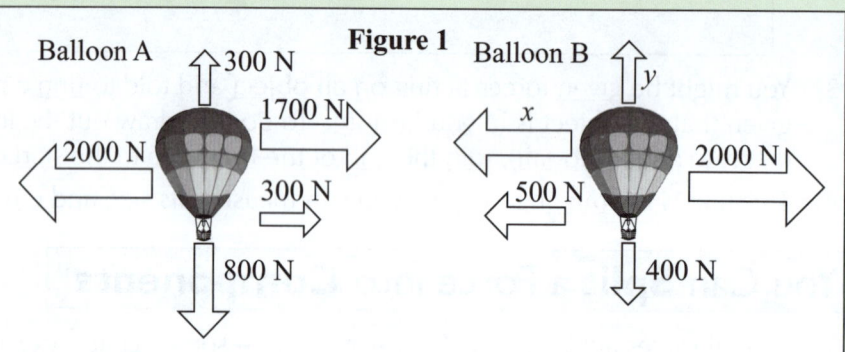

Figure 1

Balloon A: 300 N up, 1700 N right, 2000 N left, 300 N right, 800 N down.
Balloon B: y up, x left, 2000 N right, 500 N left, 400 N down.

1.1 Calculate the size of the resultant force acting on Balloon A and give its direction.

[3 marks]

1.2 The resultant force acting on Balloon B is zero. Calculate the size of forces x and y.

[2 marks]

2 A train moves 700 m in a straight line along a flat track.
The resultant force acting on the train is 42 000 N forwards along the track. *Grade 6-7*

2.1 Calculate the work done by the resultant force as the train moves 700 m. Give your answer in kJ.

[3 marks]

2.2 The weight of the train is 200 000 N. The resistive force on the train is 15 000 N.
Draw a free-body diagram of the train. Model the train as a rectangle.

[4 marks]

3 A spring increases in length when masses are suspended from it, as shown in **Figure 2**. When a metal ball with a mass of 0.10 kg is suspended from the spring, the spring stretches by 3 cm. If the experiment was repeated on Mars, the spring would only be stretched by 1.1 cm. *Grade 7-9*

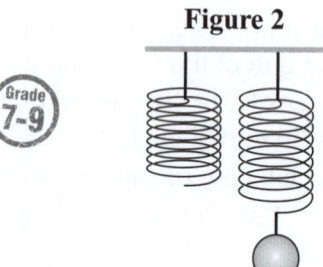

Figure 2

3.1 Suggest why the spring would stretch less on Mars than on Earth.

[3 marks]

3.2 The weight of the ball on Mars is 0.37 N. Calculate the value of g on Mars.

[3 marks]

Topic P5 — Forces

Forces and Elasticity

*Forces don't just make objects **move**, they can also make them **change shape**. Whether they change shape **temporarily** or **permanently** depends on **the object** and the forces applied.*

Stretching, Compressing or Bending Transfers Energy

1) When you apply a force to an object you may cause it to stretch, compress or bend.

2) To do this, you need more than one force acting on the object — otherwise the object would simply move in the direction of the applied force, instead of changing shape.

3) Work is done when a force stretches or compresses an object and causes energy to be transferred to the elastic potential energy store of the object.

4) If it is elastically deformed (see below), ALL this energy is transferred to the object's elastic potential energy store (see p.299).

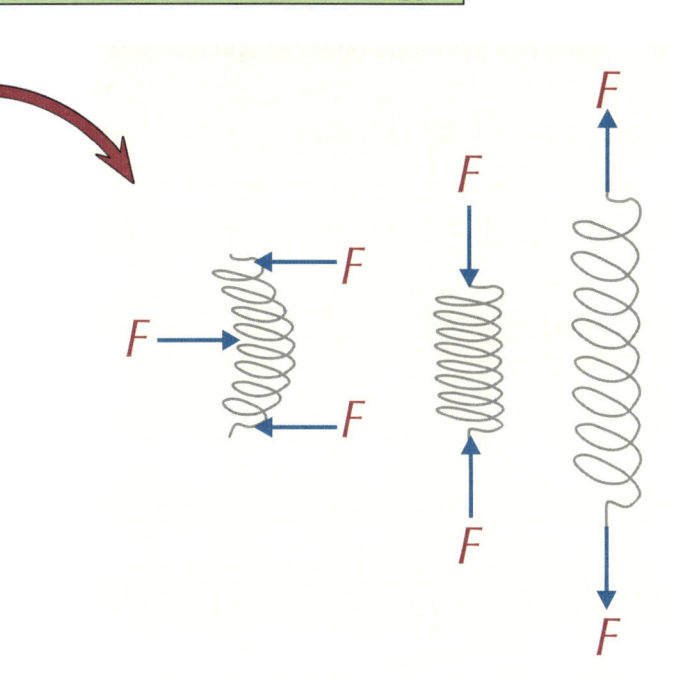

Elastic Deformation

1) An object has been elastically deformed if it can go back to its original shape and length after the force has been removed.

2) Objects that can be elastically deformed are called elastic objects (e.g. a spring).

Inelastic Deformation

1) An object has been inelastically deformed if it doesn't return to its original shape and length after the force has been removed.

Elastic objects are only elastic up to a certain point...

Remember the difference between elastic deformation and inelastic deformation. If an object has been elastically deformed, it will return to its original shape when you remove the force. If it's been inelastically deformed, its shape will have been changed permanently — for example, an over-stretched spring will stay stretched even after your remove the force.

Topic P5 — Forces

Forces and Elasticity

Springs obey a really handy little **equation** that relates the **force** on them to their **extension** — for a while at least. Thankfully, you can **plot a graph** to see where this equation is **valid**.

Extension is Directly Proportional to Force...

If a spring is supported at the top and a weight is attached to the bottom, it stretches.

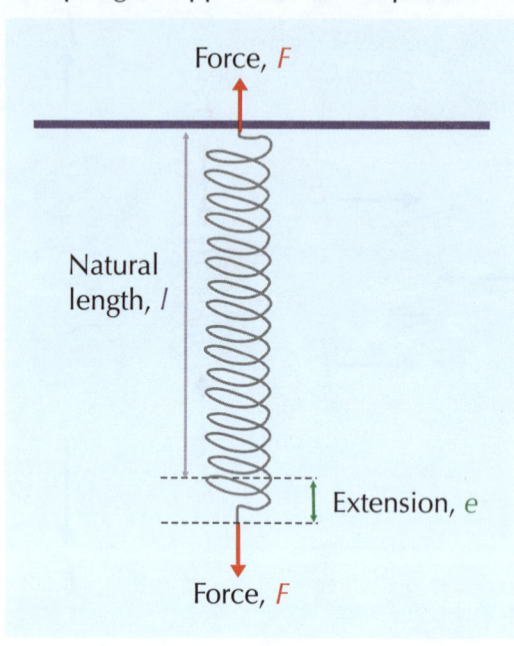

1) The extension of a stretched spring (or certain other elastic objects) is directly proportional to the load or force applied — so $F \propto e$.

2) This is the equation:

$$F = ke$$

Force (N), Spring constant (N/m), Extension (m)

3) The spring constant, k, depends on the material that you are stretching — a stiffer spring has a greater spring constant.

4) The equation also works for compression (where e is just the difference between the natural and compressed lengths — the compression).

...But this Stops Working when the Force is Great Enough

There's a limit to the amount of force you can apply to an object for the extension to keep on increasing proportionally.

1) The graph shows force against extension for an elastic object.

2) There is a maximum force above which the graph curves, showing that extension is no longer proportional to force.

3) This is known as the limit of proportionality and is shown on the graph at the point marked P.

4) You might see graphs with these axes the other way around — extension-force graphs. The graph still starts has a straight part, but starts to curve upwards once you go past the limit of proportionality, instead of downwards.

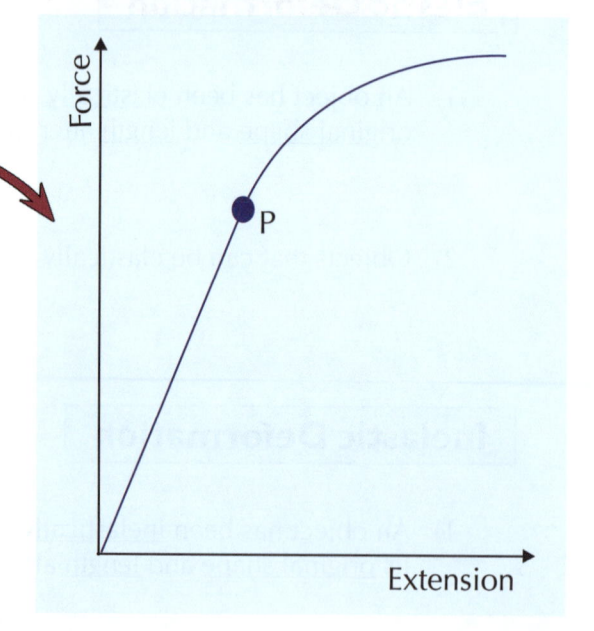

The spring constant is measured in N/m...

Be careful with units when doing calculations with springs. Your values for extension will usually be in centimetres or millimetres, but the spring constant is measured in newtons per metre. So convert the extension into metres before you do any calculations, or you'll get the wrong answer.

Q1 A spring is fixed at one end and a force of 1 N is applied to the other end, causing it to stretch. The spring extends by 2 cm. Calculate the spring constant of the spring. [4 marks]

Topic P5 — Forces

Investigating Springs `PRACTICAL`

*Oh look, here's another one of those **Required Practicals**... This one looks pretty straightforward, but there are a few ways this experiment can **stretch** you. **Read on**, so you won't be past your limits in the exam.*

You Can Investigate the Link Between Force and Extension

1) Before you start, set up the apparatus as shown in the diagram. Make sure you have plenty of extra masses.

2) It's a good idea to measure the mass of each of your masses (with a mass balance) and calculate its weight (the force applied) using $W = mg$ (p.354) at this point. This'll mean you don't have to do a load of calculations in the middle of the experiment.

Before you launch into the investigation, you could do a quick pilot experiment to check your masses are an appropriate size for your investigation:

- Using an identical spring to the one you'll be testing, load it with masses one at a time up to a total of five. Measure the extension each time you add another mass.
- Work out the increase in the extension of the spring for each of your masses. If any of them cause a bigger increase in extension than the previous masses, you've gone past the spring's limit of proportionality. If this happens, you'll need to use smaller masses, or else you won't get enough measurements for your graph.

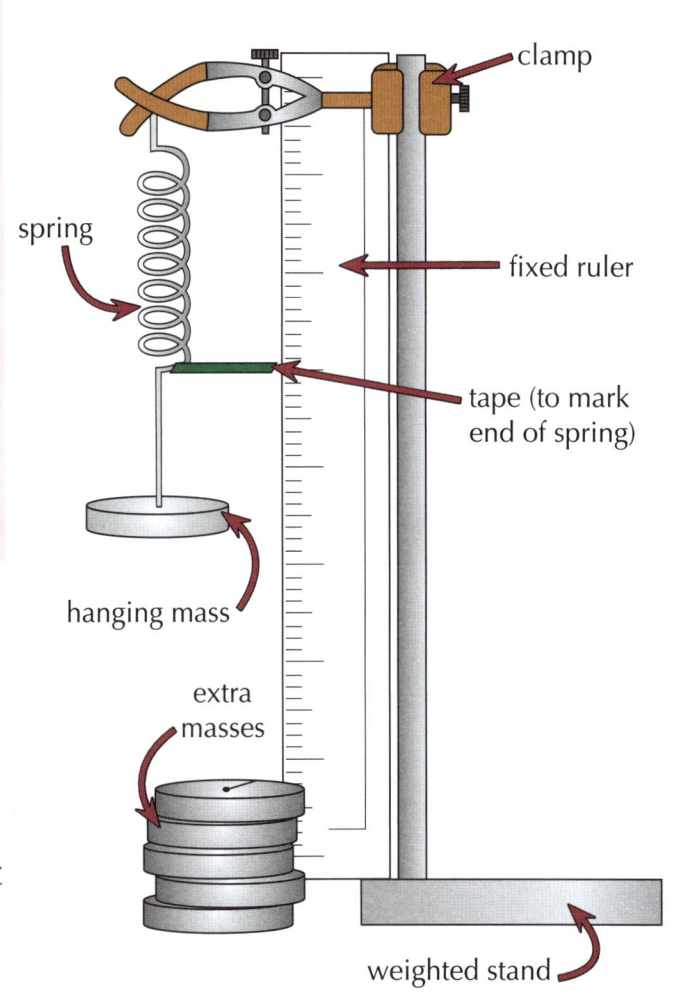

Diagram labels: clamp, spring, fixed ruler, tape (to mark end of spring), hanging mass, extra masses, weighted stand.

Method

1) Measure the natural length of the spring (when no load is applied) with a millimetre ruler clamped to the stand. Make sure you take the reading at eye level and add a marker (e.g. a thin strip of tape) to the bottom of the spring to make the reading more accurate.

2) Add a mass to the spring and allow the spring to come to rest. Record the mass and measure the new length of the spring. The extension is the change in length.

To check whether the deformation is elastic or inelastic, you can remove each mass temporarily and check to see if the spring goes back to the previous extension.

3) Repeat this process until you have enough measurements (no fewer than 6).

Extension is the change in length due to an applied force...

Make sure you know how to calculate the extension of a spring. It's not the just the length of the spring, it's the difference between the stretched length and the original, unstretched length. The extension when no force is acting on a spring should always be zero — unless the spring has been inelastically deformed.

Topic P5 — Forces

PRACTICAL: Investigating Springs

Once you've collected all your **data**, you need to know what to do with it. Fortunately this page is all about how to use the **results** from the **practical** on the last page to work out things like the **spring constant**.

You Can Plot Your Results on a Force-Extension Graph

Once you've collected your results using the method on the last page, you can plot a force-extension graph of your results. It will only start to curve if you exceed the limit of proportionality, but don't worry if yours doesn't (as long as you've got the straight line bit).

- When the line of best fit is a straight line it means there is a linear relationship between force and extension (they're directly proportional, see page 365). $F = ke$, so the gradient of the straight line is equal to k, the spring constant.
- When the line begins to bend, the relationship is now non-linear between force and extension — the spring stretches more for each unit increase in force.

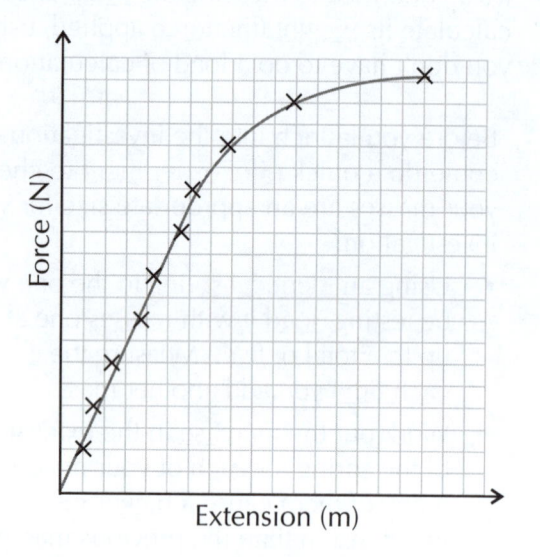

You Can Work Out Energy Stored for Linear Relationships

1) As long as a spring is not stretched past its limit of proportionality, work done in stretching (or compressing) a spring can be found using:

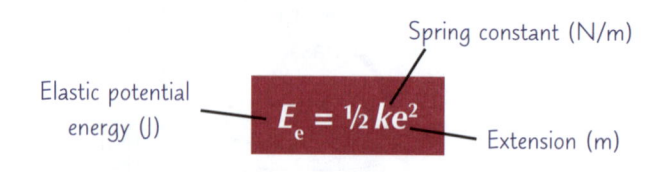

$$E_e = \frac{1}{2} k e^2$$

- Elastic potential energy (J)
- Spring constant (N/m)
- Extension (m)

2) For elastic deformation, this formula can be used to calculate the energy stored in a spring's elastic potential energy store.

3) It's also the energy transferred to the spring as it's deformed (or transferred by the spring as it returns to its original shape).

4) The energy in the elastic potential energy store of a stretched spring is equal to the area under a force-extension graph up to that point:

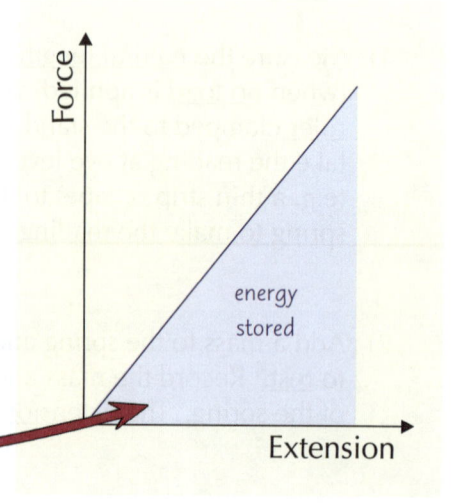

The force-extension graph curves at the limit of proportionality...

In reality, you may not always see the curved part in your force-extension graph for this experiment. Either way, you can still use the gradient of your straight line to calculate the spring constant.

Q1 A spring with a spring constant of 40 N/m extends elastically by 2.5 cm. Calculate the amount of energy stored in its elastic potential energy store. [3 marks]

Topic P5 — Forces

Warm-Up & Exam Questions

It's time to stretch those thinking muscles with another round of questions. Give these a go to test the limits of your newly extended knowledge of springs and elasticity.

Warm-Up Questions

1) True or false? An object which is elastically deformed will not return to its original shape when the force is removed.
2) State the formula linking force, extension and spring constant.
3) What is meant by the limit of proportionality of a spring?
4) Why is it a good idea to do a pilot experiment before starting an experiment on spring extension?

Exam Questions

1 A student wants to investigate how a particular spring extends when a force is applied to it. He plots a graph of force against extension, see **Figure 1**, using the results from his experiment. He then writes a summary of his results. Complete the passage below, using appropriate words to fill in the gaps.

Applying a force to the spring causes it to change ....

Up to the point **E** shown on the graph, the extension of the spring is directly .... to the applied force. In this region the spring also returns to its original shape every time the force is removed. This is known as .... behaviour.

[3 marks]

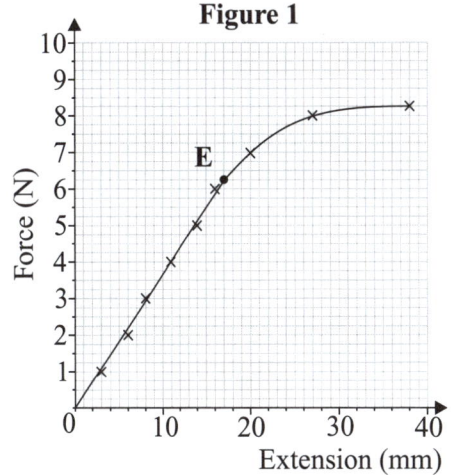

PRACTICAL

2 The teacher shows his students an experiment to show how a spring extends when masses are hung from it. He hangs a number of 90 g masses from a 50 g hook attached to the base of the spring. He records the extension of the spring and the total weight of the masses and hook each time he adds a mass to the bottom of the spring.

2.1 Give the independent variable in this experiment

[1 mark]

2.2 Give **one** control variable in this experiment.

[1 mark]

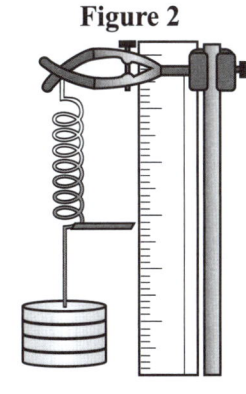

When a force of 4 N is applied to the spring, the spring extends elastically by 2.5 cm.

2.3 Calculate the spring constant of the spring.

[4 marks]

2.4 The teacher applies a 15 N force to the spring. When he removes the force, the spring is 7 cm long. The original length of the spring was 5 cm. Describe what has happened to the spring.

[1 mark]

Topic P5 — Forces

Distance, Displacement, Speed and Velocity

There are a lot of very similar **variables** on this page, but they're **different** in some **very important** ways, so prepare to pay extra close attention. It's down to whether they're a **vector** or a **scalar** quantity.

Distance is Scalar, Displacement is a Vector

1) Distance is just how far an object has moved. It's a scalar quantity (p.353) so it doesn't involve direction.
2) Displacement is a vector quantity. It measures the distance and direction in a straight line from an object's starting point to its finishing point — e.g. the plane flew 5 metres north. The direction could be relative to a point, e.g. towards the school, or a bearing (a three-digit angle from north, e.g. 035°).
3) If you walk 5 m north, then 5 m south, your displacement is 0 m but the distance travelled is 10 m.

Speed and Velocity are Both How Fast You're Going

1) Speed and velocity both measure how fast you're going, but speed is a scalar and velocity is a vector:

> Speed is just how fast you're going (e.g. 30 mph or 20 m/s) with no regard to the direction.
> Velocity is speed in a given direction, e.g. 30 mph north or 20 m/s, 060°.

2) This means you can have objects travelling at a constant speed with a changing velocity. This happens when the object is changing direction whilst staying at the same speed. An object moving in a circle at a constant speed has a constantly changing velocity, as the direction is always changing (e.g. a car going around a roundabout).
3) If you want to measure the speed of an object that's moving with a constant speed, you should time how long it takes the object to travel a certain distance, e.g. using a ruler and a stopwatch. You can then calculate the object's speed from your measurements using this formula:

$$s = vt$$ distance travelled (m) = speed (m/s) × time (s)

4) Objects rarely travel at a constant speed. E.g. when you walk, run or travel in a car, your speed is always changing. For these cases, the formula above gives the average (mean) speed during that time.

You Need to Know Some Typical Everyday Speeds

1) Whilst every person, train, car etc. is different, there is usually a typical speed that each object travels at. Remember these typical speeds for everyday objects:

> A person walking — 1.5 m/s   A car — 25 m/s
> A person running — 3 m/s   A train — 55 m/s
> A person cycling — 6 m/s   A plane — 250 m/s

2) Lots of different things can affect the speed something travels at. For example, the speed at which a person can walk, run or cycle depends on their fitness, their age, the distance travelled and the terrain (what kind of land they're moving over, e.g. roads, fields) as well as many other factors.
3) It's not only the speed of objects that varies. The speed of sound (330 m/s in air) changes depending on what the sound waves are travelling through, and the speed of wind is affected by many factors.
4) Wind speed can be affected by things like temperature, atmospheric pressure and if there are any large buildings or structures nearby (e.g. forests reduce the speed of the air travelling through them).

Speed equals distance over time...

Remember those typical speeds of objects — you might need to use them to make estimates.
Q1   A sprinter runs 200 m in 25 s. Calculate his speed.   [3 marks]

Topic P5 — Forces

Acceleration

Acceleration is the *rate of change* of *velocity*. For cases of *constant acceleration*, there's a really useful *equation* you can use to calculate all sorts of *variables* of *motion*.

Acceleration is How Quickly You're Speeding Up

1) Acceleration is definitely <u>not</u> the same as <u>velocity</u> or <u>speed</u>.
2) Acceleration is the <u>change in velocity</u> in a certain amount of <u>time</u>.
3) You can find the average acceleration of an object using:

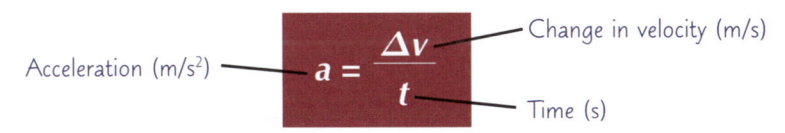

Acceleration (m/s²) — $a = \dfrac{\Delta v}{t}$ — Change in velocity (m/s), Time (s)

EXAMPLE
A cat accelerates at 2.5 m/s² from 2.0 m/s to 6.0 m/s. Find the time it takes to do this.
$t = \Delta v \div a$
$= (6.0 - 2.0) \div 2.5 = 1.6$ s

4) <u>Deceleration</u> is just <u>negative</u> acceleration (if something <u>slows down</u>, the change in velocity is <u>negative</u>).
5) You might have to <u>estimate</u> the <u>acceleration</u> (or <u>deceleration</u>) of an object. To do this, you need the <u>typical speeds</u> from the previous page:

EXAMPLE A car is travelling along a road, when it collides with a tree and comes to a stop. Estimate the deceleration of the car.

1) First, give a <u>sensible speed</u> for the car to be travelling at. — The typical speed of a car is ~25 m/s.
2) Next, <u>estimate</u> how long it would take the car to <u>stop</u>. — The car comes to a stop in ~1 s.
3) Put these numbers into the <u>acceleration equation</u>.
   $a = \Delta v \div t$
   $= (-25) \div 1$
   $= -25$ m/s²

   The ~ symbol just means it's an approximate value (or answer).

4) The question asked for the <u>deceleration</u>, so you can lose the <u>minus sign</u> (which shows the car is slowing down):
   So the deceleration is ~25 m/s²

Uniform Acceleration Means a Constant Acceleration

1) <u>Constant acceleration</u> is sometimes called <u>uniform acceleration</u>.
2) Acceleration <u>due to gravity</u> (g) is <u>uniform</u> for objects in free fall. It's roughly equal to <u>9.8 m/s²</u> near the Earth's surface and has the same value as gravitational field strength (p.354).
3) You can use this <u>equation</u> for <u>uniform</u> acceleration:

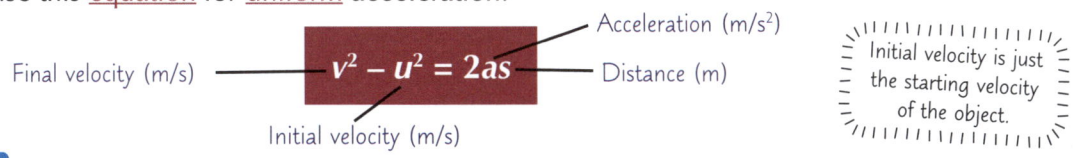

Final velocity (m/s) — $v^2 - u^2 = 2as$ — Acceleration (m/s²), Distance (m), Initial velocity (m/s)

Initial velocity is just the starting velocity of the object.

EXAMPLE A van travelling at 23 m/s starts decelerating uniformly at 2.0 m/s² as it heads towards a built-up area 112 m away. What will its speed be when it reaches the built-up area?

1) First, <u>rearrange</u> the equation so v^2 is on one side.
   $v^2 = u^2 + 2as$
2) Now put the <u>numbers</u> in — remember a is <u>negative</u> because it's a deceleration.
   $v^2 = 23^2 + (2 \times -2.0 \times 112)$
   $= 81$
3) Finally, <u>square root</u> the whole thing.
   $v = \sqrt{81} = 9$ m/s

An object is accelerating if its velocity is changing...

Don't forget — you can only use that second equation when the acceleration is <u>uniform</u>.

Q1 A ball is dropped from a height, h, above the ground. The speed of the ball just before it hits the ground is 7 m/s. Calculate the height the ball is dropped from. (acceleration due to gravity ≈ 9.8 m/s²)   [3 marks]

Topic P5 — Forces

Distance-Time Graphs

It's time for some more exciting **graphs**. **Distance-time graphs** contain a lot of **information**, but they can look a bit complicated. Read on to get to grips with the **rules** of the graphs, and all will become clear.

You Can Show Journeys on Distance-Time Graphs

If an object moves in a straight line, its distance travelled can be plotted on a distance-time graph.

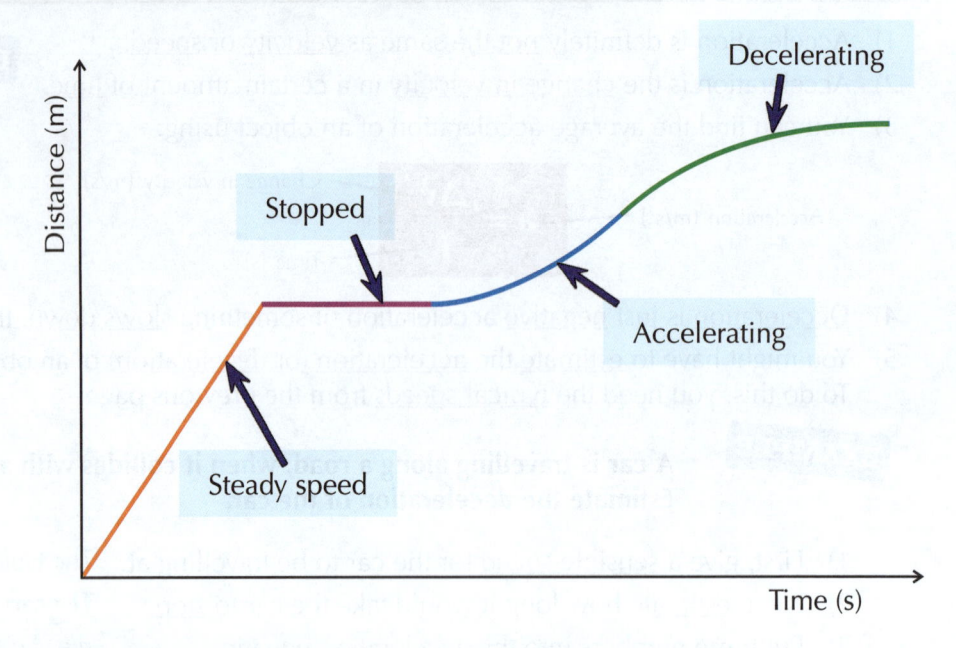

Graph labels: Distance (m) vs Time (s); Steady speed, Stopped, Accelerating, Decelerating

The Shape of the Graph Shows How the Object is Moving

1) Gradient = speed. (The steeper the graph, the faster the object is going.)
   This is because: speed = distance ÷ time = (change in vertical axis) ÷ (change in horizontal axis).

2) Flat sections are where the object's stationary — it's stopped.

3) Straight uphill sections mean it is travelling at a steady speed.

4) Curves represent acceleration or deceleration (p.365).

5) A steepening curve means the object's speeding up (increasing gradient).

6) A levelling off curve means it's slowing down (decreasing gradient).

7) If the object is changing speed (accelerating) you can find its speed at a point by finding the gradient of the tangent to the curve at that point, p.11.

Read the axes of any graph you get given carefully...

REVISION TIP: Make sure you don't get confused between distance-time graphs and velocity-time graphs. They can look similar, but tell you different things and have different rules, as you're about to find out...

Topic P5 — Forces

Velocity-Time Graphs

Even more graphs! Just like distance-time graphs, velocity-time graphs are a great way of representing journeys. There's a lot of information in them, so make sure you know how to get the most out of them.

You Can Also Show them on a Velocity-Time Graph

How an object's velocity changes as it travels can be plotted on a velocity-time graph.

1) Gradient = acceleration, since acceleration is change in velocity ÷ time.

2) Flat sections represent travelling at a steady speed.

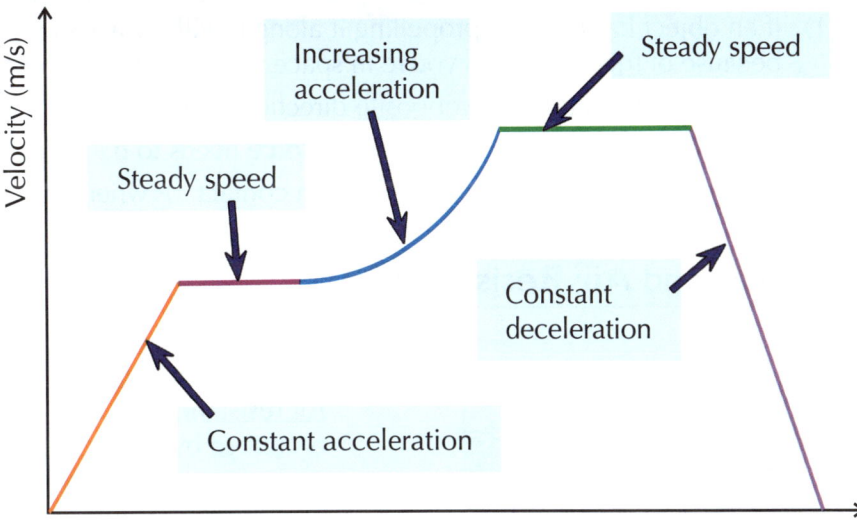

3) The steeper the graph, the greater the acceleration or deceleration.

4) Uphill sections (/) are acceleration. Downhill sections (\) are deceleration. A curve means changing acceleration.

If the graph is curved, you can use a tangent to the curve (p.11) at a point to find the acceleration at that point.

5) The area under any section of the graph (or all of it) is equal to the distance travelled in that time interval. If the section under the graph is irregular, it's easier to find the area by counting the squares under the line and multiplying the number by the value of one square.

EXAMPLE

The velocity-time graph of a car's journey is plotted and shown below.
a) Calculate the acceleration of the car over the first 10 s.
b) How far does the car travel in the first 15 s of the journey?

a) This is just the gradient of the line between 0 and 10 s:

$a = \Delta v \div t = 20 \div 10 = 2$ m/s^2

b) Split the area into a triangle and a rectangle, then add together their areas. Or find the value of one square, count the total number of squares under the line, and then multiply these two values together.

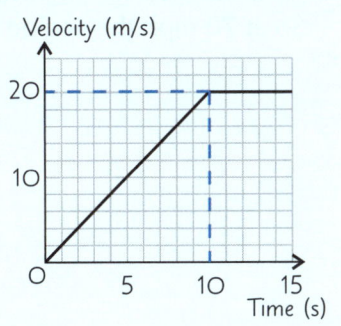

Area = (½ × 10 × 20) + (5 × 20)
= 200 m
1 square = 2 m/s × 1 s = 2 m
Area = 100 squares
= 100 × 2 = 200 m

The gradient of a velocity-time graph gives the acceleration

Q1 Sketch a velocity-time graph for an object that travels at a steady speed, then accelerates at a constant rate, then moves at a steady speed (that is different to the initial speed). [3 marks]

Q2 A stationary car starts accelerating increasingly for 10 s until it reaches a speed of 20 m/s. It travels at this speed for 20 s until the driver sees a hazard and brakes. He decelerates uniformly, coming to a stop 4 s after braking. Draw the velocity-time graph for this journey. [3 marks]

Topic P5 — Forces

Drag

*Revision can be a bit of a **drag**, but hey, you're over halfway though the topic now.
No use **slowing down** now — however, there's quite a bit of that on this page.*

Friction is Always There to Slow Things Down

1) If an object has no force propelling it along it will always slow down and stop because of friction (unless you're in space where there's nothing to rub against).
2) Friction always acts in the opposite direction to movement.
3) To travel at a steady speed, the driving force needs to balance the frictional forces.
4) You get friction between two surfaces in contact, or when an object passes through a fluid (drag).

Drag and Air Resistance

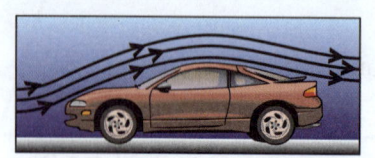

Air flows easily over a streamlined car.

1) Drag is the resistance you get in a fluid (a gas or a liquid). Air resistance is a type of drag — it's the frictional force produced by the air acting on a moving object.

2) The most important factor by far in reducing drag is keeping the shape of the object streamlined. This is where the object is designed to allow fluid to flow easily across it, reducing drag.

3) Parachutes work in the opposite way — they want as much drag as they can get.

Drag Increases as Speed Increases

Frictional forces from fluids always increase with speed.

A car has much more friction to work against when travelling at 70 mph compared to 30 mph. So at 70 mph the engine has to work much harder just to maintain a steady speed.

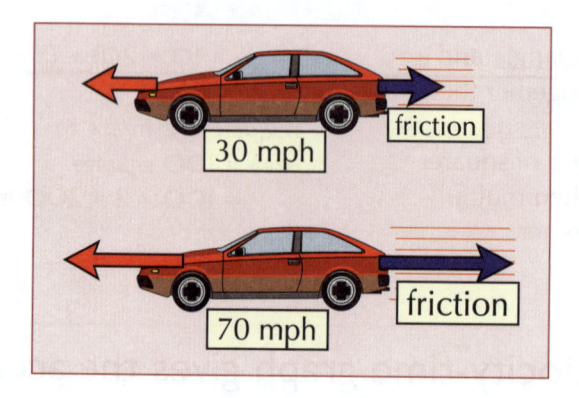

EXAM TIP

Use the right words when talking about resistive forces...
Be as specific as you can when talking about forces which act against motion (i.e. resistive forces). If an object is travelling through air, simply referring to the resistive force as 'drag' may not be enough to get you the marks — you'll need to specify the force is air resistance.

Topic P5 — Forces

Terminal Velocity

If an object **falls** for long enough, it will reach its **terminal velocity**. It's all about **balance** between **weight** and **air resistance**. **Parachutes** work by **decreasing** your terminal velocity.

Objects **Falling** Through **Fluids** Reach a **Terminal Velocity**

1) When falling objects first set off, the force of gravity is much more than the frictional force slowing them down, so they accelerate.

2) As the speed increases the friction builds up.

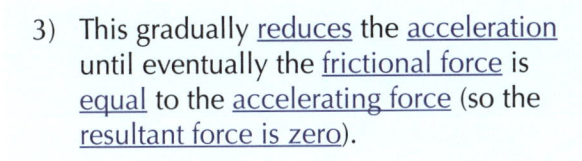

3) This gradually reduces the acceleration until eventually the frictional force is equal to the accelerating force (so the resultant force is zero).

4) It will have reached its maximum speed or terminal velocity and will fall at a steady speed.

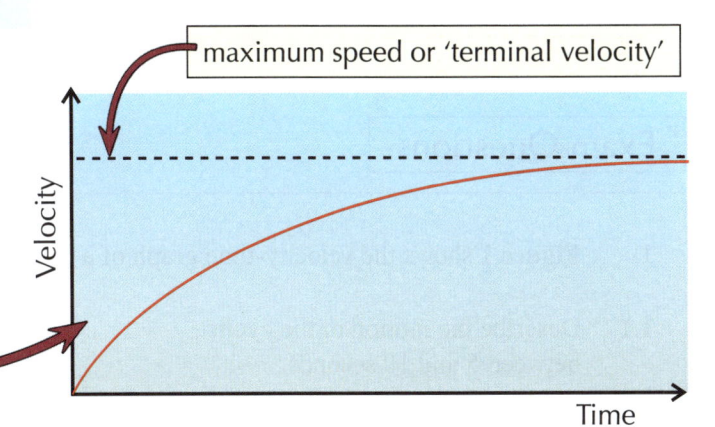

maximum speed or 'terminal velocity'

Terminal Velocity Depends on **Shape** and **Area**

1) Typically, the less streamlined an object is, the lower its terminal velocity.

2) So objects with large surface areas tend to have lower terminal velocities.

3) For example, if you dropped a marble and a beach ball off a tall building, the marble's terminal velocity would be higher than the terminal velocity of the beach ball.

4) This is because there is more air resistance acting on the beach ball, at any given speed.

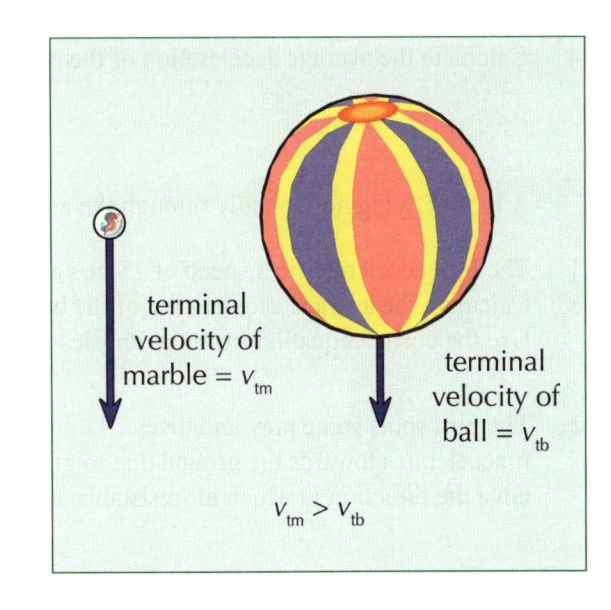

terminal velocity of marble = v_{tm}

terminal velocity of ball = v_{tb}

$v_{tm} > v_{tb}$

5) So the beach ball spends less time accelerating (and so doesn't speed up as much) before the air resistance is large enough to equal the accelerating force.

Topic P5 — Forces

Warm-Up & Exam Questions

Slow down, it's not time to move on to the next section just yet. First it's time to check that all the stuff you've just read is still running around your brain. Dive into these questions.

Warm-Up Questions

1) What is the difference between speed and velocity?
2) Suggest the typical speeds of: a) a person running,   b) a train,   c) a plane.
3) How is acceleration shown on a distance-time graph?
4) Describe the shape of the line on a velocity-time graph for an object travelling at a steady speed.
5) In general, how does the air resistance acting on a car change as the car's speed increases?

Exam Questions

1 Figure 1 shows the velocity-time graph of a cyclist. *(Grade 4-6)*

1.1 Describe the motion of the cyclist between 5 and 10 seconds.
[2 marks]

1.2 Calculate how far the cyclist travelled between 2 and 5 seconds.
[2 marks]

1.3 Calculate the acceleration of the cyclist between 2 and 5 seconds.
[2 marks]

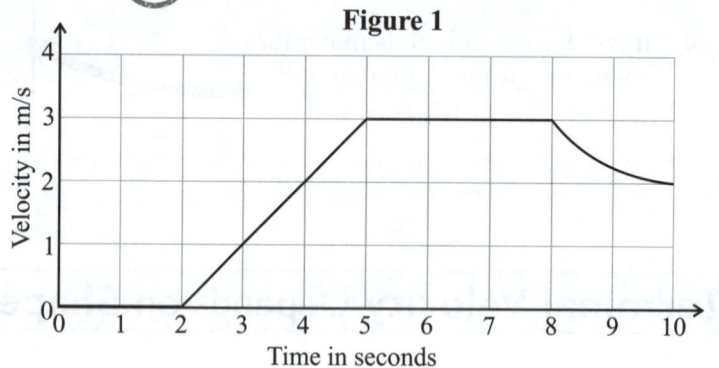

1.4 Calculate the average deceleration of the cyclist between 8 and 10 seconds.
[3 marks]

2 A bird is flying horizontally through the air at a speed of 9.0 m/s. *(Grade 6-7)*

2.1 The bird accelerates to a speed of 15 m/s across a distance of 15 m.
Calculate the average acceleration of the bird over this distance.
Use the correct equation from the Physics Equation Sheet on page 542.
[3 marks]

2.2 The bird spots some prey and dives.
It accelerates towards the ground due to gravity, and is acted on by air resistance, a resistive force.
Give the direction in which air resistance acts on the bird.
[1 mark]

2.3 The bird dives for a total of 5.00 seconds and covers a distance of 102 metres.
Calculate the average speed of the bird during the dive.
[3 marks]

2.4 When the bird dives, it pulls its wings inwards. This makes its body more streamlined.
Explain, with reference to the forces acting on the bird when it dives,
how this affects the speed at which the bird can dive.
[2 marks]

Topic P5 — Forces

Newton's First and Second Laws

*Way back in the 1660s, some clever chap named **Isaac Newton** worked out some **Laws of Motion**...*

A Force is Needed to Change Motion

This may seem simple, but it's important. Newton's First Law says that a resultant force (p.355) is needed to make something start moving, speed up or slow down:

> If the resultant force on a stationary object is zero, the object will remain stationary. If the resultant force on a moving object is zero, it'll just carry on moving at the same velocity (same speed and direction).

So, when a train or car or bus or anything else is moving at a constant velocity, the resistive and driving forces on it must all be balanced. The velocity will only change if there's a non-zero resultant force acting on the object.

1) A non-zero resultant force will always produce acceleration (or deceleration) in the direction of the force.

2) This "acceleration" can take five different forms: starting, stopping, speeding up, slowing down and changing direction.

3) On a free body diagram, the arrows will be unequal.

Acceleration is Proportional to the Resultant Force

1) The larger the resultant force acting on an object, the more the object accelerates — the force and the acceleration are directly proportional. You can write this as $F \propto a$.

2) Acceleration is also inversely proportional to the mass of the object — so an object with a larger mass will accelerate less than one with a smaller mass (for a fixed resultant force).

3) There's an incredibly useful formula that describes Newton's Second Law:

$$F = ma$$

Resultant force (N) — Acceleration (m/s^2) — Mass (kg)

You can use Newton's Second Law to get an idea of the forces involved in everyday transport. Large forces are needed to produce large accelerations:

EXAMPLE Estimate the resultant force on a car as it accelerates from rest to a typical speed.

1) Estimate the acceleration of the car, using typical speeds from page 364.
   A typical speed of a car is ~25 m/s. It takes ~10 s to reach this.
   So $a = \Delta v \div t = 25 \div 10 = 2.5$ m/s^2

   The ~ means approximately.

2) Estimate the mass of the car.
   Mass of a car is ~1000 kg.

3) Put these numbers into Newton's Second Law.
   So using $F = ma = 1000 \times 2.5 = 2500$ N
   So the resultant force is ~2500 N

Newton's second law says $F = ma$...

Sadly there's no handy equation to summarise Newton's first law. Make sure you've got your head around both laws, before moving on to Newton's third law on the next page

Q1   Find the force needed for an 80 kg man on a 10 kg bike to accelerate at 0.25 m/s^2. [2 marks]

Inertia and Newton's Third Law

Newton's Third Law and *inertia* sound pretty straightforward, but things can quickly get confusing...

Inertia is the Tendency for Motion to Remain Unchanged

1) Until acted upon by a resultant force, objects at rest stay at rest and objects moving at a steady speed will stay moving at that speed (Newton's First Law). This tendency to continue in the same state of motion is called inertia.
2) An object's inertial mass measures how difficult it is to change the velocity of an object.
3) Inertial mass can be found using Newton's Second Law of $F = ma$ (see the last page). Rearranging this gives $m = F \div a$, so inertial mass is just the ratio of force over acceleration.

Newton's Third Law — Interaction Pairs are Equal and Opposite

Newton's Third Law says: **When two objects interact, the forces they exert on each other are equal and opposite.**

1) If you push something, say a shopping trolley, the trolley will push back against you, just as hard.
2) And as soon as you stop pushing, so does the trolley. Kinda clever really.
3) So far so good. The slightly tricky thing to get your head round is this — if the forces are always equal, how does anything ever go anywhere? The important thing to remember is that the two forces are acting on different objects.

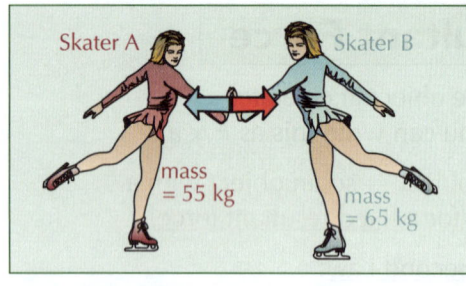

When skater A pushes on skater B, she feels an equal and opposite force from skater B's hand (the 'normal contact' force). Both skaters feel the same sized force, in opposite directions, and so accelerate away from each other.

Skater A will be accelerated more than skater B, though, because she has a smaller mass — remember $a = F \div m$.

An example of Newton's Third Law in an equilibrium situation is a man pushing against a wall. As the man pushes the wall, there is a normal contact force acting back on him. These two forces are the same size. As the man applies a force and pushes the wall, the wall 'pushes back' on him with an equal force.

It can be easy to get confused with Newton's Third Law when an object is in equilibrium. E.g. a book resting on a table is in equilibrium. The weight of the book is equal to the normal contact force. The weight of the book pulls it down, and the normal reaction force from the table pushes it up. This is NOT Newton's Third Law. These forces are different types and they're both acting on the book.

The pairs of forces due to Newton's Third Law in this case are:
1) The weight of book is pulled down by gravity from Earth (W_B) and the book also pulls back up on the Earth (W_E).
2) The normal contact force from the table pushing up on the book (N_B) and the normal contact force from the book pushing down on the table (N_T).

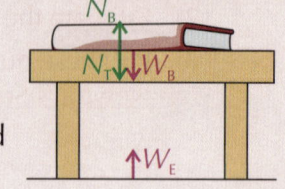

Interacting objects exert equal and opposite forces on each other

Q1 A car moves at a constant velocity along a road, so that it is in equilibrium. Give an example of a pair of forces that demonstrate Newton's Third Law in this situation. [1 mark]

Topic P5 — Forces

Investigating Motion **PRACTICAL**

*Here comes another **Required Practical**. This one's all about testing **Newton's Second Law**. It uses some nifty bits of kit that you may not have seen before, so make sure you follow the instructions closely.*

You can Investigate how Mass and Force Affect Acceleration

It's time for an experiment that tests Newton's 2nd Law, $F = ma$ (p.371).

1) Set up the apparatus shown above. Set up the trolley so it holds a piece of card with a gap in the middle that will interrupt the signal on the light gate twice. If you measure the length of each bit of card that will pass through the light gate and input this into the software, the light gate can measure the velocity for each bit of card. It can use this to work out the acceleration of the trolley.

2) Connect the trolley to a piece of string that goes over a pulley and is connected on the other side to a hook (that you know the mass of and can add more masses to).

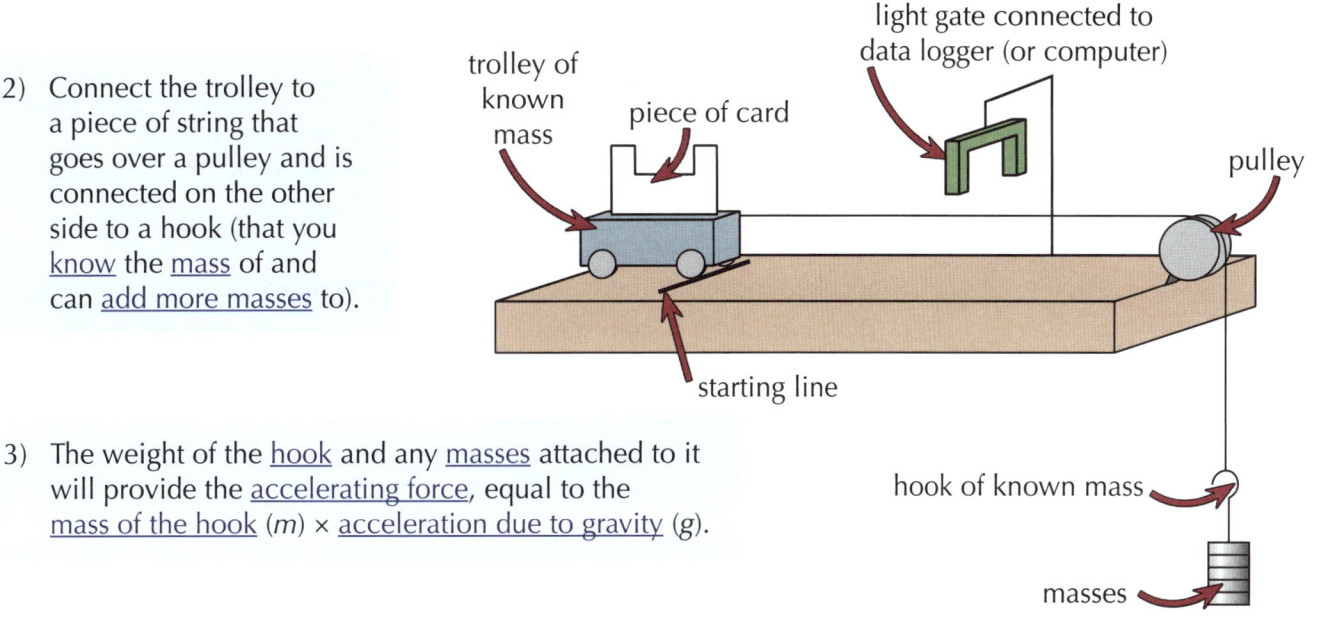

3) The weight of the hook and any masses attached to it will provide the accelerating force, equal to the mass of the hook (m) × acceleration due to gravity (g).

4) The weight of the hook and masses accelerates both the trolley and the masses, so you are investigating the acceleration of the system (the trolley and the masses together).

5) Mark a starting line on the table the trolley is on, so that the trolley always travels the same distance to the light gate.

6) Place the trolley on the starting line and hold it in place. You should let the hook and any masses on the hook hang so the string is taut (not loose and touching the table). Then, release the trolley.

7) Record the acceleration measured by the light gate as the trolley passes through it. This is the acceleration of the whole system.

8) Repeat this twice more to get an average acceleration.

Topic P5 — Forces

PRACTICAL: Investigating Motion

*Now you've set up the **equipment**, and you're used to how it works, it's time to start **adjusting** your **variables**. Take care with the **method** here — there are some important points you don't want to miss.*

Varying Mass and Force

1) To investigate the effect of mass, add masses to the trolley, one at a time, to increase the mass of the system.
2) Don't add masses to the hook, or you'll change the force.
3) Record the average acceleration for each mass.

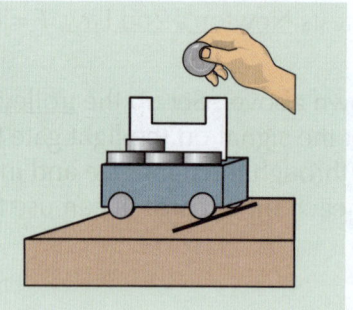

> The friction between the trolley and the bench might affect your acceleration measurements. You could use an air track to reduce this friction (a track which hovers a trolley on jets of air).

To investigate the effect of force, you need to keep the total mass of the system the same, but change the mass on the hook.

1) To do this, start with all the masses loaded onto the trolley, and transfer the masses to the hook one at a time, to increase the accelerating force (the weight of the hanging masses).
2) The mass of the system stays the same as you're only transferring the masses from one part of the system (the trolley) to another (the hook).
3) Record the average acceleration for each force.

Newton's Second Law Can Explain the Results

1) Newton's Second Law can be written as $F = ma$. Here, F = weight of the hanging masses, m = mass of the whole system and a = acceleration of the system.

2) By adding masses to the trolley, the mass of the whole system increases, but the force applied to the system stays the same. This should lead to a decrease in the acceleration of the trolley, as $a = F \div m$.

3) By transferring masses to the hook, you are increasing the accelerating force without changing the mass of the whole system. So increasing the force should lead to an increase in the acceleration of the trolley.

PRACTICAL TIP — **This experiment has a lot of steps, so don't speed through it...**
Make sure the string is the right length and there's enough space for the hanging masses to fall. There needs to be enough space so that the masses don't hit the floor before the trolley has passed through the light gate fully — if they hit the floor, the force won't be applied the whole way through the trolley's journey, so you won't get an accurate measurement for the speed.

Topic P5 — Forces

Warm-Up & Exam Questions

Now you've gotten yourself on the right side of the law(s of motion), it's time to put your knowledge on trial. Have a go at cross-examining these questions.

Warm-Up Questions

1) What is the resultant force on an object moving at a constant velocity?
2) Boulders A and B are accelerated from 0 m/s to 5 m/s in 10 s. Boulder A required a force of 70 N, and Boulder B required a force of 95 N. Which boulder has the greater inertial mass?
3) True or False? Two interacting objects exert equal and opposite forces on each other.
4) In a trolley-and-pulley system, as in the practical on page 373, where should you put masses to increase the mass of the system without increasing the force on the trolley?

Exam Questions

1 Dahlia's cricket bat has a mass of 1.2 kg.
She uses it to hit a ball with a mass of 160 g forwards with a force of 500 N.

Grade 4-6

1.1 State the force that the ball exerts on the bat. Explain your answer.

[2 marks]

1.2 Which is greater — the acceleration of the bat or the ball? Explain your answer.

[2 marks]

2 A camper van has a mass of 2500 kg. It is driven along a straight, level road at a constant speed of 90.0 kilometres per hour.

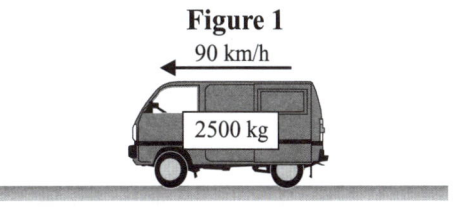

Grade 6-7

Figure 1
90 km/h
2500 kg

2.1 A headwind begins blowing with a force of 200 N, causing the van to slow down. Calculate the van's deceleration.

[3 marks]

The van begins travelling at a constant speed before colliding with a stationary 10.0 kg traffic cone. The traffic cone accelerates in the direction of the van's motion with an acceleration of 29.0 m/s².

2.2 Calculate the force applied to the traffic cone by the van.

[2 marks]

2.3 Calculate the deceleration of the van during the collision.
Assume all of the force applied by the cone to the van causes the deceleration.

[3 marks]

PRACTICAL

3* Stefan is investigating how acceleration varies with force.
He has a 1 kg trolley, attached by a pulley to a 0.5 kg hanging hook.
He also has eight 100 g masses. When the hook is released, the trolley rolls along a table, and passes through a light gate which calculates its acceleration.

Grade 7-9

Describe an experiment that Stefan can perform using this equipment to investigate the relationship between force and acceleration.

[4 marks]

Topic P5 — Forces

Stopping Distances

*Knowing what affects **stopping distances** is especially useful for everyday life, as well as the exam.*

Stopping Distance is the Sum of Two Distances

1) In an emergency (e.g. a hazard ahead in the road), a driver may perform an emergency stop. This is where maximum force is applied by the brakes in order to stop the car in the shortest possible distance. The longer it takes to perform an emergency stop, the higher the risk of crashing into whatever's in front.

2) The distance it takes to stop a car in an emergency (its stopping distance) is found by:

Stopping Distance = Thinking Distance + Braking Distance

3) The thinking distance — how far the car travels during the driver's reaction time (the time between the driver seeing a hazard and applying the brakes).

4) The braking distance — the distance taken to stop under the braking force (once the brakes are applied).

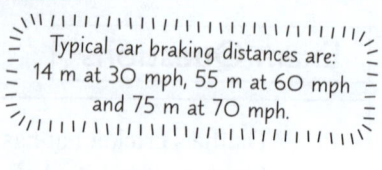

Typical car braking distances are: 14 m at 30 mph, 55 m at 60 mph and 75 m at 70 mph.

Many Factors Affect Your Total Stopping Distance

Thinking distance is affected by:
- Your speed — the faster you're going the further you'll travel during the time you take to react.
- Your reaction time — the longer your reaction time (see next page), the longer your thinking distance. This can be affected by tiredness, drugs or alcohol. Distractions can affect your ability to react.

Braking distance is affected by:
- Your speed — for a given braking force, the faster a vehicle travels, the longer it takes to stop (p.378).
- The weather or road surface — if it is wet or icy, or there are leaves or oil on the road, there is less grip (and so less friction) between a vehicle's tyres and the road, which can cause tyres to skid.
- The condition of your tyres — if the tyres of a vehicle are bald (they don't have any tread left) then they cannot get rid of water in wet conditions. This leads to them skidding on top of the water.
- How good your brakes are — if brakes are worn or faulty, they won't be able to apply as much force as well-maintained brakes, which could be dangerous when you need to brake hard.

You need to be able to describe the factors affecting stopping distance and how this affects safety — especially in an emergency.

> For example: Icy conditions increase the chance of skidding (and so increase the stopping distance) so driving too close to other cars in icy conditions is unsafe. The longer your stopping distance, the more space you need to leave in front in order to stop safely.

Speed limits are really important because speed affects the stopping distance so much.

EXAM TIP

Stopping distance = thinking distance + braking distance
The exam might ask you to give factors, other than speed, which affect thinking or braking distances, so make sure you know all the factors that affect each of these and what their effects are.

Topic P5 — Forces

Reaction Times

Reaction times are an *important factor* in *thinking distances*. They're also super easy to *test* for yourself. Read on for a simple *experiment* you can do in the lab.

You can Measure Reaction Times with the Ruler Drop Test

Everyone's reaction time is different, but a typical reaction time is between 0.2 and 0.9 s and many different factors affect it (see previous page).

You can do simple experiments to investigate your reaction time, but as reaction times are so short, you haven't got a chance of measuring one with a stopwatch. One way of measuring reaction times is to use a computer-based test (e.g. clicking a mouse when the screen changes colour). Another is the ruler drop test. Here's how to carry it out:

1) Sit with your arm resting on the edge of a table (this should stop you moving your arm up or down during the test). Get someone else to hold a ruler so it hangs between your thumb and forefinger, lined up with zero. You may need a third person to be at eye level with the ruler to check it's lined up.

2) Without giving any warning, the person holding the ruler should drop it. Close your thumb and finger to try to catch the ruler as quickly as possible.

3) The measurement on the ruler at the point where it is caught is how far the ruler dropped in the time it takes you to react.

4) The longer the distance, the longer the reaction time.

5) You can calculate how long the ruler falls for (the reaction time) because acceleration due to gravity is constant (roughly 9.8 m/s²).

> E.g. say you catch the ruler at 20 cm. From p.365 you know: $v^2 - u^2 = 2as$.
> $u = 0$, $a = 9.8$ m/s² and $s = 0.2$ m, so: $v = \sqrt{2 \times 9.8 \times 0.2 + 0}$ = 2.0 m/s (to 2 s.f.)
> v is equal to the change in velocity of the ruler.
> From page 365 you also know: $a = \Delta v \div t$ so $t = \Delta v \div a = 2.0 \div 9.8 = 0.2$ s (to 1 s.f.)
> This gives your reaction time.

6) It's pretty hard to do this experiment accurately, so you should do a lot of repeats. The results will be better if the ruler falls straight down — you might want to add a blob of modelling clay to the bottom to stop it from waving about.

7) Make sure it's a fair test — use the same ruler for each repeat, and have the same person dropping it.

8) You could try to investigate some factors affecting reaction time, e.g. you could introduce distractions by having some music playing or by having someone talk to you while the test takes place (see the previous page for more on the factors affecting reaction time).

9) Remember to still do lots of repeats and calculate the mean reaction time with distractions, which you can compare to the mean reaction time without distractions.

The further the ruler falls, the longer the reaction time

Q1 Mark's reaction time is tested using the ruler drop test. He is tested in the early afternoon and at night. In the afternoon, he catches the ruler after it has fallen a distance of 16.2 cm. At night, he catches the ruler after it has fallen 18.5 cm.
    a) Calculate Mark's reaction time in the afternoon.
       Give your answer to 2 significant figures. [5 marks]
    b) Explain why Mark's thinking distance might be longer
       when driving in the evening. [2 marks]

Topic P5 — Forces

Braking Distances

*So you know the basics of **stopping distances** now, but how do the brakes actually work to **slow down a car**? Well, it's all down to **friction** and **transferring energy** away from the wheels to the brakes.*

Braking Relies on Friction Between the Brakes and Wheels

1) When the brake pedal is pushed, this causes brake pads to be pressed onto the wheels. This contact causes friction, which causes work to be done.

2) The work done between the brakes and the wheels transfers energy from the kinetic energy stores of the wheels to the thermal energy stores of the brakes. The brakes increase in temperature.

3) The faster a vehicle is going, the more energy it has in its kinetic store, so the more work needs to be done to stop it. This means that a greater braking force is needed to make it stop within a certain distance.

4) A larger braking force means a larger deceleration. Very large decelerations can be dangerous because they may cause brakes to overheat (so they don't work as well) or could cause the vehicle to skid.

You Can Estimate the Braking Force Required to Stop

You can estimate the braking force required to make a vehicle decelerate and come to a stop. As you're only estimating the force, this is a place where you may well need to use typical values:

EXAMPLE

A car travelling at a typical speed makes an emergency stop to avoid hitting a hazard 25 m ahead.
Estimate the braking force needed to produce this deceleration.

For a refresher on typical speed values, head back to page 364.

1) Assume the deceleration is uniform, and rearrange $v^2 - u^2 = 2as$ to find the deceleration.

2) Then use $F = ma$, with $m = $ ~1000 kg.

$v = $ ~25 m/s $m = $ ~1000 kg.
$a = (v^2 - u^2) \div 2s = (0^2 - 25^2) \div (2 \times 25) = -12.5$

$F = ma$
$F = 1000 \times 12.5 = 12\,500$ N, so F is ~12 500 N

Typical values, always there when you need them...

Make sure you memorise the typical speed values on page 364. It shouldn't matter if they're slightly off, but they need to be of roughly the right size, or your calculations won't make sense. If you're asked about a vehicle that you don't know the typical speed or mass of, try to use those you do know as a guide. For example, a bus will have a greater typical mass than a car (1000 kg) but a slightly smaller typical speed than a car (25 m/s), as it's bigger and travels on slower routes.

Topic P5 — Forces

Momentum

*A **large rugby player** running very **fast** has much **more momentum** than a **skinny** bloke out for a Sunday afternoon **stroll**. Momentum's something that **all moving objects have**, so you better get your head around it.*

Momentum = Mass × Velocity

Momentum is mainly about how much 'oomph' an object has. It's a property that all moving objects have.
1) The greater the mass of an object, or the greater its velocity, the more momentum the object has.
2) Momentum is a vector quantity — it has size and direction.
3) You can work out the momentum of an object using:

$p = mv$ momentum (kg m/s) = mass (kg) × velocity (m/s)

EXAMPLE
A 50 kg cheetah is running at 60 m/s. Calculate its momentum.

$p = mv = 50 \times 60 = 3000$ kg m/s

EXAMPLE
A boy has a mass of 30 kg and a momentum of 75 kg m/s. Calculate his velocity.

$v = p \div m = 75 \div 30 = 2.5$ m/s

Momentum Before = Momentum After

In a closed system, the total momentum before an event (e.g. a collision) is the same as after the event. This is called conservation of momentum.

A closed system is just a fancy way of saying that no external forces act.

In snooker, balls of the same size and mass collide with each other. Each collision is an event where the momentum of each ball changes, but the overall momentum stays the same (momentum is conserved).

Before: The red ball is stationary, so it has zero momentum. The white ball is moving with a velocity v, so has a momentum of $p = mv$.

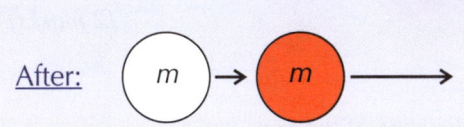

After: The white ball hits the red ball, causing it to move. The red ball now has momentum. The white ball continues moving, but at a much smaller velocity (and so a much smaller momentum). The combined momentum of the red and white ball is equal to the original momentum of the white ball, mv.

A moving car hits into the back of a parked car. The crash causes the two cars to lock together, and they continue moving in the direction that the original moving car was travelling, but at a lower velocity.

Before: The momentum was equal to mass of moving car × its velocity.
After: The mass of the moving object has increased, but its momentum is equal to the momentum before the collision. So an increase in mass causes a decrease in velocity.

If the momentum before an event is zero, then the momentum after will also be zero. E.g. in an explosion, the momentum before is zero. After the explosion, the pieces fly off in different directions, so that the total momentum cancels out to zero.

Momentum is always conserved in a closed system...

Conservation of momentum is incredibly handy, so get your head down and practise it.

Q1   Calculate the momentum of a 60 kg woman running at 3 m/s.   [2 marks]

Topic P5 — Forces

Warm-Up & Exam Questions

Time to apply the brakes for a second and put your brain through an MOT. Try out these questions. If you can handle these, your exam should be clear of hazards.

Warm-Up Questions

1) What is meant by 'thinking distance'?
2) What must be added to the thinking distance to find the total stopping distance of a car?
3) Give an example of how poor weather can affect your ability to stop a car before hitting a hazard.
4) Describe an experiment you could carry out, using a ruler, to measure the reaction time of an individual.
5) What energy transfer occurs when a car brakes?
6) Calculate the momentum of a 2.5 kg rabbit running through a garden at 10 m/s.
7) What is meant by the conservation of momentum?
8) What is the total momentum before and after an explosion?

Exam Question

1 A van is travelling along a flat road. *Grade 4-6*

1.1 The van driver spots a hazard ahead and makes an emergency stop.
The van comes to a stop in 58 m, and travels 41 m in the time between applying the brakes and stopping.
Calculate the thinking distance during this emergency stop.

[2 marks]

1.2 The next morning, there is a heavy frost on the road.
Explain how the braking distance of the van may be affected by these conditions.

[2 marks]

The van is fitted with a new set of brakes and new tyres.

1.3 State how this will affect the thinking distance and the braking distance of the van.

[2 marks]

2 In a demolition derby, cars drive around an arena and crash into each other. *Grade 6-7*

2.1 Give the equation linking momentum, velocity and mass.

[1 mark]

2.2 One car has a mass of 650 kg and a velocity of 15.0 m/s.
Calculate the momentum of the car.

[2 marks]

The car collides with the back of a stationary car with a mass of 750 kg.
The two cars stick together.

2.3 Give the momentum of the two cars after the collision.

[1 mark]

2.4 Explain how the speed of the two cars moving together after the collision differs from the speed of the moving car before the collision.

[2 marks]

Topic P5 — Forces

Topic P6 — Waves

Wave Basics

*Waves **transfer energy** from one place to another **without** transferring any **matter** (stuff).*

Waves Transfer Energy in the Direction they are Travelling

When waves travel through a medium, the particles of the medium oscillate and transfer energy between each other. BUT overall, the particles stay in the same place — only energy is transferred.

> For example, if you drop a twig into a calm pool of water, ripples form on the water's surface. The ripples don't carry the water (or the twig) away with them though.
>
> Similarly, if you strum a guitar string and create sound waves, the sound waves don't carry the air away from the guitar and create a vacuum.

Waves have Amplitude, Wavelength and Frequency

1) The amplitude of a wave is the maximum displacement of a point on the wave from its undisturbed position.

2) The wavelength is the distance between the same point on two adjacent waves (e.g. between the trough of one wave and the trough of the wave next to it).

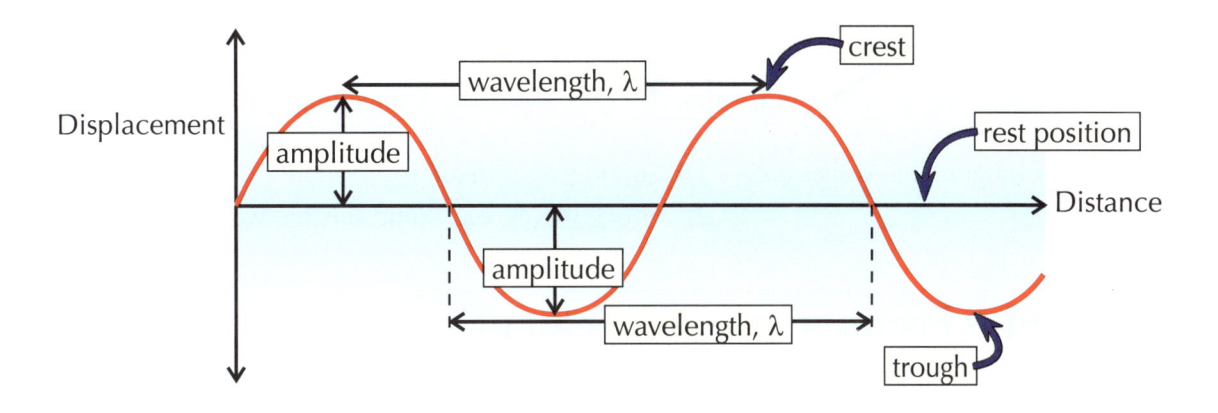

3) Frequency is the number of complete waves passing a certain point per second. Frequency is measured in hertz (Hz). 1 Hz is 1 wave per second.

The period of a wave is the amount of time it takes for a full cycle of the wave to pass a point. You can find it from the frequency of the wave using the formula:

$$T = \frac{1}{f}$$

Period (s) — Frequency (Hz)

The only thing a wave transfers is energy...

REVISION TIP It's really important that you understand this stuff really well, or the rest of this topic will simply be a blur. Make sure you can sketch the wave diagram above and can label all the features from memory. Then check you know all the definitions and the equation linking period and frequency.

Topic P6 — Waves

Transverse and Longitudinal Waves

*All waves are either **transverse** or **longitudinal**. Read on to find out more...*

Transverse Waves Have Perpendicular Vibrations

In transverse waves, the oscillations (vibrations) are perpendicular (at 90°) to the direction of energy transfer. A spring wiggled from side to side gives a transverse wave:

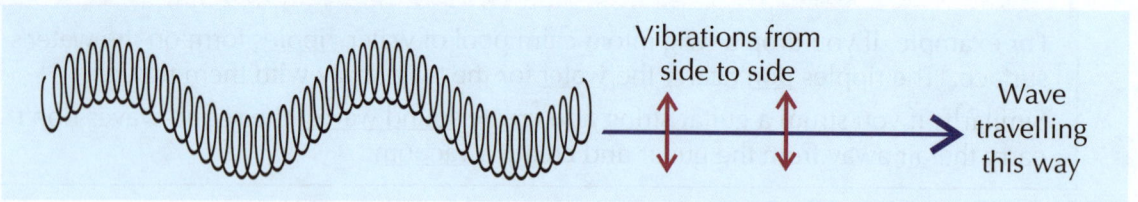

Vibrations from side to side
Wave travelling this way

Most waves are transverse, including:
1) All electromagnetic waves, e.g. light (page 388).
2) Ripples and waves in water (page 383).
3) A wave on a string (page 384).

Water waves, shock waves and waves in springs and ropes are all examples of mechanical waves.

Longitudinal Waves Have Parallel Vibrations

In longitudinal waves, the oscillations are parallel to the direction of energy transfer. If you push the end of a spring, you get a longitudinal wave.

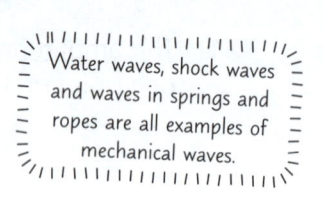

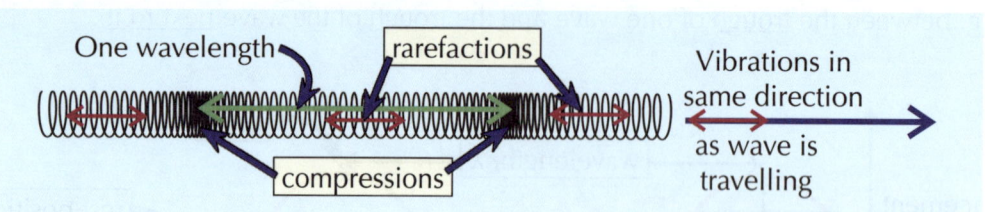

One wavelength — rarefactions — compressions
Vibrations in same direction as wave is travelling

Other examples of longitudinal waves are:
1) Sound waves in air, ultrasound.
2) Shock waves, e.g. some seismic waves.

Wave Speed = Frequency × Wavelength

The wave speed is the speed at which energy is being transferred (or the speed the wave is moving at). The wave equation applies to all waves:

$$v = f\lambda$$

Wave speed (m/s) — Wavelength (m) — Frequency (Hz)

EXAMPLE

A radio wave has a frequency of 12.0×10^6 Hz. Find its wavelength. (The speed of radio waves in air is 3.0×10^8 m/s.)

1) To find λ, you need to rearrange the equation $v = f\lambda$. $\lambda = v \div f$
2) Substitute in the values for v and f to calculate λ. $= (3.0 \times 10^8) \div (12.0 \times 10^6) =$ **25 m**

Light waves are transverse and sound waves are longitudinal...

There's a key difference between a longitudinal wave and a transverse wave — it's all to do with the direction in which the wave oscillates compared to the direction in which it transfers energy.

Q1   A wave has a speed of 0.15 m/s and a wavelength of 7.5 cm.
     Calculate its frequency.   [4 marks]

Topic P6 — Waves

Experiments with Waves

*Measuring the **speed of waves** isn't that simple. It calls for crafty methods...*

Use an Oscilloscope to Measure the Speed of Sound

By attaching a signal generator to a speaker you can generate sounds with a specific frequency. You can use two microphones and an oscilloscope to find the wavelength of the sound waves generated.

1) Set up the oscilloscope so the detected waves at each microphone are shown as separate waves.

2) Start with both microphones next to the speaker, then slowly move one away until the two waves are aligned on the display, but have moved exactly one wavelength apart.

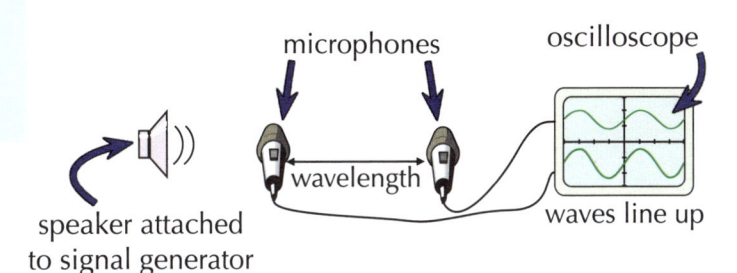

3) Measure the distance between the microphones to find one wavelength (λ).

4) You can then use the formula $v = f\lambda$ (see last page) to find the speed (v) of the sound waves passing through the air — the frequency (f) is whatever you set the signal generator to (around 1 kHz is sensible).

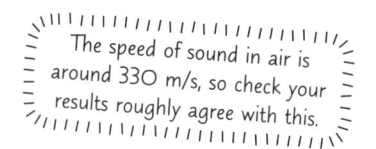

The speed of sound in air is around 330 m/s, so check your results roughly agree with this.

Measure the Speed of Water Ripples Using a Lamp

Using a signal generator attached to the dipper of a ripple tank, you can create water waves at a set frequency.

PRACTICAL

1) Dim the lights and turn on the lamp — you'll see a wave pattern made by the shadows of the wave crests on the screen below the tank.

2) The distance between each shadow line is equal to one wavelength (p.381). Measure the distance between shadow lines that are 10 wavelengths apart, then divide this distance by 10 to find the average wavelength. This is a suitable method for measuring small wavelengths.

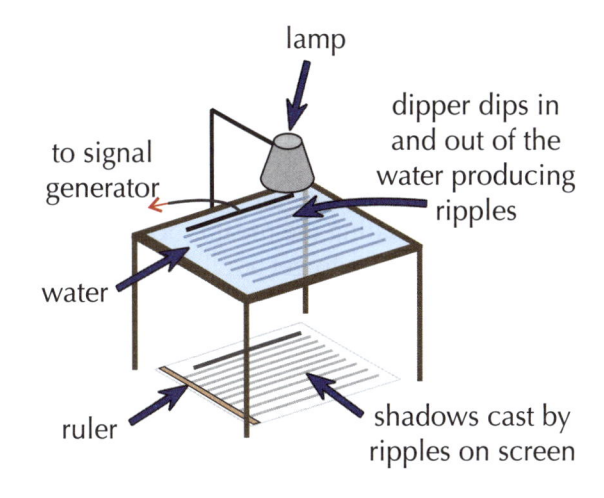

3) If you're struggling to measure the distance, you could take a photo of the shadows and ruler, and find the wavelength from the photo instead.

4) Use $v = f\lambda$ to calculate the speed of the waves.

5) This set-up is suitable for investigating waves, because it allows you to measure the wavelength without disturbing the waves.

Topic P6 — Waves

PRACTICAL: Experiments with Waves

*One more **wave experiment** coming up. This time, it's to do with **waves on strings**.*

You can Use the Wave Equation for Waves on Strings

In this practical, you create a wave on a string. Again, you use a signal generator, but this time you attach it to a vibration transducer which converts the signals to vibrations.

1) Set up the equipment shown below, then turn on the signal generator and vibration transducer. The string will start to vibrate.

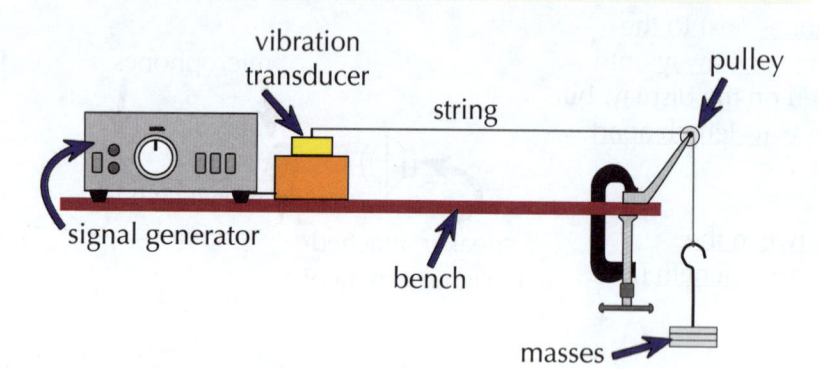

This set-up is suitable for investigating waves on a string because it's easy to see and measure the wavelength (and frequency).

2) You can adjust the frequency setting on the signal generator to change the length of the wave created on the string. You should keep adjusting the frequency of the signal generator until there appears to be a clear wave on the string. This happens when a whole number of half-wavelengths fit exactly on the string (you want at least four or five half-wavelengths ideally). The frequency you need will depend on the length of string between the pulley and the transducer, and the masses you've used.

3) You need to measure the wavelength of the wave. The best way to do this accurately is to measure the length of all the half-wavelengths on the string in one go, then divide by the total number of half-wavelengths to get the mean half-wavelength (see p.9 for more on calculating the mean). You can then double this value to get a full wavelength.

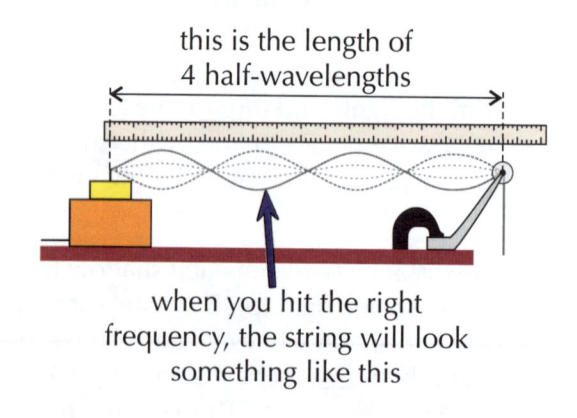

when you hit the right frequency, the string will look something like this

4) The frequency of the wave is whatever the signal generator is set to.

5) You can find the speed of the wave using $v = f\lambda$.

PRACTICAL TIP: Learn the methods for all these practicals...

These experiments seem complicated, but they all have a few things in common. First, you set the frequency on the signal generator, then find the length of the resulting wave (this tends to be the fiddly bit). You can then use the equation $v = f\lambda$ to find the wave speed. That's about it.

Topic P6 — Waves

Refraction

*Refraction is when light waves are **bent** when they enter a **new media** (which is a posh word for material).*

All Waves Can be **Absorbed**, **Transmitted** or **Reflected**

When a wave arrives at a boundary between two different materials, three things can happen:

1) The wave is absorbed by the second material — this transfers energy to the material's energy stores. Often, the energy is transferred to a thermal energy store, which leads to heating (this is how a microwave works, see page 390).

2) The wave is transmitted through the second material — the waves carry on travelling through the new material. This often leads to refraction (more on this below). This can be used in communications (p.389) as well as in the lenses of glasses and cameras.

3) The wave is reflected — this is where the incoming wave is neither absorbed nor transmitted, but instead is 'sent back' away from the second material.

What actually happens depends on the wavelength of the wave and the properties of the materials involved.

Refraction — Waves **Changing Direction** at a **Boundary**

1) When a wave crosses a boundary between two materials it changes speed.
2) If the wave is travelling along the normal it will change speed, but it's NOT refracted.
3) If the wave hits the boundary at an angle it changes direction — it's refracted.
4) The wave bends towards the normal if it slows down. It bends away from the normal if it speeds up.
5) How much it's refracted by depends on how much the wave speeds up or slows down, which usually depends on the density of the two materials (usually the higher the density of a material, the slower a wave travels through it).
6) The optical density of a material is a measure of how quickly light can travel through it — the higher the optical density, the slower light waves travels through it.
7) The wavelength of a wave changes when it is refracted, but the frequency stays the same.

If a light wave hits the boundary 'face on', it carries on in the same direction.

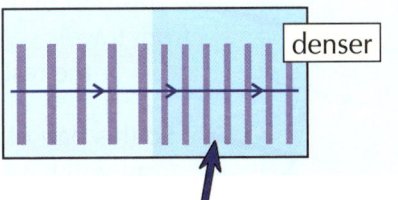

[denser]

But if a wave meets a different medium at an angle...

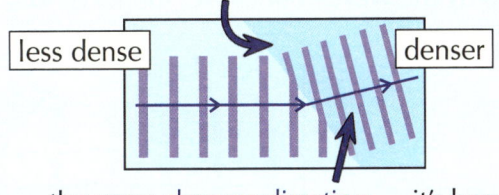

[less dense] [denser]

... the wave changes direction — it's been REFRACTED.

The wave fronts (see next page) being closer together shows a change in wavelength (and so a change in velocity).

REVISION TIP

Hitting a boundary at an angle leads to refraction...

If you can't remember which way a wave bends when it hits an optically denser material at an angle, imagine a skier skiing from some nice smooth snow onto some rough ground at an angle. The ski hitting the rough ground first slows down first, so they will swing towards that side.

Topic P6 — Waves

Refraction

Refraction is a really important **property of waves**, but it can be tricky to get your head around. Thankfully, there's a load of ways to **show** refraction in **diagrams**, to help you visualise what's going on.

You can Construct a Ray Diagram to show Refraction

Rays are straight lines that are perpendicular to wave fronts. They show the direction a wave is travelling in. You can construct a ray diagram for a refracted light ray.

1) First, draw the boundary between your two materials and the normal (a line at 90° to the boundary).

2) Draw an incident ray that meets the normal at the boundary. The angle between the ray and the normal is the angle of incidence. (If you're given this angle, make sure to draw it carefully with a protractor.)

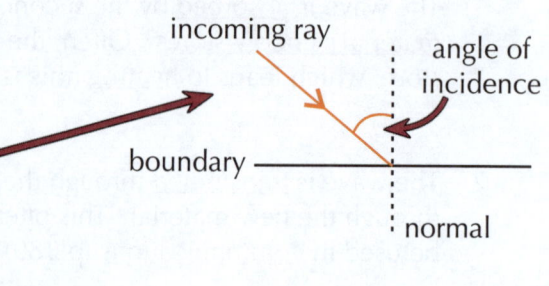

3) Now draw the refracted ray on the other side of the boundary. If the second material is optically denser than the first, the refracted ray bends towards the normal (like on the right). The angle between the refracted ray and the normal (the angle of refraction) is smaller than the angle of incidence. If the second material is less optically dense, the angle of refraction is larger than the angle of incidence.

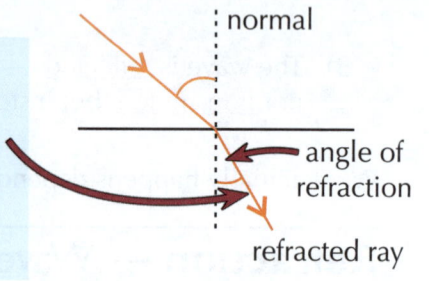

You can also Explain Refraction using Wave Front Diagrams

1) A wave front is a line showing all of the points on a wave that are in the same position as each other after a given number of wavelengths.

2) When a wave crosses a boundary at an angle, only part of a wave front crosses the boundary at first. If it's travelling into a denser material, that part travels slower than the rest of the wave front.

3) So by the time the whole wave front crosses the boundary, the faster part of the wave front will have travelled further than the slower part of the wave front.

4) This difference in distance travelled (caused by the difference in speed) by the wave front causes the wave to bend (refract).

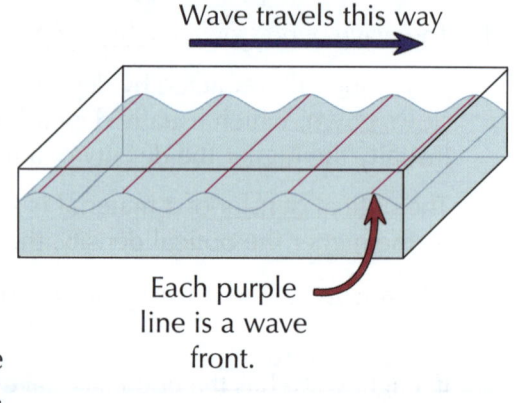

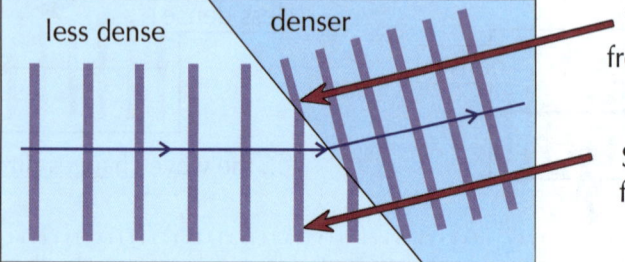

Each purple line is a wave front.

This part of the wave front travels slower than the rest.

So this part of the wave front will have travelled further by the time it crosses the boundary.

You'll need a ruler and protractor for drawing ray diagrams...

...and you'll need a nice sharp pencil too, so make sure you have all of them for the exam.

Q1 Draw a ray diagram for light entering a less optically dense medium, 40° to the normal.
[3 marks]

Topic P6 — Waves

Warm-Up & Exam Questions

Now to check what's actually stuck in your mind over the last six pages...

Warm-Up Questions

1) Describe the direction of vibrations in a longitudinal wave.
2) Give the formula for calculating the speed of a wave.
3) Outline a method you could use to measure the speed of water waves in a ripple tank.
4) True or false? A wave entering a new medium along the path of the normal won't be refracted.

Exam Questions

1 **Figure 1** shows a graph of a water wave. *Grade 4-6*

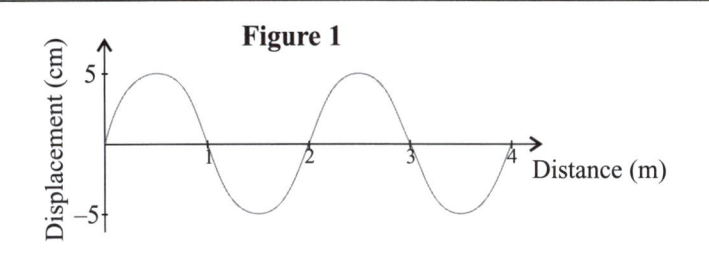

1.1 State whether water waves are transverse or longitudinal.

[1 mark]

1.2 Give the amplitude of this wave.

[1 mark]

1.3 Find the wavelength of this wave.

[1 mark]

1.4 If the frequency of the wave doubles but its speed stays the same, describe what will happen to its wavelength.

[1 mark]

2 **Figure 2** shows how an oscilloscope can be used to display sound waves by connecting microphones to it. Trace 1 shows the sound waves detected by microphone 1 and trace 2 shows the sound waves detected by microphone 2. *Grade 6-7*

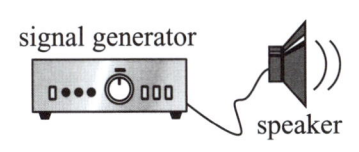

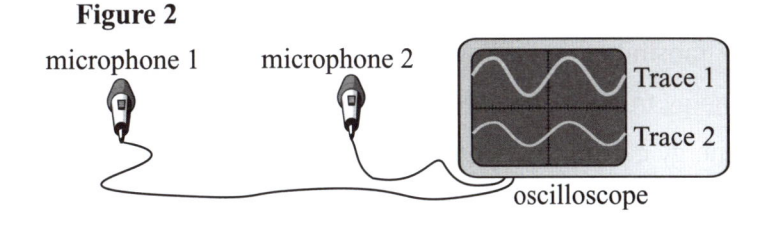

A student begins with both microphones at equal distances from the speaker and the signal generator set at a fixed frequency. He gradually moves microphone 2 away from the speaker, which causes trace 2 to move. He stops moving microphone 2 when both traces line up again as shown in **Figure 2**. He then measures the distance between the microphones.

2.1 Explain how his measurement could be used to work out the speed of sound in air.

[2 marks]

2.2 With the signal generator set to 50 Hz, the distance between the microphones was measured as 6.8 m. Calculate the speed of sound in air. Give the correct unit.

[3 marks]

Topic P6 — Waves

Electromagnetic Waves and Uses of EM Waves

The differences between types of electromagnetic (EM) waves make them useful to us in different ways.

There's a Continuous Spectrum of EM Waves

1) All EM waves are transverse waves (p.382) that transfer energy from a source to an absorber. E.g. a hot object transfers energy by emitting infrared radiation, which is absorbed by the surrounding air.

Electromagnetic waves aren't vibrations of particles, they're vibrations of electric and magnetic fields. This means they can travel through a vacuum.

2) All EM waves travel at the same speed through air or a vacuum (space).

3) Electromagnetic waves form a continuous spectrum over a range of frequencies. They're grouped into seven basic types, based on their wavelength and frequency.

RADIO WAVES	MICRO WAVES	INFRA RED	VISIBLE LIGHT	ULTRA VIOLET	X-RAYS	GAMMA RAYS
1 m – 10^4 m	10^{-2} m	10^{-5} m	10^{-7} m	10^{-8} m	10^{-10} m	10^{-15} m

Wavelength

INCREASING FREQUENCY AND DECREASING WAVELENGTH

4) The human eye can only detect a tiny part of the EM spectrum — the only part we can see is visible light.

5) There is such a large range of frequencies because EM waves are generated by a variety of changes in atoms and their nuclei. E.g. changes in the nucleus of an atom creates gamma rays (p.344). This also explains why atoms can absorb a range of frequencies — each one causes a different change.

6) EM waves travel at different speeds in different materials (which can lead to refraction).

7) Because of their different properties, different EM waves are used for different purposes.

Radio Waves are Made by Oscillating Charges

Head on over to page 328 for more on ac.

1) EM waves are made up of oscillating electric and magnetic fields.

2) Alternating currents (ac) (p.328) are made up of oscillating charges. As the charges oscillate, they produce oscillating electric and magnetic fields, i.e. electromagnetic waves.

3) The frequency of the waves produced will be equal to the frequency of the alternating current.

4) You can produce radio waves using an alternating current in an electrical circuit. The object in which charges (electrons) oscillate to create the radio waves is called a transmitter.

5) When transmitted radio waves reach a receiver, the radio waves are absorbed.

6) The energy transferred by the waves is transferred to the electrons in the material of the receiver.

7) This energy causes the electrons to oscillate and, if the receiver is part of a complete electrical circuit, it generates an alternating current (p.328).

8) This current has the same frequency as the radio waves that generated it.

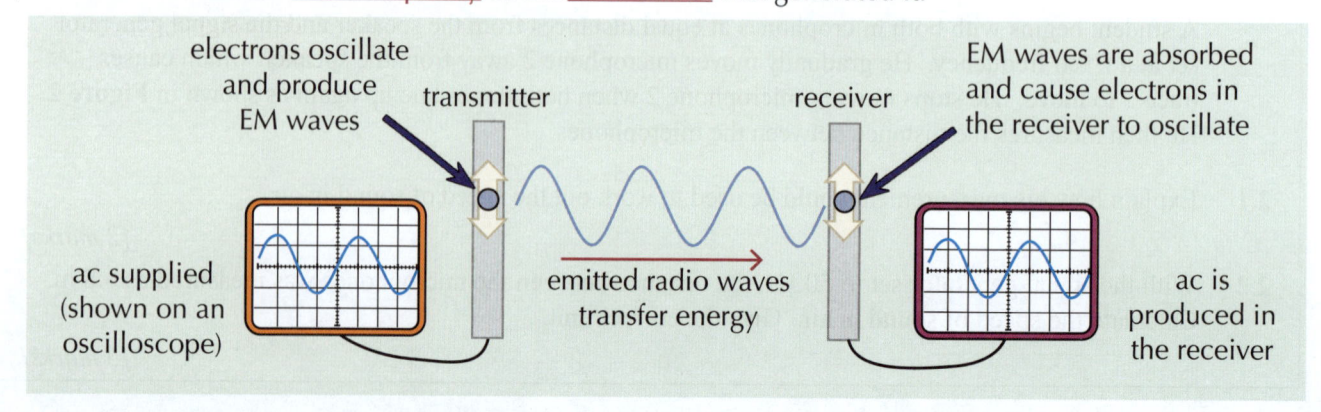

electrons oscillate and produce EM waves — transmitter
EM waves are absorbed and cause electrons in the receiver to oscillate — receiver
ac supplied (shown on an oscilloscope)
emitted radio waves transfer energy
ac is produced in the receiver

Topic P6 — Waves

Uses of EM Waves

Radio waves and *microwaves* are both types of EM waves, and they're both used for **communications**. Their exact **properties** determine which sort of communications they're used for.

Radio Waves are Used Mainly for Communication

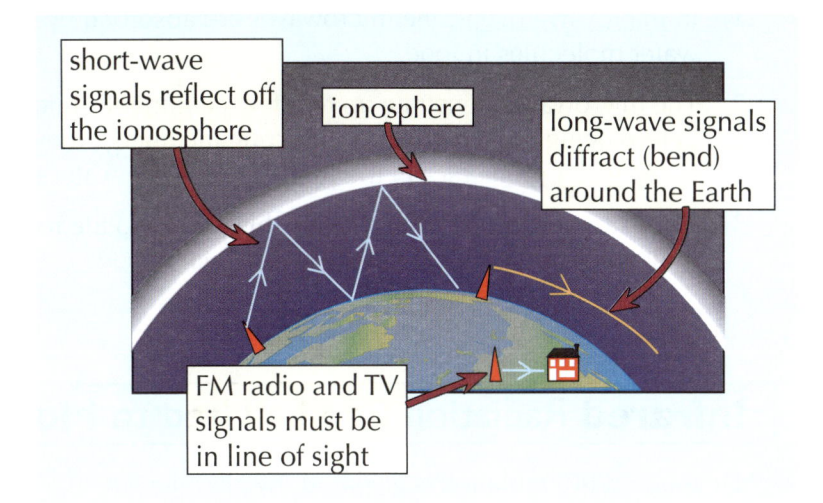

1) Radio waves are EM radiation with wavelengths longer than about 10 cm.

2) Long-wave radio waves (wavelengths of 1 – 10 km) can be transmitted from London, say, and received halfway round the world. That's because long wavelengths diffract (bend) around the curved surface of the Earth. Long-wave radio wavelengths can also diffract around hills, into tunnels and all sorts.

3) This makes it possible for radio signals to be received even if the receiver isn't in line of the sight of the transmitter.

- short-wave signals reflect off the ionosphere
- ionosphere
- long-wave signals diffract (bend) around the Earth
- FM radio and TV signals must be in line of sight

4) Short-wave radio signals (wavelengths of about 10 m – 100 m) can, like long-wave, be received at long distances from the transmitter. That's because they are reflected (see p.385) from the ionosphere — an electrically charged layer in the Earth's upper atmosphere.

5) Bluetooth® uses short-wave radio waves to send data over short distances between devices without wires (e.g. wireless headsets so you can use your phone while driving a car).

6) Medium-wave signals (well, the shorter ones) can also reflect from the ionosphere, depending on atmospheric conditions and the time of day.

7) The radio waves used for TV and FM radio transmissions have very short wavelengths. To get reception, you must be in direct sight of the transmitter — the signal doesn't bend or travel far through buildings.

Microwaves are Used by Satellites

Communication to and from satellites (including satellite TV signals and satellite phones) uses microwaves. It's best to use microwaves which can pass easily through the Earth's watery atmosphere.

For satellite TV, the signal from a transmitter is transmitted into space...

... where it's picked up by the satellite receiver dish orbiting thousands of kilometres above the Earth. The satellite transmits the signal back to Earth in a different direction...

- satellite above Earth's atmosphere
- microwaves sent to satellite
- microwaves sent back to Earth
- cloud and water vapour

... where it's received by a satellite dish on the ground. There is a slight time delay between the signal being sent and received because of the long distance the signal has to travel.

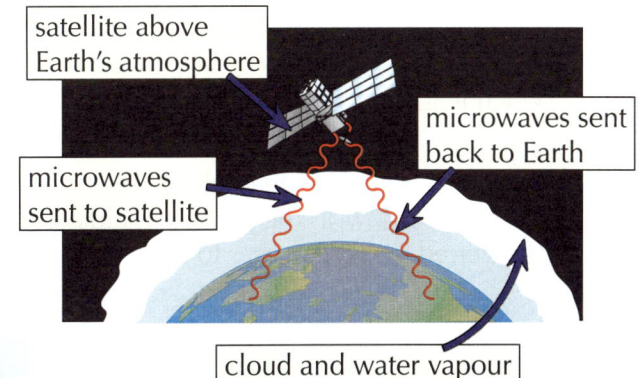

Topic P6 — Waves

Uses of EM Waves

*Each type of EM wave covers a **spectrum** of **wavelengths** and **frequencies** itself. So the **properties** of, say, a microwave from one end of the range may **differ** from those of a microwave from the **other end** of the range.*

Microwave Ovens Also Use Microwaves

1) In microwave ovens, the microwaves are absorbed by water molecules in food.

2) The microwaves penetrate up to a few centimetres into the food before being absorbed and transferring the energy they are carrying to the water molecules in the food, causing the water to heat up.

3) The water molecules then transfer this energy to the rest of the molecules in the food by heating — which quickly cooks the food.

Infrared Radiation Can be Used to Monitor Temperature...

1) Infrared (IR) radiation is given out by all objects — and the hotter the object, the more IR radiation it gives out.

2) Infrared cameras can be used to detect infrared radiation and monitor temperature. The camera detects the IR radiation and turns it into an electrical signal, which is displayed on a screen as a picture. The hotter an object is, the brighter it appears. E.g. energy transfer from a house's thermal energy store can be detected using infrared cameras.

Different colours represent different amounts of IR radiation being detected. Here, the redder the colour, the more infrared radiation is being detected.

...Or Increase it

1) Absorbing IR radiation causes objects to get hotter. Food can be cooked using IR radiation — the temperature of the food increases when it absorbs IR radiation, e.g. from a toaster's heating element.

2) Electric heaters heat a room in the same way. Electric heaters contain a long piece of wire that heats up when a current flows through it. This wire then emits lots of infrared radiation (and a little visible light — the wire glows). The emitted IR radiation is absorbed by objects and the air in the room — energy is transferred by the IR waves to the thermal energy stores of the objects, causing their temperature to increase.

The uses of EM waves depend on their properties...

Differences in wavelength, frequency and energy between types of EM wave give them different properties. For example, some types of EM wave are very harmful (see page 392). Luckily, radio waves are considered safe to beam round the world. IR radiation is generally fairly safe, although too much of it will burn you.

Topic P6 — Waves

Uses of EM Waves

*Here are just a few more uses of EM waves — complete with the all-important **reasons** why they're used.*

Fibre Optic Cables Use Visible Light to Transmit Data

1) Optical fibres are thin glass or plastic fibres that can carry data (e.g. from telephones or computers) over long distances as pulses of visible light.

2) They work because of reflection (p.385). The light rays are bounced back and forth until they reach the end of the fibre.

3) Light is not easily absorbed or scattered as it travels along a fibre.

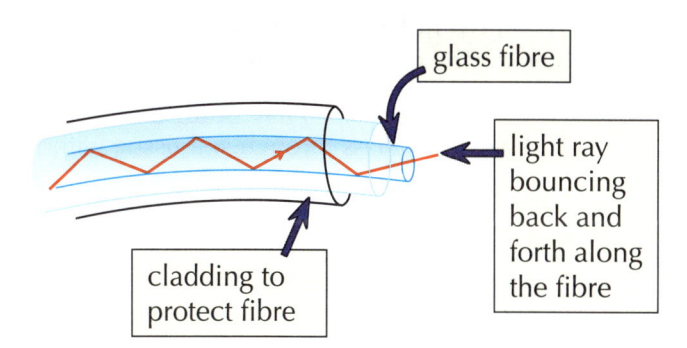

glass fibre
light ray bouncing back and forth along the fibre
cladding to protect fibre

Ultraviolet Radiation Gives You a Suntan

1) Fluorescence is a property of certain chemicals, where ultra-violet (UV) radiation is absorbed and then visible light is emitted. That's why fluorescent colours look so bright — they actually emit light.

2) Fluorescent lights generate UV radiation, which is absorbed and re-emitted as visible light by a layer of phosphor on the inside of the bulb. They're energy-efficient (p.306) so they're good to use when light is needed for long periods (like in your classroom).

3) Security pens can be used to mark property with your name (e.g. laptops). Under UV light the ink will glow (fluoresce), but it's invisible otherwise. This can help the police identify your property if it's stolen.

4) Ultraviolet radiation (UV) is produced by the Sun, and exposure to it is what gives people a suntan.

5) When it's not sunny, some people go to tanning salons where UV lamps are used to give them an artificial suntan. However, overexposure to UV radiation can be dangerous (fluorescent lights emit very little UV — they're totally safe).

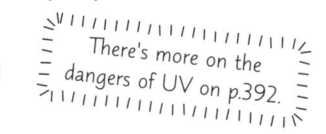

There's more on the dangers of UV on p.392.

X-rays and Gamma Rays are Used in Medicine

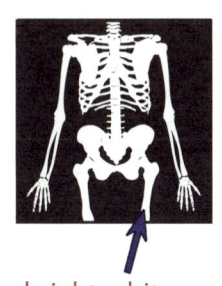

1) Radiographers in hospitals take X-ray 'photographs' of people to see if they have any broken bones.

2) X-rays pass easily through flesh but not so easily through denser material like bones or metal. So it's the amount of radiation that's absorbed (or not absorbed) that gives you an X-ray image.

3) Radiographers use X-rays and gamma rays to treat people with cancer (radiotherapy). This is because high doses of these rays kill all living cells — so they are carefully directed towards cancer cells, to avoid killing too many normal, healthy cells.

4) Gamma radiation can also be used as a medical tracer — this is where a gamma-emitting source is injected into the patient, and its progress is followed around the body. Gamma radiation is well suited to this because it can pass out through the body to be detected.

5) Both X-rays and gamma rays can be harmful to people (p.392), so radiographers wear lead aprons and stand behind a lead screen or leave the room to keep their exposure to them to a minimum.

The brighter bits are where fewer X-rays get through. This is a negative image. The plate starts off all white.

There's more on gamma rays on p.344.

Topic P6 — Waves

Dangers of Electromagnetic Waves

*Okay, so you know how **useful** electromagnetic radiation can be — well, it can also be pretty **dangerous**.*

Some EM Radiation Can be Harmful to People

1) When EM radiation enters living tissue, like you, it's often harmless, but sometimes it creates havoc. The effects of each type of radiation are based on how much energy the wave transfers.
2) Low frequency waves, like radio waves, don't transfer much energy and so mostly pass through soft tissue without being absorbed.
3) High frequency waves like UV, X-rays and gamma rays all transfer lots of energy and so can cause lots of damage.
4) UV radiation damages surface cells, which can lead to sunburn and cause skin to age prematurely. Some more serious effects are blindness and an increased risk of skin cancer.
5) X-rays and gamma rays are types of ionising radiation. (They carry enough energy to knock electrons off of atoms.) This can cause gene mutation or cell destruction, and cancer.

You Can Measure Risk Using the Radiation Dose in Sieverts

1) Whilst UV radiation, X-rays and gamma rays can all be harmful, they are also very useful (see page 391). Before any of these types of EM radiation are used, people look at whether the benefits outweigh the health risks.
2) For example, the risk of a person involved in a car accident then developing cancer from having an X-ray photograph taken, is much smaller than the potential health risk of not finding and treating their injuries.
3) Radiation dose (measured in sieverts) is a measure of the risk of harm from the body being exposed to radiation.
4) This is **not** a measure of the total amount of radiation that has been absorbed.
5) The risk depends on the total amount of radiation absorbed and how harmful the type of radiation is.
6) A sievert is pretty big, so you'll often see doses in millisieverts (mSv), where 1000 mSv = 1 Sv.

Radiation doses can be calculated for all types of radiation, not just UV, X-rays and gamma rays.

Risk can be Different for Different Parts of the Body

A CT scan uses X-rays and a computer to build up a picture of the inside of a patient's body. The table shows the radiation dose received by two different parts of a patient's body when having CT scans.

	Radiation dose (mSv)
Head	2.0
Chest	8.0

If a patient has a CT scan on their chest, they are four times more likely to suffer damage to their genes (and their added risk of harm is four times higher) than if they had a head scan.

The risks and benefits of radiation exposure must be balanced...

Ionising radiation can be dangerous, but the risk can be worth taking. From 1920-1970, X-ray machines were installed in shoe shops for use in shoe fittings. But when people realised radiation was harmful, they were phased out. The risks far outweighed the benefits of using X-rays rather than tape measures...

Topic P6 — Waves

Infrared Radiation and Temperature

*Infrared radiation is what you feel as **heat**. It's easy to think that only really hot objects, like the glowing bars on an electric fire, give out infrared radiation, but that's **not** at all true as you'll soon discover...*

Every Object Absorbs and Emits Infrared Radiation

All objects are continually emitting and absorbing infrared (IR) radiation.

1) Infrared radiation is emitted from the surface of an object.

2) The hotter an object is, the more infrared radiation it radiates in a given time.

3) An object that's hotter than its surroundings emits more IR radiation than it absorbs as it cools down (e.g. a cup of tea left on a table). And an object that's cooler than its surroundings absorbs more IR radiation than it emits as it warms up (e.g. a cold glass of water on a sunny day).

4) Objects at a constant temperature emit infrared radiation at the same rate that they are absorbing it.

5) Some colours and surfaces absorb and emit radiation better than others. For example, a black surface is better at absorbing and emitting radiation than a white one, and a matt surface is better at absorbing and emitting radiation than a shiny one.

The hot chocolate (and the mug) is warmer than the air around it, so it gives out more IR radiation than it absorbs, which cools it down.

You Can Investigate Absorption with the Melting Wax Trick

The amount of infrared radiation absorbed by different materials also depends on the material. You can do an experiment to show this, using a Bunsen burner and some candle wax.

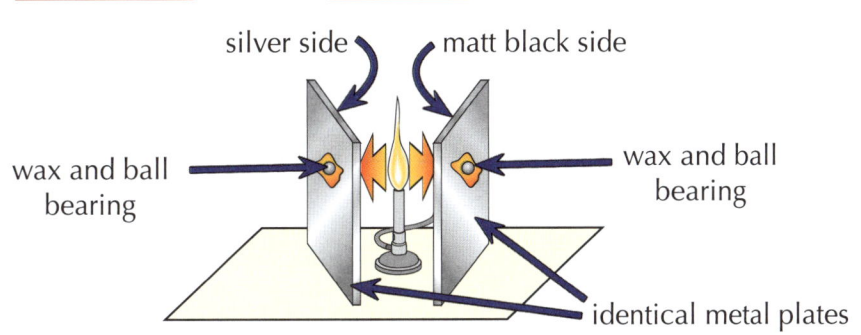

PRACTICAL

silver side — matt black side
wax and ball bearing — wax and ball bearing
identical metal plates

1) Set up the equipment as shown above. Two ball bearings are each stuck to one side of a metal plate with solid pieces of candle wax. The other sides of these plates are then faced towards the flame.

2) The sides of the plates that are facing towards the flame each have a different surface colour — one is matt black and the other is silver.

3) The ball bearing on the black plate will fall first as the black surface absorbs more infrared radiation — transferring more energy to the thermal energy store of the wax. This means the wax on the black plate melts before the wax on the silver plate.

Topic P6 — Waves

PRACTICAL: Investigating Emission

*Time for another **Required Practical**. In this one, you'll meet a fun, new piece of kit called a **Leslie Cube**. Read on to find out more about how you can use this equipment to investigate **infrared radiation emissions**.*

You Can Investigate Emission With a Leslie Cube

A Leslie cube is a hollow, watertight, metal cube made of e.g. aluminium, whose four vertical faces have different surfaces (for example, matt black paint, matt white paint, shiny metal and dull metal). You can use them to investigate IR radiation emitted by different surfaces:

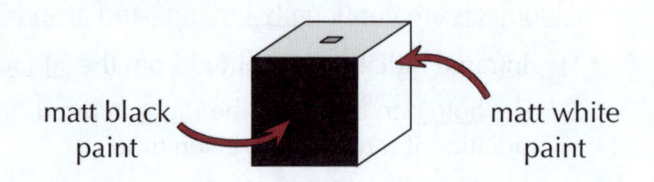

1) Place an empty Leslie cube on a heat-proof mat.

2) Boil water in a kettle and fill the Leslie cube with boiling water.

3) Wait for the cube to warm up, then hold a thermometer against each of the four vertical faces of the cube. You should find that all four faces are the same temperature.

4) Hold an infrared detector a set distance (e.g. 10 cm) away from one of the cube's vertical faces, and record the amount of IR radiation it detects.

5) Repeat this measurement for each of the cube's vertical faces. Make sure you position the detector at the same distance from the cube each time.

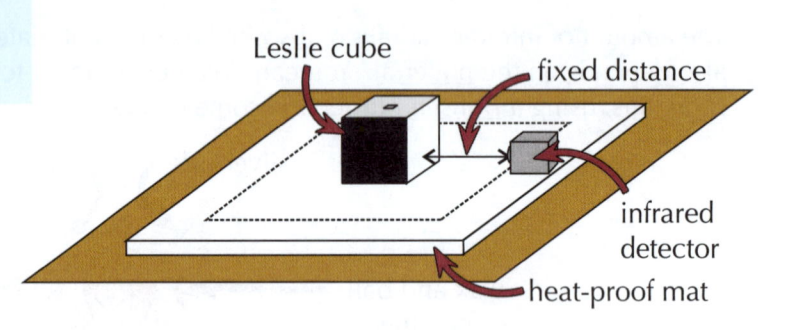

6) You should find that you detect more infrared radiation from the black surface than the white one, and more from the matt surfaces than the shiny ones.

7) As always, you should do the experiment more than once, to make sure your results are repeatable (p.7).

8) It's important to be careful when you're doing this experiment. Don't try to move the cube when it's full of boiling water — you might burn your hands. And take care if you're carrying a full kettle too.

PRACTICAL TIP: Carry out your practicals carefully...

And that means both being careful when collecting data, and careful when dealing with potential hazards. Watch out when you're pouring or carrying boiling water, and make sure any water or equipment has cooled down enough before you start handling it after your experiment is done.

Topic P6 — Waves

Warm-Up & Exam Questions

There's quite a few different sorts of electromagnetic waves — and you never know which ones might come up in the exams... So check which you're still a bit hazy on with these questions.

Warm-Up Questions

1) Which type of EM wave has the highest frequency?
2) Explain how an alternating current produces radio waves.
3) Explain how microwaves heat food.
4) What are optical fibres used for in phone lines?
5) Why is ionising radiation dangerous?
6) If an object is hotter than its surroundings, does it emit more or less IR radiation than it absorbs?
7) What specialised piece of apparatus is used to investigate IR radiation emissions from surfaces?

Exam Questions

1 EM radiation can be harmful but also useful. *(Grade 4-6)*

1.1 Give **one** practical use of ultraviolet radiation.

[1 mark]

1.2 Give **one** hazard associated with ultraviolet radiation.

[1 mark]

1.3 Gamma rays can be used in medical tracers to check that your body is working correctly. Explain how medical tracers work.

[3 marks]

1.4 Explain why gamma rays are suitable for use in medical tracers.

[1 mark]

2 **Figure 1** shows a transmitter which is transmitting a communications signal. There is a receiver for the signal inside the house. There is a mountain between the transmitter and the house. *(Grade 6-7)*

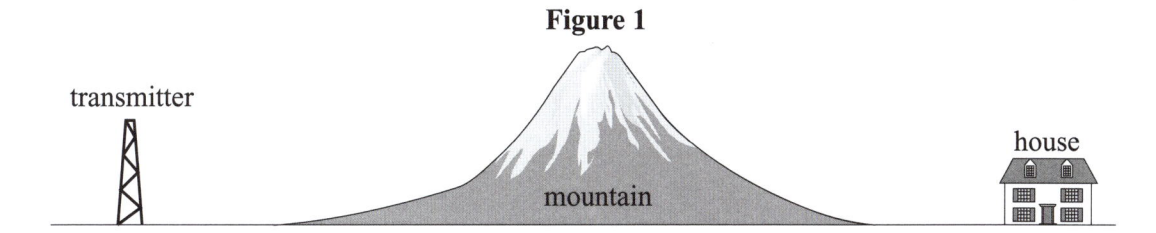

Figure 1

transmitter — mountain — house

2.1 Explain why radio waves would be more suitable than light to send the transmission.

[2 marks]

2.2 The home owner decides to get satellite TV installed. State what type of electromagnetic radiation is used to send signals to satellites and explain why it is suitable.

[2 marks]

2.3 Describe how satellite TV signals are transmitted from a transmitter on the ground to the house.

[2 marks]

Topic P6 — Waves

Exam Questions

PRACTICAL

3 A student is investigating the infrared radiation emitted by different surfaces using a Leslie Cube, as shown in **Figure 2**. The student records how long it takes the temperature on each thermometer to increase by 5 °C.

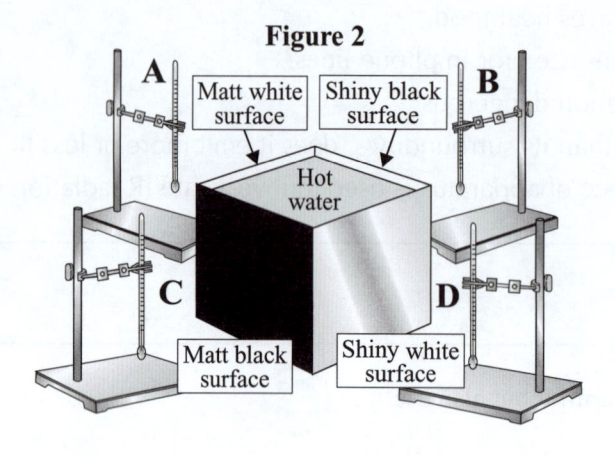

Grade 7-9

Figure 2

3.1 Suggest **one** thing the student should do to make the experiment a fair test.

[1 mark]

The student's results are displayed in **Figure 3**.

Infrared emission is affected by both the texture and colour of a surface.

3.2 Write down a conclusion from the data in **Figure 3** about how texture affects infrared radiation emission.

[1 mark]

3.3 Write down a conclusion from the data in **Figure 3** about how colour affects infrared radiation emission.

[1 mark]

3.4 The water used in the experiment was initially at boiling point, 100 °C.
The experiment is repeated using water at 60 °C.
Predict how this would affect the results.
Explain your prediction.

[2 marks]

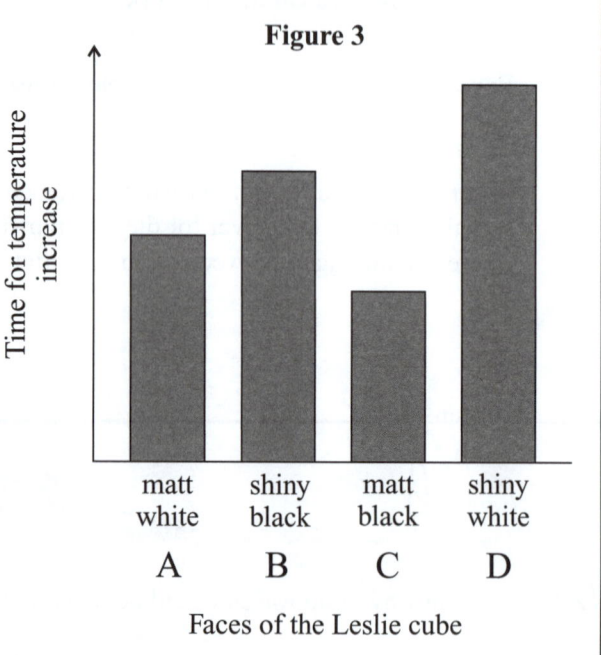

3.5 Another student suggests that using digital thermometers connected to data loggers to measure the temperatures would improve the investigation.
The digital thermometers measure temperature in °C to two decimal places.
Give **two** reasons why this student is correct.

[2 marks]

Topic P6 — Waves

Topic P7 — Magnetism and Electromagnetism

Magnets

*I think magnetism is an **attractive** subject, but don't get **repelled** by the exam — **revise**.*

Magnets Produce **Magnetic Fields**

1) All magnets have two poles — north (or north seeking) and south (or south seeking).

2) All magnets produce a magnetic field — a region where other magnets or magnetic materials (e.g. iron, steel, nickel and cobalt) experience a force. (This is a non-contact force — see page 353.)

3) You can show a magnetic field by drawing magnetic field lines.

4) The lines always go from north to south and they show which way a force would act on a north pole if it was put at that point in the field.

5) The closer together the lines are, the stronger the magnetic field. The further away from a magnet you get, the weaker the field is.

6) The magnetic field is strongest at the poles of a magnet. This means that the magnetic forces are also strongest at the poles.

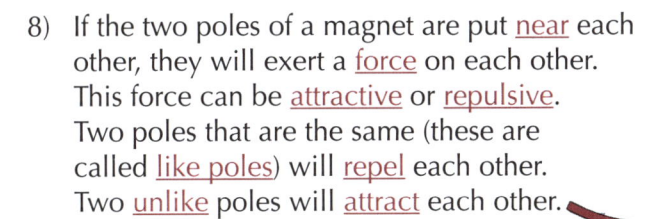

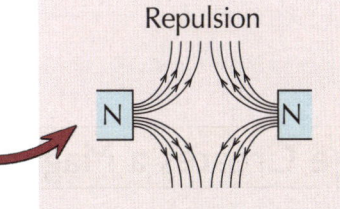

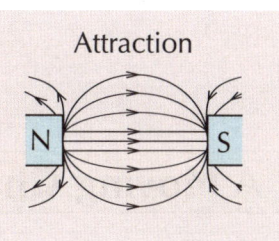

7) The force between a magnet and a magnetic material is always attractive, no matter the pole.

8) If the two poles of a magnet are put near each other, they will exert a force on each other. This force can be attractive or repulsive. Two poles that are the same (these are called like poles) will repel each other. Two unlike poles will attract each other.

Compasses Show the **Direction** of Magnetic Fields

1) Inside a compass is a tiny bar magnet (the needle). The north pole of this magnet is attracted to the south pole of any other magnet it is near. So the compass needle points in the direction of the magnetic field it is in.

2) You can move a compass around a magnet and trace the needle's position on some paper to build up a picture of what the magnetic field looks like.

3) When they're not near a magnet, compass needles always point north. This is because the Earth generates its own magnetic field, which shows that the inside (core) of the Earth must be magnetic.

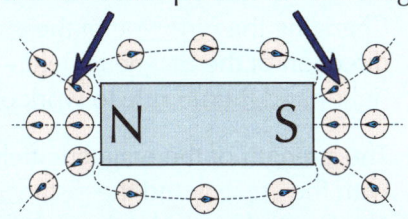

A bar magnet's magnetic field lines go from north to south...

...no matter which direction the magnet is pointing. You can see the shape of a magnetic field using compasses or iron filings. Iron filings will give you a pretty pattern — but they won't show you the direction of the magnetic field. That's where compasses really shine. They're also a lot easier to clear up.

Topic P7 — Magnetism and Electromagnetism

Magnetism

*Permanent magnets are great, but it would be **really** handy to be able to turn a magnetic field **on** and **off**. Well, it turns out that when **electric current** flows it **produces a magnetic field**...*

Magnets Can be Permanent or Induced

1) There are two types of magnet — permanent magnets and induced magnets.
2) Permanent magnets produce their own magnetic field.
3) Induced magnets are magnetic materials that turn into a magnet when they're put into a magnetic field.
4) The force between permanent and induced magnets is always attractive (see magnetic materials on the previous page).
5) When you take away the magnetic field, induced magnets quickly lose most or all of their magnetism.

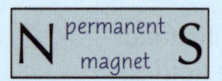

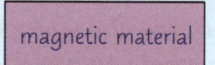

The magnetic material becomes magnetised when it is brought near the bar magnet. It has its own poles and magnetic field:

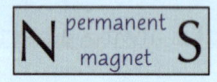

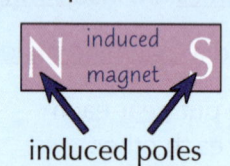

A Moving Charge Creates a Magnetic Field

1) When a current flows through a wire, a magnetic field is created around the wire.
2) The field is made up of concentric circles perpendicular to the wire, with the wire in the centre.
3) You can see this by placing a compass near a wire that is carrying a current. As you move the compass, it will trace the direction of the magnetic field.
4) Changing the direction of the current changes the direction of the magnetic field — use the right-hand thumb rule to work out which way it goes.
5) The strength of the magnetic field produced changes with the current and the distance from the wire. The larger the current through the wire, or the closer to the wire you are, the stronger the field is.

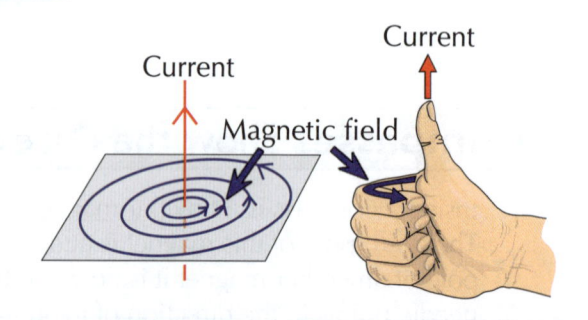

The Right-Hand Thumb Rule
Using your right hand, point your thumb in the direction of current and curl your fingers. The direction of your fingers is the direction of the field.

Just point your thumb in the direction of the current...

...and your fingers show the direction of the field. Remember, it's always your right thumb. Not your left. You'll use your left hand on page 402 though, so it shouldn't feel left out...

Q1 Draw the magnetic field for a current-carrying wire. [2 marks]

Topic P7 — Magnetism and Electromagnetism

Electromagnets

Electric currents can create *magnetic fields* (see previous page). We can use this to make magnets that can be switched on and off — these are electromagnets.

A Solenoid is a Coil of Wire

1) You can increase the strength of the magnetic field that a wire produces by wrapping the wire into a coil called a solenoid.

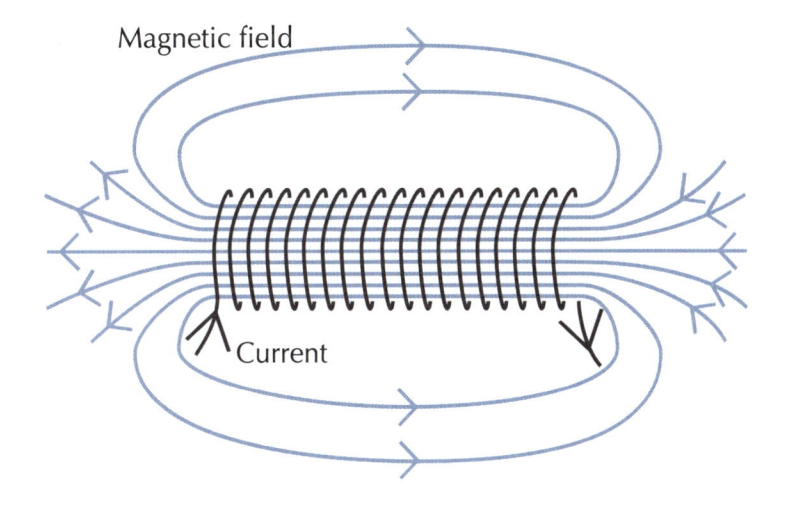

Magnetic field

Current

2) This happens because the field lines around each loop of wire line up with each other. This results in lots of field lines pointing in the same direction that are very close to each other. As you saw on page 397, the closer together field lines are, the stronger the field is.

3) The magnetic field inside a solenoid is strong and uniform (it has the same strength and direction at every point in that region).

4) Outside the coil, the magnetic field is just like the one round a bar magnet.

5) You can increase the field strength of the solenoid even more by putting a block of iron in the centre of the coil. This iron core becomes an induced magnet whenever current is flowing.

6) If you stop the current, the magnetic field disappears.

7) A solenoid with an iron core is called an ELECTROMAGNET (a magnet whose magnetic field can be turned on and off with an electric current).

Fields around electromagnets and bar magnets are the same shape

Electromagnets pop up in lots of different places — they're used in electric bells, car ignition circuits and some security doors. Electromagnets aren't all the same strength though — how strong they are depends on stuff like the number of turns of wire there are and the size of the current going through the wire.

Topic P7 — Magnetism and Electromagnetism

Warm-Up & Exam Questions

It's time for another page of questions to check your knowledge retention. If you can do the warm-up questions without breaking into a sweat, then see how you get on with the exam questions below.

Warm-Up Questions

1) Draw a diagram to show the magnetic field around a single bar magnet.
2) Describe the magnetic field around a current-carrying wire.
3) What is a solenoid?

Exam Questions

1 A student draws the magnetic field lines between four bar magnets, as shown in **Figure 1**. *(Grade 6-7)*

Figure 1

1.1 Describe an experiment that the student could have done to show this magnetic field pattern.

[2 marks]

The student arranges two of the magnets as shown in **Figure 2**.

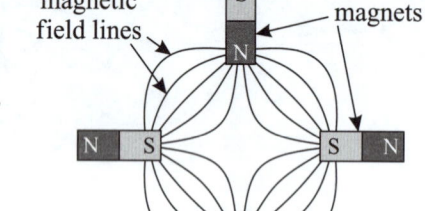

Figure 2

1.2 Describe the magnetic field lines in the shaded region between the dotted lines.

[1 mark]

1.3 State whether there will be a force of attraction, repulsion, or no force between the two magnets. Explain your answer.

[2 marks]

2 Amrita is making an electromagnet using a current-carrying solenoid and a core. *(Grade 6-7)*

2.1 Complete **Figure 3** of the solenoid to show the magnetic field inside and around it.

[2 marks]

Figure 3

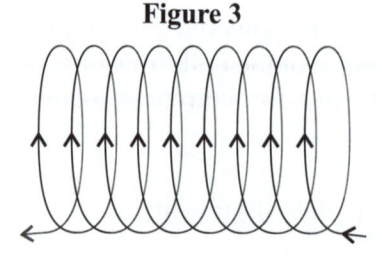

2.2 Suggest a material that would be suitable for the core.

[1 mark]

Amrita uses her electromagnet to pick up some paper clips, as shown in **Figure 4**.

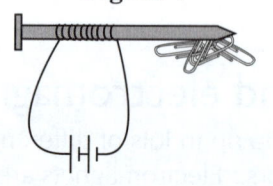

Figure 4

2.3 State what happens when the current is turned off, and explain why this happens.

[2 marks]

Topic P7 — Magnetism and Electromagnetism

The Motor Effect

*Passing an electric current through a wire produces a magnetic field around the wire (p.398). If you put that wire into a magnetic field, the **two magnetic fields interact**, which can exert a force on the wire.*

A Current in a Magnetic Field Experiences a Force

When a current-carrying wire (or any other conductor) is put between magnetic poles, the magnetic field around the wire interacts with the magnetic field it has been placed in. This causes the magnet and the conductor to exert a force on each other. This is called the motor effect and can cause the wire to move.

This is an aerial view. The red dot represents a wire carrying current "out of the page" (towards you).

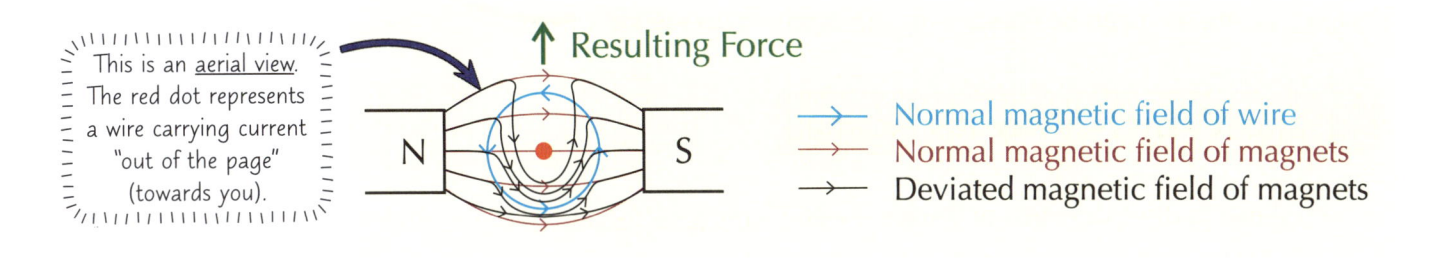

↑ Resulting Force

→ Normal magnetic field of wire
→ Normal magnetic field of magnets
→ Deviated magnetic field of magnets

1) To experience the full force, the wire has to be at 90° to the magnetic field. If the wire runs parallel to the magnetic field, it won't experience any force at all. At angles in between, it'll feel some force.

2) The force always acts at right angles to the magnetic field of the magnets and to the direction of the current in the wire.

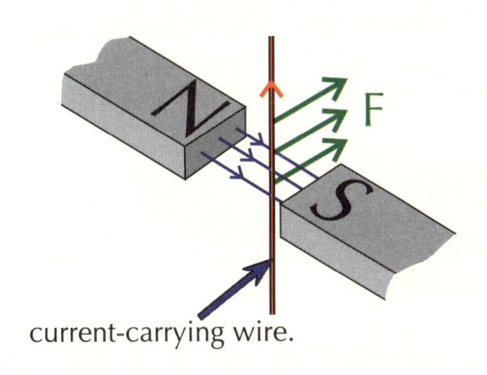

current-carrying wire.

3) A good way of showing the direction of the force is to apply a current to a set of rails inside a horseshoe magnet (shown below). A bar is placed on the rails, which completes the circuit. This generates a force that rolls the bar along the rails.

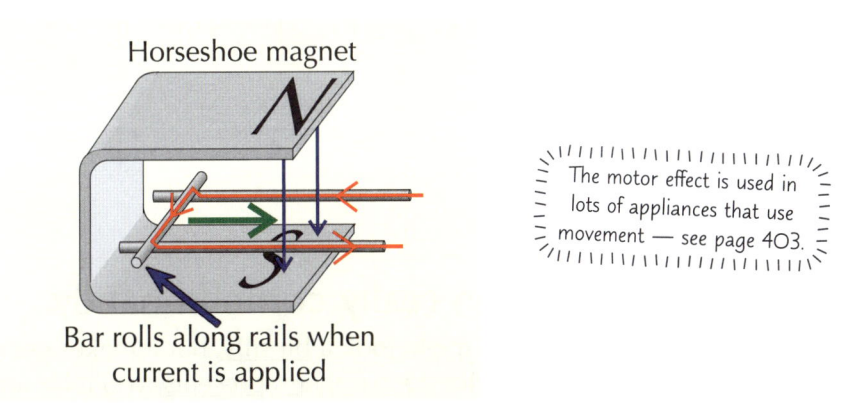

Horseshoe magnet

Bar rolls along rails when current is applied

The motor effect is used in lots of appliances that use movement — see page 403.

4) The magnitude (strength) of the force increases with the strength of the magnetic field.

5) The force also increases with the amount of current passing through the conductor.

Topic P7 — Magnetism and Electromagnetism

The Motor Effect

You Can Find the Size of the Force...

The force acting on a conductor in a magnetic field depends on three things:

1) The magnetic flux density — how many field lines there are in a region. This shows the strength of the magnetic field (p.397).
2) The size of the current through the conductor.
3) The length of the conductor that's in the magnetic field.

When the current is at 90° to the magnetic field it is in, the force acting on it can be found using the equation on the right.

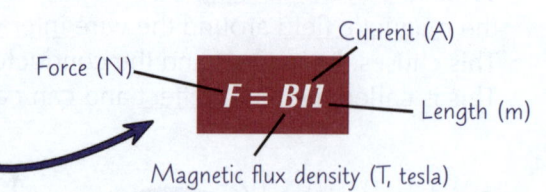

$$F = BIl$$

- Force (N)
- Magnetic flux density (T, tesla)
- Current (A)
- Length (m)

... and Which Way it's Acting

You can find the direction of the force with Fleming's left-hand rule.

1) Using your left hand, point your First finger in the direction of the Field.
2) Point your seCond finger in the direction of the Current.
3) Your thuMb will then point in the direction of the force (Motion).

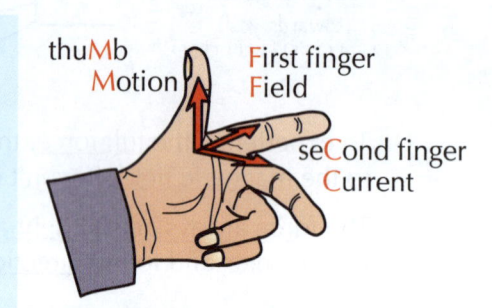

- thuMb — Motion
- First finger — Field
- seCond finger — Current

Fleming's left-hand rule shows that if either the current or the magnetic field is reversed, then the direction of the force will also be reversed. This can be used to find the direction of the force in all sorts of things — like motors, as shown on the next page.

EXAMPLE

In the diagram on the right, in which direction does the force act on the wire?

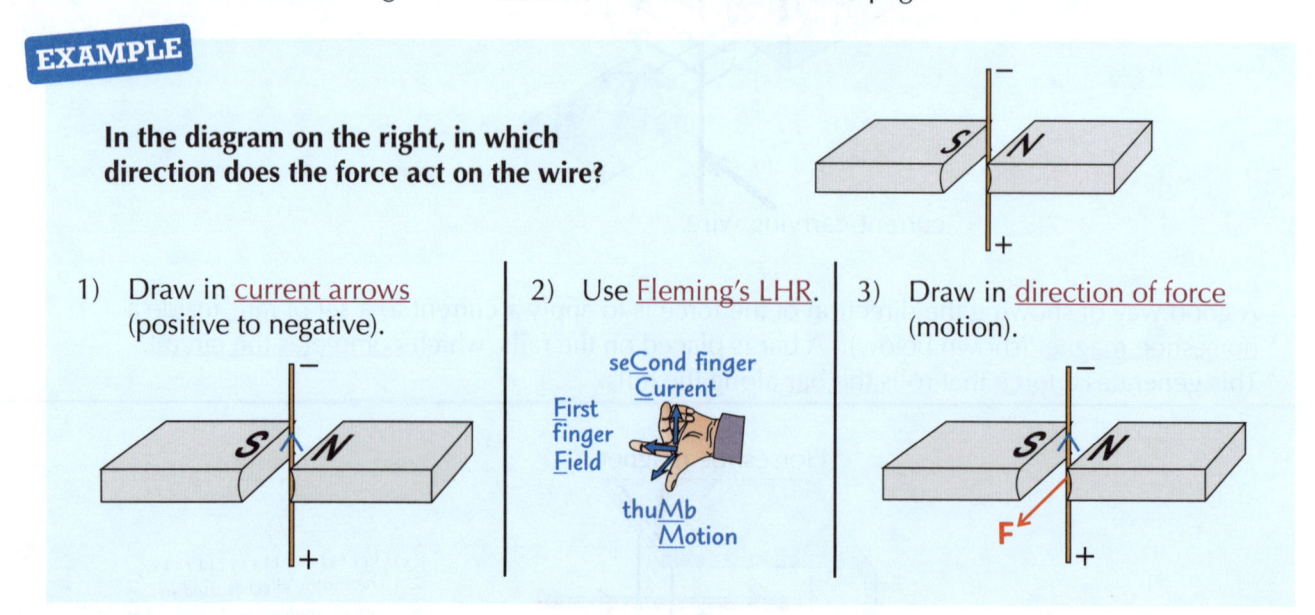

1) Draw in current arrows (positive to negative).
2) Use Fleming's LHR.
3) Draw in direction of force (motion).

Fleming's left-hand rule can really come in handy...

Use the left-hand rule in the exam. You might look a bit silly, but it makes getting those marks so much easier. As long as you know what each finger represents, you'll be sorted.

Q1 A section of a current-carrying wire is in a magnetic field, as shown in the diagram. The wire is at 90° to the magnetic field. Find the direction of the force acting on the wire. [1 mark]

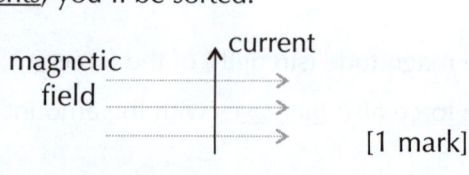

Topic P7 — Magnetism and Electromagnetism

Electric Motors

*Electric motors use the **motor effect** (see pages 401-402) to get them (and keep them) **moving**. This is one of the favourite exam topics of all time. Read it. Understand it. Learn it. Lecture over.*

A Current-Carrying **Coil** of Wire **Rotates** in a Magnetic Field

1) The diagram on the right shows a basic dc motor. Forces act on the two side arms of a coil of wire that's carrying a current.

2) These forces are just the usual forces which act on any current in a magnetic field (p.402).

3) Because the coil is on an axle and the forces act one up and one down, it rotates.

4) The split-ring commutator is a clever way of swapping the contacts every half turn to keep the motor rotating in the same direction.

5) The direction of the motor can be reversed either by swapping the polarity of the dc supply (reversing the current) or swapping the magnetic poles over (reversing the field).

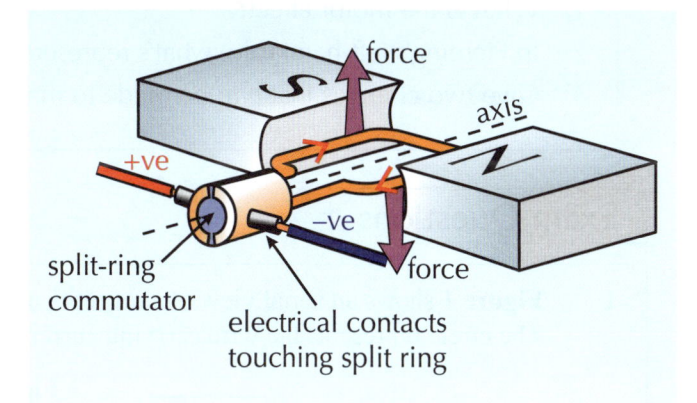

6) You can use Fleming's left-hand rule to work out which way the coil will turn.

Direct current (dc) is current that only flows in one direction.

EXAMPLE

Is the coil turning clockwise or anticlockwise?

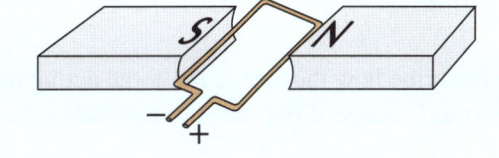

1) Draw in current arrows (positive to negative).

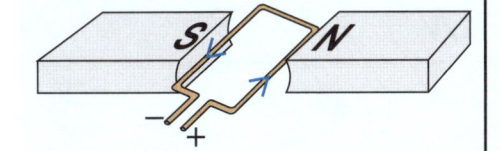

2) Use Fleming's left-hand rule on one branch (here, I've picked the right-hand branch).

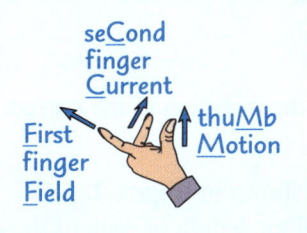

   - seCond finger — Current
   - First finger — Field
   - thuMb — Motion

3) Draw in direction of force (motion).

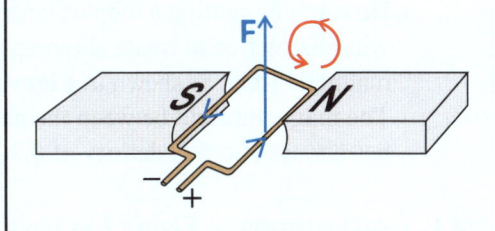

So — the coil is turning **anticlockwise**.

The motor effect has a lot of important applications...

Electric motors are important components in a lot of everyday items. Food mixers, DVD players, and anything that has a fan (hair dryers, laptops, etc) use electric motors to keep things turning.

Topic P7 — Magnetism and Electromagnetism

Warm-Up & Exam Questions

Time to test your knowledge — as usual, check you can do the basics, then get stuck into some lovely exam questions. Don't forget to go back and check up on any niggling bits you can't do.

Warm-Up Questions

1) What is the motor effect?
2) In Fleming's left-hand rule, what's represented by the first finger, the second finger and the thumb?
3) Give two changes that can be made to make a dc motor run in reverse.

Exam Questions

1 **Figure 1** shows an aerial view of a current-carrying wire in a magnetic field. The circle represents the wire carrying current out of the page, towards you.

Grade 4-6

Figure 1

N ◯ S

1.1 On **Figure 1**, draw an arrow to show the direction of the force acting on the current-carrying wire.

[1 mark]

1.2 Describe what would happen to the force acting on the current-carrying wire if the direction of the current was reversed.

[1 mark]

1.3 Describe how the size of the force acting on the wire would change if the wire was at 30° to the magnetic field.

[1 mark]

1.4 Describe how the size of the force acting on the wire would change if the wire ran parallel to the magnetic field.

[1 mark]

2 A student is building a simple dc motor. He starts by putting a loop of current-carrying wire that is free to rotate about an axis in a magnetic field, as shown in **Figure 2**. The magnetic field between the poles has a magnetic flux density of 0.2 T.

Grade 7-9

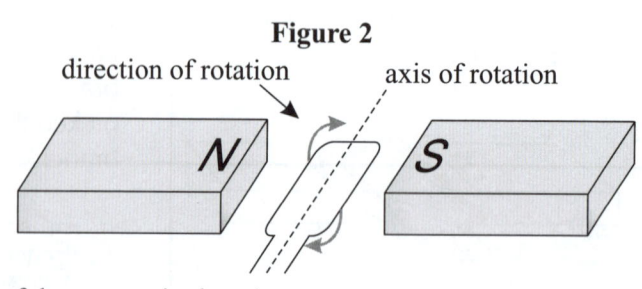

Figure 2
direction of rotation   axis of rotation
N   S

2.1 Add an arrow to **Figure 2** to show the direction of the current in the wire.

[1 mark]

2.2 The starting position of the loop is shown in **Figure 2**.
The current in the wire is 15 A, and the length of each of the two longest sides is 10 cm.
Calculate the force on one of the two sides of the coil as it starts to turn.
Use the correct equation from the Physics Equation Sheet on page 542.

[2 marks]

2.3 The motor will stop rotating in the same direction after 90° of rotation from its start position.
Suggest and explain how the student could get the motor to keep rotating in the same direction.

[2 marks]

Topic P7 — Magnetism and Electromagnetism

Revision Summary for Topics P5-7

That wraps up Topics P5-7 — time to put yourself to the test.
- Try these questions and tick off each one when you get it right.
- When you're completely happy with a topic, tick it off.

For even more practice, try the Retrieval Quizzes for Topics P5-7 — just scan the QR codes!

Topic P5 — Forces (p.353-379) ☐

1) Explain the difference between scalar and vector quantities, and contact and non-contact forces.
2) What is the formula for calculating the weight of an object?
3) Describe the forces acting on an object in equilibrium.
4) What is the difference between an elastic and an inelastic deformation?
5) How do you find the spring constant from a linear force-extension graph?
6) What is the area under the linear part of a force-extension graph of an object equal to?
7) What is the difference between displacement and distance?
8) Define acceleration in terms of velocity and time.
9) What does the term 'uniform acceleration' mean?
10) Why do objects reach terminal velocity?
11) State Newton's three laws of motion.
12) What is inertia?
13) What is the stopping distance of a vehicle? How can it be calculated?
14) Give two things that affect a person's reaction time.
15) Give two examples of methods that could be used to test a person's reaction time.

Topic P6 — Waves (p.381-394) ☐

16) Define the following features of a wave:
    a) amplitude, b) wavelength, c) frequency, d) period.
17) Describe the difference between transverse and longitudinal waves and give an example of each.
18) Describe an experiment to measure the speed of ripples on water.
19) A wave moves from material A into material B, and bends towards the normal as it crosses the boundary. In which material does the wave travel faster?
20) Draw a diagram showing a light ray crossing, at an angle, into a medium in which it slows down.
21) What kind of current is used to generate radio waves in an antenna?
22) Give one use of infrared radiation.
23) Name the type of radiation produced by the lamps in tanning beds.
24) What does the term 'ionising radiation' mean?
25) Compare the IR radiation absorption and emission rates for an object at constant temperature.

Topic P7 — Magnetism and Electromagnetism (p.397-403) ☐

26) What is a magnetic field?
27) True or false? The force between a magnet and a magnetic material is always repulsive.
28) Describe an electromagnet.
29) Name three ways you could increase the force on a current-carrying wire in a magnetic field.
30) Explain how a basic dc motor works.

Practical Skills

Measuring Techniques

Get your lab coat on, it's time to find out about the skills you'll need in **experiments**.

Mass Should Be Measured Using a Balance

1) To measure mass, start by putting the container you're measuring the substance into on the balance.
2) Set the balance to exactly zero and then start adding your substance.
3) It's no good carefully measuring out your substance if it's not all transferred to your reaction vessel — the amount in the reaction vessel won't be the same as your measurement. Here are a couple of methods you can use to make sure that none gets left in your weighing container...

- If you're dissolving a mass of a solid in a solvent to make a solution, you could wash any remaining solid into the new container using the solvent. This way you know that all the solid you weighed has been transferred.
- You could set the balance to zero before you put your weighing container on the balance. Then reweigh the weighing container after you've transferred the substance. Use the difference in mass to work out exactly how much substance you've transferred.

Different Ways to Measure Liquids

There are a few methods you might use to measure the volume of a liquid. Whichever method you use, always read the volume from the bottom of the meniscus (the curved upper surface of the liquid) when it's at eye level.

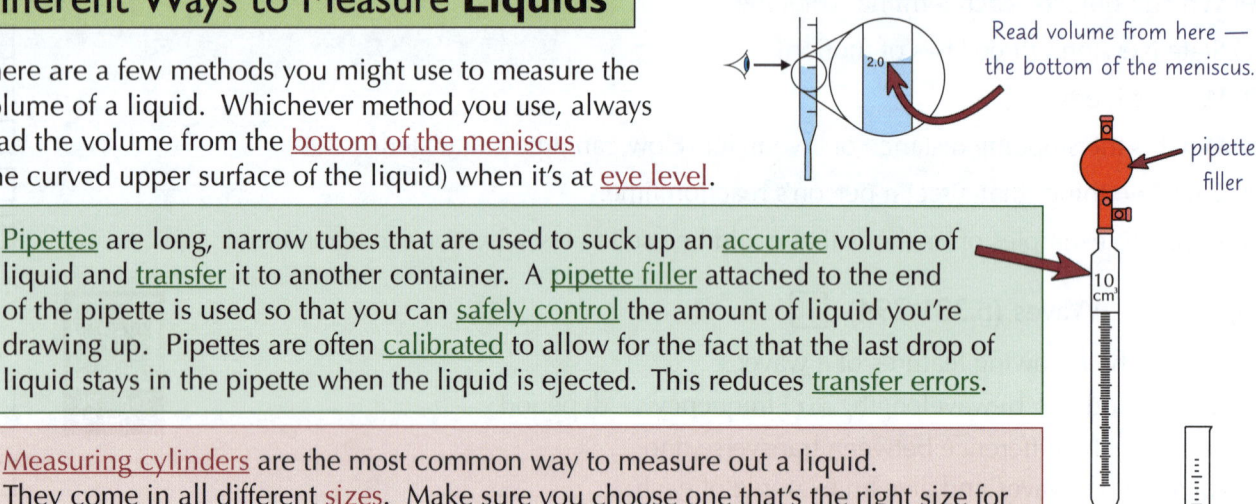

Read volume from here — the bottom of the meniscus.

pipette filler

Pipettes are long, narrow tubes that are used to suck up an accurate volume of liquid and transfer it to another container. A pipette filler attached to the end of the pipette is used so that you can safely control the amount of liquid you're drawing up. Pipettes are often calibrated to allow for the fact that the last drop of liquid stays in the pipette when the liquid is ejected. This reduces transfer errors.

Measuring cylinders are the most common way to measure out a liquid. They come in all different sizes. Make sure you choose one that's the right size for the measurement you want to make. It's no good using a huge 1000 cm³ cylinder to measure out 2 cm³ of a liquid — the graduations will be too big, and you'll end up with massive errors. It'd be much better to use one that measures up to 10 cm³.

If you only want a couple of drops of liquid, and don't need it to be accurately measured, you can use a dropping pipette to transfer it. For example, this is how you'd add a couple of drops of indicator into a mixture.

Gas Syringes Measure Gas Volumes

1) Gases can be measured with a gas syringe. They should be measured at room temperature and pressure as the volume of a gas changes with temperature and pressure. You should also use a gas syringe that's the right size for the measurement you're making. Before you use the syringe, you should make sure it's completely sealed and that the plunger moves smoothly.
2) Alternatively, you can use an upturned measuring cylinder filled with water. The gas will displace the water so you can read the volume off the scale — see page 411.
3) Other methods to measure the amount of gas include counting the bubbles produced or measuring the length of a gas bubble drawn along a tube (see p.93). These methods are less accurate, but will give you relative amounts of gas to compare results.
4) When you're measuring a gas, you need to make sure that the equipment is set up so that none of the gas can escape, otherwise your results won't be accurate.

Practical Skills

Measuring Techniques

Eureka Cans Measure the Volumes of Solids

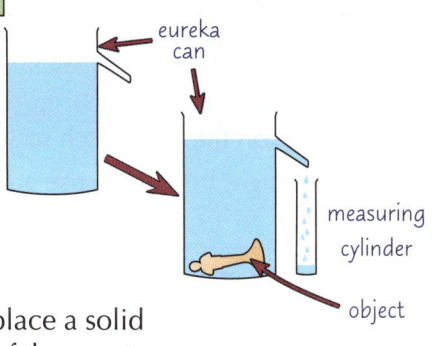

1) Eureka cans are used in combination with measuring cylinders to find the volumes of irregular solids (p.335).
2) They're essentially a beaker with a spout. To use them, fill them with water so the water level is above the spout.
3) Let the water drain from the spout, leaving the water level just below the start of the spout (so all the water displaced by an object goes into the measuring cylinder and gives you the correct volume).
4) Place a measuring cylinder below the end of the spout. When you place a solid in the beaker, it causes the water level to rise and water to flow out of the spout.
5) Make sure you wait until the spout has stopped dripping before you measure the volume of the water in the measuring cylinder. The object's volume is equal to the volume of water in the measuring cylinder.

Measure Most Lengths with a Ruler

1) In most cases a bog-standard centimetre ruler can be used to measure length. It depends on what you're measuring though — metre rulers are handy for large distances, while micrometers are used for measuring tiny things like the diameter of a wire.
2) The ruler should always be parallel to what you want to measure.
3) If you're dealing with something where it's tricky to measure just one accurately (e.g. water ripples, p.383), you can measure the length of ten of them and then divide to find the length of one.
4) If you're taking multiple measurements of the same object (e.g. to measure changes in length) then make sure you always measure from the same point on the object. It can help to draw or stick small markers onto the object to line up your ruler against. 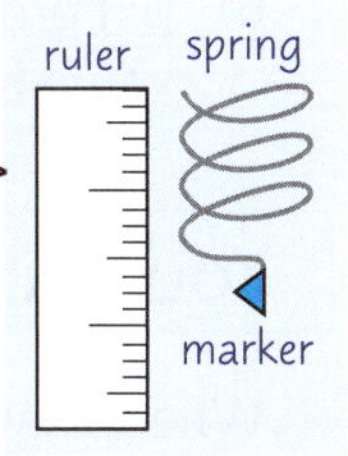
5) Make sure the ruler and the object are always at eye level when you take a reading. This stops parallax affecting your results.

Parallax is where a measurement appears to change based on where you're looking from. The blue line is the measurement taken when the spring is at eye level. It shows the correct length of the spring.

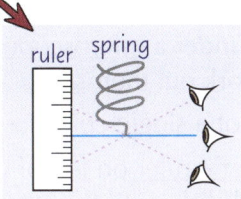

Use a Protractor to Find Angles

1) First align the vertex (point) of the angle with the mark in the centre of the protractor.
2) Line up the base line of the protractor with one line that forms the angle and then measure the angle of the other line using the scale on the protractor.
3) If the lines creating the angle are very thick, align the protractor and measure the angle from the centre of the lines. Using a sharp pencil to trace light rays or draw diagrams helps to reduce errors when measuring angles.
4) If the lines are too short to measure easily, you may have to extend them. Again, make sure you use a sharp pencil to do this.

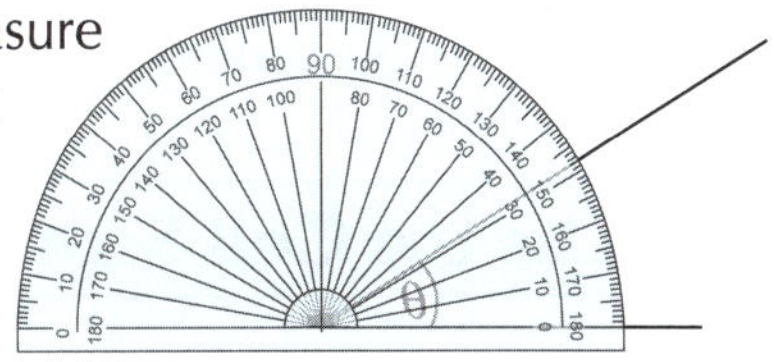

Measure Temperature Accurately

1) You can use a thermometer to measure the temperature of a substance:
2) Make sure the bulb of your thermometer is completely submerged in any mixture you're measuring.
3) If you're taking an initial reading, you should wait for the temperature to stabilise first.
4) Read your measurement off the scale on a thermometer at eye level to make sure it's correct.

Practical Skills

Measuring Techniques

You May Have to Measure the Time Taken for a Change

1) You should use a stopwatch to time experiments. These measure to the nearest 0.1 s, so are sensitive.
2) Always make sure you start and stop the stopwatch at exactly the right time. Or alternatively, set an alarm on the stopwatch so you know exactly when to stop an experiment or take a reading.
3) You might be able to use a light gate instead (p.413). This will reduce the errors in your experiment.

Measure pH to Find Out How Acidic or Alkaline a Solution Is

1) You need to be able to decide the best method for measuring pH, depending on what your experiment is.
2) Indicators are dyes that change colour depending on whether they're in an acid or an alkali. You use them by adding a couple of drops of the indicator to the solution you're interested in.
3) Universal indicator is a mixture of indicators that changes colour gradually as pH changes. It doesn't show a sudden colour change. It's useful for estimating the pH of a solution based on its colour.
4) Indicators can be soaked into paper and strips of this paper can be used for testing pH. If you use a dropping pipette to spot a small amount of a solution onto some indicator paper, it will change colour depending on the pH of the solution.

> Litmus paper turns red in acidic conditions and blue in basic conditions. Universal indicator paper can be used to estimate the pH based on its colour.

5) Indicator paper is useful when you don't want to change the colour of all of the substance, or if the substance is already coloured so might obscure the colour of the indicator. You can also hold a piece of damp indicator paper in a gas sample to test its pH.
6) pH probes are attached to pH meters which have a digital display that gives a numerical value for the pH of a solution. They're used to give an accurate value of pH.

You Can Measure the Size of a Single Cell

When viewing cells under a microscope, you might need to work out their size.

To work out the size of a single cell:

1) Place a clear, plastic ruler on top of your microscope slide. Clip the ruler and slide onto the stage.
2) Select the objective lens that gives an overall magnification of x 100.
3) Adjust the focus to get a clear image of the cells.
4) Move the ruler so that the cells are lined up along 1 mm. Then count the number of cells along this 1 mm sample.
5) 1 mm = 1000 μm. So to calculate the length of a single cell in μm, you just need to divide 1000 μm by the number of cells in the sample. E.g. if you counted 4 cells in 1 mm, the length of a single cell would be: 1000 ÷ 4 = 250 μm

> You can read all about using a microscope on pages 20-21.

Use the Cell Size to Work out the Length of a Scale Bar

1) If you draw a diagram of a cell you've observed under a microscope, you might want to include a scale bar.
2) Once you know the size of one cell, you can use it to calculate how long your scale bar should be.
3) To draw a 500 μm scale bar, just use this formula:

$$\text{scale bar length (μm)} = \frac{\text{drawn length of cell (μm)} \times 500}{\text{actual length of cell (μm)}}$$

Practical Skills

Safety and Ethics

Before you start any experiment, you need to know what **safety precautions** you should be taking. And they depend on your **method**, your **equipment**, and the **chemicals** you're using.

Make Sure You're **Working Safely** in the **Lab**

1) Make sure that you're wearing sensible clothing when you're in the lab (e.g. open shoes won't protect your feet from spillages). When you're doing an experiment, you should wear a lab coat to protect your skin and clothing. Depending on the experiment, you may need to also wear safety goggles and gloves.
2) You also need to be aware of general safety in the lab, e.g. keep anything flammable away from lit Bunsen burners, don't directly touch any hot equipment, handle glassware carefully so it doesn't break, etc.
3) You should follow any instructions that your teacher gives you carefully. But here are some basic principles for dealing with chemicals and equipment...

Be Careful When You're Using **Chemicals**...

1) The chemicals you're using may be hazardous — for example, they might be flammable (catch fire easily), or they might irritate or burn your skin if it comes into contact with them.
2) Make sure you're working in an area that's well ventilated and if you're doing an experiment that might produce nasty gases (such as chlorine), you should carry out the experiment in a fume hood so that the gas can't escape out into the room you're working in.
3) Never directly touch any chemicals (even if you're wearing gloves). Use a spatula to transfer solids between containers. Carefully pour liquids between containers, using a funnel to avoid spillages.
4) Be careful when you're mixing chemicals, as a reaction might occur. If you're diluting a liquid, add the concentrated substance to the water (not the other way around) or the mixture could get very hot.

...and **Equipment**

1) Stop masses and equipment falling by using clamp stands. Make sure masses are of a sensible weight so they don't break the equipment they're used with, and use pulleys of a sensible length. That way, any hanging masses won't hit the floor during the experiment.
2) When heating materials, make sure to let them cool before moving them, or wear insulated gloves while handling them. If you're using an immersion heater to heat liquids, you should always let it dry out in air, just in case any liquid has leaked inside the heater.
3) If you're using a laser, there are a few safety rules you must follow. Always wear laser safety goggles and never look directly into the laser or shine it towards another person. Make sure you turn the laser off if it's not needed to avoid any accidents.
4) When working with electronics, make sure you use a low enough voltage and current to prevent wires overheating (and potentially melting) and avoid damage to components, like blowing a filament bulb.

You Need to Think About **Ethical Issues** In Your Experiments

1) Any organisms involved in your investigations need to be treated safely and ethically.
2) Animals need to be treated humanely — they should be handled carefully and any wild animals captured for studying (e.g. during an investigation of the distribution of an organism) should be returned to their original habitat.
3) Any animals kept in the lab should also be cared for in a humane way, e.g. they should not be kept in overcrowded conditions.
4) If you are carrying out an experiment involving other students (e.g. investigating the effect of caffeine on reaction time), they should not be forced to participate against their will or feel pressured to take part.

Practical Skills

Setting Up Experiments

*Setting up the equipment for an experiment correctly is **important**. These pages cover some of the experimental set-ups that you could be asked about in your **exams**. So you'd better get on and learn them.*

You May Have to Identify the Products of Electrolysis

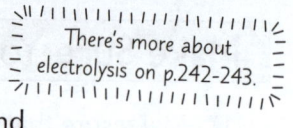

There's more about electrolysis on p.242-243.

1) When you electrolyse an aqueous solution, the products of electrolysis will depend on how reactive the ions in the solution are compared to the H^+ and OH^- ions that come from water.
2) At the cathode you'll either get a pure metal coating the electrode or bubbles of hydrogen gas.
3) At the anode, you'll get bubbles of oxygen gas unless a halide ion is present, when you'll get the halogen.
4) You may have to predict and identify what's been made in an electrolysis experiment. To do this, you need to be able to set up the equipment correctly so that you can collect any gas that's produced. The easiest way to collect the gas is in a test tube.
5) Here's how to set up the equipment...

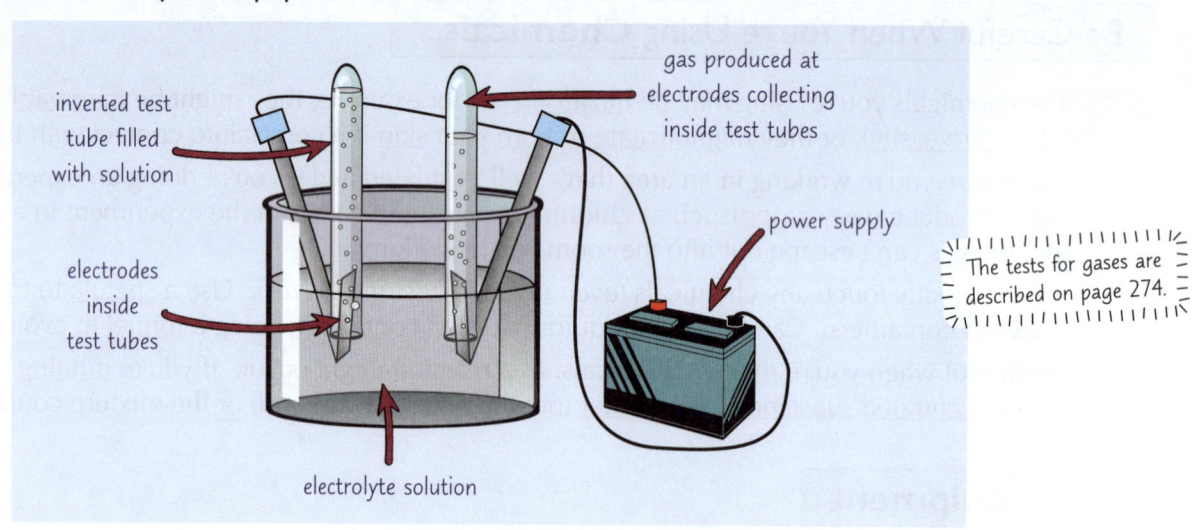

The tests for gases are described on page 274.

Potometers Should Be Set Up Underwater

A potometer is a special piece of apparatus used to measure the water uptake by a plant. Here's how to set one up:

If there are air bubbles in the apparatus or the plant's xylem it will affect your results.

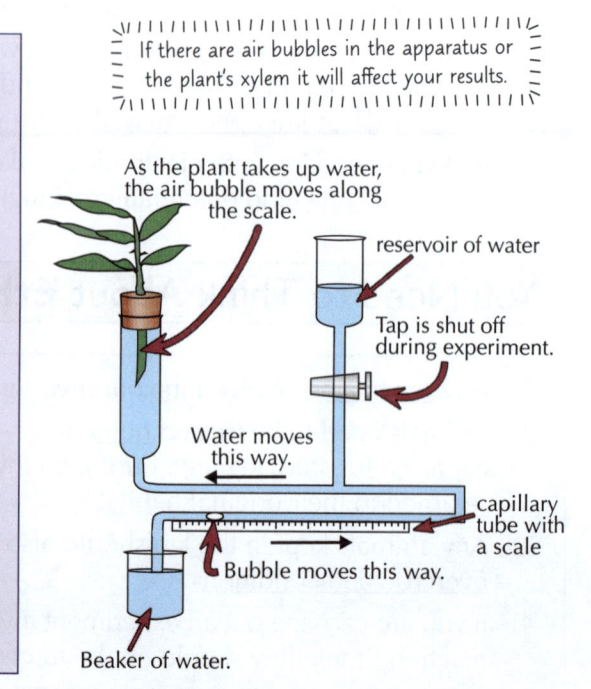

1) Cut a shoot underwater to prevent air from entering the xylem. Cut it at a slant to increase the surface area available for water uptake.
2) Assemble the potometer in water and insert the shoot under water, so no air can enter.
3) Remove the apparatus from the water but keep the end of the capillary tube submerged in a beaker of water.
4) Check that the apparatus is watertight and airtight.
5) Dry the leaves, allow time for the shoot to acclimatise and then shut the tap.
6) Remove the end of the capillary tube from the beaker of water until one air bubble has formed, then put the end of the tube back into the water.
7) A potometer can be used to estimate the transpiration rate of a plant. There's more about this on page 72.

Practical Skills

Setting Up Experiments

To Collect Gases, the System Needs to be Sealed

1) There are times when you might want to collect the gas produced by a reaction. For example, to investigate the rate of reaction.
2) The most accurate way to measure the volume of a gas that's been produced is to collect it in a gas syringe (see page 406).
3) You could also collect it by displacing water from a measuring cylinder. Here's how you do it...

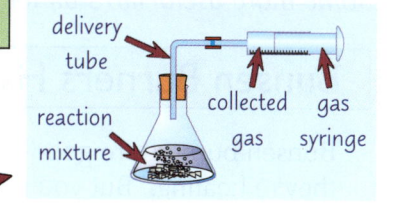

- Fill a measuring cylinder with water, and carefully place it upside down in a container of water. Record the initial level of the water in the measuring cylinder.
- Position a delivery tube coming from the reaction vessel so that it's inside the measuring cylinder, pointing upwards. Any gas that's produced will pass through the delivery tube and into the measuring cylinder. As the gas enters the measuring cylinder, the water is pushed out.
- Record the level of water in the measuring cylinder and use this value, along with your initial value, to calculate the volume of gas produced.

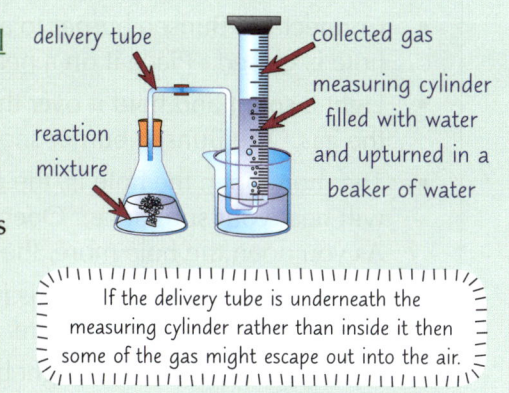

If the delivery tube is underneath the measuring cylinder rather than inside it then some of the gas might escape out into the air.

4) This method is less accurate than using a gas syringe to measure the volume of gas produced. This is because some gases can dissolve in water, so less gas ends up in the measuring cylinder than is actually produced.
5) If you just want to collect a sample to test (and don't need to measure a volume), you can collect it over water, as above, using a test tube. Once the test tube is full of gas, you can stopper it and store the gas for later.

Remember — when you're measuring a gas, your equipment has to be sealed or some gas could escape and your results wouldn't be accurate.

Make Sure You Can Draw Diagrams of Your Equipment

1) When you're writing out a method for your experiment, it's always a good idea to draw a labelled diagram showing how your apparatus will be set up.
2) The easiest way to do this is to use a scientific drawing, where each piece of apparatus is drawn as if you're looking at its cross-section. For example:

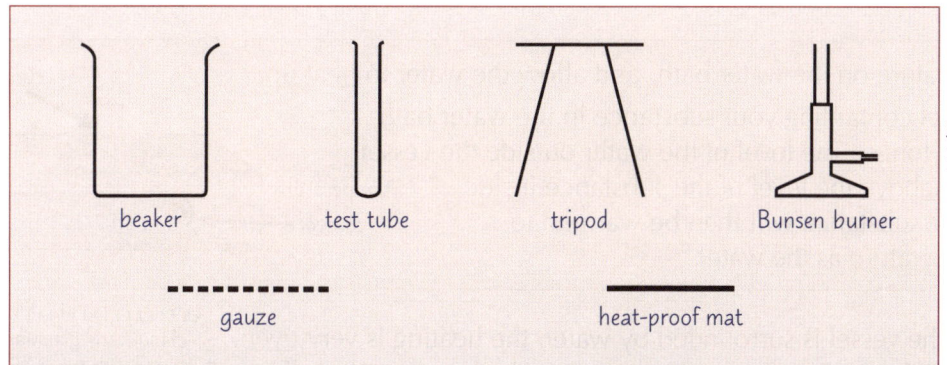

beaker   test tube   tripod   Bunsen burner
gauze   heat-proof mat

The pieces of glassware are drawn without tops so they aren't sealed. If you want to draw a closed system, remember to draw a bung in the top.

These simple diagrams are clear and easy to draw

Have a go at drawing out some of the practical diagrams on these pages using a simplified cross-section drawing of each piece of equipment. It'll give you some practice at doing them and you can revise how to set up the experiments as well. Win-win.

Practical Skills

Heating Substances

*Some more useful lab stuff for you now — a bit about **heating things up**.*

Bunsen Burners Have a Naked Flame

Bunsen burners are good for heating things quickly. You can easily adjust how strongly they're heating. But you need to be careful not to use them if you're heating flammable compounds as the flame means the substance would be at risk of catching fire.

Here's how to use a Bunsen burner...

- Connect the Bunsen burner to a gas tap, and check that the hole is closed. Place it on a heat-proof mat.
- Light a splint and hold it over the Bunsen burner. Now, turn on the gas. The Bunsen burner should light with a yellow flame.
- The more open the hole is, the more strongly the Bunsen burner will heat your substance. Open the hole to the amount you want. As you open the hole more, the flame should turn more blue.
- The hottest part of the flame is just above the blue cone, so you should heat things here.
- If your Bunsen burner is alight but not heating anything, make sure you close the hole so that the flame becomes yellow and clearly visible.
- If you're heating something so that the container (e.g. a test tube) is in the flame, you should hold the vessel at the top, furthest away from the substance (and so the flame) using a pair of tongs.
- If you're heating something over the flame (e.g. an evaporating dish), you should put a tripod and gauze over the Bunsen burner before you light it, and place the vessel on this.

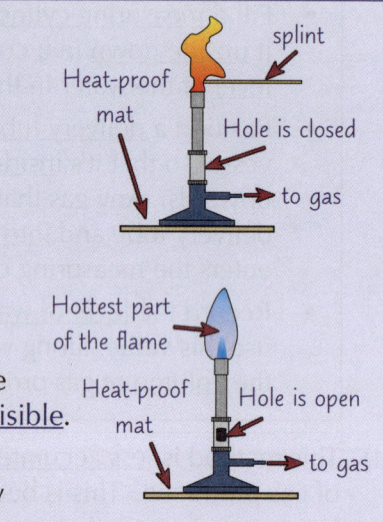

The Temperature of Water Baths & Electric Heaters Can Be Set

1) A water bath is a container filled with water that can be heated to a specific temperature. A simple water bath can be made by heating a beaker of water over a Bunsen burner and monitoring the temperature with a thermometer. However, it is difficult to keep the temperature of the water constant.

2) An electric water bath will monitor and adjust the temperature for you. Here's how you use one:

- Set the temperature on the water bath, and allow the water to heat up.
- Place the vessel containing your substance in the water bath using a pair of tongs. The level of the water outside the vessel should be just above the level of the substance inside the vessel. The substance will then be warmed to the same temperature as the water.

As the substance in the vessel is surrounded by water, the heating is very even. Water boils at 100 °C though, so you can't use a water bath to heat something to a higher temperature than this — the water won't get hot enough.

Handle any glassware you've heated with tongs until you're sure it's cooled down.

3) Electric heaters are often made up of a metal plate that can be heated to a certain temperature. The vessel containing the substance you want to heat is placed on top of the hot plate. You can heat substances to higher temperatures than you can in a water bath but, as the vessel is only heated from below, you'll usually have to stir the substance inside to make sure it's heated evenly.

Practical Skills

Working with Electronics

Electrical devices are used in a bunch of **experiments**, so make sure you know how to use them.

You Have to Interpret Circuit Diagrams

Before you get cracking on an experiment involving any kind of electrical devices, you have to plan and build your circuit using a circuit diagram. Make sure you know all of the circuit symbols on page 316 so you're not stumped before you've even started.

There Are a Couple of Ways to Measure Potential Difference and Current

Voltmeters Measure Potential Difference

1) If you're using an analogue voltmeter, choose the voltmeter with the most appropriate unit (e.g. V or mV). If you're using a digital voltmeter, you'll most likely be able to switch between them.
2) Connect the voltmeter in parallel (p.325) across the component you want to test. The wires that come with a voltmeter are usually red (positive) and black (negative). These go into the red and black coloured ports on the voltmeter. Funnily enough.
3) Then simply read the potential difference from the scale (or from the screen if it's digital).

Ammeters Measure Current

1) Just like with voltmeters, choose the ammeter with the most appropriate unit.
2) Connect the ammeter in series (p.324) with the component you want to test, making sure they're both on the same branch. Again, they usually have red and black ports to show you where to connect your wires.
3) Read off the current shown on the scale or by the screen.

Turn your circuit off between readings to prevent wires overheating and affecting your results (p.317).

Multimeters Measure Both

1) Instead of having a separate ammeter and voltmeter, many circuits use multimeters. These are devices that measure a range of properties — usually potential difference, current and resistance.
2) If you want to find potential difference, make sure the red wire is plugged into the port that has a 'V' (for volts).
3) To find the current, use the port labelled 'A' or 'mA' (for amps).
4) The dial on the multimeter should then be turned to the relevant section, e.g. to 'A' to measure current in amps. The screen will display the value you're measuring.

Light Gates Measure Speed and Acceleration

1) A light gate sends a beam of light from one side of the gate to a detector on the other side. When something passes through the gate, the beam of light is interrupted. The light gate then measures how long the beam was undetected.
2) To find the speed of an object, connect the light gate to a computer. Measure the length of the object and input this using the software. It will then automatically calculate the speed of the object as it passes through the beam.
3) To measure acceleration, use an object that interrupts the signal twice in a short period of time, e.g. a piece of card with a gap cut into the middle.
4) The light gate measures the speed for each section of the object and uses this to calculate its acceleration. This can then be read from the computer screen.

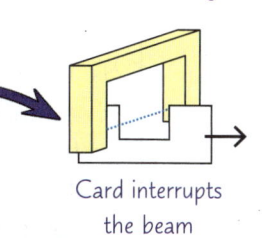

Light gate
Beam of light
Card interrupts the beam

Have a look at page 373 for an example of a light gate being used.

Practical Skills

Sampling

You need to be able to carry out **sampling** that'll give you **non-biased results**. First up **why**, then **how**...

Sampling Should be Random

1) When you're investigating a population, it's generally not possible to study every single organism in the population. This means that you need to take samples of the population you're interested in.
2) The sample data will be used to draw conclusions about the whole population, so it's important that it accurately represents the whole population.
3) To make sure a sample represents the population, it should be random.

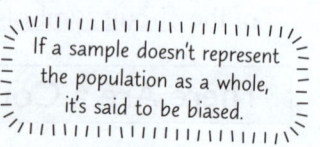

If a sample doesn't represent the population as a whole, it's said to be biased.

Organisms Should Be Sampled At Random Sites in an Area

1) If you're interested in the distribution of an organism in an area, or its population size, you can take population samples in the area you're interested in using quadrats or transects (see pages 157-158).
2) If you only take samples from one part of the area, your results will be biased — they may not give an accurate representation of the whole area.
3) To make sure that your sampling isn't biased, you need to use a method of choosing sampling sites in which every site has an equal chance of being chosen. For example:

If you're looking at plant species in a field...
1) Divide the field into a grid.
2) Label the grid along the bottom and up the side with numbers.
3) Use a random number generator (on a computer or calculator) to select coordinates, e.g. (2,6).
4) Take your samples at these coordinates.

Non-random sampling — Only looks at a small part of the field.
Random sampling — Randomly selects squares from all over the field.

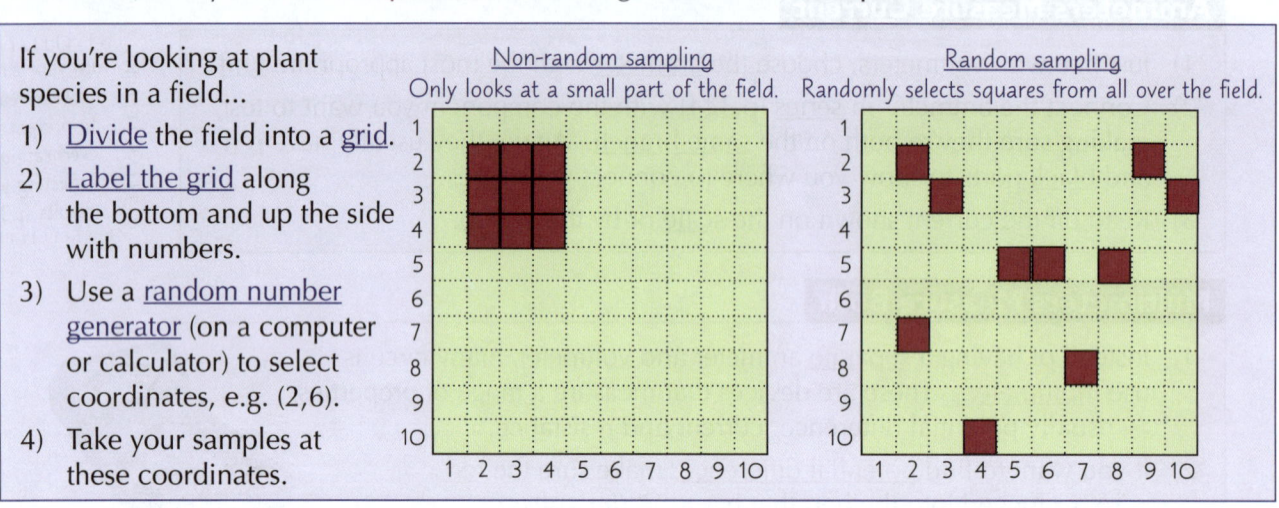

Health Data Should be Taken from Randomly Selected People

1) As mentioned above, it's not practical (or even possible) to study an entire human population.
2) You need to use random sampling to choose members of the population you're interested in. For example:

> A health professional is investigating how many people diagnosed with Type 2 diabetes in a particular country also have heart disease:
> 1) All the people who have been diagnosed with Type 2 diabetes in the country of interest are identified by hospital records. In total, there are 270 196 people.
> 2) These people are assigned a number between 1 and 270 196.
> 3) A random number generator is used to choose the sample group (e.g. it selects the individuals #72 063, #11 822, #193 123, etc.)
> 4) The proportion of people in the sample that have heart disease can be used to estimate the total number of people with Type 2 diabetes that also have heart disease.

Practical Skills

Comparing Results

*Being able to **compare** your results is really important. Here are some ways you might do it.*

Percentage Change Allows you to Compare Results

1) When investigating the change in a variable, you may want to compare results that didn't have the same initial value. For example, you may want to compare the change in mass of potato cylinders left in different concentrations of sugar solution that had different initial masses (see page 32).

2) One way to do this is to calculate the percentage change. You work it out like this:

$$\text{percentage (\%) change} = \frac{\text{final value} - \text{original value}}{\text{original value}} \times 100$$

EXAMPLE

A student is investigating the effect of the concentration of sugar solution on potato cells. She records the mass of potato cylinders before and after placing them in sugar solutions of different concentrations. The table on the right shows some of her results. Which potato cylinder had the largest percentage change?

Potato cylinder	Concentration (mol/dm³)	Mass at start (g)	Mass at end (g)
1	0.0	7.5	8.7
2	1.0	8.0	6.8

Stick each set of results into the equation:

$\% \text{ change} = \frac{\text{final value} - \text{original value}}{\text{original value}} \times 100$

1. $\frac{8.7 - 7.5}{7.5} \times 100 = 16\%$ — The mass at the start is the original value. The mass at the end is the final value.

2. $\frac{6.8 - 8.0}{8.0} \times 100 = -15\%$ — Here, the mass has decreased so the percentage change is negative.

Compare the results. **16% is greater than 15%, so the potato cylinder in the 0.0 mol/dm³ sugar solution had the largest percentage change.**

Percentiles Tell you Where in Your Data Set a Data Point Lies

1) Percentiles are useful if you want to compare the value of one data point to the rest of your data.

2) To find a percentile, you rank your data from smallest to largest, then divide it into one hundred equal chunks. Each chunk is one percentile.

3) This means that each percentile represents one percent of the data, and so the value of a percentile tells you what percentage of the data has a value lower than the data points in that percentile.

> E.g. A student is in the 90th percentile for height in his class.
> This means that 90% of the class are shorter than him.

4) Percentiles can be used to give a more realistic idea of the spread of data than the range (see p.9) — by finding the range between the 10th and 90th percentiles in a data set (the middle 80% of the data), you can look at the spread of the data while ignoring any outlying results.

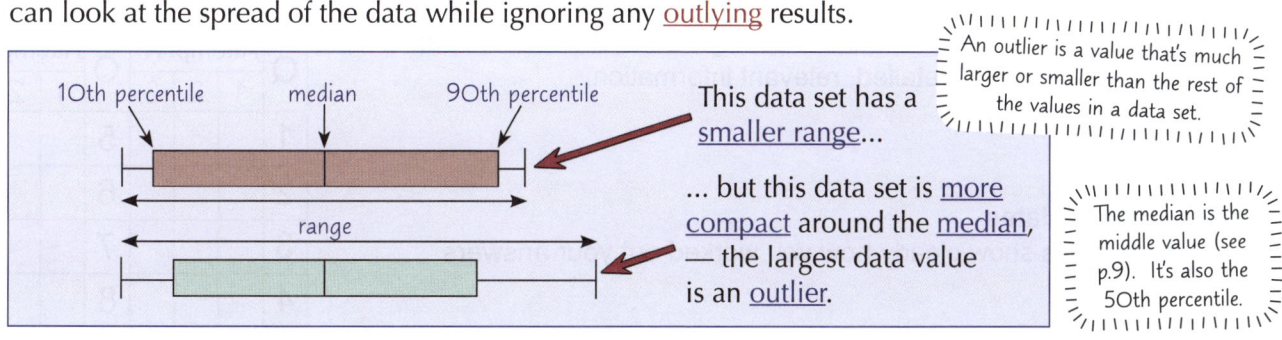

An outlier is a value that's much larger or smaller than the rest of the values in a data set.

This data set has a smaller range...

... but this data set is more compact around the median, — the largest data value is an outlier.

The median is the middle value (see p.9). It's also the 50th percentile.

Practical Skills

Practice Exams

Once you've been through all the questions in this book, you should feel pretty confident about the exams. As final preparation, here is a set of **practice exams** to really get you set for the real thing. The time allowed for each paper is 1 hour 15 minutes. These papers are designed to give you the best possible preparation for your exams.

CGP Practice Exam Paper GCSE Combined Science

GCSE Combined Science
Biology Paper 1
Higher Tier

In addition to this paper you should have:
- A ruler.
- A calculator.

Centre name

Centre number

Candidate number

Surname

Other names

Candidate signature

Time allowed:
- 1 hour 15 minutes

Instructions to candidates
- Write your name and other details in the spaces provided above.
- Answer **all** questions in the spaces provided.
- Do all rough work on the paper.
- Cross out any work you do not want to be marked.

Information for candidates
- The marks available are given in brackets at the end of each question.
- There are 70 marks available for this paper.
- You are allowed to use a calculator.
- You should use good English and present your answers in a clear and organised way.
- For Questions 1.4, 2.2, 4.5 and 7 ensure that your answers have a clear and logical structure, include the right scientific terms, spelt correctly and include detailed, relevant information.

Advice to candidates
- In calculations show clearly how you worked out your answers.

For examiner's use

Q	Attempt Nº 1 2 3	Q	Attempt Nº 1 2 3
1		5	
2		6	
3		7	
4		8	
		Total	

1 **Figure 1** shows a single-celled organism called *Euglena*, found in pond water.

Figure 1

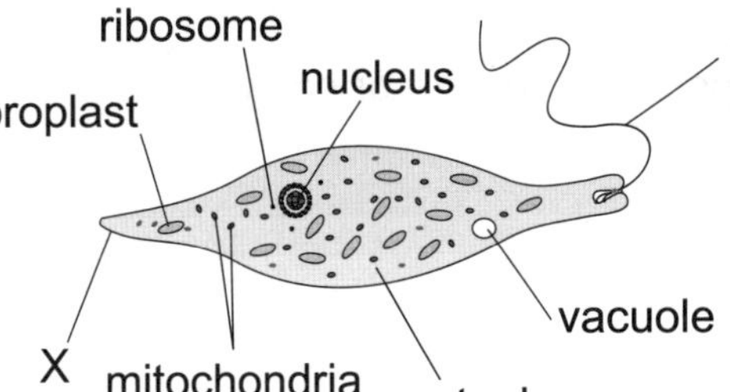

1.1 Name part **X**.

....
[1 mark]

1.2 *Euglena* is a eukaryote. Which of the following is **not** a eukaryote?
Tick **one** box.

☐ sperm cell ☐ muscle cell ☐ fruit fly ☐ *E. coli* bacteria
[1 mark]

1.3 A scientist viewed an individual *Euglena* under a microscope with × 150 magnification.
He calculated the real length of the *Euglena* to be 0.054 mm.
Calculate the length of the image of the Euglena. Use the formula:

$$\text{magnification} = \frac{\text{image size}}{\text{real size}}$$

....

.... mm
[2 marks]

1.4 When *Euglena* was first discovered, scientists disagreed over whether it was a plant or an animal.
Compare the features of plant and animal cells.
Include details of their features in your answer.

....

....

....

....

....

....

....

....

....
[6 marks]

Turn over for the next question **Turn over ▶**

2 Measles, mumps and rubella are all examples of communicable diseases.

2.1 How is measles spread between people?
Tick **one** box.

☐ By droplets from an infected person's sneeze or cough.

☐ By sexual contact.

☐ By eating contaminated food.

☐ By a vector.

[1 mark]

2.2 The MMR vaccine protects against measles, mumps and rubella.
Explain how vaccination helps to protect the body against a disease.

....

....

....

....

....

....

[4 marks]

Zika virus disease is another example of a communicable disease.
Symptoms of infection include fever, skin rashes, muscle and joint pain, and headaches.
The virus that causes the disease is spread by a mosquito vector.

2.3 Suggest **two** ways that the spread of the Zika virus disease could be reduced.

....

....

....

[2 marks]

3 Different chemical reagents can be used to test for the presence of certain molecules in samples of food.

3.1 A student prepared a food sample in order to test whether the sample contained protein.
What reagent should be used for this test?
Tick **one** box.

☐ Benedict's solution   ☐ iodine solution

☐ biuret solution   ☐ Sudan III stain solution

[1 mark]

The student tested four different food samples for reducing sugars.
She obtained the results shown in **Table 1**.

Table 1

Sample	A	B	C	D
Colour of sample	blue	brick-red	yellow	green

3.2 Name the reagent that the student would have used to test for reducing sugars.

....
[1 mark]

3.3 Which of the samples in **Table 1** didn't contain reducing sugars?
Tick **one** box.

☐ A   ☐ B   ☐ C   ☐ D

[1 mark]

Lactose is a reducing sugar commonly found in dairy products, such as milk and cheese. An enzyme called lactase breaks down lactose during digestion. The resulting products are the sugars glucose and galactose. These are absorbed into the blood from the small intestine.

3.4 Describe how the small intestine is adapted to absorb molecules such as glucose.

....
....
....
[3 marks]

3.5 Lactose intolerance is a digestive problem caused by insufficient production of lactase.

To test a person for lactose intolerance, they are given a drink of lactose solution.
A blood sample is then taken from them every 30 minutes for two hours.
The blood is tested to see how much sugar it contains.
Suggest what will happen to the blood sugar level of a person who is lactose intolerant during the test. Explain your answer.

....
....
....
[2 marks]

Turn over for the next question   **Turn over ▶**

4 **Figure 2** shows a human heart.

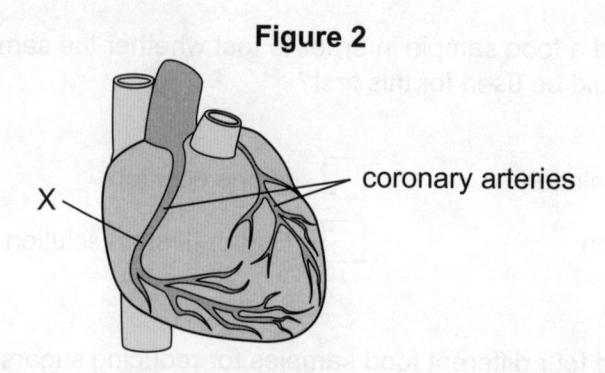

Figure 2

X — coronary arteries

4.1 Explain what would happen if the coronary artery was blocked at the point labelled **X**.

....

....
[2 marks]

A patient has fatty deposits in the walls of one of his coronary arteries.
The patient's doctor recommends that the patient is treated using a stent.

4.2 Explain how having a stent fitted could help the patient.

....

....
[1 mark]

Statins are a type of drug used to reduce the risk of coronary heart disease.

A new statin has been developed and was initially put through preclinical testing. Following this, the drug was given to thirty healthy volunteers in a clinical trial.

A trial was then carried out on 2000 patients who had previously had a heart attack — half were given the drug and half were given a placebo.

Figure 3 shows the results after five years of treatment.

Figure 3

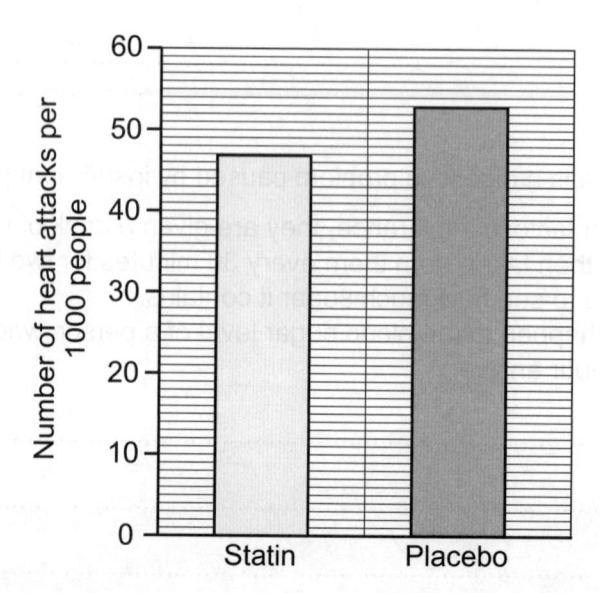

4.3 During the clinical trial, what was the main reason for giving the drug to healthy human volunteers?

....

[1 mark]

4.4 Give **one** reason why the results of the trial could be considered valid.

....

....

[1 mark]

4.5 A person with heart failure may need to have their heart replaced.
The replacement heart can either be from a donor or it can be an artificial heart.

Evaluate the treatment of heart failure using a heart transplant from a donor and using an artificial heart. Include a justified conclusion in your evaluation.

....

....

....

....

....

....

....

....

....

....

....

....

[6 marks]

Turn over for the next question

Turn over ▶

5 A student did an experiment to investigate the effect of temperature on the action of the enzyme amylase. The method used is shown below.

> 1. Add a set volume of starch solution to a test tube and the same volume of amylase solution to another.
> 2. Place the test tubes in a water bath at 10 °C.
> 3. Allow the starch and amylase solutions to reach the temperature of the water bath, then mix them together and return the mixture to the water bath.
> 4. Take a small sample of the mixture every ten seconds and test for starch.
> 5. Stop the experiment when starch is no longer present in the sample.
> 6. Repeat the experiment at different temperatures.

5.1 What happens to the starch solution during the experiment?

....

[1 mark]

5.2 Suggest how the student could have tested for the presence of starch in **Step 4**.

....

....

....

....

[3 marks]

Figure 4 shows a graph of the student's results.

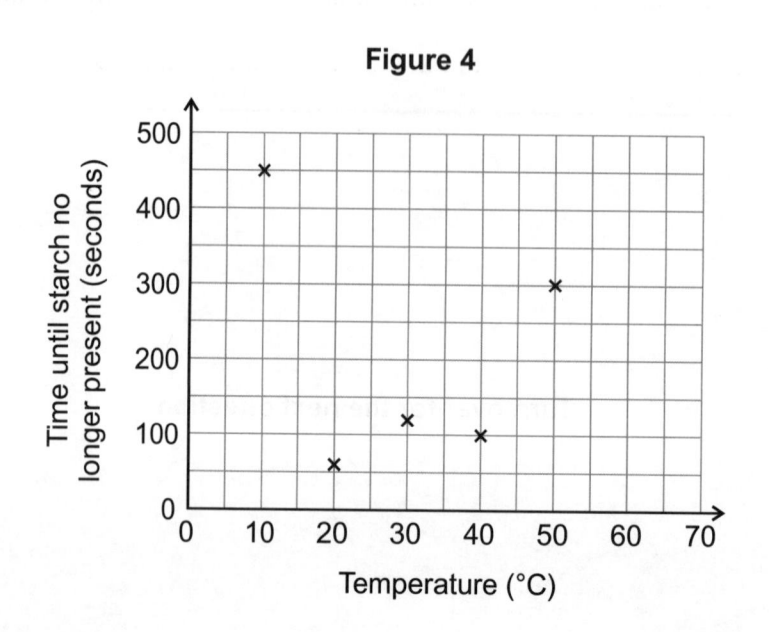

Figure 4

[Graph: Time until starch no longer present (seconds) vs Temperature (°C). Points approximately at (10, 450), (20, 50), (30, 120), (40, 100), (50, 300).]

5.3 Calculate the rate of the reaction at 40 °C.
Use the formula:

Rate = $\dfrac{1000}{\text{time}}$

....

....

.... s^{-1}
[2 marks]

5.4 At 60 °C, the amount of starch in the mixture did not decrease.
Explain why.

....

....

....

....
[3 marks]

5.5 The student thinks that one of the results shown in **Figure 4** is likely to be anomalous. Explain which is the anomalous result and suggest what the student might have done to cause this anomalous result.

....

....

....
[3 marks]

The student plans to alter the experiment in order to investigate the effect of pH on the action of amylase.

5.6 Describe how the pH could be altered in the experiment.

....

....
[1 mark]

Turn over for the next question

Turn over ▶

6 A scientist measured the rate of transpiration in two plants over 48 hours. The results are shown in **Figure 5**.

Figure 5

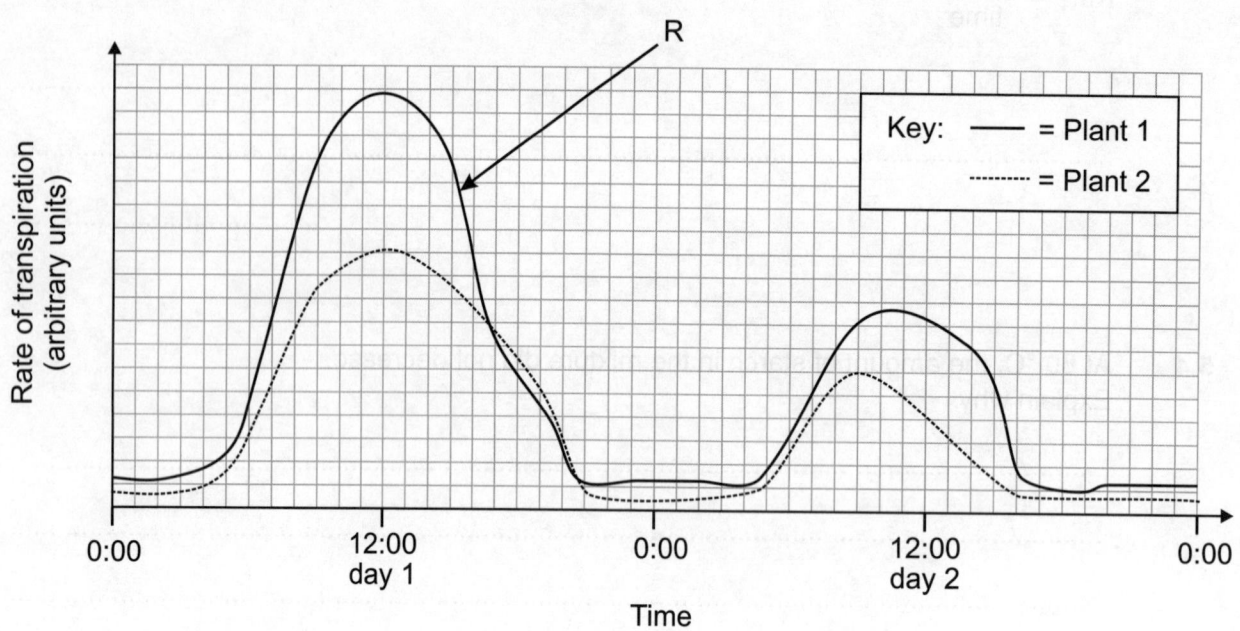

6.1 The rate of transpiration for both plants was slower on **day 2** than on **day 1**. Suggest **one** explanation for this.

....
....
....

[2 marks]

6.2 At time **R** on the graph, **plant 1** was wilting. Suggest **one** explanation for this.

....
....

[1 mark]

6.3 Describe how a transpiration stream moves water through a plant.

....
....
....
....
....

[3 marks]

7 Herbicides are chemicals that are used to kill unwanted plants.
Some herbicides work by disrupting the cell cycle within plants.

Describe the stages of the cell cycle and suggest why disrupting the cell cycle by using herbicides can kill plants.

[6 marks]

Turn over for the next question

8   A student is investigating how his heart rate changes during and after exercise.
He measures his heart rate using a portable heart rate monitor.
He takes his resting heart rate before running around the school track
for two minutes. Then he rests again. His results are shown in **Table 2**.

Table 2

Time after first heart rate measurement taken (min)	First run — Heart rate (beats/min)
0	72
1	118
2	132
3	129
4	116
5	98
6	84
7	76
8	72
9	72

8.1 Complete **Figure 6** using the data from **Table 2**.
- Complete the *x*-axis. Include a label and use a suitable scale.
- Plot the heart rate.
- Draw a curve of best fit.

Figure 6

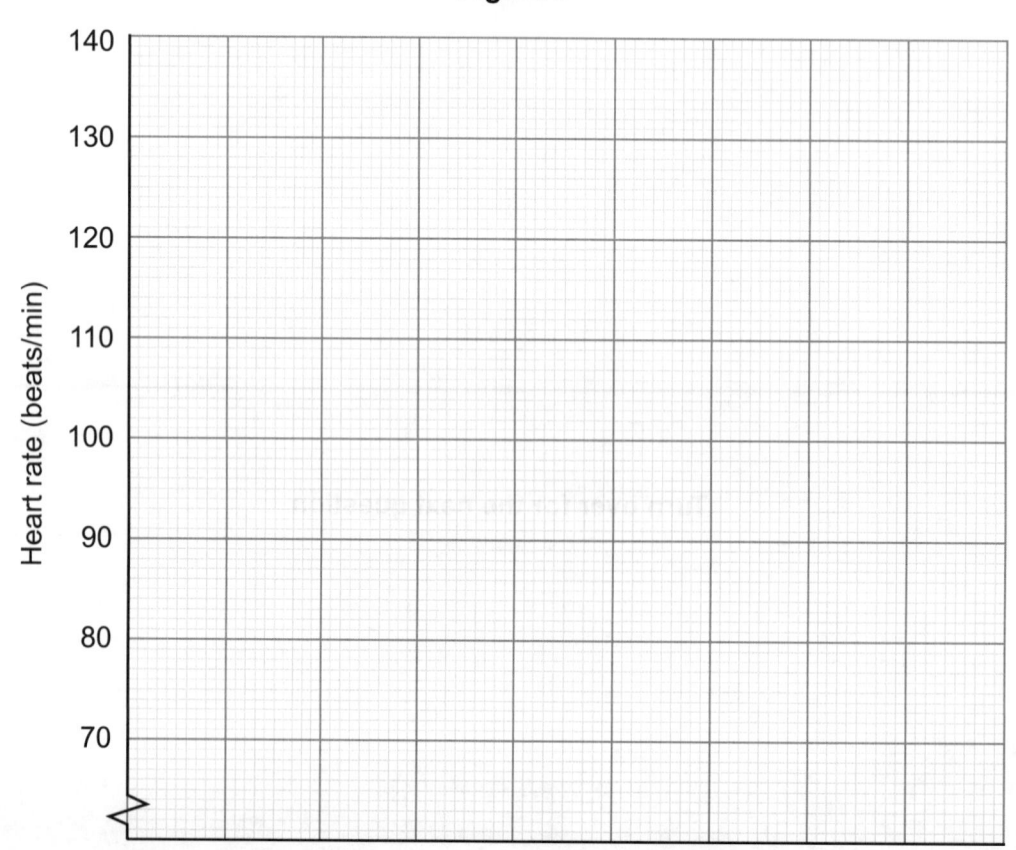

8.2 Use your graph in **Figure 6** to estimate the student's heart rate after thirty seconds.

heart rate = ... (beats/min)

[1 mark]

8.3 Describe how the student's heart rate changes with exercise.
Explain why this change occurs.

....

....

....

....

....

[4 marks]

END OF QUESTIONS

GCSE Combined Science
Biology Paper 2
Higher Tier

In addition to this paper you should have:
- A ruler.
- A calculator.

Centre name

Centre number

Candidate number

Surname

Other names

Candidate signature

Time allowed:
- 1 hour 15 minutes

Instructions to candidates
- Write your name and other details in the spaces provided above.
- Answer **all** questions in the spaces provided.
- Do all rough work on the paper.
- Cross out any work you do not want to be marked.

Information for candidates
- The marks available are given in brackets at the end of each question.
- There are 70 marks available for this paper.
- You are allowed to use a calculator.
- You should use good English and present your answers in a clear and organised way.
- For Questions 2.5, 4.7 and 6.2 ensure that your answers have a clear and logical structure, include the right scientific terms, spelt correctly and include detailed, relevant information.

Advice to candidates
- In calculations show clearly how you worked out your answers.

For examiner's use

Q	Attempt Nº 1	2	3	Q	Attempt Nº 1	2	3
1				5			
2				6			
3				7			
4				8			
				Total			

1 The endocrine system is important for regulating many different processes in the body.

Figure 1 shows some of the glands in the endocrine system.

Figure 1

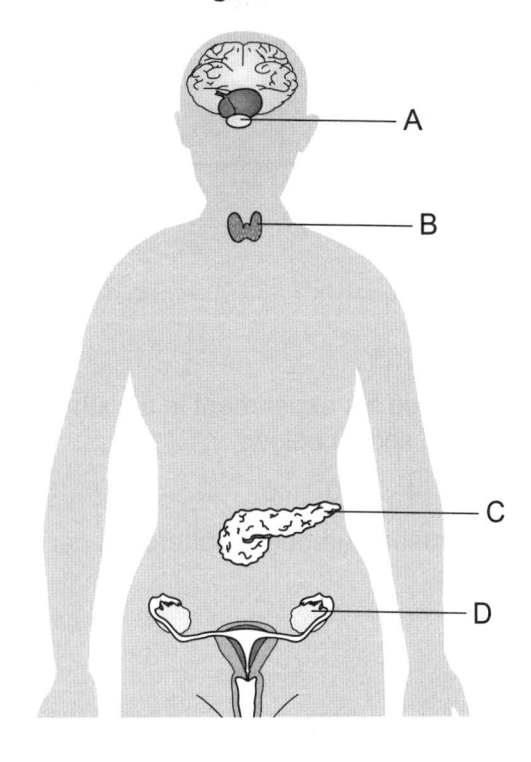

The thyroid gland releases a hormone called thyroxine. One way in which thyroxine affects the body is by increasing the strength of the heart beat.

1.1 Which label on **Figure 1** points to the thyroid gland? Tick **one** box.

☐ A   ☐ B   ☐ C   ☐ D

[1 mark]

1.2 Describe how thyroxine is able to directly affect cells in the heart.

....
....
....

[2 marks]

The pituitary gland is an important part of the endocrine system.

1.3 Explain why the pituitary gland is often referred to as the 'master gland'.

....
....
....

[2 marks]

Turn over for the next question

2 A student was investigating the distribution of buttercups in an area around his school. He counted the number of buttercups in 10 quadrats in five different fields. His quadrat measured 1 m². His results are shown in **Table 1**.

Table 1

Field	A	B	C	D	E
Mean number of buttercups per quadrat	10	35	21	37	21

2.1 What is the median of the data in **Table 1**?

....
[1 mark]

2.2 A week later, the student repeated his experiment in a sixth field, Field **F**. His results for each quadrat are shown below:

6   15   9   14   20   5   3   11   10   7

Using this data, calculate the mean number of buttercups per m² in Field **F**.

....

Mean = ... buttercups per m²
[2 marks]

2.3 Field **F** measures 90 m by 120 m.
Estimate the population of buttercups in Field **F**.

....

Estimated population = ... buttercups
[2 marks]

The student observed that the distribution of buttercups changed across Field **A**. Buttercups grow well in damp soil, so the student thinks that the change in the distribution of buttercups is due to variability in the moisture level of the soil across the field. The student wants to investigate this.

2.4 Suggest a hypothesis about the distribution of buttercups in Field **A**, based on the student's observations.

....
[1 mark]

2.5 Describe how the student could investigate this hypothesis.

....

....

....

....

....
[4 marks]

3 The peppered moth is an insect that lives on the trunks of trees in Britain.
The moths are prey for birds such as thrushes.

The peppered moth exists in two varieties:
- A light-coloured variety that is better camouflaged on tree trunks in unpolluted areas.
- A dark-coloured variety that is better camouflaged on sooty tree trunks in badly polluted areas.

Figures 2 and **3** show these two varieties of moths on different tree trunks.

Figure 2

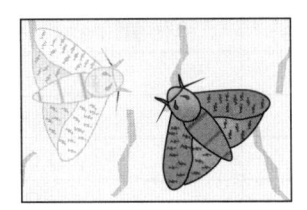

Figure 3

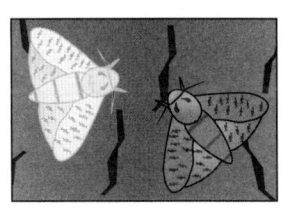

The dark variety of the moth was first recorded in the North of England in 1848.

It became increasingly common in polluted areas until the 1960s, when the number of soot covered trees declined because of the introduction of new laws.

3.1 The binomial name of the peppered moth is *Biston betularia*.
What is the moth's genus?

....
[1 mark]

3.2 Which variety of moth has a better chance of survival in a soot polluted area?

....
[1 mark]

3.3 Using the idea of natural selection, explain why the variety of moth given in **3.2** became more common in soot polluted areas.

....
....
....
....
[3 marks]

Turn over for the next question

Turn over ▶

4 A scientist was investigating the reflex actions of males and females.

The scientist made the following hypothesis: **'Males have faster reaction times than females.'**

The reaction times of eight participants were tested in the investigation.
Each participant was tapped just below the knee with a small rubber hammer.
When the leg was tapped it automatically kicked outwards at the knee.

The scientist recorded how long it took each participant to respond to the stimulus of the tap on the leg. Each participant did the test 20 times, and a mean reaction time was calculated (to 2 decimal places). The results are shown in **Table 2**.

Table 2

Sex	Participant	Age (years)	Mean reaction time (s)
Female	1	29	0.05
	2	26	0.06
	3	24	0.06
	4	27	0.04
Male	5	19	0.05
	6	22	0.04
	7	25	0.04
	8	20	0.05

4.1 How can you tell that the participants' response was a reflex? Give **two** reasons.

....

....

....
[2 marks]

4.2 What was the dependent variable in this experiment?
Tick **one** box.

☐ age   ☐ stimulus   ☐ reaction time   ☐ sex
[1 mark]

4.3 What was the independent variable in this experiment?
Tick **one** box.

☐ age   ☐ stimulus   ☐ reaction time   ☐ sex
[1 mark]

4.4 **Figure 4** shows the mean reaction times for males and females in the investigation.

Figure 4

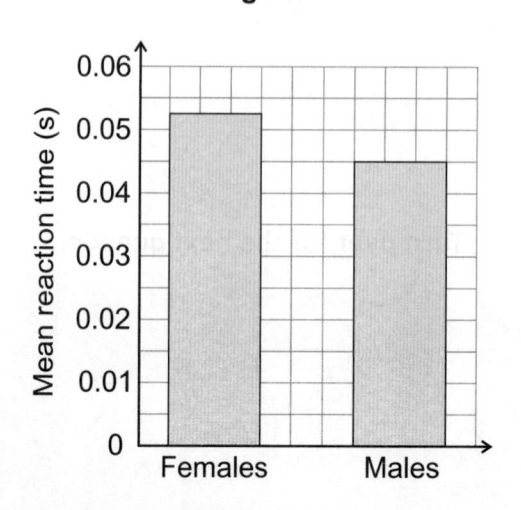

What can be concluded from the data in **Figure 4**?
Refer back to the scientist's hypothesis in your answer.

....

....

[2 marks]

4.5 Suggest **one** variable that the scientist should have controlled in this experiment.

....

....

[1 mark]

Another example of a reflex is the Babinski reflex, in which a baby curls its big toe upwards when the sole of its foot is stroked. **Figure 5** shows the parts of the nervous system involved in this reflex.

Figure 5

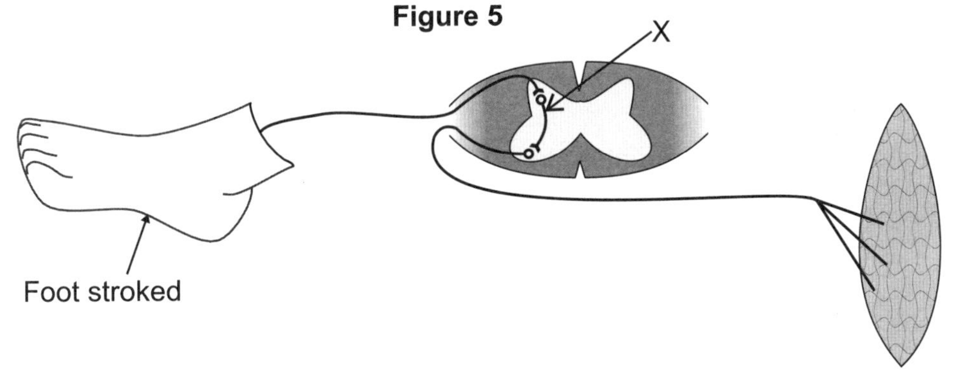

Foot stroked

4.6 Name part **X** shown in **Figure 5**.

....

[1 mark]

4.7 The touch stimulus is detected by receptors in the skin and causes a reflex response. Describe the path taken by a nervous impulse in this reflex, beginning at the receptors.

....

....

....

....

....

....

....

....

....

[6 marks]

Turn over for the next question   **Turn over ▶**

5   Various research programmes aim to improve human health through research into the human genome.

5.1 What is meant by the term 'genome'?

....

[1 mark]

Cystic fibrosis is an inherited disorder caused by a recessive allele.

5.2 How could research into the human genome have the potential to help people with cystic fibrosis?

....

....

[1 mark]

A couple have a baby boy. The doctor tells them that the baby has inherited cystic fibrosis. Neither parent shows signs of the disorder.

5.3 Construct a Punnett square to show how the baby inherited cystic fibrosis. Use the diagram to work out the probability of any future child of the couple inheriting cystic fibrosis.

Use **F** to represent the dominant allele and **f** to represent the recessive allele.

Probability = ...

[4 marks]

5.4 Is the baby homozygous or heterozygous for cystic fibrosis?
Explain your answer.

....

....

[1 mark]

6 Hepatitis B is a viral disease that can severely damage the liver. The disease can be prevented in people who have been vaccinated against it. Being vaccinated involves being deliberately exposed to antigens carried by the hepatitis B virus. Scientists have successfully genetically engineered potatoes so that they can be used as a vaccine against hepatitis B.

6.1 Production of the genetically engineered potatoes involves the introduction of the HBsAg gene into the potatoes. Suggest the role of the HBsAg gene.

....

....

[1 mark]

6.2 Describe the process involved in producing genetically engineered organisms.

....

....

....

....

....

....

....

[4 marks]

Turn over for the next question

Turn over ▶

7 Reproduction can be sexual or asexual.

7.1 Give **three** differences between sexual and asexual reproduction.

....

....

....

....
[3 marks]

In humans, sexual reproduction involves the reproductive system.

7.2 The male reproductive system includes the testes.
What hormone is produced by the testes?

....
[1 mark]

7.3 The female reproductive system includes the ovaries.

The ovaries produce the hormone oestrogen.
Describe the role of oestrogen in the menstrual cycle.

....

....
[2 marks]

Figure 6 shows the fluctuations in the levels of four different hormones during one 28 day menstrual cycle.

Figure 6

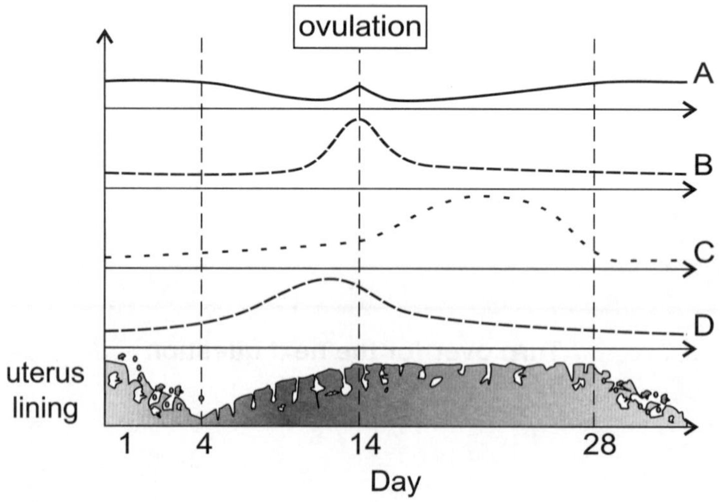

7.4 Which line in **Figure 6** represents progesterone?
Explain your answer.

Line ....

Explanation ....

....
[2 marks]

Some methods of contraception use reproductive hormones to control fertility.
One such method is the contraceptive implant, shown in **Figure 7**.

Figure 7

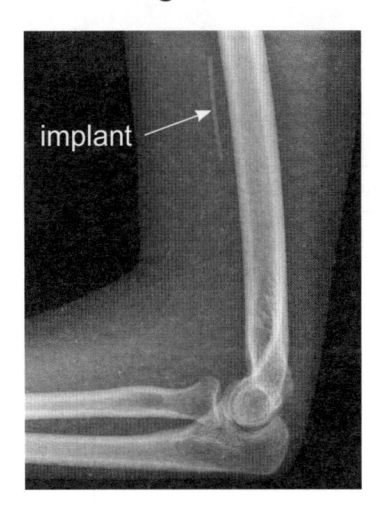

The contraceptive implant:

- is a small, plastic rod that is inserted by a doctor or nurse
- releases progesterone, which reduces fertility
- is effective for three years
- is over 99% effective at preventing pregnancy
- can cause side effects such as headaches and nausea
- can be made less effective by certain medications

Figure 8 shows a condom. The condom is a barrier method of contraception.

Figure 8

The condom:

- is worn over the penis during intercourse
- prevents sperm from entering the vagina
- can only be used once
- is 98% effective at preventing pregnancy when used correctly
- protects against sexually transmitted disease (STDs)

7.5 Use the information to evaluate the implant and condom as methods of contraception.
Give a conclusion of which you think is the better method of contraception.
Justify your conclusion.

....

....

....

....

....

....

....

....

....

[4 marks]

Turn over for the next question

Turn over ▶

8   **Figure 9** shows the carbon cycle.

Figure 9

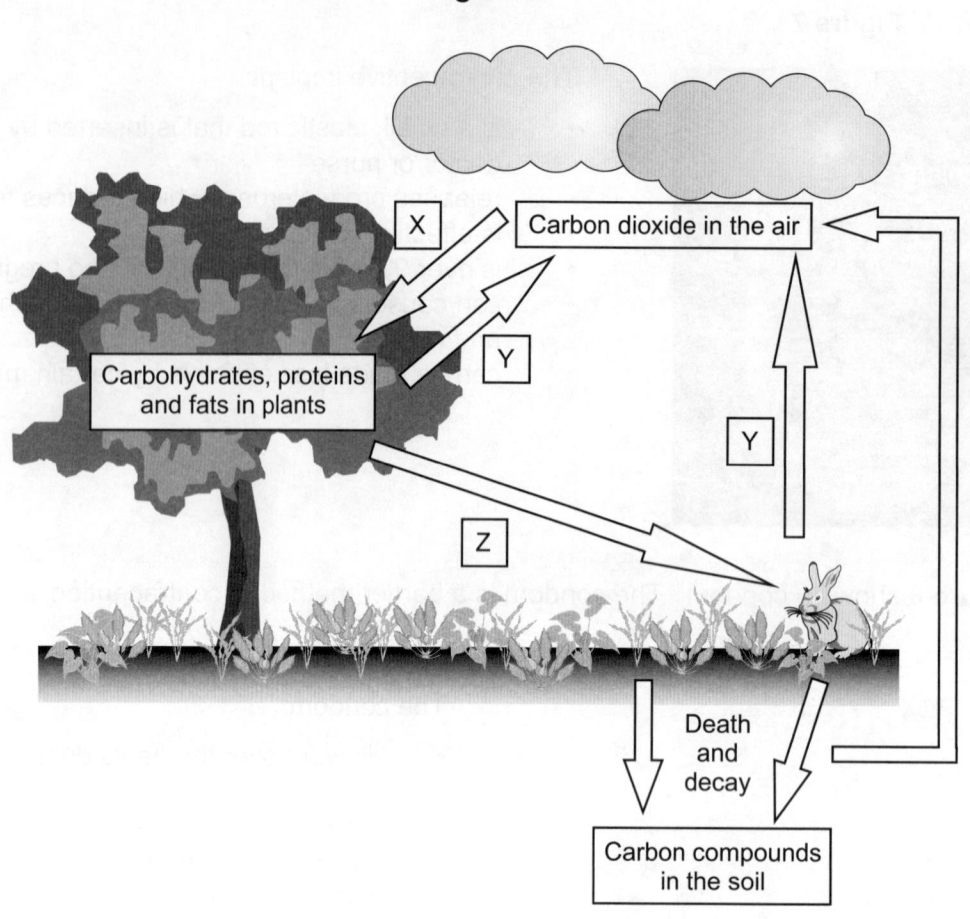

8.1 Describe what is occurring at points **X**, **Y** and **Z** in the cycle.

....

....

....

....

....
[3 marks]

8.2 How are microorganisms involved in the carbon cycle?

....

....

....
[2 marks]

A scientist was examining some data to see if there is a link between the global human population and the carbon dioxide concentration in the atmosphere.

Figure 10 shows the two graphs that the scientist examined.

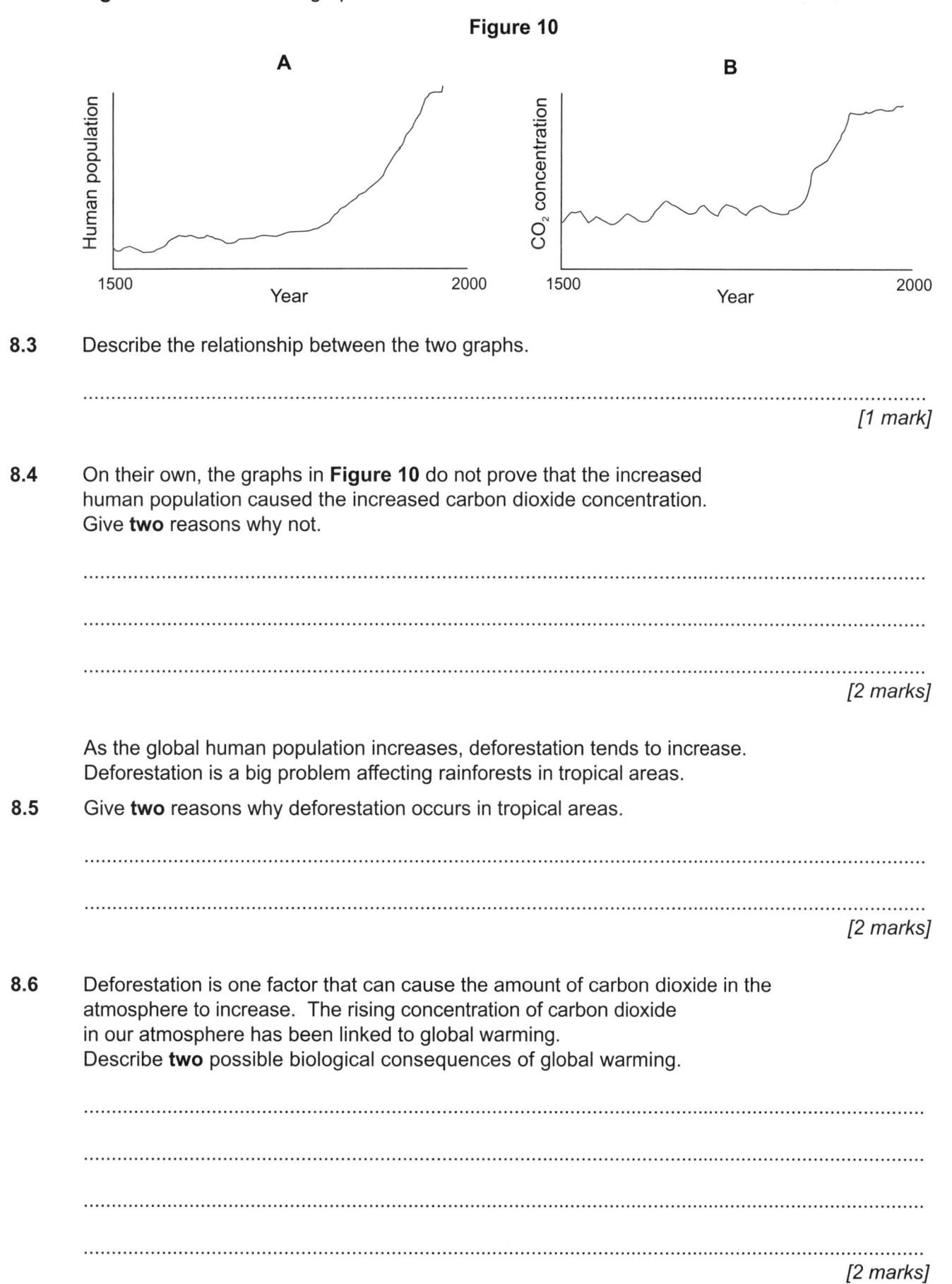

Figure 10

A — Human population vs Year (1500–2000)

B — CO_2 concentration vs Year (1500–2000)

8.3 Describe the relationship between the two graphs.

....

[1 mark]

8.4 On their own, the graphs in **Figure 10** do not prove that the increased human population caused the increased carbon dioxide concentration.

Give **two** reasons why not.

....

....

....

[2 marks]

As the global human population increases, deforestation tends to increase. Deforestation is a big problem affecting rainforests in tropical areas.

8.5 Give **two** reasons why deforestation occurs in tropical areas.

....

....

[2 marks]

8.6 Deforestation is one factor that can cause the amount of carbon dioxide in the atmosphere to increase. The rising concentration of carbon dioxide in our atmosphere has been linked to global warming.

Describe **two** possible biological consequences of global warming.

....

....

....

....

[2 marks]

END OF QUESTIONS

GCSE Combined Science
Chemistry Paper 1
Higher Tier

In addition to this paper you should have:
- A ruler.
- A calculator.
- A periodic table (on page 542).

Centre name
Centre number
Candidate number

Time allowed:
- 1 hour 15 minutes

Surname
Other names
Candidate signature

Instructions to candidates
- Write your name and other details in the spaces provided above.
- Answer **all** questions in the spaces provided.
- Do all rough work on the paper.
- Cross out any work you do not want to be marked.

Information for candidates
- The marks available are given in brackets at the end of each question.
- There are 70 marks available for this paper.
- You are allowed to use a calculator.
- You should use good English and present your answers in a clear and organised way.
- For Questions 2.4 and 5.2, ensure that your answers have a clear and logical structure, include the right scientific terms, spelt correctly, and include detailed, relevant information.

Advice to candidates
- In calculations show clearly how you worked out your answers.

For examiner's use

Q	Attempt Nº 1	2	3	Q	Attempt Nº 1	2	3
1				4			
2				5			
3				6			
				7			
				Total			

1 The elements in Group 1 of the periodic table are known as the alkali metals.

1.1 Group 1 metals can react with non-metals to form ionic compounds.
What is the charge on a Group 1 ion in an ionic compound?
Tick **one** box.

☐ +2

☐ +3

☐ −1

☐ +1

[1 mark]

A student watched his teacher carefully place small pieces of lithium, sodium and potassium into cold water. His observations are recorded in **Table 1**.

Table 1

Metal	Observations
lithium	Fizzes, moves across surface.
sodium	Fizzes strongly, moves quickly across surface, melts.
potassium	Fizzes violently, moves very quickly across surface, melts and a flame is seen.

He decides that the order of reactivity of the three metals is:

- potassium (most reactive)
- sodium
- lithium (least reactive)

1.2 Give **two** pieces of evidence from **Table 1** that support the student's conclusion.

....

....

....

....

[2 marks]

Question 1 continues on the next page

Turn over ▶

1.3 Explain the pattern of reactivity that the student has noticed in terms of the outer electrons of the atoms.

....

....

....

....

[3 marks]

1.4 Complete and balance the chemical equation for the reaction between lithium and water.

2Li + 2H$_2$O → .... + ...

[2 marks]

1.5 Choose the statement that explains why the solution produced when lithium reacts with water is alkaline.
Tick **one** box.

☐ It contains lithium ions.

☐ It contains water.

☐ It contains an ionic compound.

☐ It contains hydroxide ions.

[1 mark]

1.6 The nuclear symbol for an atom of fluorine is shown below.

$$^{19}_{9}F$$

How many protons, neutrons and electrons are there in this atom of fluorine?

Protons = ...

Neutrons = ...

Electrons = ...

[3 marks]

2 The structure and bonding of elements and compounds affects their properties.

2.1 Sodium and chlorine can react together to form an ionic compound (sodium chloride).
Figure 1, below, is a dot and cross diagram illustrating this reaction.

Complete the right-hand side of **Figure 1** by adding the charges of both ions and adding the electrons to the outer shell of the chloride ion.

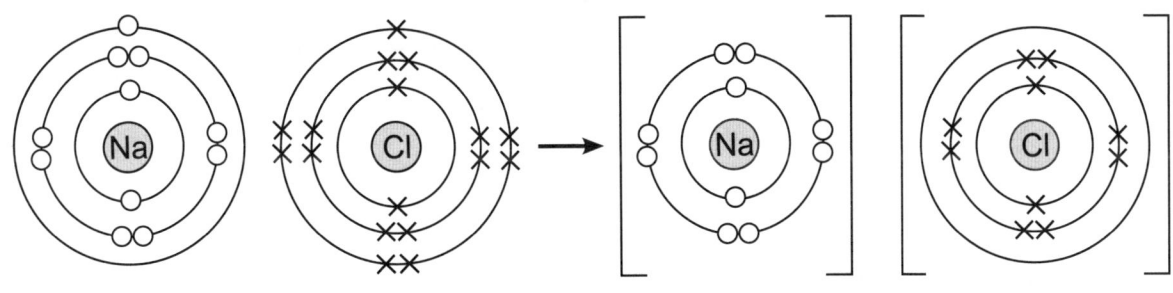

Figure 1

[2 marks]

Table 2 shows some properties of five substances, **A-E**.

Table 2

Substance	Melting point in °C	Boiling point in °C	Does it conduct electricity when solid?	Does it conduct electricity when dissolved or molten?
A	−210	−196	No	No
B	−219	−183	No	No
C	801	1413	No	Yes
D	115	445	No	No
E	1083	2567	Yes	Yes

2.2 Substance **A** consists of small, covalently bonded molecules.
Explain why it has a relatively low melting point.

....

....
[2 marks]

2.3 Look at **Table 2**. One of the substances, **A-E**, is an ionic compound.
Use the information in the table to suggest which of the substances is ionic.
Explain your answer.

....

....

....
[2 marks]

Question 2 continues on the next page

Turn over ▶

2.4 **Table 3** contains information about some of the properties of diamond and graphite.

Table 3

	Hardness	Melting point	Conducts electricity?
Diamond	Hard	High	No
Graphite	Soft	High	Yes

Explain these properties of diamond and graphite in terms of their structure and bonding.

....
....
....
....
....
....
....
....
....
....

[6 marks]

3 **Figure 2** shows the apparatus used by a student to measure the temperature change that occurred when she added a piece of magnesium ribbon to dilute hydrochloric acid.

Figure 2

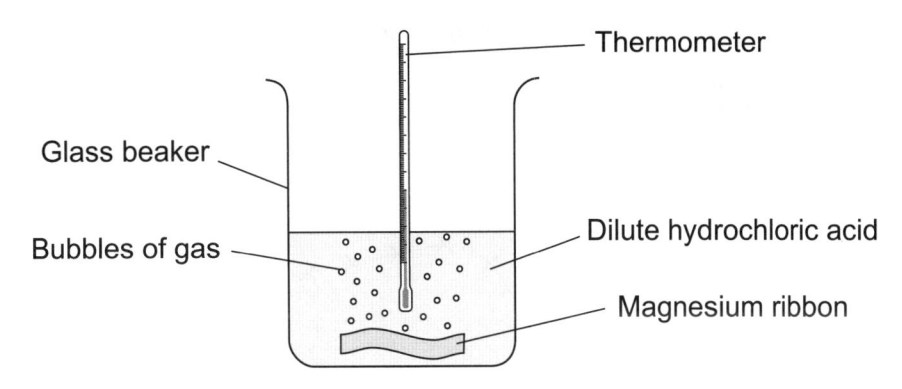

3.1 Suggest **two** changes that the student could make to the apparatus in order to reduce heat loss from her experiment.

....

....

....

....
[2 marks]

3.2 A close up of the thermometer used during the experiment is shown in **Figure 3**.

Figure 3

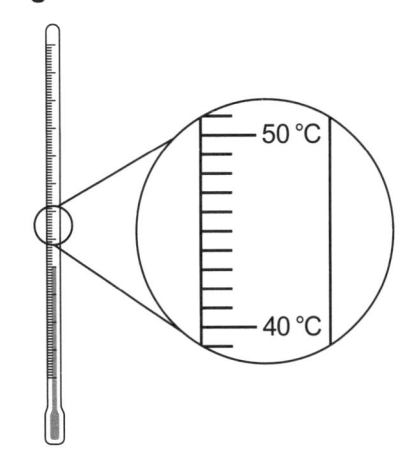

What value does each **small division** on the scale of the thermometer represent?
Tick **one** box.

☐ 0.1 °C

☐ 10 °C

☐ 1 °C

☐ 2 °C

[1 mark]

Question 3 continues on the next page

Turn over ▶

The student recorded the initial temperature of the dilute hydrochloric acid.
She added the magnesium ribbon to the acid. She then measured
the temperature of the reaction mixture every 10 seconds.
The student's results are shown on the graph in **Figure 4**.

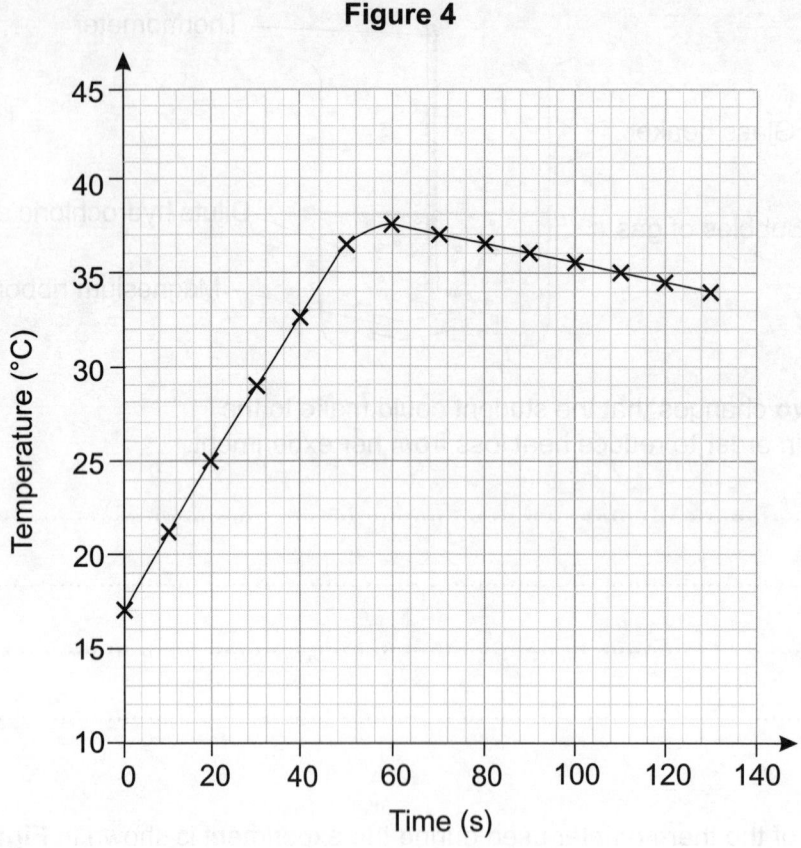

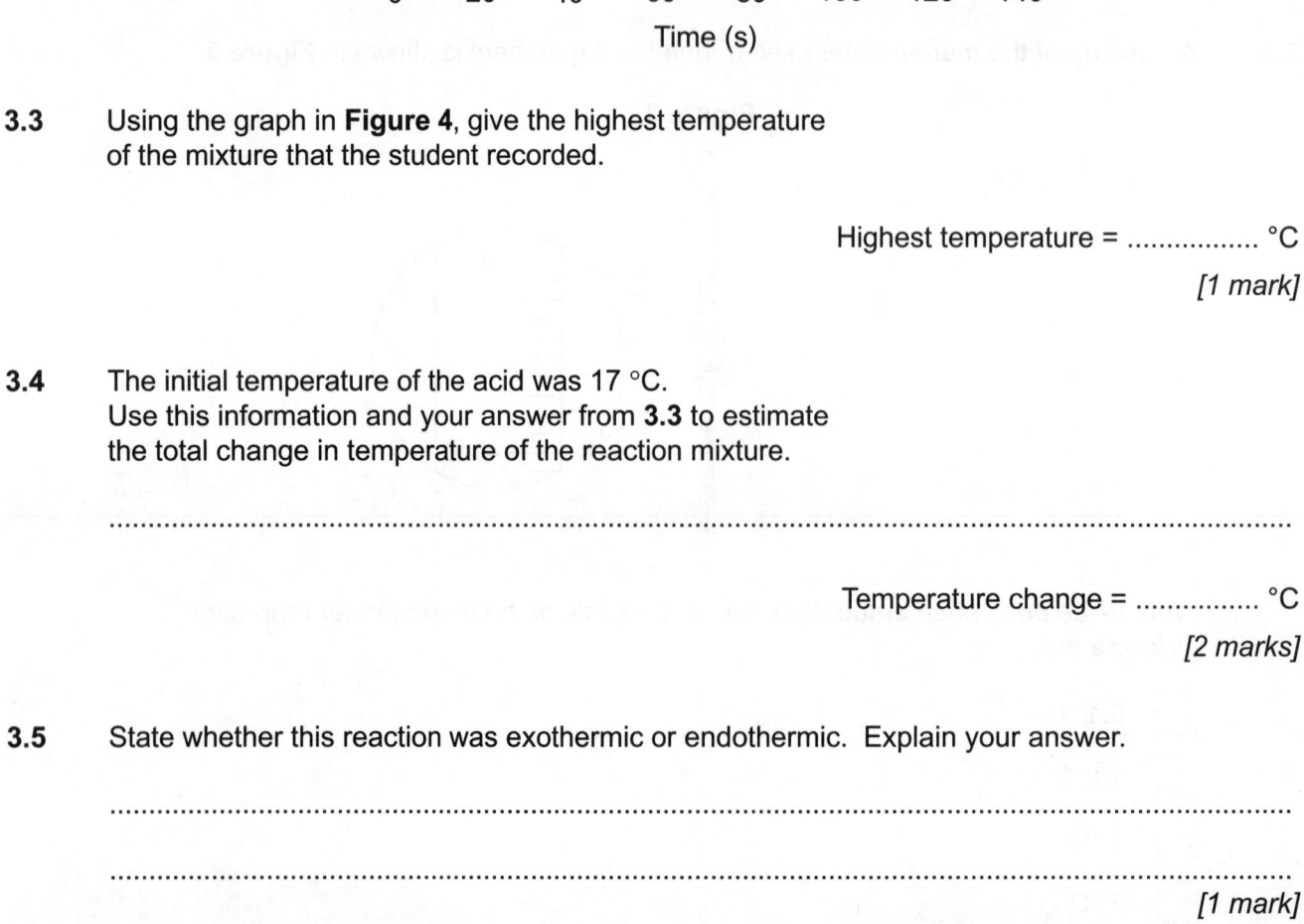

Figure 4

3.3 Using the graph in **Figure 4**, give the highest temperature
of the mixture that the student recorded.

Highest temperature = ... °C

[1 mark]

3.4 The initial temperature of the acid was 17 °C.
Use this information and your answer from **3.3** to estimate
the total change in temperature of the reaction mixture.

....

Temperature change = ... °C

[2 marks]

3.5 State whether this reaction was exothermic or endothermic. Explain your answer.

....

....

[1 mark]

4 A student reacts four different metals with dilute sulfuric acid.
She controls all other variables to make sure that the test is fair.
She collects the hydrogen gas given off by each reaction in a gas syringe.
Figure 5 shows all four reactions after 30 seconds.

Figure 5

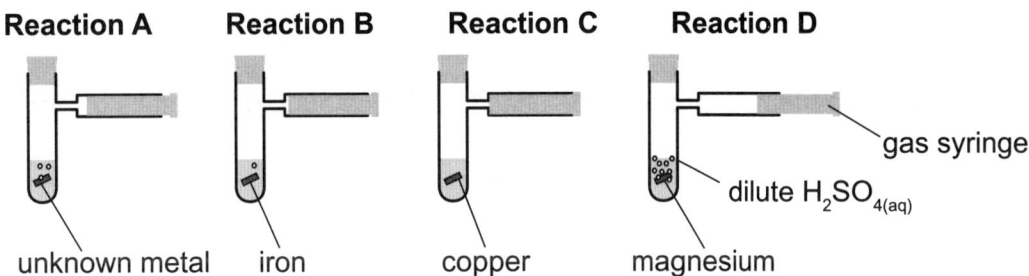

Reaction A — unknown metal
Reaction B — iron
Reaction C — copper
Reaction D — magnesium, dilute $H_2SO_{4(aq)}$, gas syringe

4.1 Which reaction, **A**, **B**, **C**, or **D**, contains the **most reactive** metal?
Explain how you can tell.

....

....

....
[3 marks]

4.2 Use your knowledge of the reactivity series to suggest a possible identity for the unknown metal used in reaction **A**.

....
[1 mark]

4.3 In another experiment, the student placed pieces of different metals in metal salt solutions.
She left them for 10 minutes. The student then recorded whether any reaction had occurred.
The results of this experiment are shown in **Table 4**.

Table 4

	Did any reaction occur with:		
	iron sulfate	magnesium sulfate	copper sulfate
iron	No	No	....
magnesium	....	No	Yes
copper	No	No	No

Complete **Table 4** by filling in the gaps.
[2 marks]

4.4 The equation for the reaction between magnesium and copper sulfate solution is:

$$Mg_{(s)} + CuSO_{4(aq)} \rightarrow MgSO_{4(aq)} + Cu_{(s)}$$

Write the ionic equation for this reaction.

....
[2 marks]

Turn over for the next question   **Turn over ▶**

5 A student added zinc oxide (ZnO) to dilute hydrochloric acid (HCl).
   They reacted to produce zinc chloride, a soluble salt.

5.1 Give the chemical formula of zinc chloride.

....
[1 mark]

5.2 Describe a method that could be used to produce pure, dry crystals of zinc chloride.

....
....
....
....
....
....
....
....
....
....
[6 marks]

5.3 Another student added solid sodium carbonate (Na_2CO_3) to dilute hydrochloric acid.
     Name the salt formed by this reaction.

....
[1 mark]

5.4 Which gas was given off by the reaction described in 5.3?
     Tick **one** box.

☐ Hydrogen   ☐ Chlorine   ☐ Oxygen   ☐ Carbon Dioxide
[1 mark]

5.5 The solution formed at the end of the reaction described in 5.3 is neutral.
     Suggest a method you could use to test the pH of the solution.
     State what you would expect to observe.

....
....
[2 marks]

6 Iron can be extracted from iron(III) oxide, Fe_2O_3, by reduction, using carbon.
Here is the equation for this reaction:

$$2Fe_2O_3 + 3C \rightarrow 4Fe + 3CO_2$$

6.1 Give **one** reason why this reaction is described as a reduction reaction.

....
[1 mark]

6.2 Calculate the mass of iron that could be extracted from 40 g of iron(III) oxide.
Relative atomic masses, A_r: Fe = 56, O = 16.

....

....

....

....

....

Mass of iron = ... g
[4 marks]

6.3 Explain why reduction with carbon isn't used to extract aluminium from its ore.

....

....
[2 marks]

6.4 Small amounts of carbon can be added to iron to make an alloy called steel.
Explain why steel is harder than pure iron.

....

....

....

....

....

....

....
[4 marks]

Turn over for the next question

Turn over ▶

7 A student carried out an experiment to investigate the electrolysis of copper sulfate solution, CuSO₄ (aq), using inert carbon electrodes.
The diagram in **Figure 6** shows how his experiment was set up.

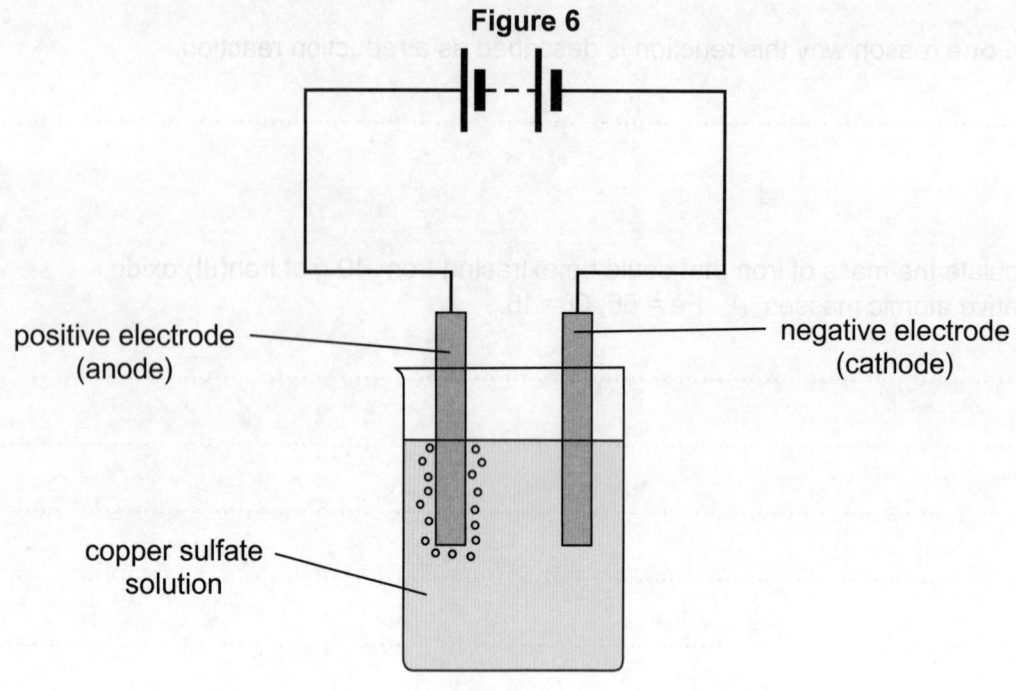

Figure 6

7.1 Explain why a solution of copper sulfate can conduct electricity, but solid copper sulfate cannot.

....

....
[2 marks]

7.2 List all **four** of the ions that are present in aqueous copper sulfate solution.

....

....
[1 mark]

7.3 Complete the half equation shown below for the reaction taking place at the positive electrode (anode).

.... OH⁻ → O₂ + ... H₂O + 4 ....

[1 mark]

The student repeated the experiment three times, running the electrolysis for exactly 30 minutes each time. He weighed the dry electrodes before starting each run.
At the end of each run, he dried both electrodes and weighed them again.

Table 5 shows the change in mass of both electrodes for each of the three runs.

Table 5

	Change in mass of electrode in g			
	Run 1	Run 2	Run 3	Mean
Positive electrode (anode)	0.00	0.00	0.00	0.00
Negative electrode (cathode)	2.36	2.71	2.55	....

7.4 Complete **Table 5** by finding the mean change in mass for the negative electrode.

[1 mark]

7.5 Explain why the negative electrode increased in mass in this experiment. Your answer should include the half equation for the reaction taking place at the negative electrode.

....

....

....

....

....

[3 marks]

7.6 The student decided to run the experiment for 60 minutes instead of 30 minutes. Predict the effect that this would have on the change in mass of the negative electrode.

....

[1 mark]

END OF QUESTIONS

GCSE Combined Science
Chemistry Paper 2
Higher Tier

In addition to this paper you should have:
- A ruler.
- A calculator.
- A periodic table (on page 542).

Centre name

Centre number

Candidate number

Time allowed:
- 1 hour 15 minutes

Surname

Other names

Candidate signature

Instructions to candidates
- Write your name and other details in the spaces provided above.
- Answer **all** questions in the spaces provided.
- Do all rough work on the paper.
- Cross out any work you do not want to be marked.

Information for candidates
- The marks available are given in brackets at the end of each question.
- There are 70 marks available for this paper.
- You are allowed to use a calculator.
- You should use good English and present your answers in a clear and organised way.
- For Questions 3.3 and 6.1, ensure that your answers have a clear and logical structure, include the right scientific terms, spelt correctly, and include detailed, relevant information.

Advice to candidates
- In calculations show clearly how you worked out your answers.

For examiner's use

1 Alkanes are hydrocarbon compounds found in crude oil. **Table 1** shows how the boiling points of some alkanes change as the molecules get bigger.

Table 1

Alkane	Molecular formula	Boiling point (°C)
Propane	C_3H_8	−42
Butane	C_4H_{10}	−0.5
Pentane	C_5H_{12}	
Hexane	C_6H_{14}	69
Heptane	C_7H_{16}	98

1.1 Using the data in **Table 1**, plot a graph of the number of carbon atoms in an alkane molecule against boiling point on the axes below.
Draw a smooth curve through the points you have plotted.

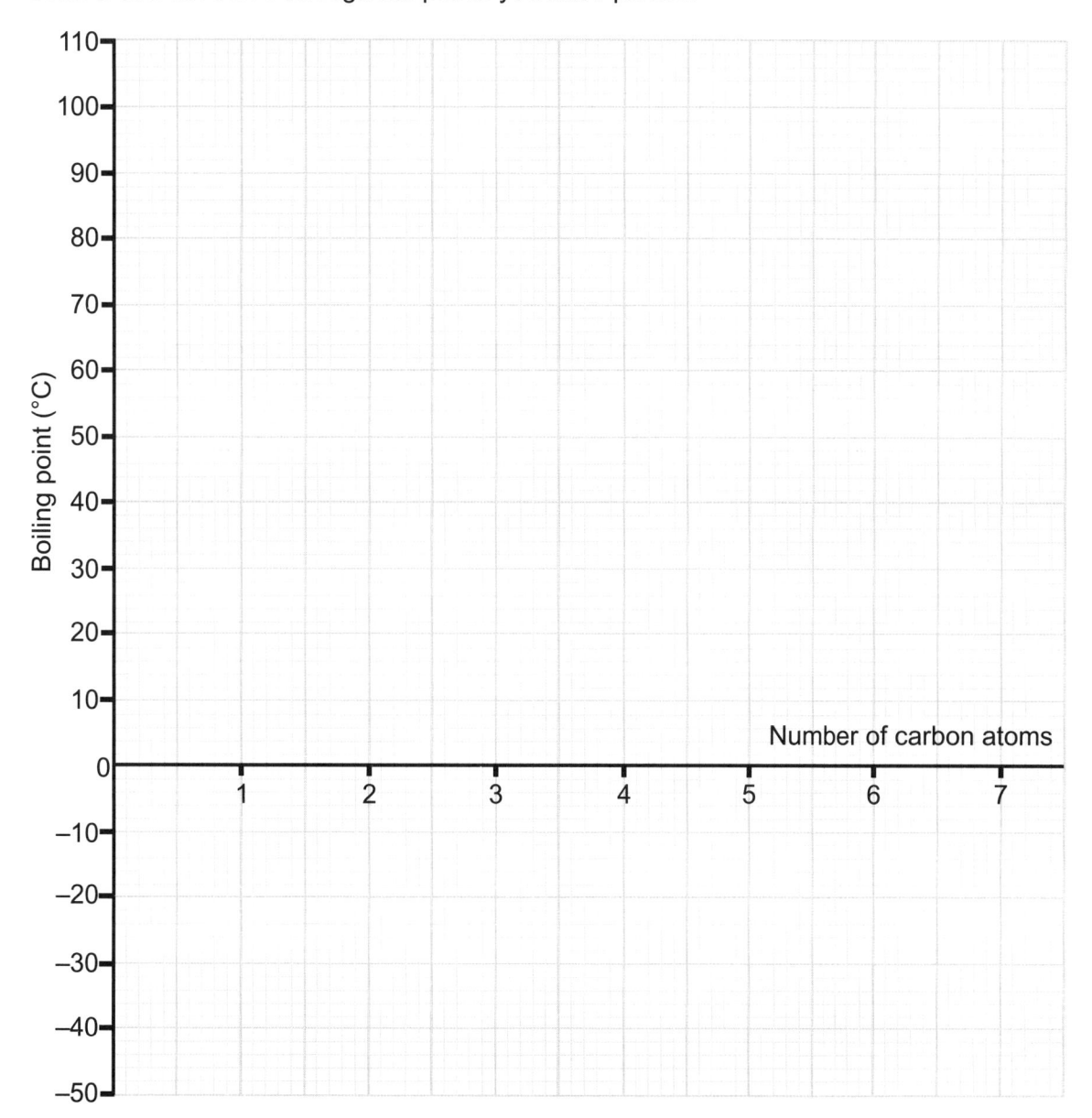

[2 marks]

Question 1 continues on the next page

Turn over ▶

1.2 Use your graph to estimate the boiling point of pentane.

.... °C

[1 mark]

1.3 What is the general formula of the alkanes? Tick **one** box.

☐ C_nH_{2n}

☐ C_nH_{2n+1}

☐ C_nH_{2n+2}

☐ C_nH_{2n-1}

[1 mark]

1.4 Propane is an alkane with three carbon atoms.
Draw the displayed formula of propane.

[1 mark]

1.5 Propene is an alkene with three carbon atoms.
Describe a test you could use to distinguish between propene and propane.
Say what you would observe in each case.

....

....

....

[3 marks]

1.6 Propane burns in the presence of oxygen.
Complete this equation for the complete combustion of propane.

$$C_3H_8 + 5O_2 \rightarrow 3CO_2 + ...$$

[2 marks]

2 Nitrogen dioxide is an atmospheric pollutant that irritates the respiratory system. It is thought that there is a link between exposure to nitrogen dioxide and the severity of asthma attacks in people with asthma.

Figure 1 shows the results of a study carried out by a group of scientists that compared atmospheric nitrogen dioxide levels with the severity of asthma attacks suffered by men under the age of 40 working in a city centre.

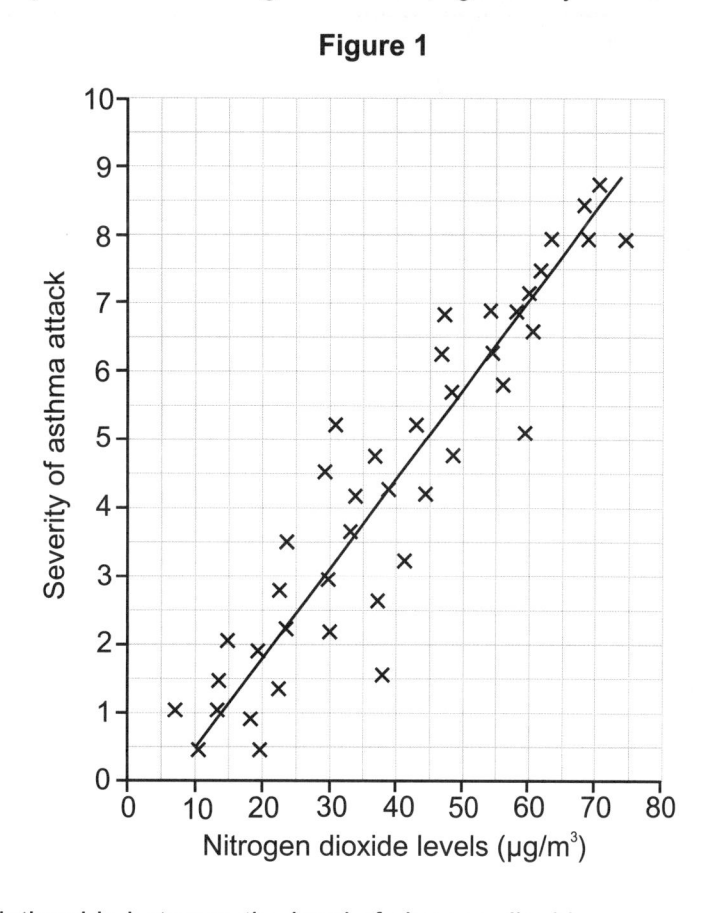

Figure 1

[Scatter graph: Severity of asthma attack (y-axis, 0–10) vs Nitrogen dioxide levels (µg/m³) (x-axis, 0–80), showing a positive linear correlation.]

2.1 Describe the relationship between the level of nitrogen dioxide in the air and the severity of asthma attacks shown in **Figure 1**.

....

....
[1 mark]

2.2 The scientists decided they could not draw a general conclusion about the link between nitrogen dioxide levels and the severity of asthma attacks that would apply to everyone.
Which of these reasons **does not** describe why this might be the case? Tick **one** box.

☐ The scientists would need to collect data from women too.

☐ The severity of asthma attacks might be affected by another pollutant which happens to be abundant in the same areas as nitrogen dioxide.

☐ The sample of people that the scientists collected data from was too big.

☐ The scientists would need to collect data from other age groups too.

[1 mark]

Question 2 continues on the next page

Turn over ▶

2.3 Where do the oxides of nitrogen in the air come from?
Suggest why levels of nitrogen oxides can be particularly high in cities.

....

....

....

....
[3 marks]

2.4 Nitrogen dioxide dissolves in water to form acid rain.
Name **one** other pollutant gas that can cause acid rain.

....
[1 mark]

3 In the UK, the majority of our drinking water is produced from treating groundwater or surface water. Drinking water can also be made by treating sea water or waste water.

3.1 Producing water that is safe to drink from sea water is expensive.
Suggest why some countries produce drinking water by this method.

....
[1 mark]

3.2 What is the name of the process used to remove salt from sea water?
Tick **one** box.

☐ Filtration ☐ Desalination ☐ Sterilisation ☐ Cracking
[1 mark]

3.3 A teacher gives a student a sample of sea water, and asks her to produce a sample of pure water from it.
Outline a method that the student could use to remove the salt from the sea water.

....
....
....
....
....
....
....
....
....
[6 marks]

3.4 Sewage treatment plants process sewage and release clean, treated water back into the environment. The first step in the treatment of sewage is screening.
What happens in the screening step?
Tick **one** box.

☐ Chlorine is added to the sewage to kill microorganisms.

☐ The sewage is placed into large storage tanks and allowed to settle.

☐ Anaerobic digestion is used to break down the sewage.

☐ Large bits of material (such as grit) are removed from the sewage.
[1 mark]

3.5 Following screening, sedimentation is used to separate the effluent from the sludge.
Describe what happens to the effluent before it can be returned to the environment.

....
....
[2 marks]

Turn over for the next question **Turn over ▶**

4 This question is about the evolution of the atmosphere.

The pie charts in **Figure 2** show the composition of Earth's atmosphere as it may have been 4 billion years ago and as it is at the present time.

Figure 2

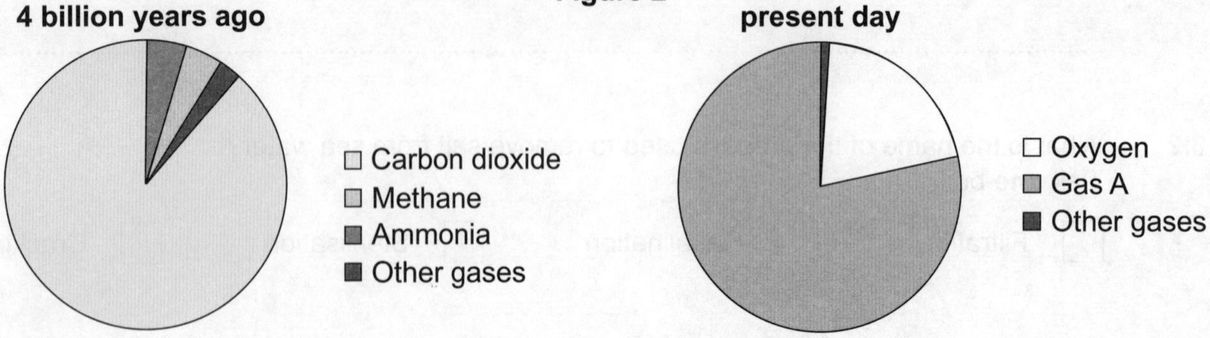

4 billion years ago
- Carbon dioxide
- Methane
- Ammonia
- Other gases

present day
- Oxygen
- Gas A
- Other gases

4.1 Name Gas A.

....
[1 mark]

4.2 The evolution of algae and plants affected the composition of gases in the atmosphere.
Explain how algae and plants changed the atmosphere.

....
....
....
[3 marks]

4.3 Human activity is affecting the composition of the atmosphere.
Suggest **one** reason why each of the following factors affects the level of carbon dioxide in the atmosphere.

Deforestation ....

....

Increased energy consumption ....

....

Increasing population ....

....
[3 marks]

4.4 A student says:

"I think that if the amount of carbon dioxide in the atmosphere continues to rise, this may lead to a drop in global food production in the future."

Explain why the student may be correct.

....
....
....
....
[3 marks]

5 A student is investigating how the rate of the reaction between calcium carbonate and hydrochloric acid is affected by the concentration of the acid.

The student uses the following method:

- Weigh out 0.7 g of calcium carbonate.
- Add the calcium carbonate to an excess of 7.3 g/dm³ hydrochloric acid in a conical flask.
- Use a gas syringe to collect the gas given off by the reaction.
- Measure and record the volume of gas produced every 10 s.
- Repeat the experiment using hydrochloric acid with a concentration of 14.6 g/dm³.

5.1 Suggest **two** variables other than the mass of calcium carbonate that the student would have to keep the same for each run to make it a fair test.

....

....

[2 marks]

Figure 3 shows the student's results for the first experiment, using 7.3 g/dm³ hydrochloric acid.

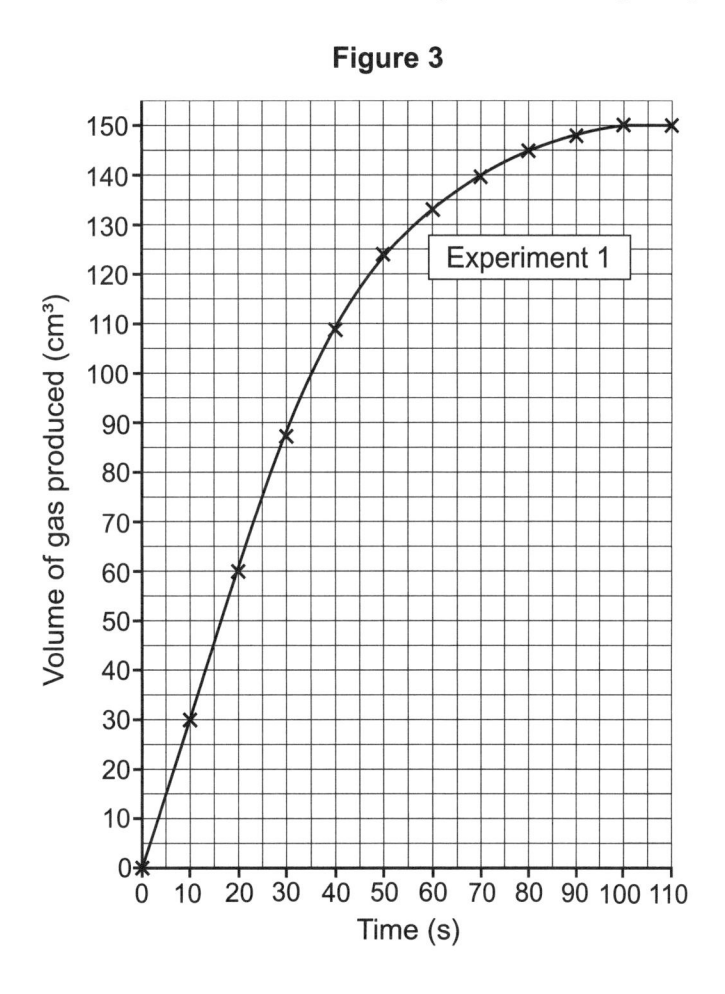

Figure 3

Question 5 continues on the next page

Turn over ▶

5.2 Draw a tangent to the graph in **Figure 3** at 50 seconds.
Using the gradient of the tangent, find the rate of the reaction at this time.
Include the units of the rate in your answer.

....
....
....
....

Rate of reaction = ... Unit = ...

[4 marks]

The first student added the results of his second experiment, using 14.6 g/dm³ hydrochloric acid, to his graph. This graph is shown in **Figure 4**, below.

Figure 4

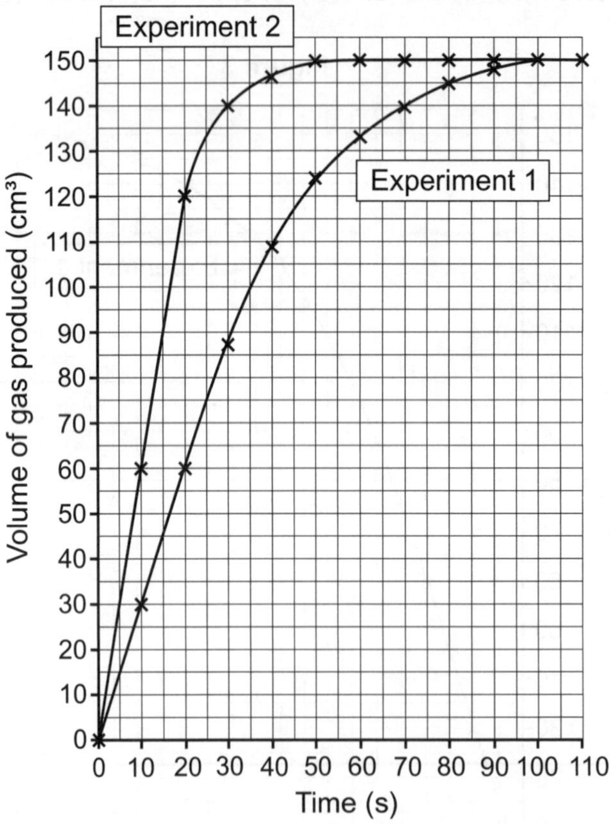

5.3 Explain how the student could tell from his graph that increasing the concentration of the acid had increased the reaction rate.

....

[1 mark]

5.4 In terms of collision theory, explain why concentration affects the rate of a reaction.

....
....
....

[2 marks]

A second student is investigating the properties of vinegar. Ethanoic acid is found in vinegar.
The student reacted some vinegar with solid sodium carbonate.
The apparatus that he used is shown in **Figure 5**.

Figure 5

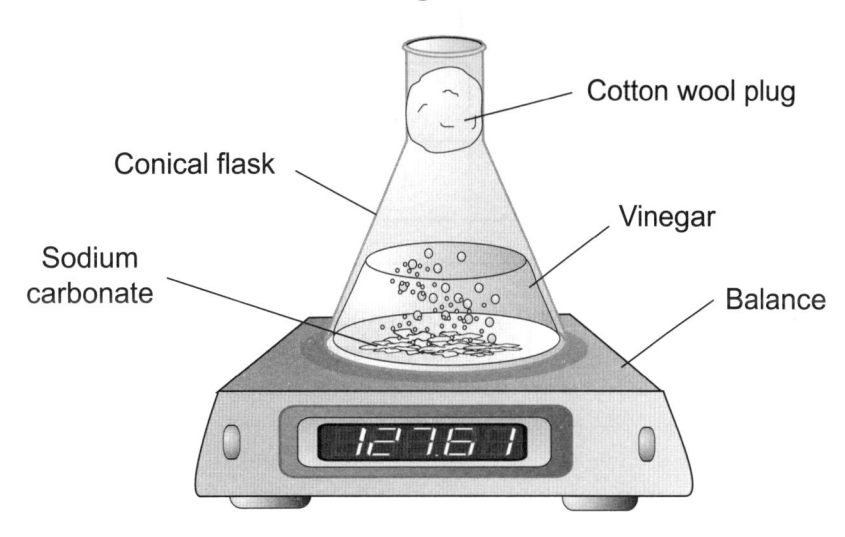

The student recorded the initial mass of the flask and then recorded it again after 60 s.
He repeated the experiment three times. His results are shown in **Table 2**.

Table 2

	Initial Mass in g	Final Mass in g	Loss of Mass in g
Run 1	128.00	127.61	0.39
Run 2	128.50	127.95	0.55
Run 3	128.35	127.90	0.45

5.5 Calculate the mean loss of mass after 60 s.

....

mean mass lost = ... g

[2 marks]

5.6 The student repeats the experiment a fourth time, but this time
he collects the gas released by the reaction in a gas syringe.
Name the gas that the student collects.
Describe a test that he could use to confirm the identity of the gas.

....

....

....

[3 marks]

Turn over for the next question

Turn over ▶

6 The extraction and use of metals in modern life can have a damaging effect on the environment.

The extraction of aluminium from ores requires the electrolysis of aluminium oxide.
Table 3 shows the average energy consumption per kilogram of aluminium produced by the electrolysis of aluminium oxide and recycling.

Table 3

	Average energy consumption (kWh/kg)
Extraction using electrolysis	15
Recycling	0.75

6.1 Using the information in **Table 3** and your own knowledge, discuss why it is more sustainable to recycle, where possible, than to mine and extract new metals.

....

[6 marks]

6.2 Copper, like aluminium, can be extracted from ores using a process that requires a large amount of electricity. However, a lower energy alternative called phytomining can be used to extract copper from low-grade ores. Describe how copper is extracted from low-grade ores using phytomining.

....

[4 marks]

7 A company uses a process called the contact process to make sulfuric acid.
The first step of the process is the exothermic reaction of sulfur dioxide and oxygen to form sulfur trioxide. The equation for the reaction is shown below.

$$2SO_{2(g)} + O_{2(g)} \rightleftharpoons 2SO_{3(g)}$$

7.1 This reaction can reach equilibrium.
When a reaction is at equilibrium, what does this tell you about the forward and reverse reactions?

....

....
[1 mark]

7.2 You can predict how changing the conditions will affect this reaction using Le Chatelier's principle.
What is Le Chatelier's principle?

....

....
[1 mark]

7.3 State what will happen to the yield of sulfur trioxide in this reaction if the pressure inside the reaction vessel is increased.
Explain your answer.

....

....

....

....
[3 marks]

7.4 A measured mass of vanadium oxide was added to the reaction vessel at the start of the process. The same mass of vanadium oxide is present at the end of the reaction.
Suggest what role vanadium oxide is playing in this reaction.

....
[1 mark]

7.5 The company used to produce 7500 kg of sulfur trioxide each day.
After modifying the plant to allow the sulfur trioxide to be removed from the reaction vessel as soon as it is made, the yield of the plant increased by 15%.
How much sulfur trioxide can the plant make in five days now?

....

....

....

mass made in five days = ... kg
[3 marks]

END OF QUESTIONS

GCSE Combined Science
Physics Paper 1
Higher Tier

In addition to this paper you should have:
- A ruler.
- A calculator.
- The Physics Equations sheet (on page 542).

| Centre name |
| Centre number |
| Candidate number |

Time allowed:
- 1 hour 15 minutes

| Surname |
| Other names |
| Candidate signature |

Instructions to candidates
- Write your name and other details in the spaces provided above.
- Answer **all** questions in the spaces provided.
- Do all rough work on the paper.
- Cross out any work you do not want to be marked.

Information for candidates
- The marks available are given in brackets at the end of each question.
- There are 70 marks available for this paper.
- You are allowed to use a calculator.
- You should use good English and present your answers in a clear and organised way.
- For Questions 1.6 and 5.5, ensure that your answers have a clear and logical structure, include the right scientific terms, spelt correctly and include detailed, relevant information.

For examiner's use

Q	Attempt Nº 1 2 3	Q	Attempt Nº 1 2 3
1		4	
2		5	
3		6	
		Total	

Advice to candidates
- In calculations show clearly how you worked out your answers.

1 Table 1 gives details of some isotopes.

Table 1

Isotope	Symbol	Type of decay
Radium-226	$^{226}_{88}Ra$	alpha
Radon-222	$^{222}_{86}Rn$	alpha
Radon-224	$^{224}_{86}Rn$	beta
Bismuth-210	$^{210}_{83}Bi$	alpha, beta
Bismuth-214	$^{214}_{83}Bi$	alpha, beta
Lead-210	$^{210}_{82}Pb$	beta

1.1 Calculate the number of neutrons in a bismuth-214 nucleus.

....
[1 mark]

1.2 Using data from **Table 1**, complete the equations in **Figure 1** to show how the following isotopes decay.

Figure 1

$$^{226}_{88}Ra \longrightarrow \boxed{\text{......}Rn} + \boxed{^{4}_{2}He}$$

$$^{210}_{82}Pb \longrightarrow \boxed{\text{......}Bi} + \boxed{^{0}_{-1}e}$$

[2 marks]

Question 1 continues on the next page

Turn over ▶

Figure 2 shows the activity-time graph of a sample of polonium-210.

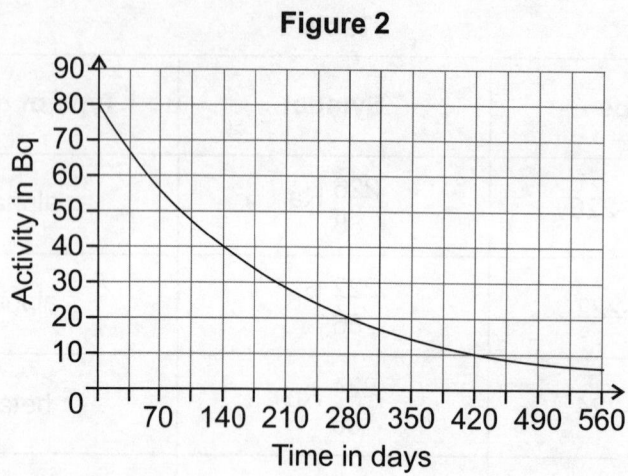

Figure 2

[Graph showing activity in Bq (y-axis, 0-90) versus time in days (x-axis, 0-560), with an exponential decay curve starting at 80 Bq.]

1.3 Using the graph in **Figure 2**, determine the time it takes for the activity of the sample to drop from 80 Bq to 10 Bq.

Time taken = ... days
[1 mark]

1.4 Determine the half-life of polonium-210.

Half-life = ... days
[1 mark]

Polonium-210 emits alpha radiation. Scientists who work with it must be particularly careful to avoid radioactive contamination.

1.5 Define the term radioactive contamination.

....
....
....
[1 mark]

1.6 Explain and compare the dangers of radioactive contamination with radioactive irradiation by an alpha source, such as polonium-210.

....
....
....
....
....
....
....
....
[4 marks]

2 A student is investigating the two electrical circuits shown in **Figure 3**.
All the lamps and batteries used are identical.

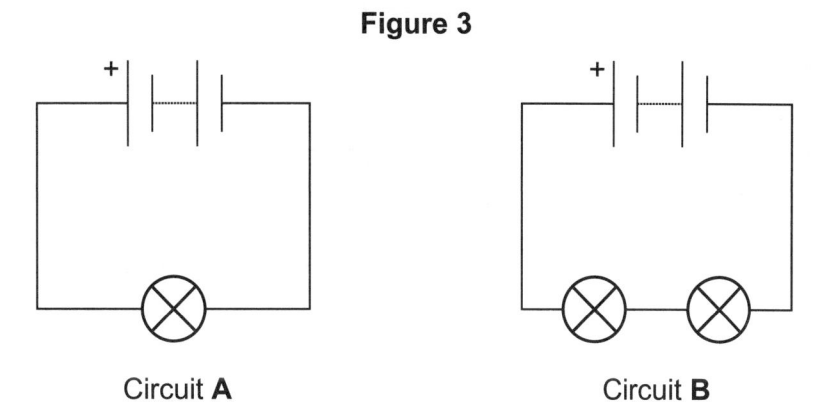

Figure 3

Circuit **A**   Circuit **B**

2.1 Compare the current and total resistance in circuits **A** and **B**.

....

....

....
[2 marks]

2.2 The student adds an ammeter and a voltmeter to circuit **A**.
They show readings of 0.30 A and 11 V respectively.
State the equation that links power, current and potential difference.

....
[1 mark]

2.3 Calculate the power of the lamp.

....

....

....

Power = ... W
[2 marks]

2.4 Compare the potential difference across the bulb in circuit **A** with the potential difference across one of the bulbs in circuit **B**.
Explain your answer.

....

....

....

....
[2 marks]

Question 2 continues on the next page

Turn over ▶

The student considers adding one of the components in **Figure 4** to circuit **A**.

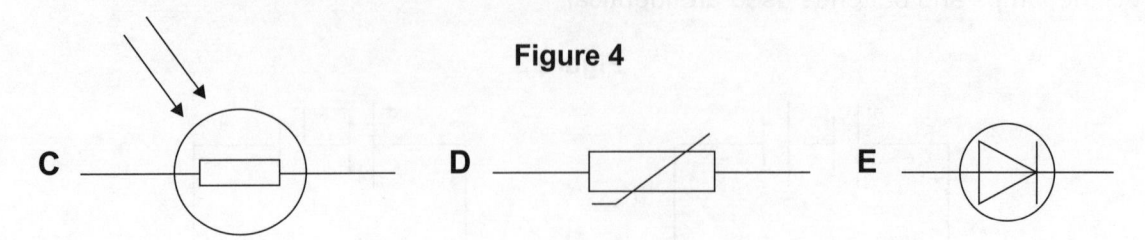

Figure 4

C ———⊗———   D ———[⌿]———   E ———▷|———

2.5 What happens to the resistance of component **C** as the intensity of light that falls on it increases?
Tick **one** box.

The resistance increases. ☐

The resistance remains constant. ☐

The resistance decreases. ☐

[1 mark]

2.6 Give an application for component **D**.

....

....
[1 mark]

2.7 On the axes in **Figure 5**, sketch the *I-V* characteristic of component **E**.

Figure 5

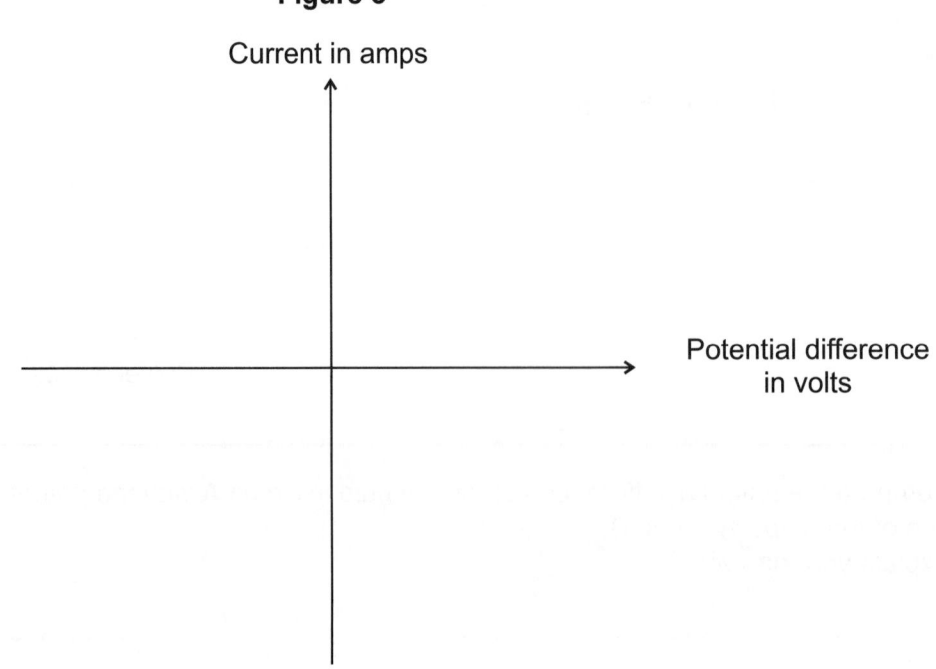

[2 marks]

3 A representation of the particles of a substance is shown in **Figure 6**.

Figure 6

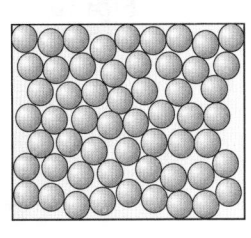

3.1 Name the state of matter of the substance shown in **Figure 6**.

....
[1 mark]

3.2 The substance in **Figure 6** is heated.
Describe what happens to the internal energy of the substance when it is heated.
Explain why this occurs.

....

....

....
[2 marks]

The student wishes to find the density of the substance.
A sample of the substance has a mass of 0.36 kg, and a volume of 4×10^{-4} m^3.

3.3 Write down the equation that links mass, volume and density.

....
[1 mark]

3.4 Calculate the density of the substance.

....

....

Density = ... kg/m^3
[2 marks]

Question 3 continues on the next page

Turn over ▶

Figure 7 shows a graph of temperature against time for the substance as it is being continually heated.

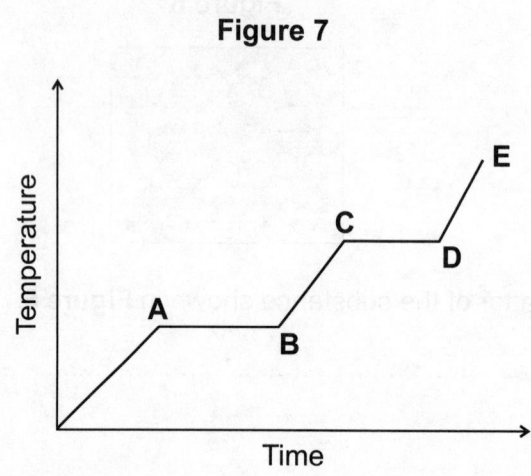

Figure 7

3.5 Which point represents the **boiling point**?
Tick **one** box.

☐ A
☐ B
☐ C

[1 mark]

3.6 Explain the shape of the line in **Figure 7** between points **A** and **B**.

....
....
....
....

[2 marks]

3.7 69 000 J of energy is transferred to a 1.5 kg solid sample of the substance to completely melt it without changing its temperature.
Calculate the specific latent heat of fusion of the substance.
Use the correct equation from the Physics Equation Sheet on page 542.

....
....
....

Specific latent heat of fusion = ... J/kg

[3 marks]

4 A student wanted to know how the current flowing through a filament lamp changes with the potential difference across it. She set up the circuit shown in **Figure 8**.

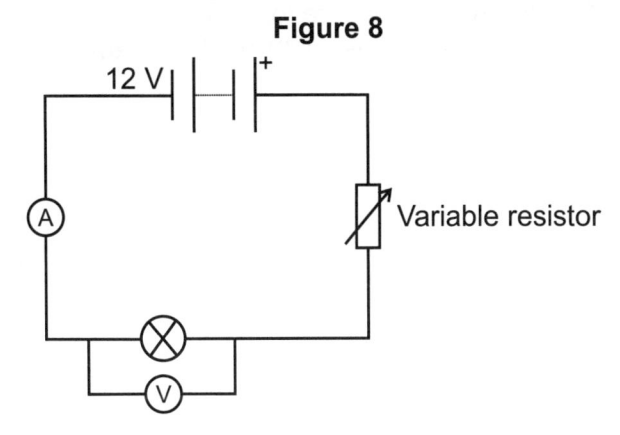

Figure 8

She used the variable resistor to change the potential difference across the lamp. For each setting of the variable resistor, the student recorded the readings of the voltmeter and the ammeter. Her results are plotted on the graph in **Figure 9**.

Figure 9

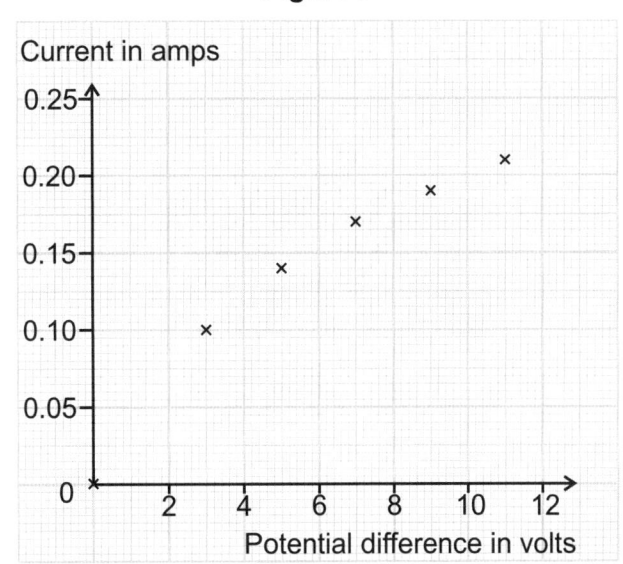

4.1 Draw a curve of best fit on the graph in **Figure 9**.

[1 mark]

4.2 The student took multiple readings of the current at each voltage.
Give **two** reasons as to why she did this.

....

....

....

[2 marks]

4.3 Explain, with reference to energy transfers, what happens to the resistance of the lamp as the current through it increases.

....

....

....

....

[4 marks]

Question 4 continues on the next page   **Turn over ▶**

4.4 The lamp is disconnected from the test circuit, and is connected to a 16 V power supply.
At this potential difference the lamp has a resistance of 64 Ω.
The lamp operates at this potential difference for 180 s.
Calculate the amount of charge which passes through the lamp in this time.

....

....

....

....

....

Charge = ... C

[5 marks]

Figure 10 shows the inside of the three-pin plug for an electric desk lamp.

Figure 10

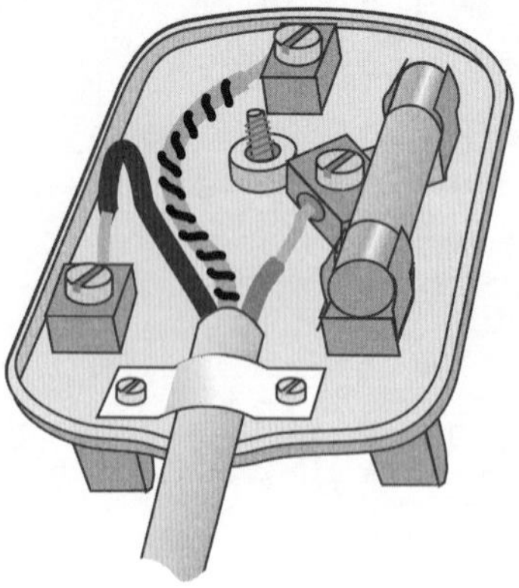

4.5 What colour is the live wire?
Tick **one** box.

blue ☐

brown ☐

yellow and green ☐

[1 mark]

4.6 The lamp's thee-core cable is frayed, so that the metal core of the live wire is exposed.
Explain what would happen if someone touched the exposed live wire of the desk lamp when it is plugged in.

....

....

....

....

....

[3 marks]

5 **Figure 11** shows the amount of electricity generated by different renewable energy resources in the UK each season between 2012 and 2015.
A kilowatt hour (kWh) is a unit of energy equal to 3.6×10^6 J.

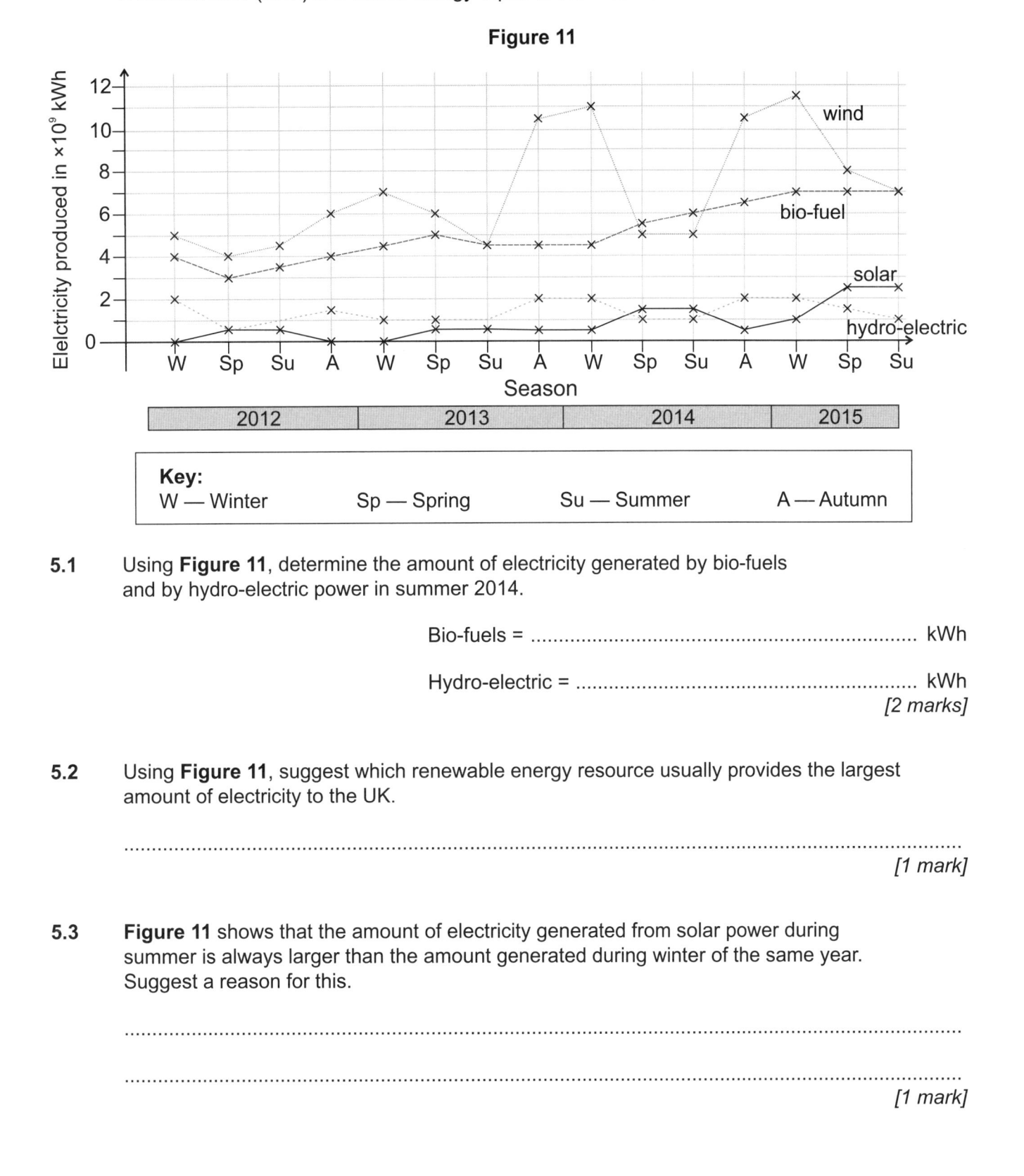

Figure 11

[Graph showing electricity produced in ×10⁹ kWh vs Season from 2012 to 2015, with curves for wind, bio-fuel, solar, and hydro-electric]

Key:
W — Winter   Sp — Spring   Su — Summer   A — Autumn

5.1 Using **Figure 11**, determine the amount of electricity generated by bio-fuels and by hydro-electric power in summer 2014.

Bio-fuels = ... kWh

Hydro-electric = ... kWh

[2 marks]

5.2 Using **Figure 11**, suggest which renewable energy resource usually provides the largest amount of electricity to the UK.

....

[1 mark]

5.3 **Figure 11** shows that the amount of electricity generated from solar power during summer is always larger than the amount generated during winter of the same year. Suggest a reason for this.

....

....

[1 mark]

Question 5 continues on the next page

Turn over ▶

5.4 Some electricity in the UK is generated from non-renewable energy resources.
Give **one** advantage and **one** disadvantage of using non-renewable energy resources to generate electricity.

Advantage = ...

....

Disadvantage = ...

....
[2 marks]

A homeowner is considering installing solar panels on their roof, to generate electricity for their home. She currently pays £650 a year for electricity from the national grid.

The homeowner contacts a solar panel supplier, who gives her information on costs, and advises her to have annual maintenance work on the solar panels.
Table 2 shows information about the solar panels that the supplier provided.

Table 2

Set-up costs (£)	8000
Annual maintenance cost (£)	250
Typical lifetime (years)	30

5.5 Explain, using data from **Table 2**, whether solar panels or the national grid would be a cheaper source of electricity during the 30-year life span of the solar panels.
Your answer should take into account set-up costs, and annual costs.
You should assume that the home owner uses exactly the amount of electricity that is generated by the solar panels.

....

....

....

....

....

....

....
[4 marks]

6 Two divers, **A** and **B**, are stood on diving boards, as shown in **Figure 12**.
Both divers have a mass of 65 kg.

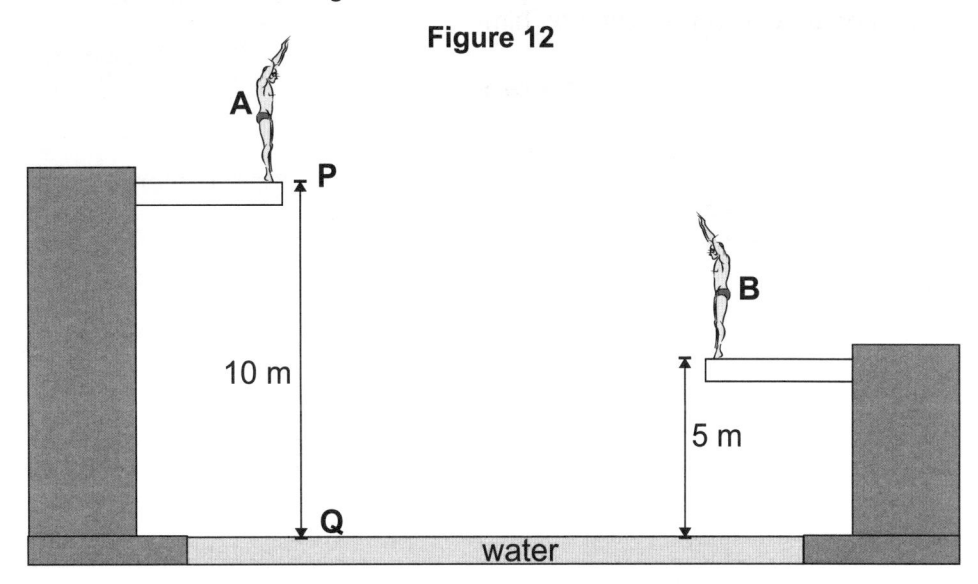

Figure 12

6.1 Which diver has more energy in their gravitational potential energy store?

....
[1 mark]

6.2 Diver **A** jumps off the diving board and falls into the water.
State the energy transfer which occurs during the fall.
You can ignore air resistance and friction.

....

....
[1 mark]

6.3 Write down the equation which links gravitational potential energy, mass, gravitational field strength and height.

....
[1 mark]

6.4 Calculate the energy transferred from Diver **A**'s gravitational potential energy store during the fall from point **P** to point **Q**.
The gravitational field strength is 9.8 N/kg.
Give your answer to 2 significant figures.

....

....

....

Energy transferred = ... J
[2 marks]

Question 6 continues on the next page

Turn over ▶

Figure 13 shows a graph of the energy in Diver A's gravitational potential energy store and kinetic energy store as he falls from the diving board, P, to the pool surface, Q, assuming there is no friction or air resistance acting on him.

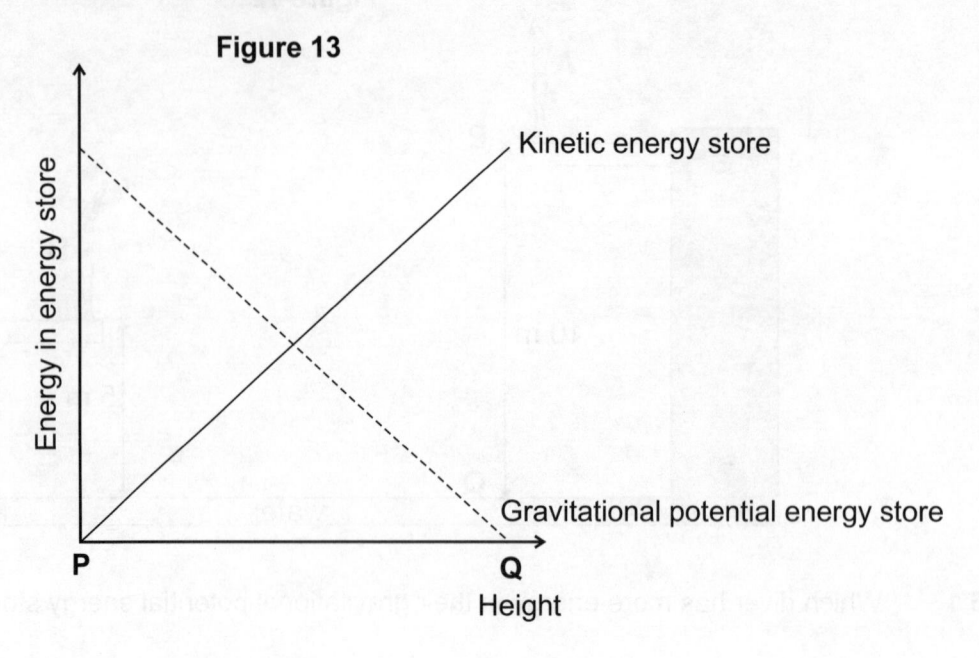

6.5 Explain the shape of the lines in **Figure 13** in terms of energy transfer and conservation of energy.

....

....

....

....
[2 marks]

6.6 Calculate the speed of Diver A as he enters the water, assuming there is no friction or air resistance acting on him.
Use your unrounded answer from **6.4**.

....

....

....

....

Speed of Diver **A** at point **Q** = ... m/s
[4 marks]

END OF QUESTIONS

GCSE Combined Science
Physics Paper 2
Higher Tier

In addition to this paper you should have:
- A ruler.
- A calculator.
- The Physics Equations sheet (on page 542).

Centre name			
Centre number			
Candidate number			

Time allowed:
- 1 hour 15 minutes

Surname
Other names
Candidate signature

Instructions to candidates
- Write your name and other details in the spaces provided above.
- Answer **all** questions in the spaces provided.
- Do all rough work on the paper.
- Cross out any work you do not want to be marked.

Information for candidates
- The marks available are given in brackets at the end of each question.
- There are 70 marks available for this paper.
- You are allowed to use a calculator.
- You should use good English and present your answers in a clear and organised way.
- For Question 3.2, ensure that your answer has a clear and logical structure, includes the right scientific terms, spelt correctly and includes detailed, relevant information.

Advice to candidates
- In calculations show clearly how you worked out your answers.

1   X-rays can be used in hospitals for medical treatments and diagnoses.
    Figure 1 shows X-ray images used for diagnoses.
    X-rays are directed at a body part being examined.
    A detector is placed behind the body part to detect the X-rays that reach it.

Figure 1

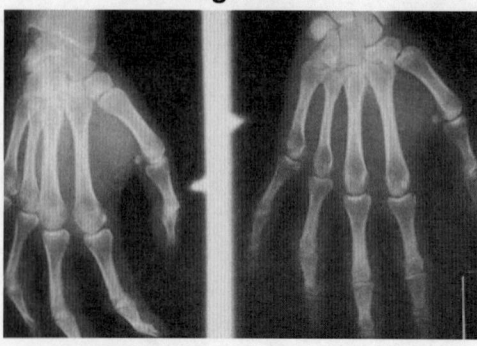

1.1   Explain how X-ray images, like those shown in **Figure 1**, are formed.

....

....
[2 marks]

1.2   Give **one** medical condition that X-rays can be used to either treat or diagnose.

....
[1 mark]

X-rays are part of the electromagnetic spectrum. Electromagnetic waves are a type of transverse wave. Transverse waves have a number of distinct properties. A trace of a transverse wave is displayed in **Figure 2**.

Figure 2

1.3   Calculate the amplitude of the wave in **Figure 2**.

....

Amplitude = ... m
[1 mark]

1.4   Define the 'frequency' of radiation.

....
[1 mark]

1.5   Draw and label a line on **Figure 2** to indicate the wavelength of the wave.
[1 mark]

2 Two swimmers, **A** and **B**, are having a race. They each swim a length of a 20 m swimming pool. The distance-time graph in **Figure 3** shows swimmer **A**'s motion.

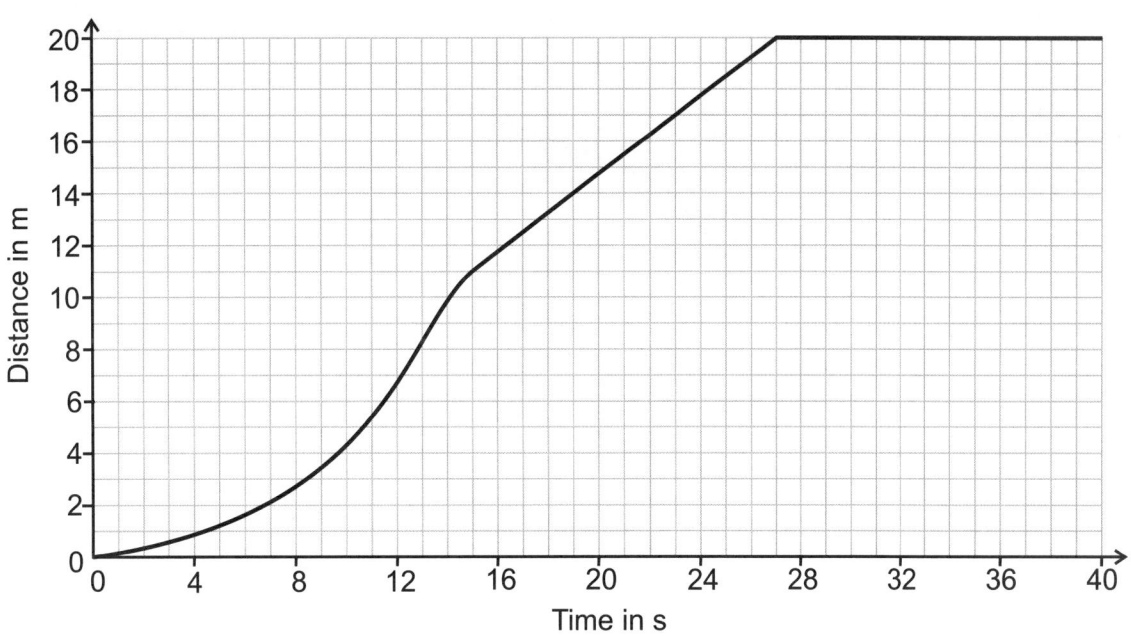

Figure 3

2.1 State **one** contact force which acts on swimmer **A** while she is swimming.

....
[1 mark]

2.2 For part of her swim, swimmer **A** is travelling at a constant speed.
Work out the time she spends travelling at a constant speed.

....

Time = ... s
[1 mark]

2.3 Determine the resultant force on swimmer **A** when she is travelling at a constant speed.

Force = ... N
[1 mark]

2.4 Using the graph in **Figure 3**, calculate the speed of swimmer **A** when she is travelling at a constant speed.

....

Speed = ... m/s
[2 marks]

2.5 Between which of the following distances was swimmer **A** travelling fastest?
Tick **one** box.

☐ Between 14 m and 15 m.

☐ Between 9 m and 10 m.

☐ Between 0 m and 1 m.

[1 mark]

Question 2 continues on the next page

Turn over ▶

Figure 4 shows the distance-time graph of swimmer B's motion.

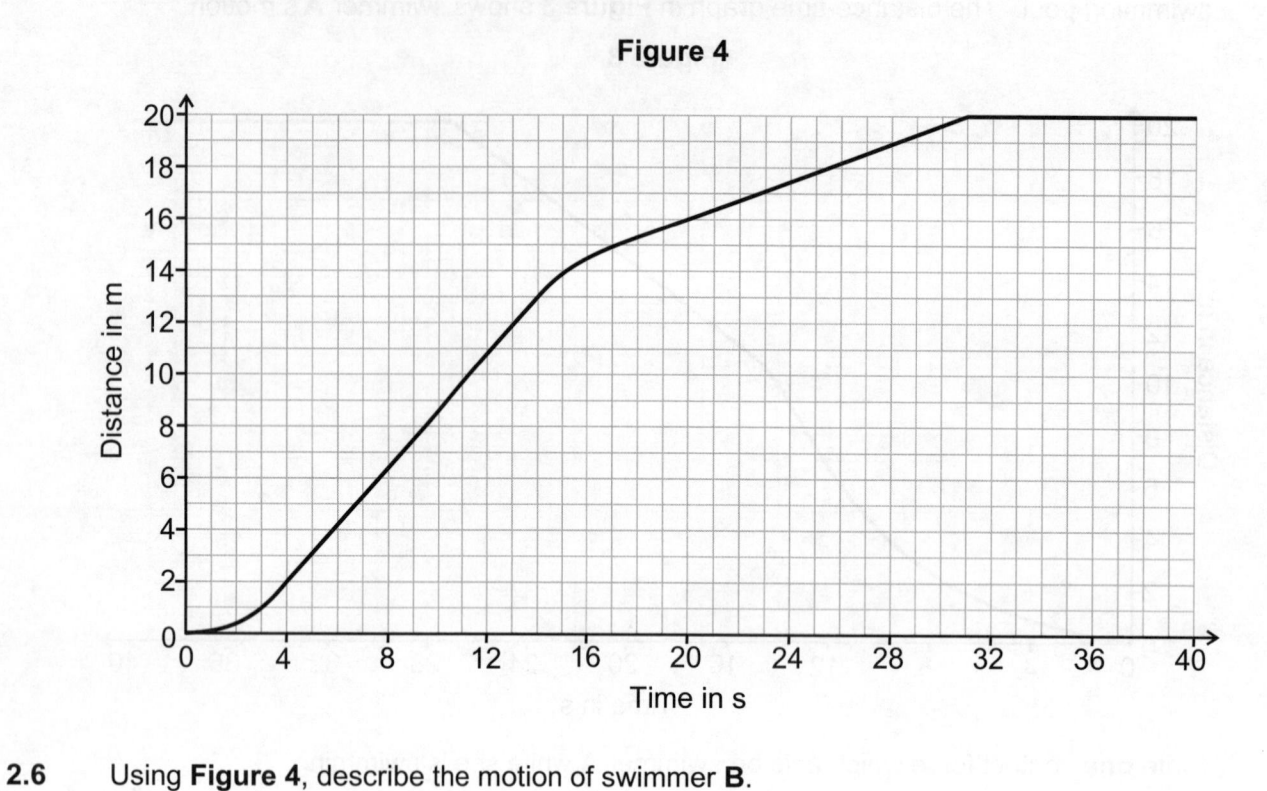

Figure 4

[Distance-time graph showing: curve starts at origin, accelerates from 0 to about 4s, then straight line with steady increase reaching ~14m at 14s, then less steep straight line to ~20m at 31s, then flat horizontal line from 31s to 40s at 20m.]

2.6 Using **Figure 4**, describe the motion of swimmer **B**.

....
....
....
....
....
....
....
....
....
....

[5 marks]

2.7 State whether swimmer **A** or swimmer **B** won the race.

....

[1 mark]

3 A student is given a set of apparatus, set up as shown in **Figure 5**.

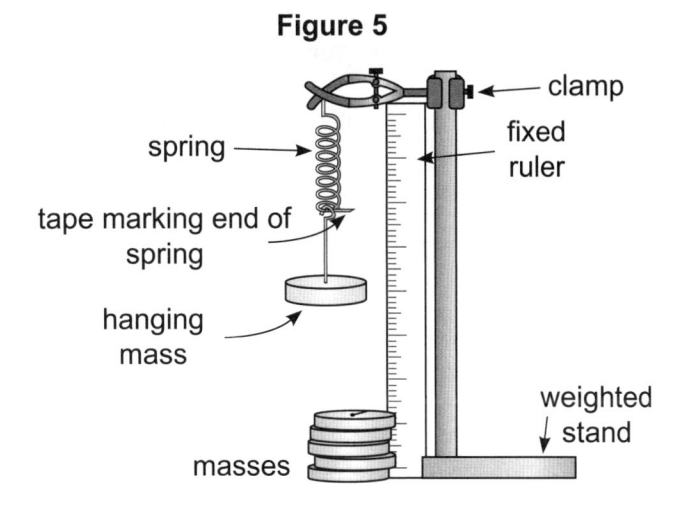

Figure 5

3.1 Name the type of error which may be reduced by the use of the tape marker at the end of the spring.

....

[1 mark]

3.2 Describe how the student could use the apparatus in **Figure 5** to plot a force-extension graph for the spring and find the spring constant.

[6 marks]

Question 3 continues on the next page

The student used the apparatus in **Figure 5** to produce the graph shown in **Figure 6**. She marked the limit of proportionality, and labelled it **A**.

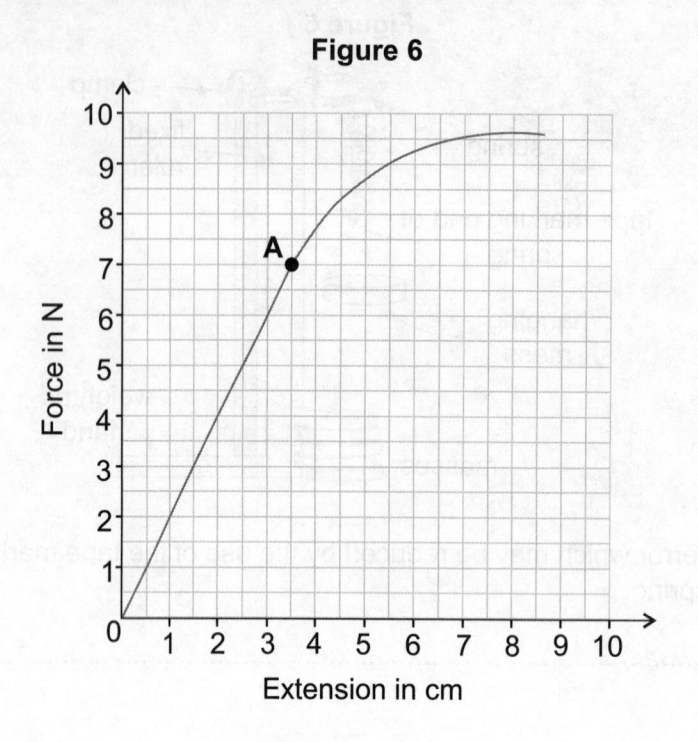

Figure 6

3.3 State what is meant by the 'limit of proportionality'.

....

....

[1 mark]

3.4 Using **Figure 6**, calculate the spring constant of the spring used in the experiment.

....

....

....

....

....

Spring constant = ... N/m

[3 marks]

4 A skydiver jumps from an aeroplane and his motion is recorded.
Figure 7 shows the velocity-time graph of his fall.

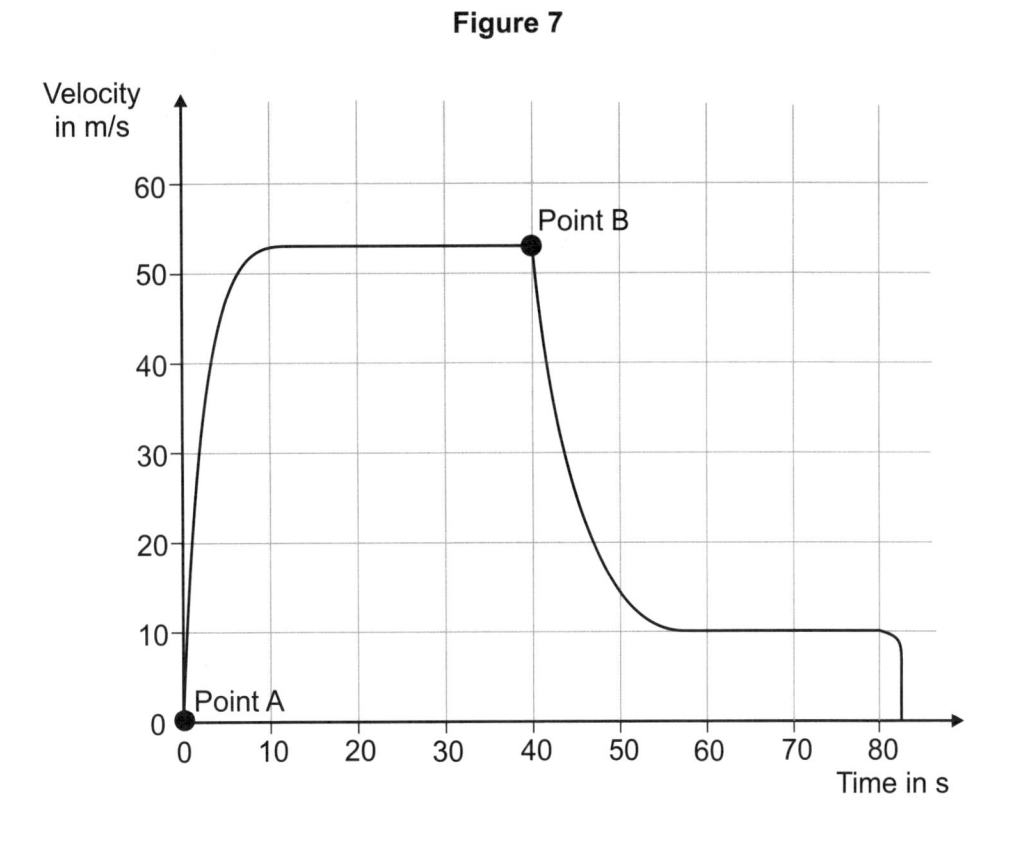

Figure 7

4.1 Write down the equation that links weight, mass and the gravitational field strength.

....
[1 mark]

4.2 The skydiver has a mass of 80.0 kg. Calculate his weight.
Use gravitational field strength = 9.8 N/kg.

....

....

Weight = ... N
[2 marks]

Question 4 continues on the next page

Turn over ▶

4.3 Using **Figure 7**, estimate the total distance travelled by the skydiver.

....

....

....

....

Distance = ... m

[4 marks]

4.4 When the skydiver jumps from the plane, the plane is travelling at a constant speed, at a constant height above the Earth.
Complete the free body diagram for the plane shown in **Figure 8**.
Label any arrows you draw with the name of the force they represent.

Figure 8

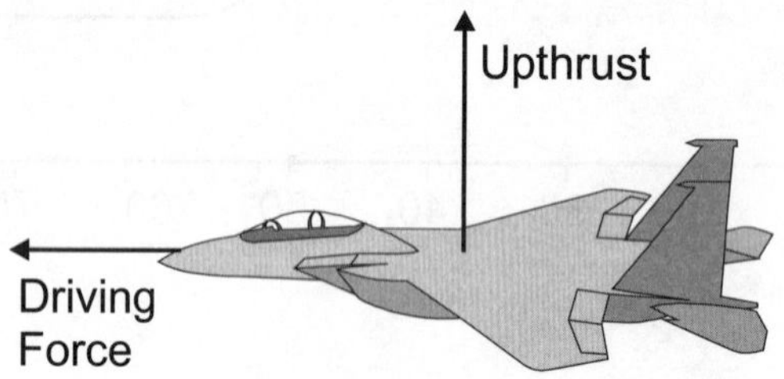

[4 marks]

4.5 Once the skydiver has jumped, the plane accelerates away.
Write down the equation which links force, mass and acceleration.

....

[1 mark]

4.6 The plane experiences a resultant driving force of 48 000 N as it accelerates.
The plane has a mass of 4000 kg.
Calculate the acceleration of the plane.

....

....

....

Acceleration = ... m/s²

[3 marks]

5 A driving instructor is looking at the Highway Code. He finds the data shown in **Table 1** about stopping distances for a well-maintained car travelling on dry roads at various speeds.

Table 1

Speed (km/h)	Thinking distance (m)	Braking distance (m)	Stopping distance (m)
32	6	6	12
48	9	14	
64	12	24	
80	15	38	53
96	18	55	
112	21	75	96

5.1 Complete **Table 1** by calculating the remaining stopping distances.

[1 mark]

5.2 The data in **Table 1** was obtained by observing a large number of drivers.
Explain why it was sensible to use a large sample of people.

[2 marks]

5.3 Describe the thinking distance and braking distance of a car, and the different factors (other than speed) that can increase them.

[5 marks]

Question 5 continues on the next page

Turn over ▶

5.4 A 1000 kg car is travelling at 30.0 m/s.
Write down the equation that links momentum, mass and velocity.

....
[1 mark]

5.5 Calculate the momentum of the car.

....

....

....

Momentum = ...kg m/s
[2 marks]

5.6 The car makes an emergency stop to avoid hitting a hazard.
The driver applies the brakes when he is 100 m away from the hazard.
Calculate the minimum deceleration required for the car to stop before hitting the hazard.
Use the correct equation from the Physics Equation Sheet on page 542.

....

....

....

....

Deceleration = ... m/s^2
[3 marks]

6 **Figure 9** shows the magnetic field around a bar magnet.

Figure 9

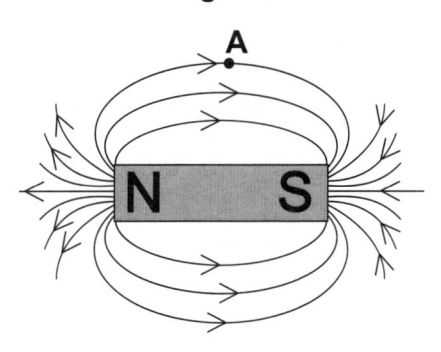

6.1 Identify the position of the compass needle if a compass was placed at point **A**.
Tick **one** box.

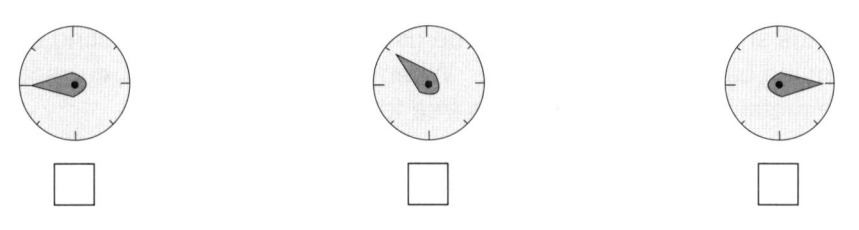

[1 mark]

Figure 10 shows two bar magnets being brought together.

Figure 10

6.2 Draw field lines on **Figure 10** to show the magnetic field between the two magnets.

[2 marks]

Current-carrying wires also have a magnetic field around them.
A current-carrying wire can be used to make a solenoid, as shown in **Figure 11**.

Figure 11

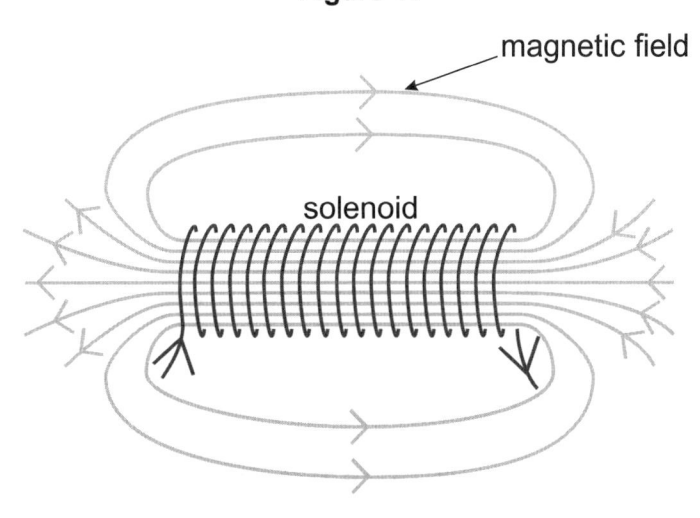

Question 6 continues on the next page

Turn over ▶

6.3 Explain how coiling a current-carrying wire into a solenoid affects the strength of the magnetic field around the wire.

[3 marks]

The apparatus shown in **Figure 12** can be used to show the force acting on a current-carrying bar in a magnetic field. When the switch is closed, current flows through the metal bar. The metal bar is free to move.

Figure 12

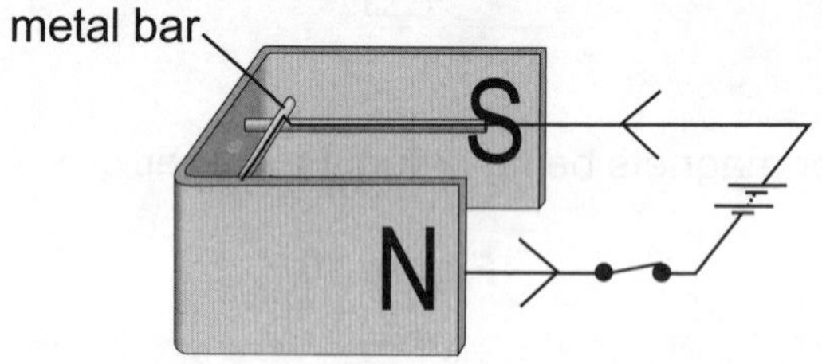

6.4 Suggest whether a force will act on the bar when the switch is closed.
Give a reason for your answer.

[2 marks]

6.5 Another magnet, with magnetic flux density of 1.5 T is set up. A current-carrying wire, carrying a 4.0 A current, is placed within the magnetic field, at right angles to the field.
It experiences a force 0.45 N.
Calculate the length of wire inside the magnetic field.
Use the correct equation from the Physics Equation Sheet on page 542.

Length of wire = ... cm
[4 marks]

END OF QUESTIONS

Answers

Topic B1 — Cell Biology

Page 19
Microscopy
Q1 real size = image size ÷ magnification
= 2.4 mm ÷ 40
= 0.06 mm *[1 mark]*
0.06 × 1000 = **60 μm** *[1 mark]*

Page 22
Warm-Up Questions
1) mitochondria
2) Plant cells have a rigid cell wall, they have a permanent vacuole and they contain chloroplasts.
3) Any two from: e.g. prokaryotic cells are smaller than eukaryotic cells. / Prokaryotic cells don't have mitochondria but eukaryotic cells do. / Prokaryotic cells don't have a true nucleus but eukaryotic cells do. / Prokaryotic cells have circular DNA but eukaryotic cells don't.
4) electron microscope
5) 4.5×10^{-4} μm

Exam Questions
1 nucleus *[1 mark]*
Remember, DNA in prokaryotic cells floats freely in the cytoplasm — it's not stored in a nucleus.
2.1 C *[1 mark]*
2.2 They absorb light needed for photosynthesis to make food for the plant *[1 mark]*.
2.3 They're where proteins are made in the cell *[1 mark]*.
3.1 How to grade your answer:
    Level 0: There is no relevant information. *[No marks]*
    Level 1: There is a brief explanation of how to prepare a slide or how to use a light microscope. *[1 to 2 marks]*
    Level 2: There is some explanation of how to prepare a slide and use a light microscope. *[3 to 4 marks]*
    Level 3: There is a clear and detailed explanation of how to prepare a slide and use a light microscope. *[5 to 6 marks]*

Here are some points your answer may include:
To prepare a slide:
Add a drop of water to the middle of a clean slide.
Cut up an onion and separate it out into layers.
Use tweezers to peel off some epidermal tissue from the bottom of one of the layers.
Use tweezers to place the epidermal tissue into the water on the slide.
Add a drop of iodine solution/stain.
Place a cover slip on top by standing it upright on the slide, next to the water droplet, then carefully tilting and lowering it so it covers the onion tissue without trapping any air bubbles.
To use a light microscope:
Clip the slide onto the stage.
Select the lowest-powered objective lens.
Use the coarse adjustment knob to move the stage up to just below the objective lens (without looking down the eyepiece).
Look down the eyepiece and use the coarse adjustment knob to move the stage downwards until the image is roughly in focus.
Adjust the focus with the fine adjustment knob, until a clear image of the cells is visible.
To see the cells with greater magnification, swap to a higher-powered objective lens and refocus.

3.2 E.g. real size = 75 μm ÷ 1000 = 0.075 mm
magnification = image size ÷ real size
= 7.5 mm ÷ 0.075 mm = **× 100**
[2 marks for correct answer, otherwise 1 mark for correct working.]
You could have converted the image size to μm here instead — the important thing is that both values have the same units before you stick them in the formula.

Page 28
Chromosomes and Mitosis
Q1 a) 11 ÷ (62 + 11) = 0.150...
0.150... × 100 = **15%** *[1 mark]*
b) E.g. she could see the X-shaped chromosomes in the middle of the cells. / She could see the arms of the chromosomes being pulled apart *[1 mark]*.

Page 29
Warm-Up Questions
1) It's the process by which a cell changes to become specialised for its job.
2) The cell has a hair-like shape, which gives it a large surface area to absorb water and minerals from the soil.
3) Copies of the plant can be made by taking stem cells from the meristem and growing them into new, genetically identical plants (clones).
4) in the nucleus
5) True

Exam Questions
1.1 The amount of DNA is doubling *[1 mark]* so that there is one copy for each new cell *[1 mark]*.
1.2 The two new cells separate *[1 mark]*.
1.3 two *[1 mark]*
2.1 They could be grown into a particular type of cell, which can then be used to replace faulty cells *[1 mark]*.
2.2 Embryonic stem cells have the potential to develop into any kind of cell, whereas adult stem cells can only develop into certain types of cell *[1 mark]*.
2.3 E.g. bone marrow *[1 mark]*

Page 30
Diffusion
Q1 a) The ink will diffuse / spread out through the water *[1 mark]*. This is because the ink particles will move from where there is a higher concentration of them (the drop of ink) to where there is a lower concentration of them (the surrounding water) *[1 mark]*.
b) The ink particles will diffuse / spread out faster *[1 mark]*.

Page 32
Osmosis
Q1 Water will move out of the piece of potato by osmosis *[1 mark]*, so its mass will decrease *[1 mark]*.

Page 34
Exchanging Substances
Q1 Surface area:
(2 × 2) × 2 = 8
(2 × 1) × 4 = 8
8 + 8 = 16 μm² *[1 mark]*
Volume:
2 × 2 × 1 = 4 μm³ *[1 mark]*
So the surface area to volume ratio is **16 : 4, or 4 : 1** *[1 mark]*.

Page 36
More on Exchanging Substances
Q1 The flat shape of the leaf increases the area of the underside of the leaf (where gas exchange takes place) *[1 mark]*. This increases the rate at which carbon dioxide can diffuse into the leaf, and therefore the rate at which the plant can photosynthesise *[1 mark]*.
Q2 The damage to the villi is likely to reduce the surface area for absorption *[1 mark]*. Therefore, less iron can be absorbed from the digested food in the small intestine into the blood *[1 mark]*.

Pages 38-39
Warm-Up Questions
1) The higher the temperature, the faster the rate of diffusion because the particles have more energy and so move around faster.
2) A partially permeable membrane only allows small molecules (e.g. water) to diffuse through it.
3) Osmosis and active transport.
4) They're thin, they have a large surface area, they have lots of blood vessels and they're often ventilated.

Answers

5) E.g. alveoli (in the lung) and villi (in the small intestine).
6) Any two from: e.g. it is made up of gill filaments which give a large surface area. / Each gill filament is covered in lamellae, which further increases the surface area. / The lamellae have a thin surface layer of cells. / The lamellae have lots of capillaries. / A large concentration gradient is maintained between the water and the blood.

Exam Questions
1 The time taken will decrease *[1 mark]*. There will be more ammonia gas particles at the end of the tube where they are injected, meaning a greater concentration gradient between that end and the end where the litmus paper is *[1 mark]*. This means an increased rate of diffusion, so the gas particles will reach the litmus paper more quickly *[1 mark]*.
2.1 The potato cylinder in tube D, because this tube contains the most concentrated sugar solution so this cylinder will have lost the most water *[1 mark]* by osmosis *[1 mark]*.
2.2 Tube A contained distilled water, so some of the water moved by osmosis into the potato cylinder *[1 mark]* from an area of high water concentration to an area of low water concentration *[1 mark]*.
3.1 By diffusion down their concentration gradients into the blood *[1 mark]*, and by active transport, against their concentration gradient *[1 mark]*.
3.2 E.g. they increase the surface area to maximise absorption *[1 mark]*. They have a thin wall/a single layer of surface cells to reduce the distance across which diffusion occurs *[1 mark]*. They have a good blood supply for the uptake of substances *[1 mark]*.
4.1 diffusion *[1 mark]*
The acid must by moving by diffusion here as it is moving from a region of higher concentration (outside the cubes) to a region of lower concentration (inside the cubes, which don't contain any acid to start with).
4.2 $(835 + 825 + 842 + 838) \div 4 =$ **835 s**
[2 marks for correct answer, otherwise 1 mark for correct working.]
4.3 Surface area: $(10 \times 10) \times 6 = 600$ mm^2
Volume: $10 \times 10 \times 10 = 1000$ mm^3
So the surface area to volume ratio is 600 : 1000, which simplifies to **3 : 5**
[3 marks for correct answer, otherwise 1 mark for correct surface area and 1 mark for correct volume.]
600 and 1000 are both divisible by 200. If you don't spot this straight away, you could simplify the ratio by first dividing both sides by 100, then by 2.
4.4 As the size of the gelatine cube increases, the time taken for the cube to become yellow increases *[1 mark]*. This is because there is a greater distance for the acid to travel in the bigger cubes / the bigger cubes have a smaller surface area to volume ratio *[1 mark]*, which decreases the rate of diffusion *[1 mark]*.

Topic B2 — Organisation

Page 44
Investigating Enzymatic Reactions
Q1 2 minutes = 2 × 60 = 120 seconds
$36 \div 120 =$ **0.3 cm^3/s** *[1 mark]*

Pages 49-50
Warm-Up Questions
1) A group of organs working together to perform a particular function.
2) The pH at which the enzyme works best.
3) a) amylase
b) protease
c) lipase
Carbohydrases (e.g. amylase) break down carbohydrates, such as starch. Proteases break down proteins, and lipases break down lipids (fats).
4) a) (simple) sugars
b) amino acids
c) glycerol and fatty acids
5) stomach, pancreas, small intestine

6) E.g. break up the food using a pestle and mortar. Then transfer the ground up food to a beaker and add some distilled water. Next, stir the mixture with a glass rod, and finally filter the solution using a funnel lined with filter paper.

Exam Questions
1.1 *[1 mark]* (Place where bile is produced)
1.2 It neutralises the hydrochloric acid from the stomach *[1 mark]*.
1.3 It emulsifies fats *[1 mark]* to give a much bigger surface area of fat for the enzyme lipase to work on *[1 mark]*.
2.1 The enzyme has a specific shape which will only fit with one type of substrate *[1 mark]*.
2.2 It would break the bonds in the enzyme and change the shape of the enzyme's active site/denature the enzyme *[1 mark]*. This would mean the substrate would no longer fit into it so the enzyme wouldn't work anymore *[1 mark]*.
A similar thing happens when the pH or the temperature is too high — the bonds are disrupted and the shape of the active site may change.
3.1 Accept answers between 38 °C and 40 °C *[1 mark]*.
3.2 Enzyme B, because it has an unusually high optimum temperature which it would need to work in the hot vent *[1 mark]*.
4 The food sample contains starch *[1 mark]* and lipids *[1 mark]*, but no proteins *[1 mark]*.
5.1 To prevent the starch coming into contact with amylase in the syringe, which would have started the reaction before he had started the stop clock *[1 mark]*.
5.2 Rate = $1000 \div 60 =$ **17 s^{-1}** (2 s.f.) *[1 mark]*
5.3 Repeat the experiment using buffers with a range of different pH values and compare the results *[1 mark]*.

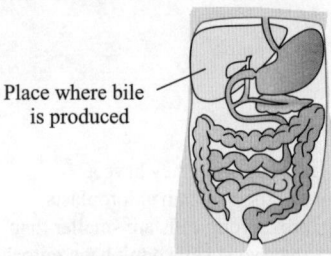

Page 54
Circulatory System — Blood Vessels
Q1 2.175 l × 1000 = 2175 ml *[1 mark]*
$2175 \div 8.7 =$ **250 ml/min** *[1 mark]*

Page 55
Circulatory System — Blood
Q1 They help the blood to clot at a wound *[1 mark]*.
Q2 To carry oxygen from the lungs to all the cells in the body *[1 mark]*.

Pages 56-57
Warm-Up Questions
1) bronchi
2) They supply oxygenated blood to the heart itself.
3) A device that is implanted under the skin and has a wire going to the heart. It produces an electric current to keep the heart beating regularly.
4) They carry blood back to the heart.
5) platelets

Exam Questions
1.1 $495 \div 12 =$ **41 breaths per minute** *[1 mark]*
You might be wondering why the answer has been rounded to 41 when the calculator said 41.25. That's because you can't get a quarter of a breath.
1.2 Resting heart rate is controlled by a group of cells in the right atrium wall that act as a pacemaker *[1 mark]*.
2.1 It is biconcave, which gives it a large surface area for absorbing oxygen *[1 mark]*.
2.2 E.g. it contains haemoglobin *[1 mark]* which binds with oxygen so it can be carried to the body tissues *[1 mark]*. /
It has no nucleus *[1 mark]* so there is space to carry oxygen *[1 mark]*.

2.3 White blood cells *[1 mark]*. They defend the body against infection *[1 mark]*.
2.4 They have permeable walls *[1 mark]*, so substances can diffuse in and out *[1 mark]*. Their walls are usually only one cell thick *[1 mark]*, which increases the rate of diffusion by decreasing the distance over which it occurs *[1 mark]*.
2.5 150 s ÷ 60 = 2.5 min
1155 ÷ 2.5 = **462 ml/min** *[2 marks for correct answer, otherwise 1 mark for correct working.]*

Make sure you read the question carefully — if you gave your answer in ml/second you wouldn't have got all the marks available.

3.1 A — aorta, B — vena cava, C — left atrium *[1 mark]*
3.2 It pumps blood around the body *[1 mark]*.
3.3 To prevent the backflow of blood *[1 mark]*.
3.4 How to grade your answer:
Level 0: There is no relevant information. *[No marks]*
Level 1: There are some relevant points describing how deoxygenated blood passes through the heart to reach the lungs but the answer is missing some detail. *[1 to 2 marks]*
Level 2: There is a clear, detailed description of how deoxygenated blood passes through the heart to reach the lungs. *[3 to 4 marks]*
Here are some points your answer may include:
Deoxygenated blood enters the right atrium through the vena cava.
The right atrium contracts.
The blood passes through a valve into the right ventricle.
The right ventricle contracts, forcing the blood through the pulmonary artery and out of the heart towards the lungs.
4.1 E.g. the vein has a bigger lumen/thinner wall/valves *[1 mark]*. / The artery has a smaller lumen/thicker wall/no valves *[1 mark]*.

To answer this question, you needed to think about how the structure of veins and arteries differ — and how you could tell them apart by just looking at them.

4.2 The vein, because it has a thinner wall/less muscle in its wall/ isn't as strong *[1 mark]*.

Page 61
Warm-Up Questions
1) the coronary arteries
2) a) a stent
   b) E.g. complications during the operation, infection from surgery and developing a blood clot/thrombosis.
3) A mechanical device that is put into a person to pump blood if their own heart fails.

Exam Questions
1.1 fatty material *[1 mark]*
1.2 The fatty material causes the coronary arteries to become narrow, so blood flow to the heart muscle is restricted *[1 mark]*. This reduces (or stops) the delivery of oxygen to the heart muscle *[1 mark]*.
2.1 It could mean that blood flows in both directions rather than just forward *[1 mark]*, so the blood wouldn't circulate as effectively as normal *[1 mark]*.
2.2 Biological valves *[1 mark]* — these are replacement valves that can be taken from humans or other mammals *[1 mark]*. Mechanical valves *[1 mark]* — these are man-made replacement valves *[1 mark]*.
2.3 E.g. it requires surgery, which could lead to bleeding/infection. / There could be problems with blood clots *[1 mark]*.
3.1 Statins are drugs that can reduce the amount of 'bad' cholesterol present in the bloodstream *[1 mark]*. This slows down the rate of fatty deposits forming, which reduces the likelihood of coronary heart disease developing *[1 mark]*.
3.2 E.g. the patient has to remember to take them every day. / Statins can sometimes cause negative side effects. / The effect of taking statins isn't instant *[1 mark]*.

Page 67
Warm-Up Questions
1) The state of physical and mental wellbeing.
2) It can be spread from person to person or between people and animals.
3) E.g. money is needed to research/treat the diseases. / People with non-communicable diseases may be unable to work, which may reduce the country's economy.
4) The presence of certain substances in the body. / The presence of certain substances in the environment.

Exam Questions
1.1 A risk factor is something that is linked to an increase in the likelihood that a person will develop a certain disease during their lifetime *[1 mark]*.
1.2 E.g. smoking *[1 mark]*
1.3 E.g. ionising radiation *[1 mark]*
2.1 Uncontrolled cell division *[1 mark]*.
2.2 malignant *[1 mark]*
2.3 Tumour cells can break off and spread to other parts of the body by travelling in the bloodstream *[1 mark]*. The malignant cells then invade healthy tissues elsewhere in the body and form secondary tumours *[1 mark]*.
3.1 A disease that cannot spread between people or between animals and people *[1 mark]*.
3.2 Because of the problem with their immune system, their body is less likely to be able to defend itself against the pathogen that causes influenza *[1 mark]*.

Page 72
Measuring Transpiration and Stomata
Q1 Aloe vera, because the transpiration rate will be higher in the hot, dry area *[1 mark]*, so the aloe vera will have fewer stomata to help conserve water *[1 mark]*.

Pages 73-74
Warm-Up Questions
1) Meristem tissue is found at the growing tips of roots and shoots and is able to differentiate into lots of different types of plant cell.
2) palisade mesophyll tissue
3) False
4) light intensity, temperature, air flow, humidity

Exam Questions
1 spongy mesophyll tissue *[1 mark]*
2.1 xylem vessels *[1 mark]*
2.2 They are made of dead cells joined end to end *[1 mark]* with no end walls between them and therefore a hole down the middle *[1 mark]*. They're strengthened with a material called lignin *[1 mark]*.
2.3 transpiration *[1 mark]*
3.1 phloem *[1 mark]*
3.2 They are made of columns of elongated living cells with small pores in the end walls *[1 mark]* to allow cell sap to flow through *[1 mark]*.
3.3 translocation *[1 mark]*
4.1 The water level in the vase would decrease more slowly *[1 mark]*, as the rate of transpiration would be lower *[1 mark]*. This is because water molecules have less energy at lower temperatures, meaning they don't diffuse/ evaporate as quickly from the leaves *[1 mark]*.
4.2 How to grade your answer:
Level 0: There is no relevant information. *[No marks]*
Level 1: The correct diagram is identified and the answer links the shape of the guard cell to the closing of the stomata at night. *[1 to 2 marks]*
Level 2: The correct diagram is identified and the answer clearly explains how the shape of the guard cell changes at night, allowing the stomata to close to reduce water loss when gas exchange is not required. *[3 to 4 marks]*
Here are some points your answer may include:
A, because the guard cell is most flaccid.
Flaccid guard cells mean that the stomata would be closed.
The stomata close at night as they don't need to be open for gas exchange as photosynthesis doesn't happen in the dark.
The closing of the stomata at night prevents water being lost through transpiration.
5.1 (10 + 11 + 9) ÷ 3 = **10%** *[2 marks for correct answer, otherwise 1 mark for correct working]*

5.2 The movement of air from the fan sweeps away water vapour, maintaining a low concentration of water outside the leaf *[1 mark]* and increasing the rate at which water is lost through diffusion *[1 mark]*. This means that the plants next to the fan would lose more water (and therefore more mass) than the plants in a still room in the same amount of time *[1 mark]*.

5.3 The rate of transpiration would be slower *[1 mark]* since most water loss occurs through the stomata, which are on the underside of the leaves *[1 mark]*.

5.4 E.g. you could put a new group of 3 basil plants in a separate room *[1 mark]* and increase the humidity in the room by misting/spraying the air with water *[1 mark]*.

If you've thought of another sensible way to increase or decrease the humidity around the plants, you'd still get the mark in the exam.

Topic B3 — Infection and Response

Page 80
Warm-Up Questions
1) A communicable disease is a disease that is easily spread.
2) E.g. measles, HIV and tobacco mosaic virus.
3) A red skin rash.
4) It causes purple or black spots to develop on the leaves, which can then turn yellow and drop off.
5) By sexual contact.
6) Vaccinations stop people from developing the disease, so that they cannot pass it on to someone else.

Exam Questions
1.1 Initial symptoms are flu-like *[1 mark]*.
1.2 Pain when the infected person urinates *[1 mark]*. Thick yellow or green discharge from the vagina or penis *[1 mark]*.
1.3 Any two from: e.g. fever / stomach cramps / vomiting / diarrhoea *[2 marks]*.
2.1 A microorganism that can cause disease *[1 mark]*.
2.2 The tobacco mosaic virus *[1 mark]*. It can reduce the growth of the plant *[1 mark]*.
2.3 By sexual contact *[1 mark]*, or by exchanging bodily fluids such as blood *[1 mark]*.
3.1 To prevent the contamination of food by disease-causing pathogens that may be on the chefs' hands *[1 mark]*.
3.2 Malaria is spread by vectors *[1 mark]* and not through contaminated food/surfaces / skin to skin contact *[1 mark]*.
3.3 E.g. mosquitoes are the vectors of malaria, so destroying mosquitoes will prevent malaria being spread between people *[1 mark]*.

Page 82
Fighting Disease — Vaccination
Q1 Basia's white blood cells recognise the antigens on the flu virus and rapidly produce antibodies, which kill the pathogen *[1 mark]*. Cassian's white blood cells don't recognise the antigens, so it takes a while for them to produce antibodies and he becomes ill in the meantime *[1 mark]*.

Pages 87-88
Warm-Up Questions
1) The skin acts as a barrier to pathogens and secretes antimicrobial substances that kill them.
2) To destroy pathogens that enter the body.
3) foxgloves
4) Whether the drug works and produces the effect you're looking for.
5) A placebo is a substance that's like the real drug but doesn't do anything.
6) Using a placebo allows the doctor to see the actual difference the drug makes (to a patient's illness/symptoms).

Exam Questions
1.1 They trap particles that could contain pathogens *[1 mark]*.
1.2 They waft the mucus up to the back of the throat where it can be swallowed *[1 mark]*.
1.3 (hydrochloric) acid *[1 mark]*.
2.1 human volunteers *[1 mark]*
Drugs are tested on human cells, live animals and human tissue in pre-clinical trials. If a drug makes it through the pre-clinical trials, it's then tested on human volunteers in a clinical trial.
2.2 In a double blind trial neither the patient nor the doctor *[1 mark]* knows who is receiving the drug and who is receiving the placebo until all the results have been gathered *[1 mark]*.
2.3 dosage *[1 mark]*, efficacy/how well the drug works *[1 mark]*
2.4 Peer review is where other scientists check the work to make sure it is valid/has been carried out rigorously *[1 mark]*. It's done help to prevent false claims being made about the results *[1 mark]*.
3.1 Engulfing foreign cells and digesting them / phagocytosis *[1 mark]*.
3.2 A particular antibody will only lock onto a specific type of antigen from one type of pathogen *[1 mark]*.
4.1 *Penicillium* mould / *Penicillium notatum* *[1 mark]*
4.2 Overuse of antibiotics may increase the rate of development of resistant strains of bacteria *[1 mark]*. This will make bacterial infections harder to treat in the future *[1 mark]*.
4.3 Antibiotics cannot kill viruses *[1 mark]*.
5.1 E.g. a painkiller/aspirin *[1 mark]*
5.2 Rubella is a virus and viruses reproduce using your body cells *[1 mark]*, which makes it very difficult to develop drugs that destroy just the virus without killing the body's cells *[1 mark]*.
5.3 How to grade your answer:
Level 0: There is no relevant information. *[No marks]*
Level 1: There is a brief explanation of how vaccination against rubella can prevent a person catching the disease or how having a large proportion of vaccinated individuals in a population reduces the risk of rubella for people who are not vaccinated. *[1 to 2 marks]*
Level 2: There is some explanation of how vaccination against rubella can prevent a person catching the disease and how having a large proportion of vaccinated individuals in a population reduces the risk of rubella for people who are not vaccinated. *[3 to 4 marks]*
Level 3: There is a clear and detailed explanation of how vaccination against rubella can prevent a person catching the disease and how having a large proportion of vaccinated individuals in a population reduces the risk of rubella for people who are not vaccinated. *[5 to 6 marks]*
Here are some points your answer may include:
When a person is vaccinated against rubella, they are injected with dead or inactive rubella viruses.
The dead or inactive viruses carry antigens, which cause the body to produce antibodies to attack them.
If live rubella viruses infect the body after this, white blood cells can rapidly mass produce antibodies to defeat the virus.
If a large proportion of the population is vaccinated against rubella, then there are fewer people who are able to pass the disease on.
This means that even someone who hasn't been vaccinated is less likely to catch the disease.
5.4 E.g. they may be worried that they will have a bad reaction to a vaccine. / Vaccines don't always work and so the person might not be given immunity *[1 mark]*.

Topic B4 — Bioenergetics

Page 94
Measuring the Rate of Photosynthesis
Q1 Light intensity becomes four times smaller *[1 mark]*.
Q2 light intensity $\propto \dfrac{1}{\text{distance}^2}$
$1 \div 15^2 = 0.00444...$ a.u. *[1 mark]*
$1 \div 5^2 = 0.04$ a.u. *[1 mark]*
$0.04 \div 0.00444... = 9$ *[1 mark]*

Pages 96-97
Warm-Up Questions
1) glucose
2) A limiting factor is something that stops photosynthesis from happening any faster.
3) If the temperature's too high, the plant's enzymes will be denatured, so the rate of photosynthesis rapidly decreases.

Remember, if the temperature is too high for an enzyme, the bonds holding it together may break. This can cause the shape of the enzyme's active site to change, denaturing the enzyme.

4) E.g. oxygen production.
5) light intensity $\propto \dfrac{1}{\text{distance}^2}$
6) To increase the plants' growth so that more/bigger tomatoes are produced and a bigger profit can be made from selling them.

Exam Questions
1.1 carbon dioxide + water *[1 mark]* $\xrightarrow{\text{light}}$ glucose + oxygen *[1 mark]*
1.2 cellulose *[1 mark]*
1.3 Any two from: e.g. for respiration. / For storage as lipids/oils or fats. / For storage as insoluble starch. / For making amino acids, which are then made into proteins. *[2 marks]*
2.1 By counting the number of bubbles produced / by measuring the volume of gas produced, in a given time/at regular intervals *[1 mark]*.
2.2 Dependent variable — rate of photosynthesis/number of bubbles in a given time/volume of gas in a given time *[1 mark]*.
Independent variable — light intensity *[1 mark]*.
2.3 E.g. carbon dioxide concentration in the water/temperature/the plant being used *[1 mark]*
3.1 At low light intensities, increasing the CO_2 concentration has no effect *[1 mark]*, but at higher light intensities, increasing the concentration of CO_2 increases the maximum rate of photosynthesis *[1 mark]*.
3.2 The rate of photosynthesis does not continue to increase because temperature or the level of carbon dioxide becomes the limiting factor *[1 mark]*.

You don't know if the temperature was kept constant or not, so either the level of carbon dioxide or temperature could have been the limiting factor here — there's no way of knowing.

4.1
[1 mark]

4.2 Plants need both chlorophyll and light to photosynthesise and produce starch — there is only chlorophyll in the green area of the plant *[1 mark]*, and light can only reach parts of the leaf not covered by black paper *[1 mark]*.
5 light intensity = $\dfrac{1}{d^2}$
= $\dfrac{1}{7.5^2}$
= **0.018 a.u. (2 s.f.)**
[2 marks for correct answer, otherwise 1 mark for correct working.]

Page 101
Exercise
Q1 Running *[1 mark]*. It raises the pulse rate the most, so it is the most vigorous type of exercise *[1 mark]*. The more vigorous the exercise, the more anaerobic respiration will be taking place in the muscles *[1 mark]*. Anaerobic respiration produces lactic acid, so running will lead to the greatest build up of lactic acid in the blood *[1 mark]*.

Page 102
Warm-Up Questions
1) Any two from: e.g. to build up larger molecules from smaller ones. / To contract muscles. / To keep body temperature steady.
2) The sum of all of the reactions that happen in a cell or the body.
3) Glucose and oxygen.
4) fermentation
5) Breathing rate increases, breath volume increases and heart rate increases.

Exam Questions
1.1 Any two from: e.g. aerobic respiration uses oxygen, anaerobic respiration does not. / Glucose is broken down fully during aerobic respiration but is only partially broken down during anaerobic respiration. / Aerobic respiration doesn't produce lactic acid, anaerobic respiration does. / Aerobic respiration releases more energy than anaerobic respiration. *[2 marks]*
1.2 glucose + oxygen *[1 mark]* → carbon dioxide + water *[1 mark]*
2.1 glucose → lactic acid *[1 mark]*
2.2 During vigorous exercise, the body can't supply enough oxygen to the muscles *[1 mark]*. It uses anaerobic respiration to provide energy without using oxygen, which keeps the muscles going for longer *[1 mark]*.
3.1 Because during exercise the muscles need more energy from respiration *[1 mark]*, and this respiration requires oxygen *[1 mark]*.
3.2 Because there is an oxygen debt / oxygen is needed to react with the lactic acid that has built up *[1 mark]*.
4 E.g. during vigorous exercise, the muscles use glucose rapidly *[1 mark]*. Blood glucagon level may rise so that some of the glycogen stored in the liver can be converted back to glucose to provide more energy for respiration *[1 mark]*.

Topic B5 — Homeostasis and Response

Page 107
Reflexes
Q1 A rapid, automatic response to a stimulus that doesn't involve the conscious part of the brain *[1 mark]*.
Q2 a) muscle *[1 mark]*
b) The heat stimulus is detected by receptors in the hand *[1 mark]*, which send impulses along a sensory neurone to the CNS *[1 mark]*. The impulses are transferred to a relay neurone *[1 mark]*. They are then transferred to a motor neurone and travel along it to the effector/muscle *[1 mark]*.

Page 108
Investigating Reaction Time
Q1 a) 242 + 256 + 253 + 249 + 235 = 1235 *[1 mark]*
1235 ÷ 5 = **247 ms** *[1 mark]*
b) Any two from: e.g. the hand each person used to click the mouse / the computer equipment/programme used / the amount of energy drink they consumed / the type of energy drink used / the time between consuming the energy drink and taking the test *[2 marks]*.

Page 109
Warm-Up Questions
1) The maintenance of a stable internal environment in response to changes in both internal and external conditions.
2) E.g. body temperature, blood glucose level, water content.
3) synapse
4) sensory neurone, relay neurone, motor neurone
5) E.g. age / gender / drugs / caffeine.

Exam Questions
1.1 Stimulus: appearance of red triangle *[1 mark]*
Receptors: cells in the eye / light receptor cells *[1 mark]*
Effectors: muscles (in hand controlling mouse) *[1 mark]*
1.2 343 × 3 = 1029
1029 − 328 − 346 = **355 ms** *[2 marks for the correct answer, otherwise 1 mark for the correct calculation]*

2.1 motor neurone *[1 mark]*
2.2 Muscle *[1 mark]*, which contracts to move the baby's finger *[1 mark]*.
2.3 When the electrical impulse reaches the end of the neurone, it stimulates the release of a chemical *[1 mark]*. The chemical diffuses across the synapse to activate an electrical impulse in the next neurone *[1 mark]*.
2.4 In a baby older than 6 months, the pathway will involve conscious parts of the brain, whereas in a newborn baby it won't. / In a baby older than 6 months, the response will not be produced as rapidly as in the newborn baby *[1 mark]*.

The response in the baby older than 6 months is not a reflex — it chooses whether it wants to grasp an object. Remember, reflexes are automatic — they don't involve conscious parts of the brain, which makes the response much faster.

Page 112
Controlling Blood Glucose
Q1 Curve 1, because the secretion rate is high when the blood glucose level is low / the secretion rate decreases as the blood glucose level rises *[1 mark]*. Glucagon increases the blood glucose level, so it is secreted when the blood glucose level becomes too low *[1 mark]*.

Page 114
Warm-Up Questions
1) In the blood.
2) E.g. pituitary gland, thyroid gland, adrenal gland, pancreas, testes.
3) Removes glucose from the blood. / Makes the liver turn glucose into glycogen for storage.
4) A condition in which the body becomes resistant to its own insulin.

Exam Questions
1.1 Organ A is the pancreas *[1 mark]*.
Organ B is the liver *[1 mark]*.
1.2 Eating carbohydrates *[1 mark]*.
1.3 The pancreas/organ A produces little or no insulin *[1 mark]*. This means that the liver/organ B is unable to remove glucose from the blood for storage *[1 mark]*. So the blood glucose level is able to rise to a dangerously high level *[1 mark]*.
1.4 It makes the liver/organ B turn glycogen into glucose for release into the blood *[1 mark]*.
2 The pituitary gland releases hormones that act on other glands, directing them to release hormones *[1 mark]*. If a pituitary hormone that acts on the thyroid gland is not released *[1 mark]*, then the thyroid gland may also stop releasing hormones, resulting in the symptoms described *[1 mark]*.
3.1 in the muscles *[1 mark]*
3.2 Eating releases glucose into the bloodstream *[1 mark]*. Excess glucose cannot be converted into glycogen since there's not enough functioning glycogen synthase *[1 mark]*, so the blood glucose level increases *[1 mark]*.

Page 121
Warm-Up Questions
1) FSH/follicle-stimulating hormone
2) Any three from: e.g. progesterone-only pill / contraceptive implant / contraceptive injection / plastic IUD.
3) E.g. it doesn't always work. / It can be expensive. / Too many eggs can be stimulated, resulting in multiple pregnancies.
4) They stimulate several eggs to mature.
5) thyroid

Exam Questions
1.1 It inhibits it *[1 mark]*.
1.2 progesterone *[1 mark]*
1.3 day 14 *[1 mark]*
2.1 Keeping oestrogen levels permanently high inhibits production of FSH *[1 mark]*, so no eggs mature / so egg development and production stop *[1 mark]*.
2.2 E.g. by stimulating the production of thick cervical mucus *[1 mark]*, which prevents any sperm getting through and reaching the egg *[1 mark]*.

2.3 E.g. the contraceptive implant *[1 mark]*, as this is effective for three years once inserted and so does not have to be thought about on a daily basis *[1 mark]*. / The contraceptive injection *[1 mark]*, as this is effective for 2 to 3 months and so does not have to be thought about on a daily basis *[1 mark]*. / The contraceptive patch *[1 mark]*, as each patch lasts one week, so does not have to be thought about on a daily basis.
2.4 E.g. male/female sterilisation *[1 mark]*.
3 The cat's heart rate would increase *[1 mark]* because adrenaline is released *[1 mark]*. The increased heart rate increases the rate of delivery of glucose and oxygen *[1 mark]* to the brain and muscle cells *[1 mark]*, which prepares the cat to escape danger/the dog by fight or flight *[1 mark]*.

Topic B6 — Inheritance, Variation and Evolution

Page 125
Meiosis
Q1 23 *[1 mark]*

Page 128
Warm-Up Questions
1) A small section of DNA found on a chromosome that codes for a particular sequence of amino acids that are put together to make a specific protein.
2) Because there are two parents, the offspring contain a mixture of their parents' genes. This mixture of genetic information produces variation.
3) two
4) XX

Exam Questions
1.1 A polymer made up of two strands. *[1 mark]*
1.2 Its genome. *[1 mark]*

Remember, an organism's genome is its entire set of genetic material. A gene is a short section of DNA and a chromosome is a really long structure, which contains genes.

1.3 DNA contains genes *[1 mark]*. Each gene codes for a particular sequence of amino acids *[1 mark]*, which are put together to make a specific protein *[1 mark]*.
2.1 asexual *[1 mark]*
2.2 They will be genetically identical *[1 mark]*.

Remember, asexual reproduction produces clones — offspring are exactly the same as the parent.

3.1 three *[1 mark]*

When a cell undergoes meiosis, each new cell ends up with half the number of chromosomes as in the original cell.

3.2 four *[1 mark]*

Remember, when a cell undergoes meiosis, four gametes are produced — it doesn't matter whether you're talking about human cells or mosquito cells.

3.3 Meiosis produces gametes that are genetically different to each other *[1 mark]*. A male gamete and a female gamete then combine at fertilisation *[1 mark]*, so the offspring inherits a mixture of chromosomes from both parents *[1 mark]*.

Page 132
More Genetic Diagrams
Q1

	R	r
r	Rr	rr
r	Rr	rr

round peas : wrinkly peas
    1   :   1

[1 mark for correct gametes, 1 mark for correct offspring genotypes and 1 mark for correct ratio.]

Pages 135-136
Warm-Up Questions
1) Different versions of the same gene.
2) The combination of alleles an organism has.

Answers

3) Because the allele which causes cystic fibrosis is recessive, so you have to have two recessive alleles to have the disorder. Heterozygous people have one dominant and one recessive allele.
4) It's a genetic disorder where a baby is born with extra fingers or toes.
5) Taking a cell from an embryo and analysing its genes in order to detect genetic disorders.

Exam Questions

1.1

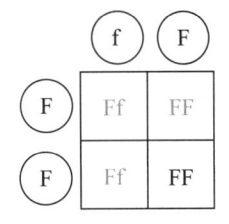

	f	F
F	Ff	FF
F	Ff	FF

[1 mark for correct genotype of offspring, 1 mark for correct genotypes of gametes]

1.2 1 in 2 / 50% *[1 mark]*
1.3 One is unaffected *[1 mark]* and the other is a carrier of cystic fibrosis *[1 mark]*.
2.1 E.g.

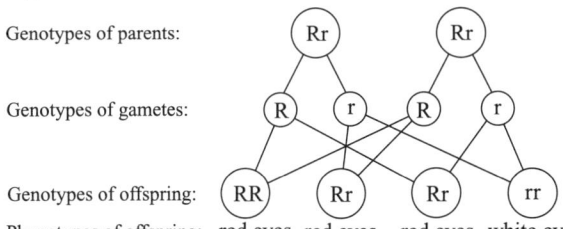

Genotypes of parents: Rr, Rr
Genotypes of gametes: R, r, R, r
Genotypes of offspring: RR, Rr, Rr, rr
Phenotypes of offspring: red eyes, red eyes, red eyes, white eyes

[1 mark for correct genotypes of the parents, 1 mark for correct genotypes of offspring, 1 mark for correct phenotypes of offspring]

You could have drawn a Punnett square instead here.

2.2 1 in 4 / 25% *[1 mark]*
3 Dd *[1 mark]*. Polydactyly is a dominant disorder, so if she was DD all of her children would be affected *[1 mark]*.
4.1
Chromosomes of parents: female XX, male XY
Chromosomes of gametes: X, X, X, Y
Chromosomes of offspring: XX, XX, XY, XY
Sex of offspring: female, female, male, male

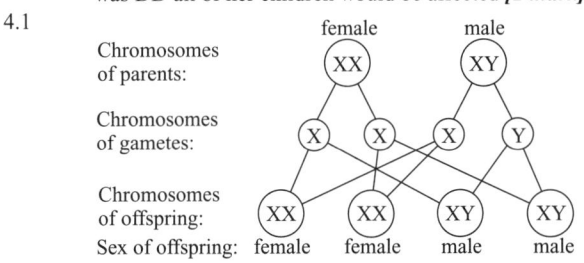

[1 mark for correct chromosomes in parents, 1 mark for correct chromosomes in offspring, 1 mark for correct sex of offspring]

4.2 Male children will not inherit the colour blindness allele because they don't inherit an X chromosome from their father *[1 mark]*.
4.3 0 / 0% *[1 mark]*

A daughter of this couple would inherit the recessive colour blindness allele from her father, but also a dominant allele from her mother, so she would not be colour blind.

5.1 AA, Aa *[1 mark]*
5.2 E.g.

Genotypes of parents: aa, Aa
Genotypes of gametes: a, a, A, a
Genotypes of offspring: Aa, Aa, aa, aa

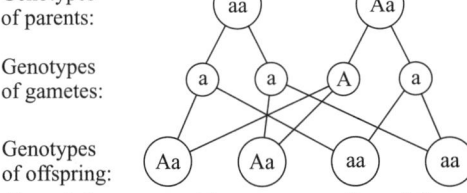

[1 mark for parent with genotype aa, 1 mark for parent with genotype Aa, 1 mark for correct genotypes of offspring]

5.3 50% *[1 mark]*

Offspring with the genotype aa will have albinism.

5.4 Fertilisation is random/the genetic diagram only shows the probability of the outcome, so the numbers of offspring produced will not always be exactly in those proportions *[1 mark]*.

Page 139
Evolution

Q1 There was a variety of tongue lengths in the moth population *[1 mark]*. Moths with longer tongues got more food/nectar and were more likely to survive *[1 mark]*. These moths were more likely to reproduce and pass on the genes responsible for their long tongues *[1 mark]*. So, over time, longer tongues became more common in the moth population *[1 mark]*.

Page 141
Warm-Up Questions

1) Differences between members of the same species that have been caused by the environment/conditions something lives in.
2) Simple life forms that first started to develop over three billion years ago.
3) Any three from: e.g. the environment changes too quickly. / A new predator kills all the individuals. / A new disease kills all the individuals. / They can't compete with another species for food. / A catastrophic event (e.g. a volcanic eruption or collision with an astroid) kills all the individuals.

Exam Questions

1.1 The difference in weight must be caused by the environment *[1 mark]*, because the twins have exactly the same genes *[1 mark]*.

In this case, the environment can mean the amount of food each twin eats or the amount of exercise they each do.

1.2 No, because if they were caused by genes both twins should have the birthmark *[1 mark]*.
2.1 Variation that is caused by differences in genotype *[1 mark]*.
2.2 Mutations change an organism's DNA *[1 mark]*, which can change the protein produced by a gene *[1 mark]* and lead to new characteristics / a new phenotype, increasing variation *[1 mark]*.
2.3 E.g. if the environment changes, some mutations may give individuals a phenotype that makes them more suited to the new environment *[1 mark]*. This would make them more likely to survive (than individuals without the phenotype) *[1 mark]*.
3 How to grade your answer:
Level 0: There is no relevant information. *[No marks]*
Level 1: There are some relevant points describing how the stingray has evolved but the answer is missing some detail. *[1 to 2 marks]*
Level 2: There is a clear, detailed explanation of how the stingray has evolved through natural selection. *[3 to 4 marks]*

Here are some points your answer may include:
Ancestors of this stingray showed variation in their appearance.
The stingrays that looked more like flat rocks were better camouflaged and so less likely to be seen and eaten by predators/more likely to survive.
This means they were more likely to reproduce.
As a result, the genes that caused the stingrays to look more like flat rocks were more likely to be passed on to the next generation.
Over time, the flat rock appearance became more common in the population and the stingray evolved.

Page 142
Selective Breeding

Q1 Select rabbits with floppy ears *[1 mark]* and breed them together to produce offspring *[1 mark]*. Select offspring with floppy ears and breed them together *[1 mark]*. Repeat this over many generations until all of the offspring have floppy ears *[1 mark]*.

Q2 Selective breeding reduces the gene pool *[1 mark]*. This causes an increased chance of organisms inheriting harmful genetic defects *[1 mark]*. There is also an increased chance that a population could be wiped out by a new disease *[1 mark]*.

Answers

Page 145
Warm-Up Questions
1) E.g. to produce plants with large or unusual flowers.
2) During selective breeding, organisms are bred with other organisms that they're closely related to. This reduces the gene pool, meaning any genetic defects present in the population are more likely to be passed on.
3) E.g. insulin.

Exam Questions
1.1 E.g. to isolate/cut the gene out of the organism's DNA *[1 mark]*
1.2 E.g. to improve the size/quality of their fruit. / To make them make them resistant to disease/insects/herbicides *[1 mark]*
1.3 Any two from: e.g. some people are not convinced that GM crops are safe and are concerned that we might not fully understand the effects of eating them on human health. / Some people say that growing GM crops will negatively affect the number of wild flowers and insects that live in and around the crops. / There is concern that the transplanted genes could get out into the natural environment, which could lead to the creation of 'superweeds'. *[2 marks]*
2 The tall and dwarf wheat plants could be bred together *[1 mark]*. The best of the offspring/the offspring with the highest grain yield and highest bad weather resistance could then be bred together *[1 mark]*, and this process repeated over several generations *[1 mark]*.
3.1 Yes, because the average milk yield has increased over the generations *[1 mark]*.
3.2 $\frac{(5750 - 5000)}{5000} \times 100$
= **15%** *[2 marks for the correct answer, otherwise 1 mark for correct working.]*

Page 149
Classification
Q1 B and C *[1 mark]*.

Page 150
Warm-Up Questions
1) The microbes that cause decay can't survive in low oxygen conditions, so the dead organisms are preserved rather than decayed.
2) Any one from: e.g. when the illness is only minor. / When the infection is being caused by a virus.
3) Taking the complete course makes sure that all the bacteria are destroyed. This means that there are none left to mutate and develop into antibiotic-resistant strains.
4) *fiber*

Exam Questions
1.1 Species C *[1 mark]*
1.2 Yes, you would expect Species D to look similar to Species E because they share a recent common ancestor, so they are closely related/have similar genes *[1 mark]*.
2.1 C, B, D, A *[2 marks for correct answer, otherwise 1 mark for three stages in the correct order]*
2.2 E.g. people in hospital are more likely to have weakened immune systems than people in the rest of society *[1 mark]*, and so are more likely to develop serious illness as a result of MRSA infection *[1 mark]*.
2.3 E.g. it can lead to infections becoming more widespread/difficult to control *[1 mark]*.
2.4 When antibiotics are used, resistant bacteria have an advantage over non-resistant bacteria *[1 mark]*, so they will increase in number meaning the resistance spreads *[1 mark]*. Reducing the use of antibiotics will slow/reduce the spread of antibiotic resistance *[1 mark]*.

Topic B7 — Ecology
Page 151
Competition
Q1 Any three from: light / space / water / mineral ions *[1 mark for each correct answer, up to 3 marks]*.
Q2 E.g. the frog population might increase as there might be more water spiders available for them to eat *[1 mark]* because there will be fewer sticklebacks to eat the water spiders / less competition for food *[1 mark]*. /
The frog population might decrease as they are more likely to be eaten by pike *[1 mark]* because there will be fewer sticklebacks for the pikes to eat *[1 mark]*.

Page 154
Adaptations
Q1 a) A behavioural adaptation *[1 mark]*.
b) E.g. it has flippers *[1 mark]* so it can swim for food *[1 mark]*. / A thick layer of fat *[1 mark]* so it retains heat *[1 mark]*. / A low surface area to volume ratio *[1 mark]* so it retains heat *[1 mark]*.

Page 155
Food Chains
Q1 a) grass *[1 mark]*
b) three *[1 mark]*
c) grasshopper *[1 mark]*
d) The population of grasshoppers could increase *[1 mark]* as there's nothing to eat them *[1 mark]*. The population of snakes could decrease *[1 mark]* as there's nothing for them to eat *[1 mark]*.

Page 156
Warm-Up Questions
1) a community
2) The interaction of a community of living organisms (biotic) with the non-living (abiotic) parts of their environment.
3) Any four from: moisture level / light intensity / temperature / carbon dioxide level / wind intensity / wind direction / soil pH / mineral content of soil.
4) Structural adaptations are features of an organism's body structure that allow an organism to live in an environment.
5) A producer is an organism that makes its own food using energy from the Sun.

Exam Questions
1.1 tertiary consumer *[1 mark]*
1.2 The algae are producers *[1 mark]*. They are the source of biomass /energy for the food chain *[1 mark]*.
2.1 It doesn't sweat *[1 mark]*.
2.2 E.g. it lives in burrows *[1 mark]* so it can avoid the heat above ground *[1 mark]*. / It holds its tail over its head *[1 mark]* so it can shelter from the sun *[1 mark]*. / It lies in the shade *[1 mark]* so it can shelter from the sun *[1 mark]*. / It lies with its limbs spread out wide *[1 mark]* so it can lose more heat (as its surface area to volume ratio is increased) *[1 mark]*.
3.1 At first the population size of the cutthroat trout would decrease *[1 mark]*, as the lake trout would eat the cutthroat trout *[1 mark]*. This would lead to a decline in the population of the lake trout (as they'd have less to eat) *[1 mark]*, allowing an increase in the population of the cutthroat trout *[1 mark]*. The population size of the lake trout would then increase (as they'd have more to eat) and the cycle would start again *[1 mark]*.
3.2 Any two from: availability of food / competition for resources / new pathogens *[1 mark for each correct answer, up to 2 marks]*.

Page 157
Using Quadrats
Q1 $0.75 \times 4 = 3$ buttercups per m^2 *[1 mark]*.
$3 \times 1200 =$ **3600 buttercups in total** *[1 mark]*.

Pages 161-162
Warm-Up Questions
1) A line used to help find out how organisms are distributed across an area.
2) $(14 + 11 + 11 + 12 + 12) \div 5 = 12$
3) To break down/decay dead matter and animal waste.
4) Through burning.

Exam Questions
1.1 eating *[1 mark]*
1.2 respiration *[1 mark]*
1.3 Detritus feeders and microorganisms break down/decay the dead matter *[1 mark]* and return carbon to the air as carbon dioxide through respiration *[1 mark]*.
1.4 photosynthesis *[1 mark]*
2.1 By the process of transpiration / water evaporates from the plants *[1 mark]*.
2.2 Energy from the Sun evaporates water from the ocean *[1 mark]*, so the water molecule enters the atmosphere as water vapour *[1 mark]*. The warm water vapour rises, then cools and condenses into clouds *[1 mark]*. The water molecule then falls from the clouds as precipitation/rain/snow/hail into a garden pond *[1 mark]*.
3.1 E.g. they could have placed quadrats at regular intervals *[1 mark]* along a transect/in a straight line from the wood to the opposite side of the field *[1 mark]*, and counted the number of poppies in each quadrat *[1 mark]*.
3.2 E.g. the number of poppies increases with increasing distance from the wood *[1 mark]*.
3.3 Any two from: e.g. moisture level / soil pH / soil mineral content / wind intensity / wind direction. *[2 marks — 1 mark for each correct answer.]*
3.4 Species A = 47 squares out of 100
= $(47 \div 100) \times 100 = 47\%$ *[1 mark]*
Species B = 48 squares out of 100
= $(48 \div 100) \times 100 = 48\%$ *[1 mark]*

Remember, to calculate percentage cover of an organism in a quadrat you count the number of squares which are more than half covered by the organism.

3.5 E.g. because there may have been too many blades of grass to count each one individually / it's hard to count individual blades of grass *[1 mark]*.
4 How to grade your answer:
Level 0: There is no relevant information. *[No marks]*
Level 1: There is a brief description of one or two ways in which carbon stored in the vegetation could be returned to the atmosphere. *[1 to 2 marks]*
Level 2: There is some description of more than two of the ways carbon stored in the vegetation could be returned to the atmosphere. *[3 to 4 marks]*
Level 3: There is a clear and detailed description of all the ways carbon stored in the vegetation could be returned to the atmosphere. *[5 to 6 marks]*
Here are some points your answer may include:
Carbon stored in the small branches will be returned to the atmosphere as carbon dioxide when the branches are burnt.
The green plants could be eaten by animals, which will release some carbon as carbon dioxide during respiration.
The green plants could also be broken down by microorganisms/detritivores which will release carbon as carbon dioxide during respiration.
The wood that is taken away to be made into furniture will eventually return the carbon to the atmosphere through decay/burning when its lifespan as furniture is over.

Page 171
Warm-Up Questions
1) The variety of different species of organisms on Earth, or within an ecosystem.
2) E.g. carbon dioxide, methane.
3) Breeding programmes breed endangered animals in captivity to make sure the species survives if they die out in the wild. Individuals can sometimes be released into the wild to boost or re-establish a population.
4) Hedgerows and field margins can be reintroduced around single-crop fields. These provide a habitat for organisms that would otherwise be unable to live in the area.

Hedgerows and field margins mean that more species of wild plants can grow. Remember, plants are often the producers in food chains — so the more variety there is in the plants that are growing, the more organisms that will be able to survive in the area.

Exam Questions
1.1 E.g. smoke *[1 mark]*, acidic gases *[1 mark]*.
1.2 E.g. sewage/toxic chemicals from industry can pollute lakes/rivers/oceans. / Fertilisers/pesticides/herbicides/toxic chemicals used on land can be washed into water *[1 mark]*.
1.3 E.g. the human population size is increasing *[1 mark]*, people around the world are demanding a higher standard of living *[1 mark]*.
2.1 E.g. changes in species distributions *[1 mark]*, changes in migration patterns *[1 mark]*.
2.2 Governments have introduced regulations and programmes to reduce deforestation *[1 mark]*. They have also introduced regulations to limit the amount of carbon dioxide released by businesses *[1 mark]*.
3.1 When peat is drained, it comes into more contact with air and some microorganisms start to decompose it *[1 mark]*. This releases carbon dioxide *[1 mark]*. Carbon dioxide is also released when peat is burned as a fuel *[1 mark]*. Carbon dioxide is a greenhouse gas, which contributes to global warming *[1 mark]*.
3.2 E.g. destroying peat bogs reduces biodiversity *[1 mark]*, as it destroys the habitats of the organisms that live in the bog *[1 mark]*.
4.1 E.g. protecting wetlands will protect the habitats of species that live there *[1 mark]*. This will help to preserve the level of biodiversity in the ecosystem *[1 mark]*. A high level of biodiversity is important for humans to survive *[1 mark]*.
4.2 Any two from: e.g. people may disagree with the amount of money that is spent on conserving the wetlands. / People may think it would be better to use the land for farming, which would help to protect food security. / People may worry about the effect on the local economy if the wetlands are protected, because the area couldn't be used for human activities such as farming. / People may think that the land could be better used for developing society, e.g. by using it to build houses on. *[2 marks]*

Topic C1 — Atomic Structure and the Periodic Table

Page 173
Atoms
Q1 protons = atomic number = 31 *[1 mark]*
electrons = protons = 31 *[1 mark]*
neutrons = mass number − atomic number
= 70 − 31 = 39 *[1 mark]*

Page 175
Isotopes
Q1 E.g. it's the number of protons in an atom that determines what type of atom it is, so if all the atoms have the same number of protons then the substance is an element *[1 mark]*.
Q2 Relative atomic mass =
$\dfrac{(92.2 \times 28) + (4.7 \times 29) + (3.1 \times 30)}{92.2 + 4.7 + 3.1}$ *[1 mark]*
$= \dfrac{2581.6 + 136.3 + 93}{100} = \dfrac{2810.9}{100}$
$= 28.109 =$ **28.1** *[1 mark]*

Page 177
Formulas and Equations
Q1 $(2 \times Na) + (1 \times C) + (3 \times O) = 6$ *[1 mark]*
Q2 Aluminium — 2 atoms, sulfur — 3 atoms and oxygen — 12 atoms *[1 mark]*.

Page 178
Formulas and Equations
Q1 $2Fe + 3Cl_2 \rightarrow 2FeCl_3$ *[1 mark]*
Q2 a) water → hydrogen + oxygen *[1 mark]*
    b) $2H_2O \rightarrow 2H_2 + O_2$
    [1 mark for correct products and reactants, 1 mark for being balanced correctly]

Pages 179-180
Warm-Up Questions
1) The total number of protons and neutrons.
2) An element is a substance that consists of only one type of atom.
3) A compound is a substance made from two or more elements in fixed proportions throughout the compound and they're held together by chemical bonds.
4) ions
5) $C_6H_{12}O_6 + 6O_2 \rightarrow 6CO_2 + 6H_2O$

Exam Questions
1.1
Name of particle	Relative charge
Proton	+1
Neutron	0

[2 marks — 1 mark for each correct charge]
1.2 nucleus *[1 mark]*
1.3 8 *[1 mark]*
1.4 1 *[1 mark]*
2.1 7 *[1 mark]*
2.2 The number of protons is the same as the atomic number *[1 mark]*
2.3 N *[1 mark]*
3.1 methane and oxygen *[1 mark]*
3.2 carbon dioxide and water *[1 mark]*
3.3 oxygen/O_2 *[1 mark]*
3.4 $CH_4 + 2O_2 \rightarrow CO_2 + 2H_2O$
[1 mark for correct missing reactant, 1 mark for correctly balancing the equation]
4.1 $H_2SO_4 + 2NH_3 \rightarrow (NH_4)_2SO_4$ *[1 mark for each correct reactant, 1 mark for correctly balancing the equation]*
4.2 15 *[1 mark]*
There are eight atoms of hydrogen, one atom of sulfur, four atoms of oxygen, and two atoms of nitrogen.
4.3 8
There are 4 hydrogen atoms in NH_4 and there are two of these.
5.1 An isotope is a different atomic form of the same element *[1 mark]*, which has the same number of protons *[1 mark]* but a different number of neutrons *[1 mark]*.
5.2 Protons = 6 *[1 mark]*, neutrons = 7 *[1 mark]*, electrons = 6 *[1 mark]*
5.3 It has a different atomic number from carbon *[1 mark]*.
5.4 $(79 \times 13) + (21 \times 14) = 1321$
Relative atomic mass = $1321 \div 100 = 13.21 =$ **13.2**
[4 marks for correct final answer, otherwise give 1 mark for each correct stage of working]

Page 186
Distillation
Q1 Ethanol *[1 mark]*. Ethanol has the second lowest boiling point and will be collected once all the methanol has been distilled off and the temperature increased *[1 mark]*.

Page 187
Warm-Up Questions
1) Two or more elements or compounds mixed together.
2) evaporation / crystallisation
3) fractional distillation

Exam Questions
1.1 E.g. put the paper in a beaker of solvent, e.g. water *[1 mark]*.
1.2 Pencil marks are insoluble (so won't dissolve into the solvent) *[1 mark]*.

2.1 E.g. mix the lawn sand with water to dissolve the ammonium sulfate *[1 mark]*. Filter the mixture using filter paper to remove the sharp sand *[1 mark]*. Pour the remaining solution into an evaporating dish and slowly heat it to evaporate the water until you have a dry product *[1 mark]*.
2.2 E.g. the products were not completely dry *[1 mark]*.
3.1 The boiling points of water and methanoic acid are too close together to allow them to be separated by simple distillation *[1 mark]*.
3.2
Temperature on thermometer	Contents of the flask	Contents of the beaker
30 °C	both liquids	no liquid
65 °C	water	propanone
110 °C	no liquid	both liquids

[3 marks for whole table correct otherwise 1 mark for each correct row]

Page 190
Electronic Structures
Q1 2,8,3 or [diagram] *[1 mark]*
Q2 2,8,8 or [diagram] *[1 mark]*

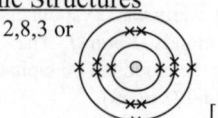

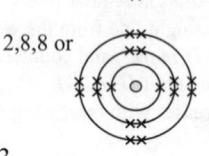

Page 193
Warm-Up Questions
1) The 'plum pudding model' — a ball of positive charge with electrons stuck in it.
2) a) 2
   b) 8
3) The discovery of isotopes.

Exam Questions
1.1 [diagram of Na electron structure] *[1 mark]*
1.2 Any one of: lithium / potassium / rubidium / caesium / francium *[1 mark]*
1.3 1 *[1 mark]*
2.1 By atomic weight *[1 mark]*
2.2 By atomic number *[1 mark]*
2.3 Similar chemical properties due to having the same number of electrons in their outer shell *[1 mark]*.
3 How to grade your answer:
Level 0: No description is given. *[No marks]*
Level 1: Brief description of how the theory of atomic structure has changed. *[1 to 2 marks]*
Level 2: Some detail given of how the theory of atomic structure has changed. *[3 to 4 marks]*
Level 3: A clear and detailed description of how the theory of atomic structure has changed. *[5 to 6 marks]*
Here are some points your answer may include:
At the start of the 19th century John Dalton described atoms as solid spheres that make up the different elements.
In 1897 JJ Thomson concluded that atoms weren't solid spheres and that an atom must contain smaller, negatively charged particles (electrons). He called this the 'plum pudding model'.
In 1909 Ernest Rutherford conducted a gold foil experiment, firing positively charged particles at an extremely thin sheet of gold. Most of the particles went straight through, so he concluded that there was a positively charged nucleus at the centre, surrounded by a 'cloud' of negative electrons.

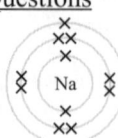

Niels Bohr proposed a new model of the atom where all the electrons were contained in shells. He suggested that electrons can only exist in fixed orbits, or shells.

Further experimentation by Rutherford and others showed that the nucleus could be divided into smaller particles, each with the same charge as a hydrogen atom, these became known as protons.

James Chadwick carried out an experiment which provided evidence of the existence of neutral particles within the nucleus, which became known as neutrons.

Page 196
Group 1 Elements
Q1   lithium + water → lithium hydroxide + hydrogen *[1 mark]*

Page 198
Group 7 Elements
Q1 $Br_2 + 2NaI \rightarrow 2NaBr + I_2$ *[1 mark]*

Pages 200-201
Warm-Up Questions
1) positive ions
2) Any three of: e.g. strong / can be bent or hammered into different shapes / conduct heat / conduct electricity / high melting point / high boiling point.
3) lithium oxide / Li_2O
4) negative
5) Group 0

Exam Questions
1.1 Highest (X): fluorine *[1 mark]*. Lowest (Y): iodine *[1 mark]*.
1.2 iodine *[1 mark]*
2.1 alkali metals/Group 1 elements *[1 mark]*
2.2 To the right of the line *[1 mark]*. Since it does not conduct electricity, it must be a non-metal *[1 mark]*.
3.1 ionic bonds *[1 mark]*
3.2 E.g. displacement reaction *[1 mark]*
3.3 iodine/I_2 *[1 mark]* as it is displaced from potassium iodide *[1 mark]*.
3.4 The products of the reaction will be aqueous potassium chloride/$KCl_{(aq)}$ *[1 mark]* and bromine gas/$Br_{2(g)}$ *[1 mark]*. Chlorine is more reactive than bromine as its outer shell is closer to the nucleus *[1 mark]*. This results in chlorine displacing bromine from potassium bromide *[1 mark]*.
3.5 Group 0 elements are generally inert *[1 mark]*. This is because they are energetically stable and don't need to lose or gain electrons to have a full outer shell *[1 mark]*.
4.1 They have a single outer electron which is easily lost so they are very reactive *[1 mark]*.
4.2 As you go down Group 1, the outer electron is further from the nucleus *[1 mark]*. So the attraction between the nucleus and the electron decreases *[1 mark]*. This means the outer electron is more easily lost and the metal is more reactive *[1 mark]*.
4.3 hydrogen *[1 mark]* and potassium hydroxide *[1 mark]*
4.4 alkaline *[1 mark]*

Topic C2 — Bonding, Structure and Properties of Matter

Page 202
Ions
Q1 Noble gas electronic structures have a full shell of outer electrons *[1 mark]*, which is a very stable structure *[1 mark]*.

Page 204
Ions
Q1 The transfer of one electron from one atom to another *[1 mark]*
Q2

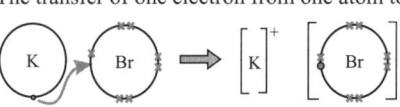

[1 mark for arrow showing electron transferred from potassium to bromine, 1 mark for correct outer shell electron configurations (with or without inner shells), 1 mark for correct charges]

Page 206
Ionic Compounds
Q1 a) It will have a high melting point *[1 mark]* because a lot of energy is needed to break the strong attraction between the ions/the strong ionic bonds *[1 mark]*.
    b) When melted, the ions are free to move, so they can carry an electric charge *[1 mark]*.
    c) The compound contains magnesium and sulfide ions. Magnesium is in Group 2 so forms 2+ ions *[1 mark]*, and sulfur is in Group 6 so forms 2– ions *[1 mark]*. The charges balance with one of each ion, so the empirical formula is MgS *[1 mark]*.

Page 207
Warm-Up Questions
1) A charged atom or group of atoms.
2) +2
3) –1
4) high
5) When ionic compounds dissolve in water, the ions separate and are all free to move in the solution, so they'll carry an electric charge.
6) $Al(OH)_3$

Exam Questions
1.1 Sodium will lose the electron from its outer shell to form a positive ion *[1 mark]*. Fluorine will gain an electron to form a negative ion *[1 mark]*.
1.2 Ionic compounds have a giant ionic lattice structure *[1 mark]*. The ions form a closely packed regular lattice arrangement *[1 mark]*, held together by strong electrostatic forces of attraction between oppositely charged ions *[1 mark]*.
2.1 lithium oxide *[1 mark]*
2.2

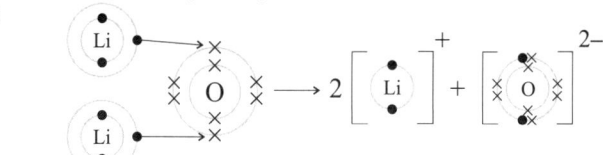

[1 mark for arrows shown correctly, 1 mark for correct electron arrangement and charge on lithium ion, 1 mark for correct electron arrangement and charge on oxygen ion]
2.3 When molten, the Li^+ and O^{2-} ions are able to move *[1 mark]*. These ions are able to carry electric charge *[1 mark]*.
2.4 The formula of the compound is **LiCl** *[1 mark]*. Lithium is in Group 1, so forms +1 ions. Chlorine is in Group 7, so forms –1 ions. Therefore there needs to be one lithium ion for every chlorine ion for the compound to be neutral *[1 mark]*.

Page 208
Covalent Bonding
Q1

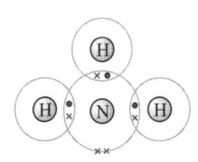

[1 mark for 3 shared pairs of electrons, 1 mark for correct number of electrons in outer shell of each atom (with our without inner shells on nitrogen)]

Page 211
Warm-Up Questions
1) A chemical bond made by the sharing of a pair of electrons between two atoms.
2) 3
3) gas or liquid
4) covalent bonds
5) intermolecular forces

500

Exam Questions

1

[1 mark for showing a pairs of shared electrons between C and H, 1 mark for no other electrons shown]

2.1

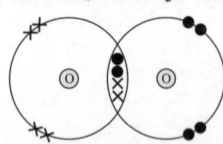

[1 mark for showing 2 pairs of shared electrons between O atoms, 1 mark for showing two non-bonding pairs of electrons on each oxygen]

2.2   3 [1 mark]

3.1   Hydrogen chloride doesn't contain any ions or delocalised electrons to carry a charge [1 mark].

3.2   E.g. a pair of electrons (one from the hydrogen atom and one from the chlorine atom) is shared between the two atoms [1 mark]. The atoms are held together by the strong attraction between this shared pair of negatively charged electrons and the positively charged nuclei of the atoms [1 mark].

3.3   Chlorine is a larger molecule than hydrogen chloride [1 mark] and therefore there are greater intermolecular forces between molecules [1 mark]. As the intermolecular forces are greater between chlorine molecules, its boiling point is higher than hydrogen chloride [1 mark].

Chlorine has three shells of electrons, whereas hydrogen only has one. So Cl_2 is a bigger molecule than HCl.

Page 212
Polymers
Q1 $(C_2H_3Cl)_n$ [1 mark]

Page 217
Warm-Up Questions
1) By covalent bonding.
2) solid
3) E.g. diamond is much harder than graphite. Diamond doesn't conduct electricity whereas graphite does.
4) Buckminsterfullerene
5) The layers of atom in metals are able to slide over each other.

Exam Questions
1.1   In a giant covalent structure, all of the atoms are bonded to each other with strong covalent bonds [1 mark]. It takes lots of energy to break these bonds and melt the solid [1 mark].

1.2   E.g. diamond / graphite / silicon dioxide [1 mark]

2.1   Graphite is formed of layers of carbon atoms that are held together weakly [1 mark]. The layers can easily slide over each other, making graphite soft and slippery [1 mark].

2.2   In diamond, each carbon atom forms four covalent bonds in a very rigid structure [1 mark]. This makes diamond very hard, so it would be good at cutting other substances [1 mark].

2.3   Any one from: e.g. delivering drugs / catalysts / lubricants / strengthening materials [1 mark]

2.4   E.g. each carbon atom has a delocalised electron that is able to carry the charge [1 mark].

3.1   E.g.

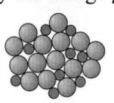

[1 mark for showing two different sizes of atoms, 1 mark for showing irregular arrangement]

3.2   The regular arrangement of atoms in iron means that they can slide over each other, resulting in iron being soft [1 mark]. Steel contains different sized atoms which distort the layers of iron atoms [1 mark] making it more difficult for them to slide over each other [1 mark].

Page 220
States of Matter
Q1   a) solid [1 mark]
      b) liquid [1 mark]
      c) liquid [1 mark]
      d) gas [1 mark]

Page 221
Warm-Up Questions
1) The material, the temperature and the pressure.
2) solid
3) weak
4) The particles move faster.
5) Lots of bonds have formed between gas particles so the gas becomes a liquid.
6) $Na^+_{(aq)}$

Exam Questions
1.1   In solids, there are **strong** [1 mark] forces of attraction between particles, which hold them in fixed positions in a **regular** [1 mark] arrangement. The particles don't **move** [1 mark] from their positions, so solids keep their shape. The **hotter** [1 mark] the solid becomes, the more the particles in the solid vibrate.

1.2   The particles gain energy, so they move faster [1 mark]. The intermolecular bonds are weakened and, when they have enough energy, they break [1 mark]. This means the particles are free to move far apart from each other and the liquid becomes a gas [1 mark].

2.1   The particles are free to move about / have virtually no forces of attraction between them [1 mark], so they move randomly, spreading out to fill the container [1 mark].

2.2   There's a weak force of attraction between the particles in a liquid [1 mark]. This means they're free to move past each other but tend to stick closely together [1 mark].

2.3   gas [1 mark]

Topic C3 — Quantitative Chemistry

Page 222
Relative Formula Mass
Q1   a) A_r of H = 1 and A_r of O = 16
        M_r of H_2O = (2 × 1) + 16 = 18 [1 mark]
      b) A_r of Li = 7, Ar of O = 16 and A_r of H = 1
        So M_r of LiOH = 7 + 16 + 1 = 24 [1 mark]
      c) A_r of H = 1, A_r of S = 32 and A_r of O = 16
        M_r of H_2SO_4 = (2 × 1) + 32 + (4 × 16) = 98 [1 mark]

Q2 A_r of K = 39, A_r of O = 16 and A_r of H = 1
      M_r of KOH = 39 + 16 + 1 = 56 [1 mark]
      $\frac{39}{56} \times 100 = $ **70%** [1 mark]

Page 224
The Mole and Mass
Q1 M_r of H_2O = 16 + (2 × 1) = 18 [1 mark]
      number of moles = mass ÷ M_r
      number of moles = 90 g ÷ 18 = **5 moles** [1 mark]

Q2 M_r of KBr = 39 + 80 = 119 [1 mark]
      mass = number of moles × M_r
      mass = 0.20 × 119 = **24 g** [1 mark]

Page 225
The Mole and Mass
Q1   Total mass on the left hand side
      = $M_r(H_2SO4) + 2 \times M_r(NaOH)$
      M_r of H_2SO4 = (2 × 1) + 32 + (4 × 16) = 98
      2 × M_r of NaOH = 2 × (23 + 16 + 1) = 80
      So total mass on the left hand side = 98 + 80 = **178**
      [2 marks for 178, 1 mark for either 98 or 80]
      Total mass on right hand side = $M_r(Na_2SO_4) + 2 \times M_r(H_2O)$
      M_r of Na_2SO_4 = (2 × 23) + 32 + (4 × 16) = 142
      2 × M_r of H_2O = 2 × [(2 × 1) + 16] = 36
      142 + 36 = **178** [2 marks for 178, 1 mark for either 142 or 36]
      The total M_r on the left-hand side is equal to the total M_r on the right-hand side, so mass is conserved [1 mark].

Page 226
Warm-Up Questions
1) relative formula mass
2) Avogadro constant
3) A mole is an amount of a substance that contains as many particles as the Avogadro constant (6.02×10^{23}).
4) 56
5) One mole of O_2 weighs $16 \times 2 =$ **32 g**

Exam Questions
1.1 M_r of $BF_3 = 11 + (19 \times 3) =$ **68** *[1 mark]*
1.2 M_r of $B(OH)_3 = 11 + (17 \times 3) =$ **62** *[1 mark]*
2 number of moles = $\dfrac{\text{mass in grams}}{M_r}$ *[1 mark]*
3 M_r of $KOH = (39 + 16 + 1) =$ **56** *[1 mark]*
Mass of 4 moles of $KOH = 4 \times 56 = 224$ g *[1 mark]*
Extra mass needed = $224 - 140 =$ **84 g** *[1 mark]*
4.1 Oxygen in the air, which previously couldn't be weighed, has now reacted with metal **X** to form a solid oxide *[1 mark]*.
4.2 $100 - 40 =$ **60%** *[1 mark]*
4.3 Mass of metal **X** in 8.0 g of mixture:
= $8.0 \times (24 \div 100) = 1.92$ g *[1 mark]*
The metal oxide contains 60% metal **X** by mass, so the mass of metal oxide used to make the mixture = $1.92 \div (60 \div 100)$
= **3.2 g** *[1 mark]*.

Page 227
The Mole and Equations
Q1 a) N_2: $\dfrac{84}{28} =$ **3.0 mol** *[1 mark]*
H_2: $\dfrac{18}{2} =$ **9 mol** *[1 mark]*
NH_3: $\dfrac{102}{17} =$ **6.0 mol** *[1 mark]*
b) Divide by the smallest number of moles (3.0):
N_2: $\dfrac{3.0}{3.0} = 1$ H_2: $\dfrac{9}{3.0} = 3$ NH_3: $\dfrac{6.0}{3.0} = 2.0$ *[1 mark]*
The balanced symbol equation is:
$N_2 + 3H_2 \rightarrow 2NH_3$ *[1 mark]*

Page 228
Concentration and Limiting Reactants
Q1 volume = $15 \div 1000 = 0.015$ dm³ *[1 mark]*
concentration = mass ÷ volume = $0.6 \div 0.015 =$ **40 g/dm³** *[1 mark]*

Page 229
Concentration and Limiting Reactants
Q1 $M_r(KBr) = 119$, $M_r(KCl) = 74.5$ *[1 mark]*
No. of moles of $KBr = 23.8 \div 119 = 0.200$ mol *[1 mark]*
From the reaction equation, 2 moles of KBr react to form 2 moles of KCl. So 0.200 moles of KBr reacts to form 0.200 moles of KCl *[1 mark]*.
Mass $KCl = 74.5 \times 0.200 =$ **14.9 g** *[1 mark]*

Page 230
Warm-Up Questions
1) The number of moles of each substance taking part in or made by the reaction.
2) To make sure that all of the other reactant reacts.
3) The amount of a substance in a certain volume of a solution.
4) It halves.

Exam Questions
1.1 Li: $3.5 \div 7 =$ **0.5 mol**
O_2: $4.0 \div 32 =$ **0.125 mol**
Li_2O: $7.5 \div 30 =$ **0.25 mol**
[2 marks for all three correct answers, otherwise 1 mark for two correct answers]
1.2 Divide by the smallest number of moles (0.125):
Li: $\dfrac{0.5}{0.125} = 4$ H_2: $\dfrac{0.125}{0.125} = 1$ Li_2O: $\dfrac{0.25}{0.125} = 2$ *[1 mark]*
The balanced symbol equation is:
$4Li + O_2 \rightarrow 2Li_2O$ *[1 mark]*

2.1 M_r of $NaHCO_3 = 23 + 1 + 12 + (3 \times 16) = 84$ *[1 mark]*
no. of moles of $NaHCO_3 = 6.0 \div 84 = 0.0714...$ mol *[1 mark]*
1 mole of Na_2SO_4 is made for every 2 moles of $NaHCO_3$ that reacts, so no. of moles of $Na_2SO_4 = 0.0714... \div 2$
= $0.0357...$ mol *[1 mark]*
M_r of $Na_2SO_4 = (2 \times 23) + 32 + (4 \times 16) = 142$ *[1 mark]*
Mass of $Na_2SO_4 = 142 \times 0.0357... = 5.071...$
= **5.1g** (2 s.f.) *[1 mark]*
2.2 The limiting reactant is the reactant that gets used up and therefore limits the amount of product formed *[1 mark]*.
3.1 $160 \div 1000 = 0.160$ dm³
concentration = mass ÷ volume
= $24.5 \div 0.160 =$ **153.125 g/dm³**
= **153 g/dm³** (to 3 s.f.) *[1 mark]*
3.2 $200 \div 1000 = 0.20$ dm³
mass = concentration × volume = $75 \times 0.2 =$ **15 g** *[1 mark]*
3.3 640 g = 0.640 kg *[1 mark]*
concentration = 56 kg per 100 dm³ = 0.56 kg/dm³ *[1 mark]*
volume = mass ÷ concentration = $0.640 \div 0.56$
= **1.14285... dm³** *[1 mark]*
= **1.14 dm³** (3 s.f.) *[1 mark]*

Topic C4 — Chemical Changes

Page 232
Strong Acids, Weak Acids and their Reactions
Q1 Any one of, e.g. sulfuric acid / nitric acid / hydrochloric acid *[1 mark]*.
Q2 Change in pH = $3 - 6 = -3$
Change in concentration of $H^+ = 10^{-(-3)} = 10^3 = 1000$
So, the concentration of H^+ is 1000 times greater at pH = 3 than at pH = 6 *[1 mark]*.

Page 234
Strong Acids, Weak Acids and their Reactions
Q1 calcium carbonate + hydrochloric acid →
calcium chloride + carbon dioxide + water *[1 mark for calcium chloride, 1 mark for carbon dioxide and water]*
$CaCO_3 + 2HCl \rightarrow CaCl_2 + CO_2 + H_2O$
[1 mark for the correctly balanced equation]

Page 235
Warm-Up Questions
1) 0-14
2) neutral
3) Strong acids ionise completely in water, so all of the acid particles dissociate to release H^+ ions. Weak acids do not fully ionise, so only some of the acid particles dissociate to release H^+ ions.
4) Difference in pH = $5 - 2 = 3$
Factor H^+ ion concentration changes by = $10^{-3} =$ **0.001**
You could give your answer here as '10^{-3}', '0.001' or 'it decreased by a factor of 1000' — they all mean the same thing.
5) Copper nitrate and water.

Exam Questions
1.1 H^+ ions/hydrogen ions *[1 mark]*
1.2 neutralisation *[1 mark]*
2.1 alkalis *[1 mark]*
2.2 $2HNO_3 + Mg(OH)_2 \rightarrow Mg(NO_3)_2 + 2H_2O$
[1 mark for formulas of both products correct, 1 mark for putting a 2 in front of H_2O to balance the equation]
3.1 E.g. the excess silver carbonate will sink to the bottom of the flask and stay there / the mixture will stop producing bubbles (of carbon dioxide) *[1 mark]*.
3.2 filtration *[1 mark]*
3.3 Heat the silver nitrate solution gently using a water bath/ electric heater to evaporate some of the water *[1 mark]*.
Leave the solution to cool until crystals form *[1 mark]*.
Filter out the crystals and dry them *[1 mark]*.

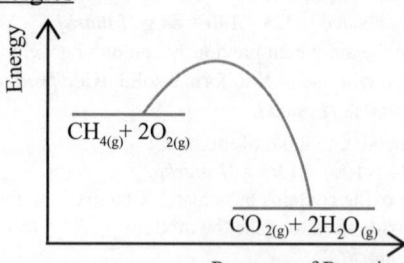

Page 237
Metals and their Reactivity
Q1 $2Na_{(s)} + 2H_2O_{(l)} \rightarrow 2NaOH_{(aq)} + H_{2(g)}$
[1 mark for correct reactants and products, 1 mark for balancing, 1 mark for state symbols]

Page 238
Metals and their Reactivity
Q1 $2PbO + C \rightarrow 2Pb + CO_2$
[1 mark for the correct products, 1 mark for the correctly balanced equation]

Q2 Carbon is less reactive than calcium and therefore will not reduce calcium oxide / Calcium is more reactive than carbon, so calcium oxide won't be reduced by carbon *[1 mark]*.

Page 240
Redox Reactions
Q1 a) $Zn_{(s)} + Fe^{2+}_{(aq)} \rightarrow Zn^{2+}_{(aq)} + Fe_{(s)}$ *[1 mark]*
    b) $Zn_{(s)}$ is being oxidised *[1 mark]*.
    $Fe^{2+}_{(aq)}$ is being reduced *[1 mark]*.

Page 241
Warm-Up Questions
1) How easily it loses electrons to form positive ions.
2) magnesium chloride
3) A metal hydroxide and hydrogen.
4) a) $Zn_{(s)} + Cu^{2+}_{(aq)} \rightarrow Zn^{2+}_{(aq)} + Cu_{(s)}$
   b) zinc / Zn

Exam Questions
1.1 Any one from: potassium / sodium / calcium *[1 mark]*.
1.2 copper *[1 mark]*
Metals below hydrogen in the reactivity series don't react with acids.
1.3 E.g. iron and dilute acid would produce bubbles of hydrogen gas *[1 mark]* more slowly than zinc and dilute acid / very slowly *[1 mark]*.
You don't need to use these exact words — the two points you need to cover are that it would still produce hydrogen gas, but at a slower rate than the zinc.
2.1 $2Fe_2O_3 + 3C \rightarrow 4Fe + 3CO_2$
[1 mark for formulas of all reactants and products correct, 1 mark for correctly balancing the equation]
2.2 Oxygen is being lost from iron oxide / the iron(III) ions in the iron oxide are gaining electrons *[1 mark]*.
3 In A there will be no charge *[1 mark]*. In B the solution will have changed from blue to green *[1 mark]* and the grey metal will be coated in orange metal *[1 mark]*. Iron is more reactive than copper *[1 mark]*. So in A, the copper cannot displace the iron from iron sulfate *[1 mark]*, but in B, the iron does displace the copper from copper sulfate *[1 mark]*.

Page 242
Electrolysis
Q1 a) chlorine gas/Cl_2 *[1 mark]*
    b) calcium atoms/Ca *[1 mark]*

Page 245
Electrolysis of Aqueous Solutions
Q1 a) bromine gas/Br_2 *[1 mark]*
    b) copper atoms/Cu *[1 mark]*

Page 246
Warm-Up Questions
1) the cathode / negative electrode
2) zinc and chlorine gas
3) reduced
4) hydrogen gas

Exam Questions
1.1 To lower the melting point of the aluminium oxide *[1 mark]*.
1.2 $Al^{3+} + 3e^- \rightarrow Al$ *[1 mark]*
1.3 $2O^{2-} \rightarrow O_2 + 4e^-$ *[1 mark]*
1.4 The oxygen made at the positive electrode reacts with the carbon to make carbon dioxide *[1 mark]*, wearing the electrode away *[1 mark]*.

2.1 hydrogen *[1 mark]*
2.2 $2H^+ + 2e^- \rightarrow H_2$ *[1 mark]*
2.3 chlorine *[1 mark]*
2.4 $2Cl^- \rightarrow Cl_2 + 2e^-$ / $2Cl^- - 2e^- \rightarrow Cl_2$ *[1 mark]*
2.5 Sodium is more reactive than hydrogen, so the sodium ions from the sodium chloride stay in solution *[1 mark]*. Hydroxide ions are also left in solution when hydrogen is produced from water *[1 mark]*.
2.6 Copper is less reactive than hydrogen *[1 mark]*.

Topic C5 — Energy Changes
Page 249
Bond Energies
Q1
[1 mark for correct axes, 1 mark for correct energy levels of reactants and products, 1 mark for correct shape of curve linking the reactants to the products]

Page 250
Bond Energies
Q1 Energy required to break original bonds:
$(1 \times N \equiv N) + (3 \times H-H)$
$= 941$ kJ/mol $+ 1308$ kJ/mol $= 2249$ kJ/mol *[1 mark]*
Energy released by forming new bonds:
$(6 \times N-H) = 2346$ kJ/mol *[1 mark]*
Overall energy change:
$= 2249$ kJ/mol $- 2346$ kJ/mol $= -97$ **kJ/mol** *[1 mark]*

Page 251
Warm-Up Questions
1) An exothermic reaction is one which transfers energy to the surroundings.
2) An endothermic reaction is one which takes in energy from the surroundings.
3) When bonds are formed.
4) The activation energy is the minimum amount of energy the reactants need to collide with each other and react.

Exam Questions
1 B *[1 mark]*
2.1 Exothermic, because the temperature of the mixture has increased *[1 mark]*, therefore the particles have transferred energy to the reaction mixture *[1 mark]*.
2.2 A lid was placed on the cup to reduce energy lost to the surroundings (by evaporation) *[1 mark]*.
3.1 $C-H$ and $O=O$ *[1 mark]*
3.2 $(4 \times 414) + (2 \times 494) = 2644$ kJ/mol
This is the amount of energy required to break the bonds in CH_4 and $2O_2$.
$(2 \times 800) + (4 \times 459) = 3436$ kJ/mol
This is the amount of energy released by forming the bonds in CO_2 and $2H_2O$.
$2644 - 3436 = -792$ **kJ/mole** *[3 marks for correct answer, otherwise 1 mark for finding the energy needed to break the bonds in the reactants, 1 mark for finding the energy released by forming bonds in the products.]*

Topic C6 — The Rate and Extent of Chemical Change

Page 260
Finding Reaction Rates from Graphs

Q1 a) E.g.

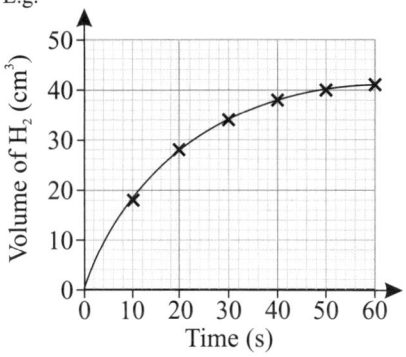

[1 mark for correctly marking on all 6 points, 1 mark for choosing a sensible scale for the axes, 1 mark for drawing a line of best fit]

b) E.g.

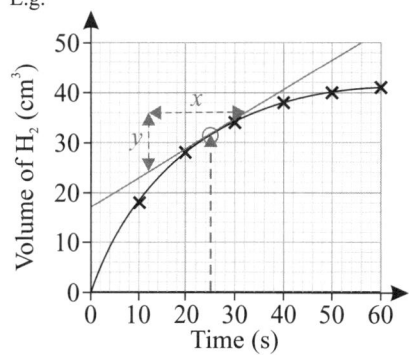

change in y = 36 − 24 = 12,
change in x = 32 − 12 = 20,
rate = change in y ÷ change in x
= 12 ÷ 20 = **0.6 cm³/s**

[1 mark for drawing a tangent at 25 s, 1 mark for correctly calculating a change in y from the tangent, 1 mark for correctly calculating a change in x from the tangent and 1 mark for a rate between 0.5 cm³/s and 0.7 cm³/s]

Pages 261-262
Warm-Up Questions

1) E.g. the rusting of iron is a reaction that happens very slowly. Explosions are very fast reactions.
2) They must collide with enough energy.
3) There will be more particles in the same volume, which will lead to more frequent collisions, so the rate of reaction will increase.
4) g/s
5) E.g. observe a mark through the solution in which the precipitate forms and measure how long it takes for it to disappear.

Exam Questions

1.1 stopwatch/stopclock/timer *[1 mark]*
1.2 gas syringe *[1 mark]*
1.3 E.g. place a conical flask on a mass balance *[1 mark]* and record the change in mass at regular intervals as the gas leaves the flask *[1 mark]*.
2.1 Any two from: e.g. the concentration of sodium thiosulfate / hydrochloric acid / the depth of liquid / the person judging when the black cross is obscured / the black cross used (size, darkness etc.). *[2 marks — 1 mark for each correct answer.]*

Judging when a cross is completely obscured is quite subjective — two people might not agree on exactly when it happens. You can try to limit this problem by using the same person each time, but you can't remove the problem completely. The person might have changed their mind slightly by the time they do the next experiment — or be looking at it from a different angle, be a bit more bored, etc.

2.2

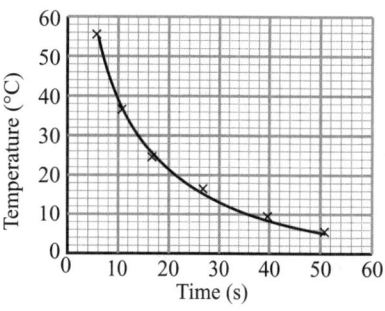

[1 mark for correctly drawn axes with a sensible scale, 2 marks for all points plotted correctly, otherwise 1 mark if 5 of 6 points plotted correctly, 1 mark for a suitable line of best fit]

2.3 As the temperature decreases the time decreases, meaning that the reaction is slower as the temperature decreases *[1 mark]*.
2.4 At each temperature it would take longer for the reaction to complete *[1 mark]*.
2.5 A lower concentration of reactant means there are fewer particles in the same volume of solution *[1 mark]*. This makes collisions between the reactant particles less frequent *[1 mark]*, and therefore decreases the rate of reaction *[1 mark]*.
2.6 E.g. by repeating the experiment *[1 mark]*. If the results gained are similar then the experiment is repeatable *[1 mark]*.
3.1 A *[1 mark]*
3.2

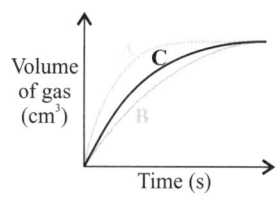

Curve C, as above. The curve should be between curves A and B *[1 mark]*.
3.3 The variables are controlled so that you can tell if the variable you're changing/the dependent variable is causing the results seen *[1 mark]*.
3.4 E.g. yes, because the same volume of gas was produced in each experiment *[1 mark]*.
This suggests that the same concentration and volume of acid (or an excess of acid) was used in both experiments.
3.5 Measuring how quickly the reaction loses mass *[1 mark]*.
4.1 Mean rate = amount of product formed ÷ time
= 40 ÷ 60 = **0.67 cm³/s** *[2 marks for correct answer, otherwise 1 mark for correct working]*
4.2 E.g.

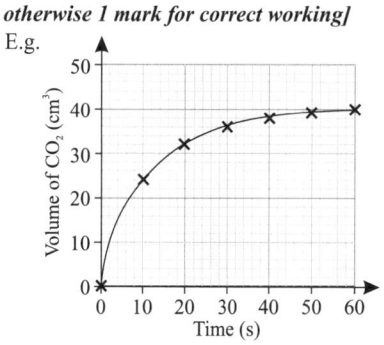

[1 mark for correctly drawn axes with a sensible scale, 2 marks for correctly marking on all 6 points, otherwise 1 mark if 5 of 6 points plotted correctly, 1 mark for a suitable line of best fit.]

4.3 E.g.

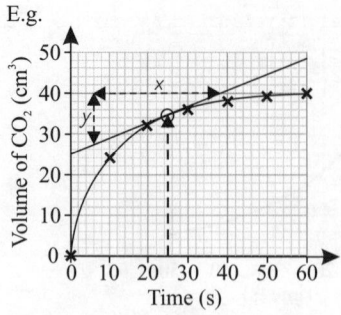

change in y = 40 − 27 = 13, change in x = 38 − 6 = 32,
rate = change in y ÷ change in x = 13 ÷ 32 = **0.4 cm³/s**
[1 mark for drawing a tangent at 25 s, 1 mark for correctly calculating a change in y from the tangent, 1 mark for correctly calculating a change in x from the tangent and 1 mark for a rate between 0.3 cm/s and 0.5 cm/s]

5 How to grade your answer:
Level 0: No relevant information is given. *[No marks]*
Level 1: One or two ways of increasing the rate are described and there's reference to collision theory. *[1 to 2 marks]*
Level 2: At least two ways of increasing the rate are given with appropriate reference to collision theory. *[3 to 4 marks]*
Level 3: There is a clear and detailed discussion of three ways by which the rate can be increased, which includes relevant references to collision theory. *[5 to 6 marks]*

Here are some points your answer may include:
Collision theory says that the rate of reaction depends on how often and how hard the reacting particles collide with each other.
If the particles collide hard enough (with enough energy) they will react.
Increasing the temperature makes particles move faster, so they collide more often and with greater energy. This will increase the rate of reaction.
If the surface area of the nickel catalyst is increased then the particles around it will have more area to work on. This increases the frequency of successful collisions and will increase the rate of reaction.
Increasing the pressure of the hydrogen will mean the particles are more squashed up together. This will increase the frequency of the collisions and increase the rate of reaction.

Page 265
Le Chatelier's Principle
Q1 a) More $H_2CO_{3(aq)}$ would be produced *[1 mark]*.
b) Less $NH_{3(g)}$ and $HCl_{(g)}$ would be produced *[1 mark]*.
c) More $CO_{2(g)}$ would be produced *[1 mark]*.

Page 266
Warm-Up Questions
1) They are the same.
2) The equilibrium will move to the left/towards reactants and the amount of reactants will increase.
3) It would have no effect (because there are equal numbers of gas molecules on both sides).

Exam Questions
1.1 The reaction is reversible *[1 mark]*.
1.2 Both (the forward and reverse) reactions are taking place at exactly the same rate *[1 mark]*.
2.1 Less $NO_{2(g)}$ will be produced *[1 mark]*, because there are more molecules of gas on the right hand side of the equation *[1 mark]*.
2.2 It will have no effect *[1 mark]*, because there are the same number of molecules of gas on both sides of the equation *[1 mark]*.
3.1 It gives out energy *[1 mark]*, because it's exothermic *[1 mark]*.
As the forward reaction is endothermic you know that the reverse reaction is exothermic and therefore gives out energy.

3.2 A reversible reaction is always exothermic in one direction and endothermic in the other direction *[1 mark]*, so a change in temperature will always favour one reaction more than the other *[1 mark]*.
3.3 It would move to the right *[1 mark]*.

Topic C7 — Organic Chemistry
Page 268
Hydrocarbons
Q1 $C_2H_6 + 3½O_2 \rightarrow 2CO_2 + 3H_2O$ or
$2C_2H_6 + 7O_2 \rightarrow 4CO_2 + 6H_2O$
[1 mark for correct reactants and products, 1 mark for correctly balancing]
Q2 a) $C_{10}H_{22}$ is more viscous than C_5H_{12} *[1 mark]*.
b) $C_{10}H_{22}$ has a higher boiling point than C_5H_{12} *[1 mark]*.
c) $C_{10}H_{22}$ is less flammable than C_5H_{12} *[1 mark]*.

Page 269
Fractional Distillation
Q1 The hydrocarbons in petrol have a shorter chain length than the hydrocarbons in diesel *[1 mark]*. This means that petrol has a lower boiling point than diesel *[1 mark]*.

Page 270
Uses and Cracking of Crude Oil
Q1 $C_5H_{12} \rightarrow C_2H_4 + C_3H_8$ *[1 mark]*

Pages 271-272
Warm-Up Questions
1) methane, ethane, propane, butane
2) single covalent bonds
3) When burnt they release energy.
4) e.g. fuel for transport / feedstock for making new compounds
5) long-chain hydrocarbons

Exam Questions
1 ethane *[1 mark]*
2.1 butane *[1 mark]*
2.2 C_4H_{10} *[1 mark]*
2.3 Any two from: e.g. polymers / solvents /lubricants / detergents *[2 marks — 1 mark for each correct answer]*
3 Flammability — Decreases as the molecules get bigger
Viscosity — Increases as the molecules get bigger
Boiling point — Increases as the molecules get bigger
[1 mark for each correctly drawn line]
4.1 F *[1 mark]*
4.2 A *[1 mark]*
4.3 Inside the fractionating column there is a temperature gradient with the hottest part at the bottom and coolest at the top *[1 mark]*. Crude oil that is gaseous moves up the column and when hydrocarbons in the gas reach a part of the column where the temperature is lower than their boiling points they condense and drain out of the column *[1 mark]*. Hydrocarbons with longer chain lengths have higher boiling points so condense lower down the column whereas hydrocarbons with shorter chain lengths have lower boiling points so condense higher up the column *[1 mark]*.
5.1 carbon dioxide/CO_2 *[1 mark]* and water/H_2O *[1 mark]*
5.2 $C_3H_8 + 5O_2 \rightarrow 3CO_2 + 4H_2O$ *[1 mark for correct reactants and products, 1 mark for correct balancing]*
5.3 oxidation *[1 mark]*
6.1 Because shorter-chain hydrocarbons generated by cracking tend to be more useful than longer ones *[1 mark]*.
6.2 $C_8H_{18} \rightarrow \mathbf{C_2H_6} + 2C_3H_6$ *[1 mark for correct products, 1 mark for correct balancing]*

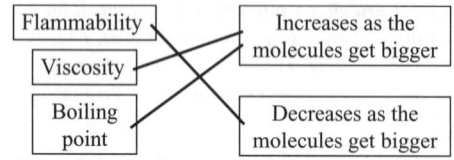

6.3 E.g. catalytic cracking is where long-chain hydrocarbons are vaporised *[1 mark]* and then passed over a hot powdered aluminium catalyst *[1 mark]*. Or they can be cracked by steam cracking which is where long-chain hydrocarbons are vaporised and mixed with steam *[1 mark]*. They are then heated to a very high temperature *[1 mark]*.

You don't have to mention the names of the different cracking methods (catalytic and steam) but it might help structure your answer.

Topic C8 — Chemical Analysis

Page 276
Paper Chromatography
Q1 $R_f = \frac{6.3}{8.4} = 0.75$ *[1 mark]*.

Page 277
Warm-Up Questions
1) A pure substance is a substance that only contains one compound or one element.
2) Impurities in a substance will increase the boiling point of the substance and may result in it boiling over a wider temperature range.
3) E.g. paint / drugs / cleaning products / fuels / cosmetics / fertilisers / metal alloys / food / drink.
4) Chromatography separates out the substances in a mixture.

Exam Questions
1.1 Light the gas with a lighted splint *[1 mark]*. Hydrogen will burn with a squeaky pop *[1 mark]*.
1.2 Place a glowing splint in the sample of gas *[1 mark]*. Oxygen will relight it *[1 mark]*.
2.1 D *[1 mark]*
2.2 A *[1 mark]*
2.3 C *[1 mark]*
2.4 R_f = distance travelled by substance in sunrise yellow ÷ distance travelled by solvent
$R_f = 9.0 \div 12.0 = \mathbf{0.75}$
[2 marks for correct answer, otherwise 1 mark for using the correct formula to calculate R_f]

Topic C9 — Chemistry of the Atmosphere

Page 280
Climate Change and Greenhouse Gases
Q1 The sun gives out short wavelength radiation *[1 mark]* which is reflected back by the Earth as long wavelength/thermal radiation *[1 mark]*. The thermal radiation is absorbed by greenhouse gases in the atmosphere *[1 mark]*. Greenhouse gases give out the thermal radiation in all directions including back towards the Earth, causing the temperature to rise *[1 mark]*.

Page 285
Warm-Up Questions
1) volcanic activity
2) E.g. limestone / coal
3) E.g. coal / crude oil / natural gas
4) E.g. walk, cycle, or take public transport instead of using their car for a journey / reduce their use of air travel / turn down their heating at home.
5) Any two from: e.g. carbon monoxide / soot / unburned hydrocarbons / particulates.

Exam Questions
1 Once green plants had evolved, they thrived in Earth's early atmosphere which was rich in **carbon dioxide** *[1 mark]*. These plants also produced **oxygen** *[1 mark]* by the process of **photosynthesis** *[1 mark]*. Some of the **carbon** *[1 mark]* from dead plants eventually became 'locked up' in fossil fuels.
2.1 When sulfur dioxide gas reacts with water in clouds *[1 mark]* it forms dilute sulfuric acid, which falls as rain *[1 mark]*.
2.2 E.g. it kills plants / damages buildings and statues / makes metals corrode *[1 mark]*.
2.3 Incomplete combustion of fossil fuels produces particulates *[1 mark]*. Particulates (and the clouds they help to produce) reflect sunlight back into space *[1 mark]* so less light reaches the Earth *[1 mark]*.
2.4 Short wavelength radiation from the sun passes through the Earth's atmosphere *[1 mark]*. It hits the Earth's surface and is reflected back as long wavelength radiation *[1 mark]*. This long wavelength radiation is absorbed by greenhouse gases in the atmosphere *[1 mark]*. They re-radiate it in all directions, including back towards the Earth, warming its surface *[1 mark]*.
3.1 A measure of the amount of carbon dioxide and other greenhouse gases released over the full life-cycle of a product, service or event *[1 mark]*.
3.2 How to grade your answer:
   Level 0: There is no relevant information. *[No marks]*
   Level 1: There is a brief description of at least one potential effect of an increase in global temperature. Some attempt is made to explain what impact this effect could have on humans. *[1 to 2 marks]*
   Level 2: There is some description of at least two potential effects of an increase in global temperature and an explanation of the potential impact of these effects on humans. *[3 to 4 marks]*
   Level 3: There is a clear and detailed explanation of at least three effects of an increase in global temperature and a clear explanation of the potential impact of these effects on humans. *[5 to 6 marks]*
Here are some points your answer may include:
Effect: An increase in global temperature could lead to polar ice caps melting. This could cause a rise in sea levels.
Impacts: Rising seas levels could cause flooding in coastal areas and cause coastal erosion.
Flooding and coastal erosion could make people who live near the coast homeless / cause costly damage to buildings and roads / pose a threat to human life.
Effect: Climate change could lead to changes in rainfall patterns.
Impacts: Some regions may have too much or too little water. Having too little water may affect the ability of certain regions to produce enough food for the human population. This could lead to famine or even starvation.
Too much water could lead to flooding.
Flooding could make people homeless / cause costly damage to buildings and roads / pose a threat to human life.
Effect: Climate change may lead to an increase in both the frequency and severity of storms.
Impacts: Storms can cause damage to buildings and roads and can pose a direct threat to human life.
Effect: Rising temperatures can directly affect the human and wildlife populations in an area.
Impacts: An increase in temperature may affect what food plants can be grown in a certain region.
This could lead to famine or even starvation.

Topic C10 — Using Resources

Page 291
Warm-Up Questions
1) E.g. natural rubber
2) Development that takes account of the needs of present society while not damaging the lives of future generations.
3) E.g. saves energy needed to extract metals from the earth / conserves limited supplies of metals from the earth / cuts down on the amount of waste going to landfill.
4) E.g. getting the raw materials / manufacturing and packaging / using the product / product disposal.

Exam Questions
1.1 A natural resource that doesn't renew itself quick enough to be considered replaceable *[1 mark]*.
1.2 Any two from: e.g. reuse the cans / recycle the aluminium / use fewer cans *[2 marks]*.

2.1 E.g. because the supply of copper-rich ores is limited *[1 mark]*
2.2 Bacteria convert copper compounds in the ore into soluble copper compounds which separate out from the ore *[1 mark]*. This produces a (leachate) solution containing copper ions, from which copper can be extracted by electrolysis/displacement with a more reactive metal e.g. scrap iron *[1 mark]*.
2.3 E.g. these processes have a smaller environmental impact *[1 mark]*.
2.4 E.g. these processes are slower *[1 mark]*.
3.1 The effect of some pollutants produced in the life cycle of a product can be difficult to quantify *[1 mark]*.
3.2 E.g. the person carrying out the company's LCA may have purposefully not included details of the disposal of the product *[1 mark]*, because the company wanted to use the LCA to support that their product was environmentally friendly for advertising reasons *[1 mark]*.

Page 292
Potable Water and Water Treatment
Q1 E.g. the water is filtered using a wire mesh, and then using filter beds *[1 mark]*. The filtered water is then sterilised using chlorine / ozone / ultraviolet light *[1 mark]*.

Page 294
Potable Water and Water Treatment
Q1 Screening — sewage is screened to remove any large bits of material and grit *[1 mark]*.
Sedimentation — heavier solids sink to the bottom to form sludge, while the lighter effluent floats on the top *[1 mark]*.

Page 295
Warm-Up Questions
1) Any two from: e.g. the levels of dissolved salts in the water aren't too high / the water has a pH of between 6.5 and 8.5 / there aren't any bacteria or other microbes in the water.
2) filtration
3) harmful chemicals
4) effluent and sludge

Exam Questions
1.1 Potable water contains dissolved substances whereas pure water only contains water molecules *[1 mark]*.
1.2 First, large bits of material are removed by a wire mesh *[1 mark]*, then sand and gravel beds filter out any other solid bits *[1 mark]*.
1.3 E.g. chlorine / ozone / ultraviolet light *[1 mark for each correct answer up to a maximum of three marks.]*
2.1 screening *[1 mark]*
2.2 The effluent undergoes aerobic digestion *[1 mark]*. During aerobic digestion air is pumped through the effluent which encourages aerobic bacteria to break down any organic matter in the water *[1 mark]*.
2.3 E.g. processes used to treat waste and sea water use more energy than treating fresh water and are therefore more expensive *[1 mark]*. People may not like the idea of drinking treated waste water *[1 mark]*.
3.1 E.g. sodium ions can be tested for by carrying out a flame test using a sample of water *[1 mark]*. If sodium ions are present the flame will turn yellow *[1 mark]*. To test for chloride ions a few drops of dilute nitric acid should be added to a sample of water, followed by a few drops of silver nitrate solution *[1 mark]*. If chloride ions are present, a white precipitate will form *[1 mark]*.
3.2 E.g. the pH of the water would need to be tested to see if it is between 6.5 and 8.5 *[1 mark]*.

Topic P1 — Energy

Page 298
Work Done
Q1 Energy is transferred mechanically *[1 mark]* from the kinetic energy store of the wind *[1 mark]* to the kinetic energy store of the windmill *[1 mark]*.

Page 299
Kinetic and Potential Energy Stores
Q1 The change in height is 5.0 m. So the energy transferred from the gravitational potential energy store is:
$E_p = mgh = 2.0 \times 9.8 \times 5.0 = 98$ J *[1 mark]*
This is transferred to the kinetic energy store of the object, so $E_k = 98$ J *[1 mark]*
$E_k = \frac{1}{2}mv^2$ so
$v^2 = 2E_k \div m$ *[1 mark]*
$= (2 \times 98) \div 2.0$ *[1 mark]*
$= 98$ m^2/s^2
$v = \sqrt{98} = 9.899... =$ **9.9 m/s (to 2 s.f.)** *[1 mark]*

Page 300
Specific Heat Capacity
Q1 $\Delta E = mc\Delta\theta$ so
$\Delta\theta = \Delta E \div (m \times c)$ *[1 mark]*
$= 50\,000 \div (5 \times 4200)$
$= 2.380...$ °C *[1 mark]*
So the new temperature $= 5 + 2.380...$
$= 7.380... =$ **7 °C (to 1 s.f.)** *[1 mark]*

Page 302
Warm-Up Questions
1) Any two from: e.g. mechanically (by a force doing work) / electrically (work done by when a current flows) / by heating / by radiation.
2) Energy is transferred from the chemical energy store of the person's arm to the kinetic energy stores of the arm and the ball (and the gravitational energy store of the ball). Once the ball is released, energy is transferred from the kinetic energy store of the ball to its gravitational potential energy store.
3) kinetic energy = ½ × mass × (speed)^2 / $E_k = \frac{1}{2}mv^2$
4) A lorry travelling at 60 miles per hour.

Exam Questions
1.1 gravitational potential energy = mass × gravitational field strength × height / $E_p = mgh$ *[1 mark]*
So, $h = E_p \div (m \times g)$ *[1 mark]*
$= 137.2 \div (20 \times 9.8)$ *[1 mark]*
= **0.7 m** *[1 mark]*
1.2 Energy is transferred from the gravitational potential energy store *[1 mark]* to the kinetic energy store of the load *[1 mark]*.
1.3 Some of the energy would also be transferred to thermal energy store of the air (and the thermal energy store of the load) *[1 mark]*.
2.1 change in thermal energy = mass × specific heat capacity × temperature change / $\Delta E = mc\Delta\theta$
So, $c = \Delta E \div (m \times \Delta\theta)$ *[1 mark]*
$\Delta\theta = 100 - 20 = 80$ °C *[1 mark]*
$c = 36\,000 \div (0.5 \times 80)$ *[1 mark]* = **900 J/kg °C** *[1 mark]*
2.2 Concrete has a higher specific heat capacity *[1 mark]* and so will be able to store a lot more energy in its thermal energy store *[1 mark]*.
Even if you got the answer to 2.1 wrong, if your conclusion is correct for your answer to 2.1, you'd get the marks for this question.
3.1 Reading values from the start and end of the linear point on the graph:
E.g. $\Delta E = 3 - 1 = 2$ kJ = 2000 J
$\Delta\theta = 2.4 - 0.4 = 2$ °C
[1 mark for any values accurately calculated from a pair of points on the linear part of the graph]
change in thermal energy = mass × specific heat capacity × temperature change / $\Delta E = mc\Delta\theta$,
So, $c = \Delta E \div (m \times \Delta\theta)$ *[1 mark]*
$= 2000 \div (1 \times 2)$ *[1 mark]* = **1000 J/kg °C** *[1 mark]*
3.2 Lower *[1 mark]*. In the investigation, some of the energy transferred by the heater would have been transferred to the thermal energy stores of the surroundings rather than the block *[1 mark]*. For the same temperature change to have occurred for a smaller amount of energy transferred, the specific heat capacity must be smaller *[1 mark]*.
It's important to be able to spot reasons why the results of an investigation aren't perfectly accurate.

Page 303
Conservation of Energy and Power
Q1 $P = E \div t$
      $t = 2 \times 60 = 120$ s *[1 mark]*
      $P = 4800 \div 120$ *[1 mark]* = **40 W** *[1 mark]*

Page 306
Efficiency
Q1   efficiency
      = useful output energy transfer ÷ total input energy transfer
      = 225 ÷ 300 *[1 mark]* = **0.75** *[1 mark]*
Q2   efficiency = useful power output ÷ total power input
                = 900 ÷ 1200 = 0.75 *[1 mark]*
      useful output energy transfer
      = efficiency × total input energy transfer *[1 mark]*
      = 0.75 × 72 000 *[1 mark]*
      = **54 000 J** *[1 mark]*

Page 307
Warm-Up Questions
1) Energy can be transferred usefully, stored or dissipated, but can never be created or destroyed.
2) Power is the rate of doing work. The units are watts.
3) conduction, convection
4) E.g. lubrication
5) The higher the thermal conductivity, the greater the rate of the energy transfer (i.e. the faster energy is transferred) through it.
6) Some energy is always dissipated, so less than 100% of the input energy transfer is transferred usefully.

Exam Questions
1.1   power = work done ÷ time / $P = W \div t$ *[1 mark]*
      $P = 1000 \div 20$ *[1 mark]*
          = **50 W** *[1 mark]*
1.2   Less energy is transferred to the thermal energy store of the motor's parts and the surroundings *[1 mark]*, so more is transferred to the scooter's kinetic energy store *[1 mark]*.
1.3   It will be faster / complete the course in less time *[1 mark]* because the motor transfers the same amount of energy, but over a shorter time *[1 mark]*.
2.1   efficiency = useful output energy transfer ÷
                   useful input energy transfer *[1 mark]*
2.2   efficiency = useful output energy transfer ÷
                   useful input energy transfer
                = 480 ÷ 1200 *[1 mark]*
                = **0.4 (or 40%)** *[1 mark]*
2.3   power = energy transferred ÷ time / $P = E \div t$
      1 minute = 60 seconds
      So, output power = 600 ÷ 60 *[1 mark]*
                       = **10 W** *[1 mark]*
2.4   efficiency = useful output power ÷ total output power
      So, total input power = useful output power
                              ÷ efficiency *[1 mark]*
      total input power = 10 ÷ 0.55 *[1 mark]*
                        = 18.181... = **18 W (to 2 s.f.)** *[1 mark]*
2.5   Disagree *[1 mark]*. Torch B has a lower input energy transfer than torch A, i.e. it transfers less energy per minute than torch A (as 18 × 60 = 1080, and 1080 < 1200) *[1 mark]*.

Even if you got the answer to 2.4 wrong, if your conclusion is correct for your answer to 2.5, you'd get the marks for this question. You could also answer this question by comparing the input powers of the torches.

Page 315
Warm-Up Questions
1) Any three from: coal / oil / natural gas / nuclear fuel (plutonium or uranium).
2) Advantage: E.g. they'll never run out.
   Disadvantage: Any one from: e.g. energy output often depends on outside factors which cannot be controlled / they can't respond to immediate increases in energy demands.
3) Any one from: e.g. Bio-fuels can be used to run vehicles / electricity generated using renewable resources can be used to power vehicles.
4) Any two from: e.g. it releases greenhouse gases and contributes to global warming / it causes acid rain / coal mining damages the landscape.
5) Any two from: e.g. renewable resources don't currently provide enough energy / energy from renewables cannot be relied upon currently / it's expensive to build new renewable power plants / it's expensive to switch to cars running on renewable energy.

Exam Questions
1.1   Any two from: e.g. wave / tidal / geothermal / bio-fuels *[1 mark for each correct renewable energy resource]*.
1.2   Any one from: e.g. flooding a valley for a dam destroys animal habitats / carbon dioxide is released by rotting vegetation in flooded valley *[1 mark]*.
2.1   From the gravitational potential energy store of the water *[1 mark]* to its kinetic energy store *[1 mark]*.
2.2   E.g. they cause no pollution / they use a renewable energy source *[1 mark for each correct advantage, up to a maximum of two]*.
3.1   power = energy transferred ÷ time / $P = E \div t$
      So, $E = P \times t$ *[1 mark]*
      seconds in 5 hours = 5 × 60 × 60 = 18 000 s
      Energy provided by 1 m² solar panel
                      in 5 hours = 200 × 18 000 *[1 mark]*
                                 = 3 600 000 J *[1 mark]*
      Number of panels needed = energy needed ÷ energy provided
      = 32 500 000 ÷ 3 600 000 *[1 mark]*
      = 9.027... = **10 panels (to next whole number)** *[1 mark]*

Remember, because you have to have a set number of whole panels, if you get a decimal answer, you need to round up to the next whole number to be able to provide the right amount of energy.

3.2   Ten 1 m² solar panels are needed, and they have 10 m² of space on their roof (10 × 1 m² = 10 m²), so the family can install sufficient solar panels *[1 mark]*.
3.3   E.g. Solar panels are less reliable than coal-fired power stations *[1 mark]*. The energy output of the solar panels will vary based on the number of hours of good sunlight, and may not be able to provide enough energy on a given day *[1 mark]*. The energy output of coal-fired power stations is not influenced by environmental factors like weather, and energy output can be increased to meet demand *[1 mark]*.

Topic P2 — Electricity

Page 316
Current and Circuit Symbols
Q1 $Q = It$ so $t = Q \div I$ *[1 mark]*
                  = 28 800 ÷ 8 *[1 mark]*
                  = 3600 s *[1 mark]*
      $t = 3600 \div 60$ = **60 minutes** *[1 mark]*

Page 317
Resistance
Q1 $V = IR$ so $R = V \div I$ *[1 mark]*
                    = 230 ÷ 5.0 *[1 mark]*
                    = **46 Ω** *[1 mark]*

Page 319
I-V Characteristics
Q1   As the current through the lamp increases, the temperature of its filament increases *[1 mark]* causing its resistance to increase *[1 mark]*. A larger resistance means less current can flow per unit potential difference, and so the graph gets shallower *[1 mark]*.

Page 320
Warm-Up Questions
1) Ohms / Ω
2) The greater the resistance, the smaller the current / the smaller the resistance, the greater the current.
3)
4) Any one from: e.g. a wire / a fixed resistor
5) In parallel.

6) A graph that shows how the current flowing through a component changes as the potential difference across it varies.

Exam Questions
1.1 potential difference = current × resistance / $V = IR$
So, $R = V \div I$ *[1 mark]*
= 1.5 ÷ 0.30 *[1 mark]*
= **5.0 Ω** *[1 mark]*
1.2 charge = current × time / $Q = It$
= 0.30 × 35 *[1 mark]*
= **10.5 C** *[1 mark]*
1.3 The amount of current flowing through the circuit will decrease *[1 mark]*.
1.4

[1 mark]

1.5 The resistance of the filament lamp increases as the temperature increases *[1 mark]*.
2.1 Potential difference (across the component) *[1 mark]*.
2.2 Diodes only allow current to flow in one direction *[1 mark]*.
2.3 At point A, $V = 6$ V, $I = 3$ A *[1 mark]*
potential difference = current × resistance / $V = IR$
$R = V \div I$ *[1 mark]*
= 6 ÷ 3 *[1 mark]*
= **2 Ω** *[1 mark]*

Page 324
Series Circuits
Q1 $R_{total} = 4 + 5 + 6 = 15$ Ω *[1 mark]*
$V = I \times R = 0.6 \times 15$ *[1 mark]* = **9 V** *[1 mark]*

Page 325
Parallel Circuits
Q1 The total current through the circuit decreases *[1 mark]* as there are fewer paths for the current to take *[1 mark]*. The total resistance of the circuit increases *[1 mark]* as, using $V = IR$, a decrease in the total current means an increase in the total resistance *[1 mark]*.

Page 327
Warm-Up Questions
1) Any one from: e.g. in automatic night lights / outdoor lighting / burglar detectors.
2) The resistance decreases.
3) E.g.

4) Any one from: e.g. if you remove or disconnect one component, then the whole circuit is broken / you can't switch components on or off independently.
5) The total resistance is the sum of all the resistances.
6) Two resistors connected in series.
7) E.g.

Exam Questions
1.1 total resistance = $R_1 + R_2 + R_3$
= 2 + 3 + 5 *[1 mark]*
= **10 Ω** *[1 mark]*
1.2 The current will be 0.4 A *[1 mark]* because in a series circuit, the same current flows through all parts of the circuit *[1 mark]*.

1.3 V = source pd
$V_3 = V - V_1 - V_2$
= 4 – 0.8 – 1.2 *[1 mark]*
= **2 V** *[1 mark]*
2.1 **15 V** *[1 mark]*
Potential difference is the same across each branch in a parallel circuit.
2.2 potential difference = current × resistance / $V = IR$
$I = V \div R$ *[1 mark]*
= 15 ÷ 3 *[1 mark]*
= **5 A** *[1 mark]*
2.3 $I_2 = 5 + 3.75$ *[1 mark]*
= **8.75 A** *[1 mark]*
Even if you got the answer to 2.2 wrong, award yourself the marks for 2.3 if you did the sum above correctly.

Page 329
Power of Electrical Appliances
Q1 $P = E \div t = 6000 \div 30$ *[1 mark]*
= **200 W** *[1 mark]*
Q2 $E = P \times t$ *[1 mark]*
= 250 × (2 × 60 × 60)
= **1 800 000 J** *[1 mark]*
$E = 375 \times (2 \times 60 \times 60) = 2\,700\,000$ J *[1 mark]*
So change in energy is
2 700 000 – 1 800 000 = **900 000 J** *[1 mark]*

Page 330
More on Power
Q1 $E = Q \times V = 10\,000 \times 200$ *[1 mark]*
= **2 000 000 J** *[1 mark]*
Q2 $P = V \times I = 12 \times 4.0$ *[1 mark]* = **48 W** *[1 mark]*
Q3 $R = P \div I^2$ *[1 mark]* = $2300 \div 10.0^2$ *[1 mark]*
= **23 Ω** *[1 mark]*

Page 333
Warm-Up Questions
1) The live wire, neutral wire, and earth wire.
2) Energy is transferred electrically to the thermal energy store of the heating element.
3) power = (current)^2 × resistance / $P = I^2R$
4) The network of cables and transformers that distributes electricity across the country.

Exam Questions
1 The live wire is at a potential difference of around 230 V *[1 mark]*. Touching the wire forms a low-resistance path from the wire to the earth through your body *[1 mark]*, causing a large current to flow through you, which is an electric shock *[1 mark]*.
2.1 power = potential difference × current / $P = V \times I$ *[1 mark]*
2.2 $I = P \div V$ *[1 mark]*
= (2.8 × 1000) ÷ 230 *[1 mark]*
= 12.17... A = **12** *[1 mark]* **A** *[1 mark, allow 'amps']*
2.3 She should choose kettle B because it has the higher power rating *[1 mark]*. This means that it transfers more energy usefully / to heat the water per unit time, so it will boil the water faster *[1 mark]*.
3.1 Step-up transformers increase the potential difference *[1 mark]* of the electricity supply, allowing the electricity to be transmitted at a high potential difference, and so a low current *[1 mark]*. This reduces the energy lost through heating in the cables *[1 mark]*.
3.2 Rearrange $V_sI_s = V_pI_p$ for I_s:
$I_s = \dfrac{V_p I_p}{V_s}$ *[1 mark]*
$= \dfrac{4.00 \times 10^5 \times 2.00 \times 10^3}{2.75 \times 10^5}$ *[1 mark]*
= 2.909... × 10^3 A
= **2.91 × 10^3 A (to 3 s.f.)** *[1 mark]*
4.1 power = potential difference × current / $P = IV$
$P = 0.5 \times 3.0$ *[1 mark]*
= **1.5 W** *[1 mark]*
energy transferred = power × time / $E = Pt$
$t = 0.5$ hours = (30 × 60) s = 1800 s
$E = 1.5 \times 1800$ *[1 mark]*
= **2700 J** *[1 mark]*

4.2 energy transferred = charge flow × potential difference / $E = QV$
So, $Q = E \div V$ *[1 mark]*
$Q = 2700 \div 3.0$ *[1 mark]*
 = **900 C** *[1 mark]*
In the exam, you'd probably get all the marks for 4.2 if you did the sum above correctly, even if you got the answer to 4.1 wrong.

Topic P3 — Particle Model of Matter

Page 335
Density
Q1 Gemstone's mass = 0.019 kg = 0.019 × 1000
  = 19 g *[1 mark]*
Gemstone's volume = volume of water pushed out of eureka can = 7.0 cm³
$\rho = m \div V$
 = 19 ÷ 7.0 *[1 mark]*
 = 2.714...
 = **2.7 g/cm³ (to 2 s.f.)** *[1 mark]*

Page 337
Specific Latent Heat
Q1 $E = m \times L = 0.25 \times 120\,000$ *[1 mark]*
  = **30 000 J** *[1 mark]*

Pages 339-340
Warm-Up Questions
1) In a liquid, the particles are held close together, but can move past each other. They form irregular arrangements. The particles move in random directions at low speeds.
2) Density is a measure of the amount of mass in a given volume / compactness.
3) Cooling a system decreases its internal energy.
4) The specific latent heat of vaporisation of a substance is the amount of energy needed to change 1 kg of that substance from a liquid to a gas.
5) J/kg

Exam Questions
1.1 Particles are held close together in a fixed, regular pattern *[1 mark]*. They vibrate about fixed positions *[1 mark]*.
1.2 melting *[1 mark]*
1.3 evaporation *[1 mark]*
2.1 The densities of each of the toy soldiers are the same, but their masses may vary *[1 mark]*.
2.2 The volume of the toy soldier / the volume of water displaced by the toy soldier *[1 mark]*.
The mass of the toy soldier *[1 mark]*.
2.3 How to grade your answer:
  Level 0: There is no relevant information. *[No marks]*
  Level 1: There is a brief explanation of an experiment to measure the density of the toy soldier. The answer lacks coherency. *[1 to 2 marks]*
  Level 2: There is an explanation of an experiment to measure the density of the toy soldier, with reference to the equipment needed. The answer has some structure. *[3 to 4 marks]*
  Level 3: There is a clear and detailed explanation of an experiment to measure the density of the toy soldier. The method includes details of the equipment needed and how to process the results to work out the density of the toy soldier. The answer is well structured. *[5 to 6 marks]*
Here are some points your answer may include:
Measure and record the mass of the toy soldier using the mass balance.
Fill a eureka can with water.
Place an empty measuring cylinder beneath the spout of the eureka can.
Submerge the toy soldier in the eureka can.
Measure the volume of water displaced from the eureka can using the measuring cylinder.

The volume of water displaced is equal to the volume of the soldier.
Use the equation 'density = mass ÷ volume / $\rho = m \div V$' to calculate the density of the toy soldier.
With questions where you have to describe a method, make sure your description is clear and detailed.
3.1 specific latent heat of fusion *[1 mark]*
3.2 thermal energy for a change of state =
   mass × specific latent heat / $E = mL$
So, $L = E \div m$ *[1 mark]*
40.8 g = (40.8 ÷ 1000) kg = 0.0408 kg
$L = 47.7 \div 0.0408$ *[1 mark]*
 = **1170 J/kg (to 3 s.f.)** *[1 mark]*
3.3 The internal energy of the system increases as it's heated *[1 mark]*. This is because heating a system transfers energy from thermal energy stores to the kinetic stores of the particles in the system *[1 mark]*.
3.4 When a system is heated, energy is transferred to the particles in the system, causing them to gain energy in their kinetic stores/move faster *[1 mark]*. If the substance is heated enough, the particles will have enough energy in their kinetic stores to break the bonds holding them together, so they change state *[1 mark]*.
4.1 The particles in a gas have high energies *[1 mark]*, move in random directions at high speeds *[1 mark]* and are not arranged in any pattern *[1 mark]*.
4.2 In a sealed container, the gas particles collide with the container walls *[1 mark]* and exert a force on the walls, (creating an outward pressure) *[1 mark]*.
4.3 density = mass ÷ volume / $\rho = m \div V$ *[1 mark]*
4.4 $\rho = 8.2 \div 6.69$ *[1 mark]*
 = **1.2 g/cm³**
[3 marks for correct answer, including units. Deduct 1 mark if reported to an incorrect number of significant figures and deduct 1 mark if incorrect units given]
4.5 The pressure of the gas within the container increases as the container is heated *[1 mark]*. This is because the increase in temperature causes the particles to move faster / increases the energy in the kinetic energy stores of the particles, meaning more force is exerted on the walls of the container when the particles collide with it *[1 mark]*. The increased speed / average energy in kinetic stores of the particles also means there are more collisions, which also increases the total force exerted on the container *[1 mark]*.
5 density = mass ÷ volume / $\rho = m \div V$
So, $m = \rho \times V$ *[1 mark]*
volume of cube = 1.5 × 1.5 × 1.5 = 3.375 cm³ *[1 mark]*
The cube's density is 3500 kg/m³.
1 g/cm³ = 1000 kg/m³, so this is
3500 ÷ 1000 = 3.5 g/cm³ *[1 mark]*
$m = 3.5 \times 3.375$ *[1 mark]*
 = 11.8125 = **12 g (to 2 s.f.)** *[1 mark]*

Topic P4 — Atomic Structure

Page 344
Ionising Radiation
Q1 E.g. Alpha would not be suitable because it is stopped by a few cm of air or a sheet of paper *[1 mark]*. It would not be able to pass through the packaging to sterilise the equipment *[1 mark]*.

Page 345
Nuclear Equations
Q1 Beta particles *[1 mark]*
Q2 $^{219}_{86}\text{Rn} \rightarrow {}^{215}_{84}\text{Po} + {}^{4}_{2}\text{He}$
[1 mark for correct layout, 1 mark for correct symbol for an alpha particle, 1 mark for total atomic and mass numbers being equal on both sides]

Page 347
Half-Life
Q1 After one half-life the count-rate will be
$40 \div 2 = 20$ cps *[1 mark]*
After a second: $20 \div 2 = 10$ cps
After a third: $10 \div 2 = 5$ cps *[1 mark]*
So the ratio is $5:40 = 1:8$ *[1 mark]*

Pages 350-351
Warm-Up Questions
1) The nuclear model of the atom contains a tiny nucleus which contains protons and neutrons. The rest of the atom is mostly empty space. Electrons exist in fixed energy levels round the outside of the nucleus.
2) Isotopes of an element are atoms with the same number of protons / the same atomic number but a different number of neutrons / a different mass number.
3) alpha particles
4) Beta emitters are not immediately absorbed, like alpha radiation, and do not penetrate as far as gamma rays. Therefore variations in the thickness of the sheet significantly affect the amount of radiation passing through.
5) beta radiation
6) gamma rays
7) Radioactive contamination is caused when radioactive atoms get into or onto an object. Radioactive irradiation occurs when objects are exposed to radiation from a radioactive source.
8) Alpha radiation can't penetrate the skin and is easily blocked by a small air gap, so cannot damage tissue inside the body through irradiation. If a person is contaminated with alpha radiation however, it is very dangerous as alpha sources are highly ionising and do lots of damage to nearby tissue.

Exam Questions
1.1 Beta (particles) *[1 mark]*, because the radiation passes through the paper, but not the aluminium, so it is moderately penetrating in comparison to the other two *[1 mark]*.
1.2 E.g. a Geiger-Muller tube/counter *[1 mark]*
2.1 The time taken for the number of radioactive nuclei in a sample to halve / the time taken for the count-rate or activity to fall to half of its initial level *[1 mark]*.
2.2 4 minutes is equivalent to $4 \div 2 = 2$ half-lives *[1 mark]*. After 1 half-life, there will be ½ of the unstable nuclei left. So, after 2 half-lives, there will be $½ \div 2 = ¼$ / **one quarter** of the unstable nuclei left *[1 mark]*.
3.1 $2 \times 60 = 120$ seconds
$120 \div 40 = 3$ half-lives *[1 mark]*
$8000 \div 2 = 4000, 4000 \div 2 = 2000,$
$2000 \div 2 = \textbf{1000 Bq}$ *[1 mark]*
3.2 $8000 \div 2 = 4000, 4000 \div 2 = 2000, 2000 \div 2 = 1000,$
$1000 \div 2 = 500, 500 \div 2 = 250.$
So it takes **5 half-lives** to drop to 250 Bq
[2 marks for correct answer, otherwise 1 mark for attempting to halve values to find number of half-lives].
3.3 $(100 \div 8000) \times 100$ *[1 mark]* = **1.25%** *[1 mark]*
4.1 Protons *[1 mark]* and neutrons *[1 mark]*.
4.2 The total number of protons and neutrons in the nucleus/atom *[1 mark]*.
4.3 Atom A and atom B *[1 mark]* because isotopes of the same element have the same atomic number, but different mass numbers *[1 mark]*.
5.1 E.g. $_{-1}^{0}e$ / $_{-1}^{0}\beta$ *[1 mark]*
5.2 The atomic number increases by 1 *[1 mark]* and the mass number stays the same *[1 mark]*.
5.3 The atomic number doesn't change *[1 mark]* and neither does the mass number *[1 mark]*.
5.4 $_{84}^{209}\text{Po} \rightarrow {}_{82}^{205}\text{Pb} + {}_{2}^{4}\text{He}$
[1 mark for both the mass number and atomic number of He, 1 mark for the atomic number of Po, 1 mark for the mass number of Pb]

Topic P5 — Forces
Page 354
Weight, Mass and Gravity
Q1 a) $W = mg = 5 \times 9.8$ *[1 mark]* = **49 N** *[1 mark]*
    b) $W = 5 \times 1.6$ *[1 mark]* = **8 N** *[1 mark]*

Page 356
Resultant Forces
Q1 20 cm = 0.2 m *[1 mark]*
$W = Fs = 20 \times 0.2$ *[1 mark]* = **4 J** *[1 mark]*

Page 357
More on Forces
Q1 Draw the given forces to scale and tip-to-tail. The third force is found by joining the end of the second force to the start of the first force. E.g.

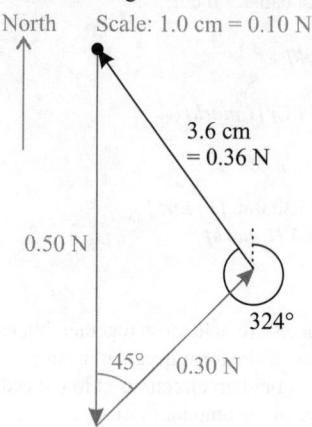

Third force = 0.36 N on a bearing of 324°.
[1 mark for a correct scale drawing with a sensible scale, 1 mark for a magnitude between 0.35 and 0.37 N, 1 mark for a bearing between 323 and 325°]

Page 358
Warm-Up Questions
1) Contact force: e.g. air resistance
Non-contact force: e.g. gravitational attraction
2) Vector quantity: e.g. velocity / momentum / force
Scalar quantity: e.g. mass / speed / volume
3) a) N/kg
   b) kg
   c) N
4) If all force arrows placed tip-to-tail form a closed loop, the forces are balanced.

Exam Questions
1.1 Total force to the right = 1700 + 300 = 2000 N
Total force to the left = 2000 N
Total horizontal force = 2000 − 2000 = 0 N *[1 mark]*
Resultant force = downwards force − upwards force
= 800 − 300
= **500 N** *[1 mark]* **downwards** *[1 mark]*
1.2 Total vertical force = 0 N
so, y = **400 N** *[1 mark]*
Total horizontal force = 0 N
so, $x + 500$ N = 2000 N
$x = 2000 − 500 = $ **1500 N** *[1 mark]*
2.1 work done = force × distance moved along the line of action of the force / $W = Fs$
$W = 42\,000 \times 700$ *[1 mark]*
= 29 400 000 J *[1 mark]*
= **29 400 kJ** *[1 mark]*

Answers

2.2

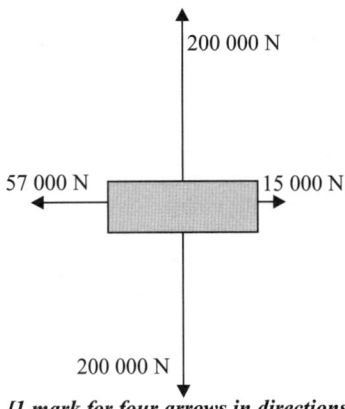

[Diagram: rectangle with four arrows — 200 000 N up, 200 000 N down, 57 000 N left, 15 000 N right]

[1 mark for four arrows in directions shown, 1 mark for upwards arrow same length as downwards arrow, 1 mark for driving force arrow bigger than resistive force arrow, 1 mark for all arrows labelled correctly]

You'd still get the marks if you've drawn the driving force to the right, and the resistive force to the left, as the direction that the train was travelling in was not specified in the question.

3.1   The spring would stretch less on Mars because the gravitational field strength on Mars is less than that on Earth *[1 mark]*, so the ball would weigh less *[1 mark]* and the force on the spring would be lower *[1 mark]*.

3.2   weight = mass × gravitational field strength / $W = mg$
so $g = W ÷ m$ *[1 mark]*
= 0.37 ÷ 0.10 *[1 mark]*
= **3.7 N/kg** *[1 mark]*

Page 360
Forces and Elasticity
Q1   2 cm = 0.02 m *[1 mark]*
$F = ke$ so $k = F ÷ e$ *[1 mark]*
= 1 ÷ 0.02 *[1 mark]*
= **50 N/m** *[1 mark]*

Page 362
Investigating Springs
Q1   2.5 cm = 0.025 m *[1 mark]*
$E_e = ½ke^2 = ½ × 40 × (0.025)^2$ *[1 mark]*
= **0.0125 J** *[1 mark]*

Page 363
Warm-Up Questions
1) false
2) Force = spring constant × extension / $F = ke$
3) The limit of proportionality is the point at which the spring stops behaving according to $F = ke$ / F is no longer proportional to e.
4) E.g. to check that the masses to be used in the experiment are appropriate.

Exam Questions
1   shape / length / size *[1 mark]*, proportional *[1 mark]*, elastic *[1 mark]*.

There are quite a few things you could write for the first word — as long as your answer seems sensible give yourself the mark.

2.1   The mass on the bottom of the spring / the force applied to the bottom of the spring *[1 mark]*.
2.2   Any one from: e.g. the spring used throughout the experiment / the temperature the experiment is carried out at *[1 mark]*.
2.3   extension = 2.5 cm = 0.025 m *[1 mark]*
force = spring constant × extension / $F = ke$
so $k = F ÷ e$ *[1 mark]*
= 4 ÷ 0.025 *[1 mark]*
= **160 N/m** *[1 mark]*

Remember to convert the measurement of extension from cm into m before you do your calculation.

2.4   The spring has been inelastically deformed *[1 mark]*.

Page 364
Distance, Displacement, Speed and Velocity
Q1 $s = vt$ so $v = s ÷ t$ *[1 mark]*
= 200 ÷ 25 *[1 mark]* = **8 m/s** *[1 mark]*

Page 365
Acceleration
Q1 $u = 0$ m/s, $v = 7$ m/s, $a = g = 9.8$ m/s^2,
$s = (v^2 – u^2) ÷ 2a$ *[1 mark]*
= (49 – 0) ÷ (2 × 9.8) *[1 mark]*
= **2.5 m** *[1 mark]*

Page 367
Velocity-Time Graphs
Q1   E.g.

[Graph: Velocity (m/s) vs Time (s) — horizontal line, then positive gradient, then horizontal line at higher velocity]

[1 mark for a straight, horizontal line representing steady speed, 1 mark for a straight line with a positive gradient representing constant acceleration, 1 mark for a straight, horizontal line at a different velocity to the initial velocity to represent a different steady speed]

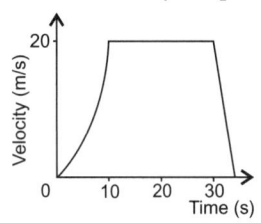

Q2

[Graph: Velocity (m/s) vs Time (s) — upward curve to 20 m/s, horizontal line, then decreasing line; axis marks at 10, 20, 30]

[1 mark for an upwards curved acceleration line to 20 m/s, 1 mark for a straight line representing steady speed, 1 mark for a straight line representing deceleration]

Page 370
Warm-Up Questions
1) Speed is scalar, velocity is a vector / velocity has a direction, speed does not.
2) a) E.g. 3 m/s
    b) E.g. 55 m/s
    c) E.g. 250 m/s

Your answers may be slightly different to these, but as long as they're about the same size, you should be fine to use them in the exam.

3) An upwards curved line / a curve with increasing gradient.
4) A straight, horizontal line.
5) As the speed of the car increases, air resistance on the car increases.

Exam Questions
1.1   The cyclist travels at a constant speed (of 3 m/s) between 5 s and 8 s *[1 mark]*, then decelerates between 8 s and 10 s *[1 mark]*.
1.2   Area of triangle = 0.5 × width × height
Width = 5 – 2 = 3 s
Height = 3 m/s
Distance = 0.5 × 3 × 3 = **4.5 m**
[2 marks, otherwise 1 mark for an attempt to calculate the area under the graph between 2 and 5 seconds]
1.3   Acceleration is given by the gradient of a velocity-time graph.
change in $y = 3 – 0 = 3$ m/s
change in $x = 5 – 2 = 3$ s
acceleration = 3 ÷ 3 = **1 m/s^2**
[2 marks, otherwise 1 mark for an attempt to calculate the gradient of the line between 2 and 5 seconds]

You could also have used $a = Δv ÷ Δt$ here.

1.4   average acceleration = change in velocity ÷ change in time / $a = Δv ÷ Δt$
velocity at 8 s = 3 m/s; velocity at 10 s = 2 m/s
so $Δv = 2 – 3 = –1$ m/s *[1 mark]*
So, $a = –1 ÷ 2$ *[1 mark]*
= –0.5 m/s^2
= **0.5 m/s^2** *[1 mark]*

Your answer should be positive since the question asks for deceleration, rather than acceleration.

2.1 (final velocity)² − (initial velocity)² = 2 × acceleration × distance / $v^2 - u^2 = 2as$
So, $a = (v^2 - u^2) \div 2s$ *[1 mark]*
$a = (15^2 - 9^2) \div (2 \times 15)$ *[1 mark]*
= **4.8 m/s²** *[1 mark]*

2.2 upwards / in the opposite direction to the direction of motion *[1 mark]*

2.3 distance travelled = average speed × time / $s = vt$
So, $v = s \div t$ *[1 mark]*
$v = 102 \div 5.00$ *[1 mark]*
= **20.4 m/s** *[1 mark]*

2.4 Its (average) speed will be higher *[1 mark]* as the air resistance acting on the bird will be lower *[1 mark]*.

Page 371
Newton's First and Second Laws
Q1 $F = ma = (80 + 10) \times 0.25$ *[1 mark]*
= **22.5 N** *[1 mark]*

Page 372
Inertia and Newton's Third Law
Q1 Any one from: e.g the gravitational force of the Earth attracts the car and the gravitational force of the car attracts the Earth *[1 mark]* / the car exerts a normal contact force down against the ground and the normal contact force from the ground pushes up against the car *[1 mark]* / the car (tyres) pushes the road backwards and the road pushes the car (tyres) forwards *[1 mark]*.

Page 375
Warm-Up Questions
1) 0 N
2) boulder B
Boulder B needs a greater force to accelerate it by the same amount as Boulder A.
3) true
This is Newton's Third Law.
4) Masses should be added to the trolley.

Exam Questions
1.1 The ball exerts a force of −500 N on the bat *[1 mark]*, because, due to Newton's Third Law, if the bat exerts a force on the ball, the ball exerts an equal force on the bat in the opposite direction *[1 mark]*.

1.2 The acceleration of the ball is greater *[1 mark]* because it has a smaller mass, but is acted on by the same size force (and $F = ma$) *[1 mark]*.

2.1 force = mass × acceleration / $F = ma$
So, $a = F \div m$ *[1 mark]*
Set direction of van's motion to be positive, so F = −200 N
$a = -200 \div 2500$ *[1 mark]*
= −0.08 m/s²
So, deceleration = **0.08 m/s²** *[1 mark]*
The question asked for deceleration, so you should really quote your answer without the minus sign. However, you should get the marks either way.

2.2 force = mass × acceleration / $F = ma$
$F = 10.0 \times 29.0$ *[1 mark]*
= **290 N** *[1 mark]*

2.3 By Newton's Third Law, force on van in collision is −290 N *[1 mark]*.
force = mass × acceleration / $F = ma$
So, $a = F \div m$
$a = -290 \div 2500$ *[1 mark]*
= −0.116 m/s²
So deceleration = **0.116 m/s²** *[1 mark]*
You'd still get the marks here, even if you got 2.2 wrong, as long as your method's correct.

3 How to grade your answer:
Level 0: There is no relevant information. *[No marks]*
Level 1: A simple experiment to investigate force and acceleration which can be performed with the given equipment is partly outlined. How to process the results is not explained or is explained poorly. The answer lacks coherency. *[1 to 2 marks]*
Level 2: An experiment to investigate force and acceleration which can be performed with the given equipment is outlined in detail. How to process the results to find the spring constant is described clearly and in detail. The answer is well structured. *[3 to 4 marks]*

Here are some points your answer may include:
Place all of the masses in the trolley.
Calculate and record the weight of the trolley.
Place the trolley on the starting line.
Release the trolley, so that it moves through the light gate, and record the acceleration measured.
Take one of the masses from the trolley, and attach it to the hook.
Calculate and record the new total weight of the hook and the new total weight of the trolley.
Reset the position of the trolley on the starting line.
Release the trolley again so that it moves through the light gate, and record the acceleration measured.
Repeat these steps until all the masses from the trolley have been moved to the hook.
Plot your results on a graph of acceleration against weight, and draw a line of best fit.

Page 377
Reaction Times
Q1 a) $v^2 - u^2 = 2as$
$v^2 = 2 \times 9.8 \times 0.162 + 0$ *[1 mark]* = 3.1752 m²/s²
$v = \sqrt{3.1752} = 1.781...$ m/s *[1 mark]*
$a = \Delta v \div t$ so
$t = \Delta v \div a$ *[1 mark]*
= 1.781... ÷ 9.8 *[1 mark]* = 0.181... s
= **0.18 s (to 2 s.f.)** *[1 mark]*

b) His reaction time is longer in the evening *[1 mark]* so whilst driving, he may take longer to react to a hazard, meaning his thinking distance would be longer *[1 mark]*.

Page 379
Momentum
Q1 $p = mv = 60 \times 3$ *[1 mark]* = **180 kg m/s** *[1 mark]*

Page 380
Warm-Up Questions
1) The thinking distance is the distance travelled during your reaction time (the time between seeing a hazard, and applying the brakes).
2) The braking distance.
3) Any one from: e.g. poor grip on the roads increases braking distance / poor visibility delays when you see the hazard / distraction by the weather delays when you see the hazard.
4) Get the individual to sit with their arm resting on the edge of a table. Hold a ruler end-down so that the 0 cm mark hangs between their thumb and forefinger. Drop the ruler without warning. The individual must grab the ruler between their thumb and forefinger as quickly as possible. Measure the distance at which they have caught the ruler.
Use $v^2 - u^2 = 2as$, $a = 9.8$ m/s² and $a = \Delta v \div t$ to calculate the time taken for the ruler to fall that distance. This is their reaction time.
5) Energy is transferred from the kinetic energy stores of the wheels to the thermal energy stores of the brakes.
6) $p = mv = 2.5 \times 10 =$ **25 kg m/s**
7) In a closed system, the total momentum before an interaction must equal the total momentum after the interaction.
8) The momentum is zero.

Exam Question
1.1 stopping distance = braking distance + thinking distance,
So, thinking distance = stopping distance − braking distance *[1 mark]*
thinking distance = 58 − 41
= **17 m** *[1 mark]*

1.2 Their braking distance may increase *[1 mark]*, because the frost on the road will decrease the friction between the tyres and the road, causing them to decelerate at a lower rate and travel further whilst braking *[1 mark]*.

1.3 thinking distance = unchanged *[1 mark]*
braking distance = decreases *[1 mark]*
2.1 momentum = mass × velocity / $p = mv$ *[1 mark]*
2.2 $p = mv$
$p = 650 × 15.0$ *[1 mark]*
= **9750 kg m/s** *[1 mark]*
2.3 9750 kg m/s *[1 mark]*
Due to conservation of momentum, the total momentum after the collision is equal to the total momentum before the collision.
2.4 The two cars will move away at a speed lower than that of the initially moving car *[1 mark]* as the momentum is the same as before the collision, but the mass has increased (so the velocity must decrease) *[1 mark]*.

Topic P6 — Waves

Page 382
Transverse and Longitudinal Waves
Q1 $7.5 ÷ 100 = 0.075$ m *[1 mark]*
wave speed = frequency × wavelength, so frequency
= wave speed ÷ wavelength *[1 mark]*
= $0.15 ÷ 0.075$ *[1 mark]*
= **2 Hz** *[1 mark]*

Page 386
Refraction
Q1

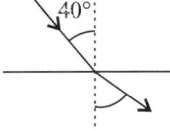

[1 mark for a correct diagram showing rays and the normal, 1 mark for an angle of incidence of 40°, 1 mark for an angle of refraction greater than 40°]

Page 387
Warm-Up Questions
1) In a longitudinal wave, the vibrations are parallel to the direction of travel/energy transfer.
2) wave speed = frequency × wavelength / $v = f\lambda$
3) E.g. Set up and turn on a ripple tank. Then, dim the lights and turn on the lamp so a wave pattern can be seen on the screen below the ripple rank. From the screen, measure the distance between the shadow lines that are a certain number of wavelengths apart, e.g. ten wavelengths. Divide the distance by this number of wavelengths to find the average wavelength. Use the equation wave speed = frequency × wavelength / $v = f\lambda$ to find the speed of the waves.
4) true

Exam Questions
1.1 transverse *[1 mark]*
1.2 5 cm *[1 mark]*
1.3 2 m *[1 mark]*
1.4 It will halve *[1 mark]*.
$v = f\lambda$, so if f doubles, then λ must halve, so that v stays the same.
2.1 The distance he measures is 1 wavelength *[1 mark]*. This can be used, together with the frequency of the signal, in the formula for wave speed, wave speed = frequency × wavelength / $v = f\lambda$ *[1 mark]*.
2.2 wave speed = frequency × wavelength / $v = f\lambda$
So $v = 50 × 6.8$ *[1 mark]*
= **340** *[1 mark]* **m/s** *[1 mark]*

Pages 395-396
Warm-Up Questions
1) gamma rays
2) Alternating current is made up of oscillating charges, which produce oscillating electric and magnetic fields in the form of radio waves.
3) The microwaves penetrate a few centimetres into the food before being absorbed by water molecules. The energy from the absorbed microwaves causes the food to heat up.
4) E.g. to carry data over long distances.

5) It has enough energy to knock electrons off atoms — this can cause gene mutations, cell destruction and cancer.
6) It emits more IR radiation than it absorbs.
7) Leslie cube

Exam Questions
1.1 Any one from: e.g. fluorescent light bulbs / tanning lamps *[1 mark]*.
1.2 Any one from: e.g. sunburn / premature ageing of skin / blindness / increased risk of skin cancer *[1 mark]*.
1.3 A gamma ray emitter is injected into/swallowed by the patient *[1 mark]* and the gamma rays emitted are detected by an external detector *[1 mark]*. By seeing where the gamma rays come from, they can track the progress of the tracer around the body and check it is functioning correctly *[1 mark]*.
1.4 Gamma rays can pass out of the body without being absorbed *[1 mark]*.
2.1 Radio waves can bend around / pass through objects so the signal can reach the inside of the house *[1 mark]*. Light waves would be blocked by the mountain / walls, and so would not be able to reach the receiver inside the house *[1 mark]*.
2.2 Microwave radiation *[1 mark]*. It passes through Earth's watery atmosphere without being absorbed, so can reach the satellites *[1 mark]*.
2.3 They are transmitted through the atmosphere into space, where they are picked up by a satellite receiver orbiting Earth *[1 mark]*. The satellite transmits the signal back to Earth in a different direction, where it is received by a satellite dish connected to the house *[1 mark]*.
3.1 Any one from: e.g. place the thermometers at equal distances away from the cube / place the thermometers at the same height as each other / make sure no thermometers are in direct sunlight/a draught *[1 mark]*.
3.2 Matt surfaces are better infrared radiation emitters then shiny surfaces *[1 mark]*.
3.3 Black surfaces are better infrared radiation emitters than white surfaces *[1 mark]*.
3.4 The times recorded would be longer *[1 mark]*. Cooler objects emit infrared radiation at a lower rate *[1 mark]*.
3.5 E.g. the resolution of the digital thermometer is higher, so there will be less uncertainty in the results (the results will be more accurate) / the student is less likely to misread the temperature (human error is less likely) *[1 mark for each correct reason, up to a maximum of 2]*.

Topic P7 — Magnetism and Electromagnetism

Page 398
Magnetism
Q1 E.g. for current out of the page:

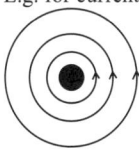

[1 mark for concentric circles getting further apart, 1 mark for arrows on field lines with correct direction]

Page 400
Warm-Up Questions
1)

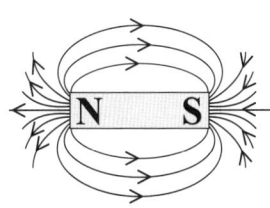

2) It's made up of concentric circles around the wire (with the wire at the centre).
3) A coil of current-carrying wire, often used to make electromagnets.

Exam Questions
1.1 E.g. Put the magnets on a piece of paper and place many compasses in different places between the magnets to show the magnetic field at those points *[1 mark]*. The compass needles will line up with the magnetic field lines *[1 mark]*.
They could also use iron filings to show the pattern.
1.2 The field lines point straight across from the north pole towards the south pole *[1 mark]*.
1.3 Attraction *[1 mark]*, as opposite poles are facing each other and opposite poles attract *[1 mark]*.
2.1

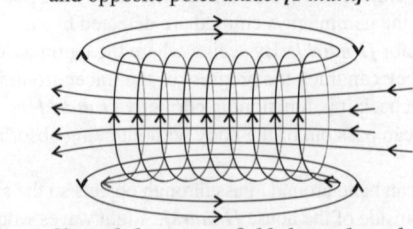

[1 mark for correct field shape, 1 mark for direction]

2.2 E.g. iron *[1 mark]*
2.3 The paperclips will fall *[1 mark]*, because an electromagnet only has a magnetic field if a current is flowing *[1 mark]*.

Page 402
The Motor Effect
Q1 Into the page *[1 mark]*.

Page 404
Warm-Up Questions
1) When a current-carrying wire in a magnetic field experiences a force.
2) First finger — magnetic field
Second finger — current
Thumb — force (motion)
3) Swapping the polarity of the dc supply (reversing the current), or swapping the magnetic poles over (reversing the field).

Exam Questions
1.1

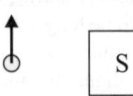

[1 mark]

1.2 The direction of the force would be reversed too *[1 mark]*.
1.3 The force would be lower *[1 mark]*.
1.4 There would be no force on the wire *[1 mark]*.
2.1 E.g.

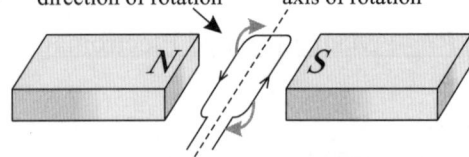

[1 mark for any indication that the current goes anticlockwise]

2.2 force = magnetic flux density × current × length of conductor inside field / $F = BIl$
$F = 0.2 \times 15 \times 0.1$ *[1 mark]*
= **0.3 N** *[1 mark]*
2.3 By swapping the direction of the current/contacts every half turn (using a split-ring commutator) *[1 mark]* so the forces on the loop always act in a way that keeps the loop rotating *[1 mark]*.

Biology Practice Paper 1
1.1 cell membrane *[1 mark]*
1.2 *E. coli* bacteria *[1 mark]*
1.3 image size = magnification × real size
= 150 × 0.054
= **8.1 mm**
[2 marks for correct answer, otherwise 1 mark for correct working]

1.4 How to grade your answer:
Level 0: No relevant information is given. *[No marks]*
Level 1: There is a brief comparison of plant and animal cells, including at least one similarity and one difference. *[1 to 2 marks]*
Level 2: There is a comparison of plant and animal cells, including at least two similarities and two differences. Some descriptions of subcellular structures are included. *[3 to 4 marks]*
Level 3: There is a detailed comparison of plant and animal cells, including at least three similarities and three differences. Detailed descriptions of subcellular structures are included.
[5 to 6 marks]
Here are some points your answer may include:
Similarities:
Both plant and animal cells have a nucleus, which controls the cell's activities.
Both plant and animal cells contain cytoplasm, which is where most of the cell's chemical reactions take place.
Plant cells and animal cells both have a cell membrane, which controls what goes in and out of the cell.
Mitochondria are found in both plant cells and animal cells — these are where most of the reactions for aerobic respiration take place.
Both plant cells and animal cells have ribosomes, which are where proteins are made.
Differences:
Chloroplasts, the site of photosynthesis, are present in plant cells, but not in animal cells.
Plant cells have a cell wall, which supports and strengthens the cell, but animal cells do not.
Plant cells contain a permanent vacuole, containing cell sap, but animal cells do not.
2.1 By droplets from an infected person's sneeze or cough *[1 mark]*.
2.2 How to grade your answer:
Level 0: There is no relevant information. *[No marks]*
Level 1: There are some relevant points explaining how vaccination helps to protect the body against disease but the answer is missing some detail.
[1 to 2 marks]
Level 2: There is a clear, detailed explanation of how vaccination helps to protect the body against disease. *[3 to 4 marks]*
Here are some points your answer may include:
The body is injected with small amounts of dead or inactive pathogens (which are harmless).
These carry antigens, which cause the white blood cells in the body to produce antibodies.
Antibodies attack/kill the pathogens.
If live pathogens of the same type appear again, the white blood cells can rapidly mass-produce antibodies to kill the pathogens so the person doesn't get ill.
2.3 Any two from: e.g. stop the mosquitoes from breeding / protect people from mosquito bites using mosquito nets / protect people from mosquito bites by using insecticides (to kill the mosquitoes) *[2 marks]*.
3.1 biuret solution *[1 mark]*
3.2 Benedict's solution *[1 mark]*
3.3 A *[1 mark]*
3.4 It is covered in many villi that provide a large surface area for diffusion (and active transport) to occur across *[1 mark]*. The villi have a thin wall/single layer of surface cells, which decreases the distance for diffusion to occur across *[1 mark]*. They also have a good blood supply to assist quick absorption *[1 mark]*.
3.5 Their blood sugar level will not rise very much or not rise at all *[1 mark]*. This is because a person with lactose intolerance has little or no lactase to break down the lactose in the drink, so there will be little or no sugar to be absorbed from the small intestine *[1 mark]*.

Answers

4.1 The blood supply to the area below the blockage would be cut off/reduced *[1 mark]*. Not enough oxygen would reach this part of the heart muscle, resulting in cells being unable to respire/damage/death of the muscle tissue/a heart attack *[1 mark]*.

4.2 A stent will keep the coronary artery open, making sure that enough blood can reach the heart muscle *[1 mark]*.

4.3 To make sure it did not cause any harmful side effects when the body is working normally *[1 mark]*.

4.4 E.g. a control/placebo was used *[1 mark]*.

4.5 How to grade your answer:
Level 0: No relevant information is given. *[No marks]*
Level 1: At least one advantage or disadvantage of each treatment method is given. No logical conclusion has been made. *[1 to 2 marks]*
Level 2: At least one advantage and disadvantage of each treatment method is clearly described. An attempt has been made to come to a logical conclusion. *[3 to 4 marks]*
Level 3: There is a detailed description of the advantages and disadvantages of each treatment method. A clear and justified conclusion has been made. *[5 to 6 marks]*

Here are some points your answer may include:
Advantages of a donor heart:
A donor heart is likely to work better than an artificial heart.
A donor heart may be more of a permanent treatment than an artificial heart.
Disadvantages of a donor heart:
There may be a long wait for a suitable donor heart to become available.
There is a greater risk that a donor heart will be rejected by the immune system, compared to an artificial heart.
There is a risk of bleeding and infection due to the transplant surgery.
Advantages of an artificial heart:
An artificial heart can be used as a temporary fix, which may mean that the person's heart can continue to be used once it has had time to rest and heal.
An artificial heart can be available as soon as a person needs it.
An artificial heart is less likely to be rejected by the immune system compared to a donor heart.
Disadvantages of an artificial heart:
There is a risk of bleeding and infection due to the surgery needed to fit an artificial heart.
An artificial heart doesn't work as well as a healthy natural heart — for example, parts of it may wear out or the electrical motor could fail.
Blood doesn't flow as smoothly through an artificial heart as it does through a natural heart. This increases the risk of blood clots, which can lead to strokes.
Blood thinning drugs have to be taken after treatment with an artificial heart, which can cause problems with bleeding if the person is hurt in an accident.

5.1 It is broken down into sugars/maltose *[1 mark]*.

5.2 E.g. they could have added the sample to a drop of iodine solution (e.g. in a well of a spotting tile) *[1 mark]*. If starch was present the iodine solution would have changed to blue-black *[1 mark]*. If starch was no longer present, the iodine solution would have remained browny-orange *[1 mark]*.

5.3 Time of reaction at 40 °C = 100 s.
Rate = 1000 ÷ 100 = **10 s^{-1}** *[2 marks for correct answer, otherwise 1 mark for correct working.]*

5.4 The temperature was too high *[1 mark]*, causing the enzyme to denature / the shape of the enzyme's active site to change *[1 mark]*. This means the starch could no longer fit in the active site of the enzyme, so it could not be broken down *[1 mark]*.

5.5 The result for 20 °C is anomalous *[1 mark]* because the time taken until starch is no longer present is quicker than expected/quicker than at 30 or 40 °C *[1 mark]*. To cause this result, the student may not have used the correct volume of starch/amylase solution. / The student may have started timing the experiment too late. / The student may have stopped the experiment too early *[1 mark]*.

5.6 By using buffer solutions with a range of different pH values *[1 mark]*.

6.1 E.g. day 2 was less bright, so the stomata weren't fully open and so less water could move out of the leaves. / Day 2 was colder, so the water evaporated/diffused more slowly. / Day 2 was less windy, so the water vapour was carried away more slowly, meaning that diffusion couldn't happen as quickly. / Day 2 was wetter/more humid, so there was a smaller diffusion gradient between the inside and outside of the leaf so diffusion couldn't happen as quickly *[1 mark for reason, 1 mark for explanation]*.

The rate of transpiration varies throughout the day due to the changing light intensity, but it can also be affected by the temperature, the air flow and the humidity around the leaves.

6.2 The plant has lost too much water/has lost water faster than it could be replaced through the roots *[1 mark]*.

6.3 Transpiration creates a slight shortage of water in the leaf *[1 mark]*. More water is drawn up from the rest of the plant through the xylem vessels to replace it *[1 mark]*. This in turn means that more water is drawn up from the roots, and so there's a constant transpiration stream of water through the plant *[1 mark]*.

7 How to grade your answer:
Level 0: No relevant information is given. *[No marks]*
Level 1: There is a basic description of at least two of the stages of the cell cycle or a suggestion of why disrupting the cell cycle may kill plants is stated. *[1 to 2 marks]*
Level 2: There is a clear description of at least two stages of the cell cycle and a suggestion of why disrupting the cell cycle may kill plants is stated. *[3 to 4 marks]*
Level 3: There is a detailed description of each stage of the cell cycle and a suggestion of why disrupting the cell cycle may kill plants is stated. *[5 to 6 marks]*

Here are some points your answer may include:
The cell cycle involves the division of cells to form two identical cells.
Before division takes place the cell grows and increases the amount of subcellular structures it has, such as mitochondria and ribosomes.
It then duplicates its DNA so there's one copy for each new cell.
Next, mitosis takes place. The chromosomes line up at the centre of the cell and cell fibres pull them apart. The two arms of each chromosome go to opposite ends of the cell. Membranes form around each of the sets of chromosomes to become the nuclei of the two new cells. Finally the cytoplasm and cell membrane divide so two identical daughter cells are formed.
Disrupting the cell cycle can kill plants as plants are multicellular organisms which use mitosis to grow and to replace damaged cells. If they can no longer do this, they may die.

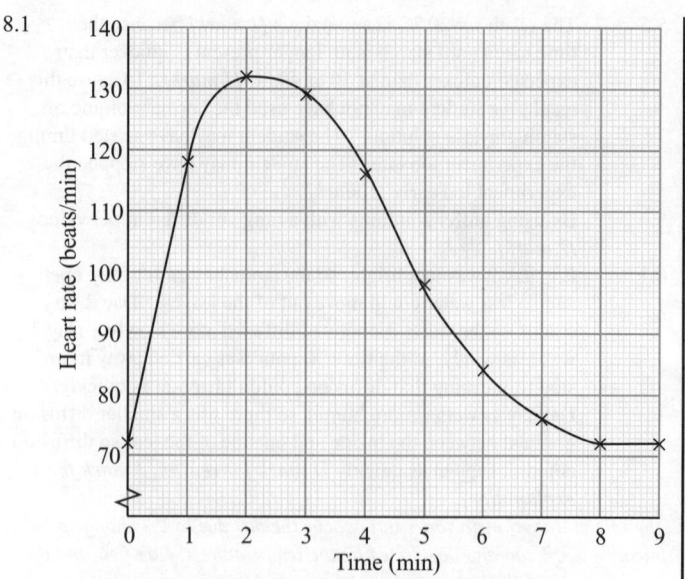

8.1 [Graph: Heart rate (beats/min) vs Time (min). Curve rises from ~70 at 0 min to peak ~132 at 2 min, then decreases through ~130 at 3, ~117 at 4, ~98 at 5, ~84 at 6, ~76 at 7, ~72 at 8 and 9 min.]

[1 mark for label and suitable scale for the x-axis, 2 marks for all points correctly plotted (or 1 mark for 8 points plotted correctly), 1 mark for a smooth curve of best fit.]

8.2 95 beats/min *[1 mark. Allow any value correctly read from 30 seconds on your own graph.]*

8.3 The student's heart rate increases during exercise *[1 mark]*. This is because when he exercises he needs more energy, so he respires more *[1 mark]*. Increased respiration means that his cells need more oxygen *[1 mark]*, so his heart rate increases so that the blood flows more quickly to the cells to deliver oxygen *[1 mark]*.

Biology Practice Paper 2

1.1 B *[1 mark]*
1.2 The thyroid gland releases thyroxine directly into the blood *[1 mark]*. Thyroxine then travels in the bloodstream to its target organ/the heart *[1 mark]*.
1.3 It produces hormones that act on other glands *[1 mark]*, which directs them to release hormones that bring about change *[1 mark]*.
2.1 21 *[1 mark]*
To find the median, you write out all the results from lowest to highest, e.g. 10, 21, 21, 35, 37. 21 is in the middle of the list, so it is the median.
2.2 (6 + 15 + 9 + 14 + 20 + 5 + 3 + 11 + 10 + 7) ÷ 10
= 100 ÷ 10
= **10 buttercups per m²** *[2 marks for correct answer, otherwise 1 mark for correct working.]*
2.3 90 × 120 = 10 800 m² *[1 mark]*
10 × 10 800 = **108 000 buttercups** *[1 mark]*
Allow incorrect value from 2.2.
2.4 E.g. more buttercups grow where there is a higher moisture level in the soil *[1 mark]*.
2.5 How to grade your answer:
Level 0: There is no relevant information. *[No marks]*
Level 1: There is a brief description of how the student could investigate whether the change in distribution of buttercups is due to variability in the moisture level of the soil. *[1 to 2 marks]*
Level 2: There is a detailed description of how the student could investigate whether the change in distribution of buttercups is due to variability in the moisture level of the soil. *[3 to 4 marks]*
Here are some points your answer may include:
He could use a transect across Field A.
To do this he should mark out a line across the field.
Then he should record the number of buttercups in quadrats placed next to each other/at intervals along the line.
He should also measure the moisture level of the soil at each sampling point (e.g. with a probe).
3.1 *Biston* *[1 mark]*
3.2 the dark variety *[1 mark]*
3.3 The dark variety is less likely to be eaten by predators in soot polluted areas (because they are better camouflaged) *[1 mark]* so they are more likely to survive to reproduce *[1 mark]*, meaning that the genes for the characteristics that made them successful / genes for dark colouring are more likely to be passed on to the next generation and become more common in the population *[1 mark]*.
4.1 Their reaction time was very fast *[1 mark]*.
Their response was involuntary/automatic *[1 mark]*.
If you have to think about what response to give then it's not a reflex action.
4.2 reaction time *[1 mark]*
4.3 sex *[1 mark]*
4.4 The males in this experiment had a faster mean reaction time than the females *[1 mark]*, so the data supports the scientist's hypothesis *[1 mark]*.
4.5 E.g. the age of the participants *[1 mark]*. / The strength of the tap on the knee *[1 mark]*. / Caffeine consumption of the participants prior to the investigation *[1 mark]*.
4.6 relay neurone *[1 mark]*
4.7 How to grade your answer:
Level 0: There is no relevant information. *[No marks]*
Level 1: There is a brief description of some parts of the path taken by a nervous impulse in the reflex. *[1 to 2 marks]*
Level 2: There is some description of the path taken by a nervous impulse in the reflex, but some detail is missing. *[3 to 4 marks]*
Level 3: There is a clear and detailed description of the path taken by a nervous impulse in the reflex. *[5 to 6 marks]*
Here are some points your answer may include:
The impulse travels along a sensory neurone to the central nervous system/spinal cord.
When the impulse reaches a synapse between the sensory neurone and a relay neurone, it triggers chemicals to be released.
These chemicals cause impulses to be sent along the relay neurone.
When the impulse reaches a synapse between the relay neurone and a motor neurone, chemicals are released again which cause impulses to be sent along the motor neurone. The impulse then reaches the muscle, which contracts to curl the big toe upwards.
5.1 The entire set of genetic material in an organism *[1 mark]*.
5.2 Knowing more about the cystic fibrosis gene could help us to understand the disorder better / develop effective treatments for it *[1 mark]*.
5.3 E.g.

mother's alleles

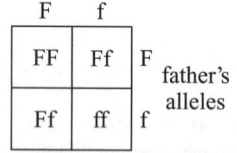

	F	f
F	FF	Ff
f	Ff	ff

father's alleles

ff offspring has cystic fibrosis.
Probability = 0.25 / 25% / 1:3 / 1 in 4 / ¼
[1 mark for correctly identifying parents' genotypes, 1 mark for correctly identifying possible genotypes of the offspring, 1 mark for correctly identifying cystic fibrosis genotype, 1 mark for identifying the correct probability of a child having cystic fibrosis.]
The parents must both be carriers, since neither of them show any sign of the disorder. This means they both have one copy of the recessive allele for cystic fibrosis — so they're both Ff.
5.4 Homozygous, because he has two alleles the same / both of his alleles are recessive *[1 mark]*.
6.1 The HBsAg gene codes for the hepatitis B antigen *[1 mark]*.
6.2 How to grade your answer:
Level 0: There is no relevant information. *[No marks]*
Level 1: There are some relevant points describing the process by which organisms are genetically engineered but the answer is missing some detail. *[1 to 2 marks]*

7.1 Any three from: e.g. sexual reproduction involves the fusion of male and female gametes whereas asexual reproduction doesn't involve gametes. / Sexual reproduction involves two parents whereas asexual reproduction only involves one parent. / Sexual reproduction produces offspring that are genetically different to their parents whereas asexual reproduction produces offspring that are genetically identical to their parents (clones). / Sexual reproduction produces offspring that are genetically different to each other whereas asexual reproduction produces offspring that are genetically identical. *[3 marks]*

Level 2: There is a clear, detailed description of the process by which organisms are genetically engineered. *[3 to 4 marks]*
Here are some points your answer may include:
Enzymes are used to isolate/cut the useful gene from one organism's genome.
The gene is then inserted into a vector such as a virus or a bacterial plasmid.
When the vector is introduced to a target organism, the useful gene is inserted into its cells.

7.2 testosterone *[1 mark]*
7.3 It causes the lining of the uterus to grow *[1 mark]*. It also stimulates the release of luteinising hormone (LH) and inhibits the release of follicle stimulating hormone (FSH) *[1 mark]*.
7.4 C *[1 mark]* — e.g. because the level corresponds to the thickness of the uterus lining, which is maintained by progesterone *[1 mark]*.
There are a few different ways that you can tell that this line represents progesterone. As long as you're able to justify your answer, you'll get the marks.
7.5 Advantages of the implant: e.g. it works for three years / protection is always available / you do not have to remember to take a pill every day / it is highly effective.
Disadvantages of the implant: e.g. it has to be inserted by a doctor or nurse which may be painful/inconvenient / if certain medications are taken, a different contraceptive method would have to be used / you could suffer from side effects / it does not protect against STDs.
Advantages of the condom: e.g. it protects against STDs / there are no side effects / it is highly effective if used correctly / it is not affected by medication.
Disadvantages of the condom: e.g. it needs to be available at the time of intercourse / if it isn't used correctly it may not be effective / it can only be used once.
[3 marks for at least one advantage and one disadvantage of each method, otherwise 2 marks for at least two advantages or disadvantages of either method or 1 mark for one advantage or disadvantage of either method. 1 mark for giving a justified conclusion that refers to at least one advantage and one disadvantage of the chosen method.]

8.1 At point X, CO_2 is being removed from the atmosphere by photosynthesis *[1 mark]*. At point Y, CO_2 is being released into the atmosphere by plants and animals respiring *[1 mark]*. At point Z, carbon compounds in the plants are being transferred to animals as they eat the plants *[1 mark]*.
8.2 Microorganisms break down waste products and dead organisms *[1 mark]* and release carbon dioxide into the atmosphere as they respire *[1 mark]*.
8.3 The two sets of data show the same pattern/increase at the same time *[1 mark]*.
8.4 Any two from: e.g. the two things may follow similar patterns by chance. / Some other factor may have caused both increases. / The concentration of carbon dioxide varied even when human population was low/fairly constant. *[2 marks]*
8.5 Any two from: e.g. to increase the amount of land available for farming cattle. / To increase the amount of land available for rice crops. / To increase the amount of land available for growing crops from which biofuels are produced *[2 marks]*.
8.6 Any two from: e.g. habitats in low-lying areas will be lost due to rising sea levels *[1 mark]*. / The distribution of organisms could change due to changes in temperature and rainfall *[1 mark]*. / Biodiversity could be reduced *[1 mark]*. / There could be changes in migration patterns (e.g. some birds may migrate further north) *[1 mark]*.

Chemistry Practice Paper 1

1.1 +1 *[1 mark]*
1.2 Any two from: e.g. potassium fizzes more than sodium, which fizzes more than lithium / potassium moves more quickly than sodium, which moves more quickly than lithium / potassium melts and a flame is seen, sodium melts but no flame is seen and lithium does not melt *[1 mark for each correct observation]*.
1.3 As you go down Group 1 the outer electron gets further from the nucleus *[1 mark]*. This means that the outer electron is more easily lost because it feels less attraction from the nucleus *[1 mark]*. So reactivity increases as you go down Group 1/from lithium to sodium to potassium *[1 mark]*.
1.4 $2Li + 2H_2O \rightarrow$ **$2LiOH + H_2$**
[1 mark for formulas of both products correct, 1 mark for correct balancing]
1.5 It contains hydroxide ions *[1 mark]*.
1.6 Protons = 9 *[1 mark]*
Neutrons = 19 − 9 = 10 *[1 mark]*
Electrons = 9 *[1 mark]*
Remember: number of protons = atomic number, number of neutrons = mass number − atomic number, number of electrons (in a neutral atom) = number of protons.

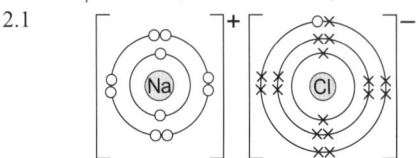

2.1 *[1 mark for adding seven crosses and one dot to outer shell of Cl⁻ ion, 1 mark for correct charge on both ions.]*
2.2 The molecules in substance A are only attracted to each other by weak intermolecular forces *[1 mark]* which don't need much energy to break/overcome *[1 mark]*.
2.3 Substance C *[1 mark]*. It has a high melting and boiling point and can conduct electricity when molten or dissolved but not when solid *[1 mark]*.
2.4 How to grade your answer:
Level 0: There is no relevant information. *[No marks]*
Level 1: A brief attempt is made to explain one or two of these properties in terms of structure and bonding. *[1 to 2 marks]*
Level 2: Some explanation of three or four of the properties, in terms of their structure and bonding, is given. *[3 to 4 marks]*
Level 3: Clear and detailed explanation of all three of the properties, in terms of their structure and bonding, is given. *[5 to 6 marks]*
Here are some points your answer may include:
Diamond
Each carbon atom in diamond forms four covalent bonds in a rigid giant covalent structure/tetrahedral lattice, making it very hard.
Because it is made up of lots of covalent bonds, which take a lot of energy to break, diamond has a very high melting point.
There are no free/delocalised electrons in the structure of diamond, so it can't conduct electricity.
Graphite
Each carbon atom in graphite forms three covalent bonds, creating sheets of carbon atoms that can slide over each other.
The carbon layers are only held together weakly, which is what makes graphite soft and slippery.
The covalent bonds between the carbon atoms take a lot of energy to break, giving graphite a very high melting point.
Only three out of each carbon's four outer electrons are used in bonds, so graphite has lots of free/delocalised electrons and can conduct electricity.

3.1 Any two from: e.g. have a lid on the beaker / use insulation (e.g. cotton wool) around the beaker / use a polystyrene beaker *[1 mark for each correct answer]*.
3.2 1 °C *[1 mark]*
3.3 37.5 °C *[1 mark]*

3.4 Temperature change = final temperature − initial temperature
= 37.5 − 17 = **20.5 °C**
[2 marks for correct answer, otherwise 1 mark for writing a correct expression for calculating the temperature change.]
If your answer to 4.3 was wrong, you can still have both marks for correctly subtracting 17 from it to find the temperature change.

3.5 The reaction was exothermic as the temperature of the surroundings increased during the reaction *[1 mark]*.

4.1 Reaction D *[1 mark]*. The most reactive metal will react fastest with the acid *[1 mark]*. In reaction D the largest volume of gas has been collected in the syringe / the most bubbles are being given off *[1 mark]*.

4.2 e.g. zinc *[1 mark]*
You would get this mark if you named any metal between magnesium and iron in the reactivity series (for example, aluminium would be fine here too).

4.3

	Did any reaction occur with:		
	iron sulfate	magnesium sulfate	copper sulfate
iron	No	No	Yes
magnesium	Yes	No	Yes
copper	No	No	No

[1 mark for each correct answer]

4.4 $Mg_{(s)} + Cu^{2+}_{(aq)} \rightarrow Mg^{2+}_{(aq)} + Cu_{(s)}$
[1 mark for the correct reactants, 1 mark for the correct products]

5.1 $ZnCl_2$ *[1 mark]*

5.2 How to grade your answer:
Level 0: There is no relevant information *[No marks]*
Level 1: Statements showing some understanding of the method with some techniques named.
[1 to 2 marks]
Level 2: Brief description of the main steps of preparation in order, including filtration, evaporation/crystallisation and drying.
[3 to 4 marks]
Level 3: Detailed description of all correct steps in order.
[5 to 6 marks]
Here are some points your answer may include:
Addition of zinc oxide to hydrochloric acid
Gently warm the dilute hydrochloric acid using a Bunsen burner, then turn off the Bunsen burner.
Add the zinc oxide a bit at a time until no more reacts.
The zinc oxide is now in excess.
Filtration to remove excess zinc oxide
Pour the mixture into a filter funnel lined with filter paper and collect the aqueous solution of zinc chloride.
Crystallisation
Heat the solution using a water bath or an electric heater to evaporate some of the water.
Leave the solution to cool, allowing crystals of zinc chloride to form.
Drying
Filter the zinc chloride crystals out of the remaining solution and leave the crystals to dry.

5.3 sodium chloride *[1 mark]*

5.4 carbon dioxide *[1 mark]*

5.5 E.g. test a sample of the solution using universal indicator paper / test the solution using a pH probe. If the paper turns green / the probe shows a pH of seven, then the solution is neutral.
[1 mark for any sensible method you could use to test the pH of the solution, 1 mark for a correct, matching observation of what that method would show if the solution was neutral.]

6.1 Oxygen is being removed from the metal oxide / Fe^{3+} ions (iron(III) ions) are gaining electrons *[1 mark]*.

6.2 M_r of $Fe_2O_3 = (2 \times 56) + (3 \times 16) = 160$
Moles of Fe_2O_3 = mass ÷ M_r = 40 ÷ 160 = 0.25
From the balanced equation you know that 2 moles of Fe_2O_3 produce 4 moles of Fe. So 0.25 moles of Fe_2O_3 will produce $0.25 \times 2 = 0.50$ moles of Fe.
Mass of Fe = moles × A_r = 0.50×56 = **28 g**
[4 marks for correct answer, otherwise 1 mark for M_r of Fe_2O_3, 1 mark for number of moles of Fe_2O_3, 1 mark for number of moles of Fe.]

6.3 Aluminium is more reactive than carbon/above carbon in the reactivity series *[1 mark]*. Reduction with carbon can only be used to extract metals that are less reactive than carbon/below carbon in the reactivity series *[1 mark]*.

6.4 In pure iron, the atoms are arranged in layers *[1 mark]*. These layers can slide over each other freely *[1 mark]*. Steel also contains carbon atoms, which are a different size to the iron atoms *[1 mark]*. The carbon atoms distort the layers, so they can't slide over one another so easily *[1 mark]*.

7.1 In a solution of copper sulfate, the ions are free to move and carry an electric charge *[1 mark]*. When copper sulfate is solid, the ions are held in fixed positions and can't move *[1 mark]*.

7.2 Cu^{2+}, SO_4^{2-}, H^+, OH^- *[1 mark]*
The Cu^{2+} and SO_4^{2-} ions come from the ionic compound. The H^+ and OH^- ions come from the water.

7.3 $4OH^- \rightarrow O_2 + 2H_2O + 4e^-$ *[1 mark]*

7.4 Mean change of mass for negative electrode
= $(2.36 + 2.71 + 2.55) \div 3$ = **2.54** *[1 mark]*

7.5 At the negative electrode, copper ions/Cu^{2+} ions are being reduced to copper metal/Cu *[1 mark]*. The half equation for this reaction is: $Cu^{2+} + 2e^- \rightarrow Cu$ *[1 mark]*. So a layer of copper metal forms on the negative electrode during the electrolysis *[1 mark]*.

7.6 The negative electrode would change in mass by twice as much *[1 mark]*.

Chemistry Practice Paper 2

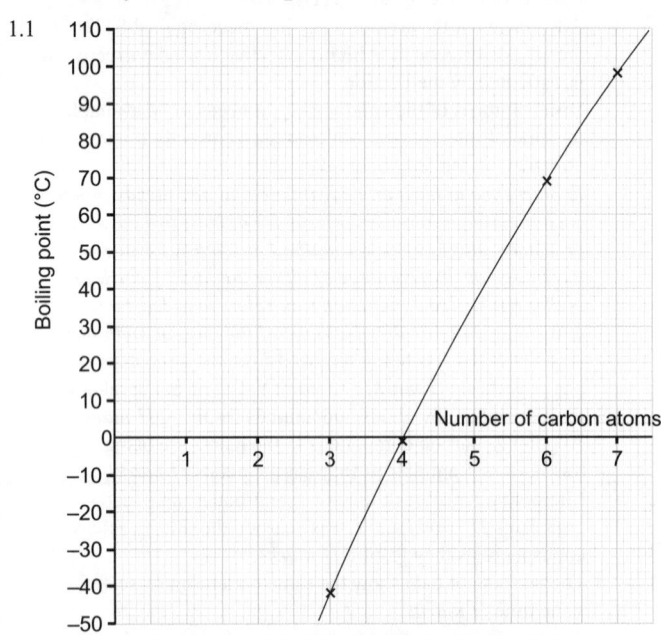

1.1 [graph of boiling point vs number of carbon atoms, points plotted at approximately (3, −42), (4, 0), (6, 69), (7, 98)]

[1 mark for all four points correctly plotted, 1 mark for a smooth curve that passes through all the points]

1.2 36 °C *[1 mark for any answer in the range 34-38 °C]*

1.3 C_nH_{2n+2} *[1 mark]*

1.4
```
    H H H
    | | |
H − C−C−C − H
    | | |
    H H H
```
[1 mark]

1.5 Add a few drops of bromine water to both compounds and shake *[1 mark]*. With propane, nothing will happen *[1 mark]*. Propene will decolourise the bromine water / turn the solution from orange to colourless *[1 mark]*.

1.6 $C_3H_8 + 5O_2 \rightarrow 3CO_2 + $ **4H$_2$O**
[1 mark for correctly giving H$_2$O as the missing product, 1 mark for correct number of moles of H$_2$O.]

2.1 As the level of nitrogen dioxide increases, the severity of asthma attacks increases / there is a positive correlation between nitrogen dioxide levels and severity of asthma attacks *[1 mark]*

2.2 The sample of people that the scientists collected data from was too big *[1 mark]*.

2.3 Oxides of nitrogen are formed when nitrogen and oxygen from the air react at high temperatures *[1 mark]*. This happens in car engines (which operate at high enough temperatures for nitrogen oxides to form) *[1 mark]*. In cities, there are lots of cars, so the levels of nitrogen oxides tend to be higher *[1 mark]*.

2.4 e.g. sulfur dioxide *[1 mark]*

3.1 E.g. they don't have enough fresh water / groundwater / surface water to treat and use as drinking water *[1 mark]*.

3.2 Desalination *[1 mark]*

3.3 How to grade your answer:
 Level 0: There is no relevant information *[No marks]*
 Level 1: There is a brief description of the method to distil seawater, but many details are missing or incorrect. *[1 to 2 marks]*
 Level 2: There is some explanation of the method used to distil sea water. Most of the information is correct, but a few small details may be incorrect or missing. *[3 to 4 marks]*
 Level 3: There is a clear, detailed and fully correct explanation of the method used to distil sea water in the lab. *[5 to 6 marks]*
Here are some points your answer may include:
Pour the sea water into a (round bottom) flask.
Attach the flask to a condenser and secure both with clamps.
Connect a supply of cold water to the condenser.
Place a beaker under the condenser to collect the fresh water.
Place a Bunsen burner under the round bottom flask and heat the sea water slowly.
The water will boil and form steam.
The steam will condense back to pure liquid water in the condenser and be collected in the beaker as it runs out.
Continue to heat the (round bottom) flask until you have collected a reasonable amount of pure water.

3.4 Large bits of material (such as grit) are removed from the sewage *[1 mark]*.

3.5 The effluent undergoes aerobic biological treatment *[1 mark]*. Air is added to encourage aerobic bacteria to break down any organic matter that is present *[1 mark]*.

4.1 nitrogen *[1 mark]*

4.2 Algae and plants evolved to carry out photosynthesis *[1 mark]*. During photosynthesis carbon dioxide is absorbed, so the amount of carbon dioxide in the atmosphere decreased *[1 mark]*. Photosynthesis also produces oxygen, so the amount of oxygen in the atmosphere increased *[1 mark]*.

4.3 Deforestation — e.g. plants take carbon dioxide out of the atmosphere, so removing trees causes carbon dioxide levels to rise *[1 mark]*.
Increased energy consumption — e.g. burning fossil fuels releases carbon dioxide into the atmosphere *[1 mark]*.
Increasing population — any one from: e.g. more people will be respiring and releasing carbon dioxide / more energy will be used (and carbon dioxide is released when fuels are burnt) / more land will be needed, so trees will have to be cut down, and less carbon dioxide will be removed from the air *[1 mark]*.

4.4 E.g. carbon dioxide is a greenhouse gas *[1 mark]*, so an increase in carbon dioxide in the atmosphere could lead to an increase in global temperatures/global warming *[1 mark]*. As temperatures rise, global food production could decrease due to more extreme weather events / loss of farming land available / water shortages *[1 mark]*.

5.1 Any two from: e.g. volume of acid / size of solid particles / temperature *[1 mark for each correct answer]*

5.2 Draw a tangent to the graph at 50 s, e.g.:

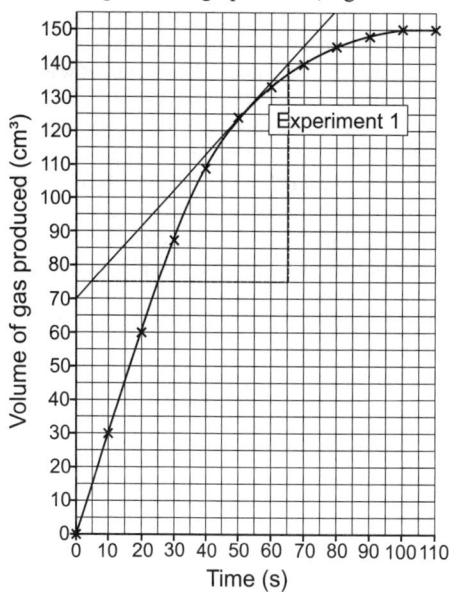

Then find the gradient of your tangent, e.g.:
Gradient of tangent = $\dfrac{\text{change in } y}{\text{change in } x} = \dfrac{(140 - 75)}{(65 - 5)}$
$= 65 \div 60 = 1.08...$
units = cm$^3 \div$ s = cm^3/s
rate of reaction at 50 s = **1.1 cm^3/s** (2 s.f.)
[4 marks in total — 1 mark for a correctly drawn tangent, 1 mark for gradient calculation, 1 mark for correct answer in the range 1 - 1.2, 1 mark for correct units]

5.3 The gradient of the graph at the start of the reaction is steeper for Experiment 2 *[1 mark]*.

5.4 Increasing the concentration of a reactant increases the number of particles of that substance in the reaction mixture *[1 mark]*. This increases the frequency of collisions between particles of the reactants, increasing the rate of the reaction *[1 mark]*.

5.5 $((0.39 + 0.55 + 0.45) \div 3) =$ **0.46 g** (2 s.f.)
[2 marks for correct answer, otherwise 1 mark for writing a correct expression that could be used to find the mean.]

5.6 The gas is carbon dioxide *[1 mark]*. The student should bubble the gas through/shake the gas with an aqueous solution of calcium hydroxide/lime water *[1 mark]*. If carbon dioxide is present the solution will turn cloudy *[1 mark]*.

6.1 How to grade your answer:
 Level 0: No relevant information. *[No marks]*
 Level 1: Response shows a basic understanding that more energy is used in mining and extracting metals from ores compared to recycling metals. An attempt is made to explain why recycling metals is more sustainable. *[1 to 2 marks]*
 Level 2: Response gives a clear understanding that more energy is used in mining and extracting metals from ores compared to recycling metals. Clear reasons are given for why recycling metals is more sustainable. *[3 to 4 marks]*
 Level 3: A clear and detailed response is given which demonstrates a clear understanding that more energy is used in mining and extracting metals from ores compared to recycling metals. The response gives clear and detailed ideas that support why recycling metals is more sustainable. *[5 to 6 marks]*.
Here are some points your answer may include:
Recycling of metals such as aluminium uses only a fraction of the energy required to extract new metals from ores.
Energy used to extract and recycle metals can come from burning fossil fuels which releases gases that contribute to global warming.
As the recycling of metals uses less energy than mining and extracting new metal it can result in less pollution being released into the environment.

6.1 Recycling metals conserves the amount of metal ores, which are finite resources, in the earth and this means the use of these metals is more sustainable. Recycling metals also reduces the amount of waste which goes to landfill.
6.2 Plants are grown in soil that contains copper *[1 mark]*. The plants can't use or get rid of the copper so it accumulates in their leaves *[1 mark]*. The plants can then be dried and burnt, which produces ash containing soluble copper compounds *[1 mark]*. Copper can then be extracted from these compounds by electrolysis / displacement using scrap iron *[1 mark]*.
7.1 The forward and reverse reactions are happening at exactly the same rate *[1 mark]*.
7.2 Le Chatelier's principle states that if you change the conditions of a reversible reaction at equilibrium the system will try to counteract that change *[1 mark]*.
7.3 The yield of sulfur trioxide will increase *[1 mark]*. When pressure is increased the position of equilibrium moves towards the side with fewer gas molecules *[1 mark]*. There are two molecules of gas on the right, compared to three on the left, so the position of equilibrium will move to the right *[1 mark]*.
7.4 catalyst *[1 mark]*
7.5 E.g. 15% of 7500 kg = 7500 × 0.15 = 1125 kg
new mass made in a day = 7500 + 1125 = 8625 kg
new mass made in 5 days = 8625 × 5 = **43 125 kg**
[3 marks for correct answer, otherwise 1 mark for finding the new mass made in a day and 1 mark for multiplying it by five to find the new mass made in five days.]

Physics Practice Paper 1

1.1 214 − 83 = **131 neutrons** *[1 mark]*
1.2 $^{222}_{86}$Rn *[1 mark]*
$^{210}_{83}$Bi *[1 mark]*
1.3 420 days *[1 mark]*
1.4 Half-life when activity drops to half original total.
Activity after 1 half-life = 80 ÷ 2 = 40 Bq
Using **Figure 2**, when activity = 40 Bq, time = 140 days.
Therefore, half-life = **140 days** *[1 mark]*
1.5 Contamination is when unwanted radioactive atoms are on or inside an object *[1 mark]*.
1.6 How to grade your answer:
Level 0: There is no relevant information. *[No marks]*
Level 1: There is a brief explanation on the dangers of alpha contamination and irradiation, but little to no comparison between them. The answer has little or no clear structure. *[1 to 2 marks]*
Level 2: There is a clear explanation and comparison of the dangers of contamination and irradiation by alpha sources. The answer is well structured. *[3 to 4 marks]*
Here are some points your answer may include:
Alpha radiation is strongly ionising.
If alpha radiation enters living cells, it can kill or damage them and cause cancer.
Contamination on the outside of the body by an alpha source could result in the ingestion of the alpha source.
If an alpha source is ingested, inside the body it is almost certain to be absorbed by living cells and cause damage.
The alpha radiation will do a lot of damage to a very localised area.
Irradiation by an alpha source is less dangerous than contamination by an alpha source.
Alpha radiation is easily absorbed by thin barriers (e.g. skin) or the air, so is unlikely to reach the body's delicate organs if the source is outside the body.
2.1 E.g. the current is higher in circuit A *[1 mark]*.
The total resistance is higher in circuit B *[1 mark]*.
2.2 power = potential difference × current / $P = VI$ *[1 mark]*
2.3 $P = 11 \times 0.30$ *[1 mark]* = **3.3 W** *[1 mark]*
2.4 The bulb in circuit A has a greater potential difference across it *[1 mark]* because in a series circuit, the potential difference from the power supply is shared between components *[1 mark]*.
2.5 The resistance decreases *[1 mark]*.
2.6 E.g. a car engine temperature sensor *[1 mark]*.
2.7

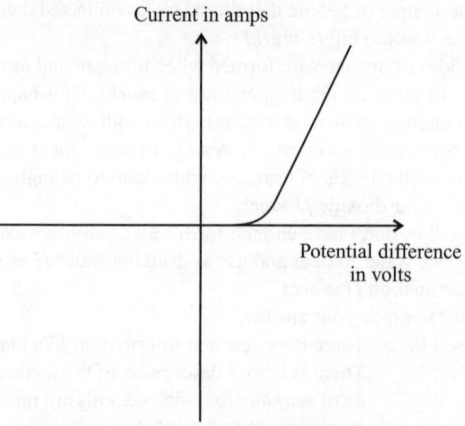

[1 mark for zero current at negative potential differences, 1 mark for curve into positive-gradient at a non-zero positive potential difference]

3.1 liquid *[1 mark]*
3.2 The internal energy of the substance increases *[1 mark]* as energy is transferred by heating to the (kinetic and potential) energy stores of the particles *[1 mark]*.
3.3 density = mass ÷ volume / $\rho = m \div V$ *[1 mark]*
3.4 $\rho = 0.36 \div (4 \times 10^{-4})$ *[1 mark]* = **900 kg/m³** *[1 mark]*
3.5 C *[1 mark]*
3.6 The line is flat because a change of state is occurring *[1 mark]* and all energy transferred to the substance is being used to break intermolecular bonds and change the state of the substance, and not increase its temperature *[1 mark]*.
3.7 thermal energy for a change of state = mass × specific latent heat / $E = mL$
So, $L = E \div m$ *[1 mark]*
$L = 69\,000 \div 1.5$ *[1 mark]* = **46 000 J/kg** *[1 mark]*

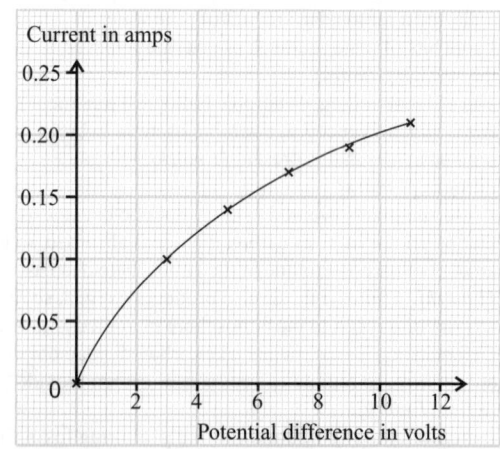

4.1

[1 mark for curved line close to all points and through the origin]

4.2 Any two of: e.g. to make sure her results were repeatable / to allow her to calculate a mean and obtain more precise results / to allow her to spot any anomalous results *[1 mark for each correct reason]*.
4.3 As an electrical charge flows through the lamp, energy is transferred to its thermal energy store *[1 mark]*. As the current increases, more energy is transferred electrically to the thermal energy store of the component, increasing the temperature *[1 mark]*. Resistance increases with temperature *[1 mark]*, and so resistance increases with increasing current *[1 mark]*.
4.4 potential difference = current × resistance / $V = IR$
So, $I = V \div R$ *[1 mark]* = $16 \div 64$ *[1 mark]* = 0.25 A *[1 mark]*
charge flow = current × time / $Q = It$
$Q = 0.25 \times 180$ *[1 mark]* = **45 C** *[1 mark]*

4.5 brown *[1 mark]*
4.6 If someone touches the live-wire, a large potential difference is produced across their body *[1 mark]* which causes a large current to flow through their body *[1 mark]*. This causes an electric shock which can severely injure them *[1 mark]*.
5.1 Bio-fuels = 6×10^9 kWh *[1 mark]*
Hydro-electric = 1×10^9 kWh *[1 mark]*
[Allow 1 mark only if the answers are 6 kWh and 1 kWh and ×10^9 is omitted]
5.2 wind power *[1 mark]*
5.3 Any one from: e.g. there are more hours of daylight in summer than in winter, so more electricity can be generated from solar power / there are generally more clear days during summer so more electricity can be generated from solar power *[1 mark]*.
5.4 Advantage: any one from: e.g. non-renewables are reliable / we can easily alter energy output to meet demand *[1 mark]*.
Disadvantage: any one from: e.g. non-renewables will eventually run out / burning some non-renewables, e.g. fossil fuels, produces pollutants / burning some non-renewables, e.g. fossil fuels, can contribute to global warming *[1 mark]*.
5.5 How to grade your answer:
Level 0: There is no relevant information. *[No marks]*
Level 1: Some comparison is made between the two sources, which indicates the use of some numerical analysis of the data provided. Any conclusions made may not be consistent with calculations shown. *[1 to 2 marks]*
Level 2: A coherent argument is made, showing clear comparison of the sources through use of numerical analysis of the data provided. A logical conclusion is drawn, which is supported by calculations. *[3 to 4 marks]*
Here are some points your answer may include:
Solar panels have a set up cost of £8000, while the national grid has no set-up cost.
Each year, solar panels maintenance costs £400 less than purchasing electricity from the national grid (£650).
After 20 years, the amount saved by using solar panels instead of buying electricity from the national grid will equal the solar panel's set-up cost.
Total maintenance cost over 30 years of solar panels
= 30 × 250 = £7500
Total cost of solar panels over 30 years = 7500 + 8000
= £15 500
Total cost of electricity from the national grid over 30 years
= 30 × 650 = £19 500
Solar panels will save 19 500 – 15 500 = £4000 in 30 years.
Solar panels are a cheaper source of electricity over the 30 year lifetime
OR
During the 30-year life span of the solar panels:
Total cost of solar panels = set-up cost +
(30 × annual maintenance cost)
= 8000 + (30 × 250) = £15 500
Total cost of electricity from national grid = 30 × annual cost
= 30 × 650
= £19 500
£15 500 < £19 500, so solar panels are a cheaper source of electricity.
6.1 diver A *[1 mark]*
6.2 From diver A's gravitational potential energy store to their kinetic energy store *[1 mark]*.
6.3 gravitational potential energy = mass × gravitational field strength (g) × height / $E_p = mgh$ *[1 mark]*
6.4 E_p = 65 × 9.8 × 10 *[1 mark]*
= 6370 J = **6400 J (to 2 s.f.)** *[1 mark]*
6.5 As the diver falls, energy is transferred from his gravitational potential energy store to his kinetic energy store, so the kinetic energy store graph slopes upwards as the g.p.e store graph slopes downwards *[1 mark]*. Due to conservation of energy, and as there are no resistive forces, the sum of the energy in the gravitational potential and kinetic energy stores at any given point between P and Q is constant (so the lines have the same, but opposite, gradient) *[1 mark]*.

6.6 kinetic energy = 0.5 × mass × (speed)^2 / $E_k = \frac{1}{2}mv^2$
No resistive forces, so by conservation of energy, all energy transferred from g.p.e. store goes to the kinetic energy store.
So, $E_p = E_k$ = 6370 J *[1 mark]*
So, $v = \sqrt{\frac{2E_k}{m}}$ *[1 mark]* = $\sqrt{\frac{2 \times 6370}{65}}$ *[1 mark]*
= **14 m/s** *[1 mark]*

Physics Practice Paper 2

1.1 X-rays aren't easily absorbed by tissues, but are absorbed by denser materials like bones and metal *[1 mark]*. The detector detects the X-rays transmitted at each point and creates a picture showing areas of tissue and bone *[1 mark]*.
1.2 Any one from, e.g. X-rays can be used to treat cancers / X-ray photographs can be used to diagnose bone fractures / X-ray photographs can be used to diagnose dental problems (problems with your teeth) *[1 mark]*.
1.3 amplitude = 7 squares tall
one square = 1 cm tall
amplitude = 7 × 1 = **7 cm** *[1 mark]*
1.4 E.g. frequency is the number of complete waves passing a certain point per second / the number of waves produced by a source each second *[1 mark]*.
1.5 E.g.

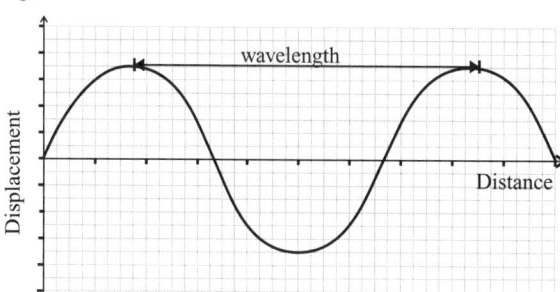

[1 mark for straight horizontal line drawn from a point on the wave to an equivalent point on the wave, labelled 'wavelength' or 'λ']
2.1 E.g. drag *[1 mark]*
2.2 Graph is linear between 15 s and 27 s.
27 – 15 = **12 s** *[1 mark]*
2.3 0 N *[1 mark]*
When an object is travelling at a constant speed in a fixed direction, all the forces are balanced and so the resultant force will be zero.
2.4 Speed is the gradient of a distance time graph.
change in y = 20 – 11 = 9 m
change in x = 27 – 15 = 12 s
speed = 9 ÷ 12 *[1 mark]* = **0.75 m/s** *[1 mark]*
2.5 Between 9 m and 10 m *[1 mark]*.
The swimmer is travelling fastest when the gradient of the graph is steepest. Of the options given, the graph is steepest between 9 m and 10 m. You can draw a tangent to see this more clearly.
2.6 Swimmer B accelerates during the first 2 m / between 0 m and 2 m / for the first 4 seconds *[1 mark]*.
They swim at a constant speed for the next 11 m / between 2 and 13 m / for the next 10 seconds *[1 mark]* and then undergo a period of deceleration for the next 2 m / between 13 m and 15 m / for the next 3 seconds *[1 mark]*.
They then swim at a slower constant speed than before for the next 5 m / between 15 m and 20 m / for the next 14 seconds *[1 mark]*. They then remain stationary, having reached the end of the pool (in 31 s) *[1 mark]*.
2.7 Swimmer A won the race *[1 mark]*.
3.1 Random errors *[1 mark]*
3.2 How to grade your answer:
Level 0: There is no relevant information. *[No marks]*
Level 1: There is a brief description of an experiment using the equipment shown. The answer lacks coherency. *[1 to 2 marks]*

Level 2:	There is a good description of an experiment which can be performed with the equipment shown, and some description of how the results should be processed to calculate the spring constant. The answer has some structure. *[3 to 4 marks]*	
Level 3:	There is a clear and detailed description of an experiment which can be performed using the equipment show, and of how the to calculate the spring constant from the resulting force-extension graph. The answer is well structured. *[5 to 6 marks]*	

Here are some points your answer may include:
Measure the mass of each of the masses using a mass balance.
Calculate the weight of each of the masses using weight = mass × gravitational field strength / $W = mg$.
Using the ruler, measure the length of the spring when it has no masses hanging from it (the unstretched length).
Hang a mass from the spring.
Record the force applied by the mass (the weight of the mass) and the new length of the spring.
Calculate the extension of the spring by subtracting the unstretched length from the new length.
Repeat these steps, increasing the mass hanging from the spring, recording the new weight and calculating the extension each time.
After you have a suitable number of points, plot your results on a force-extension graph, with force on the *y*-axis, and tension on the *x*-axis.
Draw a line of best fit on your results.
Identify the linear part of your graph.
Since force applied to spring = spring constant × extension / $F = ke$, $k = F \div e$, so the gradient of the linear part of the graph is equal to the spring constant.
Calculate the spring constant by calculating the gradient of the linear part of the graph.

3.3 The point beyond which the spring no longer obeys the relation force applied to spring = spring constant × extension / $F = ke$ *[1 mark]*.

3.4 Below the limit of proportionality (where the graph is linear) the spring obeys:
force applied to spring = spring constant × extension / $F = ke$
So, k = gradient = change in y ÷ change in x
change in y = 7.0 − 0 = 7.0 N
change in x = 3.5 − 0 = 3.5 cm = 0.035 m
[1 mark for an attempt to work out a change in x and y between points on the linear part of the graph]
k = 7.0 ÷ 0.035 *[1 mark]* = **200 N/m** *[1 mark]*

You'd get the marks here for using any values for the change in y and x, as long as they're from the linear part of the graph.

4.1 Weight = mass × gravitational field strength / $W = mg$ *[1 mark]*
4.2 W = 80.0 × 9.8 *[1 mark]* = **784 N** *[1 mark]*
4.3 Area under the graph = ~16 squares
(Allow between 15 and 17) *[1 mark]*
Each square = 30 × 10 = 300 m *[1 mark]*
Distance fallen = 16 × 300 *[1 mark]*
= **4800 m**
[1 mark, allow between 4500 m and 5100 m]

4.4
[1 mark for arrow pointing to the right, from the right side of the plane, the same length as the Driving Force arrow, 1 mark for labelling the right-pointing arrow 'Air Resistance', 1 mark for arrow pointing downwards from the middle of the plane, the same length as the Upthrust arrow, 1 mark for the downwards arrow labelled as 'Weight']

4.5 force = mass × acceleration / $F = ma$ *[1 mark]*
4.6 $F = ma$
so, $a = F \div m$ *[1 mark]*
= 48 000 ÷ 4000 *[1 mark]* = **12 m/s²** *[1 mark]*

5.1 23
36
73 *[1 mark for all three correct]*

5.2 Reaction times vary from person to person *[1 mark]*.
A sample needs to be large to be representative of the population *[1 mark]*.
To get a single representative value, it's a good idea to take an average from a large number of results.

5.3 The thinking distance is the distance the vehicle travels during the driver's reaction time *[1 mark]*.
The braking distance is the distance the car travels under the braking force *[1 mark]*.
Any three from: e.g. the thinking distance is increased if the driver is tired / the thinking distance is increased if the driver is under the influence of drugs or alcohol / the braking distance is increased in poor weather conditions / the braking distance is increased if the surface of the road has reduced friction (due to rain, snow, ice, etc) / the braking distance is increased by having worn or faulty brakes / the braking distance is increased by having worn or faulty tyres
[1 mark for each correct factor].

5.4 momentum = mass × velocity / $p = mv$ *[1 mark]*
5.5 p = 1000 × 30.0 *[1 mark]*
= **30 000 kgm/s²** *[1 mark]*

5.6 (final velocity)² − (initial velocity)² = 2 × acceleration × distance / $v^2 − u^2 = 2as$
So, $a = (v^2 − u^2) \div 2s$ *[1 mark]*
= (0 − 30²) ÷ (2 × 100) *[1 mark]*
= −4.5 m/s²
so deceleration = **4.5 m/s²** *[1 mark]*
Since the question asked for deceleration, you should ignore the minus sign when you give your answer.

6.1 *[1 mark]*

6.2
[1 mark for correct shape of field lines, 1 mark for at least 2 field lines, all correctly labelled with arrows, and no field lines crossing each other]

6.3 Coiling the wire into a solenoid brings the magnetic field lines around the wire close together, so that they all line up and are pointing in the same direction *[1 mark]*. The closer the magnetic field lines are, the stronger the magnetic field *[1 mark]* so the strength of the magnetic field around the wire is increased *[1 mark]*.

6.4 The metal bar won't feel any force *[1 mark]* because the current through it is parallel to the magnetic field *[1 mark]*.

6.5 force = magnetic flux density × current × length of conductor inside field / $F = BIl$
So, $l = F \div (BI)$ *[1 mark]*
= 0.45 ÷ (1.5 × 4.0) *[1 mark]*
= 0.075 m = (0.075 × 100) cm *[1 mark]*
= **7.5 cm** *[1 mark]*

Answers

Glossary

Abiotic factor	A non-living factor of the environment.
Acceleration	A change in velocity in a certain amount of time.
Accurate result	A result that is very close to the true answer.
Acid	A substance with a pH of less than 7 that forms H$^+$ ions in water.
Activation energy	The minimum amount of energy that reactant particles must have when they collide in order to react.
Active transport	The movement of particles against a concentration gradient (i.e. from an area of lower concentration to an area of higher concentration) using energy transferred during respiration.
Activity (radioactive)	The number of nuclei of a sample that decay per second.
Adaptation	A feature or characteristic that helps an organism to survive in its natural environment.
Aerobic respiration	Respiration taking place in the presence of oxygen.
Air resistance	The frictional force caused by air on a moving object.
Alkali	A substance with a pH of more than 7 that forms OH$^-$ ions in solution.
Alkali metal	An element in Group 1 of the periodic table. E.g. sodium, potassium etc.
Alkane	A saturated hydrocarbon with the general formula C_nH_{2n+2}. E.g. methane, ethane etc.
Alkene	An unsaturated hydrocarbon that contains a carbon-carbon double bond and has the general formula C_nH_{2n}. E.g. ethene, propene etc.
Allele	An alternative version of a gene.
Alloy	A metal that is a mixture of two or more metals, or a mixture involving metals and non-metals.
Alpha decay	A type of radioactive decay in which an alpha particle is given out from a decaying nucleus.
Alpha particle	A positively-charged particle made up of two protons and two neutrons (a helium nucleus).
Alpha particle scattering experiment	An experiment in which alpha particles were fired at gold foil to see if they were deflected. It led to the plum pudding model being abandoned in favour of the nuclear model of the atom.
Alternating current (ac)	Current that is constantly changing direction.
Alveolus	A tiny air sac in the lungs, where gas exchange occurs.
Amino acid	A small molecule that is a building block of proteins.
Ammeter	A component used to measure the current through a component. It is always connected in series with the component.
Amplitude	The maximum displacement of a point on a wave from its undisturbed position.
Anaerobic respiration	Respiration taking place in the absence of oxygen.
Angle of incidence	The angle the incoming ray makes with the normal at a boundary.
Angle of refraction	The angle a refracted ray makes with the normal when a wave refracts at a boundary.
Anion	A particle with a negative charge, formed when one or more electrons are gained.
Anomalous result	A result that doesn't seem to fit with the rest of the data.
Antibiotic	A drug used to kill or prevent the growth of bacteria.
Antibiotic resistance	When bacteria aren't killed by an antibiotic.
Antibody	A protein produced by white blood cells in response to the presence of an antigen.
Antigen	A molecule on the surface of a cell or a pathogen. Foreign antigens trigger white blood cells to produce antibodies.
Antitoxin	A protein produced by white blood cells that counteracts toxins made by invading bacteria.
Artery	A blood vessel that carries blood away from the heart.
Asexual reproduction	Where organisms reproduce by mitosis to produce genetically identical offspring.
Atmosphere	The layer of air that surrounds a planet.

Glossary

Atom	A neutral particle made up of protons and neutrons in the nucleus, with electrons surrounding the nucleus.
Atomic number	The number of protons in the nucleus of an atom. It's also known as proton number.
Avogadro constant	The number of particles in one mole of a substance, which is 6.02×10^{23}.
Base	A substance that reacts with acids in neutralisation reactions.
Behavioural adaptation	A way in which an organism behaves that helps it to survive in its environment.
Beta decay	A type of radioactive decay in which a beta particle is given out from a decaying nucleus.
Beta particle	A high-speed electron emitted in beta decay.
Bias	Unfairness in the way data is presented, possibly because the presenter is trying to make a particular point (sometimes without knowing they're doing it).
Binomial system	The system used in classification for naming organisms using a two-part Latin name.
Bio-fuel	A renewable energy resource made from plant products or animal dung.
Biodiversity	The variety of different species of organisms on Earth, or within an ecosystem.
Bioleaching	The process by which a metal is separated from its ore using bacteria.
Biotic factor	A living factor of the environment.
Bond energy	The amount of energy required to break a bond (or the amount of energy released when a bond is made).
Braking distance	The braking distance is the distance a vehicle travels after the brakes are applied until it comes to a complete stop, as a result of the braking force.
Calibrate	Measure something with a known quantity to see if the instrument being used to measure that quantity gives the correct value.
Capillary	A type of blood vessel involved in the exchange of materials at tissues.
Carbohydrase	A type of digestive enzyme that catalyses the breakdown of a carbohydrate into sugars.
Carbon footprint	A measure of the amounts of greenhouse gases released by a product, a service or an event.
Cardiovascular disease	Disease of the heart or blood vessels.
Catalyst	A substance that increases the speed of a reaction, without being changed or used up.
Categoric data	Data that comes in distinct categories, e.g. blood type (A+, B–, etc.), metals (copper, zinc, etc.).
Cation	A particle with a positive charge, formed when one or more electrons are lost.
Cell membrane	A membrane surrounding a cell, which holds it together and controls what goes in and out.
Cell wall	A structure surrounding some cell types, which gives strength and support.
Cellulose	A molecule which strengthens cell walls in plants and algae.
Central Nervous System (CNS)	The brain and spinal cord. It's where reflexes and actions are coordinated.
Chemical bond	The attraction of two atoms for each other, caused by the sharing or transfer of electrons.
Chlorophyll	A green substance found in chloroplasts which absorbs light for photosynthesis.
Chloroplast	A structure found in plant cells and algae. It is the site of photosynthesis.
Chromatogram	The pattern of spots formed as a result of separating a mixture using chromatography.
Chromatography	An analytical method used to separate the substances in a mixture based on how the components interact with a mobile phase and a stationary phase.
Chromosome	A long molecule of DNA found in the nucleus. Each chromosome carries many genes.
Climate change	A change in the Earth's climate. E.g. global warming, changing rainfall patterns etc.
Clinical trial	A set of drug tests on human volunteers.
Clone	An organism that is genetically identical to another organism.

Glossary

Closed system	A system where neither matter nor energy can enter or leave. The net change in total energy in a closed system is always zero.
Collision theory	The theory that in order for a reaction to occur, particles must collide with sufficient energy.
Combustion	An exothermic reaction between a fuel and oxygen.
Communicable disease	A disease that can spread between individuals.
Community	The populations of different species living in a habitat.
Compound	A substance made up of atoms of at least two different elements, chemically joined together.
Concentration	The amount of a substance in a certain volume of solution, given in units of 'units of amount of substance'/'units of volume'.
Conduction	A method of energy transfer by heating where vibrating particles transfer energy through a material by colliding with neighbouring particles and transferring energy between their kinetic energy stores.
Conservation of energy principle	Energy can be transferred usefully from one energy store to another, stored or dissipated — but it can never be created or destroyed.
Conservation of momentum	In a closed system, the total momentum before an event is the same as the total momentum after the event.
Contamination (radioactive)	The presence of unwanted radioactive atoms on or inside an object.
Continuous data	Numerical data that can have any value within a range (e.g. length, volume or temperature).
Contraceptive	A method of preventing pregnancy, which can be hormonal or non-hormonal.
Control experiment	An experiment that's kept under the same conditions as the rest of the investigation, but where the independent variable isn't altered.
Control variable	A variable in an experiment that is kept the same.
Convection	A method of energy transfer by heating in liquids and gases in which energetic particles move away from hotter regions to cooler regions.
Conversion factor	A number which you must multiply or divide a unit by to convert it to a different unit.
Coordination centre	An organ (e.g. the brain, spinal cord or pancreas) that processes information from receptors and organises a response from the effectors.
Coronary artery	A blood vessel which supplies blood to the heart muscle.
Coronary heart disease	A disease in which the coronary arteries are narrowed by the build up of fatty deposits.
Correlation	A relationship between two variables.
Covalent bond	A chemical bond formed when atoms share a pair of electrons.
Covalent substance	A substance where the atoms are held together by covalent bonds.
Cracking	The process that is used to break long-chain hydrocarbons down into shorter, more useful hydrocarbons. Two types of cracking are catalytic cracking and steam cracking.
Crystallisation	The formation of solid crystals as water evaporates from a solution. For example, salt solutions undergo crystallisation to form solid salt crystals.
Current	The flow of electric charge. The size of the current is the rate of flow of charge. Measured in amperes (A).
Cystic fibrosis	An inherited disorder of the cell membranes caused by a recessive allele.
Cytoplasm	A gel-like substance in a cell where most of the chemical reactions take place.
Deforestation	The cutting down of forests (large areas of trees).
Delocalised electron	An electron that isn't associated with a particular atom or bond and is free to move within a structure.
Density	A substance's mass per unit volume.
Dependent variable	The variable in an experiment that is measured.

Glossary

Diabetes	A condition that affects the body's ability to control its blood glucose level.
Differentiation	The process by which a cell becomes specialised for its job.
Diffusion	The spreading out of particles from an area of higher concentration to an area of lower concentration.
Diode	A circuit component that only allows current to flow through it in one direction. It has a very high resistance in the other direction.
Direct current (dc)	Current that always flows in the same direction.
Discrete data	Numerical data that can only take a certain value, with no in-between value (e.g. number of people).
Displacement	The straight-line distance and direction from an object's starting position to its finishing position.
Displacement reaction	A reaction where a more reactive element replaces a less reactive element in a compound.
Displayed formula	A chemical formula that shows the atoms in a covalent compound and all the bonds between them.
Distance-time graph	A graph showing how the distance travelled by an object changes over a period of time.
Distillation	A way of separating out a liquid from a mixture. You heat the mixture until the bit you want evaporates, then cool the vapour to turn it back into a liquid.
Distribution	Where organisms are found in a particular area.
DNA	Deoxyribonucleic acid. The molecule in cells that stores genetic information.
Dominant allele	The allele for the characteristic that's shown by an organism if two different alleles are present for that characteristic.
Double-blind trial	A clinical trial where neither the doctors nor the patients know who has received the drug and who has received the placebo until all the results have been gathered.
Drag	The frictional force caused by any fluid (a liquid or gas) on a moving object.
Earth wire	The green and yellow wire in an electrical cable that only carries current when there's a fault. It stops exposed metal parts of an appliance from becoming live.
Ecosystem	The interaction of a community of living organisms with the abiotic parts of their environment.
Effector	Either a muscle or gland which responds to nervous impulses.
Efficacy	Whether something, e.g. a drug, works or not.
Efficiency	The proportion of input energy transfer which is usefully transferred. Also the proportion of input power which is usefully output.
Elastic deformation	An object undergoing elastic deformation will return to its original shape and length once any forces being applied to it are removed.
Elastic object	An object which can be elastically deformed.
Elastic potential energy store	Anything that has been stretched or compressed, e.g. a spring, has energy in its elastic potential energy store.
Electrode	An electrical conductor which is submerged in the electrolyte during electrolysis.
Electrolysis	The process of breaking down a substance using electricity.
Electrolyte	A liquid or solution used in electrolysis to conduct electricity between the two electrodes.
Electromagnet	A solenoid with an iron core.
Electromagnetic (EM) spectrum	A continuous spectrum of all the possible wavelengths of electromagnetic waves.
Electron	A subatomic particle with a relative charge of -1.
Electron shell	A region of an atom that contains electrons. It's also known as an energy level.
Electronic structure	The number of electrons in an atom (or ion) of an element and how they are arranged.
Electrostatic force	A force of attraction between opposite charges.

Glossary

Element	A substance that is made up only of atoms with the same number of protons.
Empirical formula	A chemical formula showing the simplest possible whole number ratio of atoms in a compound.
Endothermic reaction	A reaction which takes in energy from the surroundings.
Energy level	A region of an atom that contains electrons. It's also known as an electron shell.
Energy store	A means by which an object stores energy. There are different types of energy store: thermal (or internal), kinetic, gravitational potential, elastic potential, chemical, magnetic, electrostatic and nuclear.
Enzyme	A protein that acts as a biological catalyst.
Equilibrium (physics)	A state in which all the forces acting on an object are balanced, so the resultant force is zero.
Equilibrium (reversible reactions)	The point at which the rates of the forward and backward reactions in a reversible reaction are the same, and so the amounts of reactants and products in the reaction container don't change.
Eukaryotic cell	A complex cell, such as a plant or animal cell.
Evolution	The changing of the inherited characteristics of a population over time.
Excretion	The removal of waste products from the body.
Exothermic reaction	A reaction which transfers energy to the surroundings.
Extinction	When no living individuals of a species remain.
Extremophile	An organism that's adapted to live in extreme conditions.
Fair test	A controlled experiment where the only thing that changes is the independent variable.
Family tree	A diagram that shows how a characteristic is inherited in a group of related people.
Feedstock	A raw material used to produce other substances through industrial processes.
Fermentation	The process of anaerobic respiration in yeast cells.
Fertilisation	The fusion of male and female gametes during sexual reproduction.
Fertility	The ability to conceive a child.
Filtration	A physical method used to separate an insoluble solid from a liquid.
Finite resource	A resource that isn't replaced at a quick enough rate to be considered replaceable.
Flammability	How easy it is to ignite a substance.
Fleming's left-hand rule	The rule used to work out the direction of the force produced by the motor effect. Your first finger points in the direction of the magnetic field, your second finger points in the direction of the current and your thumb points in the direction of the force (or motion).
Fluid	A substance that can flow — either a liquid or a gas.
Food security	Having enough food to feed the population.
Force	A push or a pull on an object caused by it interacting with something.
Formulation	A useful mixture with a precise purpose made by following a formula.
Fossil	The remains of an organism from many years ago, which is found in rock.
Fossil fuel	The fossil fuels are coal, oil and natural gas. They're non-renewable energy resources that we burn to generate electricity.
Fossil record	The history of life on Earth preserved as fossils.
Fraction	A group of hydrocarbons that condense together when crude oil is separated using fractional distillation. E.g. petrol, naphtha, kerosene etc.
Fractional distillation	A process that can be used to separate substances in a mixture according to their boiling points.
Free body diagram	A diagram that shows all the forces acting on an isolated object, the direction in which the forces are acting and their (relative) magnitudes.
Frequency	The number of complete waves passing a certain point per second. Measured in hertz, Hz.
Friction	A force that opposes an object's motion. It acts in the opposite direction to motion.

Glossary

Functional adaptation	Something that goes on inside an organism's body that helps it to survive in its environment.
Gamete	A sex cell, e.g. an egg cell or a sperm cell in animals.
Gamma decay	A type of radioactive decay in which a gamma ray is given out from a decaying nucleus.
Gamma ray	A high-frequency, short-wavelength electromagnetic wave.
Geiger-Müller tube	A particle detector that is used with a counter to measure count rate.
Gene	A short section of DNA, found on a chromosome, which contains the instructions needed to make a protein (and so controls the development of a characteristic).
General formula	A formula that can be used to find the molecular formula of any member of a homologous series.
Genetic engineering	The process of cutting out a useful gene from one organism's genome and inserting it into another organism's cell(s).
Genetically modified (GM) crop	A crop which has had its genes modified through genetic engineering.
Genome	All of the genetic material in an organism.
Genotype	What alleles you have, e.g. Tt.
Geothermal power	A renewable energy resource where energy is transferred from the thermal energy stores of hot rocks underground and is used to generate electricity or to heat buildings.
Giant covalent structure	A large molecule made up of a very large number of atoms held together by covalent bonds (also known as a macromolecule).
Gland	An organ that hormones are produced and secreted from.
Global dimming	The decrease in the amount of sunlight reaching the Earth's surface due to an increase in the amount of particulates in the atmosphere.
Global warming	The increase in the average temperature of the Earth.
Glucagon	A hormone produced and secreted by the pancreas when blood glucose level is too low.
Glycogen	A molecule that acts as a store of glucose in liver and muscle cells.
Gradient	The slope of a line graph. It shows how quickly the variable on the y-axis changes with the variable on the x-axis.
Gravitational potential energy (g.p.e.) store	Anything that has mass and is in a gravitational field has energy in its gravitational potential energy store.
Greenhouse effect	When greenhouse gases in the atmosphere absorb long wavelength radiation and re-radiate it in all directions, including back towards Earth, helping to keep the Earth warm.
Greenhouse gas	A gas that can absorb long wavelength radiation.
Group	A column in the periodic table.
Guard cell	A type of cell found on either side of a stoma. A pair of these cells control the stoma's size.
Habitat	The place where an organism lives.
Haemoglobin	A red pigment found in red blood cells that carries oxygen.
Half equation	An equation which shows how electrons are transferred when a substance is reduced or oxidised. E.g. at an electrode during electrolysis.
Half-life	The time it takes for the number of nuclei of a radioactive isotope in a sample to halve. OR The time it takes for the count rate (or activity) of a radioactive sample to fall to half its initial level.
Hazard	Something that has the potential to cause harm (e.g. fire, electricity, etc.).
Heterozygous	Where an organism has two alleles for a particular gene that are different.
Homeostasis	The regulation of conditions inside your body (and cells) to maintain a stable internal environment, in response to changes in both internal and external conditions.
Homologous series	A group of chemicals that react in a similar way because they have the same functional group. E.g. the alcohols or the carboxylic acids.

Glossary

Homozygous	Where an organism has two alleles for a particular gene that are the same.
Hormone	A chemical messenger which travels in the blood to activate target cells.
Hydrocarbon	A compound that is made from only hydrogen and carbon.
Hypothesis	A possible explanation for a scientific observation.
***I-V* characteristic**	A graph of current against potential difference for a component.
In excess	A reactant that is not used up during a reaction.
Inbreeding	When closely related animals or plants are bred together.
Incomplete combustion	When a fuel burns but there isn't enough oxygen for it to burn completely. Products can include carbon monoxide and carbon particulates. Also known as partial combustion.
Independent variable	The variable in an experiment that is changed.
Indicator	A substance that changes colour above or below a certain pH.
Induced magnet	A magnetic material that turns into a magnet when it is placed inside another magnetic field.
Inelastic deformation	An object undergoing inelastic deformation will not return to its original shape and length once the forces being applied to it are removed.
Inertia	The tendency of an object to remain stationary or continue travelling at a constant velocity.
Inertial mass	The ratio between the resultant force acting on an accelerating object and its acceleration.
Infrared (IR) radiation	A type of electromagnetic wave that is given out by all objects. It can also be absorbed by objects which makes the object hotter.
Inherited disorder	A disorder caused by a faulty allele, which can be passed on to an individual's offspring.
Insoluble	A substance is insoluble if it does not dissolve in a particular solvent.
Insulin	A hormone produced and secreted by the pancreas when blood glucose level is too high.
Interdependence	Where, in a community, each species depends on other species for things such as food, shelter, pollination and seed dispersal.
Intermolecular force	A force of attraction that exists between molecules.
Internal energy	The total energy that a system's particles have in their kinetic and potential energy stores.
Ion	A charged particle formed when one or more electrons are lost or gained from an atom or molecule.
Ionic bond	A strong attraction between oppositely charged ions.
Ionic compound	A compound that contains positive and negative ions held together in a regular arrangement (a lattice) by electrostatic forces of attraction.
Ionic equation	An equation that shows only the particles that react and the products they form.
Ionic lattice	A closely-packed regular arrangement of particles held together by electrostatic forces of attraction.
Ionising radiation	Radiation that has enough energy to knock electrons off atoms.
Irradiation	Exposure to radiation.
Isotope	A different form of the same element, which has atoms with the same number of protons (atomic number), but a different number of neutrons (and so different mass number).
IVF	*In vitro* fertilisation. The artificial fertilisation of eggs in the lab.
Joules	The standard unit of energy.
Kinetic energy store	Anything that's moving has energy in its kinetic energy store.
Lattice	A closely-packed regular arrangement of particles.
Le Chatelier's principle	The idea that if the conditions of a reaction are changed when a reversible reaction is at equilibrium, the system will try to counteract the change.
Life cycle assessment	An assessment of the environmental impact of a product over the course of its life.
Light-dependent resistor (LDR)	A resistor whose resistance is dependent on light intensity. The resistance decreases as light intensity increases.

Glossary

Limit of proportionality	The point beyond which the force applied to an elastic object is no longer directly proportional to the extension of the object.
Limiting factor	A factor which prevents a reaction from going any faster.
Limiting reactant	A reactant that gets completely used up in a reaction, so limits the amount of product that's formed.
Linear graph	A straight line graph.
Lipase	A type of digestive enzyme that catalyses the breakdown of lipids into fatty acids and glycerol.
Litmus	A single indicator that's blue in alkalis and red in acids.
Live wire	The brown wire in an electrical cable that carries an alternating potential difference from the mains.
Longitudinal wave	A wave in which the oscillations are parallel to the direction of energy transfer.
Lubricant	A substance (usually a liquid) that can flow easily between two objects. Used to reduce friction between surfaces.
Macromolecule	A large molecule made up of a very large number of atoms held together by covalent bonds (also known as a giant covalent structure).
Magnetic field	A region where magnetic materials (like iron and steel) and current-carrying wires experience a force.
Magnetic flux density	The number of magnetic field lines per unit area. Its symbol is B and it is measured in tesla, T.
Magnetic material	A material (such as iron, steel, cobalt or nickel) which can become an induced magnet while it's inside another magnetic field.
Mass number	The number of neutrons and protons in the nucleus of an atom.
Mean (average)	A measure of average found by adding up all the data and dividing by the number of values there are.
Median (average)	A measure of average found by selecting the middle value from a data set arranged in ascending order.
Medical tracer	A radioactive isotope that can be injected into or swallowed by people. Their progress around the body can be followed using an external detector and can diagnose medical conditions.
Meiosis	A type of cell division where a cell divides twice to produce four genetically different gametes. It occurs in the reproductive organs.
Menstrual cycle	A monthly sequence of events during which the body prepares the lining of the uterus (womb) in case it receives a fertilised egg, and releases an egg from an ovary. The uterus lining then breaks down if the egg has not been fertilised.
Meristem tissue	Tissue found at the growing tips of plant shoots and roots that is able to differentiate.
Metabolism	All the chemical reactions that happen in a cell or the body.
Metal ore	Rocks that are found naturally in the Earth's crust containing enough metal to make the metal profitable to extract.
Metal	An element that can form positive ions when it reacts.
Metallic bond	The attraction between metal ions and delocalised electrons in a metal.
Microwave	A type of electromagnetic wave that can be used for cooking and satellite communications.
Mitochondria	Structures in a cell which are the site of most of the reactions for aerobic respiration.
Mitosis	A type of cell division where a cell reproduces itself by splitting to form two identical offspring.
Mixture	A substance made from two or more elements or compounds that aren't chemically bonded to each other.
Mobile phase	In chromatography, the mobile phase is a gas or liquid where the molecules are able to move.
Mode (average)	A measure of average found by selecting the most frequent value from a data set.
Model	Something used to describe or display how an object or system behaves in reality.
Mole	A unit of amount of substance — the mass of one mole of a substance is equal to the value of the relative formula mass of that substance in grams, and contains 6.02×10^{23} particles of the substance.

Glossary

Molecular formula	A chemical formula showing the actual number of atoms of each element in a compound.
Molecule	A particle made up of at least two atoms held together by covalent bonds.
Momentum	A property of a moving object that is the product of its mass and velocity.
Motor effect	When a current-carrying wire in a magnetic field experiences a force.
Motor neurone	A nerve cell that carries electrical impulses from the CNS to effectors.
MRSA	A strain of antibiotic-resistant bacteria. (Meticillin-resistant *Staphylococcus aureus*.)
Mutation	A random change in an organism's DNA.
National grid	The network of transformers and cables that distributes electrical power from power stations to consumers.
Natural resource	A resource formed without human input.
Natural selection	The process by which species evolve.
Negative feedback	A mechanism that restores a level back to optimum in a system.
Nervous system	The organ system in animals that allows them to respond to changes in their environment.
Neurone	A nerve cell. Neurones transmit information around the body, including to and from the CNS.
Neutral substance	A substance with a pH of 7.
Neutral wire	The blue wire in an electrical cable that current in an appliance normally flows through. It is around 0 V.
Neutralisation reaction	The reaction between acids and bases that leads to the formation of neutral products — usually a salt and water.
Neutron	A subatomic particle with a relative charge of 0.
Newton's First Law	An object will remain at rest or travelling at a constant velocity unless it is acted on by a resultant force.
Newton's Second Law	The acceleration of an object is directly proportional to the resultant force acting on it, and inversely proportional to its mass.
Newton's Third Law	When two objects interact, they exert equal and opposite forces on each other.
Non-communicable disease	A disease that cannot spread between individuals.
Non-contact force	A force that can act between objects that are not touching.
Non-metal	An element that doesn't form positive ions when it reacts with the exception of hydrogen.
Non-renewable energy resource	An energy resource that is non-renewable cannot be made at the same rate as it's being used, so it will run out one day.
Normal (at a boundary)	A line that's perpendicular (at 90°) to a surface at the point of incidence (where a wave hits the surface).
Nuclear model	A model of the atom that says that the atom has a small, central positively-charged nucleus with negatively-charged electrons moving around the nucleus, and that most of the atom is empty space. The nucleus is made up of protons and neutrons.
Nucleus (atom)	The centre of an atom, containing protons and neutrons.
Nucleus (of a cell)	A structure found in animal and plant cells which contains the genetic material.
Obesity	A condition where a person has an excessive amount of body fat, to the point where it poses a risk to their health.
Ohmic conductor	A conductor with resistance that is constant at a constant temperature. It has a linear *I-V* characteristic.
Optimum dose	The dose of a drug that is most effective and has few side effects.
Optimum level (in the body)	A level of something (e.g. water, ions or glucose) that enables the body to work at its best.
Organ	A group of different tissues that work together to perform a certain function.

Glossary

Organ system	A group of organs working together to perform a particular function.
Organic compound	A chemical compound that contains carbon atoms.
Osmosis	The movement of water molecules across a partially permeable membrane from a region of higher water concentration to a region of lower water concentration.
Oxidation	A reaction where electrons are lost or oxygen is gained by a species.
Oxygen debt	The amount of extra oxygen your body needs after exercise to react with the build up of lactic acid and remove it from cells.
Paper chromatography	An analytical technique that can be used to separate and analyse coloured substances.
Parallel circuit	A circuit in which every component is connected separately to the positive and negative ends of the battery.
Partially permeable membrane	A membrane with tiny holes in it, which lets some molecules through it but not others.
Pathogen	A microorganism that causes disease, e.g. a bacterium, virus, protist or fungus.
Peer-review	The process in which other scientists check the results and explanations of an investigation before they are published.
Period (chemistry)	A row in the periodic table.
Period (of a wave)	The time taken for one full cycle of a wave to be completed.
Periodic table	A table of all the known elements, arranged in order of atomic number so that elements with similar chemical properties are in groups.
Permanent magnet	A magnetic material that always has its own magnetic field around it.
Permanent vacuole	A structure in plant cells that contains cell sap.
pH scale	A scale from 0 to 14 that is used to measure how acidic or alkaline a solution is.
Phagocytosis	The process by which white blood cells engulf foreign cells and digest them.
Phenotype	The characteristics you have, e.g. brown eyes.
Phloem	A type of plant tissue which transports dissolved sugars around the plant.
Photosynthesis	The process by which plants use energy to convert carbon dioxide and water into glucose and oxygen.
Physical change	A change where you don't end up with a new substance — it's the same substance as before, just in a different form. (A change of state is a physical change.)
Phytomining	The process by which a metal is extracted from soil by using plants.
Placebo	A substance that is like a drug being tested, but which doesn't do anything.
Plasma	The liquid component of blood, which carries blood cells and other substances around the body.
Platelet	A small fragment of a cell found in the blood, which helps blood to clot at a wound.
Plum pudding model	A disproved theory of the atom as a ball of positive charge with electrons inside it.
Polydactyly	An inherited disorder, caused by a dominant allele, where a person has extra fingers or toes.
Polymer	A long chain molecule that is formed by joining lots of smaller molecules (monomers) together.
Potable water	Water that is safe for drinking.
Potential difference	The driving force that pushes electric charge around a circuit, measured in volts (V). Also known as pd or voltage.
Power	The rate of transferring energy (or doing work). Normally measured in watts (W).
Precipitate	A solid that is formed in a solution during a chemical reaction.
Precise result	When all the data is close to the mean.
Predator	An animal that hunts and kills other animals for food.
Prediction	A statement based on a hypothesis that can be tested.

Glossary

Pressure	The force per unit area exerted on a surface.
Prey	An animal that is hunted and killed by another animal for food.
Primary consumer	An organism in a food chain that feeds on a producer.
Producer	An organism at the start of a food chain that makes its own food using energy from the Sun.
Product	A substance that is formed in a chemical reaction.
Prokaryotic cell	A small, simple cell, e.g. a bacterium.
Protease	A type of digestive enzyme that catalyses the breakdown of proteins into amino acids.
Protein	A large biological molecule made up of long chains of amino acids.
Protist	A type of pathogen. Protists are often transferred to other organisms by a vector.
Proton	A subatomic particle with a relative charge of +1.
Punnett square	A type of genetic diagram.
Pure substance	A substance that only contains one compound or element throughout.
Quadrat	A square frame enclosing a known area. It is used to study the distribution of organisms.
Radiation dose	A measure of the risk of harm to your body due to exposure to radiation.
Radio wave	A type of electromagnetic wave mainly used for radio and TV signals.
Radioactive decay	The random process of a radioactive substance giving out radiation from the nuclei of its atoms.
Radioactive substance	A substance that spontaneously gives out radiation from the nuclei of its atoms.
Radiotherapy	A treatment of cancer that uses ionising radiation (such as gamma rays and X-rays) to kill cancer cells.
Random error	A difference in the results of an experiment caused by unpredictable events, e.g. human error in measuring.
Range	The difference between the smallest and largest values in a set of data.
Rate of reaction	How fast the reactants in a reaction are changed into products.
Ray	A straight line showing the path along which a wave moves.
Reactant	A substance that reacts in a chemical reaction.
Reaction profile	A graph that shows how the energy in a reaction changes as the reaction progresses (also known as an energy level diagram).
Reaction time	The time taken for a person to react after an event (e.g. seeing a hazard).
Reactivity series	A list of elements arranged in order of their reactivity. The most reactive elements are at the top and the least reactive at the bottom.
Receptor	A group of cells that are sensitive to a stimulus (e.g. receptor cells in the eye detect light).
Recessive allele	An allele whose characteristic only appears in an organism if there are two copies present.
Redox reaction	A reaction where one substance is reduced and another is oxidised.
Reduction	A reaction where electrons are gained or oxygen is lost.
Reflection	When a wave bounces back as it meets a boundary between two materials.
Reflex	A fast, automatic response to a stimulus.
Refraction	When a wave changes direction as it passes across the boundary between two materials at an angle to the normal.
Relative atomic mass (A_r)	The average mass of the atoms of an element measured relative to the mass of one atom of carbon-12. The relative atomic mass of an element is the same as its mass number in the periodic table.
Relative formula mass (M_r)	All the relative atomic masses (A_r) of the atoms in a compound added together.
Relay neurone	A nerve cell that carries electrical impulses from sensory neurones to motor neurones.
Reliable result	A result that is repeatable and reproducible.

Glossary

Renewable energy resource	An energy resource that is renewable is one that is being, or can be, made at the same rate (or faster) than it's being used, and so will never run out.
Repeating unit	The shortest repeating section of a polymer.
Reproducible result	A result that will come out the same if someone different does the experiment, or a slightly different method or piece of equipment is used.
Resistance	Anything in a circuit that reduces the flow of current. Measured in ohms, Ω.
Resolution	The smallest change a measuring instrument can detect.
Respiration	The process of breaking down glucose to transfer energy, which occurs in every cell.
Resultant force	A single force that can replace all the forces acting on an object to give the same effect as the original forces acting altogether.
Reversible reaction	A reaction where the products of the reaction can themselves react to produce the original reactants.
R_f value	In chromatography, the ratio between the distance travelled by a dissolved substance and the distance travelled by a solvent.
Ribosome	A structure in a cell, where proteins are made.
Right-hand thumb rule	The rule to work out the direction of the magnetic field around a current-carrying wire. Your thumb points in the direction of the current, and your fingers curl in the direction of the magnetic field.
Risk	The chance that a hazard will cause harm.
Risk factor	Something that is linked to an increased likelihood that a person will develop a certain disease.
S.I. unit	A standard unit of measurement, recognised by scientists all over the world.
Scalar	A quantity that has magnitude but no direction.
Scaling prefix	A word or symbol which goes before a unit to indicate a multiplying factor (e.g. 1 km = 1000 m).
Secondary consumer	An organism in a food chain that eats a primary consumer.
Selective breeding (artificial selection)	When humans artificially select the plants or animals that are going to breed, so that the genes for particular characteristics remain in the population.
Sensory neurone	A nerve cell that carries electrical impulses from a receptor in a sense organ to the CNS.
Series circuit	A circuit in which every component is connected in a line, end to end.
Sex chromosome (humans)	One of the 23rd pair of chromosomes, X or Y. Together they determine whether an individual is male or female.
Sexual reproduction	Where two gametes combine at fertilisation to produce a genetically different new individual.
Significant figure	The first significant figure of a number is the first non-zero digit. The second, third and fourth significant figures follow on immediately after it.
Simple distillation	A way of separating a liquid out from a mixture if there are large differences in the boiling points of the substances.
Simple molecule	A molecule made up of only a few atoms held together by covalent bonds.
Solar cell	A device that generates electricity directly from the Sun's radiation.
Solenoid	A coil of wire often used in the construction of electromagnets.
Solute	A substance dissolved in a solvent to make a solution.
Solution	A mixture made up of one substance (the solute) dissolved in another (the solvent).
Solvent	A liquid in which another substance (a solute) can be dissolved.
Solvent front	The point the solvent has reached up the filter paper during paper chromatography.
Species	A group of similar organisms that can reproduce to give fertile offspring.
Specific heat capacity	The amount of energy (in joules) needed to raise the temperature of 1 kg of a material by 1 °C.
Specific latent heat (SLH)	The amount of energy needed to change 1 kg of a substance from one state to another without changing its temperature. (For cooling, it is the energy released by a change in state.)

Glossary

Specific latent heat of fusion	The specific latent heat for changing between a solid and a liquid (melting or freezing).
Specific latent heat of vaporisation	The specific latent heat for changing between a liquid and a gas (evaporating, boiling or condensing).
Split-ring commutator	A ring with gaps in it that swaps the electrical contacts of a device every half-turn.
Stable community	A community where all the species and environmental factors are in balance, so that the population sizes are roughly constant.
Standard form	A number written in the form $A \times 10^n$, where A is a number between 1 and 10.
State of matter	The form which a substance can take — e.g. solid, liquid or gas.
State symbol	The letter, or letters, in brackets that are placed after a substance in an equation to show what physical state it's in. E.g. gaseous carbon dioxide is shown as $CO_{2(g)}$.
Statins	A group of medicinal drugs that are used to decrease the risk of heart and circulatory disease.
Stationary phase	In chromatography, the stationary phase is a solid or really thick liquid where molecules are unable to move.
Stem cell	An undifferentiated cell which has the ability to become one of many different types of cell, or to produce more stem cells.
Stent	A wire mesh tube that's inserted inside an artery to help keep it open.
Stimulus	A change in the environment.
Stoma	A tiny hole in the surface of a leaf.
Stopping distance	The distance covered by a vehicle in the time between the driver spotting a hazard and the vehicle coming to a complete stop. It's the sum of the thinking distance and the braking distance.
Strong acid	An acid which fully ionises in an aqueous solution.
Structural adaptation	A feature of an organism's body structure that helps it to survive in its environment.
Sustainable development	An approach to development that takes into the account the needs of present society while not damaging the lives of those in the future.
Synapse	The connection between two neurones.
System	The object, or group of objects, that you're considering.
Systematic error	An error that is consistently made throughout an experiment.
Tangent	A straight line that touches a curve at a particular point without crossing it.
Terminal velocity	The maximum velocity a falling object can reach without any added driving forces. It's the velocity at which the resistive forces (drag) acting on the object match the force due to gravity (weight).
Tertiary consumer	An organism in a food chain that eats a secondary consumer.
Theory	A hypothesis which has been accepted by the scientific community because there is good evidence to back it up.
Thermal conductivity	A measure of how quickly an object transfers energy by heating through conduction.
Thermal decomposition	A reaction where one substance chemically changes into at least two new substances when it's heated.
Thermal insulator	A material with a low thermal conductivity.
Thermistor	A resistor whose resistance is dependent on the temperature. The resistance decreases as temperature increases.
Thinking distance	The distance a vehicle travels during the driver's reaction time (before the brakes have been applied).
Three-core cable	An electrical cable containing a live wire, a neutral wire and an earth wire.
Tissue	A group of similar cells that work together to carry out a particular function.
Toxicity	How harmful something is, e.g. a drug.
Toxin	A poison. Toxins are often produced by bacteria.

Glossary

Transect	A line which can be used to study the distribution of organisms across an area.
Transformer	A device which can change the potential difference of an ac supply.
Translocation	The movement of dissolved sugars around a plant.
Transpiration stream	The movement of water from a plant's roots, through the xylem and out of the leaves.
Transverse wave	A wave in which the oscillations are perpendicular (at 90°) to the direction of energy transfer.
Tumour	A growth of abnormal cells.
Ultraviolet (UV) radiation	A type of electromagnetic wave, the main source of which is sunlight.
Uncertainty	The amount by which a given result may differ from the true value.
Universal indicator	A wide range indicator that changes colour depending on the pH of the solution that it's in.
Urea	A waste product produced from the breakdown of amino acids in the liver.
Vaccination	The injection of dead or inactive microorganisms, in order to produce an immune response that will help to protect you against a particular pathogen in the future.
Valid result	A result that is repeatable, reproducible and answers the original question.
Valve	A structure within the heart or a vein which prevents blood flowing in the wrong direction.
Variation	The differences that exist between individuals.
Vector (in disease)	An organism that transfers a disease from one animal or plant to another, which doesn't get the disease itself.
Vector (in genetic engineering)	Something used to transfer DNA into a cell, e.g. a virus or a bacterial plasmid.
Vector (physics)	A quantity which has both magnitude (size) and a direction.
Vein	A blood vessel that carries blood to the heart.
Velocity	The speed and direction of an object.
Velocity-time graph	A graph showing how the velocity of an object changes over a period of time.
Virus	A tiny pathogen that can only replicate within host body cells.
Viscosity	How runny or gloopy a substance is.
Visible light	The part of the electromagnetic spectrum that we can see with our eyes.
Voltmeter	A component used to measure the potential difference across a component. Always connected in parallel with the component.
Wave	An oscillation that transfers energy without transferring any matter.
Wavelength	The length of a full cycle of a wave, e.g. from a crest to the next crest.
Weak acid	An acid which partially ionises in an aqueous solution.
Weight	The force acting on an object due to gravity.
White blood cell	A blood cell that is part of the immune system, defending the body against disease.
Work done	The energy transferred when a force moves an object through a distance, or by a moving charge.
X-ray	A high-frequency, short-wavelength electromagnetic wave. It is mainly used in medical imaging and treatment.
Xylem	A type of plant tissue which transports water and mineral ions around the plant.
Zero error	A type of systematic error caused by using a piece of equipment that isn't zeroed properly.

Index

A

abiotic factors 152
absorption 385, 393
  of infrared 393
abstinence 118
acceleration 365, 371
  due to gravity
      298, 369, 373, 377
  measuring 373
  on distance-time graphs 366
  on velocity-time graphs 367
  uniform 365
accuracy (of results) 7, 8
acids 231-234, 237
activation energy
      249, 254, 255
active sites 42
active transport 33
activity (radioactivity)
      346, 347
adaptations 154
adrenal glands 110, 120
adrenaline 120
aerobic digestion 294
aerobic respiration 100
air resistance 368, 369
alkali metals 195, 196
alkalis 231-233
alkanes 267-270
alkenes 270
alleles 129, 130
allotropes of carbon 213-215
alloys 216
alpha radiation 344, 345
alpha scattering experiment 341
alternating currents (ac) 328, 388
alveoli 35, 51, 52
ammeters 318, 413
amplitude 381
amylase 44-46
anaerobic digestion 294
anaerobic respiration 100
ancestors 149
angle of incidence 386
angle of refraction 386
animal cells 17
anions 203
anodes 242-245
anomalous results 8
antibiotic resistance 84, 147
antibiotics 84, 147
antibodies 55, 81
antimicrobials 81
antiretroviral drugs 77
antitoxins 55, 81
aorta 53
apparatus 406, 407
Archaea 148
area under a graph 362, 367
arteries 54
artificial blood 60
artificial hearts 59
asexual reproduction 124
aspirin 85
atomic models
  development of 341, 342
  nuclear 342
  plum pudding 341
atomic number 173, 175, 191, 192, 343, 345
atoms 173-177, 341-345
atria 53
Avogadro constant 223

B

bacteria 18, 75, 78, 148
balances 406
balancing equations 178, 227
ball and stick models 205
bar charts 10
barrier methods
      (of contraception) 118
basal metabolic rate 120
bases 231, 233, 234
behavioural adaptations 154
Benedict's reagent 47
benign tumours 66
beta radiation 344, 345
bias 3
bile 45
binomial system 149
biodiversity
      163, 164, 166-170
  maintenance of 169, 170
bio-fuels 312
bioleaching 287
biological heart valves 60
biotic factors 153
Biuret test 48
blind studies 86
Bohr, Niels 189
boiling 219, 336, 337
bond energies 249, 250
brakes 376, 378
braking distances 376, 378
breathing rate 52
bromine water
bronchi 51
bronchioles 51
Buckminsterfullerene 215
Bunsen burners 183, 412

C

caffeine (effect on reaction time) 108
cancer 66, 391, 392
capillaries 54
carbohydrases 45
carbon cycle 160
carbon dioxide
  in the atmosphere 278-283
  test for 274
carbon footprints 282, 283
carbon neutral 312
catalysts 42, 255, 270
categoric data 10
cathodes 242-245
cations 203
cavity wall insulation 305
cell
  cycle 27, 28
  division 27, 28
  membranes 17, 30
  walls 18
cells 17, 18
  drawing 21
  specialised 23, 24
central nervous system (CNS) 105-107
centre of mass 354
Chadwick, James 189
changes of state
      219, 336, 337
charge
  electric 316, 330
  ions 342
  of a nucleus 341-343, 345
  relative charges of particles 342
chemical equations 177
chlorophyll 18, 89, 90
chloroplasts 18, 89, 90
cholesterol 59
chromatography
      182, 275, 276
chromosomes 27, 28, 122
  X and Y 126, 127
cilia 81
circuit diagrams 316
circuits 316, 318, 319, 322-326
circuit symbols 316
class (classification) 148
classification 148, 149
climate change 165, 166
clinical trials 86
closed systems 297
coal 308, 313
collision theory 254, 255
combustion reactions 247, 268, 284
communicable diseases 62, 75, 76
communities 151
compasses 397, 398
components
  electrical 316, 319
  of a force 357
compounds 176, 177
compression (of springs) 359, 360
compressions (in waves) 382
computational models 3
concentration gradients 30
concentrations 228
conclusions 14
condensation 159
condensing 219, 336, 337
condoms 78, 118
conduction 304
conservation of energy 303
conservation of mass 224, 225, 336
conservation of momentum 379
contact forces 353
contamination 348, 349
contraception 117, 118
control variables 6
convection 304
copper extraction 287
coronary arteries 53
coronary heart disease 58, 59
correlation 11, 14
count-rate 346
covalent bonding 176, 208-210
cover slips (slides) 20
cracking (of hydrocarbons) 270
crude oil 269, 270
crystallisation 183, 184, 234
current 316-319, 324, 325
  alternating 328, 388
  direct 328
  in parallel 325
  in series 324
  I-V characteristics 319
  magnetism 398, 401-403
current-carrying wires 398, 401, 403
cystic fibrosis 133
cytoplasm 17

D

Dalton, John 188
dangers of ionising radiation 349, 391, 392
Darwin, Charles 139
decay 160
deceleration 365, 378
  on distance-time graphs 366
  on velocity-time graphs 367
deforestation 168
delocalised electrons 216
density 335
dependent variables 6
detritus feeders 160
diabetes 113
diamond 213, 214
diaphragm (thorax) 51
diaphragms (contraception) 118
differentiation 23, 40
diffusion 30, 31, 34-37
digestive enzymes 45
digestive system 41, 46
digitalis 85
diodes 317, 319
direct currents (dc) 328
discrete data 10
displacement (distance) 364
displacement (waves) 381
displacement reactions 198, 240
dissipated energy 303, 305
distance 364

Index

distance-time graphs 366
distillation
   fractional 186, 269
   of water 293
   simple 185
distribution of organisms 157, 158
DNA 27, 28, 122, 123
dosage 86
dot and cross diagrams 204, 208-210
double-blind studies 86
double bonds 209
double circulatory systems 53
double-glazing 305
drag 368, 369
draught excluders 305
drugs 84-86
   development of 86
dynamic equilibria 263

E

earth wires 328
ecosystems 151
   maintenance of 169, 170
effectors 104-106
efficacy (of drugs) 86
efficiency 306
elastic deformation 359, 362
elastic objects 359
elastic potential energy stores 299, 359, 362
electric cars 314
electric heaters 306, 390, 412
electricity 316-319, 321-326, 328-332
   supply and demand 331
   usage 313
electric motors 403
electric shocks 328
electrolysis 242-245, 410
   aluminium oxide 243
   aqueous solutions 244
   copper(II) sulfate 244
   extraction of metals 238
electrolytes 242
electromagnetic spectrum 388
electromagnetic waves 388
   dangers 392
   gamma rays 344, 345, 391, 392
   infrared 390, 393
   microwaves 389
   uses 388-391
   UV 391, 392
   visible light 391
   X-rays 391, 392
electromagnetism 399
electronic structure 190, 194
electron microscopes 19
electrons 173, 341, 342, 344
electron shells 189, 190
elements 174, 343, 345
embryo screening 134

emission (infrared) 393, 394
empirical formulas 206
endocrine system 110
endothermic reactions 89, 247, 249
energy 297-301, 303-306, 308-314
   conservation 303
   internal 336
   stores 297
   transfers 297, 298, 304, 305
energy resources 308-314
   non-renewables 308, 313
   renewables 308-312
   transport 308, 314
   trends in use 314
energy stores 297
   elastic potential 299, 359, 362
   gravitational potential 298, 299
   kinetic 299
   thermal 297, 300, 304, 390
energy transfers 297-299, 304, 306, 356
   by heating 304, 305, 336, 338
   by waves 381
   efficiency 306
   electrical 329, 330
   rate of 303
   reducing 305
   work done 356
environmental impact (of energy resources) 309-314
environmental variation 137, 138
enzymes 42-46, 255
epidermal tissue 68
equations
   balancing 178
   symbol 177, 178
equilibria 263-265
equilibrium (forces) 357, 372
errors 8
estimating 365, 371, 378
ethics (in investigations) 409
Eukaryota 148
eukaryotes 17, 76
eureka cans 335, 407
evaluations 16
evaporation 159, 183, 184, 336, 337
evolutionary trees 149
evolution by natural selection 139, 140
exchange surfaces 34-37
exercise 101
exothermic reactions 98, 247, 249
experimental safety 409
extension (of springs) 359-362
extinction 140
extraction of metals 238, 243

F

fair tests 6
falling objects 369
family (classification) 148
family trees 132
fatty acids 45
fermentation 100
fertility 117-119
fertility treatments 118, 119
field lines 397
fields
   gravitational 299, 354
   magnetic 397-399, 401-403
field strength
   gravitational 299, 354
   magnetic 397, 399, 402
fight or flight response 120
filament lamps 317, 319
filtration 183, 184
finite resources 286
Fleming, Alexander 85
Fleming's left-hand rule 402, 403
follicle-stimulating hormone (FSH) 116, 118, 119
food chains 155
food poisoning 78
force-extension graphs 360, 362
forces 353-357, 359-362, 364-369, 371-374, 378
   contact 353
   free-body diagrams 355
   frictional 305, 368, 369, 378
   gravitational 298, 354
   interaction pairs 353, 372
   magnetic 397-399, 401-403
   Newton's laws 371, 372
   non-contact 353, 397
   normal contact 298, 353, 372
   resolving 357
   resultant 355, 356, 371
   weight 354
formulas 177
formulations 273
fossil fuels 269, 279, 282, 284, 308, 313
fossils 146
fractional distillation 186, 269
free-body diagrams 355
freezing 219, 336, 337
frequency 381
   of EM waves 388
   of mains supply 328
friction 305, 368, 369, 378
fullerenes 215
functional adaptations 154
fungi 76, 77

G

gall bladder 46
gamete fusion 125
gametes 124, 125
gamma radiation 344, 345, 349, 388
   dangers of 392
   uses of 391
gases 218-220, 406
   gas pressure 338
   particle motion 334, 338
   state of matter 334
gas exchange 35-37
gas syringes 406
Geiger-Muller tube 346
gene pools 142
genes 27, 123
genetic
   diagrams 127, 130-133
   disorders 133, 134
   engineering 143, 144
   variants 138
   variation 137, 138
genetically modified crops 143, 144
genomes 123
genotypes 129
genus 148, 149
geothermal power 310
giant ionic lattices 205
gills 37
glands 110
glass recycling 288
global warming 165, 166, 313
glucagon 112
glucose
   in the blood 112, 113
   test for 47
   uses in plants 89
glycerol 45
glycogen 112
gonorrhoea 78
government targets 314
gradients 11, 260
graphene 214
graphite 213, 214
graphs 10, 11
   distance-time 366
   force-extension 360, 362
   for rate of reaction 253, 260
   heating and cooling 337
   radioactive decay 347
   velocity-time 367
gravitational fields 299, 354
gravitational field strength 354
gravitational force 298, 354
gravitational potential energy stores 298, 299
greenhouse gases 165
greenhouses 95
Group 0 elements 199
Group 1 elements 195, 196
Group 7 elements 197, 198
groups (of the periodic table) 192
guard cells 72
gullet 46

Index

H
habitats 151
haemoglobin 55
half equations 245
half-life 346, 347
halogens 197, 198
hazards 5, 8, 409
heart 53
heart valves 60
heating 297, 300, 336
heating substances 412
helium nucleus 344, 345
heterozygous organisms 129
HIV 77
homeostasis 104
homologous series 267
homozygous organisms 129
hormones 110, 111
hybrid cars 314
hydrocarbons 267-270, 284
hydro-electric power 310
hypotheses 2, 6

I
immune system 81
incomplete combustion 284
independent variables 6
indicators 231
'induced fit' model 42
induced magnets 398
inelastic deformation 359
inertia 372
inertial mass 372
infertility 118, 119
infrared cameras 390
infrared radiation
　　390, 393, 394
　investigating 393, 394
insulation 305
insulin 112, 113
interaction pairs 353, 372
intercepts (on a graph) 11
interdependence (of species)
　　151
intermolecular forces 210
internal energy 336
intrauterine devices (IUDs)
　　117
inverse
　correlations 11
　proportion 94
　square law 94
investigating
　IR absorption 393
　IR emission 393, 394
　I-V characteristics 319
　motion 373, 374
　resistance 318, 326
　specific heat capacity 301
　springs 361, 362
　wave speed 383, 384
in vitro fertilisation (IVF) 119

iodine test (for starch) 44
ionic bonding 176, 198,
　　202-205
ionic equations 240, 242-245
ionisation 342-344, 349, 392
ionising power 343, 349
ionising radiation 344, 349
　alpha 344, 345, 349
　beta 344, 345, 349
　dangers of
　　348, 349, 391, 392
　gamma 344, 345, 349
　uses of 391
ions 176, 202-204, 342, 343
irradiation 348, 349
isotopes 175, 191, 343, 346
IVF 119

K
kinetic energy stores 299
kingdom (classification) 148

L
lactic acid 100, 101
lamellae 37
large intestine 46
laws of motion 371, 372
leaves
　gas exchange 36
　tissues in 68
Le Chatelier's principle 265
Leslie cubes 394
Life Cycle Assessments (LCAs)
　　289, 290
light-dependent resistors (LDR)
　　321, 322
light gates 373, 413
light microscopes 19-21
limiting factors (of
　　photosynthesis) 90-92
limiting reactants 228, 229
limit of proportionality
　　360, 362
linear components 319
line graphs 10, 11
lines of best fit 10, 11
Linnaean system 148
Linnaeus, Carl 148
lipases 45
lipids (test for) 48
liquids 218-220, 334, 406
　density of 335
liver 46, 112
live wires 328
'lock and key' model 42
loft insulation 305
longitudinal waves 382
lubricants 305, 306
lungs 51, 52
luteinising hormone (LH)
　　116, 118, 119

M
magnetic fields
　　397-399, 401-403
　field lines 397
　field strength 397, 399, 402
　flux density 402
　of the Earth 397
magnetic forces
　　397-399, 401-403
magnetic materials 397
magnification 19
malaria 78
malignant tumours 66
Marsden, Ernest 188
mass 354
　inertial mass 372
mass number
　　173, 175, 343, 345
matter
　particle model
　　334, 336, 338
mean (average) 9
measles 77
measuring
　mass 406
　pH 408
　time 408
　volume 406, 407
mechanical energy transfers
　　297
mechanical heart valves 60
median 9
medical imaging 391
medical tracers 391
meiosis 125
melting 219, 336, 337
Mendeleev, Dmitri 191
menstrual cycle 115, 116
meristem tissue 68
metabolism 99
metal carbonates 234
metal hydroxides 233
metallic bonding 216
metal ores 238
metal oxides 233
metals 176, 194, 236-240
　bonding of 216
　extraction of 238, 243
micrometers 407
microorganisms 75
microscopes 19-21
microwave ovens 390
microwaves 389, 390
migration patterns 166
　human 123
mitochondria 17
mitosis 27, 28, 125
mixtures 181
mode 9
models (scientific) 3
molecular formulas 208
moles 223, 224, 227, 229
momentum 379
motor effect 401, 402
motor neurones 105-107

motors 403
MRSA 84, 147
mucus 81
muscle cells 24
muscle fatigue 101
mutations 138

N
nanotubes 215
national grid 331, 332
natural resources 286
natural selection 139
negative correlations 11
negative feedback systems 104
　blood glucose 112
　thyroxine 120
nerve cells 23
nervous system 105-107
neurones 105-107
neutralisation reactions
　　231, 247, 248
neutral wires 328
neutrons 173-175, 342,
　　343, 345
Newton's First Law 371
Newton's Second Law
　　371, 373, 374
Newton's Third Law 372
noble gases 199
non-communicable diseases 62
non-contact forces 353
non-linear components 319
non-metals 176, 194, 208
non-renewable resources 286
non-renewables energy
　　resources 308, 313
north poles 397
nuclear equations 345
nuclear fuels 308, 313
nuclear model (of atom)
　　188, 189, 342
nuclear power 313
nuclear symbols 173, 174
nuclear waste 313
nuclei (of atoms) 173, 188,
　　342, 343, 345, 346
nuclei (of cells) 17

O
oestrogen 115-117
ohmic conductors 317
oil (energy resource) 308, 313
optical density 385
optical fibres 391
order (classification) 148
organs 40, 41
organ systems 40, 41
osmosis 31, 32
ovaries 110, 115, 116
ovulation 115, 116
oxidation 238-240, 242,
　　243, 247
oxygen debt 101

Index

P
pacemakers 53
painkillers 85
palisade mesophyll tissue 68
pancreas 46, 110, 112
paper chromatography 182, 275, 276
parallax 407
parallel circuits 325, 326
parasites 76
partially permeable membranes 31
particle model of matter 334, 336, 338
particle theory 218
pathogens 75, 76
peat bogs 167
peer review 2, 86
pepsin 45, 46
percentage
  change 415
  cover 158
  masses 222
periodic table 191, 192
periods (of the periodic table) 192
periods (of waves) 381
permanent magnets 398
pH 231-233, 408
phagocytosis 55, 81
phenotypes 129
phenotype variation 139
phloem cells 24
phloem tubes 68, 69
photosynthesis 89-95
  rate of 90-94
phylum (classification) 148
physical changes 336
phytomining 287
pilot experiments 361
pipettes 406
pituitary gland 110, 116, 120
placebo effect 86
plant cells 18
plasma 55
plasmids 18, 143
platelets 55
pleural membranes 51
plum pudding model 188, 341
plutonium 308
pollution 164
polydactyly 133
polymers 212
population (human) 163, 164
positive correlations 11
potable water 292, 293
potatoes 32
potential difference 316, 317
  energy transferred 330
  in parallel 325
  in series 323
  I-V characteristics 319
  measuring 413
  national grid 332
potometers 72, 410

power 303
  electrical 329, 330
power ratings 329
precipitation 159
precision (of results) 7, 8
preclinical testing 86
predator-prey cycles 155
predators 155
pressure
  gas 338
prey 155
primary consumers 155
producers 155
progesterone 116, 117
prokaryotes 17, 18
proteases 45
proteins (test for) 48
protists 76, 78
protons 173-175, 342, 343, 345
puberty 115
pulmonary artery 53
pulmonary vein 53
Punnett squares 127, 130
purity 273

Q
quadrats 157, 158

R
radiation 343-349
  alpha 344, 345, 349
  beta 344, 345, 349
  gamma 344, 345, 349, 388
radiation dose 392
radioactive decay 343-349
radiotherapy 391
radio waves 388, 389
radius (of an atom) 342
random
  errors 8
  sampling 414
range (of data) 9
rarefactions 382
rates of reaction 44, 253-260
  graphs 253, 258, 260
  measurements of 256-258
ray diagrams 386
reaction times 108, 376, 377
reactivity series 236, 238
receptors 104-106
rectum 46
recycling 288
  glass 288
  metals 288
  waste water 294
red blood cells 55
reducing energy transfers 305
reduction (reaction) 238-240, 242, 243
reflection 385
reflex arcs 107
refraction 385, 386
relative atomic mass (A_r) 175, 191, 222

relative formula mass (M_r) 222
relay neurones 107
reliability (of energy resources) 309-314
renewable resources 286
renewables 308-312
repeatability (of data) 6, 7
repeating units 212
representational models 3
reproducibility (of data) 6, 7
resistance (air) 368, 369
resistance (electrical) 316, 317
  in parallel 325, 326
  in series 324, 326
resistors 321, 322
  in parallel 325
  in series 324
resolution (microscopes) 19
resolving (a force) 357
respiration 98, 100
resultant forces 355, 356, 371
reversible reactions 263-265
R_f values 276
ribcage 51
ribosomes 17
right-hand thumb rule 398
ripple tanks 383
risk factors 64, 65
risks 5, 8
  of using radiation 349, 391, 392
root hair cells 24, 33
rose black spot 77
rounding numbers 9
ruler drop test 377
Rutherford, Ernest 188

S
safety 8
  during experiments 409
  handling radioactive sources 348, 349
salivary glands 46
Salmonella 78
salts 205, 233, 234, 237
  experiments with 183-185
sample size 7
sampling 414
satellites 389
saturated compounds 267
scalar quantities 353
scale drawings 356
secondary consumers 155
secondary sexual characteristics 115
selective breeding 142
sensing circuits 322
sensory neurones 105-107
series circuits 323, 324, 326
sewage treatment 293, 294
sex hormones 115-119
sexually transmitted diseases 78
sexual reproduction 124
significant figures 9
simple distillation 185

simple molecular substances 209, 210
S.I. units 12
skin cancer 392
slides (microscope) 20
small intestine 46
smoke detectors 344
solar cells 309
solar power 309, 314
solenoids 399
solids 218-220, 334
  density of 335
sound waves 383
source potential 323
south poles 397
specialised cells 23, 24
speciation 140
species 149
  in classification 148
specific heat capacity 300, 301
specific latent heat 337
speed 299, 364-367
  braking distances 376
  of sound in air 383
  of waves 382-386
  typical speeds 364
sperm cells 23, 115
spermicide 118
spongy mesophyll tissue 68
spring constant 360
springs 359-362
stains (microscopes) 20
standard form 19
starch 44
  test for 47
states of matter 219, 334, 336, 337
state symbols 220
statins 59
stem cells 25, 26
stents 58
step-down transformers 332
step-up transformers 332
sterilisation (contraception) 118
stomach 46
stomata 36, 72
stopping distances 376
streamlining 306, 368
strong acids 232-234
structural adaptations 154
subcellular structures 17, 18, 23
sublimation 336
Sudan III 48
sugars (test for) 47
sunburn 392
superbugs 147
surface area to volume ratios 34, 35
survival of the fittest 139
sustainable development 287
symbol equations 177, 178
synapses 106, 107
systematic errors 8
systems 297

Index

T
tables (of data) 9
taking measurements 413
tangents 260
target organs 110
temperature
　internal energy 338
　specific heat capacity
　　300, 301
　specific latent heat 337
temperature detectors 321
terminal velocity 369
tertiary consumers 155
testes 110, 115
testosterone 115
tests for
　alkenes 270
　gases 274
theoretical yields 229
theories 2
thermal conductivity 304
thermal decomposition 247
thermal energy stores
　　297, 300, 304, 390
thermal insulation
　　301, 305, 306
thermistors 321, 322
thermometers 407
thermostats 321
thinking distance 376
Thomson, J J 188
thorax 51
three-core cables 328
three-domain system
　　of classification 148
thyroid gland 110, 120
thyroid stimulating hormone
　　(TSH) 120
thyroxine 120
tidal barrages 311
tissues 40, 41
tobacco mosaic virus 77
toxicity (of drugs) 86
tracers 391
trachea 51
transects 158
transformers 332
transmission 385
transpiration 69-72, 159
　rate of 71, 72
transverse waves 382
trends in electricity use 331
trends in energy resources
　　314
triple bonds 209
tumours 66
TV signals 389
Type 1 diabetes 113
Type 2 diabetes 113
typical speeds 364

U
UK mains supply 328
ultraviolet (UV) 391, 392
uncertainty 15
uniform acceleration 365
uniform fields 399
units 12, 13
universal indicator 231
uranium 308, 313

V
vaccination 79, 82, 83
vacuoles 18
valid results 6
valves (heart) 53, 60
variables 6
variation 137, 138
vectors 76, 79, 143, 353
veins 54
velocity 364, 365, 367
　momentum 379
　terminal 369
velocity-time graphs 367
vena cava 53
ventricles 53
villi 36
viruses 75, 77
voltmeters 318, 413
volume of a gas 338

W
wasted energy 303, 306
waste management 164
water baths 412
water cycle 159
water treatment 292-294
wave equation 382
wave front diagrams 385, 386
wavelength 381, 388
wave power 311
waves 381-386, 388-394
　electromagnetic 388-392
　investigating 383, 384
　longitudinal 382
　refraction 385, 386
　speed 382-386
　transverse 382
wave speed 382-386
weak acids 232
weight 354
white blood cells 55, 81
wind power 309
wind turbines 309
Woese, Carl 148
word equations 177
work 298, 303, 329,
　　356, 359

X
X and Y chromosomes
　　126, 127
X-rays 391, 392
xylem cells 24
xylem tubes 68, 69

Y
yeast cells 100

Z
zero errors 8

The Periodic Table

Periods	Group 1	Group 2											Group 3	Group 4	Group 5	Group 6	Group 7	Group 0
1						1 **H** Hydrogen 1												4 **He** Helium 2
2	7 **Li** Lithium 3	9 **Be** Beryllium 4											11 **B** Boron 5	12 **C** Carbon 6	14 **N** Nitrogen 7	16 **O** Oxygen 8	19 **F** Fluorine 9	20 **Ne** Neon 10
3	23 **Na** Sodium 11	24 **Mg** Magnesium 12											27 **Al** Aluminium 13	28 **Si** Silicon 14	31 **P** Phosphorus 15	32 **S** Sulfur 16	35.5 **Cl** Chlorine 17	40 **Ar** Argon 18
4	39 **K** Potassium 19	40 **Ca** Calcium 20	45 **Sc** Scandium 21	48 **Ti** Titanium 22	51 **V** Vanadium 23	52 **Cr** Chromium 24	55 **Mn** Manganese 25	56 **Fe** Iron 26	59 **Co** Cobalt 27	59 **Ni** Nickel 28	63.5 **Cu** Copper 29	65 **Zn** Zinc 30	70 **Ga** Gallium 31	73 **Ge** Germanium 32	75 **As** Arsenic 33	79 **Se** Selenium 34	80 **Br** Bromine 35	84 **Kr** Krypton 36
5	85 **Rb** Rubidium 37	88 **Sr** Strontium 38	89 **Y** Yttrium 39	91 **Zr** Zirconium 40	93 **Nb** Niobium 41	96 **Mo** Molybdenum 42	[98] **Tc** Technetium 43	101 **Ru** Ruthenium 44	103 **Rh** Rhodium 45	106 **Pd** Palladium 46	108 **Ag** Silver 47	112 **Cd** Cadmium 48	115 **In** Indium 49	119 **Sn** Tin 50	122 **Sb** Antimony 51	128 **Te** Tellurium 52	127 **I** Iodine 53	131 **Xe** Xenon 54
6	133 **Cs** Caesium 55	137 **Ba** Barium 56	139 **La** Lanthanum 57	178 **Hf** Hafnium 72	181 **Ta** Tantalum 73	184 **W** Tungsten 74	186 **Re** Rhenium 75	190 **Os** Osmium 76	192 **Ir** Iridium 77	195 **Pt** Platinum 78	197 **Au** Gold 79	201 **Hg** Mercury 80	204 **Tl** Thallium 81	207 **Pb** Lead 82	209 **Bi** Bismuth 83	[209] **Po** Polonium 84	[210] **At** Astatine 85	[222] **Rn** Radon 86
7	[223] **Fr** Francium 87	[226] **Ra** Radium 88	[227] **Ac** Actinium 89	[261] **Rf** Rutherfordium 104	[262] **Db** Dubnium 105	[266] **Sg** Seaborgium 106	[264] **Bh** Bohrium 107	[277] **Hs** Hassium 108	[268] **Mt** Meitnerium 109	[271] **Ds** Darmstadtium 110	[272] **Rg** Roentgenium 111	[285] **Cn** Copernicium 112	[286] **Nh** Nihonium 113	[289] **Fl** Flerovium 114	[289] **Mc** Moscovium 115	[293] **Lv** Livermorium 116	[294] **Ts** Tennessine 117	[294] **Og** Oganesson 118

Relative atomic mass (top number); Atomic (proton) number (bottom number).

The Lanthanides (atomic numbers 58-71) and the Actinides (atomic numbers 90-103) are not shown in this table.

Physics Equations Sheet

In each physics paper you have to sit for GCSE Combined Science, you'll be given an equations sheet listing some of the equations you might need to use. That means you don't have to learn them, but you still need to be able to pick out the correct equations to use and be really confident using them. The equations sheet won't give you any units for the equation quantities — so make sure you know them inside out.

The equations you'll be given in the exam are all on this page. You can use this page as a reference when you're doing the exam questions in each topic, and the Practice Papers at the end of the book.

elastic potential energy = ½ × spring constant × (extension)²	$E_e = \frac{1}{2}ke^2$
change in thermal energy = mass × specific heat capacity × temperature change	$\Delta E = mc\Delta\theta$
thermal energy for change of state = mass × specific latent heat	$E = mL$
(final velocity)² − (initial velocity)² = 2 × acceleration × distance	$v^2 - u^2 = 2as$
period = $\frac{1}{\text{frequency}}$	
force (on a current-carrying conductor) = magnetic flux density × current × length	$F = BIl$
potential difference across primary coil × current in primary coil = potential difference across secondary coil × current in secondary coil	$V_p I_p = V_s I_s$